Chinese Legal Family

Qinhua He · Yonghong Qian · Chunhai Zhang · Guanghong Wu

Chinese Legal Family

商務印書館
SINCE1897 The Commercial Press

Springer

Qinhua He
Institute of Legal Civilization History
East China University of Political Science and Law
Shanghai, China

Chunhai Zhang
Law School
Nanjing University
Nanjing City, Jiangsu, China

Yonghong Qian
School of Political Science and Law
Zhengzhou University of Light Industry
Zhengzhou, Henan, China

Guanghong Wu
Law School
Guangxi Minzu University
Nanning, Guangxi, China

Translated by
Linan Tian
Law School
People's Public Security University of China
Beijing, China

ISBN 978-981-96-6521-1 ISBN 978-981-96-6522-8 (eBook)
https://doi.org/10.1007/978-981-96-6522-8

Jointly published with The Commercial Press, Ltd.
The print edition is not for sale in China (Mainland). Customers from China (Mainland) please order the print book from: The Commercial Press, Ltd.

This book is published with financial support from Chinese Fund for the Humanities and Social Sciences.

Translation from the Chinese Simplified language edition: "《法律文明史(第7卷):中华法系》" by Qinhua He et al., © The Commercial Press 2019. Published by The Commercial Press. All Rights Reserved.

This Springer imprint is published by the registered company Springer Nature Singapore Pte Ltd.
The registered company address is: 152 Beach Road, #21-01/04 Gateway East, Singapore 189721, Singapore

Preface

The book *Chinese Legal Family* was completed by our team of 10 members, led primarily by several professors, including myself, over nearly a decade. It was written based on over a century of research on the Chinese legal family since the early 20th century and represents a comprehensive work.

In the past decade, research on the Chinese legal family has been steadily increasing. Multiple works have been published, continuous publications have been released under the title "Chinese Legal Family," and numerous papers have been published. While many of these works do not strictly focus on the Chinese legal family in its true sense since the Chinese legal family includes not only China but also neighboring countries like Vietnam, Korea, and Japan, those that concentrate on traditional Chinese legal studies in the name of the "Chinese Legal Family" are still valuable. They contribute to our understanding of the origins and development of the Chinese legal family and help us grasp its essential characteristics. After all, the Chinese legal family is based on the foundation of Chinese legal culture and its zenith during the Sui and Tang dynasties.

Therefore, we can understand that the Chinese legal family is not merely a concept confined to one nation but encompasses several countries, even an international cultural concept. It is the result of legal and cultural exchanges and integration among several countries, centered on China, and is a product of internationalization and convergence of legal cultures in medieval East Asia. One crucial feature of the Chinese legal family, in addition to characteristics like written legal codes, a combination of ritual and law, family ethics, a blurred line between civil and criminal law, and the integration of various laws, is its international character. It not only represents the outcome of legal and cultural exchanges between countries but also serves as a powerful force driving such exchanges between nations.

So, what are the unique characteristics of the Chinese legal family compared to other legal systems like Sharia, Common Law, and Civil Law? We believe that, first, the Chinese legal family has a long history, a large population under its influence, and a relatively stable geographical scope, maintaining its continuity without interruption. Second, it is relatively comprehensive, comprising legal concepts (with Confucian legal thought as its core), legal codes such as China's Tang Code and Ming

Code, Japan's Taiho Code and Yoro Code, Korea's Gyŏngguk Daejeon (*Great Code of the National Governance*), Vietnam's Quốc triều hình luật (the *Le Code*), legal systems including the bureaucratic system, criminal system, and civil system, legal procedures and institutions, numerous legal figures, as well as legal scholarship and education. Third, the formation of the Chinese legal family serves as an excellent example of human legal civilization because unlike other legal systems such as the Islamic, Anglo-American, and Continental legal systems, which developed through war and colonial expansion, the Chinese legal family was established through voluntary and peaceful exchanges, with subsidiary legal countries genuinely respecting and admiring the mother legal country, China.

Given these distinct features of the Chinese legal family, when Professor TIAN Linan of PPSUC proposed to translate our book "Chinese Legal Family" into English and applied for funding from The National Social Science Fund of China to publish it abroad, my fellow authors and I were thrilled and fully supportive. If this book is published in the English-speaking world, it can introduce the Chinese legal family to a wider international audience. Moreover, it can help more countries and people understand the outstanding traditional Chinese legal culture represented by the Chinese legal family, thereby making a valuable contribution to human legal civilization.

As for the characteristics of this book, I have summarized them into three aspects:

First, it is comparatively systematic and comprehensive. It provides analyses and discussions on various aspects of the Chinese legal family, including the legal system of the mother legal country China, the legal systems of subsidiary legal countries Japan, Korea, and Vietnam, the relationship between legal systems, the worldviews of the Chinese legal family, legal scholarship (legal studies), legal education, legal professionals, the formation, growth, development, and eventual collapse of the Chinese legal family, its historical legacy, and the academic history of Chinese legal family research.

Second, it offers new insights and content in the study of the legal systems of member countries. Authors responsible for Japan, Korea, and Vietnam are experts in Japanese, Korean, and Vietnamese languages. They have not only extensively used original language source materials but have also provided detailed and innovative introductions and evaluations of the legal systems of member countries. Compared to similar books, this book provides the most substantial and exciting discussions of the legal systems of the three member countries, making it a standout feature of the book.

Third, the book presents new explanations of fundamental concepts, categories, and core content related to the Chinese legal family. It offers fresh perspectives on terms such as Chinese, legal system, the Chinese legal family, legal studies (legal scholarship), legal professionals, Lv Boshi (doctor of law), Mingfa, Myobodo, and more. It provides extensive discussions of the codification achievements within the Chinese legal family, in-depth analyses and interpretations of legal commentarial studies (legal hermeneutics) within the Chinese legal family, detailed examinations and discussions of legal education within the Chinese legal family, as well as a thorough examination and research into the activities and contributions of legal professionals, especially the lineages of legal families within the Chinese legal family.

These aspects not only distinguish this book from similar works but also represent new contributions to current research on the Chinese legal family.

Due to these characteristics and innovations, the book's target audience primarily falls into two categories: those interested in traditional Chinese legal culture and the legal cultures of East Asian countries such as Japan, Korea, and Vietnam, and those who wish to conduct further in-depth research on the legal concepts, legal systems, legal institutions, legal procedures, legal education, and legal research of China and East Asian countries, as well as their characteristics and essence. This book, with its comprehensive content on the Chinese legal family, serves as an encyclopedia dedicated to the topic.

The keywords for this book could include: Chinese legal family; ancient East Asian law; legal studies (Lv Xue, *Myobodo* in Japan)/jurisprudence; legal professionals/legal scholars (jurists, *Myobo Hakase* in Japan); *Tang Lv Shu Yi* (*Commentary on Tang Code*).

Finally, we would like to express our heartfelt gratitude to Professor TIAN Linan of PPSUC and their team for their exceptionally hard and diligent work in translating this book. We also extend our appreciation to the publishing house and its editors for their contributions to the translation and publication of this book. We hope that this book will receive attention and recognition from readers abroad. Of course, the book may contain errors in its information and viewpoints, and we welcome feedback and corrections from international readers.

August 2023

Qinhua He
Institute of Legal Civilization History
of East China University of Political
Science and Law
Shanghai, China

Competing Interests The authors have no competing interests to declare that are relevant to the content of this manuscript.

Summary

In 2011, "History of Legal Culture," a Major Project of the Chinese Fund for the Humanities and Social Sciences, chaired by Professor Qinhua He of the East China University of Political Science and Law, was officially launched. It produced the book series *History of Legal Culture*, consisting of 16 independent volumes. In 2019, Volume 7, *Chinese Legal Family*—with almost 850,000 Chinese characters—was published. Picking up from Volume 3 of the series, *Ancient Far Eastern Law*, this volume continues the discussion of the development of ancient Chinese law after the Wei, Jin, and Southern and Northern Dynasties, from the Sui and Tang Dynasties to the end of the Qing Dynasty. As the development of Chinese law in the Sui and Tang Dynasties reached its peak in history and spread to neighboring countries, such as Korea, Japan, and Vietnam, a huge legal family was formed—the Chinese Legal Family—covering entire East Asia, including part of South Asia. Hence, Volume 7 focuses on this legal family and discusses the related academic issues. The present work is the English translation of *Chinese Legal Family*, completed under the Translation Project of Chinese Academic Works sponsored by the Chinese Fund for the Humanities and Social Sciences (2021) (with some chapters or sections abbreviated).

This book mainly discusses the origin, essence, characteristics, and the fundamental content of the Chinese Legal Family, the development of the laws as they were instituted in other countries in the Chinese Legal Family—such as Japan, Korea, and Vietnam—the impact of the Chinese Legal Family on the development of China's Fengjian (the political ideology and governance system in ancient China, 封建) society, and the historical status of the Chinese Legal Family.

Chapter 1 elucidates what legal families are, what the Chinese Legal Family is, the formation and development of the Chinese Legal Family, its content and characteristics, the disintegration of the Chinese Legal Family, and the social background and historical reasons for the disintegration.

Chapter 2 provides a systematic review of the legal philosophy—legal views and thoughts—and jurisprudence developed in the Chinese Legal Family, as well as legal studies (Lv Xue, 律学, which is called *Myobodo* in Japan), legal scholars (jurists, who are called *Myobo Hakase* in Japan), and legal education (*Myobo* subject in Japan).

Chapter 3, with selected text translated, is about the laws of the mother country of the Chinese Legal Family, represented by the Tang Dynasty. Two aspects are discussed, namely the forms of law in the Chinese Legal Family—such as Lv, Ling, Ge, Shi, and Ge Hou Chi—and the legal system. In the criminal law area, the legal system covers the names of crimes and punishments and the principles for the punishments. In civil law, it addresses the rules concerning ownership, contract, marriage, family, and succession, among others. In administrative law, it includes the central and local administrative management system, the management of officials, and the administrative supervision system. It also addresses the judicial litigation system, including the judicial organs and litigation and trial systems.

Chapter 4, with selected text translated, is on the laws of countries that adopted the Chinese legal system. It discusses the formation and development of the law and jurisprudence in three countries, namely Japan, Korea, and Vietnam. The primary focus of this chapter is to examine how the Chinese Legal Family and Chinese laws have influenced the legal systems in these countries. For example, Japan went through a process of adoption, decline, and subsequent adoption once again with the Lv (criminal code) and Ling (administrative and civil regulations) systems, which were named the Ritsuryo system in Japan. Korea's legal development has been marked by distinct phases including reliance on local customs, a blend of Chinese laws and indigenous practices, and a more comprehensive adoption of Chinese legal ideas and institutions. Vietnam's legal institutions have been influenced by the Chinese Legal Family for a long time in its history from the earliest foundation of various Fengjian dynasties to their consolidation and development, and their eventual decline.

Chapter 5 examines in two parts the disintegration of the Chinese Legal Family: a general discussion and a detailed analysis. The former attempts to define the time frame for the dismantle of the Chinese Legal Family and look into the reasons behind its collapse (i.e. the conflict and integration of legal systems). The latter elaborates on the process of the Chinese Legal Family's disintegration in China, including its initial phase during the period of legal reforms at the end of the Qing Dynasty, the process of a gradual disintegration during the construction of legal systems by the Nanjing Provisional Government and the Beiyang Government, and then its final and complete disintegration with the promulgation of the Six Codes by the Nanjing Nationalist Government between 1928 and 1937. This chapter also explores the process and manifestations of the Chinese Legal Family's disintegration in Japan, Korea and Vietnam, and the new patterns of law and legal studies in East Asia that emerged after the disintegration. Put differently, it discusses how these countries departed from the Chinese Legal Family and adopted the Civil Law system under the influence of Western legal culture as they took on a path towards modernization and westernization.

In conclusion, the last chapter provides a summary of the historical legacy of the Chinese Legal Family, covering its understanding of law, the tradition of codified laws, commentaries on the legal provisions, prudence in imposing punishments, principles and institutions of criminal law developed with time, as well as values such as the protection of the environment and resources, respect for the elderly and care for the young and the sick and disabled, and a preference for resolving issues without going through litigation. These historical legacies continue to play an important role in the development of the legal systems and jurisprudence in contemporary China and other Asian countries.

Division of Writing Tasks by Chapter

Chapter 1 by Qinhua He. Chapter 2.1 by Qinhua He, Xiaoxia Jiang; Chapter 2.2 by Qinhua He; Chapter 2.3 by Qinhua He; Chapter 2.4 by Qinhua He, Ye Yuan, Jing Kong. Chapter 3 by Yonghong Qian. Chapter 4.1 by Min Wei; Chapter 4.2 by Chunhai Zhang; Chapter 4.3 by Guanghong Wu; Chapter 5 by Ying Liu. Epilogue by Qinhua He. Appendix by Qin Li.

Contents

Chapter 1
Introduction

The Chinese Legal Family is one of the longest-lasting and largest legal families, together with Hindu Law, Sharia, Common Law, and Civil Law. It occupies an important position in the history of human legal culture. When was the Chinese Legal Family formed? What were the historical and cultural conditions for its formation? How did it rise, develop, evolve, and eventually decline? What was the status of legal philosophy, jurisprudence, legal scholars, and legal education in the Chinese Legal Family? What forms of law and legal systems were included? What were its characteristics and styles? How did it affect the laws of modern China and East Asian countries, such as Japan, Korea, and Vietnam? These are the issues to be discussed in detail in this book, *The Chinese Legal Family,* which constitutes Volume 7 of the book series *History of Legal Culture.*

1 Overview

In China, the study of the Chinese Legal Family started as early as the late nineteenth century to the early twentieth century.

The original version of the chapter has been revised. A correction to this chapter can be found at https://doi.org/10.1007/978-981-96-6522-8_6

Q. He et al., *Chinese Legal Family*, https://doi.org/10.1007/978-981-96-6522-8_1

1.1 Discussions on the Chinese Legal Family in the Late Qing and Early Republic Years

In China, Gong Fazi was the first person to propose the concept of the Chinese Legal Family. In 1884, Professor Hozumi Nobushige (1855–1926) from the Faculty of Law of the University of Tokyo, Japan, put forward the theory that there were five major *legal families* in the world. This divided the legal systems of various countries into five families, namely the Hindu family, Chinese family, Muslim family, British family, and Roman family. The Chinese family referred to here is the Chinese Legal Family we will discuss. On January 28, 1903, *Zhengfa Xuebao* (政法学报, *Political Science and Law Quarterly*) (Issue 2 of Guimao Year, i.e., 1903) published an article written by Gong Fazi, "Comparative Study of the Five Legal Families in the World." This was a detailed discussion on the formation, historical evolution, main content, basic characteristics, and influence of the world's five major legal families, based on the work of Hozumi Nobushige. In this article Gong Fazi also provided a short introduction to the Chinese Legal Family.[1]

In 1904, Liang Qichao (1873–1929), a giant in the Hundred Days' Reform, further discussed the concept and status of the Chinese Legal Family in world legal history in his article "The Development of the Chinese Jurisprudence." He said that "recent legal scholars proposed that there are four world legal families, and the Chinese Legal Family is one of them. The other legal families either developed earlier than the Chinese one and disappeared a long time ago or prosper today but were only formed in recent years. There is a good reason to be proud of the Chinese Legal Family. As extraordinary things are created in uncommon places, China has a population of hundreds of millions and has established an empire that has lasted for thousands of years. It should have such an independent and great legal system." (Liang, 1936, 42).

Subsequently, various legal journals in China began to publish research articles on the Chinese Legal Family. For example, Lu Fu's "Theories Concerning the Chinese Legal Family" (published in Volume 1, Issue 1 of *Fazheng Xuebao* [法政学报, *Journal of Law and Political Science*] in 1918); Meng Zhiying's "Comparative Views of the Five Legal Families" (published in Volume 3, Issue 1 of *Zhengfa Yuekan* [政法月刊, *The Monthly of Political Science and Law*] in 1923); Gao Weijun's "Establishment of a Chinese Legal Family" (published in Volume 2, Issue 8 of *Faxue Jikan* [法学季刊, *The China Law Review*] in 1926); and Xue Siguang's "Characteristics of the Chinese Legal Family and Its Future" (published in Volume 1, Issue 4 of *Shehui Kexue Luncong Yuekan* [社会科学论丛月刊, *The Monthly* of *Social Science Series*] in 1929).

The above works show that the discussion on the Chinese Legal Family in the Late Qing and Early Republic Years mostly concentrated on its concepts—by comparing

[1] Regarding the life stories of Gong Fazi, Professor Chen Linghai of East China University of Political Science and Law and Associate Professor Lai Junnan of Law School at Shanghai Jiaotong University provided the latest detailed research. See Chen (2017, 189–206), Lai (2008, 416–455).

the similarities and differences of the five major legal families in the world, emphasizing the long history of the Chinese Legal Family—and characteristics, and how the Chinese Legal Family could overcome its collapse and revitalize itself.

1.2 Research After the 1930s

In the 1930s, the number of treatises on the Chinese Legal Family further increased. Some examples are Li Cishan's "The Chinese Legal Family in the World Legal Families" (published in Volume 1, Issue 4 of *Faxue Congkan* [法学丛刊, *China Law Journal*] in 1930); Ma Cunkun's "Establishing a New Chinese Legal Family" (published in Volume 7, Issue 39 of *Falv Pinglun* [法律评论, *Chaoyang Law Review*] in 1930); Jiao Yitang's "The New Chinese Legal Family and the Great Harmony of the World" (published in Volume 1, Issue 1 of *Faxue Jikan* in 1930); Ding Yuanpu's "Formation of the Chinese Legal Family and Its Future" (published in Volume 1, Issues 4–5 of *Xiandai Faxue* [现代法学, *Modern Law*] in 1931); Wang Ruqi's "Revitalization of the Chinese Legal Family" (published in Volume 1, Issue 10 of *Fuxing Yuekan* [复兴月刊, *The Monthly of Renaissance*] in 1933); Liu Zhe's "Civil and Criminal Law in Classical Japan Dominated by the Chinese Legal Family" (published in Volume 2, Issue 4 of *Faxue Congkan* in 1933) (He & Li, 2003, from 793); Ju Zheng's "Re-establishment of the Chinese Legal Family" (published in Volume 3, Issue 1 of *Zhonghua Faxue Zazhi* [中华法学杂志, *Republic of China Journal of Law*] in 1944); Zhang Tianquan's "The Chinese Legal Family" (published in Volume 4, Issue 8 of *Zhonghua Faxue Zazhi* in 1945); and Cao Decheng's "Exploration of the Chinese Legal Family: Objects and Tasks of the Research" (published in Volume 7, Issue 4 of *Zhonghua Faxue Zazhi* in 1948).

Among these, the works of Ding Yuanpu, Cheng Shude, Jiang Liquan, Chen Guyuan, Ju Zheng, and Yang Honglie are of special significance. In 1931, Ding Yuanpu raised the question concerning the Chinese Legal Family in his article "Formation of the Chinese Legal Family and Its Future," saying, "In summary, the spirit of the Chinese Legal Family is rooted in the concept of a combination of Li (Ritual Propriety, 礼) and Xing (Punishment, 刑), and the path of its evolution is actually expanded from the law of patriarchal clans to the law of the nation. … In our country, criminal law is particularly developed, while the Roman-style codes focus on Civil Law. They have a different history and environment. This should not be criticized" (Ding, 1931).

In 1934, an article by Cheng Shude, "A Discussion of the Chinese Legal System," was published by Falv Pinglun. The article emphasized that "the rise and fall of the legal families are directly related to the strength of the country. When China is weak, the Chinese Legal Family also wanes. It is not because of deficiencies in the legal system" (Cheng, 1934).

Jiang Liquan, a jurist in the same period, elaborated on the Chinese Legal Family in his article "Evolution of the Legislation of the Chinese Legal Family" in 1935. He carried out an analysis from the aspects of the legal families, evolution and status of the Chinese Legal Family, background and core of past legislation of the Chinese Legislation, characteristics and transformation of the Chinese Legal Family, theoretical basis of the evolution of the Chinese Legal Family, differences between the legislation of the Chinese Legal Family and that of European and American countries, and a comparison of these legislation before and after the evolution. He pointed out that the "evolution of law should be suitable for the evolution of the society. When the conditions for maintaining the existence of the social change, the form of society should change accordingly." The same is true of the Chinese Legal Family. The preconditions for legal evolution are to seek social stability, economic development, and balance of the various practical interests of society. "The legislation of the Chinese Legal Family often has norms that are full of creativity and transformation. They become the primary rules for a society to exist and evolve" (Jiang, 2009).

Chen Guyuan published his book *The History of the Chinese Legal System* in 1934, which mentioned the Chinese Legal Family.[2] From 1936–1937, he continued to publish articles, including "Relationship between Confucian Jurisprudence and China's Inherent Legal System—A Review of China's Inherent Legal System I," "Relationship between the Family System and China's Inherent Legal System—A Review of China's Inherent Legal System II," and "Relationship between Natural Law and China's Inherent Legal System—A Review of China's Inherent Legal System III," wherein he emphasized that to do research on the Chinese Legal Family, Confucianism, the family system, and the concepts of natural law must be studied. In 1964 and 1969, Chen Guyuan published two books based on a summary and review of his own works: *Essentials of Chinese Legal History* and *Chinese Culture and Chinese Legal System* (both published by San Min Book Co., Ltd., Taiwan). These books provide an in-depth discussion of the cultural background, core spirit, value orientation, and structural characteristics of the Chinese Legal Family.[3]

In 1937, Yang Honglie published his masterpiece, *The Influence of Chinese Law in East Asian Countries*, which clarified the theories concerning legal families advanced by Hozumi Nobushige and affirmed the statement that the Chinese Legal Family is one of the largest legal families in the world (Yang, 1999, 1). He clearly pointed out that "comparing the history of various legal families, the Chinese Legal Family has been continuously developed over thousands of years. Its life is longer than the most ancient legal families, such as Egyptian and Mesopotamian legal systems. Its influence spread to East Asian countries such as Korea, Japan, Ryukyu, Annam, and Xiyu (Western Regions). Egyptian or Mesopotamian legal systems, which were limited to a narrow area, are not comparable to the Chinese Legal Family. Therefore, to say that the Chinese Legal Family is one of the largest legal families in the world is not inappropriate" (Yang, 1999, 4). He believes that the Chinese Legal Family is the

---

[2] In the main body of this book, Chen Guyuan did not list the Chinese Legal Family in the contents (chapters, sections, and headings) but clearly pointed out in the preface that the Chinese Legal Family is one of the legal families in the world. Its development depends on the Chinese people. See Chen (1988, 1).

[3] *Essentials of Chinese Legal History* (2011) has been reprinted by The Commercial Press.

earliest in history, longest in existence, largest in the world, and most widely spread legal family, so it has uncontestable value.

The achievements in research on the Chinese Legal Family by the legal scholars of the Republic of China in the 1930s—also including a small number of works finished in the 1940s—can be summarized. Although scholars have paid attention to the existence of the Chinese Legal Family and its important position in world legal history, identified the origins and evolution of Chinese legal thought, clarified the significance of academic research to promote legal reforms and revolution (Zhang, 2010, 7), and initially identified the characteristics of the Chinese Legal Family, generally the research in this period still focused on emphasizing that the Chinese Legal Family was an important legal family in the world (Ding Yuanpu, and others); thus, refuting the view that the Chinese Legal Family has died out and expecting to establish a new Chinese Legal Family (Jiang Liquan, Chen Guyuan, Ju Zheng, and others).

1.3 Continuation of Research on the Chinese Legal Family in the 1980s and 1990s

After the founding of the People's Republic of China, because of the influence of leftist thoughts and historical nihilism and since the concept of legal families originates from the West and therefore belongs to the category of "bourgeois jurisprudence," for a long time, the Chinese Legal Family was basically ignored. It was not until the end of 1978, when China implemented the national policy of emancipating the mind, reforming and opening up, that research on the Chinese Legal Family received further attention from academic circles anew.

In 1980, Chen Chaobi, a professor from the Law School of Xiamen University, published his article "A Preliminary Study of the Characteristics of the Chinese Legal Family" in the first issue of *Faxue Yanjiu* (法学研究, *Chinese Journal of Law*) and led in expounding the essence and characteristics of the Chinese Legal Family. A series of works appeared soon afterward. For example, Liu Hainian and Yang Yifan's "Formation of the Chinese Legal Family and Its Characteristics" (published in Issue 1 of *Renmin Sifa* [人民司法, *People's Judicature*] in 1983); Qiao Wei's "Basic Characteristics of the Chinese Legal Family" (published in Issue 2 of *Wenshizhe* [文史哲, *Literature, History, and Philosophy*] in 1986); and Zhao Jianhua's "Brief Discussion on the Chinese Legal Family" (published in Issue 2 of *Xuexi yu Fudao* [学习与辅导, *Learning and Guidance*] in 1987). In the 1990s, research on the Chinese Legal Family became more abundant. A group of legal historians, including Ma Xiaohong, Zhang Zhongqiu, Li Shuguang, Xu Zhongming, Fan Zhongxin, Chen Guoguang, Xu Xiaoguang, Hou Wenfu, Zhang Libo, Jia Guofa, Zeng Hui, Peng Fenglian, Sun Xiao, Nan Yuquan, Yang Zhenhong, Li Gang, and Li Xin, expressed their opinions on the Chinese Legal Family.

Among these researchers, Zhang Jinfan was outstanding. In 1980, he published his article "Origins of the Features of the Chinese Legal Family" in Issue 4 of *Faxue Yanjiu*, summarizing the characteristics of the Chinese Legal Family from five aspects. In 1984, he published another article, "Re-Discussion on Several Issues of the Chinese Legal Family," in Issue 2 of *Zhongguo Zhengfa Daxue Xuebao* (中国政法大学学报, *Journal of China University of Political Science and Law*), which further summarized the characteristics of the Chinese Legal Family from six aspects. In discussing the characteristics of the Chinese Legal Family, the emphasis on the multiple sources of the Chinese Legal Family in culture, the distinction between the compiling styles of the code and legal system, and the emphasis on the joint creation of multiple ethnic groups were three aspects proposed by Zhang Jinfan independently, which were not covered by the research carried out during the period of the Republic of China (Zhang, 2010, 4–5).

In 1999, Zhang Jinfan published "Some Thoughts on the Rebuilding of the Chinese Legal Family: Discussion on the Chinese Legal Family for the Third Time" (in *Nanjing Daxue Falv Pinglun* [南京大学法律评论, *Nanjing University Law Review*] Spring 1999). In this article, the author changed his views from his previous two articles. That is, "by the beginning of the twentieth century, with the disintegration of Fengjian society, the Chinese Legal Family had lost the basis for its independent existence. At the end of the Qing Dynasty, the government reformed and revised the laws and began to incorporate capitalist laws. Particularly, Civil Law was imported from Japan and gradually became dominant. The concept of the Chinese Legal Family collapsed eventually." But "certain traces" were retained, such as the emphyteusis, pawning rights, parental rights, and ancestral inheritance rights (Chen & Zhang, 1996, 236). Instead, he now began to emphasize that "the Chinese Legal Family did not disappear. It is undergoing difficult changes, transformation, renewal, and reshaping. … The Chinese Legal Family cannot be understood as a purely historical phenomenon or a rigid concept that has lost its vitality. On the contrary, combining the modern and historical aspects and unifying the global and national aspects to reshape the Chinese Legal Family is an important subject worth serious consideration for improving the Chinese socialist legal system" (Zhang & Li, 2000, 169–170). Hence, the author elaborated on the four basics of reshaping the Chinese Legal Family: unification of legal and family obligations, emphasis on the role of law in governing the state and the combination of law and officials, integration of education and punishment, and the complementarity of statutory and case law.

Meanwhile, with the publication of a large number of papers, monographs also appeared. Among these, the most influential book is *Research on the Chinese Legal Family,* written by Hao Tiechuan in 1997 (Hao, 1997). This was the first research work in mainland China concentrating on the subject of the Chinese Legal Family and included three parts. The Introduction summarizes the research achievements of the academic circles concerning the Chinese Legal Family since modern times, involving research on the characteristics and stages of development of the Chinese Legal Family and the research ideas of the book. Part I is about the characteristics of the Chinese Legal Family. It comprises four chapters and pays special attention to the influences of Legalism on the codes, Confucianism on the judges, and mythology on public consciousness. Part II concentrates on the collapse of the Chinese Legal Family and its impacts. This part comprises four chapters: observations on the relationship between identities and contracts in ancient China based on *Fanshan Pan Du* (Judicial Records Collected by Fanshan, 樊山判牍), the choice of the Civil Law system in modern China, the influence of traditional thinking on contemporary Chinese legislative skills, and cultural traditions and the formation of the characteristics of contemporary Chinese legislation.

From the perspective of relevance, Part I of the book is very distinctive and insightful. The author's point of view is very different from the traditional point of view in the field of legal history. Traditionally, when talking about the characteristics of the Chinese Legal Family, the combination of various laws, "mandatory penalties for actions failing to follow Li (Ritual Propriety)," laws being made by the emperor, familism, integration of laws of various ethnic groups, and others are often highlighted. When talking about the features of ancient Chinese laws, Qu Tongzu's view was generally accepted, and the influence of Confucius on ancient Chinese laws was always mentioned. In Hao Tiechuan's book, the generally accepted theory was modified, proposing that the Chinese Legal Family had three distinctive features: the legalization of the codes, the influence of Confucius on the judges, and the mythology of the public consciousness. In this author's opinion, Hao Tiechuan's view is very reasonable, albeit not comprehensive. The codes of various dynasties after the Tang Dynasty fundamentally followed the Legalist ideology, although they were regarded as "taking Li as the only standard." Therefore, Hao Tiechuan's work occupies a very important position in the research results concerning the Chinese Legal Family in mainland China.

1.4 New Progress in the Research on the Chinese Legal Family in the 21st Century

Since the start of the twenty-first century, research on the Chinese Legal Family in China has made new progress. In 2001, Guo Chengwei took the lead in editing and publishing a book, *The Spirit of the Chinese Legal Family* (Guo, 2001). This book summarized the spirit of the Chinese Legal Family into three aspects: the spirit of legislation, administration, and judiciary. The spirit of legislation includes a long and splendid history, including the divine rights of emperors, law making by emperors, family law being the key, the importance of the family, combined Li and Fa (law, 法), hierarchy laws, moral guidance and additional punishment, more importance attached to criminal law than to Civil Law, and an emphasis on harmony and a preference for resolving issues without going through litigation. The spirit of administration includes agriculture-based countries, precocious administration, autocratic monarchy, centralized powers, rule of man and law, strengthening of administration and officials, reinforced household registration management, guarantee of taxation, emphasis on agriculture, and suppression of commerce. The spirit of the judiciary includes prohibiting and preventing conflicts, emphasizing results and understating formats, being prudent in imposing punishments, having a clear hierarchy and strict responsibility, mediating disputes and settling lawsuits, sacrificing benefit for the sake of righteousness, focusing on people instead of divinities, wise listening and discriminating, invoking laws to decide punishments, considering both feelings and reasons, using politics to lead laws, special power granted to supervisory departments, guaranteeing imperial power as the goal of the law, prohibiting and preventing heresies, born in springs and dead in autumns (following the *heavenly principles*), making decisions based on people's specific situations.

It is fair to say that the book reveals the spirit of the Chinese Legal Family in detail and analyzes it from three angles, namely legislation, administration, and the judiciary. It provides appropriate information on ancient Chinese society. Although the book focuses on the *spirit* of the Chinese Legal Family, it actually analyzes its *features*. Meanwhile, the book is not limited to exploring the origin and evolution of the Chinese Legal Family (a long history with far-reaching influence) and elaborating on the institutions in the Chinese Legal Family (broad and profound essence). It also goes deep into the spiritual aspects of the Chinese Legal Family, which provides refreshing ideas. The author further expounds on the essence and contribution of the Chinese Legal Family in the Preface of the book. He holds that the Chinese Legal Family is "a regional legal family with Confucian characteristics, which takes the Chinese Fengjian system as its essence and the contemporaneous legal systems of the neighboring Fengjian countries such as Japan, Korea, and Vietnam as its extension." This induction is concise and well-reasoned. The author believes that due to the broad and profound essence of the Chinese Legal Family, a legal spirit had been formed through long-term legal practice, which not only contributed to the world legal culture but also contributed to China's contemporary "law-based governance and establishment of a socialist country with the rule of law." Of course, the author also pointed out that the spirit of the Chinese Legal Family contained some negative and outdated content, such as cultural absolutism and national policies, such as emphasizing agriculture and suppressing commerce.

In 2002, Liu Guang'an published *Re-understanding of the Chinese Legal Family*, expounding on the concept, characteristics, and significance of the Chinese Legal Family in the author's mind. He holds that "there is no unified view in academic circles concerning the concept, characteristics, and significance of the Chinese Legal Family. Different conclusions can be drawn from different perspectives. Considering the root of the Chinese Legal Family, it can be said that the Chinese Legal Family is a legal tradition created and developed on the basis of Chinese culture" (Liu, 2002, preface 1–5). The author discussed the features and basis of the Chinese Legal Family from three aspects: family law and customary folk law, ethnic groups, imperial power and legislation, and Confucianism and jurisprudence. He believes that "understanding the concept of the Chinese Legal Family from the perspective of the Chinese cultural tradition is a development of the previous understanding. It makes the concept of the Chinese Legal Family more inclusive and open" (Liu, 2010, 34–35). In his later treatise, he discussed this issue further (Liu, 2011).

Zhang Jinfan wrote a series of articles concerning the Chinese Legal Family, some of which are "Humanism—One of the Features of the Chinese Legal Family" (published in Issue 9 of *Hebei Faxue* [河北法学, *Hebei Law Science*] in 2005); "New Theory on the Chinese Legal Family" (published in Issue 1 of *Nanjing Daxue Xuebao* [南京大学学报, *Journal of Nanjing University*] in 2007); "The Development of My Understandings of the Chinese Legal Family" (in Volume 1 of *Chinese Legal Family* edited by Zhu Yong); "Interpretation of the Locality of the Chinese Legal Family" (published in Issue 5 of *Zhengfa Luntan* [政法论坛, *Tribune of Political Science and Law*] in 2010); "The Chinese Legal Family Condenses the Legal Wisdom of Ethnic Minorities" (published in Issue 6 of *Minzu Yanjiu* [民族研究, *Ethno-National Studies*] in 2011); and "Revival of Legal Culture and Rethinking of the Chinese Legal Family" (in *Lessons Learned: Past and Present in the Research of Legal History*, Xiamen University Press, 2012). These works further illuminated the Chinese Legal Family (especially its features) and forwarded the idea of "reshaping the Chinese Legal Family" (Zhang, 2012, 300). He also edited the book *Retrospect and Prospect of the Chinese Legal Family* (China University of Political Science and Law Press, 2007), which reviews and sorts out the research on the Chinese Legal Family. Additionally, Zhang Jinfan revised his monograph, *The Tradition and Modern Transformation of Chinese Law*, adding Chapter 15, "The Chinese Legal Family Created by Various Ethnic Groups," which provides an elaboration of the viewpoint that "the Chinese Legal Family was created by various ethnic groups in China" that he previously proposed (Zhang, 2009, 348).

In addition to the achievements of the above-mentioned scholars, Rao Ai's "New Thoughts on the Chinese Legal Family: A Comparative Study with Civil Law and Common Law" (published in Issue 1 of *Xi'nan Jiaotong Daxue Xuebao* [西南交通大学学报, *Journal of Southwest Jiaotong University*] in 2000); Wang Limin's "Another Discussion on the Chinese Legal Family" (published in Issue 5 of *Huadong Zhengfa Xueyuan Xuebao* [华东政法学院学报, *ECUPL Journal*] in 2001); Ai Yongming's "Chinese Legal Family Is Not Punishment Based" (published in Issue 1 of *Zhongguo Faxue* [中国法学, *China Legal Science*] in 2004); Yu Ronggen and Long Daxuan's "Summary of Study on the Chinese Legal Family" (published in Issue 4 of *Shanghai Zhengfa Xueyuan Xuebao* [上海政法学院学报, *Journal of Shanghai University of Political Science and Law*] in 2005); and He Qinhua and Kong Jing's "The Birth of a New Chinese Legal System? From the Three Legal Families to an East Asian Common Law" (published in Issue 4 of *Faxue Luntan* [法学论坛, *Legal Forum*] in 2005) among others all contributed to the increasing research interest on the Chinese Legal Family in the new century. Scholars such as Zhang Xibo, Chen Hongyi, Shao Fang, Zeng Daiwei, Qu Chaoli, Li Qing, Yang Zhengrong, Xu Xiangmin, Chen Chen, Liu Yuanzheng, Zhang Hongjie, Shi Guangquan, Liu Gaoyong, Wang Xuwei, and Xu Xiaozhuang also published their own research on the Chinese Legal Family, laws and jurisprudence in ancient China, and relations between the law of Han ethnicity and the laws of various ethnic minorities.

Among the above works, the most influential is Yang Yifan's "A Major Misunderstanding in the Study of the Chinese Legal Family—Questioning the Doctrine of 'Integration of All Laws and No Differentiation of Civil and Criminal Laws'" (published in Issue 6 of *Zhongguo Shehui Kexue* [中国社会科学, *Social Sciences in China*] in 2002). This article raises doubts about the doctrine of "integration of all laws and no differentiation between civil and criminal laws." It was clearly pointed out that "this paper has carried out a comparative study of various forms of law and the contents and style structures of a large number of representative laws in ancient China. It concludes that from the pre-Qin Dynasty to the Ming and Qing Dynasties, there were various forms of law, each of which had its own specific functions. There were differences between civil and criminal laws, and criminal laws were different from various non-criminal laws. These legislative principles have been consistent throughout the ages. Lv Dian (律典, legal codes) was criminal codes, and its contents made it criminal law. It was by no means a compilation of various criminal, administrative, military, civil, and other legal norms. Lv Dian and the other forms of law worked in both a separated and coordinated way, all laws being used and complementing each other. Whether considering the contents or style structures of the various forms of law, the doctrine of 'integration of all laws and no differentiation between civil and criminal laws' is untenable" (Yang, 2002).

In 2010, the Law Press launched a multi-volume book series, *Chinese Legal Family*, edited by Zhu Yong. As a serial publication, the book conducts thematic and continuous research on the Chinese Legal Family.[4] Aside from the specific legal institutions and principles adopted in different periods of the Chinese Legal Family, the book also provides general topics, such as the development, evolution, and features of the Chinese Legal Family. For example, in Volume 1, articles by five scholars who specialized in the Chinese Legal Family were collected, including Zhang Jinfan's "The Development of My Understandings of the Chinese Legal Family," Gao Mingshi's "Analysis of the Basic Legislative Principles of the Chinese Legal Family," Liu Guang'an's "Re-understanding of the Chinese Legal Family," Wang Tao's "Keywords of Modern Western Philosophy and Research on the Chinese Legal Family," and Li Qing's "Socio-Historical Roots of East Asian Countries' Acceptance of the Chinese Legal Family—From the Perspective of Korea." Articles on the features of traditional Chinese law from the perspective of different fields of law, written by Zhang Zhongqiu, Li Dianrong, Huang Yuansheng, and others, were also collected.

In Volume 2, the topics include academic research, academic focus, legal figures, academic new talents, and academic dynamics. It includes articles by Chen Huixin, Li Xiandong, Li Ming, Shan Chun, Hu Xingdong, Lin Qian, and Ye Penghuang. This volume explores the traditional elements of the laws of various departments in different periods in China from different angles.

Volume 3 deals with the general issues of the Chinese Legal Family and includes two articles, Yang Jing's "Literature Review of the Chinese Legal Family" and Ruan Zhigang's "The Landscape of the Chinese Legal Family Created by Yang Honglie." The latter provides a detailed analysis and review discussing the principles, timelines, spatial scope, nature, features, and implicit aims of the Chinese Legal Family proposed in the 1930s by Yang Honglie in three of his works: *History of Chinese*

[4] As of April 2017, 9 volumes have been published.

Legal Development, *History of Chinese Legal Thoughts*, and *The Influence of Chinese Law on East Asian Countries.*

Yang Jing's "Literature Review of the Chinese Legal Family" provides a detailed review of the history and achievements of the research on the Chinese Legal Family conducted by scholars over more than 100 years. The academic research was divided into three stages: the early 1900s, the 1920s to the 1940s, and the 1980s and thereafter. In the first stage, Liang Qichao's works and academic viewpoints are highlighted. In the second stage, the views and theories of Cheng Shude, Yang Honglie, Ju Zheng, Chen Guyuan, Ding Yuanpu, and others are assessed. In the third stage, the works of Chen Chaobi, Zhang Jinfan, Rao Ai, Nan Yuquan, Yu Ronggen, Long Daxuan, Yang Zhenhong, Ma Xiaohong, and other scholars are recommended. The article also provides an introduction and some comments on various issues covered by those works, including the essence, features, reasons for formation and disintegration, and the process of the disintegration of the Chinese Legal Family, as well as the integration of the legal culture of the Han ethnicity and other ethnic groups in the Chinese Legal Family.

Aside from Yang Jing's article, two other sources are also important in the summary and review of the academic research on the Chinese Legal Family: Yu Ronggen and Long Daxuan's "Summary of Study on the Chinese Legal Family" (published in Issue 4 of *Shanghai Zhengfa Xeuyuan Xuebao* in 2005); and *Retrospect and Prospect of the Chinese Legal Family* edited by Zhang Jinfan (China University of Political Science and Law Press, 2007). The first article holds that the Chinese Legal Family has lasted for thousands of years. With this historical fact, coupled with more than a hundred years of academic research, it is fair to say that a study has been formed; thus, "to name it a study is fair" (Yu & Long 2005). The author then elaborates on the study of the Chinese Legal Family from five aspects: legal families and the Chinese Legal Family as well as its study, the origin, development, revival and prosperity, and trend of the study.

The second book involves five chapters, providing a systematic discussion on the research situation of the Chinese Legal Family in the Republic of China and the People's Republic of China, the legal culture of the Chinese Legal Family and the neighboring countries in East Asia, a comparative study between the Chinese Legal Family and other legal families in the world, and the thinking concerning the value and in-depth research of the Chinese Legal Family.

At the end of the book, there are 14 articles on the Chinese Legal Family written by scholars who were active during the Republic years: Ju Zheng, Gao Weilian, Li Cishan, Ma Cunkun, Ding Yuanpu, Wang Ruqi, Cheng Shude, Jiang Liquan, Liu Lumin, Chen Guyuan, Chen Peng, Li Jingxi, Zhang Tianquan, and Cao Decheng.

Another book published in this period concentrating on the Chinese Legal Family is *The Form and Soul of the Chinese Legal Family*, edited by Li Yufu (Li, 2010). The book includes four chapters covering theories, institutions, judiciary, and extraterritorial laws. The main content of the book covers Chinese legal history and the history of legal thought, as well as some subjects of comparative law and legal culture. In the preface, the author expresses strong concern for the legal modernization carried out in China since the twentieth century, saying, "the legal modernization is characterized by large-scale legal transplant. However, the social effect of the laws is modest. The nearly completely westernized legal system that has been painstakingly constructed only remains on paper, and it is difficult for it to take root in the land of China. The reason for this is that the Western legal culture has been regarded as the main object of the legal transplant and the main criterion for deciding the effectiveness of legal reforms. Traditional Chinese legal culture has been ignored, neglected, or even criticized and attacked. Forcing the modernization of Chinese law in a quick but rough way has proven to be a failure." (Li, 2010).

This author will not comment too much on whether the above conclusions and viewpoints are justified because in a country with an outdated legal system, to realize the modernization of law, complete and systematic transplant and absorption of the legal systems of the advanced Western countries—including the awareness, ideas and institutions—are perhaps necessary. In modern times, China is not the only country that has modernized its law by transplanting the advanced legal culture of the West. Japan, India, South Korea, the Philippines, Malaysia, and all other countries with outdated legal systems have also experienced a similar process. However, Li Yufu believes that "from the perspective of ideological inheritance, the traditional Chinese legal culture did not die out with the collapse of the Chinese Legal Family. On the contrary, in the modernization of the traditional Chinese law, the traditional Chinese legal culture is still playing either a positive or negative role" (Li, 2010, preface 1–5); he is undoubtedly correct.

2 Essence and Characteristics of the Chinese Legal Family

2.1 Essence of the Legal System

The legal system or law system, sometimes called the legal family, is a system composed of the laws of several states that share a common historical origin, contents, features, and discourse. Since the formation of the Sumerian legal system—the first legal family in human history—in ancient Mesopotamia around 2100 BC, various legal families were developed, such as the Ancient Egyptian Law, Hindu Law, Chinese Legal Family, Greek Law, Roman Law, Slavonic Law, Celtic Law, Maritime Law, Canon Law, Sharia, Common Law, and Civil Law. Most of these legal families have been lost in history, except for Sharia, Common Law, and Civil Law. Among them, the Chinese Legal Family was undoubtedly the largest in range (involving hundreds of millions of people) and longest in duration (more than 1300 years). Thus, it has left an enormous footprint in the history of human legal culture.

The above definition of legal families makes it very clear that laws can only become a legal family when they meet the following conditions. First, the laws of not only one state but several states can constitute a legal family. The core of the concept is that a legal family is formed by the laws of several states.[5] Second, these laws of several states must share a common historical origin. For instance, the historical origin of the Chinese Legal Family was the laws of the Sui and Tang Dynasties in ancient China. The historical origin of Greek Law was the laws of the Athenian city-states. Third, common contents can be found in a legal family. For example, in the various states of the Chinese Legal Family, Confucianism was the common legal guiding ideology. Their common legal principles and institutional contents include moral guidance and additional punishment, tempering justice with mercy, balancing severe punishment and leniency according to social situations, and attaching importance to family law and moral orders. Fourth, the laws must have common features. For example, one feature of the Common Law system is that it is based on cases, and judgments are made according to precedents. Fifth, a common discourse can be found. For instance, in Civil Law systems, the provisions of the legal codes, their interpretation, and the definitions of the terms are very similar, sometimes almost identical. Thus, the implementation of the laws has a considerable number of commonalities.

From the above, it is clear that the Chinese Legal Family is typical in terms of the features of a legal family. States that adopt this legal family system are consistent in various aspects, such as legal ideology, principles, and institutions. It is also very stable in terms of the range. In its more than 1300 years of existence, its geographic range has always been in East Asia, including China, Japan, Korea, and Vietnam. From the implicit features of a legal family, it can be found that the Chinese Legal Family mentioned in the previous works of some Chinese scholars was not the Chinese Legal Family in its strict sense because their discussion focused on the legal system of ancient China, or of the Qin Dynasty, Han Dynasty, Sui Dynasty, or Tang Dynasty. The laws of a single state cannot constitute a legal family—although the domestic laws of ancient China also include different laws of various ethnic groups, they do not accord with the concept of a modern legal system. To exemplify the Chinese Legal Family, it must go beyond China as a single country. Even if the discussion cannot include all members of the Chinese Legal Family because of the language issue and limited materials, it must include at least two states—e.g., China and Japan, China and Korea, or China and Vietnam.

2.2 *Essence of the Chinese Legal Family*

There are different elaborations in academic circles on the essence of the Chinese Legal Family.

---

[5] In the book, *The Tradition and Modern Transformation of the Chinese Law*, Zhang Jinfan expressed the same view: "As an independent legal system, it must not only have unique features, but also be accepted and adopted by some other countries and regions. Otherwise, it is not enough to be called an independent legal system." See Zhang (2009, 351).

For example, Chen Chaobi believes that the inherent features or concepts of the Chinese Legal Family are very rich. "It has created an extremely rich and colorful ancient culture in the history of more than 4.000 years; our motherland has stood tall among the ancient civilizations of the world as a great country; its legal system and thoughts have maintained a unique internal connection and have been continuously developed, forming a self-contained legal system with national characteristics. … The Chinese Legal Family, in a broad sense, should include three historical stages of laws but with fundamental differences: a 3000-year-old Fengjian legal system, a short-lived semi-Fengjian legal system in modern Chinese history, and a socialist legal system after the establishment of the People's Republic of China. Compared with the former two, the socialist legal system is fundamentally the opposite. It is the Chinese nation that connects the three different legal systems into a whole, which constitute the Chinese Legal Family in a broad sense."[6]

Actually, this concept, in a broad sense, has many problems. It not only extends the denotation of *Chinese Law*[7] without limit, which causes "great confusion" concerning the concept but also deviates from the basic requirement that it "must be composed of the laws of several states" (Zhang, 1984). It is because Korea, Japan, Vietnam, and some other states fully transplanted Chinese laws and joined this legal system after the Sui and Tang Dynasties in the early seventh century. In the late modern period, because of several reasons—such as the spread of Western Laws to the East and China's economic, political, and legal reforms—the Chinese Legal Family began to disintegrate during the late Qing Dynasty when the government revised the laws. This also happened in Korea and Vietnam around the same time. In Japan, this legal system already ceased developing as early as 1880, shortly after the outbreak of the *Meiji Restoration*, when Japan promulgated a Westernized Criminal Code, which was the result of learning from French criminal law.[8] As some scholars pointed out, "observing the fate of the Chinese Legal Family in East Asian countries, the revision of laws in the late Qing Dynasty could be considered to be the final disintegration of the legal system in its home country" (Zhang, 1999a, 1999b).

Most scholars hold that the Chinese Legal Family is a collective term for the Chinese laws represented by *Tang Lv Shu Yi* (Commentary on Tang Code, 唐律疏议) and the laws following them, adopted by various countries (Yang, 2012, 282). Rao Ai deems that "compared with Civil Law and Common Law, the Chinese Legal Family can be defined as a general term for the laws represented by the Tang Code, based on the ancient Chinese ethical law, and adopted by a series of Fengjian countries in East

---

[6] However, Chen Chaobi did not mention what "Chinese Law in a narrow sense" is. See Chen (1980).

[7] Similar to Chen Chaobi who holds that the Chinese Legal Family also includes the socialist law after the foundation of the PRC, Hao Tiechuan also holds that "in terms of the nature, current Chinese legal system is socialist law, but considering the culture, the existing Chinese legal system has its unique features. It is suitable to call it the Chinese Legal Family." See Hao (1997, 15).

[8] In 1873, when enacting *Kaitei Ritsurei* (Criminal Code Amendment, 改定律例), Japan learnt from the Chinese criminal code. But when enacting criminal law in 1880, Japan invited Boissonade (1825–1910), a French legal scholar to lead the work and introduced comprehensively the Western legislative achievements.

Asia and Southeast Asia. Therefore, just as the definitions of Western Common Law and Civil Law conform to the theory concerning the concept of the legal family, the definition of the Chinese Legal Family also conforms to the theory concerning the concept of the legal system" (Rao, 2000). He Qinhua and Kong Jing also say that "The so-called Chinese Legal Family is a collective term for the legal systems developed during the Fengjian period under the specific social and historical conditions in ancient China, fundamentally featuring a combination of Li (Ritual Propriety) and Fa (law), with written criminal codes as the core content, and represented by *Tang Lv Shu Yi*, and the legal systems imitating the Chinese legal systems adopted by East Asian countries" (He & Kong, 2005).[9]

Overall, the Chinese Legal Family is an international or regional concept, not just a single-country concept. Although its origin, prosperity, and maturity are all based on its development in its home country, China, the analysis and elaboration of its essence cannot be limited to only China but would have to include Korea, Japan, and Vietnam. This is a prerequisite for analyzing and determining the essence of the Chinese Legal Family.

2.3 *Features of the Chinese Legal Family*

The features of the Chinese Legal Family are probably the most commonly discussed topic in the articles concerning the Chinese Legal Family. However, as mentioned above, the features of the Chinese Legal Family discussed by many scholars are actually the features of ancient Chinese laws. Although it is the foundation and backbone of the Chinese Legal Family, they are not the same. For example, Chen Guyuan holds that the formation of the Chinese Legal Family can date back to the legislative reform conducted by Li Kui (455BC–395BC), the regent adviser to Marquess Wen of Wei. He promulgated *Fa Jing* (Law Classics, 法经). It can also date back to Emperor Yao, around 2300 BC. The features of the Chinese Legal Family can be summarized into eight aspects: centering on the ethics and rites, duty-based, attachment to families, emphasizing childcare and education facilities, advocating Ren (benevolence, 仁) and Shu (empathy, 恕), reduction of litigation burden, flexible law, and judicial accountability (Chen, 2011, 46 + 54–59).

Since the 1980s, Chinese scholars such as Chen Chaobi, Hou Wenfu, Zhang Libo, Jia Guofa, Liu Hainian, Yang Yifan, Qiao Wei, Xu Zhongming, Ai Yongming, Peng Fenglian, Wang Limin, Liu Guang'an, Yang Zhengrong, Zhu Yong, Zhang Zhongqiu, Ma Xiaohong, Xu Xiangmin, Chen, Liu Yuanzheng, Zhang Hongjie, He Qinhua, and Kong Jing, gradually became unanimous about the features of the Chinese Legal Family. These features include highlighting the statutory codes, combining Li and Fa, emphasizing family ethics, no differentiation between civil and criminal laws, and integrating laws of all areas. Some scholars further emphasized and analyzed

---

9 Some scholars also define the Chinese Legal Family from the geographic range; for instance, Wang Limin. See Wang (2001).

a certain aspect of the features of the Chinese Legal Family. For example, Zeng Hui and Li Xin hold that a distinctive feature of the Chinese Legal Family is that it is closed and analyzed the reasons for this (Zeng, 1987; Li, 1994). Fan Zhongxin holds that the features of the Chinese Legal Family are rooted in its inner spirit, the family ethics. They are special ethics that differentiate between the civil ethics in Common Law and Civil Law and the religious ethics in Hindu Law and Sharia (Fan, 1999). Hao Tiechuan proposes the more novel views that the features of the Chinese Legal Family can be summarized in three points: legalized (Legalism, 法家) codes, Confucianized (Confucianism, 儒家) judges, and mythologized public consciousness (Hao, 1997, 25 + 57 + 87).

In conducting research on the features of the Chinese Legal Family, Zhang Jinfan is one of the hardest-working scholars. He devoted several decades to it. In 1980, He pointed out in an article that there are five features of the Chinese Legal Family: (1) the law was decided by the rulers, (2) the law was influenced by Confucian ethics and legal concepts, (3) family values were adopted, (4) civil and criminal laws were not divided and all laws were integrated, and (5) apart from codes, some law existed in other forms (Zhang, 1980). In 1984, Zhang Jinfan published another article adding to and enriching the features of the Chinese Legal Family. The added features included that actions failing to follow Li were penalized, legislative and judicial powers were both exercised by the central government, administrative and judicial institutions were unified, the laws of various ethnic groups were integrated, and the forms of law were diversified (Zhang, 1984). In 1999, in an article elucidating the features of the Chinese Legal Family, Zhang Jinfan expressed the view that the features and merits also include that the legal obligations were unified with family obligations, the governance function of the law was based on a combination of the law and the officials, education and punishment were comprehensively used, and statutory law and case law were complementary (Zhang, 1999a, 1999b). In 2005, he again wrote an article discussing the features of the Chinese Legal Family. This time, he proposed eight features, adding two others to the previous list: (1) the legal system centered on physiocracy, and (2) the legal model featured an absolute monarchy (Zhang, 2005). In a recent speech, Zhang Jinfan proposed some further ideas about the features and merits of the Chinese Legal Family, including people-oriented thoughts, the experience of comprehensive governance, and emphasis on both ruling the people and ruling the officials (Zhang, 2017, 6–7).

3 Formation and Development of the Chinese Legal Family

The formation of the Chinese Legal Family was a process by which the laws of ancient China were adopted by other countries and became the main content and form of their own national laws. Ancient Chinese laws are the core of the legal family. Several countries transplanted Chinese laws and thus became members of the Chinese Legal Family.

3.1 Formation of the Chinese Legal Family

When did the above-mentioned process happen? Currently available materials suggest that the formation of the Chinese Legal Family can be dated to the late sixth century and early seventh century when the Sui and Tang legal systems were mature and exported to neighboring countries, such as Korea, Japan, and Vietnam.

In 581 AD, Emperor Yang Jian (541–604) founded the Sui Dynasty and ended the Southern Dynasty Chen in 589. China was once again united by one ruler. He made great achievements in legislation and institutionalization in a short time by inheriting the legislative achievements of the Northern Qi Dynasty and Northern Zhou Dynasty. In 583, he promulgated *Sui Lv* (Sui Code, 隋律), which is also called *Kaihuang Lv* (Kaihuang Code, 开皇律), laying the foundation for the formation of the Chinese Legal Family. After the rise of the Tang Dynasty, using *Kaihuang Lv* as a blueprint, Emperor Gaozu Li Yuan (566–635) made the first law of the Tang Dynasty, *Wude Lv* (Wude Code, 武德律). Subsequently, Emperor Taizong Li Shimin (598–649) and Emperor Gaozong Li Zhi (628–683) promulgated *Zhenguan Lv* (Zhenguan Code, 贞观律) and *Yonghui Lv* (Yonghui Code, 永徽律), respectively. Later, because the provisions in *Yonghui Lv* were too simple, Emperor Gaozong Li Zhi ordered Zhangsun Wuji and some other officials to interpret and give commentaries on each provision of the Code. As a result, *Tang Lv Shu Yi* was promulgated in 653, which was the earliest and most complete existing Fengjian code in ancient China (including 12 Chapters, 30 volumes, and 500 articles). During the Kaiyuan Era (713–741) in the reign of Emperor Xuanzong (685–762) of the Tang Dynasty, *Tang Lv* was revised and improved.

In addition to Lv (Code, 律), several other forms of law were adopted, such as Ling (Decree, 令), Ge (Rules, 格), and Shi (Regulations, 式). For example, during the Wude Era (618–626), Emperor Li Yuan ordered the officials to draft laws (Liu, 1975, 2134), which were improved later by multiple revisions in the Zhenguan (627–649), Yonghui (650–655), Chuigong (685–688), Shenlong (705–707), and Kaiyuan Eras. The two revisions during the Zhenguan and Kaiyuan Eras were of special importance. According to *Jiu Tang Shu: Xing Fa Zhi* (The Old Book of Tang: Treatise on Punishment and Law, 旧唐书·刑法志), when Emperor Taizong reigned, he ordered Fang Xuanling and some other officials to "make Ling of 1,590 articles in 30 volumes, which were promulgated in the first lunar month of the 11th year of the Zhenguan Era (637)" (Liu, 1975, 2138). In the 22th year of the Kaiyuan Era (734), Emperor Xuanzong ordered Li Linfu, Niu Xianke, and Wang Jingcong to "revise Ge and Ling … complement, delete, and compile the old Ge, Shi, Lv, Ling, and Chi (Imperial Orders, 敕), in total 7026 articles. … Among them, 1324 articles were deleted, 2180 articles were revised according to the context, and 3594 articles remained unchanged. … [as a result] 12-volume Lv, 30-volume Lv Shu (Commentary on Lv, 律疏), and 30-volume Ling were made" (Liu 1975, 2150). According to Volume VI, Shang Shu Xing Bu (Ministry of Justice in the Department of State Affairs, 尚书刑部) of *Tang Liu Dian* (Six Codes of Tang Dynasty, 唐六典), there were 27 types of Ling; in total, 30 volumes (Li, 2014, 183). The Ling of the Tang Dynasty basically was lost to history in China. Fortunately, there are two books, *Ryo-no-gige* (Commentary on the Administrative Code, 令义解) and *Ryo-no-shuge* (Collected Commentaries on the Administrative Codes, 令集解), compiled by Japanese scholars in the eighth century. Tang Ling has been well preserved in Japan. Professor Niida Noboru (1904–1966) of the University of Tokyo worked on the two books and restored 715 articles of Ling.[10] In 1933, he published a book, *Tang Ling Shi Yi* (Gleanings of Tang Ling, 唐令拾遗), which presents a general picture of Tang Ling.[11]

In the Tang Dynasty, besides Lv and Ling, Ge and Shi were also important sources of law. Generally, Ge was the compilation of the imperial edicts. According to Volume VI, Shang Shu Xing Bu of the *Tang Liu Dian*, "there were three sections of *Lv Ling Gu Shi* (Compilation of Rules, 律令故事) developed in the Jianwu Era of the Han Dynasty (25–56), all of which were about the penalty system. Jia Chong and some others of the Jin Dynasty drafted Lv and Ling and compiled the articles of Zhi (Imperial Orders, 制) and Zhao (Imperial Orders, 诏). They summarized them into *Gu Shi* (Rules, 故事) of 30 volumes. It was implemented together with Lv and Ling. The Liang Dynasty modified *Gu Shi* and made it 30 volumes of *Liang Ke* (The Rules of the Liang Dynasty, 梁科). The compilation work was done by Cai Fadu. The Chen Dynasty followed the Liang Dynasty. The Northern Wei Dynasty chose 'Ge' to replace 'Ke' and created *Linzhi Ge* (麟趾格). It was so named because it was made in the Linzhi Palace. The Northern Qi Dynasty followed the Northern Wei and created *Quan Ge* (权格), implemented together with Lv and Ling" (Li, 2014, 185). Ge was first called Gu Shi, then Ke, and later replaced by Ge. Its origins were the Zhi and Zhao (imperial orders) by the emperors. At the beginning of the Tang Dynasty, in 619, Emperor Gaozu made 53 articles of Ge. Since the Yonghui Era, Ge was divided into Liusi Ge (Ge that was not issued publicly but only available for officials, 留司格) and Sanban Ge (Ge that was publicly issued, 散颁格). The latter was used more often (Ma, 1987). After the Kaiyuan Era, the Tang Dynasty developed a new form of law, the Gehou Chi (Compilation of Imperial Orders to Supplement Ge, 格后敕), which became the main form of the law of Ge during the late Tang Dynasty.

In the Tang Dynasty, the Shi were the rules governing the activities of the national administrative agencies at all levels and the legal provisions concerning official documents and procedures between superiors and subordinates. According to *Tang Liu Dian*, in the 10th year of the Datong Era of the Western Wei Dynasty (544), Shangshu (Minister in ancient China, 尚书) Su Chuo (498–546) was ordered to collect the general rules of various government departments. "The 36 articles were amended, tailored and complemented to 5 volumes and named *Datong Shi* (大统式)." (Li, 2014, 185). In the Yonghui Era of the Tang Dynasty (650–655), the 14 volumes of *Yonghui Shi* (永徽式) were made, and later the 20 volumes of *Chuigong Shi* (垂拱式), *Shenlong Shi* (神龙式), and *Kaiyuan Shi* (开元式) separately. The "names of the subordinate departments of Shangshu Department, Mishu (division in charge

[10] This equals a half of the total articles of Tang Ling. According to *Jiu Tang Shu* (volume 50)—Xing Fa Zhi, and *Tang Liu Dian* (volume 6)—Shang Shu Xing Bu, there were 1590 articles of Ling in the Zhenguan Era, and 1546 articles of Ling in the Kaiyuan Era.

[11] The Book has been translated into Chinese. See Niida (1989).

of writing history,秘书), Taichang (division in charge of etiquette and ceremony,太常), Sinong (division of agriculture,司农), Guanglu (division in charge of cookery,光禄), Taipu (division in charge of horse breeding,太仆), Taifu (division in charge of storage and trade,太府), Shaofu (division in charge of crafts,少府), Jianmen (division in charge of palace security,监门), Suwei (division in charge of military defense of the capital,宿卫), Jizhang (division in charge of accountancy,计帐) were adopted as the headings of the sections, and in total it included 33 sections" (Li, 2014, 185). In the Tang Dynasty, Shi was normally revised with the amendment of Lv and Ling. However, after the Kaiyuan Era, it was no longer revised. The Shi had a certain degree of coercive power. People who violated it would not only be subject to administrative punishment but might also be accused of conducting a "crime of violating Shi" and be punished with 40 floggings according to Lv (Zhangsun, 2008, 344). Different opinions exist in academic circles regarding the nature of the Tang Shi. The traditional view is that the Shi were the implementation rules and official documents and procedures of the national agencies. Some scholars hold that the Tang Shi was the rule implementing the Lv, Ling, and Ge (Feng, 1992). Some other scholars hold that the Shi were not official documents and procedures. Instead, the Ling and Shi were both rules with the nature of administrative law instead of being guidelines and implementation rules, respectively. This book holds that the Tang Shi was the rule implementing Ling. The contents of Shi included detailed rules for the national agencies to conduct administrative management and judicial activities. Official documents and procedures were not covered by the Shi.

In the Tang Dynasty, in addition to the Lv, Ling, Ge, and Shi, the *Tang Liu Dian* was also compiled and finalized between the 10th year (722) and 26th year (738) of the Kaiyuan Era. The nature of the *Tang Liu Dian* has been the subject of great controversy in modern times. Some scholars believe that the *Tang Liu Dian* was the administrative code of the Tang Dynasty, while other scholars do not agree.[12] In our view, from the perspective of the legislative procedure of the Tang Dynasty or its contents, the *Tang Liu Dian* is not the administrative code of the Tang Dynasty. It is not even a law at all. The *Tang Liu Dian* is only an officially compiled classic borrowing the style and layout of the *Zhou Li* (Rites of the Zhou Dynasty, 周礼) for the purpose of demonstrating the grand system of the Tang Dynasty (Qian & Li, 1989).[13]Therefore, the Dian (*Tang Liu Dian*) is not a form of legislation of the Tang Dynasty (Li, 2011, 177–178).

With the formation of the legal system, legal education and research also fully developed. After the establishment of the Sui Dynasty, a system of selecting officials through imperial examination in different categories and an investigation of policies was established, abolishing the nine-rank system. In the central government, the Guozijian (国子监)—an administrative agency specializing in the management of education—was established, and legal studies became part of it (Xu, 1975, 182). After the establishment of the Tang Dynasty, Keju (科举), the imperial examination system for selecting officials, was formally established. At that time, there were two types

---

[12] For a brief review of the different opinions on the nature of *Tang Liu Dian*, see Xu (1998).

[13] For further discission, see Qian (1996a, 1996b), from 157; Li (2004).

of examination, the Changke (Regular Examination, 常科) and Zhiju (Additional Examination, 制举). In the Changke, there is an examination called the *Mingfa* (Knowledge of the Law, 明法). An independent and mature official legal education system was formed.[14] Although legal education in the Tang Dynasty was intermittent, its perfect and thorough system design laid the foundation for more than 1300 years of legal education in the Chinese Legal Family. It was in such an atmosphere that the country attached great importance to legislation, the judiciary, and legal education, and the famous book and code of law, *Tang Lv Shu Yi*, was finally issued. This marked the heyday of jurisprudence in ancient China and laid a solid foundation for the legal studies of the Chinese Legal Family.

The Sui and Tang Dynasties developed a legal system with the Lv, Ling, Ge, and Shi as the sources of law and an educational and scholarly system concentrating on the education of law and legal studies. Its influence quickly spread to neighboring countries such as Korea, Japan, and Vietnam. As a result, the Chinese Legal Family was established, with Chinese laws as the core and adopted by the neighboring countries as the basis for formulating their own laws. For instance, adopting the codified laws of the ancient Chinese Sui and Tang Dynasties, Japan made their *Taiho Code* (大宝律令) (701) and *Yoro Code* (养老律令) (718). Vietnam was called Annan in the Tang Dynasty. "The laws adopted by Annan in this era are probably based on the law of the Tang Dynasty" (Tatsumi, 1999, 417). Simultaneously, following the legal education system of the Sui and Tang Dynasties of China, legal education based on the *Mingfa* examination (明法科) was also fostered in Japan and Korea. For example, Japan established its system of the *Myobo* examination in the fifth year of the Jinki Era (728) during the reign of Emperor Shomu.[15] Borrowing from the legal hermeneutics in ancient China, Japan developed its own jurisprudence, compiled, and created high-level results, such as *Ryo-no-gige* (834) and *Ryo-no-shuge* (868). Meanwhile, a number of families of legal scholars formed, such as the Sanuki family, Koremune family, Sakagami family, and Nakahara family, which brought the Japanese law study (*Myobodo*) into its heyday around the tenth century. In Korea, according to the *San Guo Shi Ji: Xin Luo Ben Ji* (Samguk Sagi: the Silla Record, 三国史记·新罗本纪), "in the 17th year of King Gyeongdeok, two Doctors of Law (officials of legal education) were arranged" (Yang, 1999, 28). It was reasonable for Korea to develop a Chinese-style legal study.

---

[14] Volume 15 titled Selection of Officials of *Tong Dian* (Comprehensive Statutes, 通典) records that "the regular exams include Xiucai (秀才), Mingjing (明经), Jinshi (进士), *Mingfa* (明法), Shu (书), Suan (算). Schools can be found from the capital to counties." See Du (1988, 353).

[15] According to the general opinion in Japanese academic circles, Japan set the *Mingfa* (*Myobo*) Examination in the 5th year of the Jinki Era of Emperor Shomu (728). However, Mitsuo Riko holds that *Mingfa* (*Myobo*) Examination was set in the Wado Era in the reign of Empress Genmei, based on the fact that in the historical records of the Wado Era (708–715), the term *Myobo Hakase* (officials of legal study in Japan, 明法博士) had already appeared here and there, as well as the related terms Ryoshi (Teachers for Ling, 令师) and Ritsushi (Teachers for Lv, 律师). See Riko (1967, 117).

3.2 Development of the Chinese Legal Family

The Chinese Legal Family formed in the Sui and Tang Dynasties continued to develop after the establishment of the Song Dynasty.

In terms of legal concepts, the basic thoughts were formed in the Sui and Tang Dynasties, such as people-oriented thoughts, emphasis on educating and transforming people, moral guidance and punishment, tempering justice with mercy, simplifying laws and limiting prohibitions, prudent and light punishments, fairly deciding the punishment and rewards, governing officials according to the law, and adapting laws to the times. After the establishment of the Song Dynasty, the legal concepts continued to develop. For example, the rulers of the early Song Dynasty and a group of important officials such as Bao Zheng (999–1062) attached great importance to people-oriented thoughts. Bao Zheng repeatedly emphasized that "the country owns the whole world, and therefore should nurture the people" (Bao, 2008, 160). "People are the foundation of the country. They are where the money should be used and can affect the safety of the country. At present, the most important thing is to comfort them" (Bao, 2008, 144). "Rulers should treat people with leniency to consolidate the foundation of the country. Without a solid foundation, the country will not be peaceful" (Bao, 2008, 91). Wang Anshi (1021–1086) elaborated on this issue more fully. He believed that in order to reach good governance of the country, there must be "good laws." To decide whether a law was good or bad, the key was to observe whether it benefited the people, the economic development, and the prosperity of the country with a powerful army. If a law "seizes what people want and makes them unable to feed themselves," it would be a failure (Wang, 1999, 274). These legal concepts centering on people-oriented thoughts were later recognized and emphasized by the rulers of the early Ming and Qing Dynasties and became the basic legal worldview for them to maintain and consolidate their rule.

In terms of the form of law, the Song Dynasty inherited Lv, Ling, Ge, and Shi from the Tang Dynasty and Xing Lv Tong Lei (Code, 刑律统类, also called Xing Tong, 刑统), Bianchi (Compiled Imperial Orders, 编敕), Zhi (Official Documents, 制), Chi (Imperial Orders, 敕), and Xuan (Announcements, 宣) from the late Tang Dynasty and the Five Dynasties. It further developed Yubi (Emperor's Decision, 御笔), Duanli (Judgments, 断例), Shenming (Interpretations, 申明), Tiaoli (Regulations, 条例), and Tiao Fa Shi Lei (Compiled Orders and Interpretations, 条法事类).[16] Among them, Bianchi and Tiao Fa Shi Lei were the most important. Bianchi was the compilation of the emperors' edicts and orders to facilitate judicial trials. It was a kind of legislative activity and an important form of law. It normally had supremacy over Lv. The frequency, number, and variety of the amendments to Bianchi in the

[16] On the 24th day of the 6th lunar month of the 2nd year of the Yuanfeng Era (1079), Emperor Shenzong provided a new definition for (Bian) chi, Ling, Ge, and Shi. That is, "Ge sets standards for people to adjust their activities, Shi sets regulations for people to follow, Ling stipulates forbidden matters that have not been carried out, and Chi stipulates punishments for violations that have been done. Officials to amend laws should keep this in mind and follow these principles to benefit posterity." See Xu (2014, 8223). For more detailed comments, see Dai (2003, 83–87).

Song Dynasty were unprecedented. According to the incomplete records of *Song Shi: Yi Wen Zhi* (History of Song: Treatise on Literature, 宋史·艺文志), there were more than 80 variations of Bianchi in the Song Dynasty.[17] Tiao Fa Shi Lei was another form of law, which categorized legal norms by matters—Chi, Ling, Ge, and Shi were compiled into different volumes. Bianchi comprehensively compiled Chi in chronological order but faced the problem that provisions on the same matter appeared in different sections. Hence, it was inconvenient to use. Therefore, in the Southern Song Dynasty, the government categorized the related Chi, Ling, Ge, and Shi into different volumes based on matters. Tiao Fa Shi Lei, a new form of law, was created. It not only helped improve the internal coordination of Chi, Ling, Ge, and Shi but also facilitated the judicial officials' retrieval and application of the law. Sequentially, *Chunxi Tiao Fa Shi Lei* (Tiao Fa Shi Lei of Chunxi Era [1174–1189], 淳熙条法事类), *Qingyuan Tiao Fa Shi Lei* (Tiao Fa Shi Lei of Qingyuan Era [1195–1201], 庆元条法事类), and *Chunyou Tiao Fa Shi Lei* (Tiao Fa Shi Lei of Chunyou Era [1241–1252], 淳佑条法事类) were issued in the Song Dynasty. So far, only the Qingyuan Tiao Fa Shi Lei that was promulgated by Emperor Ningzong of the Song Dynasty (1168–1224) during his reign has been preserved. It was mainly composed of laws and regulations concerning administrative, fiscal, tax, economic, and criminal issues. There were 80 volumes in the original, but only 36 volumes remain (Zang, 2003, 64–65).

In the Yuan Dynasty, when making laws, they followed the guiding ideology that "the ancient and modern times are different, so it is not necessary to follow the former laws, but the ones that are suitable for the present should be adopted" (Song, 1976, 430). Based on this ideology, there were no systematic and large-scale activities to draw up codes of law. The Yuan Dynasty inherited the forms of law, such as the Lv, Ling, Ge, and Duanli, from the Tang and Song Dynasties and sequentially promulgated *Zhiyuan Xin Ge* (New Ge of the Zhiyuan Era, 至元新格)[18] and *Fengxian*

[17] Note: The collections of Chi, Ling, Ge, and Shi, as well as the separated Ling, Ge, and Shi that were made after the Yuanfeng Era in the Song Dynasty were not included. See Dai (2003, 77).

[18] In the 28th year of the Zhiyuan Era (1291) in the reign of Emperor Shizu, Zhiyuan Xin Ge was promulgated. This is the first code enacted after the unification of the Yuan Dynasty, as well as the basic law of the Yuan Dynasty, which is a combination of various laws. "In general, it just adopted the rules that were applied at that time and compiled the articles into Tiao Ge, not comparing them with the old laws." The full text of Zhiyuan Xin Ge has been lost. Only 96 articles remained in Tong Zhi Tiao Ge (Tiao and Ge in Da Yuan Tong Zhi, 通制条格) and Yuan Dian Zhang. In addition, basic contents of Zhiyuan Xin Ge such as the "ten matters" can be seen from the Guidebook for Officials by Xu Yuanrui of the Yuan Dynasty. "Ten matters" include Gonggui(公规), Xuange(选格), Zhimin(治民), Licai(理财), Fuyi(赋役), Kecheng(课程), Cangku(仓库), Zaozuo(造作), Fangdao(防盗), and Chayu(察狱). Gonggui means regular rules that have to be followed by the government and officials; Xuange means standards for selecting officials; Zhimin means governance and nurture of the people and settlements of disputes; Licai means to guarantee the finance and stabilize commodity prices; Fuyi means to collect the tax and guarantee appropriate corvee; Kecheng means to manage the tax on salt and aspergillus oryzae; Cangku means to carefully manage the income and expenses and follow the law to store materials; Zaozuo means to supervise construction and verify materials; Fangdao means to forbid and eliminate crimes; Chayu means to make judgments and put criminals in jail. See Xu (2012, 199).

Hong Gang (Framework of Legal Institutions, 风宪宏纲).[19] Later, based on the above two codes, the government compiled the Tiaoge (Articles of Ge, 条格), Zhaoling (Imperial Orders, 诏令), and Duanli under Emperor Shizu of the Yuan Dynasty (1215–1294). During the reign of Emperor Yingzong (1320–1323), the *Da Yuan Sheng Zheng Guo Chao Dian Zhang* (Statutes of the Sacred Governed the State of the Great Yuan Dynasty, 大元圣政国朝典章, abbreviated as *Yuan Dian Zhang,* 元典章) (1320–1323) and *Da Yuan Tong Zhi* (General Regulations of the Great Yuan Dynasty, 大元通制) (1323), two great codes of law, were completed. The former was a compilation of Zhaoling, Tiaoge, and precedents concerning the political, economic, military, and legal issues of the more than 50 years since Emperor Shizu. It was categorized into different titles and subtitles, comprised of *Qianji* (the Previous Volume, 前集) and *Xinji* (the New Volume, 新集). The latter, *Da Yuan Tong Zhi,* includes 20 sections and 2539 articles. It can be divided into four main parts: Tiaoge, Duanli, Zhizhao (Imperial Orders, 制诏), and Bielei (Other Categories, 别类), among which, Tiaoge and Duanli being the most important. Tiaoge was equivalent to Ling and Duanli to Lv. These two codes, especially *Yuan Dian Zhang*, adopted a method of categorizing the law based on the six ministries in ancient China. It directly affected *Da Ming Lv* (The Great Ming Code, 大明律), which also divided the code into six sections and was later adopted into *Da Qing Lv Li* (The Great Qing Code, 大清律例).

In the Ming and Qing Dynasties, the form of law underwent changes. In addition to the Lv, Ling, and Dian, there was now also Gao (Imperial Orders, 诰). Li (Regulations, 例) was placed in a more important position. For example, during the 18th year and 20th year of the Hongwu Era of the Ming Dynasty (1385–1387), Emperor Zhu Yuanzhang formulated *Da Ming Lv*. Furthermore, to manage the officials, warn the subjects, and improve the social atmosphere, he personally compiled and promulgated *Yuzhi Dagao* (Imperial Orders, 御制大诰), *Yuzhi Dagao Xubian* (Imperial Orders II, 御制大诰续编), *Yuzhi Dagao Sanbian* (Imperial Orders III, 御制大诰三编) and *Dagao Wuchen* (Imperial Orders IV: Military, 大诰武臣). There were a total of 236 articles on Gao. Since Gao was made by the emperor himself, it had supremacy over the other laws and was an important source of law in the early Ming Dynasty. Compared with *Da Ming Lv*, the distinctive characteristics of Dagao are heavy punishments, extra punishments not provided by the law, various kinds of torture, and management of officials by strict rules. Another example is that in the Qing Dynasty, Lv and Li were combined into one code, *Da Qing Lv Li,* which elevated the Li (例, also called Tiaoli, 条例) to its highest position in history. Li was now formal legal norms created by certain procedures and no longer precedents or

[19] When Emperor Renzong reigned (1312–1320), Fengxian Hong Gang was produced. It is a Fengjian supervision law concerning the legal institutions and official management. Fengxian means legal institutions in origin, which was used to indicate the management of officials for supervisory officers in ancient China. In the 2nd year of the Yanyou Era (1315), laws were made following the Tiao and Ge made by former generations of Yuan Dynasty, including three parts, Zhaozhi, Tiaoge, and Duanli. It was finished in the second year but not applied. Later, the then applied rules and provisions concerning conduct and discipline were compiled, and Fengxian Hong Gang was produced. It was promulgated as specialized supervision law.

judgments. When the relevant departments deemed it necessary to make new Tiaoli, they would draw up Chengong Tiaozou (memorials to the throne, 臣工条奏), such as Zouben (奏本) and Tiben (题本), and submit them to the emperor. After obtaining the emperor's approval or authorization, they would formally draft the text of Tiaoli and issue it to the world. Occasionally, the government would sort out, delete, and revise Tiaoli promulgated in the previous periods. The provisions that had proved to have matured with time and practice were incorporated into codes and became part of the main law of the country. Therefore, Liang Qichao (1873–1929) held that "Lv is the fundamental law that never changes, while Li is the detailed law that can be adapted at any time" (Liang, 1936, 37).

In other countries of the Chinese Legal Family, namely Korea, Vietnam, and Japan, the laws were also developing and changing. For instance, in the Goryeo Dynasty (after 918) founded by Wang Geon (877–943), both their legal system and legal research generally imitated the Tang Dynasty. In addition, *Tang Lv Shu Yi* was applied in the Goryeo Dynasty simultaneously. According to the preamble of the *Gaoli Shi: Xing Fa Zhi* (History of Goryeo: Treatise on Punishment and Law, 高丽史·刑法志), "the institution of the first generation of the Goryeo mostly imitated the Tang Dynasty; as for the punishment and law, the Goryeo adopted Tang Lv as well, applying it according to the specific situations" (Zhang, 2016, 43). In Vietnam, Le Loi (1385–1433) established the Ly Dynasty in 1428. It was also influenced by Tang Lv. The laws of the Ly Dynasty were significantly affected by *Tang Lv Shu Yi*, particularly in the legal framework, penalty system, and criminal law principles (Yang 1999, 418). In Japan, the Ritsuryo system began to falter in the late tenth century and was further less effective after the establishment of the Kamakura shogunate in 1192, since it promulgated its own codes such as the *Goseibai Shikimoku* (the Code of Conduct for Samurai, 御成敗式目) (1232). However, from the perspective of legal theory, the Ritsuryo system established by the *Taiho Code* and *Yoro Code* was still the legal basis in Japan. In the Edo period (1603–1867), Japan developed its own bakuhan legal system (Japanese feudal political system in the Edo period, 幕藩体制) based on the adoption of *Da Ming Lv* and *Da Qing Lv Li* from China. A number of codes, such as the *Kujikata Osadamegaki* (The Tokugawa Law Code, 公事方御定書) (1742), were issued. Until the Meiji Restoration in 1868, when Japan formulated and promulgated the *Shinritsu Koryo* (Outline of the New Criminal Code, 新律綱領) (1870) and *Kaitei Ritsurei* (Criminal Code Amendment, 改定律例) (1873), it still imitated and learned from the Chinese legal system (Hiroshi et al., 2010, 108 + 212 + 290–291). Therefore, after the Middle Ages, although the form of law in Japan had changed with the appearance of Shikimoku (式目), Osadamegaki (御定書), and others, the contents of the law were still greatly influenced by the law of China, the mother country of the Chinese Legal Family. In terms of legal education and jurisprudence, Japan also fully absorbed and borrowed Chinese legal education and legal hermeneutics in the Edo period.

4 Disintegration of the Chinese Legal Family

The Opium War that broke out in 1840 ended with the defeat of China. Since then, Western thoughts, concepts, and various institutions and cultures, including laws, began to be introduced into China and eventually contributed to the disintegration of the Chinese Legal Family.[20] The specific process and contents are discussed in detail in Chapter 4. Here, only some clues and issues of the collapse are provided, which mainly include four aspects.

4.1 Spread of Western Legal Concepts in China

Western legal concepts are the basic views on the law of the Western enlightenment philosophers in the bourgeois age. The core includes: the law is the embodiment of the public will; the purpose of the law is to seek happiness for the people; the law is supreme (the rule of law); states are the product of social contract and are created by the people; the people are the masters of the government (sovereignty rests with the people); all people are born equal and free and enjoy inalienable natural rights; everyone is equal before the law; freedom is to do what is permitted by law; power must be separated and mutually restricted; crimes and punishments are legally prescribed; crimes and punishments should be compatible; punishments must be humane; judicial independence should be respected; everyone who has been charged shall be presumed innocent until proved guilty. These legal concepts have been propagated, confirmed, and provided by classic legal documents, such as the *American Declaration of Independence* (1776), the *American Constitution* (1787), the *French Declaration of the Rights of Man and of the Citizen* (1789), the *French Civil Code* (1804), and the *French Criminal Code* (1810). They began to take root in European and American countries and spread to other countries and regions in the world. China has also been affected by these concepts since the 1830s.

In the 12th year of the Daoguang Era (1832), the American missionary W. Milne (1785–1822) publicized the concepts of equality before the law and rights of defense by lawyers in his book *Brief Account of the English Character* (Chinese version).[21] In July 1833, in Guangzhou, Prussian missionary K.F.A. Gutzlaff (1803–1851) launched the first Chinese periodical in mainland China, the *Dongxiyang Kao Meiyue Tongji Zhuan* (东西洋考每月统记传, *Eastern Western Monthly Magazine*).

---

[20] The disintegration of the Chinese Legal Family was mainly caused by the decline of Chinese law. It fell behind compared with the advanced countries in the world and therefore, countries that yearned for Chinese laws have stopped following China. Instead, they began to follow the Western countries or other more advanced countries. As a result, in the Chinese Legal Family, there was only one country, China. It can no longer exist as a legal family. Moreover, the former member countries in the Chinese Legal Family surpassed the mother country concerning the legal institution after it abandoned the old legal system and learned from the laws of other countries; for example, Japan.

[21] The copy of the book was provided by Mr. Xiong Yuezhi from the Institute of History of the Shanghai Academy of Social Science.

It further introduced and disseminated Western concepts, such as the rule of law, separation of powers, equality before the law, judicial independence, and juries (Aihanzhe et al., 1997). In 1864, American missionary A. P. William Martin (1872–1916) translated and published the book *Elements of International Law*, written by an American international law scholar, Henry Wheaton (1785–1848).[22] In this book, Martin introduced the concepts of natural law and rights to China.[23] In 1868, the *Jiaohui Xinbao* (教会新报, *The Church News*) by American missionary Young John Allen (1836–1907) started its publication in Shanghai—later, the newspaper changed its name to Wanguo Gongbao (万国公报, *The Chinese Globe Magazine*) in September 1874—which also published a large number of articles introducing Western concepts of constitutionalism, the rule of law, and judicial independence.

Influenced by Western missionaries and the eastward spread of Western culture, progressive Chinese began to pay attention to, advocate, and expound on Western legal concepts. For example, Lin Zexu (1785–1850) once organized staff to translate some chapters of the book *The Law of Nations*, written by the famous Swiss international jurist E. De Vattel (1714–1767), into Chinese.[24] The concepts of sovereignty and the rule of law can be found in this book. Later, in 1842, Wei Yuan (1794–1857) finished his book *Hai Guo Tu Zhi* (海国图志, Atlas and Annals of Overseas Countries). Liang Tingzhan (1796–1861) finalized *Heshengguo Shuo* (合省国说, Introduction to the United States) in 1844. Xu Jiyu's (1795–1873) *Ying Huan Zhi Lue* (瀛寰志略, World Geography) (1848),[25] Feng Guifen's (1809–1874) *Xiaobinlu Kang Yi* (校邠庐抗议, Comments in Xiaobinlu) (1861), Wang Tao's (1828–1897)

---

[22] wheaton's original work is *Elements of International Law*, published in 1836, and Ding Weiliang named it *The Public Law of Nations* when he translated it.

[23] Regarding the term "权利 (right)" used in Chinese, most Chinese and Japanese scholars believe that it came from Japan and was created by Japanese in modern times, corresponding to "regt" in Dutch and "right" in English. For example, the famous Japanese jurist Takeyoshi Kawashima holds this viewpoint in his book *Legal Consciousness of the Japanese People* (Iwanami Shoten, 1967). When I edited Ding Weiliang's translation of the book *Elements of International Law,* I have compared the translation with Wheaton's original English work. I felt that although Ding Weiliang did not define the Chinese word "权利," it is very clear, that "权利" corresponded with the English word "right". After its publication in 1864, *Elements of International Law* was quickly introduced to Japan, and was widely translated and spread. In Japan, the Chinese term "权利" appeared after this. Therefore, although there is no concrete evidence, it is logically plausible that Japanese scholars learned the word "权利" from *Elements of International Law* and introduced it to China at the end of the nineteenth century. As for the response to this discussion in the Chinese academic circles and the analysis of the usage of the word "权利" in Ding Weiliang's work, Li Guilian has provided a more detailed discussion. I will not go into it here. See Li (2002, 437–447).

[24] The book was published in 1758 in French. Its full name is *The Law of Nations: Or Principles of the Law of Nature Applied to the Conduct and Affairs of Nations and Sovereigns* (*Le Droit des Gens* as French abbreviation). It was translated into English in 1759. By 1839, the book had become popular in Western legal circles, and there were more than 10 and 7 versions of translation in Britain and the US, respectively. Lin Zexu organized the translation of Section 94 of Chapter 8 of Volume 1, Sections 100 to 102 of Chapter 8 of Volume 2, Sections 1 and 2 of Chapter 1 of Volume 3, and the related notes of an English version. See Wang (1985).

[25] The title page reads, "Engraved in Wushen Year of Daoguang period (1848), Sir Bi Xingquan and Sir Liu Yupo checked and corrected, Ying Huan Zhi Lue," now kept in the Shanghai Library.

Taoyuan Wen Lu Wai Bian (弢园文录外编, Compilation of Articles in Taoyuan) (1883), Zheng Guanying's (1842–1921) *Sheng Shi Wei Yan* (盛世危言, Warnings in a Flourishing Age), among others, are all representative of this field. Before and after the 1898 Hundred Days' Reform, three giants, Kang Youwei (1858–1927), Liang Qichao (1873–1929), and Yan Fu (1854–1921), also vigorously spread Western legal concepts. By 1901, Shen Jiaben (1840–1913), the official amending laws in the Qing government, finally provided more comprehensive publicity, introduction, and elaboration of Western legal concepts, such as judicial independence, statutory crime and punishment, the presumption of innocence, equality before the law, the rule of law, jury system, public trial, and lawyer defense in a series of memorials to the throne, prefaces and postscripts to various translated codes and legal works, and his writings and treatises.[26] He further fixed these concepts through reforms and revisions of the law, which replaced the traditional legal philosophy concepts in the Chinese Legal Family.

4.2 *Transplant and Localization of the Western Legal Systems*

While adopting Western legal concepts, Shen Jiaben and other legal reformers also began the work of transplanting and localizing the Western legal systems. On the one hand, after Shen Jiaben presided over the Enactment Office (1904) until the 1st of the Xuantong Era (1909), he translated dozens of laws and legal academic works from more than a dozen countries. These included German Criminal Law, Court Law, Civil Procedure Law, Maritime Law, and Nationality Law, Russian Criminal Law, Japanese Criminal Law, Corrected Criminal Law, Army Criminal Law, Naval Criminal Law, Criminal Procedure Law, Tribunal Constitution Law, Commercial Law, Negotiable Instrument Law, and Prison Law, French Criminal Law, Printing Law, and Nationality Law, Dutch Criminal Law, Italian Criminal Law, British Nationality Law, US Nationality Law and Bankruptcy Law, Austrian Nationality Law, Portuguese Nationality Law, and Spanish Nationality Law. Through this approach, Shen Jiaben and others introduced the Western legal systems into China for the reference of the legislature and judicature.

On the other hand, the Enactment Office began to delete old laws and formulate new codes for China. For example, the *Imperial Commercial Law of the Qing Dynasty*, *Trial Regulations for Company Registration*, *Bankruptcy Law*, and *Regulations for Bank Registration* were promulgated in the 29th year of the Guangxu Era (1903). The *Draft Criminal and Civil Procedure Law* was enacted in the 32nd year of the Guangxu Era (1906), and the *Law on Violation of Police Orders* was promulgated in the 34th year of the Guangxu Era. The *Organic Law of Courts*, *Nationality Regulations*, and *Existing Criminal Law of the Qing Dynasty* were promulgated in

[26] Regarding the spread and localization of Western legal concepts in China in the late Qing Dynasty, see He (2006, 3–45).

the 1st year of the Xuantong Era (1909). The *New Criminal Law of the Qing Dynasty*, *Draft Criminal Procedure Law of the Qing Dynasty*, and *Draft Civil Procedure Law of the Qing Dynasty* were promulgated or completed in the 2nd year of the Xuantong Era (1910). The *Draft Civil Law of the Qing Dynasty* was completed in the 3rd year of the Xuantong Era (1911). Through these codes and draft codes, various modern Western legal institutions, such as the rule of law, lawyers, jury, free evaluation of evidence, open trial, judicial independence, recusal, no punishment without law, and presumption of innocence, were introduced and incorporated into the codes.[27]

The government of the Republic of China, established in 1912, further pushed legal reforms. By the 1930s, China finally incorporated the above-mentioned legislative achievements in the late Qing Dynasty and the legal institutions transplanted from the West into the *Complete Book of Six Codes*, formulated and promulgated between 1928 and 1935. The localization of Western laws was primarily completed to lay the foundation for a modern Chinese legal system and, at the same time, marked the collapse of the long-existing Chinese Legal Family.

4.3 Discussion on the **New Chinese Legal Family**

In the face of the collapse of the Chinese Legal Family, many scholars feel it is a pity that such a legal family that has survived and developed for more than 1,300 years just disintegrated and disappeared. Therefore, they argue from various angles that the Chinese Legal Family can continue to exist or nourish the development of Chinese law in modern times. This attempt began as early as the 1930s, as shown in Jiao Yitang's "New Chinese Legal System and the Great Harmony of the World" (Jiao, 1930), and Wang Ruqi's "The Revival of the Chinese Legal Family" (Wang, 1933). In 1946, Ju Zheng published the book *Why the Chinese Legal Family Needs to be Reconstructed*. The idea of reconstructing the Chinese Legal Family was advanced from six aspects. He further expressed four views concerning the specific reconstruction. First, the transition from the rule of Li (Ritual Propriety) in ancient times to the rule of law in modern times. Second, the transition from an agricultural country to an agro-industrial country. Third, the transition from a family-oriented life to a nation-oriented life. Fourth, embrace the Three Principles of the People as the highest guiding principles (Ju, 2007, Appendix 289–316).

---

[27] For the detailed process and contents of the revision of laws, the introduction of Western legal systems, and the formulation of China's own codes in the late Qing Dynasty, see Li (2000, 277–299). For China's transplant of Western laws and creation of laws after the 1930s, see He and Li (2003).

A more direct and detailed discussion of this issue can be found in "The Birth of a New Chinese Legal System? From the Three Legal Families to an East Asian Common Law," written by He Qinhua and Kong Jing (He & Kong, 2005). In this article, the authors first reviewed the glory of the Chinese Legal Family, further explained the essence of the Chinese Legal Family, discussed the historical basis and features of the Chinese Legal Family, explored the invasion of the Western legal systems and the disintegration of the Chinese Legal Family, analyzed the disintegration and its reasons, and emphasized the transplant of Western legal systems by the East Asian countries. The authors clearly pointed out that the Chinese Legal Family has died, but this does not mean that the Chinese Legal Family has disappeared without a trace. It has left a huge footprint and a rich historical and cultural heritage. On the basis of this heritage, combined with the development needs of today's East Asian society, we can build a *new Chinese Legal Family.*

The authors further expounded on the co-existence and competition of the three legal systems, the Chinese Legal Family, Common Law, and Civil Law, as well as the formation of the East Asian Common Law. They believe that in the context of the new era, the East Asian countries not only imitated the model of Civil Law and drew lessons from Common Law but also inherited the tradition of the Chinese Legal Family. Through competition and cooperation between the three legal systems, a unique *mixed law* form can be developed. Thus, an East Asian Common Law that not only reflected the Western legal tradition but also conformed to the interests and historical and cultural traditions of East Asian countries began to take shape. This East Asian Common Law was the *new Chinese Legal Family.* There were some favorable conditions for its creation. First, there was the interconnected nature of the historical and cultural traditions in East Asian countries, and the *Confucian cultural circle* still exists. Second, the development of the East Asian regional economic integration laid the economic foundation of the East Asian Common Law. Third, the establishment and improvement of the "10 + 3" cooperation mechanism between the ASEAN and China, Japan, and South Korea constituted the political guarantee for the formation of the East Asian Common Law. Fourth, the various instances of incompatibility when East Asian countries borrow and transplant the Western legal systems could directly drive the emergence of East Asian Common Law. Fifth, the common problems and threats faced by East Asian countries were the external driving force of the East Asian Common Law. At the end of the article, the authors analyzed and expounded on the definition, characteristics, and restrictive factors of the East Asian Common Law.

4.4 *Status of the Chinese Legal Family in the History of Human Legal Culture*

As discussed in Volume 1 of this book series, *The Origin of Legal Culture*, human legal culture first appeared as early as 3200 BC. Since then, Cuneiform law developed in the two river basins in West Asia (Mesopotamia) from 3200 BC to the sixth century BC, created by the Sumerians, Akkadians, Babylonians, Assyrians, Hittites and Neo-Babylonians. This includes the Egyptian legal system created by the Egyptians from 3100 BC to the third century BC as the core, Greek Law from the twenty-first century BC to the second century BC, Roman Law from the twelfth century BC to the sixth century AD, Hindu Law from the eighth century BC to the seventh century AD, Christian Law from the 1st to the fifteenth century, Sharia from the seventh century to the present, Common Law from the seventeenth century to the present, and Civil Law from the early nineteenth century to the present.

Among the above-mentioned legal families, except for Sharia, Common Law, and Civil Law, which still maintain their vitality, all the other legal families have died out. Although the Chinese Legal Family has disintegrated in modern times, it occupies an important position in the history of human legal culture. On the one hand, the Chinese Legal Family is one of the longest-standing legal families. It existed for more than 1300 years, from its formation in the seventh century to its disintegration in the early twentieth century. If we count the legal systems of Xia, Shang, and Zhou, which were the origins of Chinese law, the mother country of the Chinese Legal Family, the Chinese Legal Family has a history of more than 4000 years. On the other hand, the Chinese Legal Family also had one of the widest effects among legal families. Although it has a limited number of the states besides China—only Korea, Japan, Vietnam, Ryukyu, etc.—the area covered is large, accounting for almost the entire Asian continent. Additionally, the legal culture created by the Chinese Legal Family is very rich. It left a huge legacy in terms of legal concepts, legal institutions, legal procedures, legal academics, legal scholars, and legal education. Therefore, the Chinese legal system is an important part of the history of human legal culture and is one of the legal systems with the richest legacy. It is an important historical resource for modern legal professionals in building a country under the rule of law.

Definitely, in terms of the overall relationship between the Chinese Legal Family and the history of human legal culture, the Chinese Legal Family deserves more attention. On the one hand, as mentioned above, the Chinese Legal Family has left a rich historical legacy in the history of legal culture. Compared with the urban commercial civilization of ancient Mesopotamia, pharaoh theocratic civilization of ancient Egypt, religious civilization of ancient India, and city-state civilization of ancient Greece and Rome, ancient China was mainly a farming civilization. It was based on the blood relationship of individual families, clans, and religions, and its basic characteristics were consistent inheritance and continuation. Based on the farming civilization, the basic legal ethics, the three cardinal guides and the five constant virtues were created. They guided and regulated the development of law and jurisprudence in China for more than 2000 years (Zhang, 2015, 35). On the other hand, due to the long-term autocracy and centralization of power in ancient China, resistance to the progress of civilization was very strong, and sometimes there may have even been some regression. For instance, in the development of the criminal law system, progress was made step-by-step, abolishing corporal punishment and reducing the death penalty. The execution of Jiayiliu (加役流, a commutation of the death penalty, a combination of banishment and hard labor duty) is a good example.[28] Before the Tang Dynasty, the death penalty was used. During the Wude Era of the Tang Dynasty (618–626), it was changed to toe-cutting punishment (corporal punishment). In the 6th year of the Zhenguan Era (632), Jiayiliu was adopted (Zhangsun, 1983, 35). However, in order to maintain an autocratic and centralized society, when the rulers thought that something would endanger their governance and the political and ethical foundations—such as the three cardinal guides and the five constant virtues—they would never make concessions or tolerate it. In addition to literary inquisitions and suppression of intellectuals' freedom of thought and speech to strictly control their thoughts on political issues, severe suppression of the freedom of human nature and behavior was also imposed concerning family ethics. For instance, regarding the crime of rape, whether between normal people or relatives, the punishment became heavier with time. In the Tang Dynasty, rape offenders were sentenced to imprisonment; after the Yuan Dynasty, they were sentenced to death. Adultery by consent deserved 1000 km of exile, and in Ming and Qing Dynasties, death by hanging was imposed. In the same kind of behavior, the punishment did not become lighter with the progress and development of human society but became more serious. This was inconsistent with the trend and development of human legal culture (Zhang, 2015, 21). Some (inverse civilization) characteristics of the concepts and institutions of the Chinese Legal Family that have been demonstrated brought many negative comments on the subsequent development of Chinese law, and its influence continues to this day.

References

Aihanzhe, et al. (Eds.). (1997 photocopy version). *Eastern western monthly magazine* (Huang, Shijian collated). Zhonghua Book Company.

Bao, Z. (2008 photocopy version). Bao Xiaosu Zou Yi Ji (Collection of Bao Zheng's Memorial to the Throne, 包孝肃奏议集): Lun She En Bu Ji Xia (Discussion on the Amnesty Not Able to Reach the Lower Levels, 论赦恩不及下) + Qing Ba Tianxia Kelv (Plea for the Decrease of Taxation for the People, 请罢天下科率) + Yan Shanxi Yan Fa (Discussion on the Salt Law of Shanxi Province, 言陕西盐法), In *Si Ku Quan Shu* (四库全书) (Book 427, p. 91+144+160). The Commercial Press.

[28] Jiayiliu is a punishment based on the usual banishment. It includes one more year of hard labor duty than the normal two-year hard labor duty imposed in the normal banishment. For example, in *Tang Lv Shu Yi*, Article of Banishment in General Provisions "the three kinds of banishment all include one-year hard labor duty. Note: Jiayiliu, 1500 km banishment and three-year hard labor duty." Volume 6, Xingbu Langzhong Yuanwailang (officials of Ministry of Justice, 刑部郎中员外郎) of *Tang Liu Dian* provides that "Jiayili, it is named so because the usual banishment includes one-year hard labor duty and it includes three-year hard labor duty." See Liu (1996, 141).

Chen, C. (1980). Preliminary exploration of the features of the Chinese legal family. *Chinese Journal of Law, 1*, 48–53.
Chen, G. (1988 photocopy version). *The history of the Chinese legal system*. China Bookstore Publishing House (Original work published 1934, The Commercial Press).
Chen, G. (2011). *Essentials of Chinese legal history*. The Commercial Press.
Chen, J., & Zhang, Z. (1996). *Collection of seeking the knowledge—Zhang Jinfan and 40 years of the research on Chinese legal history*. Nanjing University Press.
Chen, L. (2017). The introduction of Gong Fazi and the concept of legal family into China—A milestone in the history of modern legal history. In *Collection of the 3rd modern legal history forum*. East China University of Political Science and Law.
Cheng, S. (1934). A discussion of the Chinese legal system. *Chaoyang Law Review, 11*(19).
Dai, J. (2003). Preliminary research on Bianchi of the Song dynasty. In Y. Yang & S. You (Eds.), *Textual research on the history of the Chinese legal system* (Vol. 5: Research on the legal systems of the past dynasties—Song, Liao, Jin, and Yuan dynasties; Book 1). China Social Sciences Press.
Ding, Y. (1931). Formation of the Chinese legal family and its future. *Modern Law, 1*(4–5).
Du, Y. (1988). *Tong Dian* (Comprehensive Statutes, 通典) (Volume 15: selection; Book 1) (checked and revised by Wang, Wenjin et al.). Zhonghua Book Company.
Fan, Z. (1999). *Family ethics in the Chinese legal family: A comparative study with the Ius Quiritium in western legal systems* (pp. 105–111). Nanjing University Law Review, Spring.
Feng, Z. (1992). Observing Shi—A form of law in the Tang dynasty—From several Dunhuang and Turfan documents. *Chinese Journal of Law, 3*, 69–75.
Guo, C. (Ed.). (2001). *The spirit of the Chinese legal family*. China University of Political Science and Law Press.
Hao, T. (1997). *Research on the Chinese legal family*. Fudan University Press.
He, Q. (2006). *History of science of law in China* (Vol. 3). Law Press·China.
He, Q., & Kong, J. (2005). The birth of a new Chinese legal system? From the three legal families to an East Asian common law. *Legal Forum, 4*, 44–52.
He, Q., & Li, X. (2003). *Foreign law and Chinese law: Reflections on China's transplant of foreign laws in the 20th century*. China University of Political Science and Law Press.
He, Q., & Li, X. (Eds.). (2003). *The essence of the legal papers of the republic of China* (Volume 1: Basic Laws, appendix). Law Press China.
Hiroshi, A., Ito, T., Ueda, N., & Jimbo, F. (Eds.). (2010). *History of Japanese legal system*. Seirin Shoin.
Jiang, L. (2009). Evolution of the legislation of the Chinese legal family. *Research on Legal Culture, 5*, 580–591 (checked by Zhang, Jing). [Original work published 1935, *Republic of China Journal of Law, 6*(7)].
Jiao, Y. (1930). New Chinese legal system and the great harmony of the world. *The China Law Review, 1*(1).
Ju, Z. (2007). Why the Chinese legal family needs to be reconstructed. In J. Zhang (Ed.), *Retrospect and prospect of the Chinese legal family*. China University of Political Science and Law Press.
Lai, J. (2008). Constructing the Chinese legal family—Theory, nationalism, discourse and practice (1900–1949). *Peking University Law Review*, 9(2). Peking University Press.
Li, G. (2000). *Biography of Shen Jiaben*. Law Press China.
Li, G. (2002). Discussion on right. In G. Li (Ed.), *The legal system and Jurisprudence in Modern China*. Peking University Press.
Li, L., et al. (2014). *Tang Liu Dian* (Six Codes of Tang Dynasty, 唐六典) (Volume 6: Shang Shu Xing Bu; Book 1) (checked and revised by Chen, Zhongfu). Zhonghua Book Company.
Li, X. (1994). The closedness of the Chinese legal family and its reasons. *Science of Law, 6*, 28–33.
Li, Y. (Ed.). (2010). *The form and soul of the Chinese legal family*. People's Public Security University of China Press.
Li, Y. (2004). Research on the legal system in the Tang dynasty. *The Jurist, 5*, 45–59.
Li, Y. (2011). A summary of the forms of law in the Tang dynasty. In Y. Yang (Ed.), *Research on the legal system in ancient China*. Social Sciences Academic Press (China).

Liang, Q. (1936). *Yinbingshi Heji* (The Collected Works from the Ice-Drinker's Studio, 饮冰室合集) (Vol. 5, p. 42; Volume 6: Discussion on the Development, Pros, and Cons of the Production of the Chinese Statutory Law, p. 37). Zhonghua Book Company.
Liu, G. (2002). *Re-understanding of the Chinese legal family*. Law Press China.
Liu, G. (2010). Re-understanding of the Chinese legal family. In Y. Zhu (Ed.), *Chinese legal family* (Vol. 1). Law Press China.
Liu, G. (2011). Re-understanding of the vitality of the Chinese legal family. *Tribune of Political Science and Law, 2*, 100–104.
Liu, J. (1996). *Tang Lv Shu Yi Jian Jie* (Notes on Tang Lv Shu Yi, 唐律疏议笺解) (Vol. 1). Zhonghua Book Company.
Liu, X., et al. (1975). *Jiu Tang Shu* (The Old Book of Tang, 旧唐书) (Volume 50: Treatise on Punishment and Law; Book 6). Zhonghua Book Company.
Ma, X. (1987). Evolution of Ge and its meaning. *Journal of Peking University, 3*, 112–120.
Niida, N. (1989). *Tang Ling Shi Yi* (Gleanings of Tang Ling, 唐令拾遗) (translated and edited by Li, Jin, Cunfu, Huo, Zhantong, Wang & Yande, Guo). Changchun Publishing House.
Qian, D. (1996a). Discussion on the legal system in the Tang dynasty and the nature of *Tang Liu Dian* again. In D. Qian (Ed.), *Research on Tang Lv and the legal system in the Tang dynasty*. Nanjing University Press.
Qian, D. (1996b). *Tang Liu Dian* is not an administrative code—reply to Mr. Ning Zhixin. *Social Sciences in China, 6*, 88–92.
Qian, D., & Li, Y. (1989). Discussion on the nature of *Tang Liu Dian*. *Social Sciences in China, 6*, 189–204.
Rao, A. (2000). New thoughts on the Chinese legal family: A comparative study with civil law and common law. *Journal of Southwest Jiaotong University, 1*, 68–72.
Riko, M. (1967). *The system of Lv and Ling and its related problems*. Keio Communications.
Song, L., et al. (1976). *Yuan Shi* (History of Yuan, 元史) (Volume 20: Emperor Chengzong III). Zhonghua Book Company.
Tatsumi, M. (1999). Family institution in the criminal law of the Ly dynasty in Annan, quoted from Yang, Honglie. In *The influence of Chinese law on East Asian countries*. China University of Political Science and Law Press.
Wang, A. (1999). Discussion on the tea law. In *Wang Anshi Quanji* (Complete Works of Wang Anshi, 王安石全集) (checked and revised by Qin, Ke, & Jun Gong). Shanghai Classics Publishing House.
Wang, L. (2001). Another discussion on the Chinese legal family. *ECUPL Journal, 5*, 3–11.
Wang, R. (1933). The revival of the Chinese legal family. *The Monthly of Renaissance, 1*(10).
Wang, W. (1985). Textual research on Lin Zexu's translation of western international law works. *Journal of Sun Yat-sen University, 1*, 58–67.
Xu, D. (1975). *Collected essays on the history of Chinese legal system*. Zhiwen Publishing House.
Xu, S. (2014). *Song Hui Yao Ji Gao* (Collection of the compendium in the song dynasty, 宋会要辑稿) (Volume 14: Punishment and Law I) (checked and revised by Liu, Lin et al.). Shanghai Classics Publishing House.
Xu, Y. (2012). Li Xue Zhi Nan (Guidebook for Officials, 吏学指南), Section Five Ke. In Y. Yang (Ed.), *Rare Judiciary literature of the past dynasties* (Book 1). Social Sciences Academic Press (China).
Xu, Z. (1998). Comments on the research concerning the legal system in the Tang dynasty and others. *Law and Social Development, 5*, 13–20.
Yang, H. (1999). *The influence of Chinese law on East Asian countries*. China University of Political Science and Law Press.
Yang, J. (2012). Literature review of the Chinese legal family. In Y. Zhu (Ed.), *The Chinese legal family* (Vol. 3). Law Press China.
Yang, Y. (2002). A major misunderstanding in the study of the Chinese legal family—Questioning the doctrine of "integration of all laws and no differentiation of civil and criminal laws". *Social Sciences in China, 6*, 78–94+206.

Yu, R., & Long, D. (2005). Summary of study on the Chinese legal family. *Journal of Shanghai University of Political Science and Law, 4*, 33–40.
Zang, J. (2003). Textual research on *Qing Yuan Tiao Fa Shi Lei*. In Y. Yang, & S. You (Eds.), *Textual research on the history of the Chinese legal system* (Volume 5: Research on the legal systems of the past dynasties—Song, Liao, Jin, and Yuan Dynasties; Book 1). China Social Sciences Press.
Zeng, H. (1987). Harm in practice of the closedness of the Chinese legal family. *Political Science and Law, 1*, 42.
Zhang, C. (2016). *Comparative research on Lv of the Tang Dynasty and Goryeo*. Law Press China.
Zhang, J. (1980). Origins of the features of the Chinese Legal family. *Chinese Journal of Law, 4*, 48–54.
Zhang, J. (1984). Re-discussion on several issues of the Chinese legal family. *Journal of China University of Political Science and Law, 2*, 6–16.
Zhang, J. (1999a). *Some thoughts on the rebuild of the Chinese legal family: Discussion on the Chinese legal family for the third time* (pp. 69–73). Nanjing University Law Review, Spring.
Zhang, J. (2005). Re-discussion on the features of the Chinese legal family. *Jiangxi Social Sciences, 8*, 47–52.
Zhang, J. (2009). *The tradition and modern transition of Chinese law*. Law Press China.
Zhang, J. (2010). The development of my understandings of the Chinese legal family. In Y. Zhu (Ed.), *The Chinese legal family* (Vol. 1). Law Press·China.
Zhang, J. (2012). Revival of legal culture and rethinking of the Chinese legal family. In *lessons learned: Past and present in the research of legal history*. Xiamen University Press.
Zhang, J. (2017). To carry on lost teachings of ancient sages. In Y. Zhu (Ed.), *The Chinese legal family* (Vol. 9). Law Press· China.
Zhang, Z. (1999b). *Some reflection and thoughts on the Chinese legal family* (pp. 79–96.). Nanjing University Law Review, Spring.
Zhang, Z. (2015). *Principles and significance: Exploring the approaches of Chinese legal culture*. China University of Political Science and Law Press.
Zhang, Z., & Li, M. (Eds.). (2000). *Collection of not finished—The 50th anniversary of Zhang Jinfan's teaching and research*. Nanjing University Press.
Zhangsun, W., et al. (1983). *Tang Lv Shu Yi* (Commentary on Tang Code, 唐律疏议) (checked and revised by Liu, Junwen). Zhonghua Book Company.
Zhangsun, W. (2008 photocopy version). Tang Lv Shu Yi: Za Lv (Other Laws, 杂律). In *Si Ku Quan Shu* (Book 672). The Commercial Press.

Chapter 2
Legal Philosophy, Jurisprudence, Legal Scholars, and Legal Education of the Chinese Legal Family

1 Legal Philosophy

1.1 Overview

1.1.1 Spirit, Soul, and Guiding Ideology of the Legal Family

For a legal family to form, develop, and maintain its vitality, it must have an independent spirit, an inner soul, and a guiding ideology that guide the law and its enforcement. This guiding ideology can be called a legal worldview, legal philosophy, or legal thought—these three terms are slightly different, but in this section, they are used interchangeably. Common Law values are manifested in thousands of cases, including the law's role in remedying social problems, the judge's role in correcting social ills, and the value of social fairness and justice. Therefore, the spirit, soul, and guiding ideology (legal philosophy) of Common Law is judicial justice. Civil Law values are embodied in systematic, complete, and mature codified laws (provisions), which reflect the legislative equality and social fairness and justice achieved by judges strictly abiding by the law. Therefore, the spirit, soul, and guiding ideology (legal philosophy) of Civil Law is legislative justice.

The original version of the chapter has been revised. A correction to this chapter can be found at https://doi.org/10.1007/978-981-96-6522-8_6

Q. He et al., *Chinese Legal Family*, https://doi.org/10.1007/978-981-96-6522-8_2

The above summary is not necessarily accurate, but it provides a general understanding of the two major legal families in the world. From this perspective, in terms of the Chinese Legal Family, a legal family that has survived for more than a thousand years, influenced entire East Asia, and left a huge historical legacy, what is its spirit, soul, guiding ideology, or legal philosophy? This book believes that the legal philosophy of the Chinese Legal Family is the orthodox legal worldview of ancient Chinese society. This legal worldview is formed based on the induction, summary, and refinement of the thoughts on the law by the sages. This section attempts to explore some of the legal philosophies of the Chinese Legal Family. Any kind of advice from the readers is welcome.

1.1.2 Formation and Evolution of the Legal Philosophy of the Chinese Legal Family

Zhang Zhongqiu pointed out that "there must be a great philosophy behind a great legal family. The reason why the Chinese Legal Family was able to stand towering in world legal families is not simply due to the rationality of the system, but also to its advanced legal philosophy" (Zhang, 2016, 3). As far as ancient China is concerned, as early as the Xia, Shang, and Zhou Dynasties, the basic concept of law and the embryo of the legal philosophy had been formed. This can be gleaned from the records of the unearthed oracle bone inscriptions, bronze inscriptions, and handed down literature such as *Shang Shu* (Book of Documents, 尚书), for example, the concepts of Xia and Shang's *heavenly punishment* and Zhou Gong's *noble morality and prudent punishment.* In the Spring and Autumn Period and Warring States Period, thoughts on legal philosophy became more abundant. Confucianists, Mohist, Daoists, and Legalists all advanced different basic concepts and propositions on the social phenomenon of law, which caused fierce debate and led to the birth of legal philosophy (He, 1997). However, before the Qin and Han Dynasties, Chinese legal philosophy was not yet mature. The maturity and finalization of ancient Chinese orthodox legal philosophy occurred during the reign of Emperor Wu of Han (156 BC–87 BC).

After more than 60 years of rule by the Huang-Lao thoughts to the time of Emperor Wu of Han, many social changes had taken place. After recovering economically and with a growing population, and with the decrease of corvee and taxes, a rich and prosperous social period was formed. "All granaries in urban and rural areas were full, and the government enjoyed a fiscal surplus. A large number of coins were accumulated in the capital so that the cords used to chain the coins were rotten, and the amount of the coins could not be calculated. Old crops in Taicang were so plentiful that they were piled up layer by layer outdoors until inedible. There were herds of horses on the streets, alleys, and fields. Those who rode on mares were so despised that they were not allowed to attend parties. Ordinary people enjoyed grain and meat. Officials took office for many years without being transferred, so that their descendants have grown up, and some officials simply used their positions as their surnames" (Sima, 1982, 1420). Politically, due to the central government's adoption of a policy of withdrawing powers from the local military forces after quelling the

Rebellion of the Seven States of Wu and Chu, the situation in which vassal states set up separatist regimes and ruled the region had basically ended. The authority of the central government was consolidated, and the whole country formed a unified community.

In terms of the law, at that time, the legal policy was guided by the Huang-Lao thoughts of following nature and governing by inaction. However, they were no longer suitable for Emperor Wu of Han's demand to be active, strengthening the autocratic imperial power, and strictly controlling subordinates. It also failed to effectively curb the tendencies of the ruling class to be increasingly arrogant and argumentative. *Shi Ji: Ping Zhun Shu* (Records of the Grand Historian: The Book of Prices Leveling Off, 史记·平准书) describes this tendency thus: "The regulation was loose and the people were rich. Some rich people were, therefore, arrogant and used their wealth to do illegal things. People annexed land, and local tyrants abused their power in the township. Clans with fiefs and officials lived extravagant life. Their houses, carriages, and clothes exceeded their class's standard without restriction." In terms of thoughts, although the Huang-Lao School was respected in the early Han Dynasty, the theories of various schools in the pre-Qin period were still circulating in various places. Therefore, there was a phenomenon that "different theories were taught and people had different opinions. Hundreds of schools had different ideas, goals, and wills. Therefore, the government was not able to unify and fix policies. Regulations and orders changed frequently. Low-ranking officials and ordinary people did not know what to follow" (Ban, 1962, 2523). These were obviously not good for the rule of the ruling class.

In particular, it must be noted that the Fengjian system, characterized by a unified state, absolute monarchy, and centralized powers, had nearly a hundred years of functioning, practicing, and accumulating experience after the Qin Dynasty. By the time of Emperor Wu of Han, the ruling group had become increasingly mature and gradually realized that relying solely on one theory of a certain school (such as Legalism) or the combination of Daoism and Legalism (Huang-Lao's school) had its flaws. They discovered that the guiding ideology for the national legal system must absorb the advantages of other schools and simultaneously be based on a core theory that was not only proactive but also emphasizes the self-cultivation of the members of the ruling group so that the goals of improving familial harmony, governing the state, and bringing peace to the world can be achieved. Dong Zhongshu's proposition of "respecting only Confucianism and dethroning a hundred schools of thought"—essentially, it was "taking Confucianism as the core and introducing all the advantages of other schools"—fit the above-mentioned requirements of social development. Therefore, this proposition became the legal worldview of the Han Dynasty after Emperor Wu of Han, and it also became the orthodox legal worldview (legal philosophy) of the Chinese Legal Family born in the Sui and Tang Dynasties. Although it experienced enrichment and derogation in the following Song, Yuan, Ming, and Qing Dynasties, there were no substantial changes until the end of the Qing Dynasty.

1.2 Essence of Orthodox Legal Philosophy of the Chinese Legal Family

Whether according to the dynasties or the characters, it is impossible to comprehensively discuss the ancient Chinese legal philosophy after the Sui and Tang Dynasties because the contents of it are too broad, and there is no clear clue. The length of this section imposes a limitation on a comprehensive discussion, and it is also not needed. Because if doing so, this book will overlap with some other works concerning the history of Chinese legal thoughts—although there are not many works on ancient Chinese legal philosophy, there are many works on the history of Chinese legal thoughts. Therefore, this section intends to summarize some main principles (consensus) of the legal philosophy. It is done by selecting the views and opinions on legal thoughts, law, and jurisprudence of the politicians, administrative and judicial officials, and scholar officials. Using these principles as a frame (consisting of several special topics), this section carries out analysis and discussion. These principles mainly include people-oriented thoughts, emphasis on educating and transforming people, guiding morality and punishment where needed, combined utilization of leniency and strictness, simplifying laws and limiting prohibitions, prudent penalties and light punishments, fairly deciding the punishment and rewards, governing officials acting according to the law, and the law changing with time. It is the Chinese Confucian ethics or patriarchal ethics that integrate these principles. The basis for its formation was the unique economic and political conditions of the Chinese farming society.

1.2.1 People-Oriented Thoughts

People-oriented thoughts have been the basic idea of the highest ruling class after the birth of the Chinese Legal Family.

Since the Northern and Southern Dynasties, due to the long-term separatist regimes and wars, the labor duty was heavy, production activities were destroyed, and the people were extremely poor. In response, Emperor Wen of Sui, Yang Jian, took a series of measures after unifying the country, such as promulgating *Xin Ling* (New Order, 新令) and allocating surplus public land, unowned wasteland, and open land to landless peasants or peasants owning little land for cultivation. At the same time, corvee and taxes were reduced, and the two national monopoly systems of wine and salt were abolished. All these legal measures manifested the *people-oriented* thoughts, which promoted the social and economic development of the early Sui Dynasty and improved the people's living standards.

After Emperor Taizong of Tang, Li Shimin, reigned, he further emphasized the extreme importance of the rulers to help the people, benefit the people, and love the people. In the early days of the Zhenguan Era, Li Shimin had said to his courtiers that "to be an emperor, you must save the people first. If you harm the people to serve yourself, it is no different from cutting your legs to feed yourself. Although you are full, you will die" (Wu, 2011, 1). Under this guiding ideology, the early Tang Dynasty further improved the corvee and taxation system, confirmed the legality of the peasants' occupation of the land of the dead and escaped landlords, and allocated a certain share of state-owned land to the peasants who had little or no land. At the same time, the taxation and corvee imposed on the peasants were reduced, the central and local government agencies were merged, the number of officials was decreased, and the national expenditures were cut to lighten the burden on the people.

The implementation of the *people-oriented* thoughts in the early Sui and Tang Dynasties enabled the rapid recovery and development of the social economy. The ruling order was quickly stabilized. Facts have proved that the implementation of the *people-oriented* legal thought was very beneficial and effective in consolidating the rule of the ruling class. Although the ruling groups of the Sui and Tang Dynasties implemented this policy mainly because of coercion and resignation, enlightened monarchs such as Li Shimin, who further compared the relationship between the monarch and the ordinary people to that between boats and water, were rarely seen in history. He believed: "The emperor is like a boat, and the ordinary people are like water. The water can carry the boat, and it can also capsize the boat" (Wu, 2011, 261). He also often warned and admonished his subjects and descendants about this profound truth. The Sui Dynasty did not always adhere to these thoughts, so it perished in the second generation. The Tang Dynasty pursued these thoughts for a long time, so it prospered for a long time, which further explained the importance of the *people-oriented* thoughts in politics and law. The rulers of the early Tang Dynasty were able to clearly realize the importance of the *people-oriented* thoughts, made theoretical explanations and practiced them, and incorporated them into legislation and the judiciary, which is exactly a manifestation of the maturity of the legal philosophy.

The rulers of the early Song Dynasty also emphasized the *people-oriented* thoughts. In the spring of the 2nd year of the Jianlong Era (961), "in Shangzhou, rats eat seedlings, and (Emperor Song Taizu) made a decree to exempt people from taxes" (Toqto'a et al., 2008, 93). In the sixth lunar month of the 5th year of the Kaibao Era (972), "The Yellow River broke the banks in Yangwu and the Dian River broke the banks in Gushu. On *dingyou* (chronometric method in ancient China) day, the emperor decreed that 'there has been heavy rain and rivers broke the banks, people along the rivers are suffering from the damage. The emperor has heard of it and commands the taxes to be lowered'" (Toqto'a et al., 2008, 108). In the middle of the Song Dynasty, the rulers continued to advocate the idea of developing the economy and caring for the people. For example, Fan Zhongyan emphasized in his memorial to Emperor Renzong, *Shi Shi Shu* (Memorial Concerning Ten Things, 十事疏), that "the government should dismiss redundant staff and reduce or exempt corvee, so as to facilitate the people's lives, benefit the people, and show mercy to the people" (Toqto'a et al., 2008, 160). Bao Zheng and Wang Anshi also fully discussed this. Under the influence of these virtuous ministers, Emperor Renzong of Song also paid great attention to economic development and was sympathetic to the people. During the reign of Emperor Renzong, he issued more than ten decrees, either to abolish the renting tax or to exempt the *qingmiao* (young crops, 青苗) tax from people living in disaster-stricken areas. Emperor Shenzong of Song did the same. In the 6th lunar month of the 4th year of the Zhiping Era (1067), "the officials all over the country need to report to the emperor about exemptions with issues of the corvee and taxes" (Toqto'a et al., 2008, 232). In the 5th lunar month of the 4th year of the Xining Era (1071), "Edict: Enzhou and Jizhou suffer from disasters, the emperor is sending envoys to relieve the people. Their taxes are exempted" (Toqto'a et al., 2008, 232). In the middle of the Northern Song Dynasty, the ruling group implemented the policy of developing the economy and caring for and benefiting the people. Although it did not completely tackle the accumulated problems of society, it changed the situation at the grassroots to a certain extent.

The ruling class of the Yuan Dynasty was originally the upper-class nobles of a nomadic tribe. Their rule was mainly maintained by following the customs of the clans, and military and killing were important means used by them. But after the founding of the dynasty, in order to consolidate the newly-born Mongolian regime and make it long-standing and stable, the ruling class of Yuan began to have a new understanding of the law. Its legal philosophy also changed. On the one hand, they began to realize that the foundation of state governance is to win the support of the people. Therefore, they must use legal means to comfort and take care of the people and relieve their various burdens. In the 2nd year of the Zhongtong Era (1261), on *yimao* (chronometric method in ancient China) day, Yuan Shizu issued an edict that "the ten envoys need to exempt the people from taxes after weighing the reasons. Local governments have to encourage farming and silk farming, discourage idleness and laziness, pay respect to the elderly, and hear the sufferings and difficulties of the ordinary people... Officials who are corrupt and people who do not follow filial piety should be punished according to the seriousness of their actions" (Song et al., 2008, 42). In the 20th year of the Zhiyuan Era (1283), droughts occurred in Hebei and Shandong. Emperor Shizu issued an edict to stop collecting taxes and grain in these areas. In the early Yuan system, if a person extracted one *liang* (liang is a measurement unit) of silver, he was exempted from the tax of five *dou* (dou is a measurement unit) of grain. An official proposed: "Today the people are struggling every day, the government should exempt the people from the tax of one *dan* (dan is a measurement unit, one dan equals ten dou) of grain for every liang of silver they made." Yuan Shizu said, "If heavy burdens are imposed, how can the people live!" He agreed to the proposal (Song et al., 2008, 35).

After the establishment of the Qing Dynasty, the rulers of Qing learned from the lesson of the rulers of the late Ming Dynasty that brutally oppressing the people would cause fierce confrontations. The rulers of the early Qing Dynasty paid great attention to using legal means to appease the people and show compassion for them. In the 8th year of the Shunzhi Era (1651), an edict was issued saying that "The bandits were originally ordinary people. They were forced to rebel against the government because of starvation and cold. Over the years, they have been attacked and suppressed many times. However, the military officials killed ordinary people to falsely claim rewards, while the real bandits were not killed. People are suffering, and I am deeply distressed. From now on, the governors should use both suppressing and comforting methods and can not use capturing robbers as an excuse to disturb people. This will make me satisfied" (Zhao et al., 1977, 83). After Emperor Kangxi reigned, he also issued edicts many times: "I have been seeking good governance day and night, and I have deep concern about what people live on. In recent years, there have been frequent floods and droughts, and thieves and bandits have not yet been wiped out. In addition, corrupt officials have been severely exploiting people, and the people's life has been greatly harmed. I am very sympathetic. Officials should report what they saw and heard concerning the people's sufferings and difficulties and provide suggestions to me about how to improve the situation." In the 43rd year of the Kangxi Era (1704), he further issued an edict saying that "I consulted the people about their sufferings and difficulties, and I was deeply aware of how difficult it is to do hard work every day. For those who cultivated 30 *mu* (mu is a measurement unit) of land, after the taxes are charged, they have around 20 dan of grain left. Their clothes, food, and corvee all come from this. If they are lucky and meet some honest officials, they can still have some remains. If the officials are greedy, they have nothing to live a life. Therefore, to monitor officials and comfort the people, the key is that the high-ranking officials have to genuinely care about people" (Zhao et al., 1977, 165).

1.2.2 Emphasis on Educating and Transforming People

Since the Han Dynasty, the rulers attached great importance to the educational role of the law, and various dynasties after the Sui and Tang Dynasties also continued similar thinking. For example, Yang Jian once explicitly pointed out that "to practice Ren (benevolence, 仁) and Yi (righteousness, 义), hierarchy and education are most important. De (Virtue, 德), Ren, and Yi cannot be implemented without Li (Ritual Propriety). To make the emperor feel secure and rule the people, nothing is better than Li" (Wei et al., 2019, 11). At that time, the Sui Dynasty had already formulated *Kaihuang Lv*, but Yang Jian still believed that the law alone was not enough and that the rule of De and education must be vigorously advocated. Therefore, he further put forward the proposition that "punishment can be adopted to assist education but not solely imposed," emphasizing that "if you want the people to be educated, replacing punishment with De" is, to a large extent, needed. Therefore, at the beginning of his ascension to the throne, he issued an edict that "people are encouraged to learn and follow Li," which constituted a precondition for the implementation of the law. We know that Yang Jian advocated Buddhism and Daoism. He once even ordered the abolition of schools at all levels other than the authorized schools to oppose Confucianism and promote the development of Buddhism. Yet, he still attached great importance to the idea of moral guidance together with punishment. This shows that moral education was a legal philosophy and legal policy that could not be abandoned by any monarch who wanted to stabilize his ruling order.

Of course, the Ming Dynasty did particularly well in propagating moral education. For example, while emphasizing the use of severe punishment to regulate subjects, Zhu Yuanzhang also did not forget the function of morality and education. He tried to maintain his rule by using both lenience and severe punishment, as well as the approach of moral guidance and supplementary punishment. Zhu Yuanzhang often said: "The way to govern the world consists of Li and Yue (ritual and music, 礼乐)." In *Yu Zhi Da Ming Lv Xu* (Imperial Law of the Great Ming, 御制大明律序), Zhu Yuanzhang further pointed out: "Clarifying Li to guide the people and enacting the law to restrain disobedience." He emphasized that "Li and Yue are the foundation for governing a peaceful country and Xing (Punishment) and Zheng (Policies) are the medicine to remedy abuses" (Hu et al., 1962, 2517). In his edict to his grandson, Zhu Yuanzhang said that *Da Ming Lv* "firstly includes pictures of the two punishments and secondly includes pictures of the eight rituals. That is to highlight Li. Considering that people are ignorant, if an order of leniency is annexed to the original provisions, people would easily choose to disobey the law. Therefore, for good intentions, it was listed in *Ming Li Lv* (the first chapter of *Da Ming Lv*, general provisions, 名例律). It is good enough if those who have expertise in applying the law know what it means" (Zhang et al., 1974, 2283). After Emperor Jianwen ascended to the throne, he also attached great importance to the role of Li. In his imperial order to the law officials, he emphasized: "Adopting the law is to establish basic national rules and adopting Li is to follow the human sentiment. Using punishment to govern the people is not as good as using Li to govern them. I order the officials to respect the education of Li and remit the suspicious punishment to fulfill my intention of giving special treatment to the world" (Zhang et al., 1974, 2285–2286). By the middle of the Ming Dynasty, the rulers put more emphasis on the role of morality and education, emphasizing the combination of Li and Fa (Law, Punishment). For example, Wang Shouren advocated that the education of Li and Yi should be the most important, and pure depending on punishment to restrain the society should be opposed. "Good governance does not concentrate on law, but concentrates on its suitability for the people" (Wang, 2020b, 789). Qiu Jun also repeatedly pointed out that "The rule of the sage is to put education in the first place." "There are two important things for governance: Li and Fa. Li is the source of education and transformation… This is the reason why Li prevents the crime before it is carried out" (Qiu, 1999a, vol. 67). "Li and Yue are the foundation of Xing and Zheng, and Xing and Zheng are supplements to Li and Yue… This is why education is important for cultivating Dao (the way things work), Dao is important for the emperor's rule, and ruling the world needs principles and laws" (Qiu, 1999a, vol. 1).

Gu Yanwu, a thinker in the late Ming Dynasty, had a good exposition of the relationship between law and moral education. He pointed out that "The emperors of ancient times could not bear to excessively punish the people to govern them. Therefore, in a family, the father and brother ruled; in a clan, the first son of the lineal descent ruled… Then, the ruler-minister relationship was added to the original father-son relationship to weigh things… How could the punishment be inappropriate then? Therefore, when the patriarchal law is established and the punishment is clear, the sons of the emperors govern their own clans to assist the rulers to rule the world, and they do not interfere with the litigation and punishment issues, people would naturally follow the rules without disobedience. Honest customs and simple rules would be automatically created" (Gu, 2007, 343). Gu Yanwu emphasized that "Li and Yi are the basic law to rule the people, honesty and shame are the ethics to accomplish a person. That is because if someone is not honest, he may take whatever he can take, and if someone is shameless, he can do whatever he wants to do. If a person is like that, he will be troubled or ruined" (Gu, 2007, 739). By cultivating the people's courtesy, righteousness, and honor, people's contention and wealth differences will be eliminated and the law can be implemented. Although Gu Yanwu's proposition was idealistic, his emphasis on the education of the people about Li, Yi, honesty, and shame, while implementing the law was the mainstream thought in the traditional Chinese legal worldview, which was progressive compared with the practice of simply using punishment and killing.

1.2.3 Moral Guidance and Punishment Where Needed

Moral guidance and additional punishment was the core view of the orthodox legal philosophy established in the Han Dynasty. Since the reign of Li Shimin in the Tang Dynasty, rulers more consciously promoted the idea of moral guidance together with punishment. For example, Li Shimin pointed out: "From what I can see, the emperors ruling with Ren (Benevolence) and Yi (Righteousness) would extend the life of their dynasties; for those who only adopt the law to control people, although they can maintain their rule for a while, failure and death come rapidly" (Wu, 2011, 314). Wei Zheng, a high-ranking official in the early Tang Dynasty, further emphasized that "Ren and Yi are the most important principles, and penalties and punishment are the least important principles." "Therefore, the sages appeared and changed the customs. They did not support strict punishment and laws, but rather advocated Ren and Yi."

Of course, that Wei Zheng regarded punishment as "the least important principle," and he emphasized Ren and Yi did not suggest that he agreed that the law can be abandoned. In fact, he believed that the law was "the balance of a country and the yardstick of the time" (Dong et al., 1990). Nevertheless, he thought that Ren, Yi, De (Virtue) and Xing (Punishment) are different concerning the priority. The primary ones are De, Ren, and Yi. Fa and Xing are of secondary importance. They are whips and tools for the rulers.

The thinkers after the Middle Tang Dynasty inherited the basic view of traditional Confucianism that morality is primary and punishment is supplementary. For example, Chen Zi'ang clearly stated that Ren and Yi should be the most important basis on which to govern the state, and Xing and Fa should be less used, saying, "I have heard that punishment is trivial in the politics. The former emperor has no choice but to use it to prevent rebellions and control riots" (Liu et al., 1975, 2141). Lu Zhi advanced that "the key to good governance is first using morality and second punishment. When Li and Yi are practiced, people know shame and standards. When education and orders are clear and appropriate, the society gains harmony and peace. Then cunning and evil are restrained, and violence and rebellion are controlled" (Lu, 2016). Han Yu also held that "Li and Fa are the starting points of benevolent governance" (Han, 2001, 848). Liu Zongyuan further pointed out that Xing and Li "are the same in their origins, but the utilization of them is different. You cannot use praise and punishment at the same time. If something deserving praise is punished, this is called abuse. Punishment is used too often. If something deserving punishment is praised, this is called overstep. Li is damaged.... Therefore, for good governance, exhausting the reasons to decide rewards and punishment and judging whether to praise or criticize based on human feelings need to be used in combination" (Liu, 2021, 322–323).

Since Tang Lv and Lv Shu fully incorporated the legal philosophy of moral guidance and with punishment supplementing it, the main significance of the abovementioned thinkers' emphasis on the idea of moral guidance and supplementary punishment was to criticize the severe punishment and indiscriminate killing of innocents in judicial practice. It also helped to clear the way for the reforms of the dark judiciary and the advocacy of the rule of De, education, and light punishment.

It should be admitted that whether it is the Li Shimin administration or the thinkers after the mid-Tang Dynasty, their elaboration of moral guidance and supplementary punishment had no major innovation in theory. However, they lived in the most prosperous time in ancient Chinese society, the Tang Dynasty, the time when the Chinese Legal Family was formed. In addition, the ruling class in the Tang Dynasty continuously practiced it. The idea of moral guidance with supplementary punishment, which was the core of the ancient Chinese orthodox jurisprudence worldview, with the development of the Tang Dynasty, became deeply rooted in ancient Chinese law. It became the soul of Tang Lv and the legal philosophy and guiding ideology of the Chinese Legal Family. It had a huge and far-reaching influence on the social development of China and the neighboring countries after the Tang Dynasty.

The rulers of the early Song Dynasty also attached great importance to moral guidance and punishment where needed and paid more attention to the practice of "punishment supplementing." For example, Emperor Taizu and Emperor Taizong of Song often offered amnesties, but normally the ten abominations, murder, and officials' corruption are not excused. The Li School of the Song Dynasty (Neo-Confucianism, 理学) appeared in the middle of the Northern Song Dynasty and was given a comprehensive expression by Zhu Xi. The School also regarded law as an important tool to maintain the normal ruling order of the Fengjian society and a means to assist the education of Confucianism. "The law clarifies the rules and prohibits illegal activities, which also contribute to the education and transformation of people" (Zhu, 1996, Da Deng Weilao). Therefore, governing a country must rely not only on *Li* but also on *Fa* and *Xing*: "Zheng is law and institutions. Without Xing, there would be no laws and institutions. Therefore, if a ruler wants to rule his people with Zheng, he has to depend on Xing to manage the people. De is righteousness and principles. Without Li, there would be no righteousness or principles. Therefore, if a ruler wants to rule his people with De, he has to depend on Li to manage the people. The competition between the two ways can decide who can be the emperor" (Zhu, 1996, Da Cheng Yunfu).

1.2.4 Combined Utilization of Leniency and Strictness

The combined utilization of leniency and strictness was first proposed by Zichan (?–522 BC) in the Spring and Autumn Period. *Zuo Zhuan* (Tradition of Zuo, 左传)*: The Twentieth Year of Zhao Gong* (i.e., 522 BC) records that "in Zheng (a state), Zichan was ill. He told Taishu: 'After I die, you are going to succeed me in my job. Only those who have good virtue can use leniency to gain people's trust. If no one can do this, the second-best option will be strictness. Fire is fierce, and people look at it and fear it, so it rarely dies. Water is weak, and people play with it; it dies easily. Therefore, leniency is harder.'" Here, Zichan explained the relationship between leniency and strictness very clearly. Later, the combined utilization of leniency and strictness became one of the core viewpoints in Chinese legal philosophy over several dynasties.

During the Sui and Tang Dynasties, the Chinese Legal Family was formed, and this legal philosophy was inherited by later dynasties. Even the ruling class of the Yuan Dynasty, who came from an outside ethnic group, from the perspective of consolidating the newly-born Mongolian regime and making it lasting and stable, realized that the fierce measure of military killing alone was not enough and governance with the law was very important. They began to focus on the role of law in governing the country. *Xin Yuan Shi: Xing Fa Zhi* (The New History of Yuan: Treatise on Punishment and Law, 新元史·刑法志), written by Ke Shaoxin, records that "in the sixth year during the reign of Taizu, he defeated the Jin people at Wushabao and captured a general who surrendered, the general Guo Baoyu. Baoyu suggested that at the beginning of the founding of the state, new laws should be enacted. The emperor followed it. Therefore, *Tiao Hua Wu Zhang* (Five Chapters of Provisions, 条画五章) was promulgated, including such rules as the army cannot allow willfully slaughter, only criminals who committed severe crimes can be sentenced to death, and other crimes can be punished with corporal punishment based on the specific positions. This was the beginning of law-making by the first generation of the Yuan Dynasty. When the Central Plains Region was first conquered, the officials killed people arbitrarily and even seized their wives and daughters. Yelv Chucai petitioned that 'the sentence of death must be reported to the emperor and the execution must be conducted with the emperor's permission. Anyone who violates it should be punished by death.' The emperor followed his petition. After Taizong reigned, Yelv Chucai further provided 18 suggestions; for example, local officials who dared to impose taxes without permission from the higher authorities would be punished, Mongolian Uighur Hexi people who farmed without paying taxes would be punished by death, and sentences of death penalties should be reported to the imperial court with detailed reasons, and after getting the reply, the death penalty can be executed. All his suggestions were issued as edicts."

In the Ming Dynasty, the rulers paid more attention to the law, believing it to be the *principle* of governance. As early as the 1st year of the Wu Era (1367), when Zhu Yuanzhang was on the throne of Wu (a region), he put forward that "at the beginning of the founding of the country, the first thing to be done is setting up the principles" (Gu, 2015, 8). He emphasized that "using the law is how the government can rule the world" (Hu et al., 1962, 1898). He ordered Li Shanchang and others to discuss the law. In the first year of the Hongwu Era (1368), four Confucian ministers were ordered to teach the criminal officials about Tang Lv, 20 provisions each day. Zhu Yuanzhang "every time went to the West Tower, he called in all the ministers, let them sit, and calmly discussed the law" (Zhang et al., 1974, 2280). Under the attention of Zhu Yuanzhang, in the early Ming Dynasty, not only were *Da Ming Lv* and *Dagao* quickly formulated, but various other laws and institutions were also improved.

Ming Shi: Taizu Ben Ji (History of Ming: Annals of Emperor Taizu, 明史·太祖本纪) records that in the 10th lunar month of the 1st year of the Hongwu Era (1368), Zhu Yuanzhang ordered that Dengwen drums (登闻鼓, should provide a channel for people to tell the emperor about any injustice which happened to them); in the 4th lunar month of the 5th year of the Hongwu Era, *xiangyinjiu* rite (a reception held by officials to entertain talents, 乡饮酒礼) was adopted. In the 6th lunar month of the same year, prohibitions on eunuchs were imposed, institutions concerning court ladies were set up, and the official positions and year-end performance appraisal methods of the six departments were established. In the 6th lunar month of the 24th year of the Hongwu Era, Zhu Yuanzhang ordered the ministers to set up institutions concerning the crown clothes, rooms, and utensils in the light of the institutions of the former dynasties. In the 4th lunar month of the 26th year of the Hongwu Era, Zhu Yuanzhang made an edict that from thereon, if there is a famine, the governments should first lend grain to the people and then report it to the emperor. It was adopted as a rule. As stated in *Ming Shi: Xing Fa Zhi*, Zhu Yuanzhang spent more than 30 years to establish the laws and institutions for the Ming Dynasty. "It took a long time and careful consideration and the laws were finally established. The laws were all promulgated in the 30 years."

1.2.5 Simplifying Laws and Limiting Prohibitions

Simplifying the law and limiting prohibitions was advocated by Daoism in the Spring and Autumn Period and the Warring States Period. It was adopted by the rulers of the early Han Dynasty. After that, it was incorporated into the orthodox legal philosophy. After the formation of the Chinese Legal Family, the rulers of the Sui and Tang Dynasties regarded it as an important idea for governing the country. They paid special attention to abolishing onerous laws to simplify laws and limit prohibitions. After Yang Jian, the Emperor Wen of Sui came to power, and he issued an edict to let Minister Gao Jiong and others formulate *Kaihuang Lv*, which greatly decreased the number of laws compared with the previous dynasty. For example, the section *Xing Ming* (Types of Punishment, 刑名) in *Kaihuang Lv* stipulates that "the previous punishment of whipping, beheading, and hanging should be eliminated and the punishment of exile and imprisonment should be reduced and lightened" (Wei et al., 2019, 132). After the establishment of the Tang Dynasty, Emperor Taizong of Tang Li Shimin and others further emphasized that legislation should be simple and lenient, and the punishment should be lightened. Especially regarding the death penalty, special caution should be exercised. In the 1st year of the Zhenguan Era,

Li Shimin pointed out that "a person cannot return to life after death and therefore the law must be lenient and simple" (Wu, 2015, 525). Under the guidance of this thought, although the previously formulated *Wude Lv* had "cut down all the excessive and strict laws of the Daye Era (605–616)," when it was revised during the Zhenguan Era, the old law was still considered too strict, so a major revision was made. As a result, the revised *Zhenguan Lv* "had uncountable simplified and lightened rules" (Liu et al., 1975, 2141).

In the Ming and Qing Dynasties, simplifying the law and limiting prohibitions was also a basic legal philosophy. When Zhu Yuanzhang summed up the lesson in how "the complicated rules and regulations enabled the officials to be corrupt and harm the governance" in the late Yuan Dynasty, he indicated to the law-makers at that time that "the value of the law depends on its simplicity, appropriateness, and ease of understanding. If one thing can have two explanations which can be either lenient or serious, officials will have chances to be dishonest. This is incompatible with the intention of law. If the net is too fine, there will be no big fish in the water. If the law is too strict, there will be no perfect people. You should carefully study it and report the detailed types of the crimes and the provisions to me soon. I will consider and discuss it with you" (Zhang et al., 1974, 2280). At the same time, in order to make the laws fully implemented, Zhu Yuanzhang also paid special attention to the prevention of crimes and the publicity of laws. When *Da Ming Lv* was completed in the 12th lunar month of the first year of the Wu Era (1367), in case "ordinary people would not know about it, Zhu Yuanzhang ordered Zhou Zhen, the head of the highest judiciary, to collect and categorize the adopted laws concerning all issues in people's life except for issues concerning Li (Ritual Propriety), Yue (Music), the institutions, money, grain, and the official selection. Also, Zhou Zhen was ordered to provide interpretations of the law and issue them to local governments, which was called *Lv Ling Zhi Jie* (Direct Interpretation on Lv and Ling, 律令直解). Zhu Yuanzhang read the document happily: 'My people can make fewer mistakes'" (Zhang et al., 1974, 2280). In the 30th year of the Hongwu Era (1397), *Da Ming Lv Gao* (Law and Orders of the Great Ming, 大明律诰) was finished. Zhu Yuanzhang clarified the purpose of making the law in-person thus: "The law is used by officials but not known by the people. Therefore, I ordered the law officials to collect the provisions of Dagao, draw the outline, and attach them to Lv... publish them worldwide so that all people can know and follow them" (Zhang et al., 1974, 2284).

Some people with insight in the ruling class in the mid-Ming Dynasty also emphasized that the law should be simple, clear, and demotic, so that ordinary people could easily know and abide by it, and the judicial officials could be restrained. For example, after examining the discussions concerning the complexity and simplicity of the laws in the previous dynasties, Qiu Jun pointed out in *Shen Xing Xian: Ding Lv Ling Zhi Zhi Xia* (Law of Prudent Punishment: Adoption of Laws and Orders II, 慎刑宪·定律令之制下) that at the beginning of the Shenlong Era (705–707), "Zhao Dongxi said: ...The most important thing for legislation is to make all people know it, then they will not dare to violate it. ...Let Lv, Ling, Ge, and Shi use direct language to describe things without embellishment, ...Let ordinary people understand it as soon as hearing it, and they will follow each other and avoid violation. How can they clearly know it and still violate it deliberately? Therefore, it is said that if the law is clear, people will believe in it, and if the law is compatible, officials will respect it." "The minister's note: do not simplify its provisions, do not decorate its literary meaning, but directly write down the things and clarify its meaning; use common and simple words to provide full and detailed information. If the punishment is allowed to be increased or reduced, it should be decided according to the facts. Clear language should be provided, for example, if someone deserves a certain sentence, or dozens of lashes; what punishment should be added or reduced. All people should be able to see, hear, and understand it... In this way, the people will know what to do and what to avoid, and will not fall into the trap."

In the Qing Dynasty, the rulers also emphasized the simplicity and appropriateness of the law concerning their basic views of the law. Emperor Shunzhi once said to his subordinates: "The emperor uses morality to educate the people and uses punishment to assist in his governance. If the strictness of the laws is inappropriate, officials would play with words and make different interpretations. How can fair governance and timely proceedings be achieved? I have read the memorials concerning the judicature and find out that the citations of laws are mostly inappropriate. You have to report to me the current laws, and I will review and modify them in-person." When reading *Zi Zhi Tong Jian* (History as a Mirror, 资治通鉴), Emperor Shunzhi once asked his ministers: Among Emperor Gaozu of Han, Emperor Wen of Han, Emperor Guangwu of Han, Emperor Taizong of Tang, Emperor Taizu of Song, and Emperor Taizu of Ming, who is better and who is worse? Chen Mingxia replied: "Emperor Taizong of Tang seems better." Shunzhi said, "No. Emperor Taizu of Ming made legislation which can last forever, and other rulers of all dynasties could not keep up with it."[1] After Emperor Kangxi came to power, he also expressed his concern for simplifying law and limiting prohibitions so that the laws could be fully implemented. He once told the Ministry of Punishment: "The state makes laws to prohibit violence and crimes in order to maintain safety and good faith. Therefore, the complexity and simplicity of the laws should be suitable for the times to accomplish the emperor's intention of taking care of people's life" (The Official of Qing, 1985, 1072–1073).

1.2.6 Prudent Penalties and Light Punishments

Prudent penalties and light punishments were an important part of the Chinese Fengjian orthodox legal worldview, and they were also advocated and practiced by the enlightened ruling classes of all dynasties. The rulers of the early Sui Dynasty attached great importance to this point. To this end, they formulated *Kaihuang Lv* with lenient punishments, and it was adopted that "all strict laws should be removed, when criminals are questioned, a punishment of up to 200 lashes should be imposed,

[1] See Zhao et al. (1977, 83). Here, Emperor Shunzhi was not advocating strict law and punishment during the reign of Emperor Taizu of Ming, Zhu Yuanzhang. From what Emperor Shunzhi did in his life, he had always opposed severe and strict punishment and advocated lenient and prudent punishment. What Emperor Shunzhi advocated here was Zhu Yuanzhang's emphasis on the law and his dedication to legislation.

… and the person who gives the beating should not be changed during the process" (Wei et al., 2019, 132). At the same time, it was also adopted that "a decision of the death penalty has to go through three levels of reports and replies before it can be executed" (Wei et al., 2019, 11).

After Emperor Taizong of Tang, Li Shimin, came to power, he further emphasized that the enforcement of the death penalty must undergo strict procedures, in view of his own experience of killing the official of the highest judiciary, Zhang Yungu, and the military governor of Jiaozhou, Lu Zushang with rage, who should not have been killed. He believed that the existing *three-time report* system of death penalty was not working well: "Recently, the execution of prisoners, although it requires three separate reports, can be done within minutes. The decision was not under careful consideration. What is the benefit of the three reports then?" (Liu et al., 1975, 2141). Therefore, a system of *five reports* was further stipulated. That is to say, two days and one day before the execution of the death penalty, it had to be reported to the emperor, and on the day of the execution, three reports also had to be carried out. Further, it was stipulated: "From now on, if someone deserves the death penalty according to the law but can be exempted based on human sentiment, the situation should be recorded and reported" (Liu et al., 1975, 2141). Thus, a procedure for obtaining leniency from death was adopted.

In the early Northern Song Dynasty, the fundamental view of the ruling class on the law was roughly the same as that of the ruling class in the early Tang Dynasty. For example, *Song Shi: Taizu Ben Ji* (Annals of Emperor Taizu, 太祖本纪) records that once, when Emperor Taizu of Song was reading *Yao Dian* (Records of Emperor Yao, 尧典) and *Shun Dian* (Records of Emperor Shun, 舜典) in *Shang Shu*, he sighed and said: "Yao and Shun punished the four demons only by exiling them. Why is the recent law so strict?" So, he said to the prime minister: "The princes of the Five Dynasties were domineering, and some of them twisted the law with overkill, but the imperial court did not question it. Human lives are very important. Is it right not to interfere? Since today, when prefectures execute death penalties, the facts have to be recorded and reported and the Punishment Department have to double-check it." Then he made it an edict. In the middle of the Song Dynasty, rulers and scholar-bureaucrats were also very prudent about imposing punishment. For example, Li Gou pointed out: "Li (rite), Yue (music), Xing (punishment), and Zheng (policies) are the great laws of the world; Ren (benevolence), Yi (righteousness), Li (propriety), Zhi (wisdom), and Xin (trustworthiness) are the best practices in the world. Using the eight together can make the rule last for a long time" (Li, 2005, 3). Bao Zheng clearly pointed out: "The law is an important instrument for the emperor. The country's peace and security depend on it. So, it must be treated prudently" (Bao, 2008, 92). *Song Shi: Shenzong Ben Ji* (Annals of Emperor Shenzong, 神宗本纪) also records: "In the 3rd lunar month of the 3rd year of the Xining Era (1070)… Emperor Shenzong ordered the reduction of punishment." In the 9th lunar month of the 10th year of the Xining Era (1077), he further issued an edict: "If there is no existing law to follow, all issues concerning summons, comments, and face-to-face edicts should be reported through the *Zhongshu* Department (the central Secretariat Department, 中

书) and *Shumi* Commission (the military affairs commission, 枢密). Those who pray for grace and forgiveness for exemption of punishment should also be reported."

Of course, the ultimate purpose of prudent punishment was to strengthen the rulers' control of the people. Once the people were not willing to bear the poverty and hardships and rose up to resist the rule, the ruling group would generally use violence to brutally suppress them. For example, in the 4th year of the Xining Era (1071), in order to strengthen the suppression of peasant uprisings, the imperial court issued a decree: "Make strict laws concerning the bandits in Jingdong and Hebei" (Toqto'a et al., 2008, 232). Therefore, on one hand, governance based on morality, education, and prudent punishment was required. On the other hand, bandits were strictly punished. This was a distinctive feature of the legal worldview of the ruling class in the early and middle periods of the Northern Song Dynasty. It was different from the era of Li Shimin in the early Tang Dynasty, and also different from the rule of Zhu Yuanzhang later in the early Ming Dynasty.

The ruling class of the Yuan Dynasty was originally the upper-class aristocracy of the nomadic nation. Their rule was mostly maintained by customs and military killings. Therefore, their views on the law were different from those of the Song Dynasty. However, after the establishment of the Yuan Dynasty, from the perspective of consolidating the newly-born Mongolian regime and making it long-term and stable, the ruling class began to absorb the thought of prudent penalty and light punishment from the legal philosophy prior to the Yuan Dynasty. They changed the practice of blindly attacking, killing, and looting. For example, massacre-after-winning was abolished, and laws were used to bind officials and soldiers. *Yuan Shi: Taizu Ben Ji* (History of Yuan: Annals of Emperor Taizu, 元史·太祖本纪) records that in the 6th lunar month of the 22nd year (1227), "the emperor (Genghis Khan) said to the ministers: 'I have promised not to kill and loot since the five-planet conjunction in last winter, and I forgot to issue an edict. Now you can make a public announcement so that ordinary people will also know what I mean.'" Emperor Shizu of Yuan, Kublai Khan, also held the same view (Song et al., 2008, 35). At the beginning of the Yuan Dynasty, the rulers also made efforts to reduce the application of the death penalty. *Yuan Shi: Xing Fa Zhi* records that once, Emperor Shizu said to his subordinate ministers: "If I am angry and order you to kill an offender, you must not kill him, but wait for one or two days to report about it to me again." Judging from the executions of death sentences every year in the early Yuan Dynasty, the number of executions was indeed small. It generally ranged from 50 to more than 130 per year. In the 4th year of the Zhongtong Era (1263), only seven people were executed, which was the smallest number in the early Yuan Dynasty, and there were more than 1.58 million households ruled by Yuan at that time (Song et al., 2008, 55).

In the Ming Dynasty, the ruling class began to realize from its practice that blindly severe punishment and repression could not eliminate crimes and lawlessness in society. In contrast, it created opportunities for judicial officials to abuse their power. Therefore, the rulers of the mid-Ming Dynasty began to correct Zhu Yuanzhang's practice and vigorously advocated the concept of prudent penalty and punishment. For example, Qiu Jun pointed out: "The prison is set up as a last resort. People who are guilty should be sent to prison. How can they be detained for a long time?" "If there is doubt about the crime, it should be presumed to be minor, and if there is doubt about the merit, it should be presumed to be great. ...The virtue of cherishing life is in line with the people's preference, so they will not commit crimes against the officials" (Qiu, 1999b). Hai Rui also emphasized that, regarding doubtful crimes, "it is better to make ignorant mistakes rather than killing innocent people; it is better to benefit the bad rather than losing the good people" (Chen, 1962, 117). Although these views of Qiu Jun and Hai Rui were not all accepted by the emperors, their ideas represented the inclination of the wise men in the highest ruling class at that time and the concept of legal philosophy that "the emperor transforms the people with virtue and punishment supplemented it."

After the Qing Dynasty replaced the Ming's rule, Emperors Shunzhi and Kangxi also attached great importance to prudent penalty and punishment. In the 6th lunar month of the twelfth year of the Shunzhi Era (1655), the emperor said: "I read the Law Department memorial. Five or six death penalties are carried out every day, sometimes more than ten. I have sympathy for those foolish people. After wars and disasters, they have to face strict laws. They deserve pity. In the future, the Law Department must clearly and prudently impose penalties to pursue fairness" (Zhao et al., 1977, 83). After Emperor Kangxi came to power, he also emphasized prudent punishment. For example, in the 11th year of the Kangxi Era (1672), he issued an edict: "Do not use severe punishment to simply kill people, and those who violate the order will be punished." In the 11th lunar month of the 40th year of the Kangxi Era, he issued an edict: "I read the serious cases in the autumn trial in detail, and there are many mistakes in the words. How could the courtiers not find them? The Law Department is especially careless. You should discuss the punishment for the related officials" (Zhao et al., 1977, 165). Of course, Emperor Shunzhi and Emperor Kangxi's emphasis on compassion for people, governance of officials, prudence in punishment, and fair usage of law were aimed at ensuring the long-term stability of the Qing Dynasty. Therefore, although the legal philosophy of the Shunzhi and Kangxi Eras was generally more enlightened and flexible than that of the Ming Dynasty, when their fundamental ruling interests were threatened, they would also not hesitate to strictly suppress the revolt. The *literary inquisition* that started from the Kangxi Era and lasted until the Qianlong Era (1736–1795), which turned into a disaster, was a prominent example.

Unlike the supreme rulers, a group of thinkers in the late Ming and early Qing Dynasties sincerely hoped that the rulers would be prudent about using penalties and punishments. For example, Gu Yanwu pointed out that although the ethnic minorities at that time were not as good as the Central Plains in terms of culture, they were better in terms of the simplicity of their legal system. The customs of Xiongnu were simple and so was the North Wei Dynasty. "Emperor Taiwu of Wei began to formulate the laws of rebellion, murder, and robbery. The orders were clear and the government affairs were simple. There was no collective inquest or punishment. The people were at ease" (Gu, 2007, 1672). Wang Fuzhi emphasized that "simple law leads to clear punishment, and clear punishment leads to punishment of real crimes. Then people are afraid of law and avoid violating it. In this way, it is good enough" (Wang, 2020a, 323). On the contrary, "the stricter the law, the greater the power of officials;

the more complicated the death penalty, the more bribes there are. Cover-ups and twists will be employed to avoid punishment, and the power of the emperor will be held by officials…" (Wang, 2020a, 34). Wang Fuzhi believed that whether the law can be implemented did not depend on its strictness, but on being simple, orderly, unchangeable once fixed, and universally implemented.

1.2.7 Fairly Deciding the Punishment and Rewards

Although the orthodox legal philosophy emphasized hierarchical principles, such as strict separation of rulers and ministers, special rewards for officials and nobles, and strict punishments for ordinary and lower class people, in actual political life, the ruling class had paid attention to controlling the rewards and punishment within a necessary limit to stabilize the ruling order. If this limit was exceeded and the fundamental interests of the ruling class were jeopardized, the rulers took measures to impartially enforce the law and punish the elites with due severity. In other words, although the orthodox Confucian legal philosophy maintained the patriarchal hierarchy, in order to safeguard the fundamental interests of the supreme ruling class, the principles advocated by the legalists such as "applying the same law to all, no matter whether noble or lowly, clear rewards and punishments, fair use of law" were also respected. In the mature legal philosophy, Confucianism and Legalism were integrated.

For example, during the reign of Emperor Wen of Sui, Yang Jian, he repeatedly issued decrees to praise officials with outstanding political achievements and severely punish the corrupt officials. Even princes and nobles who violated the law would not be pardoned, for instance, Jia Xida, Han Yan, Lu Ben. Although they were high-ranking officials and dignitaries at that time, they were punished according to law for corruption and bribery. Even his own son, Yang Jun, the King of Qin, was punished according to law by Yang Jian because he was "very extravagant and openly building palaces that overstepped the hierarchical limits," although *shangshu zuo pushe* (a minister, 尚书左仆射) Yang Su and others had tried their best to intercede with him.

Emperor Taizong of Tang, Li Shimin, did better and more consciously on this point. He paid special attention to unifying the standards of reward and punishment and doing everything in accordance with law without avoiding dealing with relatives and friends. When explaining this point, Li Shimin pointed out that "Reward someone for his credit, and those who did not contribute will shy away; punish someone for his crime, and those who have done evil will be afraid. Therefore, knowing rewards and punishments leads to prudent decisions" (Wu, 2011, 189). Consistent with Li Shimin's position, thinkers after the mid-Tang Dynasty also attached great importance to the publicity of the ideas of appropriate reward and punishment and equal punishment. Lu Zhi believed that "rewarding the good and punishing the bad, that's the foundation of contending for the throne" (Ouyang & Song, 1975, 4921), "rewarding the good and punishing the transgression must not be abolished" (Lu, 1988, 46). Bai Juyi also believed that treating the liege men, especially the meritorious liege men, a wise monarch should "measure his contribution and reward him with the rank of nobility; measure his crimes and correct him with the law" (Bai, 2006). By "rewarding him with the rank of nobility, the rank increases and he knows the honor"; only by "correcting him with the law" can "the law be applied and then he knows the grace."

After the Tang Dynasty, the rulers and scholar-bureaucrats of the successive dynasties also emphasized fair punishment and equal application of the law to ensure the effective implementation of the laws they enacted. For example, in the 4th year of the Hongzhi Era in the Ming Dynasty (1491), Emperor Xiaozong's decree to the Law Department clearly pointed out that "Previously, because the heaven warned, I ordered the officials to examine and record the offending criminals again. Thousands of people were released. I think comparing with being lenient at the end, being prudent at the beginning is better. From now on, all the criminal departments and judges in the world must be kind and forgiving, uphold the law fairly, and carefully examine what a criminal deserves based on human sentiment, hoping that the lessons from the ancient sages are followed" (Zhang et al., 2008, 166). Qiu Jun pointed out: "The punishment and reward provided by a ruler are not a matter of his own happiness or anger, but a public standard influencing the people's preferences" (Qiu, 1999a, vol. 3). Therefore, the ruler's mind must be "always confined to the etiquette." Otherwise, problems would arise. Zhang Juzheng also emphasized that "The law should be strict but not tough," and "the law should be simplified, not irritating and harsh." For the law to effectively play its role, the key lies in the fair and equal use of punishment. "When punishment should be imposed according to law, even nobles or close relatives of the emperor cannot be forgiven; When unjust treatment is given, even acquaintances or lowly people should be given remedies" (Zhang, 2019, 1).

Huang Zongxi, a thinker in the late Ming and early Qing Dynasties who stated that the law is a public facility and not for one family, pointed out that the law should be the "public facility of the world" and should not be a tool for the rulers to abuse their power: "The law established in the Xia, Shang and Zhou Dynasties was not adopted for any individual. However, when later rulers once gained the throne…the so-called law became the law of one family, not the law of the world." He believed that concerning the law of the world, "the looser the law, the fewer the crimes. This is the so-called the law without laws. The law of later dynasties…became rigorous and crimes arose from it. This is the so-called law not performing as law" (Huang, 2021, 29–31). Gu Yanwu also pointed out: "The ruler cannot rule the world alone. Ruling alone, the punishment will be harsh. Ruling together with the subjects, the law will be implemented" (Gu, 2007, 343). The law must be "for the sake of the whole world" (Gu, 2007, 496). Wang Fuzhi further emphasized: "Emperors provide rewards and impose punishments on behalf of the heaven. If personal strategies are involved, the heaven is betrayed and the world will not obey… Since the rewards and punishments are provided on behalf of the heaven, the emperor should publicize them worldwide and not include personal manipulation or 'the art of control," or in other words, "practicing the selflessness of the heaven" (Wang, 2020a, 532).

In the early Qing Dynasty, the rulers also paid special attention to the prudence and fairness of the law when using it for the long-term stability of the state. In the 6th lunar month of the 10th year of the Shunzhi Era, the emperor ordered that

"The law provides the standards for the whole world, and it cannot be twisted based on an individual's joy or anger. In the past, when a subject was convicted, it had to be discussed by the officials. The law enforcers did their jobs to make the case clear. Sometimes the enforcers had private interests in it and it was found out by the higher officials, the case would be discussed again and wait for the emperor's decision; sometimes the previous cases were cited and decorated by words to allow the draconian enforcement. I prefer to let everything freely grow and treat subjects with tolerance. Those who became bandits because of hunger and coldness are still allowed to give themselves up, and those who live far away and committed crimes are offered amnesty, not to say the commoners and the courtiers. How can I allow them to be unjustly treated? In the future the law officials must inspect the facts and invoke this law, interrogation and cook-up charges should be thoroughly reformed to reduce crimes and penalties" (Zhao et al., 1977, 83). In the 53rd year of the Kangxi Era, the emperor said that "Everything must be for the people's sake. If it is only to apply the law, what is its benefit even if the law is strictly followed?" (Zhao et al., 1977, 165).

1.2.8 Governing Officials According to the Law

An important view of the ancient Chinese orthodox legal philosophy was that "the law alone cannot be enforced on its own." Only with a group of excellent officials can the law of the highest ruling class be implemented in all aspects of social life. Therefore, both Confucianists and Legalists paid great attention to the issue of governing officials. In the Sui and Tang Dynasties when the Chinese Legal Family was formed and the law matured, the rulers paid more attention and consciously used legal means to strengthen the management and regulation of officials.

At the beginning of the reign of Emperor Wen of Sui, Yang Jian carried out a comprehensive rectification of the subordinate officials, from the system to the style of work. For example, in the central government, the *six-official* system was abolished and a system of three departments and six ministries was established; at the local level, governments were retrenched and redundant officials were eliminated. The *nine-rank system* that had been implemented for more than 300 years was abolished, changing the situation that *no one of the upper class comes from a disadvantaged background and no one of the lower class comes from an aristocratic family*. The evaluation of officials was strengthened and those who violated the law and disciplines were punished.

In the early Tang Dynasty, the ruling class paid more attention to the management of officials. Li Shimin once personally handled the selection and appointment of provincial governors. He wrote the names of the governors and military governors of each prefecture on the screen. "If they did something good during their term of office, it would also be listed under their names" (Wu, 2011, 186). If they did something wrong, they would be punished. Li Shimin also paid special attention to judicial corruption. At that time, the law stipulated the conditions for a judicial official to be charged. However, in practice, an official's wrongful conviction of innocents and heavier sentences of minor crimes were acceptable, but an official's wrongful release and lighter sentences of severe crimes were severely punished. Thus, officials were fearful and of course they would rather impose harsher punishment. In response to this situation, Li Shimin ordered that anyone who made a wrongful sentence would be strictly punished according to law. The judiciary was finally *gradually fair*.

In the early Song Dynasty, the ruling class also attached great importance to the management of officials. For example, officials who committed corruption and violated the law would be sentenced to death with execution in the public marketplace. Only *Song Shi: Taizu Ben Ji* (Annals of Emperor Taizu, 太祖本纪) records more than 30 such officials, for example, Zhang Mu (a Censor serving in the palace), Zhang Xun (serving as the right proposer), Li Renyou (an assistant of the Crown Prince), Wang Yuanji (an assistant of the Crown Prince). When Emperor Shenzong ascended to the throne, he also paid tight attention to the management of officials. In the 12th lunar month of the 4th year of the Zhiping Era (1067), he issued a decree: "Officials of prefectures and counties have been corrupt and caused many prisoners to die. At the end of this year, the number of deaths will be calculated to decide whether the officials are guilty or not. This is the order" (Toqto'a et al., 2008, 232). At that time, Bao Zheng and others theoretically expounded the importance of the management of officials: "I've heard that honest and upright officials are models for the people, and corrupt officials are traitors to the people" (Bao, 2008, 111). "A good ruler must eliminate the traitors and the people will be rich. If the traitors are not eliminated, how can good governance be achieved!" (Bao, 2008, 126). Wang Anshi also pointed out that whether officials can abide by the law and enforce the law was directly related to the rise and fall of the country. "It is the wealth that unifies the people in the world, it is the laws that manage the wealth, and it is the officials that guarantee the law. Without good officials, the law will not be enforced, and without good laws, the wealth will not be managed" (Wang, 1999, 309). Although the above theories failed to fundamentally end the corruption of the officials in the Song Dynasty, it still halted the trend of corruption to a certain extent. A large number of capable officials were employed and the social contradictions were eased.

In the early Yuan Dynasty, the ruling class also realized the fact that the implementation of law must rely on officials, so they took many measures to strengthen the management of officials. *Yuan Shi: Xianzong Ben Ji* (Annals of Emperor Xianzong, 宪宗本纪) records: Emperor Xianzong "strictly managed the officials. He once issued a decree: 'If you receive my praise and then are arrogant, how can disasters not follow? You have to be alert to it.'" In the 19th year of the Zhiyuan Era (1282), Emperor Shizu issued an edict: "If officials accept bribes and warehouse officials steal, and the inspectors know about it but do not correct them, they will be punished according to the seriousness of their conduct. Central and local officials who commit minor corruption deserve lashes, and those who commit serious corruption deserve the death penalty. If the inspectors are silent, they will also be punished together with the guilty officials." This decree was promulgated worldwide (Song et al. 2008, 155).

In the Ming Dynasty, Zhu Yuanzhang was very afraid that his subjects would seize the throne. To this end, he took all legal measures, including heavy punishment, to severely suppress forces and individuals who threatened his autocratic regime. For example, in addition to *Da Ming Lv*, Zhu Yuanzhang personally directed the formulation of the cases in *Dagao Si Bian*. Measured by *Da Ming Lv*, most of the cases were misdemeanors with heavy sentences, and some were innocent with wrong convictions (Yang, 1984, 32–35). According to historical records: "Thousands of people received the three penalties listed in Gao, *lingchi* (death by a thousand cuts), *xiaoshi* (cut off the head and displayed in public), and *zhongzhu* (family annihilation). Tens of thousands of people received the death penalty" (Zhang et al., 1974, 2318). In the middle of the Ming Dynasty, the rulers further strengthened the governance of corrupt officials. For example, in the 1st year of the Hongzhi Era (1488), Emperor Xiaozong issued an edict: "the courtiers are forbidden to bend the law on public affairs for their private interests." In the 2nd year of the Hongzhi Era, he issued an edict to "collect the land of the deceased courtiers and give the fields to the people." Hai Rui, an "honest official," also explicitly pointed out: "The Emperor has worked hard on the governance, but if the governance fails, it is because the punishment given to the corrupt officials is light" (Zhang et al., 2008, 711). Zhang Juzheng further emphasized that officials should be strictly managed by law. He believed that the "root" of national turmoil was that "officials do not show compassion to the people, and the people are driven to be bandits" (Zhang, 2019, 25). Therefore, in order to "rescue the impoverished people," the government must "eliminate the corrupt officials" (Zhang, 2019, 304).

The rulers of the Qing Dynasty also realized that in order to implement the people-oriented policy, they must punish the corrupt officials who harassed, disturbed, and harmed the people. In the 8th year of the Shunzhi Era, an edict was issued: "The effectiveness of the state law depends on honest officials. Recently, some officials were corrupt and many people have lost their houses. This is against my will. The governors' tasks and responsibilities are appropriate reports and impeachments, so that the related departments can correct and punish the officials. Today, the ones being reported are mostly improper and the ones being impeached are mostly low-ranking officials. The vile and evil ones are tolerated. How can the management of officials be better? The Ministry of Officials have to carefully research on it and report to me" (Zhao et al., 1977, 83). Emperor Kangxi also attached great importance to the management of officials by law, and repeatedly warned his subordinates: "Those who are corrupt and exhausted the people should be punished by the military law" (Zhao et al., 1977, 165).

1.2.9 Law Changes with Time

Another important principle in the orthodox legal philosophy was that the law should be amended and constantly reformed with time. For example, in the 8th year of the Qingli Era of the Song Dynasty (1048), Emperor Renzong issued an edict to some officials: "I want to know the mistakes I have made, the evils around me, the dangers and tricks in the central and local governments, the ruthless acts conducted in prefectures and counties, and the laws that are not used for the sake of people. You have to report all of them to me" (Toqto'a et al., 2008, 187). Under this guiding ideology, Emperors Renzong and Shenzong employed reformers such as Fan Zhongyan and Wang Anshi to carry out large-scale legislative reforms. During the reforms, the ruling group advanced a series of ideas that the law should be changed with time. For example, Wang Anshi clearly pointed out: "To follow the ancestors' law is to follow the intention of the ancestors (not the exact text)" (Wang, 1999, 1). "Adapting the law to suit the time, and then good governance can be achieved" (Wang, 1999, 207). He believed that the reason why the Song Dynasty was "poor and weak" was directly related to the fact that the ancestors' law was followed for generations. Therefore, in order to change this situation, the government must "change customs and establish law and institutions." It is precisely because of the above-mentioned ideas that Wang Anshi, Emperor Shenzong of Song, and others still unswervingly carried out the reforms despite the problems.

Although the rulers of the Yuan Dynasty ruled China as a minority ethnic group, they also emphasized that good laws should be established and adapted with time. Immortalization was not advocated. *Xin Yuan Shi: Xing Fa Zhi* records that in the 2nd year of the Yuanzhen Era (1296), Emperor Shizu ordered He Rongzu, the vice grand councilor under the Zhongshu Department, and others to amend and enact the law. He said: "The law is a set of good rules, and it should be determined early." He Rongzu said: "I selected three hundred and eighty rules and some of them are about three or four things." The emperor said: "The ancient and the modern are different, and there is no need to follow the old rules. Just take the rules that are suitable for the present."

In the Ming Dynasty, when dealing with the relationship between law and reality, Zhu Yuanzhang explicitly pointed out: "To govern the country, those who are accustomed to the old rules should adapt to the time, and those who are familiar with the recent customs should think about future crises. Trapped by the traditions and not knowing the current situations and wallowing in recent customs without thinking about the future are not good" (Hu et al., 1962, 2525). It can be said that Zhu Yuanzhang was a materialist and a dialecticist in this regard, and it was under the guidance of this thought that the *Da Ming Lv* broke through the structural system of Tang Lv and added more new contents that were adapted to the social and legal relations in the early Ming Dynasty. However, when dealing with *Da Ming Lv* and *Dagao*, when Zhu Yuanzhang participated in their formulation, he showed an idealistic and metaphysical worldview. He repeatedly stressed that the rules he formulated should not be changed.[2] In view of the changes in society after the mid-Ming Dynasty, Emperor Xiaozong and others adopted important legal thought that the law should change with time. However, due to Zhu Yuanzhang's prohibition of "changing the law of the ancestors," Emperor Xiaozong and others did not dare to directly amend the old law. Therefore, by compiling the regulations of the past dynasties and revising

[2] Zhu Yuanzhang had issued an edict clearly indicating that "the descendants have to follow them. If any courtier talks about changing them, he should be found guilty of changing ancestor's institutions," after the formulation of Lv and Ling in the Ming Dynasty. See Zhang et al. (1974, 2279).

and promulgating *Wen Xing Tiao Li* (Articles Concerning Penalties, 问刑条例), Emperor Xiaozong finally modified the legal system of the Ming Dynasty to suit social development and changes.

Of course, in addition to the above nine principles or propositions, the interconnection of Fa, Xing, and Lv (in this context, they all mean punishment), the combination of Li (Ritual Propriety) and Fa (Law, Punishment), concerning the origin of the law, the belief that the "sages" created Li, Yue (Music), Xing, and Fa (Law) and the circumstances created the states and laws, etc., are also considered a part of the ancient Chinese orthodox legal philosophy. In this regard, because there have been many works discussing them, no further discussion will be given here.

1.2.10 Economic and Ideological Basis Behind the Legal Philosophy

Observing the above-mentioned main principles of the legal philosophy of the Chinese Legal Family, the central idea is the ethical aspects of Chinese law. Some scholars summarize it as "Confucian ethics" or "patriarchal ethics," which is referred to as "ritualism" for short (Zhang, 2015, 2). The core of it is "the three cardinal guides and the five constant virtues." This is unique to Chinese legal culture, and is an essential attribute that distinguishes the Chinese legal culture from the other legal cultures in the world. The economic and ideological foundations that help to form the essential attribute of the Chinese legal philosophy are the long-lasting farming society characterized by the small-scale peasant economy in ancient China, as well as a series of ideological, political, and legal organisms with Chinese characteristics evolved from such a society.

On one hand, in the long-term stable and almost unchanged farming society, under the pressure of producing more food to satisfy the growing population, the farming society in ancient China adopted intensive and meticulous farming. This mode of production significantly demanded operating experience and family unity. Therefore, the elders in the family and men with strong physical strength became the main force for stabilizing and promoting social progress and development, and family unity further strengthened the original patriarchal relationship (Zhang, 2015, 29). This realistic background provided legitimacy for mature men to have a monopoly on major national activities, such as plowing land, sacrifices, and wars. It also provided grounds for the power hierarchy and rank sequence in families and clans, forming the fathers' power, the husbands' power, the parental power, and the patriarchal clans' power. The last two cardinal guides of the "three cardinal guides and the five constant virtues"—fathers guide sons and husbands guide wives—in the Confucian ethics or patriarchal ethics of the Chinese Legal Family were developed from here. According to the explanation provided in *Shuo Wen Jie Zi* (Discussing Writing and Explaining Characters, 说文解字): "Ethics are seniority ... another opinion is that ethics are the truth." Duan Yucai commented: "Ethics are the truth and rationality" (Xu, 1981, 371). Therefore, some scholars proposed that in the ancient Chinese circumstances, ethics were the principles of seniority, that is, how people should get along with each other according to their seniority. In short, the ethics were called the truth of people, the rationality of people, and the righteousness of people, which was commonly referred to as human ethics (Li, 1985, 211). The long-term stable and almost unchanged farming society in ancient China was the economic basis for the emergence and long-term effect of these human ethics and morality, which in turn became one of the foundations of ancient Chinese legal philosophy.

On the other hand, in the long-term farming society, the basic unit for the production and life of the ancient Chinese were families or slightly expanded families, and families and clans were connected by blood ties. From the perspective of the history of world civilizations, when humans evolved from a chiefdom society to states at the end of the Neolithic Age from 5000 to 3000 BC due to urbanization, wars between cities, and so on, the blood relationship of primitive people (nomad groups) was constantly broken—in the ancient Mesopotamian civilization, etc. During the period from 2100 to 500 BC when ancient Greek and Roman society entered the era of hierarchy and states, the clans and tribes developed from divisions by blood to divisions by geography. Blood ties were thus completely destroyed. In ancient China, it was different. Blood ties were not destroyed in the course of evolution. Rather, by wars among clans and tribes aiming at annexation, the winning clans and tribes became the supreme ruling group, and the defeated ones became their subjects. Blood ties were further strengthened; people adopted blood ties as the standard by which to distinguish between friends or foes, and the law adopted friends or foes as the standard by which to distinguish between punishable and not punishable. Additionally, the supreme patriarch of the winning clan tribe, because of their victory, became not only the supreme chief in the clan tribe but also the supreme leader of the entire society (the world), obtaining the power to issue orders and rule over all other clans and tribes. These wars constantly happened among the clans and tribes. With the wars and compromises, tribal alliances and chiefdoms were formed; finally, a unified state was developed. Thus, in addition to *fathers guide sons* and *husbands guide wives*, the third cardinal guide, *rulers guide subjects* was also developed. The basis for the *three cardinal guides* was formed.

In addition, in the principles of the legal philosophy of the Chinese Legal Family, De (Virtue) was a core concept. De ran through the principles such as moral guidance and additional punishment, combined the utilization of leniency and strictness, simplifying law and limiting prohibitions, prudent penalties and light punishments, fairly deciding the punishment and rewards, and governing officials according to the law. According to the viewpoint of the ancient Chinese, human society was formed by the unity of Yin and Yang. Its internal structure was that Dao (the way things work) was Yin, the outer and auxiliary aspect, and De was Yang, the inner and main aspect. Dao was the manifestation of De, and De was the basis for the existence of Dao. Dao and De united constituted things. This unity, reflected in the law, was moral guidance with punishment supplementing it and combining etiquette and punishment. Therefore, "the principles of traditional Chinese law were nothing but the extension and expression of the principles of Chinese culture in the legal sense. However, the essence of the principles has changed, from the philosophical concepts of unity of Yin and Yang and Yang dominating and Yin subordinating, to the legal concepts of unity of Li (Ritual Propriety) and Fa (Law) and moral guidance and punishment supplementing it. Therefore, from the perspective of legal philosophy, the principles of traditional Chinese law can be called moral principles" (Zhang, 2015, 47). In ancient China, De was not only in a dominant position in relation to Dao and Xing, but also constituted the main line of the *five constant virtues* in the *three cardinal guides and five constant virtues* of Confucian ethics and patriarchal ethics. The *five constant virtues*—Ren (benevolence), Yi (righteousness), Li (propriety), Zhi (wisdom), and Xin (trustworthiness) were all specific contents of De, that is, the five virtues. Constant virtues had the meaning of immutability, so these five virtues were also immutable. Among the unchanging five virtues, Ren means benevolence and fraternity, Yi means righteousness and appropriateness, Li means orderly and reasonable—this is Li in a micro sense; Li in a macro sense means the great law of the country, namely the main laws and institutions of the country—Zhi means wisdom and understanding, Xin means good faith and credit (Zhang, 2015, 53). These were all in line with the above-mentioned basic principles of ancient Chinese legal philosophy. They were the ethical basis of the latter.

Lastly, the ancient Chinese view of the unity of humans and nature was also one of the ideological foundations for the basic principles of ancient Chinese legal philosophy. The section "Mingli" (General Principles) of *Tang Lv Shu Yi* clearly declared: "De and Li are the roots of politics and education, and punishment is the instrument. The two are like morning and evening, and spring and autumn, which are complementing each other" (Liu, 1996b, 3). This passage classically shows how the Chinese Legal Family was influenced by the ancient Chinese cosmological view (Tian Dao concept [the natural law concept]). That is, from the perspective of the natural universe outlook of the ancient Chinese, the world we humans live in was a living system, a living body in which heaven, earth, and people coexisted harmoniously. It consisted of many pairs of opposite, interdependent and contradictory objects, such as light and dark, day and night, Yang and Yin, life and death. It was orderly and endless. In the operation of this living body, it was Dao (the way things work) that performed a regulating function. Those who conformed to Dao would survive and develop; those who did not conform would decline and perish. And this Dao, in terms of the relationship between people and things (the external world), was that people must produce and live in accordance with the development and changes of nature. Those who understood and mastered this Dao (the laws of nature) were the elders, the sages, the wise men, and the able men. This provided a philosophical basis for respecting the elders, the sages, wisdom, and skills in the Chinese Legal Family. In terms of the relationship between people, the key was that people had virtues. The standards of virtues were the three cardinal guides—*fathers guide sons,husbands guide wives,* and *rulers guide subjects*—and the five constant virtues—Ren, Yi, Li, Zhi, and Xin. Therefore, the ancient Chinese view of the natural orders, that man and nature were a unity, provided the ultimate legitimacy for the introduction, incorporation into codes, and implementation in daily life of the basic principles of the ancient Chinese legal philosophy. People-oriented thoughts, emphasis on educating and transforming people, moral guidance and supplementary punishment, combined utilization of leniency and strictness, simplifying law and limiting prohibitions, prudent penalties and light punishments, fairly deciding the punishment and rewards, governing officials according to the law, and adapting laws to the times were all externalization and expansion of this legitimacy.

It is worth noting that the above-mentioned overwhelming influence of Confucian ethics or patriarchal ethics on ancient China occurred not only in China, but also in the member states of the Chinese Legal Family. For example, in ancient Korea, "Confucianism, as a ruling idea, its influence on the social structure and life style, and its domination of the national consciousness, is worthy of special attention. The reason why Confucianism could have a decisive influence on the consciousness of law is mainly that the law was regarded as social norms supplementing (assisting) De or Li, and its role was also limited to this" (Gao, 2007, 31).

1.3 Combination of Chinese and Western and Inheritance of Tradition

The legal philosophy of the Chinese Legal Family, as the core of ancient Chinese legal thoughts, played a guiding and leading role in the survival and development of the Chinese Legal Family for more than 1300 years. In modern times, under the invasion of Western Common Law and Civil Law, it gradually waned. The law and legal philosophy formed in the new China, as the legal system and guiding ideology of the world's second largest economy in the twenty-first century, should originate from the Chinese Legal Family, Common Law, and Civil Law, but go beyond these three legal systems. On one hand, it is the inheritance and development of Common Law, Civil Law, and all the achievements of human legal culture—Marxist legal philosophy, German historical jurisprudence, British analytical positivism, and American social jurisprudence, etc. On the other hand, it must also fully absorb the essence of the Chinese Legal Family and traditional Chinese legal culture. The above-mentioned principles, people-oriented thoughts, emphasis on educating and transforming people, moral guidance with punishment supplementing it, combined utilization of leniency and strictness, simplification of the law and limiting of prohibitions, prudent penalties and light punishments, fair decisions on the punishment and rewards, the governing of officials according to the law, and adapting of laws to the times are the manifestations of this essence. Only on this basis can the new China's law and jurisprudence move toward a more brilliant future.

Specifically, first, the legal philosophy of the Chinese Legal Family originated from the induction, summarization, and condensing of legal thoughts in ancient China, especially after the Sui and Tang Dynasties. However, in general, the current research is still insufficient. Scholars who tend to separate the legal thoughts from the legal philosophy have not yet integrated and studied them together. Objectively speaking, the academic status of the history of Chinese legal thoughts has been declining. It was a prominent study around 1990. At that time, not only did many students like this study, but many teachers of this study were academic directors who had great influence, such as Li Guangcan, Zhang Guohua, Rao Xinxian, Liu

Hainian, Wang Hanqing, Qiao Wei, Chen Pengsheng, Yu Ronggen, Duan Qiuguan, Wu Shuchen.[3] Now, all of them have left their positions. After all, there is still an organization, namely the History of Chinese Legal Thoughts Research Association, and courses, namely the curriculum system arranged by major political and legal faculties. However, ancient Chinese legal philosophy has neither an independent organization—the current one is affiliated to the Jurisprudence Research Association—nor an independent curriculum system, and there are very few universities that arrange courses of ancient Chinese legal philosophy. This is something we must pay attention to.

Second, the research on the legal philosophy of the Chinese Legal Family has many achievements, but they have not been sorted out and are relatively scattered, and tend to be fragmented. There are no systematic results yet. For example, in his book *The Tradition and Modern Transformation of Chinese Law*, Zhang Jinfan made a detailed enumeration and exposition of Chinese legal traditions. There are as many as 15 traditions, among which the Chinese Legal Family was created by various ethnic groups and was listed as the last one. Zhang Jinfan listed the combination of Li and Fa, respect for De and careful punishment, respectful practice of natural law, law enforcement considering human sentiment, law being created by the emperor, rule of law based on ethics, etc. as the traditions of Chinese law. They should be considered as important contents of ancient Chinese legal philosophy. It was not seen as an issue of legal philosophy and given intensive discussion. In Yang Yifan's article "A Major Misunderstanding in the Study of the Chinese Legal Family—Questioning the Doctrine of 'Integration of All Laws and No Differentiation of Civil and Criminal Laws,'" he believed that from the pre-Qin period to the Ming and Qing Dynasties, ancient Chinese laws had various forms of law. Different forms of law had their own specific functions, so the civil and criminal laws were divided, and the criminal laws were different from various non-criminal laws. He further criticized the traditional doctrine of the Chinese Legal Family of "integration of all laws and no differentiation between civil and criminal laws." In addition, Ma Xiaohong conducted an in-depth analysis and elaboration on the ancient Chinese value, *Li*, and Zhang Zhongqiu on the core concept of legal philosophy in the Chinese Legal Family, *Dao* (the way things work). However, the perspective of the above author's discussion is the whole of ancient China, not just a systematic discussion of the legal philosophy of the Chinese Legal Family. Therefore, these research results should be reviewed and carefully sorted out to form a relatively complete system of the legal philosophy of the Chinese Legal Family that truly reflects Chinese characteristics.

Third, as mentioned above, the two major legal families in the West each have their own legal philosophy, guiding ideology, and spirit. But their essence is the same; that is, the traditions of justice and rule of law created by Plato (about 427 BC–347 BC) and Aristotle (384 BC–322 BC), which was further carried forward by Western thinkers and jurists. In the Chinese Legal Family, although there were some ideas that

[3] Among these seniors, Li Guangcan, a researcher at the Chinese Academy of Social Sciences, and Zhang Guohua, a professor at Peking University Law School, have already left. But their works have been integrated into the cornerstone of the study of the history of Chinese legal thoughts.

pursued fairness and justice in judicial trial activities, and emphasized the equality of punishments and value of the rule of law, there was no tradition of justice and rule of law formed as in the West. Therefore, when we emphasize the strengthening of legal philosophy research in the Chinese Legal Family, the main purpose is to discover elements of the legal philosophy traditions that have inspirational and transformative value for the modern construction of legal systems—such as the above-mentioned people-oriented thoughts and emphasis on educating and transforming people—incorporate them into modern law and jurisprudence, and combine them with the extraterritorial experience, such as the achievement of justice and rule of law in Common Law via precedents and in Civil Law via codified laws. In this way, ancient and modern, Chinese and foreign experience are integrated and all achievements of legal culture created by humans are combined. We believe this is the significance of our study of the legal philosophy of the Chinese Legal Family today, and it is also the goal of our effort to build new Chinese law and jurisprudence today.

2 Jurisprudence

As a legal family that survived for more than a thousand years, the Chinese Legal Family needed not only the spirit (such as Confucianism) but also a number of major codes as its foundation—such as *Tang Lv*, the *Yoro Code*,[4] the *Kyongguk taejon* (*Great Code of National Governance*, 经国大典),[5] and the *Le Code* (国朝刑律]),[6] the hard work of a group of professional law scholars, and the support of a solid, high-level and meticulous jurisprudence. This jurisprudence is the legal commentary studies (legal studies) in ancient China, Japan, Korea, and Vietnam. Due to space limitations and the author's background knowledge, this section mainly focuses on the legal studies in ancient China and Japan (later named *Myobodo*). It explores the formation, development, main contents, basic characteristics, and internal laws of the jurisprudence of the Chinese Legal Family. Suggestions and communication from academic circles are welcomed.

*2.1 Origin and Development of Legal Studies (*Myobodo*)*

Taking ancient law as the research object, legal studies paid attention to the establishment of legislative principles and the compilation of codes, as well as the discussion of legal theories and the interpretation and application of laws. It can be said that the development of the legal studies has provided important theoretical support for

---

[4] Japan, promulgated in 718 and implemented since 757.

[5] Korea, promulgated in 1461 and implemented after amendment in 1485.

[6] Vietnam, also called the *Hong Duc Code* or *Punishment Law of Le*. It was a code promulgated in the Le Dynasty (1428–1789).

the establishment and development of the Chinese Legal Family and building of the legal systems in China and its neighboring countries.

2.1.1 Etymology of Legal Studies (*Myobodo*)

The so-called *legal studies*, in short, are the studies of laws (including Ling, Ge, Shi and other forms of law) in ancient China. Specifically, the Chinese legal studies were uniquely developed in ancient China. It is an academic research field formed in the Qin and Han Dynasties with the emergence of codified laws and encouraged by the ruling class's need to annotate and interpret the codes to implement them. It is an important part of jurisprudence in ancient China. Although academic circles believe that the legal studies were born in the Qin and Han Dynasties, in fact, no record of the concept and research situation of law can be found in the literature of the Qin and Han Dynasties (He, 1999). Legal studies in the strict sense, that is, legal studies as an academic form and discipline, experienced its development in the Western and Eastern Han Dynasties and the Wei, Jin, Southern and Northern Dynasties, and only matured and became finalized in the Sui and Tang Dynasties.[7]

During the reign of Cao Rui, Emperor Ming of Wei of the Three Kingdoms (204–239), the minister Wei Ji wrote to the emperor that "The punishment law is what the state considers as important, but people look down on it when talking privately; the law officials are deciding people's lives but are chosen from those who are from humble origins. The drawbacks of the ruling may be due to this problem. Please arrange the position of Lv Boshi (Doctor of Law), teaching others about the law" (Chen, 1982, 611). Here, although Wei Ji's memorial was out of concern about the decline of the social legal atmosphere at that time, and the term *legal studies* did not appear in the text, legal studies received attention as a specialized knowledge. Later, in *Jin Shu: Shi Le Zhuan* (Book of Jin: Biography of Shi Le, 晋书·石勒传) and *Nan Shi: Kong (Zhi) Gui Zhuan* (History of the Southern Dynasties: Records of Kong [Zhi] Gui 南史·孔[稚]珪传), the term *legal studies* appeared respectively, thus: "In the 2nd year of the Taixing Era (319), (Shi) Le pretended to be the King of Zhao ... and (appointed) Xu Xian and Yu Jing as *Jijiu* (an official position, the head of the academy in ancient China) of the legal studies." "In the Yongming Era (483–493), Gui made 20 volumes of law texts, one volume of prefaces, and proposed to create positions of legal study assistant (Xiao, 1972, 838) and follow the example of Wu Jing. The emperor issued an edict following his suggestion, but in the end, it was not implemented." However, at that time, people did not use the concept of *legal studies*

[7] Since the topic of this section is limited to the Jurisprudence of the Chinese Legal Family, which was formed at the end of the sixth century and the beginning of the seventh century, the legal works of the periods before the birth of the Chinese Legal Family, including the Qin and Han Dynasties and the Wei, Jin and North and South Dynasties, are not analyzed in detail, unless they are closely related, such as *Fa Lv Da Wen* (Questions and Answers Concerning the Law, 法律答问), which was in the Shuihudi Qin bamboo texts excavated in the 1975 in Hubei, and "How to Manage Officials and Commoners" in *Yuelu Shu Yuan Cang Qin Jian (Yi)* (Qin Texts Collected in Yuelu Academy I, 岳麓书院藏秦简 (壹)) (published on February 23, 2013).

for the activities of interpreting the law. The term *legal studies* was used mainly referring to the academic (official) position of *Lv Boshi* (the teaching assistant).

After more than 500 years of tortuous development and evolution, in the Sui and Tang Dynasties when the Chinese Legal Family was formed, the legal studies had matured and became a specialized academic field. In the 3rd year of the Yonghui Era during the reign of Emperor Gaozong in the Tang Dynasty (652), the emperor issued an edict: "The interpretation of law has not yet been determined, and therefore, the selection of *Mingfa* (Knowledge of Law) officials every year has no clear standards. It is appropriate to widely summon the law scholars to provide interpretation and still let *Zhongshu* Department (the secretariat, in charge of making orders and policies) and *Menxia* Departments (the chancellery, in charge of verifying orders and policies) monitor and make final decisions" (Liu et al., 1975, 2141). Two points can be summarized from this edict. First, although *Yonghui Lv* was promulgated in the 2nd year of the Yonghui Era and legal studies matured, the central and local governments had different understandings of the legal provisions in the trial. The *Mingfa* subject (the subject of legal studies) in the annual imperial examinations also had no unified authoritative standard, so it was necessary to "make interpretation for the law."[8] Second, at that time, the legal studies were not purely organized and presided over by the division of legal studies in *Guozijian* (the highest department of education) and the judicial department of the central government. Various other government departments[9] and law interpreters in the private sectors also studied this knowledge. Therefore, the edict required that these people should be gathered so they could make commentaries for the codes provision-by-provision, and then the government could promulgate and implement them.[10] It was against this background that after more than a year of collective efforts by legal elites, the famous *Yonghui Lv Shu* (Interpretation of Lv in Yonghui, 永徽律疏, renamed "Tang Lv Shu Yi" after the Yuan Dynasty) was promulgated in the 10th lunar month of the 4th year of the Yonghui Era (653).

[8] Some scholars also believe that this edict was asking for a fixed interpretation. It can also be understood that the formal legal interpretation had been formed at that time in the Buddhist legal study, so this edict was urging the profane world to accept the results of the Buddhist legal study and realize the transition from the law without interpretation to the law with interpretation. See Chen (2015).

[9] This can be confirmed by the following text in this imperial edict: Wuji and others "participated in the making of the legal interpretation and produced 30 volumes of interpretation. The interpretation was submitted to the emperor in the 10th lunar month of the 4th year and was promulgated and implemented. Since then, all legal officials cited this interpretation to analyze cases." See Liu et al. (1975, 2141).

[10] Some scholars believe that at that time, legal studies were not only carried out in the governmental sectors. Moreover, there was a big chance that the folk legal studies were better than the official ones. This is why it was necessary to widely summon legal scholars. See He (2010). Whether or not there were legal interpreters in the private sector is still debatable in academic circles. However, the author believes that based on the textual research of the Japanese scholar Mitsuo Riko, it can be proved that there were law interpreters in the private sector since in the text of the legal documents introduced to Japan in the Tang Dynasty, there were not only codes but also many unofficial commentaries on the law. This is good evidence for the existence of folk law interpreters.

Meanwhile, in Japan, Empress Suiko came to the throne in 592 (592–628). She carried out political and legal reforms, and sent envoys to Sui and Tang to learn Chinese laws and jurisprudence. In the 9th year of the Jinki Era (728), the legal studies were established for legal education. In the middle of the eighth century, the legal studies were developed into *Myobodo*. The use of the term *Myobo* (*Mingfa* in Chinese) in ancient Japan was also borrowed from the ancient Chinese books. In China, the term *Mingfa* appeared frequently as early as the pre-Qin period. For example, in the book Guan Zi (Master Guan, 管子), there is a chapter on *Mingfa*, which emphasizes that there were both wise and fatuous monarchs, and there were both *Mingfa* (good laws) and *Anfa* (evil laws) to be enforced. Han Fei (280–233 BC) provided a clearer meaning of *Mingfa*: "The rulers need to utilize their courtiers wisely. Although some courtiers have wisdom and talent, they must not violate the law and seize all the power. Although some courtiers have deeds of merit, they cannot be rewarded before they have made meritorious deeds. Although some courtiers are loyal, they cannot be exempt from the law and behave without restraint; this is called *Mingfa*" (Han, 2010, 166). That is to say, even if a courtier is wise, virtuous, and faithful, he must respect the law and abide by the law. This is *Mingfa*. The word *Ming* here is a verb, which means to highlight and respect. The views of *Mingfa* by Guan Zhong, Han Fei and other legalist schools were advocated by the First Emperor of Qin, Li Si and other Qin rulers. It became the legal views and guiding ideology of the Qin Empire. *Shi Ji: Li Si Lie Zhuan* (Biography of Li Si, 李斯列传) clearly states: "Clarifying the institutions and making the laws, all started from the First Emperor of Qin" (Sima, 1982, 2546); *Shi Ji: Qin Shihuang Benji* (Annals of the First Emperor of Qin, 秦始皇本纪) also records: "In the 28th year, the First Emperor traveled eastward to the county and went to Zouyi Mountain. On the stone… it said, when the emperor came to the throne, he made clear laws" (Sima, 1982, 243). Here, "making clear laws" means "establishing institutions and manifesting the law." The basic meaning of *Mingfa* is to pay attention to and highlight the law, and implement the law fairly, equally, and strictly.

In the Jin Dynasty, *Mingfa* became an official position. For example, the 18th volume of *Tang Liu Dian* provides: "Jin set up *Cheng* (supervisor), *Zhubu* (secretary), and *Mingfayuan* (legal deputy)."[11] The setting of *Mingfayuan* was inherited by the Northern Qi Dynasty, and the position *Sizhi Mingfa* (legal officials) was also added. The chapter "Officials" of *Sui Shu* (Book of Sui, 隋书) records that in the Northern Qi, "*Dalisi* (the highest judicial body) held the power to make and review judicial decisions. There were one *Zheng*, one *Jian*, one *Ping* (all three were officials in charge of making judicial decisions in different fields), four *Lv Boshi* (officials in charge of deciding penalties), twenty-four *Mingfayuan* (legal deputies), two *Jianchedu* (monitors for carts transporting prisoners) and ten *Yuan* (assistants), two *Yucheng* (prison aides) and two *Yuan* (assistants), ten *Sizhi* (officials in charge of reviewing decisions), and ten *Mingfa* (legal officials)" (Wei et al., 1973, 756). In the Sui Dynasty, the practice of setting up *Mingfa* was inherited: Emperor Gaozu reigned

[11] That is, in the Jin Dynasty, the assistant officials of *Tingwei* (judicial officer) included *Cheng*, *Zhubu*, and *Mingfayuan*. See Li et al. (1992, 501).

and set up "a position of *Qing* (head officer) and a position of *Shaoqing* (deputy), respectively, in *Dalisi*," "There was no unified administration, and one *Zheng*, one *Jian*, one *Ping*, ten *Sizhi*, eight *Lv Boshi*, and twenty *Mingfa* were arranged" (Wei et al., 1973, 775–776). What were the duties of *Mingfayuan* and *Mingfa* at that time then? Professor Fuse Yaheiji, a Japanese expert on *Myobodo*, believes that *Mingfa* should be the court clerks of *Dalisi* (Yaheiji, 1966, 42). This conjecture can be established because Zhang Fei (active in the late Wei and early Jin Dynasties), the author of the famous legal book *Lv Zhu Biao* (Notes for Lv, 律注表) in the Jin Dynasty, had the official position of *Mingfayuan*. This should be a strong piece of circumstantial evidence.

In the Tang Dynasty, in *Dalisi*, there was no longer *Bitie* (secretary) titled *Mingfa*, and among the subordinate officials of the Ministry of Punishment, there was also no *Mingfa* set up as an independent official position. *Mingfa* became a quota for selecting and recommending officials. The second volume of *Tang Liu Dian* records: "For all the divisions to arrange *zhi* officials (a kind of specialized officials in the Tang Dynasty), there are quotas. [Small print] The divisions have to set the following *zhi* officials with ranks: ... one *Mingfa* for Menxia Department, ... one *Mingfa* for Ministry of Punishment, ... one *Mingfa* for Zhongshu Department, ... two *Mingfa* for *Dalisi*, ... officials from local governments should be selected the same as officials from the capital. Every year they can be selected from the former and regular officials at will. The quota should be discounted if they are selected from the honorary officials, the three types of guards, and rewarded officials with achievements" (Li 1992, 35). In other words, in the Tang Dynasty, *Mingfa* was mainly not an official position, but a subject in the imperial examinations. Together with the *xiucai* (exam on governance and policies), *mingjing* (exam on the classics), *jinshi* (exam on making poetries), *junshi* (cloze), *mingzi* (exam on characters), and *mingsuan* (exam on arithmetic), it was listed as one subject of the seven imperial examinations. Here, the *ming* is the same as the *ming* in "*mingjing*" and "*mingsuan*," which means knowing well. The second volume of *Tang Liu Dian* also records: "The *Mingfa* examination tests Lv and Ling once for each. If the candidate understands the meaning and reasons well and is able to answer without question or stop, he can be regarded as passed. [Small print] If the candidate only has a rough understanding of the outlines and examples and has no deep learning of the directions and reasons, he can be regarded as not passed. There are ten close tests for Lv and Ling respectively. The examination also includes ten essay questions, seven for Lv and three for Ling. If the candidate answers all the questions, he will be rated as A. Those who answered eight or more will be rated as B. Others will be rated as not passed" (Li et al., 1992, 45).

Mingfa in the Tang Dynasty spread to Japan through the Japanese envoys to Tang China (such as Kibino Makibi, Yamatono Nagaoka). However, at that time, Japan did not immediately name the interpretation of law as *Myobo*. The name evolved in a period of time. For example, the famous Japanese historian Mitsusada Inoue believes that the *Myobo* subject (the Law subject) was set up in Japan in the 2nd year of the Tenpyo Era (730) (Inoue, 2004, 245). Most scholars believe that the *Myobo* subject or *Myobodo* was renamed from the legal studies established by Emperor

Shomu in the 5th year of the Jinki Era (728),[12] *Myobo Hakase* was also "renamed from *Ritsugaku Hakase* (Boshi of legal studies)." Of course, the transition from being called *Ritsugaku Hakase* to *Myobo Hakase* did not happen all at once. It was called *Myoboshi* (master of *Mingfa*) *Ryoshi* (master of Ling) in-between and there was a period of transition when *Ritsugaku Hakase* and *Myobo Hakase* were used in a mixed way (Yaheiji, 1966, 62). However, according to the historical records, Riko Mitsuo finds that as early as the Wado Era (708–714), there were scattered words such as *Myobo Hakase*, *Ryoshi*, and *Ritsushi* that express the same meaning as *Myobo Hakase*. He holds that the establishment of the *Myobo* subject can be traced back to the Wado Era during the reign of Emperor Gemmei instead of the 5th year of the Jinki Era during the reign of Emperor Shomu (Riko, 1967, 117). The author believes that even if Riko's research results can be established and the setting of *Myobo Hakase* in Japan is advanced by more than 20 years, it has no impact on the conclusion that the *Myobo* subject or *Myobodo* was transformed from the earliest legal studies (which were introduced from the Sui and Tang Dynasties of China).[13]

The etymology of *Myobodo*, according to the explanation of Professor Fuse Yaheiji of Nihon University, originated from the profession of *Myobo*: "People who served as *Myobo Hakase* and judges were called *Myoboka* (master of Mingfa). The study specialized by these *Myoboka*, namely, the study concerning Lv, Ling, Ge, and Shi, was called '*Myobodo*.' *Myobodo*, together with *Myogyodo* (study of classics),

---

[12] Due to such a historical background, in Japanese ancient books, parentheses were normally used when discussing *Myobo Hakase*, providing the additional information "also called *Lvxue Boshi*." For example, in the *Instructions for Officials* written by Nijo Yoshimoto of Gofukouenin, there was the text: "*Myobo Hakase* (*Ritsugaku Hakase*) should be chosen from well-known legal scholars with special talents. They should specialize in Lv, Ling, Ge, and Shi and belong to judicial officials, including the head judge (head officer of *Dalisi*) who make judgements and one of them also performs as the prosecutor." See Yaheiji (1966, 61). For another example, *Ryo-no-shuge*, written in the tenth year of the Jogan Era (868) by *Myobo Hakase* Koremune no Naomoto, records, when interpreting the "Law on Official II: Shikibu Sho II" in the *Yoro Code* produced in 718: "The interpretation provides that: memorial on the 27th day of the 3rd lunar month of the second year of the Tenpyo Era (730) reported that ... Two people for *Lvxue Boshi* ...Ten people for *Myobo students* and twenty for *Monjo* students ... Simply selecting from low-ranking officials or talented commoners, no age limit should be imposed." See (1966). *Newly Updated National History Series, Volume 23, Ryo-no-shuge I*, 80. Yoshikawa Koubunkan. The second year of the Tenpyo Era is 730. That means that at least before 730, *Lvxue Boshi* in Japan was still a formal official position (academic officer) in *daigakuryo* under *Shikibu Sho*. Although students who studied law had been called *Myobo students*, the academic officer had not yet been called "*Myobo Hakase*."

[13] In fact, regarding the appearance time of "*Myobo Hakase*," the author thinks it can be regarded as a few years earlier than the one that is widely accepted now. In Volume 2 of *Continued Japanese Chronicle*, it was recorded that after the formulation of *Taiho Code*, the imperial court launched a top-down publicity campaign to better implement it. In the eighth lunar month of the first year of the Taiho Era (701), the imperial court sent "*Myobo Hakase*" to various places to explain the new order and implement it. See (1966). *Newly Updated National History Series II: Continued Japanese Chronicle*. 12. Yoshikawa Koubunkan. This record was 10 years earlier than the Wado Era proposed by Riko Mitsuo. The author believes that perhaps at that time, the position of *Myobo Hakase* that was responsible for interpreting and sorting out the provisions of the new laws had appeared. Maybe it had not been formally established, but it should have a temporal inheritance relationship with the subsequent *Myoboka*.

Kidendo (Monjodo) (study of literature) and Sando (study of arithmetic), were called the four studies at that time in Japan. The four studies were all categories of knowledge that were studied by scholars in *daigakuryo* (imperial university of Japan, 大学寮), the 'educational institution' under the *Shikibu Sho* (Ministry of Ceremonial, 式部省)[14] at that time. In a broad sense, they were called 'various studies.' Other studies include the study of medicine, the study of calendar, and the study of Onmyo (Yin-Yang). That is to say, *Myobodo* was one of the various studies, and particularly it was one of the four studies" (Yaheiji, 1966, 61). Therefore, Japanese *Myobodo* was actually the legal studies. Not only was it derived from the legal studies, but its inherent aims were also the study of interpreting Lv, Ling, Ge, and Shi.

2.1.2 Growth Background and Maturity of Legal Studies (*Myobodo*)

What, then, was the historical background for the growth and maturity of legal studies (in China) and *Myobodo* (in Japan)? I believe there are six aspects.

First, the progress of legislation provided an objective basis for the maturity of the legal studies. In China, until the Han Dynasty, the number of the laws were very large, and many single-line Lv, Ling, Ke, Bi, etc. appeared. In the 6th year of the Yongyuan Era during the reign of Emperor He of Han (94AD), there were already 610 articles concerning the death penalty, 1698 articles concerning the *nai* penalty (a punishment that punished the criminals by shaving their beard), and 2681 articles concerning the reduction of penalty or less punishment in the laws of the Han Dynasty (Fang et al., 1974, 920). Under such circumstances, on one hand, the rulers should make the legislation simpler, more concise, convenient, and practical. Xin Lv (New Law) of Wei, Taishi Lv (Law of the Taishi Era [265–274]) of Jin, and the laws of the Northern Zhou and Northern Qi Dynasties all made efforts in this regard and achieved very good results, so that the laws the of Sui and Tang Dynasties were reduced to over 500 articles. On the other hand, this progress in legislation had also facilitated the progress of jurisprudence. It provided both requirements and conditions for the meticulous and in-depth development of legal studies.

Second, the development of the judiciary provided a practical basis for the maturity of legal studies. With the establishment of the Qin Empire, judicial trials also developed under a unified state governance model. "Quoting classics to make judgments" and the "compilation of precedents" that appeared in the Eastern and Western Han Dynasties were efforts to improve the justice (morality) of judicial trials. In the Jin Dynasty, *Mingfayuan* Zhang Fei further developed the trial theory on the basis of summarizing the experience of judicial trials in the past dynasties. On the one hand, Zhang Fei complemented and developed Dong Zhongshu's subjectivist trial theory of "convicting based on the original mind," emphasizing that judicial trials cannot

[14] *Shikibu Sho* is the result of Japan's reform of the national bureaucratic system after the "Taika Reforms" in 645. In 649, Japan set up two ministers and eight ministries in the central government. One of them was *Shikibu Sho*, which was in charge of personnel, court ceremonies, and academic affairs (education). See Ando (2016, 74).

ignore the law; on the other hand, he proposed a trial principle similar to the modern trial psychology: "basing on the original mind, considering the human sentiment, and investigating the matter in detail," emphasizing that "the heart feels it and the person is moved, the feeling is expressed by words and spreads to the four branches, and people start to do things. Happiness, anger, sorrow, and joy embody in voice and appearance; insincerity, honesty, ferociousness, and weakness can be observed from the eyes and breaths. This is why the traitor is ashamed, his face is red, and his inner fear manifested in his appearance. … Raising hands looks like he is begging, dropping hands looks like he is grabbing, holding hands looks like he is thanking somebody, twisting hands looks like he is pouring out, hunching his arms looks like he is confessing, pushing up his sleeves looks like he is going to fight, being serious looks like he is solemn, being happy looks like he is blessed" (Fang et al., 1974, 930). There is no doubt that these achievements promoted the study of judicial affairs in the Sui and Tang Dynasties. It also gave birth to the first case-study work in ancient Chinese jurisprudence—*Long Jin Feng Sui Pan* (Judgments by Officials, 龙筋凤髓判) written by Zhang Zhuo in the Tang Dynasty.

Thirdly, after the Jin Dynasty, legal studies became more and more meticulous, and this formed an academic foundation for the maturity of the legal studies in the Sui and Tang Dynasties. Summarizing the essence of the legal studies in the two Han Dynasties, the legal studies in the Wei and Jin Dynasties reached a new level of sophistication. *Jin Shu: Xing Fa Zhi* included a fragment of *Lv Zhu Biao* written by Zhang Fei, a famous legal scholar of the Jin Dynasty. This is the only work by legal scholars in the Wei and Jin Dynasties that has survived in history. In this work, Zhang Fei provided a precise interpretation of 20 important legal terms: *gu* (intent), *shi* (arrogance), *man* (deceiving the ruler), *zha* (fraud), *bujing* (irreverence), *dou* (crime in a fight), *xi* (crime at play), *zei* (unreasonable killing), *guoshi* (negligence), *budao* (depravity), *eni* (patricide), *qiang* (inchoate crime), *zaoyi* (initiating), *mou* (conspiracy), *shuai* (leading), *qiang* (force), *lve* (counter-violence), *qun* (more than two people), *dao* (theft), *zang* (illegal acquisition of property). The interpretation was so high-standard that it became a model for the legal studies of the later generations. For example, the interpretation of *gu* is "knowing the result and still committing a crime"; the interpretation of *shi* is "thinking something is right"; the interpretation of *guoshi* is "not intensively but negligently committing a crime." They all concentrate on the psychological state of the criminal subjects when they act to define the criminal behavior. *Gu* is intentional, *shi* is a fault of overconfidence, and *guoshi* is a negligent fault. As a result, it provided relatively clear meanings for the legal concepts of *gu*, *shi*, and *guoshi*. Another example is the interpretation of *mou*—"Two people discussing with each other is called conspiracy." *Zaoyi* means "being the initiator and the first one to say"; it also clarifies that the mutual consultation and planning of two or more people are necessary elements for joint crimes. The first person to make a suggestion or give an idea (the first to put forward the criminal intent) is the prime culprit in the joint crime. These interpretations by Zhang Fei are indeed admirable.

Fourth, the rise of the metaphysical (Xuan studies) and Buddhist legal studies provided a methodological basis for the maturity of the studies. Xuan (studies about mystery) originally referred to a specialized study named after the study of the "Three

Mysteries" (i.e., *Lao Zi* [Lao-Tzu, 老子], *Zhuang Zi* [Chuangcius, 庄子], and *Zhou Yi* [The Book of Changes, 周易]) during the Wei and Jin Dynasties. The word *Xuan* here came from the first chapter of *Lao Zi*: "The mystery of mystery is the key to the understanding of all wonders." Later, metaphysicians used Lao Zhuang Taoism to explain the Confucian classics. They advocated naturalness, trusted the Confucian ethical code, and tried their best to combine Confucianism and Taoism. A new philosophical trend was formed. It was a kind of negation and sublation of the Eastern Han Dynasty's *chenwei* classics study (a study using theology to explain the classics). It adopted a new world outlook, methodology and a complete set of conceptual system to develop theories about the universe and human beings. It included the study of legal commentary and legal research. On the one hand, with the thinking methods of "unifying the all" and "using simplicity to control the complicated," the metaphysicians broke the Confucian (Jingxue) methods used in the legal studies since the Western Han Dynasty. It provided new methods for the transformation of the world outlook of the legal studies, that is, from complicated to simple, from vague to clear, and from cluttered to organized. On the other hand, another method of "distinguishing the names and analyzing the principles" systematically expounded by the metaphysician Guo Xiang also had an important influence on the legal studies in this period. "Distinguishing the names and analyzing the principles" means to analyze and explain the stipulations of a class of things, as well as their implications, so as to help people to understand them more deeply. The clear definition and logical analysis of the legal terms (such as Zhang Fei's above-mentioned 20 legal terms) in the legal research results during this period and the precise interpretation of the legal provisions were an outstanding achievement of this influence (Liu, 1996a). The methodology of the metaphysical world outlook was gradually integrated into the legislation and legal studies of the Southern and Northern Dynasties after the Jin Dynasty, and eventually, it bore fruit in the Sui and Tang Dynasties.

After the fifth century, Buddhist legal studies began to rise. With the translation and research of a number of Buddhist regulatory texts around 404 in Hou Qin of the Northern Dynasty and Song of the Southern Dynasty, such as *Ten Recitation Vinaya*, *Four Part Vinaya*, *Mahasamghika Vinaya*, and *Five Part Vinaya*, a class of Buddhist masters of law, composed of the translators and interpreters of Buddhist texts and precepts, gradually began to take shape. Its academic form, Buddhist legal studies, also began to take shape. According to the records in *Biography of High Monks* and *Biography of High Monks II*, "Minglv" (knowledge of the precepts) ranked fourth among the ten Buddhist subjects, and the proportion of Minglv monks ranked sixth. According to the *Biography of High Monks of the Song Dynasty*, among the high monks after the Tang Dynasty, 68 of them were Minglv monks, accounting for more than 10% of the total number, 656. To study and explain the Buddhist precepts, a master of law needed to make interpretations for the precepts. The interpretation analyzed precepts in different provisions and the masters of law were also known for their meticulous analysis, such as Huixun, Daoyan, Sengyin in Liu Song, Zhidao, Faying, Falin, and Zhicheng in Xiao Qi. After the Liu Song period, in fact, the Buddhist legal studies became popular. Not only had the first book concerning the interpretation been published, that is, Huiyou's *Shi Song Yi Shu* (Interpretation on the Ten Recitations, 十诵义疏), but also the name of the Buddhist legal studies was finally fixed after being called *Lvbu* (the law part), *Lvzang* (the law classics), *Lvjin* (the forbidding law), *Lvpin* (the law category), *Lvyuan* (the law ground), and *Lvxue* (the legal studies). In this way, before the publication of *Tang Lv Shu Yi*, the Buddhists had completed three major *shu* and five major *bu* (both shu and bu are interpretations of the classics), which provided interpretation on the Buddhist precepts and made the legal studies achieve an unprecedented degree of prosperity. Its mature and sophisticated research methods and models for interpreting the precepts also provided a methodological basis for the maturity of the secular legal studies in the Tang Dynasty (Chen, 2015).

Fifth, the requirements of the academic division provided internal motivation for the maturity of the legal studies. The citation of the classics to make notes for the law in the two Han Dynasties combined the legal studies with political ethics and made the legal studies increasingly prosperous. However, the development of the classical studies made it a study concentrating on chapters and sentences, which pursued detailed research on the hidden or tiny points. It became trivial and pedantic, nearing a dead end. In the Jin Dynasty, Du Yu (222–284), a general and a master of Confucianism and legal studies, and Zhang Fei, who served as *Mingfa* yuan during the reign of Emperor Wu of Jin, solved this problem with academic division, curing the theoretical source of the problem. They clearly pointed out that the law was not a book exhausting the reason and human nature. Zhang Fei also explained 20 special legal terms, such as *gu*, *shi*, *guoshi*, *zaoyi*, and *mou, in the Lv Zhu Biao.* It made the legal studies gradually mature and meticulous, differentiated legal studies from classical studies, clarified the distinction among legal studies, the metaphysics that prevailed in the Wei and Jin Dynasties, and the increasingly influential Buddhism, and laid the theoretical foundation for mature legal studies and independent and divided disciplines (He, 2010). This theoretical achievement promoted the development of legislation and judicial practice. It was on the basis of the development of the legal studies in the Han, Wei, and Jin Dynasties that the legal studies of the Sui and Tang Dynasties matured, and jurisprudential achievements that represented the highest level of the Chinese Legal Family, such as *Tang Lv Shu Yi*, were launched.

Sixth, the development of the gentry in society provided a talent base for the maturity of the legal studies. Aristocratic families in the Wei, Jin, Southern and Northern Dynasties were some specific social groups based on blood and families from the Han Dynasty to the Sui and Tang Dynasties. According to statistics, there were 28 appellations such as *gaomen* (high gate), *menhu* (gate and windows), *mendi* (gate areas), *mendi* (gate and house), *shijia* (powerful families), *shijia* (hereditary families), *shizhou* (hereditary descendants), *shizu* (hereditary clans), and *shizu* (aristocratic families), among which the most representative title is *shizu* (aristocratic families) (Mao, 2002, 141 note 1). "The Wei-Jin aristocratic families were mainly evolved from Confucian families and families of officials. There were many educated people, and the families' Confucian style was their biggest feature" (Yan, 2005, 304). The combination of study and officialdom enabled the power of the families of scholars to break through the pure academic field featuring apprenticeship, and schools and expand to social and political fields. This kind of prestige was not only the recognition of the individuals' character and knowledge, but also the recognition of the family style that had been passed down from generation to generation. It also prepared talents for the production of the legal studies. "Having practices of *xiao* (Chinese parental respect) and *you* (fraternity among siblings)" enabled the families to accurately grasp the general trend of Confucian ideas in law since Emperor Wu of Han. Knowledge transferred from father to son also made it no longer necessary to take the officials as the teachers, and therefore, embarked on a special path of teaching and learning. In the two Han Dynasties, Three Kingdoms, Wei, Jin, Southern and Northern Dynasties, knowledge inheritance of the four generations of Chen Xian, Chen Gong, Chen Chong, and Chen Zhong, family studies of Cui Xuanbo, Cui Hao, and Cui Zusi, and legal families such as the Feng's family, were representatives in this regard (He, 2010).

In Japan, the etymology of *Myobodo* has been mentioned above. Since Japanese legal studies were inherited from the Chinese legal studies in the Sui and Tang Dynasties, many in-between links in the formation of the legal studies were omitted. As for the introduction of legal studies to Japan and its subsequent development (destiny), it was the result of the changes in Japanese society from the eighth to the twelfth century. After Empress Suiko came to the throne in 592 AD, she appointed her nephew, Prince Shotoku (574–622) as regent in the following year and began political reforms, learning from Chinese legal culture in all directions. At the same time as the adoption of the 12 court ranks in 603 and the 17-article constitution in 604, the first batch of envoys to Sui was sent to China in 600. After that, in 607, 608, and 614, several batches of envoys to Sui were sent to the Sui Dynasty, including Ono no Imoko, Takamuko no Kuromaro, Buddhist monk Somin and other famous monks and students (Ando, 2016, 62). After the establishment of the Tang Dynasty in 618, Japan sent 19 batches of envoys to the Tang Dynasty from 630(Ando, 2016, 85). Among them, there were the aforementioned first generation famous Japanese legal scholars, such as Yamato no Nagaoka (689–769) and Kibi no Makibi (695–775).

In 701, Japan formulated *Taiho Code*, and in 718, it adopted *Yoro Code*, thus entering the era of a Ritsuryo country (a country based on the legal system of Lv and Ling). In order to make the law well implemented, from the first half of the eighth century, *Myobodo*, the knowledge of interpreting Lv, Ling, Ge, and Shi, began to enjoy a rapid development. The government came forward to promote the activities of publicizing and explaining Lv and Ling and set up *daigakuryo* (the imperial university) under *Shikibu Sho* (the Ministry of Ceremonial), specializing in the teaching and education of *Myobo* knowledge. In addition, the *Myobo* students and those who served as *Myobo Hakase* after graduation were appointed by the imperial court as important judicial officials such as deputy judges, head judges, and prosecutors,[15] participating in the practice of law. At that time, although *Myobo Hakase* did not enter the highest power center such as the imperial family, after more than 80 years of

[15] In the seventh year of the Konin Era (816), in order to maintain the security of Kyoto, the Japanese Emperor's Government established the *Kebiishi* Agency (Office of Prosecutors). The director-general of the agency was responsible for the exercise of judicial and police powers of the Police Department, the Deference Department, and the Ministry of Justice. See Ando (2016, 102).

experience in the Nara Dynasty (710–794), some outstanding *Myobo Hakase* gradually developed family inheritance of the knowledge of the legal studies (*Myobo*) in the Heian Dynasty (794–1192), such as the Sanuki family, the Koremune family, the Sakanoue family, and the Nakahara family, so that the legal studies (*Myobodo*) entered their heyday around the tenth century in Japan.

2.1.3 Development and Evolution of Legal Studies (*Myobodo*)

Legal studies, as the jurisprudence of the Chinese Legal Family, went through the embryonic stage in the Spring and Autumn Period and the Warring States Period, and emerged in the Qin and Han Dynasties. It was ignored at the beginning of the Wei, Jin, Southern and Northern Dynasties,[16] and promoted by a group of legal practitioners later. After its maturity in the Sui and Tang Dynasties, it entered a historical period of slow development and tortuous evolution in the Song Dynasty.

---

[16] There are different opinions in academic circles as to whether the legal studies were developed and reached a peak or were despised and lingered during the Wei, Jin, Southern and Northern Dynasties. Zhang Jinfan, Huai Xiaofeng, Yu Ronggen, Guo Dongxu, Shen Huiqing, Xing Yitian, and others have all expressed their good opinions. Su Yigong holds that the rise and fall of "the legal studies" should be decided not only by the prosperity of the subject, but also by whether the values embodied by it contain the core of "Ren" and "Ren governance" (social progress). It is in line with Shen Jiaben's point of view in *The Prosperity and Decline of the Legal Studies* that "Jin, Northern Qi, Sui, Tang, and Song Dynasties were all prosperous concerning the legal studies." See Su (2005, 476–480). Chen Linghai comprehensively denied the view that the Wei, Jin, Southern and Northern Dynasties were the prosperous times of Chinese legal studies, and take Wei Ji's statement during the reign of Emperor Ming of Wei as an example: "The punishment law is what the state considers as important, but people look down on it when talking privately." In the early Jin Dynasty, Jia Chong and Yang Hu consulted Zheng Chong about the amendment of law. Zheng Chong sneered at Lv and Ling as trivial matters and the legal studies as mediocre studies. In the beginning of the Eastern Jin Dynasty, Xiong Yuan made a criticism: "People are handling things without using the law, but competing for making orders, people have dissent and distort the law to suit situations and sentiments, so that the reputation of the law is damaged... the emperor dare not trust the law"; In the middle of the Eastern Jin Dynasty, Ge Hong held: "Officials today, no matter whether high-ranking or low-ranking, have no idea about the law... when officials don't know the law, they are likely to be deceived by their subordinates without knowing it"; Cui Zusi made a comment in the reign of Emperor Wu of Qi: "Today, the law students are from families of ordinary officials, not from aristocratic families such as Xian and Hong. They are lacking education." At the same time, Kong Zhigui reported to the throne that there were six reasons why "today, none of the scholars want to study law, and even if someone wants to study the law, he receives contempt from others." See Chen (2015). The author believes that for the legal studies, the Wei, Jin, Southern and Northern Dynasties were a transitional period (like the Middle Ages in Europe). The legal studies were developed at the beginning of the Eastern and Western Han Dynasties and went through more than 300 years of silence, weakness, preparation, and gradual revival, and the legal studies reached their peak in the Sui and Tang Dynasties. The sign of the accomplishment of such preparation and gradual rise was the establishment of *Lv Boshi* to teach law studies; the forms of law, Lv, Ling, Ge, and Shi began to be clearly distinguished; the chapter style and logical structure of the law were simplified and optimized; and the legal studies were separated from the Confucian classical studies and being increasingly independent.

On the one hand, the emperors, senior officials, and scholar-bureaucrats of the Song Dynasty were familiar with the law. Therefore, the legal studies, which had reached maturity and perfection in the Tang Dynasty, further developed. On the other hand, since the Song Dynasty, the emperor's autocracy and centralization gradually went to extremes, coupled with the rise of Neo-Confucianism by Zhu Xi (1130–1200), the legal studies began to be restrained and excluded. After entering the Yuan Dynasty, this situation was even worse. There were few legal works published, few legal scholars existed, the position of *Lvxue Boshi* was revoked, and the official (imperial examination) legal education was formally abolished. Later, in the Ming and Qing Dynasties, autocratic and centralized rule reached its peak, and the law became a main tool for such rule. In these circumstances, the rulers attached great importance to the legal studies, and the legal studies seemed to be *revived* and then *prosperous* in form. Some scholars believe that the laws of the Ming and Qing Dynasties expressly required "teaching and reading the law," and the rulers actively encouraged unofficial research on the law, which led to the emergence of a number of high-level unofficial legal works. These works played an important role in the judicial practice of the Ming Dynasty. In the Qing Dynasty, unofficial commentary of law reached its peak. From the perspective of content, it not only inherited the outstanding achievements of the legal studies in the Ming Dynasty, but also carried out various research and innovations, involving knowledge of commentary, collation, writing, phonology, etc., and some also involved the knowledge of modern jurisprudence, criminal law, etc. In terms of types, some were annotated with charts, some were written in verses, some specialized in case analysis, some specialized in legal research, and some concentrated on comparative research. The various forms greatly enriched China's legal studies (Wu, 1990, 375–391; Zhang, 1992, 164–176). However, some scholars believe that "in the Ming and Qing Dynasties, ideological pressure and cultural tyranny became more and more intense, and ethnic prejudice also existed in the Qing Dynasty. Disasters caused by writing were very common and scholars and students were silent. Political misconduct was extremely serious, and how was prosperity of academics possible" (Su, 2005, 479–480). The core values of *Ren* (benevolence) and *Ren governance* of the legal studies were taken away, leaving only a semblance of legal commentary. The legal studies in the Ming and Qing Dynasties entered an era of decline. The author believes that although the debate on this issue is fierce, the Ming and Qing legal studies indeed reached a very high-level in terms of the technical level of legal commentary.

In Japan, after the formation of *Myobodo* in the first half of the eighth century, it also experienced a process of development, prosperity, gradual decline, and disappearance. Marked by the compilation and publication of *Ryo-no-gige*, *Ryo-no-shuge*, and *Ritsu-no-shuge* (Collection of Interpretation of Lv, 律集解), Japan's *Myobodo* reached its peak in the 8th to tenth centuries. A large number of famous scholars of the legal studies appeared, such as Moribe no Muraji Osumi, Ochi no Hiroe, Shioya no Komaro, Yamada no Shirogane, Anou no Uchihito, Sanuki no Chitsugu, Sanuki no Hironao, Sanuki no Naganao, Sakurai Tanabe Sada Sho, Sakurai Yuhitsu, Okihara no Miniku, Nukata no Imatari, Koremune no Naomune, Koremune no Naomoto, Koremune no Kinkata, Kremune no Yoshitsune, Koremune no Tadasuke. After the establishment of the shogunate in Kamakura in 1192 by Minamoto no Yoritomo (1147–1199), the focus of the state power and the society gradually shifted to the Kamakura shogunate, which began to establish Buke shohatto (laws for samurai) to solve the emerging problems in the society. The original legal system centered on the centralized rule of the emperor began to decline, and *Myobodo* also began to wane. However, even in the era of Buke shohatto after the thirteenth century, when doing research on Buke shohatto such as *Goseibai Shikimoku*, there were still some achievements of the legal studies, such as various commentaries on the law (Ikeuchi, 1978). At the same time, *Yoro Code*, which was amended on the basis of the *Taiho Code*, was still the basic legal code in Japanese society in form during the Kamakura Shogunate, and later the Muromachi Shogunate (1336–1603) and the Tokugawa Shogunate (1603–1867). Therefore, the research activities of *Myobodo* were still ostensibly continuing (although their status was not as good as before).

In the seventeenth and eighteenth centuries, with the influence of China's *Da Ming Lv* (and later *Da Qing Lv Li*), there was a second wave of research on the law in Japan. Forms of law such as Lv, Li, Ling, and Huidian (institutions and regulations for officials) in the Ming and Qing Dynasties, as well as commentaries on the law of the Ming and Qing Dynasties, were successively introduced to Japan, such as Jin Zhi's *Da Ming Lv Zhi Jie* (Direct Interpretation of Da Ming Lv, 大明律直解), Wang Kentang's *Lv Li Jian Shi* (Interpretation of the Law, 律例笺释), Lei Menglin's *Du Lv Suo Yan* (Some Words When Reading the Law, 读律琐言) Yang Jian's *Lv Jie Bian Yi* (Discussion on the Interpretation of Law, 律解辨疑), and Lu Jian's *Da Ming Lv Guan Jian* (Humble Opinions on Da Ming Lv, 大明律管见). Japanese scholars, such as Sakakibara, Koshu (1656–1706), Ogyu Sorai (1666–1728), Takase Kiboku (1668–1749), Kada no Azumamaro (1669–1736), Ogyu Hokkei (1669–1754), Ashino Tokurin (1695–1775), and Moriyoshi Sonoda (1785–1840), all launched their own works on law. Of course, at that time, *Myobodo* was no longer mentioned, and legal scholars were no longer called *Myobo Hakase*.[17] The development and evolution of the legal studies in Japan (*Myobodo*) were different from those in China. The most fundamental reason is that China was the country of origin of the legal studies, while Japan was the successor. Therefore, the ups and downs of its development have a lot to do with the scope and strength of the introduction of Chinese law. Two waves, the absorption of the law and commentaries of the Sui and Tang Dynasties in the seventh century, and the absorption of the law of the Ming and Qing Dynasties after the sixteenth century, determined that the climax of the research on legal commentary in Japan closely followed the introduction of Chinese jurisprudence.

[17] Yaheiji, Fuse, a Japanese expert specialized in *Myobodo*, regarded the mid-fourteenth century as the ending of *Myobodo* in his monograph of *Research on Myobodo*. The last *Myobo Hakase* listed by him was Mr. Nakahara, who was active in the Jowa Era (1345–1350). See Yaheiji (1966, 301).

2.2 *Main Contents of the Legal Studies (*Myobodo*)*

—Commentary, Interpretation and Elaboration of Lv (Ling) Code, Lv (Ling) Articles, Chapters, Concepts, etc.

The development of jurisprudence in the Chinese Legal Family, although it has gone through many twists and turns, has persisted for a long time, leaving behind a considerable number of legal works with rich content and various styles. From these works, we can summarize the basic content of the jurisprudence in the Chinese Legal Family.

1. Re-organizing Lv and Ling and explaining the content, concepts, and terminology, this was the academic foundation of the legal studies and Japan's *Myobodo*. For example, *Tang Lv Shu Yi* has a detailed elaboration on the nature, inner content, and function of Lv, Ling, Ge, and Shi, as well as the internal relationship among them. It includes 12 chapters of specific provisions concerning general principles, guard of palaces, bureaucratic establishment, and family and marriage. It provides an explanation and interpretation of the five punishments: death penalty, exile, imprisonment, caning, and flogging, as well as the important criminal principles, for example, aggravation of punishment concerning the *ten abominations*, reduction and exemption for royal family members and officials, the patriarchal ethics, moral guidance and punishment where necessary, reduction and exemption for the elderly, young and disabled, the equivalent of crime and punishment, no punishment without law, comparison and analogy, precedence of specific provisions over general provisions, and false accusations leading to penalties. Eight basic characters and thirty-six important terms—vital to the implementation of *Da Qing Lv Li*—were given an explanation and elaboration in *Du Lv Pei Xi* (References for Reading Laws, 读律佩觿) by Wang Mingde of the Qing Dynasty; Japanese *Myobo Hakase*, Nukata no Imatari, Okihara no Miniku, Sanuki no Naganao and others proposed to compile *Ryo-no-gige* to provide a detailed explanation of the orders concerning the ranks and quota of the official positions.
2. Exploring the content of laws and the evolution of various institutions to understand their history. For example, *Xing Shu Shi Ming* (Interpretation of Terminology in Punishment Law, 刑书释名), a book written by Wang Jian, a legal scholar in the Song Dynasty, was a work that explains the names and methods of punishment used in the law (codes) of the past dynasties. Another legal scholar Liu Yun made a relatively systematic and complete description of the arrangements of the judicial officials and the historical evolution of them in his work *Xing Fa Xu Lve* (A Brief Introduction of the Punishment and Law, 刑法叙略). Xu Yuanrui, a legal scholar in the Yuan Dynasty, also made a clear exposition of the historical evolution of the official system, registration system, corporal punishment system, and interrogation system in his work *Li Xue Zhi Nan* (Guide to the Study of Officials, 吏学指南). Wu Tan wrote *Da Qing Lv Li Tong Kao* (General Exploration of the Great Qing Code, 大清律例通考) and Xue Yunsheng wrote *Du Lv Cun Yi* (Doubts and Questions When Reading the Laws, 读律存

疑). The two books carried out textual research of the law of the past dynasties from ancient times to the Guangxu Era in an item-by-item way, explored the source of the laws, and added notes to express their own opinions. *Ryo-no-shuge*, written by Koremuneno Naomoto, a Japanese *Myobo Hakase*, also made full use of the viewpoint of historicism. It not only fully absorbed and carried forward the previous achievements of the study of legal commentary, such as *Ryo-no-gige*, but also sorted and summarized the achievements of commentaries on law in China's various dynasties.

3. Elucidating the principles of law and highlighting the spirit of the law. American scholar E.S. Corwin quoted the words of U.S. Supreme Court Justice Oliver Wendell Holmes (1841–1935) in the first page of his book *The "Higher Law" Background of American Constitutional Law* to emphasize the importance of jurisprudence: "Theory is the most important part of the dogma of the law, as the architect is the most important man who takes part in the building of a house" (Edward, 1996, 1). Every work of the legal studies is based on a certain legal theory. One of the important features of *Tang Lv Shu Yi* is that the world-view of ancient Chinese orthodox legal studies based on Confucianism has been fully incorporated into the legal studies, reaching the realm of "using Li (Ritual Propriety) as the standards for all" in all legal texts, emphasizing that "De (Virtue) and Li are the foundation, policies and education are the tools."[18] The legal principles, spirits, and intentions of Fengjian society were also permeated everywhere in the works of legal studies after the Ming Dynasty, such as Lei Menglin's *Du Lv Suo Yan*. In the Japanese works of legal studies, these were also strongly advocated by the rulers and legal scholars. For example, in the annotation of *Household Order: National Repatriation Articles* of the above-mentioned *Ryo-no-shuge*, which is the most systematic unofficial legal commentary in ancient Japan, the author annotated the provision "disobedience to filial piety and fraternal duty is against Li and distortion of the constant virtues is not following the law." "Against Li" and "distortion of the constant virtues" were both given an interpretation: "against is not following, and distortion of the constant virtues are activities deviating from the five constant virtues. Not following the law means not following Lv, Ling, Ge, or Shi." "The Old Record provided an explanation of 'against Li'. In *Xiao Jing* (Classic of Filial Piety, 孝经), Confucius said: "People who do not love their parents but love others are violating De; People who do not respect their parents but respect others are violating Li."[19] When interpreting "against Li," the book also states: "The Interpretation provides, practice in a

---

[18] Of course, *Li* here is no longer the Li of Confucius and Mencius emphasized by early Confucianism, but the *Li* of the Tang Dynasty that has undergone thousands of years of transformation and adaption, that is, *Tang Li*. See Su (2006) and Gao (2010, 16–26). In fact, the intercommunication and integration of Li and Fa, as well as Lv and Jing (classics), were realized in the Han Dynasty. Shusun Tong made eighteen chapters of *Bang Zhang* (Additional Chapters, 傍章) and Zhao Yu made six chapters of *Chao Lv* (Etiquette for Pilgrimage, 朝律), all of which were codes of etiquette. See Qian (1979).

[19] (1966). *Newly Updated National History Series, Volume 23, Ryo-no-shuge I*, 325. Yoshikawa Koubunkan.

loving and respecting way to serve their parents, and then do the same thing to others; this is the foundation of filial piety."[20]

In addition to the above three aspects, exhausting various types of writing to publicize legal knowledge, comparing the pros and cons of the laws of different dynasties to improve the legislative capacity of the current dynasty, etc., are also important contents of ancient Chinese legal studies and Japanese *Myobodo*.

2.3 *Basic Features of Legal Studies (*Myobodo*)*

All scholars who do research on the legal studies have made some elaborations on the basic characteristics of the legal studies, such as Zhang Jinfan, Yang Yifan, Zhang Boyuan, Yu Ronggen, Wang Limin, Huai Xiaofeng, Zhu Yong, Wu Shuchen, Zhang Zhongqiu, Liu Guangan, Wang Hongzhi, Su Yigong, and He Min. In sum, it generally includes nine aspects: diverse and rich manifestations; Confucianism as the guiding ideology and commentary as the basic form; official studies and unofficial commentary complementing each other; Lv and Ling as the main research objects, in which criminal and administrative law was emphasized and Civil Law was disregarded; emphasis on practicality in the overall style without prominent theoretical analysis and elaboration; low status of the professional legal scholars without forming an independent professional class in China; a special legal education system; achievements of the legal studies directly affecting the operation and practice of law; the meticulousness of legal research. A detailed analysis of these characteristics can enable us to further understand the nature of the law. Due to space limitations and to avoid duplication with other scholars' discussions, here, we only give an analysis and discussion on three aspects: diverse and rich manifestations, official studies and unofficial commentary complementing each other, and the meticulousness of the legal research. Situations in Japan are also discussed.

First, the manifestations of the legal studies are rich and diverse. After the Sui and Tang Dynasties, with the continuous development of legal studies, its manifestations became more abundant and diverse: (1) comprehensive codified law commentaries, such as *Song Xing Tong* (Punishment Law of the Song Dynasty, 宋刑统); (2) interpretation of legal provisions and terms by phonetics and meanings, for example, Sun Shi's *Lv Fu Yin Yi* (Law with Pronunciations and Meanings, 律附音义); (3) systematic commentaries on the law, such as Lei Menglin's *Du Lv Suo Yan*, Wang Kentang's *Lv Li Jian Shi*, and Shen Zhiqi's *Da Qing Lv Ji Zhu* (Collection of Annotations to the Great Qing Code,大清律辑注); (4) poetic explanatory books of laws, such as Fu Lin's *Xing Tong Fu Jie* (Interpretation of Xing Tong, 刑统赋解), and Zong Jizeng's *Du Lv Yi De Ge* (Songs to Get the Code at Once, 读律一得歌); (5) Graphical books on legal studies, including Chen Haiyun's *Xing Lv Tu* (Drawings on the Punishment

[20] Ibid., 325–326. Professor Riko Mitsuo spoke highly of this commentary. He also explained that the provision here was from the *Taiho Code* and *The Old Record* here was a commentary book of the *Taiho Code*. See Riko (1961, 9).

Law, 刑律图) and *Ming Fa Zhi Zhang Tu* (Drawings on Criminal Laws, 名法指掌图) compiled by Shen Xintian; (6) legal works of monograph collections, such as Lan Dingyuan's *Luzhou Gong An* (Luzhou's Judgments, 鹿洲公案), and Wang Youhuai's *Ban An Yao Lve* (Outline of Case Handling, 办案要略); (7) works serving as instruments for assisting officials to understand the law, use the law, and carry out legal education, such as Zhang Tingxiang's *Xing Mu Yao Lve* (Important Points for Assisting Legal Officials, 刑幕要略), Wang Huizu's *Zuo Zhi Yao Yan* (Key Words for Assisting in Governance, 佐治药言), and Wan Weihan's Mu Xue Ju Yao (Key Points for Being Assistant, 幕学举要); (8) works on prison management, such as Zhao Shuqiao's *Ti Lao Bei Kao* (Carry Cell Test, 提牢备考); (9) works on interpretation of precedents, such as *Xing Bu Bi Zhao Jia Jian Cheng An* (Comparing the Judgments by the Ministry of Punishment with the Law, 刑部比照加减成案) by Xu Lian and Xiong E, *Xing An Hui Lan* (Collection of Criminal Cases, 刑案汇览) by Zhu Qingqi, and *Bo An Xin Bian* (New Compilation of the Reversed Cases, 驳案新编) by Quan Shichao and others; (10) legal popularization books or works on official experience, such as *Mu Ling Shu* (Book for Officials, 牧令书) edited by Xu Dong, and *Qi Min Yao Shu* (Essential Techniques for the Welfare of the People, 齐民要术) by Bao Shichen.[21] Of course, this formal classification into 10 aspects is only for the convenience of analysis because many legal works themselves may have the characteristics of various types. For instance, the systematic works often also have the characteristics of comprehensive works.

In Japan, through the learning and inheritance of various legal works in China, a variety of *Myobo* works of annotating, explaining, and expounding Lv, Ling, and other forms of law have also been developed. For example, *Ritsu-no-shuge* mainly annotated and interpreted the texts of Lv in the *Taiho Code* and *Yoro Code. Ryo-no-gige* and *Ryo-no-shuge* annotated and interpreted the texts of Ling in the *Taiho Code* and *Yoro Code.* The former is an official commentary and the latter an unofficial commentary (among all annotations collected in *Ritsu-no-shuge*, except for "The Old Record," which interpreted *Taiho Code*, all other annotations interpreted *Yoro Code).* The same is true for *Nukata's Commentary* and *Anou Commentary. Summary of Political Affairs* is a record of legal events that occurred in history and contents of laws and decrees, which is somewhat similar to *Xing Fa Zhi* (treatises on punishment and law) of ancient Chinese dynasties. *Assorted Kyaku of the Three Generations* (Kyaku is Ge in Japan) compiled the textual research on *Konin kyaku*, *Jogan kyaku*,

[21] Although the above-mentioned legal works are diverse in form and rich in content, their core values are the same. This was the orthodox legal worldview in ancient China, which was established in the Han Dynasty and synthesized by *Tang Lu Shu Yi.* Focusing on Confucianism and absorbing the traditional ideas of Legalism, Daoism, Buddhism, and various other schools, the worldview of the legal studies reflected the distinctive features of the Chinese Legal Family. The advantage of this view is that it emphasized the people-oriented thoughts and advocated the simplicity of the law, moral guidance with punishment complementing it, combined utilization of leniency and strictness, combined utilization of morality and punishment, no hierarchy being considered when imposing punishment, and prudent penalties and light punishments, etc. Its defects include that it overemphasized the function of Li and the endless power of morality, holding that Fa (law), Lv (specific rules), and Xing (punishment) were interconnected, so that the tool attribute of law was relatively strong.

and *Engi kyaku*. Since Japan was a successor in the field of the legal studies, a new form appeared in the Japanese legal studies, that is, translation and interpretation of the Chinese legal studies, such as Takase Kiboku's *Translations of Da Ming Lv Li*, and Ogyu Sorai's *Translation of Ming Lv*, Ogyu Hokkei's *Interpretation of Ming Lv in Japanese Characters*, and Sakakibara, Koshu's *Using Proverbs to Interpret Da Ming Lv Li*.

Second, official legal studies and unofficial legal studies complement each other. In ancient China, from its birth to the Sui, Tang, and Song Dynasties, although both official and unofficial studies developed, generally, official commentaries (official legal studies, with *Tang Lv Shu Yi* and *Song Xing Tong* as typical examples) were the basic form. However, from the Yuan Dynasty onwards, as the official law school (legal education) was cancelled, unofficial jurisprudence further flourished. Especially in the Ming and Qing Dynasties, the rulers began to encourage officials and their legal assistants to make unofficial commentaries on the law. The aim was to utilize their rich practical experience and have brainstorms to make up for the narrowness and inadequacy of the official commentary. At that time, unofficial jurisprudence basically became the main part of legal studies, and a number of high-level legal books during the Ming and Qing Dynasties were the results of unofficial jurisprudence. Of course, within the legal academic framework of the Chinese Legal Family, most of the unofficial commentaries could only supplement on the basis of affirming the rationale of the existing laws. They could not violate the will of the ruling class and traditional moral values. Otherwise, they would not be able to get the recognition of the court and judicial practice department. Their works would also lose their academic value.[22]

In Japan, there were more unofficial commentaries than official ones. For example, except for *Ryo-no-gige*, which was compiled by the officials, other commentaries were all compiled by the private sector, such as *Ryo-no-shuge, Ritsu-no-shuge, Anou Commentary, Kasuga's Commentary, Okihara's Commentary*. However, on one hand, these unofficial commentaries were basically repetitions, supplements, and extensions of *Ryo-no-gige*; on the other hand, even though unofficial, they were within the framework of the *Taiho Code* and *Yoro Code*. Therefore, the official and unofficial commentaries in the Japanese legal studies (*Myobodo*) were also very tacit and complementary. Especially after the thirteenth century, the national political system of Japan was not exactly the same as that of ancient China. That is, under the Japanese shogunate system, many legal works were actually compiled by legal scholars entrusted or instructed by the *han* (domains in Japan before the Meiji period) governments or the lords of the domains. It is difficult to distinguish between official and unofficial works. For example, in the eighteenth century, the legal scholar Takase Kiboku from Wakayama Domain completed his two masterpieces of legal science, *Translations of Da Ming Lv Li* (1720) and *Detailed Interpretation of Da Ming Lv Li* (1743), which were compiled at the request of the lord of the domain. The works were then kept and implemented by the *han* government. Therefore, this

[22] About the works of unofficial interpretation of law in the Qing Dynasty, see *Unofficial Interpretation of Law in the Qing Dynasty and Its Methods*. See Zhang (1992) and He (1992).

legal research not only had the attribute of an unofficial legal commentary, but was also the result of the officially organized compilation and implementation.

Third, the legal studies became meticulous. It was fully reflected in *Tang Lv Shu Yi*. After the continuous efforts of various generations of legal scholars, by the Ming and Qing Dynasties, the ancient Chinese legal sciences had been extremely meticulous at the technical level, reaching a state of near perfection. In this regard, *Du Lv Pei Xi* written by Wang Mingde, a legal scholar of the Qing Dynasty, can perform as an example for analysis. *Du Lv Pei Xi* fully absorbed the strengths of other legal works and further refined them. On one hand, the structure of *Du Lv Pei Xi* is very delicate. The meaning of the eight basic characters, the "eight methods of reading the law," and the meaning and interpretation of important characters and words (Wang Mingde called them the "eyes of the law"), such as *li* (obvious principles), *za* (no clear regulation provided by the law but have to impose punishment accordingly), *dan* (as long as), *bing* (together), *yi* (according to), *cong* (follow) and *congzhonglun* (theories on imposing more severe punishment), *leijian* (cumulative reduction), *dijian* (progressively reduction), *tingjian* (reduce after investigation), *dejian* (can be reduced), *zuitong* (the same punishment as), *tongzui* (impose the same punishment to non-criminals), are all discussed by the book. On the other hand, the interpretation style of *Du Lv Pei Xi* is original. It does not take the structural sequence of the code as the outline but is organized in different topics. Phrased differently, the book took a crime or a criminal law principle as the axis and then added the relevant texts of the law in various parts of the code to spark the discussion. In addition, most Ming and Qing legal works contain "the meaning of the eight characters in law," but except for Wang Kentang's *Lv Li Jian Shi*, all others only provide very brief explanations. Only *Du Lv Pei Xi* names these eight characters as "the basics of the law," and further gives an elaboration of them in great detail. Finally, the elaboration of the methods of reading the law in *Du Lv Pei Xi* is also very meticulous. The author called it the "eight methods of reading the law." These are "finding the key points, making an outline, searching the sources, mutual studying, identifying the differences, insisting, summarizing the understandings, and forgetting yourself." From the above discussion, it can be seen that *Du Lv Pei Xi* is not only a commentary on the texts of the laws and regulations but also an expository monograph. It represents the highest achievement of jurisprudence in the Chinese Legal Family.[23]

As far as Japan's situation is concerned, in addition to introducing and absorbing the achievements of Chinese jurisprudence, China's meticulous commentary, and guiding ideology (Confucianism) of Chinese legal studies, Japan further launched many works of its own. After the thirteenth century, legal scholars also made full use of the Chinese experience when commenting on and expounding the Japanese shogunate's code for Samurai, *Goseibai Shikimoku*. For example, within a short period of time after the formulation of *Goseibai Shikimoku*, Japanese scholars compiled as

[23] About the characteristics of legal studies, also see He (1994). In this article, He Min pointed out six characteristics of the legal studies: emphasis on induction, not deduction; emphasis on testimony, not analysis; emphasis on practical, not theoretical; emphasis on criminal, not civil; emphasis on case formation, not judgment; emphasis on good doubt to seek truth.

many as 34 kinds of commentaries on Shikimoku. Among these, Ei, Yuijyo and Rosetsu's commentaries reached a very high level in terms of system, annotation, and language (Ikeuchi, 1978, 574–576). For example, regarding "when the child who receives the letter of property transfer dies" (Article 20), the author of Yuijo's Commentary on *Goseibai Shikimoku* made an explanation thus: "Even if the child is still alive, if the father regrets, he can ask the child to return the property. Not to mention when the child dies, the dealing of the property can be done following the will of the father." Next, the author further elaborated on it based on the ancient Chinese Confucian classics: "Based on the intention of law, if the child dies and the property has been transferred, the parents cannot regret and ask the transferee to return the property. Not to mention if the child has wives and sons to inherit the property. Parents cannot just regret and ask them to return. The Shikimoku has violated this intention and lets the woman who has a husband return the property. Jia Yu (a book of sayings of Confucius and his disciples) records that Confucius said Yao's son, Danzhu, Shun's son, Shangjun, Yu's father, Gun, and Shun's father, Gu, were all unworthy. The only one who was worry-free was King Wen of Zhou. King Ji was his father. King Wu was his son. His father started a career, and his son inherited his legacy. King Wu inherited the unfinished achievements of King Tai, King Ji, and King Wen, destroyed the Yin Dynasty and gained the world. King Wu's actions did not cause him to lose his prestigious reputation in the world. On the contrary, he was respected as the Son of Heaven. The whole world was his wealth. He enjoyed sacrifices in the ancestral temple generation by generation, and the descendants made sure that such sacrifices would not stop. Therefore, if the sons are not filial, the parents shall not let them inherit their treasure, if there are other people who are filial and loyal, they shall let them inherit the treasure, just like Yao handed over the power to Shun, and Shun handed over the power to Yu" (Ikeuchi, 1978, 79–80). Reading the text here, the Confucian standpoint is extremely firm, the cited literature is very rich, the elaboration of the provisions is particularly detailed, and, more importantly, it is full of the spirit of criticism concerning the Shikimoku.

2.4 Inner Logic of Law and Its Historical Legacy

By the above re-organizing of the etymology, birth, development, main contents, and basic characteristics of legal studies, we can generally understand its internal logic, that is, its internal laws. On the one hand, legal studies arose with the emergence and development of ancient Chinese written law and gradually matured and reached its peak with the progress and prosperity of ancient Chinese legislation and judiciary, as well as the rise of professional jurists. On the other hand, legal studies also tended to cease and even die with the decline of the Chinese Legal Family—due to economic, political, and social development, as well as the impact of foreign culture and military aggression, etc. Therefore, as an academic form, the legal studies depended on the existence and operation of its research objects, Lv (Ling, Ge, Shi, and Li, etc.). When the rulers attached great importance to legislation and judiciary, and the strengthened operation of laws became an important part of the people's social life, legal studies also developed and even prospered. When the studies lost their service targets due to the transformation of the economic mode and social form and further gradually lost themselves, their development was hindered. Put differently, the legal studies of the Chinese Legal Family were an academic form based on the legal model of a small-scale peasant economy. With the transformation of the Chinese economic mode from a small-scale peasant economy to a capitalist commodity economy, Chinese social form from agriculture to industrialization, and Chinese law from ancient to modern law, legal studies naturally perished.

The same is true for the survival and development of *Myobodo* in Japan. When the rulers of the Nara (710–794) and Heian (794–1192) periods were interested and passionate in learning and introducing the Chinese legal system to formulate their own legal system (such as the *Taiho Code* and *Yoro Code*), *Myobodo* developed vigorously. Not only was the so-called "era of Ritsuryo (law)" formed, but also, a large number of legal achievements were launched, forming a relatively large group of professional legal scholars composed of *Myobo Hakase* and *Myobo* families. *Myobo*, *Myobo* education, and *Myobodo* were developed to the extreme. However, when Minamoto no Yoritomo (1147–1199) established the shogunate in Kamakura, the power of the emperor fell by the wayside, and the shogunate itself began to build a samurai legal system. The Ritsuryo system lost its foundation for development and prosperity and gradually disappeared from Japanese history. *Myobodo* also began to decline. In the middle of the nineteenth century, under the military pressure of the Western powers, Japan had to open its doors to meet social changes. Particularly, after the "Meiji Restoration" in 1868, when the society turned from a natural small-scale peasant economy to an industrialized capitalist commodity economy, *Myobodo*, or the Japanese study of legal commentary, completely ended and became merely a legal cultural heritage.

Such an internal logic makes legal studies (*Myobodo*) a jurisprudence that shares the same destiny as the Chinese Legal Family. Once the Chinese Legal Family collapsed, legal studies became a kind of cultural heritage and stepped off the stage of history; just as the saying goes, "with the skin gone, to what can the hair attach itself?" However, what needs to be further explored is that although the legal studies of the Chinese Legal Family have stopped being active, its legal academic value as a cultural heritage has not completely disappeared. It is still a local resource for the progress, development, and prosperity of law and jurisprudence in China and East Asian countries in the new era. It can be inherited, absorbed, and utilized by us. This legal heritage has much content with the contemporary significance of cultural inheritance, such as understandable legal works that can make grassroots judicial personnel attain a great sense of approval; the legal studies were closely connected with the judicial practice (the issues discussed by the legal studies all had been or would be difficult problems that needed to be solved in legal practice); and whether it is research or writing, the legal studies all have strong pertinence. Nevertheless, the following three aspects are the essence of legal studies. They have extremely important inheritance and promotion value for contemporary law and legal research.

First, the careful, rigorous, and meticulous study of legal commentary is the basic feature of legal studies and also their most important legacy value. For example, Shen Zhiqi, a jurist in the Qing Dynasty, wrote *Da Qing Lv Ji Zhu*. In it, the explanation and elaboration of the provisions and meanings of the law were carried out very delicately. Firstly, the book used the lower columns (the main part) to interpret the provisions of the Qing law term-by-term, with the relevant cases attached. Secondly, through the explanations in the upper columns, the issues were explained as follows: a) nouns used in the provisions and cases listed in the lower columns were explained; b) the cultural background and historical allusions of the provisions and interpretations listed in the lower columns were explained; c) intentions of the provisions listed in the lower columns were further discussed; d) views of the legal works from different schools were analyzed, and the author's own viewpoints were provided; e) interpretations listed in the lower columns were given a further illustration; f) the relationship between the provisions and cases listed in the lower columns were given an explanation. *Tang Lv Shu Yi*, *Song Xing Tong*, Koremune no Naomoto's *Ryo-no-shuge*, Lei Menglin's *Du Lv Suo Yan*, Wang Kentang's *Lv Li Jian Shi*, Xue Yunsheng's *Du Li Cun Yi*, as well as the above-mentioned Wang Mingde's *Du Lv Pei Xi*, and others are as high-quality as *Da Qing Lv Ji Zhu*. It was through such a step-by-step and meticulous elaboration that these legal works brought the hermeneutics of ancient Chinese legal studies to a very high level, which became an exceptionally beautiful pearl in Chinese traditional culture.

Second, rich and diverse research methods were adopted. In the legal studies, there were not only inductive and deductive methods, exegesis methods, and legal hermeneutics methods, such as expansion interpretation, limited interpretation, literal interpretation, and sentence interpretation, but also historical methods; that is, when expounding various legal provisions, their origin, development and evolution must be clearly elaborated. For example, in *Xing Fa Xu Lve*, written by a legal scholar of the Song Dynasty, Liu Yun, when explaining the origin and development of the "criminal officials," it started with the story of "Jiu Yao serving as the law official" during the reign of Emperor Shun and examined the institutions of the Xia, Shang and Zhou Dynasties, the regulations of the Spring and Autumn Period and Warring States Period, the Qin and Han systems, the changes of the Wei and Jin Dynasties, the reforms of the Southern and Northern Dynasties, the development of the Sui and Tang Dynasties, the regulations of the Five Dynasties and Ten Kingdoms, and the inheritance of the early Song Dynasty. The book provides a very detailed illustration. Sociological methods were also adopted. For example, changes and control of household registration were fully examined in "household and marriage law" of *Tang Lv Shu Yi* when explaining the legal responsibilities of the governments of prefectures or counties for "losing, omitting, increasing or decreasing of household registration without awareness"; the status quo and changes of the intermediaries were fully examined in "household law: city centers" of Wu Tan's *Da Qing Lv Li Tong Kao* when explaining "serving as intermediaries or piers without licenses." These descriptions of social situations aim at illustrating the correct meaning of the legal texts. The methods of philology were also employed. For example, in the Ming Dynasty, an anonymous author wrote a book, *Lv Xue Ji Yi Yuan Hai* (Collected Discussion and Sources of the Legal Studies, 律学集议渊海). In it, a large amount of space was used to explain the legal texts and intentions of the law, involving Broad Answers, Collection, Collected Solutions, Modest Opinions, Arguments for Questions, Some Trivial Words, and others. In *Da Xue Yan Yi Bu: Shen Xing Xian* (Additional Notes for the Explanation of Da Xue: Law of Prudent Punishment, 大学衍义补·慎刑宪), Qiu Jun cited more literature, including more than 30 books, such as *Shi Jing* (Classic of Poetry, 诗经), *Shang Shu, Zhou Yi, Chun Qiu Zuo Shi Zhuan* (Tradition of Zuo, 春秋左氏传), *Guan Zi, Zhou Li* (Rites of Zhou, 周礼), *Lun Yu* (The Analects, 论语), *Meng Zi* (Mencius, 孟子), *Shi Ji, Zhenguan Zheng Yao* (Keypoints of Politics in the Zhenguan Era, 贞观政要), *Song Shi, Tong Dian* (Comprehensive Statutes, 通典), *Zi Zhi Tong Jian*, and *Meng Xi Bi Tan* (Dream Pool Essays, 梦溪笔谈). Methods of Buddhist legal interpretation were also used (Chen, 2015). In addition, comparative study was an important method used in legal studies. Xue Yun sheng's *Tang Ming Lv He Bian* (Compilation of Tang and Ming Laws, 唐明律合编) is a model in this regard. There is still a certain gap between these adopted methods and the methods in the modern sense, as the adopted methods can only be regarded as rudiments of various modern methods, but after all, they were fully used and brought into play in ancient Chinese law.

Third, and more importantly, legal studies pursued legal justice. It is true that a large number of ancient Chinese legal academic works interpret the law provision-by-provision, sentence-by-sentence, and word-by-word, concentrating on explaining the problems that might be encountered during the implementation of the law. However, the works contain a pursuit of justice in legislation and judiciary. For example, Qiu Jun, a legal scholar in the Ming Dynasty, emphasized the point of view that "the law must be just, and the law prevails over the emperor's words" in his work *Da Xue Yan Yi Bu*, "The Ninth Point of Governing the Country and the World: the Law of Prudent Punishment." "The way of being a good emperor is nothing greater than *zhong* (moderation). *Zhong* means impartial when it comes to feeling and not overdone when it comes to doing things… The imposition of punishments should be neither too heavy nor too light. This is the so-called *zhong* and this is the so-called good at using punishment." "The law has fixed rules, and people do not often commit crimes. So, when imposing punishment in accordance with people's offenses, it must be clear and fair so that the law is fixed and unified and there is no departure or violation of the law. … In such a way of using the law, everything will be good" (Qiu, 1999b).

Wang Mingde, a legal scholar in the Qing Dynasty, emphasized the justice value of legal studies in his work *Du Lv Pei Xi*. He held, for legal practitioners, considering self-interests is wrong, and more importantly, the idea that seeking justice for the people and trying a case well can help them accumulate merits is also incorrect. "The harm of considering 'I' when practicing law has been proven. Those who are ignorant, vulgar, cruel in nature, or seeking private gain will have tragic consequences, such as Zhao Yu and Zhang Tang. That is for sure, and I do not need to discuss this further. However, even for those who are gentle, kind, easy-going in nature, and committed to spreading benefit (merit), who take preserving people's lives as their primary task, the problem of 'I' is still inevitable. … The so-called merits are actually evil deeds. Aren't merits and deeds done by people? They failed to realize that the law is justice under heaven, and even the Son of Heaven (the emperor) is not allowed to seek selfish interests. … They do not know that the sages can be successful because they only respect *zhong*. *Zhong* means empty and impartial. How can merits and deeds exist in it? If someone insists on some views, even if he is trying to be selfless, he is still selfish, as it is inevitable that there will be an 'I' in his consideration. The thought of 'I' just exists there, and the person will regard the criminal law as vulgar officials' business and cruel customs even before he reads the criminal code. The bias that is inconsistent with the law has already existed before he opens the book. Once he gets promoted to a high-ranking position and people build their hope in him, how can he decide important cases, clarify important reasons, assist the ruling of the emperor, and benefit the whole people? … Therefore, it is said that reading the law, you have to forget 'I' first" (Wang, 1997, 533–534).

As to *Myobodo* in Japan, although it began to decline after the establishment of the Kamakura shogunate and the end of the Ritsuryo system at the end of the twelfth century, its cultural value still exists. *Myobo Hakase* and *Myobodo* continued to exist after the twelfth century (such as the *Mingfa* family of Nakahara and Sakanoue). Activities of *Myobo* scholars continued until the Meiji Restoration Era after 1868 (for example, Ogyu Sorai and Kada no Arimaro were active in the eighteenth century, Moriyoshi Sonoda was a *Myobo* scholar in the nineteenth century, and Norimi Seta's legal study continued until the middle of the Meiji period in the 1890s). In addition, the essence of the study of legal commentaries contained in *Myobodo*, such as the pursuit of excellence in the interpretation of legal provisions, the historical methods, the hermeneutic methods, the comparative methods, the phonetic reading and training methods, and the philological methods (for example, in the book *Using Proverbs to Interpret Da Ming Lv Li* written by a modern Japanese legal scholar Sakakibara, Koshu, when expounding the meaning of laws and cases, the author cited 117 ancient Chinese political and legal documents), as well as the pursuit of judicial justice, have all been inherited and carried forward by Japanese legal philosophy and legal hermeneutics in modern times (He, 2003, 6).

3 Legal Scholars

The formation of the Chinese Legal Family was not only based on a number of famous codes and the above-mentioned abundant legal academics but also on a large number of famous legal scholars[24]—also known as *Myobo Hakase* in the Middle Ages in Japan. It was because of their hard work that the legal culture of the Chinese Legal Family spread from China to the neighboring countries, and the spirit of the Chinese

[24] A historian, Qian Jianfu, once expressed a view that ancient Chinese society only had Lv (concrete rules to mediate and resolve disputes) scholars, Lv studies, and the rule of Lv, but not Fa (a social institution) scholars, Fa studies, and the rule of Fa (see Qian, 1979). The author agrees with his point of view, but considering the actual situation of the current legal research, the name "legal scholar" is used to refer to the legal practitioners in the Chinese Legal Family (actually, they can also be called law scholars, or rule scholars).

Legal Family has been carried forward. These scholars wrote books, created schools, participated in the country's legislative and judicial activities, served as legal advisers, taught students, engaged in legal education, and imparted legal knowledge. During their active period, legal studies flourished, and this eventually laid a solid academic foundation for the Chinese Legal Family. Due to limited space and materials, this section only does some textual research on legal scholars in China and Japan.

3.1 Rise and Development of Legal Scholars

Legal scholars here refer to legal practitioners who presided over and participated in the formulation of Lv and Ling (in some dynasties, Ke, Ge, Shi, Li, etc. were also included) and interpreted, studied, applied, and implemented the Lv (Ling) texts during the social development of ancient China from the Qin and Han Dynasties to the end of the Qing Dynasty. It includes politicians, administrative and judicial officials, and scholar officials, who—full-time or part-time—are engaged in legal affairs. The research topic of this section is the Chinese Legal Family. Therefore, the legal scholars in China mentioned in this section refer to the formulators, interpreters, and enforcers of Lv, Ling, Ge, Shi, and Li after the Sui and Tang Dynasties—the birth of the Chinese Legal Family. In Japan, they refer to the group of legal practitioners (*Myobo Hakase*, etc.) who were engaged in the compilation, interpretation, implementation, and enforcement of Lv and Ling (including Ge and Shi) after the Taika Reforms in 645.

Judging from the situations in ancient China and Japan, on the one hand, the legislative, administrative, and judicial departments had not yet been clearly separated. Administrative officials were engaging in judicial trials, judicial officials were involved in administrative management, and both administrative and judicial officials were involved in formulating laws. These were all very common phenomena. Except for some legal families, an independent professional jurist class had not yet formed. On the other hand, both China and Japan had systems for selecting scholars through examinations.[25] The *Mingjing* (Confucian classics) examination was the main subject of the imperial examination, and writing (literature) played an important role in this. Therefore, for high-level officials in ancient China and Japan, writing and morality were compulsory subjects. In addition, because many official positions—such as Japan's *Myobo Hakase* and Kebiishi (prosecutor)[26]—were subject to the canon of inheritance (Xiyin system), many legal scholars undertook the study of law as their specialized occupations that had been and would be passed down from generation to generation, forming a tradition of continuity among generations—legal families.

[25] Although Japan did not completely transplant the imperial examination system from China, it inherited the subjects of the official education in Sui and Tang, such as Myogyo (study of classics), *Myobo* (study of law), Sho (study of calligraphy), and San (study of numbers).

[26] The Kebiishi was in charge of the public security of the capital, which was set up in the 7th year of the Konin Era (816). See Ando (2016, 102).

In this regard, the legal scholars in ancient China and Japan were not pure legalists or jurists, nor were they simply administrative or judicial officials. The vast majority were Confucianists, Legalists, Mohists, and Daoists at the same time. They were both knowledgeable in the classics and good at law. Some were also writers or poets, such as Bai Juyi, Su Shi, and Disheng Julai. Although the Chinese Legal Family was born in the Sui and Tang Dynasties, the ideological preparation and academic accumulation by legal scholars began as early as the Eastern and Western Han Dynasties and the Wei, Jin, Southern and Northern Dynasties. The splendid legal academics of the Chinese Legal Family and the rise of the group of legal scholars were the historical results of academic development from the Qin and Han Dynasties to the Sui and Tang Dynasties in China over hundreds of years.

On the one hand, in the West and East Han Dynasties, a large number of legal scholars appeared, and legal studies were prevalent. Xiao He (257 BC–193 BC), one of the founding fathers of the Western Han Dynasty, was originally a "petty official drawing up documents" (legal officials). He had an enthusiasm for the law and vast legal knowledge. When Liu Bang (256 BC–195 BC) led troops and conquered Xianyang, the capital of the Qin Dynasty, everyone else was focusing on gold and silver treasures, and only Xiao He concentrated on collecting Qin's legal documents. This point alone explains why Xiao He fully deserved to be called the founder of ancient Chinese *legal scholars*. After Xiao He, the famous legal scholars of the Han Dynasty also included the father and son from the Du's in Nanyang (Du Zhou, Du Yannian), the Zheng brothers from Taishan (Zheng Hong, Zheng Chang), the Guo family from Yingchuan (Guo Hong, Guo Gong, Guo Zhi, Guo Zhen, Guo He, Guo Zhen, Guo Xi, and some others), the Chens from Pei (Chen Xian, Chen Gong, Chen Chong, Chen Zhong, and some others) (Fan, 1965, 1543–1547), and the classics masters, Ma Rong and Zheng Xuan. In the Wei and Jin Dynasties, a group of famous legal scholars, including Zhang Fei, Du Yu, Liu Song, Zhong Yao, and Liu Shao, emerged. At that time, legal studies were as important as the study of the classics, and the two became equally important schools. *Lv Boshi* ("*Lvxue Boshi*"), which was established in the government during the Wei Dynasty, specialized in teaching legal studies and created a precedent for a special school for studying law.

On the other hand, the Chinese Legal Family was formed in the Sui and Tang Dynasties. This was also the period when ancient Chinese legal science developed to its peak. After nearly 700 years of academic accumulation, law studies had fully matured in the Tang Dynasty and thus further supported the jurisprudence of the Chinese Legal Family. To meet the needs of the highly developed centralized bureaucracy, the rulers paid special attention to the revision and study of laws. The Sui Dynasty adopted *Mingfa* as a new subject for the imperial examination. The reason why Tang Lv became a model of law for later generations is closely related to the research, education, and activities of legal scholars at that time. However, we know little about the deeds of the legal scholars in the Tang Dynasty due to the time which has lapsed. As far as the official legal notes are concerned, information about the legal scholars of the Tang Dynasty can be obtained mainly from *Tang Lv Shu Yi*. For example, the compilers of *Tang Lv Shu Yi* were a group of social elites who specialized in law, such as Zhangsun Wuji, Li Ji, Yu Zhining, Chu Suiliang, Liu Shi, Tang

Lin, Duan Baoxuan, Han Yuan, Laiji, Xin Maojiang, Liu Yanke, Pei Hongxian, Jia Minxing, Wang Huaike, Dong Xiong, Lu Li, Shi Shikui, Cao Huiguo, and Sima Rui (Zhangsun et al., 1983, 578–579). They can be regarded as legal scholars with a background of working as officials. In addition, according to the research of recent scholars such as Sun Zuji, there were also folk legal scholars in the Tang Dynasty, including Li Wenbo, Handan Chuo, Li Jingxuan, Liu Rengui, Cui Zhiti, Zhao Renben, Pei Guangting, Song Jing, Di Wumo, Liu Yuan, Zhang Kui, Li Chong, Wang Xingxian, Yuan Yong, Lu Shu, Li Baoyin, Wang Pu, and Lu Zhi (Sun, 1934).

In the Sui and Tang Dynasties, Japan actively learned from China about the legal system, including studies of law. At that time, many Japanese envoys who were sent to the Sui and Tang Dynasties frequently purchased legal works of the Sui and Tang Dynasties, especially the Tang Dynasty, and shipped them back to Japan. The academic works have been widely cited by Japanese scholars. Thus, in the preserved legal documents in Japan, such as the *Ritsu-no-shuge*, *Ryo-no-gig*e, and *Ryo-no-shuge*, some records of the activities of folk legal experts in the Tang Dynasty can be found. According to the investigation and research of Riko Mitsuo, a professor at Keio University in Japan, there were 15 kinds of unofficial legal commentary works in the Tang Dynasty cited in Japanese legal commentaries; the authors (legal scholars) that can be confirmed come from more than ten families, including the Zhang, Song, Jian, Yang, Cao, and Li families (Riko, 1959, 71). Although these clues are still relatively vague and unclear, we can generally make the judgment that the number of legal scholars in China during the Tang Dynasty was already quite large, and they were very active—not only the official ones but also the folk ones. It is with their hard work that great classics of legal studies, such as *Tang Lv Shu Yi*, were launched.

Further, after the Song Dynasty, the status of legal studies was no longer the same as before. Legal studies gradually declined, and the rulers paid more attention to the reformed Confucian classics provided by Neo-Confucian scholars such as Zhu Xi (1130–1200) in the Southern Song Dynasty. They were regarded as official studies that were incorporated into the imperial examinations. However, on the one hand, the emperors of the Song Dynasty were not only proficient in the law but also attached great importance to the law, reaching the highest level among the ancient Chinese emperors. On the other hand, the intellectuals of the Song Dynasty, namely the scholar-official class, were also proficient in the law and had very high legal capabilities. The Tang Dynasty also handed down good legal foundations, rich legal research results, and abundant academic accumulation. Therefore, Chinese legal studies still developed during the Song Dynasty, and a large number of outstanding jurists who made commentaries on the law or specialized in law emerged, such as He Ning, He Meng, Fan Zhi, Dou Yi, Zhao Pu, Zhao Kuangyin, Su Xiao, Ju Kejiu, Zhao Kuangyi, Zhang Yong, Liu Yun, Jia Changchao, Ma Liang, Wang Zhi, Ge Yuan, Bao Zheng, Ouyang Xiu, Li Gou, Su Xun, Su Shi, Qin Guan, Song Shou, Song Minqiu, Sun Shi, Sima Guang, Wang Anshi, Wanyan Yong, Zhu Xi, Chen Liang, Zheng Xingyi, Cai Shen, Gui Wanrong, Song Ci, Li Nangong, Hu Ying, Cai Hang, Weng Fu, Wu Shiqing, Liu Kezhuang, Fan Yingling, Wu Ge, Zhen Dexiu, Zhang Feng, Zheng Ke, Ye Shi, and Fu Lin.

In the Ming and Qing Dynasties, the ruling power was highly concentrated, and the attribute of law as a ruling tool received attention from the rulers anew. Although the development of Chinese society had entered a period of decline due to the very active unofficial legal commentaries during this period, the number of legal works reached its highest—with more than 260 known books—and the variety of legal works was the richest in Chinese history. Against this social background, the number and creativity of Chinese legal scholars also reached the highest level in history during the Ming and Qing Dynasties. The famous legal scholars of this time include Song Lian, Liu Ji, Li Shanchang, Zhou Zhen, Liu Weiqian, He Guang, Kuang Zhong, Wu Ne, Zhang Kai, Qiu Jun, Wang Shouren, Hu Qiong, Tang Shu, Li Zhi, Wang Qiao, Wang Kentang, Lei Menglin, Shu Hua, Hai Rui, Zhang Juzheng, Lv Kun, Yu Maoxue, Ouyang Dongfeng, Cao Yubian, Xiao Jingao, Zhang Kentang, Li Qing, Chen Longzheng, Ashdarhan, Gang Lin, Huang Zongxi, Li Yu, Gu Yanwu, Wang Fuzhi, Duikana, Xuan Ye, Chen Shikuang, Zhu Shi, Wang Mingde, Chen Fangsheng, Tan Xuan, Shen Zhiqi, Jiang Tingxi, Lan Dingyuan, Wan Weihan, Wu Tan, Wang Youhuai, Wang Huizu, Quan Shichao, Liu Heng, Bao Shichen, Xu Lian, Zhu Qingqi, Bao Shuyun, Xu Dong, Xue Yunsheng, Yang Rongxu, Zhao Shuqiao, and Gang Yi.

By the end of the Qing Dynasty, legal intellectuals were forced by the high-pressure policy of ideological and cultural autocracy to concentrate on textual research and research on basic principles, leading to the legal and classical studies parting ways. The status of law study was further lowered, and traditional legal study in ancient China came to an end. The legal reform of Shen Jiaben finally combined legal studies with imported Western law. The corresponding achievements of ancient Chinese legal studies were integrated into modern law studies, and legal scholars also transformed into modern Chinese jurists, including Shen Jiaben (1840–1913), Dong Kang (1867–1947), and Cheng Shude (1877–1944).

In Japan, Fujiwara no Fuhito (659–720), the compiler and interpreter of the *Taiho Code* and *Yoro Code*, started the tradition of legal study—renamed as *Myobodo* after the eighth century—in which the building of the Ritsuryo system and teaching of legal commentary were collaboratively conducted. After that, talented legal scholars, known as *Myobo Hakase* after the eighth century,[27] appeared in large numbers. These included Yamato no Nagaoka, Shioya no Komaro, and some others who participated

---

[27] Japan accepted China's *legal studies* and later changed its name to *Myobodo*. The original *Ritsugaku Hakase* was later renamed *Myobo Hakase*, which can be clearly seen from the commentary on Ling in *Ryo-no-shuge*. The author of the book, *Koremune no Naomoto*, clearly pointed out when commenting on the provisions of the "Law on Official Position No. 22: Shikibu Sho" concerning *daigakuryo* in the *Yoro Code* (718), that "the interpretation provides: it was proposed in the memorial to the emperor on the 27th day of the third lunar month of the second year of the Tenpyo Era ... two *Hakase* (doctors) of legal studies. ... ten *Myobo student*s, and twenty *Monjo* students. Simply selecting from low-ranking officials or talented commoners, no age limit should be imposed." See (1966). *Newly Updated National History Series, Volume 23, Ryo-no-shuge I*, 80. Yoshikawa Koubunkan. The second year of the Tenpyo Era is 730. That means that at least before 730, in Japan, *Ritsugaku Hakase* was still a formal official position (academic officer) in *daigakuryo* under *Shikibu Sho*. Although students had been called *Myobo students*, the academic officials had not yet been called *Myobo Hakase*. As for when the *Ritsugaku Hakase* were called *Myobo Hakase*, the specific time is not certain, since none of the ancient Japanese books that have been preserved so

in the compilation and interpretation of the *Taiho Code* and *Yoro Code* in the Nara period (710–794), Yamada Shirogane, Anou no Uchihito, Sanuki no Naganao, Koremune no Naomoto, Koremune no Tadasuke, Ochino Hiroe, Sakanoue no Sadashige, Sakanoue no Akikane, Nakahara no Akimoto, and some others in the Heian period (794–1192) (Yaheiji, 1966, 168–301). After the fifteenth century, a group of modern Japanese legal scholars was formed on the basis of absorbing Chinese *Da Ming Lv* and *Da Qing Lv Li,* such as Sakakibara Koshu, Ogyu Sorai, Takase Kiboku, and Kadano *Arimaro.* This all shows that the study of law was able to continue and develop continuously in Japan in the middle and modern times owing to the hard work of a group of legal scholars (*Myobo Hakase*). It has made the ancient Japanese legal studies (*Myobodo*) mature and promoted the gradual formation of the ancient Japanese legal culture.

3.2 *Status and Role of Legal Scholars*

Legal scholars undertook important missions in the legislative and judicial activities in ancient China. In addition to studying legal texts and teaching legal studies, they also directly participated in the revision of laws and directly engaged in judicial practice. It is in these respects that the ancient Chinese jurists had more influence than the glossators in medieval Europe. The School of Glossators in medieval Europe (centered around Bologna) is so named because they added commentaries on the margins and the spaces between the lines of the Roman legal books they studied. Their main purpose at that time was annotating and interpreting *Corpus Juris Civilis* in Rome for the teaching needs of the Law School of the University of Bologna so as to learn the spirit and knowledge of the law from the classic discourses of classical Roman jurists. They hoped that through their work, Roman legal literature could be used for study and research at that time. It was only in the later period that the School of Commentators gradually turned to practical purposes. In contrast, Chinese legal scholars were closely connected with the imperial power from the very beginning. They actively participated in the practice of national legislation, law enforcement, and judicial activities while researching the interpretation of laws and decrees.

The legislative and judicial activities in which ancient Chinese legal scholars participated can be summarized into the following:

1. Legal scholars participated in legislative activities, drafted, and amended the laws. It was an important task for some prominent legal scholars such as Fang Xuanling, Zhangsun Wuji, and Dou Yi. By participating in legislative practice, they implemented their own legal propositions and thus influenced the emperor's legislative guiding ideology and the general policy governing the country. These people were both legal scholars and ministers of the emperor. They were good at using historical and comparative methods to summarize the advantages and

far used the word *Lvxue Boshi.* The legal scholars that we can see since the eighth century, without exception, were all called *Myobo Hakase.* See Yaheiji (1966, 168).

disadvantages of each dynasty's legal system so that the legislation of their own dynasty could be developed based on the previous dynasties.

For example, in the Sui and Tang Dynasties, during the formation of the Chinese Legal Family, to consolidate and stabilize their rulings, the rulers frequently carried out legal revisions to achieve the best effect of rule by law. In this process, legal scholars played an important role. In particular, the revisions of *Kaihuang Lv* in the Sui Dynasty and *Wude Lv*, *Zhenguan Lv*, and *Yonghui Lv* in the Tang Dynasty had great influences and contributions to later generations. At the beginning of the Sui Dynasty, Gao Jiong, Yang Su, Su Wei, Niu Hong, and others formulated *Kaihuang Lv*, learning from the lessons of the Southern and Northern Dynasties' "stringent laws" and "excessive killing," which "fully eliminated the harsh laws" and, to a certain extent, avoided the barbaric punishments of the previous dynasties. In the early Tang Dynasty, Fang Xuanling, Zhangsun Wuji, Li Ji, Song Jing, Yu Zhining, and others formulated the *Zhenguan Lv* and *Yonghui Lv* based on *Kaihuang Lv* in the late Sui Dynasty and *Wude Lv* in the early Tang Dynasty. The two laws made major revisions to the previous codes, making them more concise and mature. For example, 92 capital crimes were eliminated. "Uncountable complicated crimes were simplified, and heavy crimes were lightened" (Liu et al., 1975, 2138).

In Japan, the earliest Lv and Ling were also launched with the full participation of legal scholars. For example, the aforementioned Fujiwara no Fuhito presided over the compilation of the *Taiho Code* and *Yoro Code*. Moribe no Muraji Osumi and Ochino Hiroe participated in the compilation of the *Taiho Code*. Yamato no Nagaoka (689–769), Shioya no Komaro (birth and death unknown), Yamada no Shirogane (birth and death unknown), Moribe no Muraji Osumi, and some others were also the main compilers of the *Yoro Code*. Kibino Makibi and Yamato no Nagaoka were famous envoys to Tang China. Although these two great codes were learned from, referred to, and borrowed largely from the laws of the Sui and Tang Dynasties in China, they still had many Japanese characteristics. For example, China's *ten abominations* were changed to *eight abuses*, and China's *eight deliberations* were changed to *six deliberations*. These were the creations of Japanese legal scholars. In China, rebellion, sedition, treason, parricide, depravity, great irreverence, unfilial piety, discord, unrighteousness, and incest were heinous crimes that could not be remitted. The two crimes that were not adopted by Japan were discord and incest because, at that time, these two would cause less serious harm to the rulers in Japan than in China; hence, they were deleted by the Japanese legal scholars in the legislation. Meanwhile, the eight deliberations in China were deliberation for relatives of the emperor, old retainers of the emperor, the morally worthy, able, high achievers, holders of high positions, the diligent, and guests of the state. The last two, namely the diligent and guests of the state, were not very prominent or important in Japan. Hence, they were also removed by Japanese legal scholars. Later, from 782 to 923, legal scholars, including Sanuki no Chitsugu, Fujiwara no Tokihira, Fujiwara no Tadahira, Okihara no Miniku, Fujiwara no Michiaki, and Koremune no Yoshitsune, were also the main compilers in the legislative activities—such as the formulation of *Enryaku kotai shiki*, *Konin shiki*, *Jogan shiki*, and *Engi shiki* (supplementary laws)—and played active and important roles.[28]

2. Legal scholars annotated and interpreted the law and solved legal problems. This was one of the main tasks and important duties of ancient Chinese legal scholars. The explanations and answers made by legal scholars, whether formal or academic, played a huge role in the judicial practice of ancient China. For example, *Tang Lv Shu Yi*, compiled by Zhangsun Wuji and others, and *Song Xing Tong*, compiled by Dou Yi and others, are official commentaries to *Yonghui Lv* of the Tang Dynasty and the laws of the Song Dynasty. They provide sentence-by-sentence interpretation, elaboration on the meaning of the text, and analysis of the implications. They also list questions and answers, supplementing the insufficient legal text through debate, explanation, and replies to questions. As an official interpretation, this had the same effect as Lv and Ling. *Song Xing Tong* also attaches the corresponding Chi (through the notes of "permit" and "the minister's petition"). In the Ming Dynasty, although Lei Menglin's *Du Lv Suo Yan*, Wang Kentang's *Lv Li Jian Shi*, Lu Jianyun's *Du Lv Guan Jian* (Humble Opinions When Reading the Law, 读律管见), Wang Mingde's *Du Lv Pei Xi* in the Qing Dynasty, Shen Zhiqi's *Da Qing Lv Ji Zhu*, and Xia Jingyi's *Du Lv Shi Zhang* (Finding the Basis of Law, 读律示掌) are only academic explanations, they also played an important guiding role in judicial practice.

In Japan, it was also the main duty of *Myobo Hakase* to annotate the law and answer questions about the law. After the *Taiho Code* and *Yoro Code* were formulated and promulgated, a group of *Myobo Hakase*, including Sanuki no Naganao and Okihara no Miniku, were appointed by the imperial court. After years of effort, they compiled *Ryo-no-gige* as the Official Commentary of the Japanese laws in 834. After more than 30 years, Koremune no Naomoto, an outstanding representative of the Koremune legal family, compiled and completed the two books *Ritsu-no-shuge* and *Ryo-no-shuge* around 868, providing a systematic and complete annotation and elaboration of the *Taiho Code* and *Yoro Code*. These brought the legal annotation and research of Japan to a new level. Simultaneously, Japan successively launched a large number of commentaries for the law; for example, Yamato no Nagaoka's *Old Answers*, Nukata no Imatari's *Nukata's Commentary*, Okihara no Miniku's *Okihara's Commentary*, Kuninomiyatsuko no Imatari's *Kasuga's Commentary*, Atoji's *Ato Commentary*, Anou no Uchihito's *Anou's Commentary*, Koremune no Tadasuke's *Summary of Political Affairs*, Sanuki no Naganao's *Sanuki's Commentary*, and some other commentaries the authors of which could not be verified, such as *Left Chapters of the Lv Book*, *Private Commentary on the New Ling*, *Interpretation of Lv*, *Interpretation of Ling*, *Five Commentaries*, *Newly Revised Interpretation of the Law*. These works effectively promoted the implementation of the laws and contributed to the construction of a Ritsuryo state.

---

[28] About the history of compilation and detailed contents of *Enryaku kotai shiki*, *Konin shiki*, *Jogan shiki*, and *Engi shiki*, see (1965). *Newly Updated National History Series, Volume 26*. Yoshikawa Koubunkan; (1972). *Newly Updated National History Series, Assorted Kyaku of the Three Generations I & II*. Yoshikawa Koubunkan.

3. Legal scholars imparted legal knowledge and trained legal professionals. Among the legal scholars of the Chinese Legal Family, the most famous ones had different numbers of students. This tradition was inherited from the Western and Eastern Han Dynasties and the Wei, Jin, Southern and Northern Dynasties and flourished in the Sui and Tang Dynasties. Famous scholars include Liu Shao (the author of *Fa Lun* [Law Theories, 法论], etc.), who was active during the era of Emperor Ming of Wei (226–239); Ji Kang (224–263), Fu Xuan (217–278), Du Yu (222–284), and Zhang Fei (the author of *Lv Zhu Biao*, etc.) of the Jin Dynasty; Kong Zhigui (447–501) and Cai Fadu (the compiler of *Liang Lv* [Liang Code, 梁律]) of the Southern Dynasties; Fengshu (compiler of *Beiqi Lv* [Northern Qi Code, 北齐律]) of the Northern Dynasty; and Wang Tong (584–617), Yang Wang, Kong Yingda (574–648), and Yan Shigu (581–645) of the Sui and Tang Dynasties. There were also Sun Shi (1019–1079) and Fu Lin (active during the early Northern Song Dynasty) of the Song Dynasty and Shen Zhongwei of the Yuan Dynasty (active during the late Yuan Dynasty), among others. Legal scholars Tang Shu (1497–1574) and Li Zhi (1527–1602) of the Ming Dynasty were once the backbone of the judicial officials. However, after offending the powerful and being demoted and dismissed, the two engaged in lecturing and teaching students. Wang Huizu (1731–1807), a famous legal scholar and legal educator of the Qing Dynasty, also made great contributions to China's legal education. His three works (trilogy), *Zuo Zhi Yao Yan*, *Xu Zuo Zhi Yao Yan* (Important Words to Assist the Governance Vol. 2, 续佐治药言), and *Xue Zhi Yi Shuo* (Some Suppositions for Learning to Govern, 学治臆说), were a summary of his long-term experience in being an assistant to magistrates for legal education. They were also the most popular textbooks of legal studies at the time. Both his in-person student teaching and elaboration on his experience as a legal assistant had huge influences on the folk legal education of his time.[29] It should be said that the long historical tradition of legal education in ancient China was inseparable from legal scholars.

In Japan, since 649, the Ministry of the Central Government of Japan was established as an institution under which there was *daigakuryo* specializing in education. Since then, legal education, namely *Myobo* education, began in daigakuryo. Most of the Japanese legal scholars, namely *Myobo Hakase*, came from *daigakuryo*. Not only did they graduate from *daigakuryo*, but they were also engaged in *Myobo* education and the work of imparting knowledge to disciples. Among them, the most famous were Sanuki no Naganao and Koremune no Naomoto. Sanuki no Naganao was a famous jurist in the early Heian period. Born in the 2nd year of the Enryaku Era (783), he entered *daigakuryo* to study law, and his grades were excellent. In the 7th year of the Tencho Era (830), he was awarded the position of *Myobo Hakase* when he was 48 years old. In the 10th year of the Tencho Era (833), he began the compilation of *Ryo-no-gige*. At that time, his official position was junior six rank, lower grade, left *Shoshi* (an official position), as well as *Myobo Hakase* and Kageyushi (supervisor/auditor). In the 3rd year of the Saiko Era (856), Naganao requested to resign on the

[29] In addition, Lei Menglin from the Ming Dynasty and Wang Mingde from the Qing Dynasty were also legal scholars and successful legal educators.

grounds of his advanced age. The emperor agreed to his other requests but denied his resignation from *Myobo Hakase*. In the 2nd year of the Ten'an Era (858), he received the consent of the emperor to teach law in his own home.[30] Koremune no Naomoto, whose date of birth and death were unknown, was a famous legal scholar in the early Heian period. In the 1st year of the Gangyo Era (877), he took up the posts of judicial officials, including as prosecutor in *Kebiishi* Agency and *Kageyushi* (auditor). At the same time, he performed as *Myobo Hakase* in *daigakuryo*. After the 1st year of the Engi Era (901), as a highly respected legal scholar, he was given the privilege of teaching the law in his own home. This practice, known as "Engi Lectures," together with the above-mentioned lecture by Sanuki no Naganao ("Jogan Lectures"), created a precedent for private lectures by *Myobo Hakase* (out of *daigakuryo*) in Japan, which was of great significance to the development of Japanese legal studies in the Middle Ages (Editing Committee of Japanese Grand Dictionary of National History, 1993, 651).

3.3 Main Doctrines and Theories of Legal Scholars

Judging from the historical records, the writings of legal scholars can be described as plentiful. For example, in the Tang Dynasty, there were *Tang Lv Shu Yi* compiled by important ministers such as Zhangsun Wuji, Chu Suiliang, Yu Zhining, and Tang Lin; *Fa Li* (Cases, 法例) written by legal scholar Cui Zhiti and others; *Tang Kaiyuan Ge Ling Ke Yao* (Key Points of Ge, Ling, and Ke of the Tang Kaiyuan Era, 唐开元格令科要) written by Pei Guangting; *Pang Tong Kaiyuan Ge* (Wide Knowledge of Ge of Kaiyuan Era, 旁通开元格) written by Song Jing; *Dazhong Xing Fa Zong Yao Gehou Chi* (Summary of Punishment and Law of the Dazhong Era [847–860]: Gehou Chi, 大中刑法总要格后敕), in 60 volumes, written by Liu Zhuan and others; *Dazhong Xing Lv Tong Lei* (Classified Punishment Law of the Dazhong Era, 大中刑律统类), in 12 volumes, written by Zhang Kui; and *Fa Jian* (Mirror of Law, 法鉴), in 8 Volumes, written by Li Chong. Some other books have not been preserved in China but were disseminated in Japan, such as *Zhang's Commentary*, *Song's Commentary*, *Jian's Commentary*, *Cao's Commentary*, *Tang Wen Da* (Tang's Questions and Answers, 唐问答), *Tang Lv Shi* (Interpretation of Tang Lv, 唐律释), and *Lv Shu Gu Geng Lu* (Framework of Commentary to Law, 律疏骨梗录).

In the Song Dynasty, there were *Song Xing Tong*, compiled by Dou Yi, the founding father of the Song Dynasty; *Lv Fu Yin Yi*, written by the legal scholar Sun Shi; *Xing Fa Yao Li* (Important Cases for the Punishment and Law, 刑法要例), in eight volumes, written by Huang Mao; *Ling Lv Shou Jian* (Indication for Following Ling and Lv, 令律守鉴), in two volumes, written by Wang Xingxian; *Xing Ming Duan Li* (Judgments According to the General Principles, 刑名断例), in three volumes, written by Zeng Min; *Xing Shu Shi Ming* written by Wang Jian; and *Xing Fa Xu Lue* written by Liu

[30] In the 4th year of the Jogan Era (862), on the 8th lunar month, day 17, Sanuki no Naganao died at the age of 80.

Yun. However, most these legal works have lost in history, except for a few, such as *Tang Lv Shu Yi*, *Song Xing Tong*, *Lv Fu Yin Yi*, and *Xing Shu Shi Ming*.

In the Ming and Qing Dynasties, the works of legal scholars that can be found in the historical records were more abundant and outstanding. In the Ming Dynasty alone, there were more than 100, and in the Qing Dynasty, there were more than 160, a total of more than 260 works (He, 2006, 235–241). Unlike in the Tang and Song Dynasties, most of the works of the legal scholars in the Ming and Qing Dynasties have been preserved and can be seen by us today. Hence, after the formation of the Chinese Legal Family, through illustration in official and unofficial legal works, the main theoretical viewpoints and research methods used in ancient times can generally be grasped, and their basic thoughts analyzed. For example, legal scholars presented some valuable insights on legislative principles, judicial principles, and types of crimes and punishments. They also made new achievements in comparative law. It is an important research subject of the Chinese Legal Family, ancient Chinese legal theories, and the history of Chinese legal thought that further investigation and cataloging of these following ideological achievements are needed.

1. Promotion of legal equality and judicial justice. This has been an important content of the memorials to the throne and interpretation of the codes. For example, Lu Zhi (754–805), a thinker in the Tang Dynasty, believed that "rewarding the good and punishing the bad, that's the foundation for contending for the throne" (Ouyang & Song, 1975, 4921). "rewarding the good and punishing those who transgress must not be abolished" (Lu, 1988, 46). Li Gou (1009–1059), a legal scholar in the Song Dynasty, advocated that the laws must be equal, saying, "Law is shared by the emperor and the people. If the people of imperial lineage who committed crimes are not punished or executed, the emperor is practicing favoritism. If the people with titles of nobility who committed crimes are not punished or executed, the officials are practicing favoritism. .... Therefore, the rulers should ignore the closeness or distance of the relations, treat the noble and the low equally, and use the unified law" (Li, 2003, 90). The great writer Su Shi (1036–1101) also advanced the idea of judicial justice that "strictly applying the laws should begin with the courtiers" propounding that "In the past, sages made punishments and rewards. They knew that the people would enjoy rewards and fear punishments. Therefore, giving a reward should start from the bottom to the top. For ordinary people who do good things, the award should follow immediately, and thus people in the world who do good things fully know that they will be rewarded. Imposing punishment should start from top to bottom. For nobles and courtiers who committed minor crimes, the punishment should follow immediately, and thus the officials who do bad things fully know that they would be punished. ... Shang Yang and Han Fei used severe punishment and torture to supervise the world. An important lesson is that they imposed punishment starting from the nobles and courtiers and spreading to the commoners. That's why Qin finally convinced the world. To strictly apply laws and prohibitions

should start from the high-ranking officials so that the lower-ranking officials will not commit violations."[31]

2. Explanations on the specific meaning of charges, types of punishment, and standards for conviction and sentence, analysis and comparison of the meaning of the law, and making comparison of the meaning of the law." For example, regarding the legal system, *Tang Lv Shu Yi* identifies four forms of law, Lv, Ling, Ge, and Shi, and makes a relatively full exposition of them. Japan inherited the Chinese tradition of "comparing the meaning of the law." In the preface of *Konin shiki*, it is clearly pointed out: "Lv is based on punishment, Ling is based on persuasion, Ge is made according to the timely demand, and Shi is made to fill the gap. The four supplement each other, and it is sufficient to set a good example."[32] In the section "Official Position of Ling the First" of *Ryo-no-shuge*, the Japanese legal scholars also elaborated on what Ling is.[33] Regarding the structure of the code, *Tang Lv Shu Yi* theoretically summarizes and explains the structure and style of the 12 chapters in its General Principles and Guardian. Regarding the penalty system, *Tang Lv Shu Yi* provides a comparison and interpretation of the death penalty, exile, imprisonment, caning, and flogging. On the main principles of criminal law, *Tang Lv Shu Yi* discusses the aggravation of punishment concerning the *ten abominations*, reduction and exemption for royal family members and officials, patriarchal ethics, moral guidance and supplementary punishment, reduction and exemption of punishment for the elderly, young, disabled, and diseased, the equivalent of the crime and punishment, no punishment without law, comparison and analogy, precedence of specific provisions over general provisions, false accusations leading to penalties, and more, to help the judicial officials understand the provisions and concepts of the codes. On the elaboration of important legal systems, *Tang Lv Shu Yi* covers issues of intent and negligence, joint crime, combined punishment for several crimes, aggravation of punishment for recidivism, reduction of punishment for voluntary surrender, and others. Regarding the interpretation of legal texts, *Tang Lv Shu Yi* is meticulous and uses different methods, such as limited, extensive, analogical, literal, sentence-by-sentence, and innovative interpretation; and interpretations by cases, differentiation and analysis, and questions and answers. On the interpretation of special terms in the code, more than 190 are listed in seven categories (He, 2006, 451). It can be

[31] See Su (1986, 734–735). In addition, after the Ming Dynasty, legal scholars also discussed judicial justice. For example, Tang Shu (1497–1574), a legal scholar in the Ming Dynasty, emphasized judicial positions such as "dealing with things without private consideration" and "seeking the truth"; Wang Kentang, Lei Menglin, and legal scholars Shen Zhiqi and Wang Mingde of the Qing Dynasty also expressed similar thoughts in their legal works. See He (2006, 479–500).

[32] (1972). *Newly Updated National History Series, Assorted Kyaku of the Three Generations I*. 1. Yoshikawa Koubunkan.

[33] "Ling was also called Jiao Ling (enlightenment and law). Enlightening people about the law so that they would not violate the law. ... In other words, question: what about using the term Xun (instruction) instead of Ling? Answer: Ling is not persuasion. Ling is telling people about right and wrong and teaching people the law rules. ... In other words, Ling is the law, the guidance, the teaching." See (1966). *Newly Updated National History Series, Volume 23, Ryo-no-shuge I*. 3–5. Yoshikawa Koubunkan.

said that *Tang Lv Shu Yi* reached the peak in terms of the comparison and interpretation of legal meanings. It established the tradition of legal interpretation in the Chinese Legal Family, which lasted until the end of the Qing Dynasty; its influence still remains today.

3. Emphasis on the simplicity of legislation and convenience and benefit for the people. Gao Jiong, Zheng Yi, and the others who formulated *Kaihuang Lv*, and Fang Xuanling, Zhangsun Wuji, and the others who participated in the compilation of *Tang Lv Shu Yi* all repeatedly emphasized the guiding ideology of legislation—laws should be simple and for the purpose of facilitating and benefiting people. For example, Gao Jiong and others drew up the "types of punishment" in *Kaihuang Lv* and only reserved the five punishments—death penalty, exile, imprisonment, caning, and flogging—to "remove the previous punishment of whipping, beheading, and hanging, and reduce and lighten the punishment of exile and imprisonment" (Fang et al., 1973, 711). Although *Wude Lv* enacted in the early Tang Dynasty had "cut down all the excessive and strict law of the Daye Era and formulated fifty-three rules to make the law lenient and simple," when the code was revised in the Zhenguan Era, the ruler still thought that the punishment adopted by the old law was excessive. Therefore, major revisions have been made. As a result, the revised *Zhenguan Lv* "had uncountably simplified and lightened rules" (Liu et al., 1975, 2134, 2138).

After the Song and Yuan Dynasties, the emphasis on the simplicity of legislation and the convenience and benefits of the people were combined with fairness and justice of the law, respect for life, people-oriented thoughts, and prudent punishment. For example, Qiu Jun (1420–1495), a legal scholar in the Ming Dynasty, in his work *Da Xue Yan Yi Bu: Shen Xing Xian*, emphasized several principles that must be adhered to when making the law, such as the law must be fair, and the law takes priority over what the emperor said[34]; life should be respected; people-oriented thoughts should be valued.[35] Another legal scholar in the Ming Dynasty, Wang Kentang (1549–1613), also emphasized that it was the basic duty of a legal practitioner to fully understand the original legislative intent—helping the people, benefiting the people, and caring for the people, to be proficient in the interpretation of the law, and to use punishment prudently. "The meaning of the law must be explained and made clear. This is not only because the language and intention are so concise, strict, profound,

[34] Qiu Jun pointed out: "The way of being a good emperor is nothing greater than *zhong* (moderation). *Zhong* means impartial when it comes to the feeling, and not overdone when it comes to doing things ... The imposition of punishments should be neither too heavy nor too light. This is the so-called *zhong* and this is the so-called good at using punishment." See Qiu (1999b).

[35] *Shen Xing Xian* has included several valuable ideas, such as humanitarianism, people-oriented thoughts, respect for every human life, and the inalienable aspect of human freedom and equality. For example, Qiu Jun pointed out: "The emperor's willingness of taking care of people is consistent with people's will. That is why Emperor Shun became Shun. Basically, people are born between heaven and earth and are able to live in the world. Once a person is born, everyone wants him/her to be alive. However, a person himself/herself knows that he/she wants to be alive, but does not know that others all want him to be alive. Therefore, there is competition, sometimes even a fight, among people. As a result, the chances of being alive decreases." See Qiu (1999b).

and wide that it is hard for people to understand but also because the purpose of implementing punishment and law is to avoid future punishment and violation of the law. The emperors had good intentions and cared for the people. It is sometimes obvious and sometimes indistinct in the 30 volumes (of the code). Nevertheless, they are not directly known to normal officials, who are limited to the sentences and words used in law. Thus, a detailed explanation must be provided. Would the legislature dare to omit words because they prefer simple words to complicated words? If officials who are handling people's lives can gain some inspiration from what I said, feel the goodwill of the emperors, and follow the instruction of the emperors, then the punishment can be good punishment" (He, 2006, 290).

In Japan, although their legal studies were inherited from China and many opinions on legislation and the judiciary were copied from the views of the Chinese legal scholars, the Japanese legal scholars still expressed some of their own opinions. For example, the Japanese legal scholars, such as Kiyohara no Natsuno, Sugawara no Kiyotomo, Fujiwara no Yutoshi, Fujiwara no Mamoru, Sanuki no Naganao, and Okihara no Miniku, explicitly declared in the preface of *Ryo-no-gige*: "Grown in spring and harvested in autumn, this punishment was born together with heaven and earth; Yin being miserable and yang being comfortable, the law is frequently used together with wind and frost. ... In the past, when people used ropes as clothes, lax instructions were easy to follow; when people drew their clothes, the sense of shame was hard to appear. The Zhou Dynasty adopted Sandian (three codes) and the law flourished; the Han Dynasty issued Jiuzhang (nine-chapter law) and more schools were introduced. Although the contents were rich, the law could hardly deal with the crimes, and although the institutions were established, some defects were fundamental and serious. Until the end of the dynasties, there were even more lengthy and jumbled rules. Both the emperors and the subjects made decisions according to their preferences. The rules were made in the morning and destroyed early in the evening, which was only a waste of effort. Rich people were given lighter punishment, poor people received heavier punishment, and the law was decided by corrupted rulers. Therefore, if the law is issued but not followed, it is better not to issue the law. If the law is not clear, it is arbitrary punishment. Our emperor is worthy and hard-working. He makes and implements the law and learns from the laws of the Qi and Qin Dynasties while removing the harshest rules. ... The production of laws should follow the principle that the language should be simple, and the scope of the law should be wide."[36] Here, the main idea is very clear, as it criticizes the cumbersome nature of the law and emphasizes the simplicity of the legislation.

4. The application of comparative law in legal research. The study of comparative law in ancient China was founded and developed by legal scholars. A classic is a book titled *Tang Ming Lv He Bian* written and edited by Xue Yunsheng (1819–1901), a minister of the Ministry of Punishment and a legal scholar in the late Qing Dynasty. In his book, more than 40 years of legal research results and judicial practice were collected. The book is based on the two famous legal

[36] (1966). *Newly Updated National History Series, Volume 22, Ryo-no-gige*, preface 1. Yoshikawa Koubunkan.

codes of the Tang and Ming Dynasties preserved in ancient China, first listing the articles found in Tang Lv and then listing the similar articles found in Ming Lv. It further indicates which articles have been inherited by Ming Lv, which have been modified by Ming Lv, and which have disappeared in Ming Lv, and then makes a full comparative analysis of the articles. By analogy, Xue Yunsheng made a thorough study of various legal systems, principles, and even conceptual terms in ancient China. As we know, until the Qing Dynasty, there were four major ancient Chinese codes: Tang Lv, Song Xing Tong, Ming Lv, and Qing Lv. Among these four codes, Song Xing Tong imitated Tang Lv, and Qing Lv inherited Ming Lv. Therefore, Xue Yunsheng's comparison of Tang Ming Lv and Ming Lv is, in fact, a comparison of the legal systems of the Tang, Song, Ming, and Qing Dynasties. Broadly speaking, in a sense, it is also a comparative study of the entire ancient Chinese law. This, both in content and method, provides precious legal cultural wealth for us.

Since Japanese legal studies came from China, they went through a process of comparison and selection upon being translated. Therefore, the Japanese legal scholars were better at comparative study. The most famous classic is the book *Ryo-no-shuge*, which is like an encyclopedia of comparative law. On the one hand, because the book mainly explains the *Yoro Code* that is inherited from the *Taiho Code*, the book often cites *The Old Record*—the annotation work of the *Taiho Code*—when expounding the implicit meaning of the provisions of the *Yoro Code*. For example, when interpreting the "Law on Monks and Nuns" in Volume 8 of *Ryo-no-shuge*, there is a stipulation about the handling of *maoming xiangdai* (imposters). When giving the interpretation, the author expressed his own point of view that "Mao means to cover, and maoming xiangdai is when person A pretends to be person B, but the public authorities know nothing about it." In addition, the author immediately quoted *The Old Record*: "Maoming xiangdai refers to the situation provided in the last provision, where a person changes his title and pretends to be a monk."[37] On the other hand, because there were many commentaries on the *Yoro Code*, in order to enhance the persuasiveness of the commentaries, the authors often compared various theories and took the preferable point of view. For example, when interpreting the article that "when the harvest is not good because of floods, droughts, locusts, or frosts, the authority should examine, completely record, and report the situation." In the "Law on Taxes and Corvees" in Volume 13 of *Ryo-no-shuge*, more than 10 different commentaries were quoted, such as the *Interpretation on Law* (a commentary book on the *Taiho Code* and *Yoro Code*, authors unknown), *Sanuki's Commentary* (a commentary book on the *Yoro Code* written by Sanuki no Naganao), *Ato Commentary* (a commentary book on the *Yoro Code* written by Atoji), *Interpretation on Ritsuryo* (a commentary book on the *Yoro Code*, authors unknown).[38] In addition, *Ryo-no-shuge* also cites the doctrines and viewpoints of Chinese legal scholars from time to time

[37] (1966). *Newly Updated National History Series, Volume 23, Ryo-no-shuge I*, 250. Yoshikawa Koubunkan.

[38] (1966). *Newly Updated National History Series, Volume 23, Ryo-no-shuge I*, 396–402. Yoshikawa Koubunkan.

when annotating the text of the law and compares Japanese and Chinese hermeneutics to clarify the special features of the text of the Japanese law. According to the research of Masajiro Takigawa, an expert on *Ryo-no-shuge, Ryo-no-shuge* quoted a number of works of Chinese legal annotations, including *Song Si Ji* (Song's Private Commentary, 宋私记), *Zhang Si Ji* (Zhang's Private Commentary, 张私记), and *Jian Ji* (Jian's Commentary, 简记) (Miura & Takikawa, 1982, 7).

3.4 Characteristics of Legal Scholars' Activities

The activities of legal scholars in the Chinese Legal Family are characterized by diverse group composition, large and long-lasting groups of legal scholars, large numbers of legal families, concentration on legal commentary, attaching great importance to practice, and aims of serving the society, among others. By grasping these characteristics, the reason why the Chinese Legal Family could reach a glorious state in the East in the Middle Ages and occupy a unique position in the history of world legal culture can be fully recognized and understood. Due to space limitations and considering that academia has published some papers on the two characteristics of the activities—centering on annotating Lv and Ling and attaching importance to practice and aiming at serving the society—this section focuses on the other three characteristics (diverse group composition, large and long-lasting groups of legal scholars, and large numbers of legal families).

3.4.1 Diverse Group Composition

Compared with Common Law and Civil Law, the legal scholars of the Chinese Legal Family have very diverse origins. Among them were founding fathers of various dynasties, such as Li Delin, Zheng Yi, Zhangsun Wuji, Pei Ji, Fang Xuanling, Du Ruhui, Fan Zhi, Zhao Pu, Liu Ji, Li Shanchang, Ashdarhan, and Gang Lin. In Japan, the legal scholars who were also founding fathers included Fujiwara no Fuhito and Yamato no Nagaoka, the compiler and commentators of the *Taiho Code* and *Yoro Code*, respectively, and Fujiwara no Tokihira, the compiler of the *Konin shiki* and *Jogan shiki*. There were also officials at the highest level equal to the position of ministers, such as Gao Jiong, Yang Wang, Yu Zhining, Dai Zhou, Song Jing, Lu Zhi, Dou Yi, Wang Anshi, Yelv Chucai, He Rongzu, Qiu Jun, Duikana, Zhu Shi, and Xue Yunsheng. In Japan, the bureaucratic group included Kibi no Makibi, Ochi no Hiroe, Koremune no Kinkata, and Sakanoue no Sadashige.

In the Chinese Legal Family, there were famous legal experts, such as Sun Shi, Song Minqiu, Fu Lin, Shen Zhongwei, Beishulu Chong, He Guang, Wu Ne, Zhang Kai, Hu Qiong, Wang Kentang, Lei Menglin, Shu Hua, Xiao Jingao, Wang Mingde, Chen Fangsheng, Shen Zhiqi, Wang Youhuai, Xu Lian, and Zhu Qingqi. In Japan, the famous legal experts included Sanuki no Naganao, Koremune no Naomoto, Koremune no Tadasuke, and Okihara no Miniku.

There were senior judicial officials in the Chinese Legal Family, such as Su Wei, Zhao Chuo, Di Renjie, Xu Yougong, Su Xiao, Ju Kejiu, Bao Zheng, Su Tianjue, Liu Weiqian, Kuang Zhong, Hai Rui, Lan Ding Yuan, Quan Shichao, and Zhao Shuqiao. In Japan, the judicial officials included Sanuki Chiji and Sakanoue no Akikane.

There were also great Confucianists, scribes, and historians, such as Wang Tong, Kong Yingda, Yan Shigu, Jia Gongyan, Sima Guang, Zhu Xi, Liu Kezhuang, Zhendexiu, and Ye Shi. Finally, there were also writers and poets, such as Chen Ziang, Han Yu, Zhang Zhuo, Liu Yuxi, Bai Juyi, Liu Zongyuan, Ouyang Xiu, Su Xun, Su Shi (Dongpo), Qin Guan, Zhao Mengfu, Li Zhi, and Li Yu. In Japan, the writers and poets included Ogyu Sorai, Kada no Azumamaro, and Kada no Arimaro.

3.4.2 Large Group of Legal Scholars and Their Long Duration

In China, there were more than 50 legal scholars in the Sui and Tang Dynasties, including Fang Xuanling, more than 60 legal scholars in the Song and Yuan Dynasties—including Ju Kejiu and Beishulu Chong—and more than 80 legal scholars in the Ming and Qing Dynasties, including Zhang Kai, Chen Shikuang, and Gang Yi. These are just the legal scholars whose works have remained to this day or who have been recorded in historical records. Not only was there a large group of legal scholars, but they were active in China for a long time. The legal studies survived nearly 1300 years, not counting the nearly 1000 years from the formation of legal studies in the Qin and Han Dynasties in the third century BC to the heyday of legal studies in the Sui and Tang Dynasties in the early seventh century AD—even only counting from the Sui and Tang Dynasties when the Chinese Legal Family was formed to the end of the Qing Dynasty in the early twentieth century.

The situation in Japan is the same. In just the two periods, Nara and Heian (710–1192), there were more than 100 famous Lv experts (*Myobo Hakase*), including Yamato no Nagaoka, Yamada no Shirogane, Sanuki no Hironao, and Sakurai Tanabe Sada Sho. After Japan entered the Kamakura shogunate society in 1192, a group of *Myobo Hakase* of each generation was still active–such as the *Myobo Hakase* Nakahara Akihito, who died in 1321. After that, although *Myobodo* declined day by day and the title of *Myobo Hakase* began to disappear gradually during the Muromachi Shogunate period after the middle of the fourteenth century, Lv experts who researched Ritsuryo still existed, such as the famous Lv expert Sakanoue no Akinari, who was active in the 1340s. In the Edo period (after the seventeenth century), legal studies were revived, and a group of famous Lv experts appeared, such as Sakakibara, Koshu (1656–1706), Ogyu Sorai (1666–1728), Takase Kiboku (1668–1749), Kada no Azumamaro (1669–1736), Ogyu Hokkei (1669–1754), Ashi no Tokurin (1695–1775), and Moriyoshi Sonoda (1785–1840).

3.4.3 Large Number of Legal Families

Legal families existed in the Han, Wei, Jin, and Southern and Northern Dynasties. In the Sui and Tang Dynasties, when the Chinese Legal Family was formed, the legal families further developed. For example, in the early Tang Dynasty, there were the father and son Han Zhongliang and Han Yuan, uncle and nephew Dai Zhou and Dai Zhide, and father and son Su Gui and Su Ting. According to historical records, when Han Zhongliang was a *Dali Shaoqing* (a deputy in *Dalisi*) at the beginning of the Wude Era, he was ordered by the emperor to create Lv and Ling together with Lang Chuzhi and others (Liu et al., 1975, 2739–2740). Zhongliang's son, Yuan, performed as a *huangmen shilang* (official position, emperor's assistant) and made the 30-volume *Lv Shu* together with Zhangsun Wuji from the 3rd to the 4th year of the Yonghui Era (651–652) (Zhangsun et al., 1983, 578). Dai Zhou came from Anyang, Xiangzhou. He not only knew Lv and Ling but also was good at strictly enforcing the law (Liu et al., 1975, 2532).

Dai Zhou had no children, and thus, he adopted the son of his elder brother, Zhide, as his descendant. Zhide was proficient in codes and enforced the law in a lenient way. During the Longshuo Era (661–663) and Yifeng Era (676–678), he actively participated in the revision of Ling, Ge, and Shi (Wang, 2006, 820).

Su Gui and Su Ting were famous legal scholars in the Tang Dynasty. Their ancestors were the famous legal scholars Su Chuo and Su Wei during the Wei, Jin, Southern and Northern Dynasties. Wei's grand great-great-grandson, Gui, was proficient in law (Liu et al., 1975, 2878). From the first year to the second year of the Shenlong Era (705–706), Gui made the 7-volume *San Ban Ge* and the 20-volume *Chui Gong Shi* together with the *shangshu zuopushe* (an official position, the head of Shangshu Department) Tang Xiujing and others (Wang, 2006, 821). His son Ting was ordered to review the unjust judgments made by Lai Junchen and others when he was serving as *jiancha yushi* (an official position, supervisory censor). Ting inspected, found, and undid the false accusations. According to historical records, Su Ting, serving as *ziwei shilang* and *zhongshu shilang*—both refer to the same official position, deputy official in Zhongshu Department—revised the Kaiyuan Ling, Ge, and Shi, together with Song Jing and others, in the 3rd year (715) and the 7th year (719) of the Kaiyuan Era.[39]

After the Song and Ming Dynasties, legal families did not disappear in China and continued to play an active role in legal studies. For example, the father and son He Ning (897–955) and He Meng (950–995), in the late Five Dynasties and early Song Dynasties, worked together and devoted all their efforts to the legal work *Yi Yu Ji* (Collection of Suspicious Judgments, 疑狱集), which created a mode of compiling precedents in ancient China. Another example is the father and son Wang Qiao and Wang Kentang in the middle of the Ming Dynasty. Wang Qiao devoted his entire life to the first draft of *Du Lv Si Jian* (Private Notes When Reading the Law, 读律

---

[39] See Wang (2006, 821–822). In addition to these legal families in the Tang Dynasty, the Di's, Di Renjie, his son Di Guangsi, his great-grandson Di Jianmo were also famous legal officials at that time. Due to the lack of space, no further discussion will be given here.

私笺). His son Wang Kentang inherited his father's career, worked hard, and finally completed the famous law book *Lv Li Jian Shi*, which became the most cited work in legal studies in the Ming and Qing Dynasties.

Another example is the legal scholar Wang Mingde, who wrote the great book *Du Lv Pei Xi* based on the essence of the previous legal works of different schools. From the preface and postscript of the book, we know that a great number of people participated in the compilation of *Du Lv Pei Xi*—38 people, including Zhan Weisheng, Chen Danchi, Zhang Weiren, and Gong Rongyu.— We also know that the book was revised by Wang Mingde's second son, Wang Xinzhan. Based on this, it can be speculated that Wang Mingde was not only an upright administrative and judicial official but also a very influential legal scholar. Moreover, legal studies became his family study, and his family was also a legal family.

In Japan, legal families were a common phenomenon in the medieval legal culture. Several families served as *Myobo Hakase*, judges, prosecutors, and other judicial positions in successive generations. For example, the legal family of Sanuki, from Sanuki no Chitsugu and Sanuki no Hironao to Sanuki no Naganao and Sanuki no Naganari, lasted for several generations.

The Koremune family had Koremune no Omune, Koremune no Naomoto, Koremune no Yoshitsune, Koremune no Kinkata, Koremune no Tadasuke, Koremune no Tadamasa, Koremune no Michinari,[40] Koremune no Kunito, and others.

The Sakanoue family had Sakanoue no Sadashige, Sakanoue no Norimasa, Sakanoue no Toshimitu, Sakanoue no Akikane, Sakanoue no Kaneshige, Sakanoue no Akimoto, Sakanoue no Shigetoshi, Sakanoue no Kanetoshi, Sakanoue no Akimasa, Sakanoue no Akimori, Sakanoue no Akizumi, Sakanoue no Akinari, Sakanoue no Akimune, and others.

The Seta family was separated from the Nakahara family because of a surname change. The Seta family counted Seta Norizumi, Seta Noriaya, Seta Akitake, Seta Norimi, and others.

The Nakahara family was separated from the Koremune family because the emperor bestowed the family name "Nakahara." The Nakahara family had Nakahara no Akihito, Nakanohara no Akizumi, and others. Among these legal families, the Nakahara family lasted for dozens of generations, and hundreds of family members served as Lv experts (*Myobo Hakase*). This legal family lasted a total of more than 300 years, which is rare and spectacular in the world.

3.5 *Contributions of Legal Scholars and Inheritance of the Chinese Legal Family*

The survival of the Chinese Legal Family for more than 1300 years is inseparable from the contributions of legal scholars. They made contributions mainly in nine

[40] Tadasuke, Tadamasa, and Michinari were all awarded the surname "Yoshimune" (meaning Master of Law) by the emperor.

aspects: (1) presiding over or participating in the country's legislative activities and establishing a large and complete legal system; (2) annotating and interpreting the law so that the established legal system could operate effectively; (3) strictly enforcing the law so that a tradition of pursuing equal, fair, and just application of laws was established; (4) expounding the legal principles and spirit of Lv and Ling in the legal system to broaden the theoretical basis of the legal studies; (5) compiling, summarizing, and researching on precedents to provide a reference for judicial practitioners; (6) recording important legal events and passed down the history of legal progress; (7) engaging in judicial inspection and developing forensic science; (8) exploring the laws of prison management and developing prison science centered on the transformation of prisoners; (9) engaging in legal education and training legal talents to serve the country. It is these contributions that helped the formation of the enduring traditions of the Chinese Legal Family, which provided a rich historical heritage for the upbringing and growth of modern jurists.

First, legal scholars presided over or participated in the country's legislative activities and established a large and complete legal system. As far as China's situation is concerned, the formation of the laws in the Sui and Tang Dynasties basically laid the foundations for the entire legal systems of ancient China and even the Chinese Legal Family. The main codes of this legal system, such as *Kaihuang Lv* in Sui, *Wude Lv*, *Zhenguan Lv*, *Yonghui Lv*, and *Kaiyuan Lv*, revised and formed during the Kaiyuan Era (713–741) in Tang, were all compiled, revised and promulgated based on the presidency and participation of a group of legal scholars. These legal scholars included Li Delin in the Sui Dynasty, Zhangsun Wuji in the Tang Dynasty, Fan Zhi and Dou Yi in the Song Dynasty, Yelv Chucai in the Yuan Dynasty, Li Shanchang in the Ming Dynasty, and Ashdarhan in the Qing Dynasty.

In Japan, the major contributors to the compilation of the *Taiho Code* and *Yoro Code*—which laid the foundation of the Japanese legal system–were Lv experts (*Myobo Hakase*), such as Fujiwara no Fuhito, Moribe no Muraji Osumi, Yamato no Nagaoka, Kibi no Makibi, Yamada no Shirogane, and Shioya no Komaro. In addition, the formulation of Ling, Ge, and Shi was also inseparable from the efforts of legal scholars.

Second, legal scholars made annotations and interpretations of the law so that the established legal system could operate effectively. This was the main work and greatest contribution of legal scholars to the legal academics of the Chinese Legal Family. For example, Zhangsun Wuji (?– 659) of the early Tang Dynasty not only participated in the revision and compilation of *Wude Lv, Zhenguan Lv, and Yonghui Lv* but also compiled and completed the great *Tang Lv Shu Yi* together with Yu Zhining and others. In the Song Dynasty, Sun Shi compiled and revised *Lv Fu Yin Yi*, together with Yang Anguo, Zhao Xiyan, Song Qi, and others, to solve the problem of the *Mingfa* examination in legal education that laws and legal interpretations did not have printed copies and it was difficult for candidates to study. The book, citing *Tang Lv Shu Yi* and other legal documents in history, made a phonetic pronunciation and interpretation of 752 nouns in Tang Lv. It contributed to the development of legal studies and the popularization of legal knowledge among the scholar-bureaucrats.

Wang Kentang (1549–1613) of the Ming Dynasty drew on the strengths of various schools and made great efforts to interpret the words of the law, annotate the law, detect the legislators' intentions, and cite precedents in the annotation of the law in his book *Lv Li Jian Shi*. The book became the most cited work by legal scholars in the late Ming and Qing Dynasties.

Shu Hua, another legal scholar in the Ming Dynasty,[41] also made great contributions to the research on legal studies. He presided over the compilation of the 7-volume *Wen Xing Tiao Li*, the 30-volume *Xing Shu Hui Ju* (Legal Basis for the Punishment Books, 刑书会据) and the 30-volume *Da Ming Lv Fu Li* (Attached Cases for Da Ming Lv, 大明律附例), which were all very influential legal works at that time.

Wang Mingde, a legal scholar in the Qing Dynasty, devoted his life to completing the book *Du Lv Pei Xi*, which pushed the legal study of the Ming and Qing Dynasties to its peak.

In Japan, the *Myobo* scholar Sanuki no Naganao (783–862) presided over the compilation of *Ryo-no-gige*, the official commentary on the *Yoro Code*, while participating in legislative and judicial activities. Another *Myobo Hakase*, Koremune no Naomoto, active in the second half of the ninth century, compiled and completed *Ryo-no-shuge*, *Ritsu-no-shuge*, and *Private Commentary of the Prosecutor* based on his strong family study of unofficial commentaries. These commentaries laid the foundations for the jurisprudence of Japan as a Ritsuryo country.

Third, legal scholars strictly enforced the law and established a tradition of pursuing the equal, fair, and just application of laws. For example, Su Wei, a legal scholar in the Sui Dynasty, long held the positions of senior judicial official, such as *Dali Qing* (the highest official in *Dalisi*) and head of the Ministry of Punishment. He insisted on being impartial when implementing the law and even prevented Emperor Sui from imposing punishment without law and killing arbitrarily. *Sui Shu: Su Wei Zhuan* (Book of Sui: Biography of Su Wei, 隋书·苏威传) records that "Once, the emperor was angry with one person and wanted to kill him. Wei entered the palace to remonstrate, but the emperor did not accept it. The emperor was so angry that he would come out of the palace and kill him in person. Wei stood in the way of stopping the emperor. The emperor got around Wei and went out. Wei stopped the emperor again. The emperor went into the palace angrily. After a long while, the emperor called Wei in and thanked him: 'If you can always be like that, I will not have worries.'"

Ju Kejiu, a legal scholar from the Five Dynasties to the Song Dynasty, was once appointed as *Dali Qing* of the Zhou Dynasty. "The wife of Li Simei from Zhengzhou went to Yushitai (the Censorate) to report her husband's private trading of salt. The crime did not deserve the death penalty, but judge Yang Ying sentenced him to death. The authority arrested Yang Ying, and Yang Ying admitted his guilt. Ju Kejiu ruled that Yang Ying had delivered appropriate judgment, reduced his punishment by three grades, and exiled him for two and a half years. Prime Minister Wang Jun wanted

---

41 Shu Hua, a successful candidate in the highest imperial examination of the 38th year of the Jiajing Era (1559).

to kill Yang Ying. He called in Ju Kejiu and said: 'The dead cannot be resurrected. Ying killed a person unjustly. How can he be forgiven?' Ju Kejiu insisted and argued for him, and Yang Ying was able to avoid dying finally" (Toqto'a et al., 2008, 897). Comments can be found in *Song Shi: Ju Kejiu Zhuan* (Biography of Ju Kejiu, 剧可久传) thus: "Kejiu worked in *Tingwei* (judicial authority) for forty years. He applied the law fairly and was famous for being benevolent."

The story of Bao Zheng in the Song Dynasty, who was not afraid of elites and strictly enforced the law, was also well-known. For example, Zhang Yaozuo, who oversaw the country's financial power at the time, relied on nepotism and was corrupt. Bao Zheng impeached him many times for his corruption. Although Emperor Renzong of Song insisted on protecting him, in the end, the emperor had to remove him from office. *Song Shi: Bao Zheng Zhuan* (Biography of Bao Zheng, 包拯传) records that Bao Zheng enforced the law fairly, stating, "Bao Zheng was famous for being resolute and steadfast among officials. The nobles and eunuchs restrained themselves because of him. Those who heard of it feared him. People considered Bao Zheng to be cleaner than the Yellow River. Even kids and women knew his reputation. People called him Bao Daizhi (an official position, an assistant to the emperor who was waiting for imperial edicts). People in the capital said that 'you do not need to bribe officials because there is Yama Raja (king of hell) Bao Zheng.'"

After the Song Dynasty, there were also many other legal scholars who strictly enforced the law, such as Wang Yu and Su Tianjue in the Yuan Dynasty, Kuang Zhong, Wu Ne, and Hai Rui in the Ming Dynasty, and Lan Dingyuan and Wang Youhuai in the Qing Dynasty.

Koremune no Kinkata, a Japanese legal scholar in the Heian period, was not only an outstanding jurist but also a judicial official with integrity and humanitarianism. For example, in a case that occurred during the Tenryaku Era (947–957), Kinkata dared to contradict the emperor and insisted on his legal claims. At that time, an old official criticized the imperial court because it wasted much money in places where it should not be spent but was miserly in places where money should be used. He thus offended the imperial court. When deciding the punishment, the court consulted Kinkata and another *Myobo* scholar, Sakurai Yuhitsu. Kinkata replied that the old official had committed a crime against Shi, while Yuhitsu replied that he had committed a crime against Chi. According to Miscellaneous Lv, a crime against Shi was punished with a flogging of forty lashes—according to the "Law on Bureaucratic Establishment"—while for a crime against Chi, he would be sentenced to two years in prison, which was much heavier. Emperor Murakami adopted the advice of Yuhitsu, who argued that the crime was against Chi. Kinkata's Kanmon (advisory report) was against the will of the emperor, and he was demoted to the official position of Deputy in the Ministry of Finance (Yaheiji, 1966, 196–198). However, his spirit of pursuing the fairness of the law won the respect of legal scholars.

Fourth, legal scholars expounded on the legal principles and spirits of Lv and Ling in the legal system to broaden the theoretical basis of legal studies. For example, Wei Zheng (580–643), a legal scholar in the Tang Dynasty, clearly advanced the idea that the emperor must enforce the law fairly and use punishment equally, and said, "The foundation of punishment and reward lies in persuading people to do good things and punishing the evil. Therefore, the emperor should make unified standards, not applying them differently because of their relationship or identity" (Wu, 2011, 538). He emphasized that the reward should be greater and the punishment should be lighter and that the law should be lenient and fair, saying, "The law is the balance of a country and the yardstick of the time. The balance helps to decide the priority, and the yardstick helps to decide right or wrong. Today, the legislature needs to pay attention to the lenience and fairness of the law" (Dong et al., 1990). Further, "When giving rewards, acquaintances should not be ignored, and when imposing punishment, relatives and nobles should not be favored. Fairness should be the rule" (Wu, 2015, 203). Other legal scholars in the Tang Dynasty, such as Sun Fujia and Yu Zhining, also held the same view as Wei Zheng.

Legal scholars in the Song Dynasty, including Li Gou (1009–1059), also emphasized the importance of governing the country according to the law (Lv and Ling) and prudently issuing orders to the people, thus: "What the people obey is not the rulers but their orders; what the rulers guard is not the country but their orders. … The rulers use orders to govern the people, and the people use orders to serve the ruler. If the orders encourage something, the people will do it; if the orders abolish something, the people will stop doing it. So, the order should be consistent and not variable" (Li, 2005, 45). He also advocated that the law must be applied equally and said, "Law is shared by the emperor and the people. If the people of imperial lineage who committed crimes are not punished or executed, the emperor is practicing favoritism. If the people with titles of nobility who committed crimes are not punished or executed, the officials are practicing favoritism. … Therefore, the rulers should ignore the closeness or distance of the relations, treat the noble and the low equally, and use unified law" (Li, 2005, 27).

Other legal scholars, such as Qiu Jun, Tang Shu, Wang Kentang, and Huang Zongxi in the Ming Dynasty; and Wang Mingde, Lan Dingyuan, Wang Youhuai, and Liu Heng in the Qing Dynasty, all expounded on the spirit of the law while researching and annotating the laws.

Fifth, legal scholars compiled, summarized, and studied precedents to provide a reference for judicial officials. Outstanding legal scholars in this field include Zhang Zhuo, the author of *Long Jing Feng Sui Pan* in the Tang Dynasty; He Ning and He Meng, the authors of *Yi Yu Ji* at the end of the Five Dynasties and the early Song Dynasty; Zheng Ke, the author of *Zhe Yu Gui Jian* (Mirrors for Making Judgments, 折狱龟鉴); Gui Wanrong, the author of *Tang Yin Bi Shi* (Compilation of Classical Judgments, 棠阴比事); Manting Zengsun, the author of Ming Gong Shu Pan Qing Ming Ji (Compilation of Just Judgments Made by Famous Judges, 名公书判清明集); Li Qing, the author of Zhe Yu Xin Yu (New Words for Making Judgments, 折狱新语); Zhu Qingqi and Bao Shuyun, the authors of *Xing An Hui Lan*, and Xu Lian, the author of *Xing Bu Bi Zhao Jia Jian Cheng An*. Among them, Zheng Ke, Zhu Qingqi, and Quan Shichao had the greatest influence on later generations.

Zheng Ke[42] carefully collected 276 stories of cases about 395 things in the Song and pre-Song periods in his book *Zhe Yu Gui Jian*. He also took the opportunity to make notes on each case to elaborate his thoughts on jurisprudence and the judicial system. For example, Zheng Ke emphasized the use of Confucian Ren (benevolence) and Yi (Righteousness), the rule of De (Virtue), and education to guide the handling of cases and litigation. He advocated that the relationship among the patriarchal ethics, the three cardinal guides, and the five constant virtues should be properly handled when dealing with cases. He criticized the darkness and corruption of the judicial system at that time. He summarized the methods of solving cases and the experience of trying cases and extracted the theories so judicial officials at all levels could follow them. He also pointed out the importance of the rule of law and emphasized that good law enforcement officials should be selected. After recording two cases, one about the deaths of two related women—in Donghai County in the Western Han Dynasty and Shangyu County in the Eastern Han Dynasty—who were wrongly killed by mediocre officials, and the other about the exoneration of a filial woman—in Linzi County in the Western Jin Dynasty—who was released by a good official, Cao Shu, Zheng Ke stressed the extreme importance of choosing law enforcement officials, saying, "If the woman of Linzi had not met Cao Xian, her fate would be no different from the women in Donghai and Shangyu. Only by acknowledgment of the possibility of avoiding the two women being wronged and punished can this prominently reflect the respectability of the Linzi woman's exoneration. That is why I put the two stories together" (Zheng, 1981).

There is no biography of Zhu Qingqi in *Qing Shi Gao* (Draft of History of Qing, 清史稿), and the details of his birth and death are unknown. His contribution to legal studies was that, together with Bao Shuyun, he compiled the most famous collection of precedents in the Qing Dynasty, the 88-volume *Xing An Hui Lan*. The book collects a total of 4045 judgments from the first year of the Qianlong Era to the 14th year of the Daoguang Era (1736–1834). Zhu Qingqi and Bao Shuyun also compiled together the 16-volume *Xu Zeng Xing An Hui Lan* (Supplement to *Xing An Hui Lan*, 续增刑案汇览). This book collects more than 1670 cases in the Daoguang Era (1821–1850).

Similarly, there is no record of Quan Shichao in *Qing Shi Gao*, and the details of his birth and death are unknown. During the Qianlong Era (1736–1795), he served as the director of the Administrative Division and Shanxi Division of the Department of Punishment. He oversaw the autumn trial of the general office, supervision of the Huguang Division, and compilation and revision of the Law, among his other functions. Quan Shichao's contribution to legal studies was that he presided over and compiled *Bo An Xin Bian* (32 volumes), which was the largest compilation of the reversed cases in the Qing Dynasty. It was ground-breaking in style. Some subsequent compilations of reversed cases were just follow-ups based on this book.

---

[42] Zheng Ke was from Kaifeng. There were no biography of him in *Song Shi*. His records can be found in *Yin Ju Tong Yi* (General Discussion on Seclusion, 隐居通议), written by Liu Xun from Yuan, *Kaiyouyi Zhai Du Shu Zhi* (Reading Books in Kaiyouyi Room, 开有益斋读书志), written by Zhu Xuzeng from Qing, and *Si Ku Ti Yao Bian Zheng* (Discussion on the Summary of the Four Categories, 四库提要辨证), written by Yu Jiaxi from modern times, etc.

Sixth, legal scholars recorded major legal events and passed down the history of legal progress. The contributions in this respect made by the legal scholars of the Chinese Legal Family inherited the tradition of the legal historical narration created by a group of authors of Xing Fa Zhi in the past dynasties, such as Ban Gu (32–92). After the Sui and Tang Dynasties, this tradition was further carried forward, and a large number of works that recorded the legal political history appeared, such as Wu Jing's *Zhenguan Zheng Yao*, Sima Guang's *Zi Zhi Tong Jian*, and Qiu Jun's *Da Xue Yan Yi Bu: Zhi Guo Ping Tian Xia Zhi Yao–Shen Xing Xian*. Among them, Wu Jing was the one who laid the ideological foundation of the Chinese Legal Family and established the universal and legal outlook of legal studies.

Wu Jing (670–749) was a famous historian in the mid-Tang Dynasty who also did a lot of research on law. Although the book *Zhenguan Zheng Yao* contains mainly records of Emperor Taizong of Tang's conversations with his ministers without Wu Jing's own discussion, it is precisely because of these conversation records that we can understand the overall picture of the legal thoughts of Li Shimin's ruling group in the early Tang Dynasty. For example, in the early Zhenguan Era, Emperor Taizong said to his servants, "To be an emperor, you must save the people first. If you harm people in order to serve yourself, it is no different from cutting off your own legs to feed yourself. Although you are full, you will die. If you want to rule the world, you must first correct your own behavior. Those who behave well will produce good influence, and if the higher-ups behave reasonably, the subordinates will follow" (Wu, 2011, 1). In the 18th year of the Zhenguan Era (644), Emperor Taizong told his courtiers, "The emperor is like a boat, and the people are like water. The water can carry the boat, and it can also capsize the boat" (Wu, 2011, 261). These words vividly demonstrated Emperor Taizong's ideas of considering the people as the foundation, performing as an example, and governing the country in accordance with the will of the people. In the 1st year of the Zhenguan Era, Taizong told his courtiers, "The dead cannot be reborn, and the usage of law must be lenient and concise" (Wu, 2011, 525). In the 10th year of the Zhenguan Era, Taizong told his courtiers, "The law of the state must be simple. It should not be allowed to stipulate several punishments for one crime. … Changing the law frequently is not reasonable" (Wu, 2011, 552). These words showed that Emperor Taizong attached great importance to the clarification and prudence of punishment, the lenient and simple use of the law, and the consistency and stability of the law that it should not be changed overnight.

Seventh, legal scholars acted as legal advisers for the government and issued legal advice and opinions. Legal scholars, such as Zheng Yi, Wang Tong, and Yang Wang in the Sui Dynasty; Pei Ji, Liu Wenjing, Wei Zheng, and Sun Fujia in the Tang Dynasty; Li Gou and Sun Shi in the Song Dynasty; Liu Ji and Tang Shu in the Ming Dynasty; Zhu Shi and Yang Rongxu in the Qing Dynasty, all actively participated in the activities of the government to make laws and establish institutions by providing advice and opinions.

Different from China's situation, where legal scholars only performed as legal advisers part-time apart from their administrative and judicial jobs, in Japan, acting as legal advisers providing legal advice to the imperial court was a professional duty for legal scholars. It was a must-do activity for *Myobo Hakase*. For example, *Myobo*

Hakase from legal families, such as Koremune no Naomoto, Koremune no Kinkata, Koremune no Tadasuke, Sanuki no Chitsugu, Sanuki no Hironao, and Sanuki no Naganao, were all such legal advisers. This kind of legal opinion provided by legal advisers was called the *Myobo* Kanmon (legal advisory report),[43] and its content involved the land system, temple management, court etiquette, the implicit aims of the bureaucratic system, the affairs of the imperial family, the marriages and funerals of the royal family members and the dignitaries, and the conviction and sentencing of various crimes. It covered a wide range of issues, and when the court consulted them, *Myobo Hakase* had to reply by making a *Myobo* Kanmon. On the one hand, it was an honor for *Myobo Hakase* to make a *Myobo* Kanmon because if the Kanmon was adopted by the government, it would be incorporated into the judge's findings, which would be enforceable, and a precedent would be formed. On the other hand, making a Kanmon could be considerable pressure on *Myobo Hakase* because if the Kanmon was not in line with the court's wishes or if the legal problems they faced could not be properly resolved, the *Myobo Hakase* who made the Kanmon would be punished. For example, the *Myobo* Kanmons provided by Koremure no Kinkata, Sugawara Makoto, Sugawara no Arizane, Sakanoue no Norimasa, and others were not accepted because they were against the court's will. Moreover, these legal scholars were dismissed from office because of this. Some of them retired from officialdom, and some died soon after because of depression.[44]

Eighth, while conducting criminal trials, legal scholars also engaged in judicial inspections and developed forensic science. For example, Song Ci (1186–1249), a legal scholar in the Southern Song Dynasty, was not only an outstanding judge but also an outstanding forensic scientist. In 1247, Song Ci completed the book *Xi Yuan Ji Lu* (Collection of Grievance Relief Stories, 洗冤集录). It is the first forensic work in the history of the world. Based on the summarization of the previous achievements, Song Ci incorporated his own practical experience of forensic examination into the book and provided a systematic illustration of the theories and techniques of forensic examination. These included the rules on autopsy, methods and matters that should be taken into account in an autopsy, postmortem phenomena, various mechanical cases of suffocation, various blunt injuries, traffic accidents in ancient times, death from high temperature, poisoning, illness and sudden cardiac death, and corpse excavation. The book pushed the level of forensic science in ancient China to the forefront of the world and made significant contributions to ancient Chinese legal studies and forensic science. Particularly, Song Ci emphasized in the preface of the book that "The most severe punishment is the death penalty. To impose a death sentence, the

---

[43] Kanmon, also called Kan Format, was a document used to record the content of the answer to the consultation of the superior. The *Myobo* Kanmon, also known as the Legalist Kanmon, was Kanmon provided by legal scholars. In the ancient and medieval times, when the Japanese imperial court, the emperor, the regent, and other supreme rulers dealt with the crimes in criminal cases or decided the disputes, in principle, they would order two Myohoka to submit the Kanmon to support their judgments.

[44] For example, Sakanoue no Norimasa was removed from his post in the second year of the Choji Era (1104) because he failed to provide appropriate Kanmon in dealing with a dispute among the temple monk community. He was depressed and died soon afterwards. See Yaheiji (1966, 220).

most important grounds should be the original facts. To find out the original facts, inspection should be decisive." These words laid the basic principles for forensic inspection in China for more than a thousand years.[45]

The ancient Chinese forensic study established by Song Ci was further developed in the Yuan Dynasty, which was marked by the publishing of *Wu Yuan Lu* (Avoidance of Injustice, 无冤录) edited by Wang Yu. Wang Yu (1260–1346), who had been engaged in prison litigation and forensic examination for a long time, further developed the theory of forensic science on the basis of *Xi Yuan Ji Lu*. For example, on the one hand, *Wu Yuan Lu* added the content of the rules on the sheets for autopsy, the cases on the sheets for autopsy, postmortem examiners' supervision of defendants' signatures, principal officials' autopsy and acceptance of murder cases, the acceptance of murder cases and the autopsy, and the rules on immediate autopsy by the provincial authority. On the other hand, Wang Yu made supplementary explanations and empirical tests on some research results advanced by Song Ci, such as testing the genetic relationship by dropping blood on bones. Additionally, Wang Yu corrected some mistakes in *Xi Yuan Ji Lu*, such as the positions of the esophagus and the throat and the theory concerning the natural childbirth after the death of the mother. Finally, *Wu Yuan Lu* preserves precious historical materials by citing the results of forensic examinations of previous dynasties and the relevant rules of the imperial court.

During the Ming and Qing Dynasties, through the efforts of legal scholars, forensic science continued to develop. In addition to the continuous reprints of Song Ci's works, dozens of works were published, such as the eight-volume *Xi Yuan Ji Shuo* (Grievance Relief Stories, 洗冤集说, written by Chen Fangsheng), *Xi Yuan Hui Bian* (Compilation of the Grievance Relief Stories, written by Lang Tingdong, 洗冤汇编), *Xi Yuan Lu Ji Zheng* (Collected Evidence of the Grievance Relief Stories, 洗冤录集证, edited by Wang Youhuai), and *Xi Yuan Lu Bian Zheng* (Examination of the Grievance Relief Stories, written by Qu Zhongrong, 洗冤录辨正). Among these, the most influential is the four-volume *Xi Yuan Lu Xiang Yi* (Detailed Discussion of the Grievance Relief Stories, 洗冤录详义) edited by Xu Lian (published in 1854) during the Xianfeng Era of the Qing Dynasty (1851–1861).

Ninth, legal scholars engaged in legal education and cultivating legal talents to serve the country. The legal education of the Chinese Legal Family was provided by both the public authorities and private sector in China's Sui, Tang, and Song Dynasties, but the official school dominated. In the Yuan, Ming, and Qing Dynasties, due to the abolition of official legal education, private legal education became the main form. In private legal education, a group of legal scholars, such as Meng Kui, Shen Zhongwei, Ma Duanlin, and Su Tianjue in the Yuan Dynasty; Tang Shu and Li Zhi in the Ming Dynasty; Wang Mingde, Wan Weihan, Wang Youhuai, Wang Huizu, and Chen Tianxi in the Qing Dynasty, made outstanding contributions. Among them, Wang Huizu, a famous legal education master and famous assistant to magistrates in Jiangnan, is worth noting.

Wang Huizu (1731–1807), despite his bumpy career, set an example for grassroots legal practitioners in later generations with his honest personality and reputation. His

[45] About the detailed contents of *Xi Yuan Ji Lu*, see Song (1981) and Jia (1984).

experience in being a legal assistant and his contribution to legal education left us with a precious historical and cultural heritage. His main works, *Zuo Zhi Yao Yan, Xu Zuo Zhi Yao Yan, and Xue Zhi Yi Shuo*, encapsulate decades of experience in legal education. Among these, *Zuo Zhi Yao Yan* not only summarized the author's career of being a legal assistant but also served as teaching material for legal education, written for young people who study law. The chapters in *Zuo Zhi Yao Yan* include the concepts of doing your best, saying what you should say, leaving if it does not fit, being frugal, restraining your family, quickly settling the lawsuit, preventing litigation, surviving, being careful with the original report, investigating the situations in murder cases, being careful about implicating innocents in robbery cases, strictly regulating the local scoundrels, being cautious about calling in a woman, investigating when the guard reported resistance of arrest, being considerate with the defendant, not carelessly citing precedents, investigating cases in a cautious way, being diligent, showing the people your reputation, not issuing notices casually, not easily persuading people to learn to be assistant to magistrates, taking into consideration the customs and human sentiment, not easily ccompromising on duty, and not excessively being in debt to your lord. The content concerning legal education is focused on the following issues. Firstly, those who study and use the laws must have a "good character." In this regard, Wang Huizu proposed that legal scholars should "be humbly minded," "maintain their dignity," and have "self-discipline." He emphasized that legal scholars should pursue justice and forget about private interests. "If someone was righteous but made some unintentional mistakes, he would finally be forgiven by public opinion; if someone made a judgment based on his private interests, even if the judgment is reasonable, he would be blamed by the heaven." Secondly, the author highlighted the importance of reading books and the laws to improve the cultural literacy and professional level of legal assistants. The author pointed out that "The assistants help the magistrates to govern the people and have the responsibility of discussing issues with the lords. In case of difficulties and major events, it is necessary to cite the classics to make judgments." Therefore, reading is "necessary." "To be a good legal assistant to magistrates, the key is studying and understanding the law. Being adopted into law, every provision has its essence. Despite the efforts devoted, it is not easy to understand them. If you cannot fully understand the similarities and differences among the provisions, you may be easily misled" (He, 2006, 378–380). Of course, another important value of *Zuo Zhi Yao Yan* is that the book reflects some vivid details of the people studying law at that time to be legal assistants to magistrates.[46]

The above contributions of legal scholars have laid the foundations for the inheritance of the Chinese Legal Family. On the one hand, legal scholars have created a soul for the jurisprudence of the Chinese Legal Family, which consisted of basic principles of Confucianism and a series of principles evolving from them. Of course, in

[46] In addition, the scholars explored the laws of prison management and developed the studies of prison, centering on the rehabilitation of prisoners. For example, Zhao Shuqiao (?–1901), an official of the Ministry of Punishment in the late Qing dynasty, created the first work in Chinese history on the studies of prison, *Ti Lao Bei Kao*. These were important contributions made by legal scholars in the Chinese Legal Family. Due to the limitation of space, I will not expound on them here.

the Sui and Tang Dynasties, when the Chinese Legal Family was founded, Confucian thoughts on law had been developed. They were not just simple theories of Confucianism and Mencius but had already involved the legal views of Legalism, Taoism, Mohism, and some other schools, evolving into a legal world outlook of the Chinese Legal Family. They were already very rich in content. Some of the basic principles are quite historically progressive, such as people-oriented thoughts, emphasis on teaching and transforming people, moral guidance and supplementary punishment, combined utilization of leniency and strictness, simplifying laws and limiting prohibitions, prudent penalties and light punishments, fairly deciding the punishment and rewards, governing officials according to the law, and the law changing with time. In modern times, these principles lost their basis for existence due to their separation from their main body—the Chinese Legal Family—because of its disintegration. However, after proper transformation, refinement, and sublimation, as an excellent historical heritage in the traditional legal worldview, the principles can be incorporated into the new modern legal system and institutions and continue to play a role.

On the other hand, legal scholars forged a main body of law—or constructed an edifice of law—for the Chinese Legal Family. The *Tang Lv*, *Song Xing Tong*, *Da Ming Lv*, *Da Qing Lv Li* of China, and the *Taiho Code* and *Yoro Code* of Japan are the basic components of this body. Moreover, in order to make this legal body (system) active and not become simply documents gathering dust, legal scholars made detailed, thorough, and practical commentaries and elaborations on the legal system. These annotations and elaborations created a bridge between the legal text and practical criteria in judicial practice. For example, the Chinese and Japanese official commentaries, *Tang Lv Shu Yi* and *Ryo-no-gige*, the unofficial commentaries, *Ritsu-no-shuge*, *Ryo-no-shuge*, *Lv Fu Yin Yi*, *Du Lv Suo Yan*, *Lv Li Jian Shi*, *Da Qing Lv Ji Zhu*, and *Du Lv Pei Xi*, are all representatives in this regard.

Furthermore, the ideal and pursuits of legal scholars for perfect personality, legal fairness and judicial justice, and the tradition formed by their continuous efforts, have enabled the inheritance of some elements in the Chinese Legal Family. Adhering to the Confucian tenet—a sense of mission—of *self-cultivation, balancing the family, and governing the country and the world*, legal scholars, as a scholar-official class, expected themselves to have a perfect personality. Li Delin, Kong Yingda, Wang Mingde, and others were the most outstanding legal scholars in this regard. Most legal scholars took the equality of law as their supreme criterion and practiced it within their capabilities, whether in their legislative activities or when annotating and interpreting the law. Fang Xuanling, Zhangsun Wuji, Dai Zhou, Wang Kentang, and others were representatives in this regard. Legal scholars were living in a social framework where power was highly centralized, the administration and the judiciary were not divided, and the emperor had the highest judicial power. Nevertheless, they did their best and strived to pursue judicial justice in each case. Maximum fairness and justice was another ideal and pursuit of legal scholars. Zhao Chuo, Wei Zheng, Bao Zheng, Hai Rui, and others were models of this. It was precisely the above ideals, pursuits, and traditions of legal scholars that enabled the Chinese Legal Family to develop and continue for more than 1300 years and maintain some essential elements that can be integrated into the modern legal system after entering the modern society; this provides rich historical resources for the development of law and legal studies in contemporary China and Japan—and South Korea and Vietnam.

4 Legal Education

In 227, during the Wei Dynasty, Shangshu Wei Ji submitted a memorial to Emperor Mingdi of Wei, Cao Rui, to set the position of Lv (studies) Boshi. This started legal education. The Eastern and Western Jin and Southern and Northern Dynasties inherited and carried forward this practice, forming a tradition of official legal education in ancient China. It laid the foundation for the maturity and finalization of legal education when the Chinese Legal Family was formed in the Sui and Tang Dynasties.

4.1 Formation and Development of Legal Education in the Chinese Legal Family

The legal education of the Chinese Legal Family was formed in the Sui and Tang Dynasties. It inherited the tradition of legal education in the Han, Wei, Jin, Southern and Northern Dynasties and experienced tremendous changes and improvements. It spread to ancient Japan, Korea, and Vietnam.

4.1.1 Formation of Legal Education

In the seventh century, when the Chinese Legal Family was finalized, Chinese legal education entered a new period of development. At the beginning of the seventh century, Emperor Wen of Sui, Yang Jian (541–604), abolished the nine-rank system.[47] Emperor Yang of Sui, Yang Guang (569–618), created a system of selecting officials through imperial examination in different categories and inquiry of policies[48]

[47] *Ci Hai* (An Unabridged, Comprehensive Dictionary, 辞海) records that "At the end of the Eastern Han Dynasty, Cao Cao was in power and advocated meritocracy. In the first year of the Yankang Era (220) during the reign of Emperor Xian, Cao Pi adopted the suggestion of Chen Qun, the minister of the Ministry of Personnel, and elected prestigious people from various counties to serve as Zhongzheng. Local scholars were rated in ninth grades (nine ranks) according to their abilities, and the government selected them according to grades. It was called the 'nine ranking officials' method in line with Cao Cao's principle that officials should be selected 'regardless of family background'." This system was used in the Jin and Six Dynasties. During the reign of Emperor Wen of Sui, this system was abolished and the imperial examination system was adopted. See (2010) *Ci Hai*, 2023.

[48] Scholars such as Yu Dagang, Tang Changru, He Zhongli, and Jin Zheng believe that the Sui Dynasty abolished the nine-rank system and began to use various imperial examinations, but it is

and established the *Guozijian*—an administrative agency specializing in education management—in the central government. The central divisions affiliated with *Guozijian* included *Guozixue* (the educational institution for the children of the highest-ranking officials), *Taixue* (the educational institution for the children of lower-ranking officials), *Simenxue* (the educational institution for the children of lowest-ranking officials and commoners), *Shuxue* (the educational institution specializing in calligraphy), and *Suanxue* (the educational institution specializing in arithmetic). *Lvxue* (legal studies) was managed by *Dalisi*, which set positions for *Lv Boshi* and *Lv Boshi* students. This followed the custom since the Wei, Jin, Southern and Northern Dynasties that *Lvxue* was in the charge of the judicial department. At the end of the Sui Dynasty, the management of legal studies was moved to *Guozijian* (Xu, 1975, 182). After the establishment of the Tang Dynasty, *jinshi* Ke (examinations on classics, policies, and poetry) was further established, thus, formally establishing the imperial examination system for selecting officials. At that time, the examinations were divided into two categories: Changke (Regular Examination) and Zhiju (Additional Examination). *Mingfa* (originated from the official position of *Mingfa* established in the Jin Dynasty) was arranged under Changke, forming an independent and mature official legal education.[49] According to the laws of the Tang Dynasty, among the subordinate officials of the Ministry of Punishment, *Mingfa* was already set as an independent official position, becoming the quota for recommending officials. The second volume of *Tang Liu Dian* records that "For all the divisions to arrange zhi officials (a kind of specialized officials in the Tang Dynasty), there are quotas. [In small print] The divisions have to set the following zhi officials with ranks: ... one *Mingfa* for *Menxia* Department, ... one *Mingfa* for Ministry of Punishment, ... one *Mingfa* for *Zhongshu* Department, ... two *Mingfas* for *Dalisi*" (Li, 1992, 35). *Mingfa* became one of the seven subjects in the imperial examination, together with *xiucai*, *mingjing*, *jinshi*, *junshi*, *mingzi*, *mingsuan*, and others. Although *Mingfa* existed before the Tang Dynasty, and the official position *Lv Boshi* (*Lvxue Boshi*) was established in the Wei Dynasty, it was an invention of the Tang Dynasty to establish the imperial examination system and adopt *Mingfa* as a subject of the imperial examination, which became the core of official legal education. This is the reason why we say that the legal education of the Tang Dynasty is essentially different from the previous ones and that the legal education of the Chinese Legal Family was formed during the Tang Dynasty.

The beginning and development of legal education in Japan, a major member of the Chinese Legal Family, were almost synchronous with the formation and development of the Chinese Legal Family. To learn about the advanced and developed legal system and culture of the Sui and Tang Dynasties, Japan sent several batches of envoys to Sui and Tang. This activity can be regarded as the earliest legal education in Japan;

---

still an inspection system in nature. It was the Tang Dynasty that established the imperial examination system, in which jinshi is the main subject for selection, the literati went to attend the examination regularly, and the government selected those with talents from among them.

[49] *Tong Dian* (Volume 15, "Selection") records that "Subjects of the Regular Examination include *xiucai*, *mingjing*, *jinshi*, *Mingfa*, *shu*, and *suan*. From the capital to the prefectures and counties, there are schools everywhere." See Du (1988, 353).

that is, having Chinese officials and legal scholars as teachers, learning Chinese Sui and Tang laws, and bringing the results of their learning back to Japan. Therefore, the earliest legal education in Japan was carried out by studying abroad. This is rare in human history.[50] Outstanding students included Yamato no Nagaoka (689–769) and Kibi no Makibi (695–775). According to the research of Japanese scholars, Japanese domestic legal education generally began in the Nara (710–794) and Heian periods (794–1192). In the *Taiho Code* and *Yoro Code*, there were already provisions on "*Myobo* (legal studies) examination of the recruitment of officials."[51] Before that, during the reign of Empress Genmei (708–715), the *Myobo* subject was founded according to Ge.[52] However, at that time, it was still in its infancy. In the fifth year of the Jinki Era (728), during the reign of Emperor Shomu, the system of the *Myobo* subject was finalized, and the education of *Myobo* (legal studies) was further developed.[53]

Therefore, when was the *Myobo* subject set in the *daigakuryo*? The regulation of the quota and the corresponding rank (Senior Seventh Rank, Lower Grade) of the *ryougenokan* (the official positions set up after Ling was made), *Ritsugaku Hakase* (*Myobo Hakase*) can be found in an explanatory report contained in *Assorted Kyaku of the Three Generations* made on the 27th day of the 11th lunar month of the 13th year of the Jogan Era (871) by a head of the Iehara Family, a *San hakase* (Doctor of arithmetic), as well as the interpretation of Ge of the 5th year of the Jinki Era in the interpretation to "laws concerning official positions." Many scholars

---

[50] In the eleventh century, in the wave of the revival of Roman Law, the University of Bologna was established in Italy with the mission of teaching and annotating Roman laws, attracting young people from all over Europe to come to study law. The maximum number of people reached more than 10,000. See Bihai et al., (1976, 85). It should also be regarded as one of the few kinds of legal education centered on studying abroad in the world history.

[51] The term *Mingfa* appears frequently in Chinese pre-Qin literature. For example, it is used many times in *Guanzi* and *Han Feizi*. In particular, *Mingfa* in *Guanzi* has become an independent article. Just as the monarch has *Ming Jun* (wise King) and *Hun Jun* (dark King), the law also has *Mingfa* (good law) and *Anfa* (bad law). In the works of general history, *Mingfa* first appeared in *Shi ji*, volume 6, "Annals of the First Emperor of Qin," which includes the wording of "Making *Mingfa*" and "Publicizing *Mingfa*." The word was inscribed in stone by the First Emperor of Qin when he toured Zouyi Mountain in Shandong Province and Bolangsha in Yangwu County, Henan Province. As for the implicit aspects of the term *Mingfa*, Section "Nan Mian" (Southern) in *Han Feizi* defined it most clearly: "The ruler needs to wisely use the ministers. Although they are intelligent, they must not violate the law and become tyrannical; although they are loyal, they cannot be exempted from the law; this is called '*Mingfa*'." In subsequent literature, such as *Jin Shu: Xing Fa Zhi* (Book of Jin: Treatise on Punishment and Law), *Sui Shu: Bai Guan Zhi* (Book of Sui: Officials), *Tang Liu Dian*, and *Taiping Yu Lan* (Book for the Emperor in the Taiping Xingguo Era [976–984], 太平御览), the term *Mingfa* can also be found.

[52] The general theory of Japanese academic circles believes that the establishment of the *Myobo* subject in Japan was the in 5th year of the Jinki Era (728), during the reign of Emperor Shomu. However, Riko Mitsuo believes that the establishment of the *Myobo* subject can date back to the Wado Era during the reign of Empress Genmei because the terms *Myobo Hakase* and *Ryoshi, Ritsushi* (which have the same meaning with *Myobo Hakase*) had appeared in books of as early as the Wado Era (708–715). See Riko (1967, 117).

[53] Inoue, Mitsusada, a Japanese historian believes that the *Myobo* subject was established in the 2nd year of the Tenpyo Era (730). See Inoue (2004, 245).

thus believe it can be inferred that the *Myobo* subject was also established in the same year. However, the Japanese scholar Riko Mitsuo believes that according to the practice of setting up *ryougenokan* in Japan, in general, a certain subject was set up in *daigakuryo*, and after a few years, the quota and rank of the *ryougenokan* of that subject could be determined. If this was the case, when the quota and corresponding rank of *Ritsugaku Hakase* were determined in the 5th year of the Jinki Era, the *Myobo* subject had, in fact, already been set up in *daigakuryo* (Yaheiji, 1966, 88). Based on this, combined with the interpretation of the "Law on Monks and Nuns" in *Ryo-no-shuge* and materials with terms such as *Myobo Hakase*, *Ryoshi*, *Ritsushi*, and *Myoboshi* appeared in Ge of the 4th year of the Yoro Era (720), Riko Mitsuo believes that the *Myobo* subject would have been set up during the Wado Era (708–715) during the reign of Empress Genmei. The system was then improved during the Tenpyo Era (729–749) (Riko, 1967, 117).

4.1.2 Development of Legal Education

According to the Records of Official Selection III in *Song Shi*, at the beginning of the Song Dynasty, there were no legal academies, and only Lv Boshi was set up to teach the law. In the 6th year of the Xining Era, during the reign of Emperor Shenzong of Song (1073), the legal academy was set up in *Guozijian* as well as four law professors. During the Yuanfeng Era (1078–1085), the positions of *Lvxue Boshi* (Doctor of legal studies) and educational supervisor were set up. In the 2nd year of the Shaosheng Era, during the reign of Emperor Zhezong of Song (1095), the position of *Lvxue Boshi* was arranged again. Some scholars have pointed out that in the historical materials of the Southern Song Dynasty, there were no records of legal academies and *Lvxue Boshi*. Therefore, they speculated that China may have stopped holding an official legal academy since the Southern Song Dynasty; thus, there was also no *Lvxue Boshi* (Xu, 1975, 185). However, the Records of Official Selection III in *Song Shi* records in detail the content, procedures, and methods of the examinations of the legal academy during the Qingyuan (1195–1200), Jiading (1208–1224), and Xianchun Eras (1265–1274) in the Southern Song Dynasty. Therefore, the author believes that the legal academy was not seemingly canceled during the Southern Song Dynasty. Shen Jiaben's view that the legal academy and *Lvxue Boshi* were abolished after the Yuan Dynasty[54] should be taken seriously.

Like the Tang Dynasty, the educational administration organization in the Song Dynasty was the *Guozijian* in the central government, with permanent subdivisions, such as *Guozixue*, *Taixue*, and *Lvxue*. At the local level, various departments were set up to promote education and select scholars. The county-level educational affairs of the Song Dynasty were concurrently under the charge of county magistrates and their assistants. At the beginning of the Northern Song Dynasty, the *Guozijian* had three divisions: *Guangwen* (literature), *Taixue*, and *Lvxue*. However, there

[54] "Since the Yuan Dynasty, such official positions were cancelled, and the legal studies were thus waning." See Shen (1985, 2060).

were no law teachers in the division of *Lvxue*. The development and improvement of legal education in the Song Dynasty were closely related to the three periods of promotion of learning in the Northern Song Dynasty. The first wave of promotion of learning happened during the Qingli Era (1041–1048) (Qingli Promotion of Learning), which was initiated by Fan Zhongyan (989–1052), aimed at improving the central school, encouraging local schools, and reforming the imperial examination system and teaching methods. The second wave took place in the Xining (1068–1077) and Yuanfeng (1078–1085) Eras (Xining-Yuanfeng Promotion of Learning), which was initiated by Wang Anshi (1021–1086) during his reform. During these two waves, legal education underwent significant development. The third wave occurred in the Chongning Era (1102–1106) (Chongning Promotion of Learning), which was initiated by Emperor Huizong of Song, Caijing, and some others. This wave also generated effects on the standardization and practical application of the law.[55]

Starting from the Yuan Dynasty, the government abolished legal educational institutions,[56] thus causing legal education to decline. After that, official legal education was never restored until the end of the Chinese Empire in 1911. However, during the Ming and Qing Dynasties, due to the advocacy of the rulers, the officials and commoners were required to have a stronger knowledge and understanding of the law. For example, the "Law on Officials: Public Procedures" of *Da Ming* Lv explicitly states that "All national laws stipulate criminal charges based on the seriousness of the matter. They are issued and enforced around the world. People should always abide by the laws. The officials of all divisions must be familiar with the laws, understand and clarify the meanings of the laws, and analyze and decide matters based on them. If an official cannot explain or understand the meanings of the law, for a first offense, he will be fined one month's salary; for a second offense, he will be sentenced to 40 lashes, as well as a demerit on his record; for a third offense he will be demoted" (Huai, 1999, 36). The "Law on Officials: Public Procedures—Reading and Understanding the Law" of *Da Qing Lv Li* further stipulates that "if people who are able to read well, explain, and understand the law, make a mistake or commit a crime due to the involvement of others, they should be exempted from punishment for once, regardless of the severity. This provision does not apply to those who are involved in rebellion or treason" (Tian & Zheng, 1999, 157). These regulations promoted the enthusiasm of incumbent officials to learn the law through various channels, and legal education played the role of making officials "understand the law."

---

55 For detailed information about the three times of promoting learning, see Tang et al. (1995, 40–42).

56 "Selection, I" in Volume 81 of *Yuan Shi* (History of Yuan) states that "Sui and Tang set examinations of xiucai, mingjing, jinshi, *Mingfa*, *mingsuan*, etc., and sometimes poetry-making was also adopted. Officials started to attend to the trivialities and neglect the fundamentals. In the Song Dynasty, governance by civil officials was advocated and subjects of imperial examination were particularly emphasized. However, although these subjects helped to select people and contributed to the prosperity, their defects led to weak writing styles and officials developed wasteful customs. People who realized it were concerned about it." See Song et al. (2008, 551). Based on this view, the Yuan Dynasty abolished the subject of *Mingfa* established in Tang and Song and the official legal education. Their attention to the imperial examinations also gradually decreased.

In the Ming and Qing Dynasties, although school education included some legal knowledge, legal education attracted little attention. In the Ming Dynasty, the decline in legal education was because of the high-pressure policy implemented on intellectuals. In the Qing Dynasty, it was because of the contempt for the laws of the majority of the Manchu upper class, except for some individuals such as Emperors Shunzhi and Kangxi, as well as the attitude of the Han officials that Confucius should be respected and Legalism should be avoided. However, society cannot work well without laws, laws cannot be implemented without an enforcer, and an enforcer cannot work well without knowing the law. Without official institutions providing formal legal education, it was carried out by the private sector and local governments, forming a type of legal education given by legal assistants to magistrates—dominated by personal assistants hired by local officials. Due to the low social status of the assistants, the information on their legal education was quite limited. The main survivors of this history are *Wanglongzhuang Yishu* (Left Letters from Mr. Wang Longzhuang, 汪龙庄遗书), written by Wang Huizu, a famous legal assistant during the Qianlong Era of the Qing Dynasty, and *Chizhuang Hui Yi Lu* (Memoirs from the Chi Retreat, 迟庄回忆录), written by Chen Tianxi, a legal assistant who served in many prefectures and counties at the end of the Qing Dynasty. Zhang Weiren, a scholar in Taiwan, collected various historical materials, sorted them, and made a systematic study on the legal education of the legal assistants in the Qing Dynasty (Zhang, 1988).

In Japan, after 99 years of development, from the 5th year of the Jinki Era (728) to the 3rd year of the Tencho Era (826), the *Myobo* subject reached a fairly developed level. However, after that, the Minfa subject began to decline. According to the view of the Japanese scholar Fuse Yaheiji, the first reason for the decline of Japanese *Myobo* education was the publication of *Ryo-no-gige* in 834. Previously, Japan's interpretation and teaching of the *Taiho Code* and *Yoro Code* were the results of a hundred schools of thought, thus promoting the prosperity of *Myobo* research and *Myobo* education. The publication of *Ryo-no-gige* combined the doctrines of various schools of thought into one, destroying the rapid development of legal education.[57] The second reason was the collapse of the Ritsuryo system itself. Although the Ritsuryo system continued until the outbreak of the *Meiji Restoration* movement in 1868, the examination of the *Myobo* subject was actually stopped after the *Engi shiki* (implemented in 908) (Yaheiji, 1966, 161). Following, official positions were all held by the gentry and nobles. After the South and North courts period (1329–1392), there were even some legal research results, such as *Copy of Ling* and *Roots of Public Affairs*, that were created by scholars who were not *Myobo Hakase*. The *Myobo* subject became the family studies of a few families, and it began to decline. Even the Sanuki and Koremune families, which had been prominent in the Middle Ages, slowly died out. Only two families remained—i.e., the Nakahara and Sakanoue clans—but they had also largely disappeared by the Edo period (1603–1867). It was

[57] This is somewhat similar to the promulgation of the *Law of Citations* in ancient Rome, in which the state gave the five great jurists, including Papinian (c. 140–212), and Ulpian (c. 170–228), the right to interpret the law with the same force as the code. It made the Roman jurists' views on the interpretation of the law uniform, but also stopped the flourishing and free competition among various schools of legal interpretation. Roman jurisprudence thus tended to decline.

only in the early Meiji period there was a slight revival. However, by this time, Western law had already spread eastward, and the *Myobo* subject could only be assimilated and absorbed by Western law and legal education (Yaheiji, 1966, 162).

4.2 Content and Characteristics of Legal Education in the Chinese Legal Family

In contrast with legal education in the ancient West and modern China, legal education in the Chinese Legal Family served the development and needs of legislation and judiciary in ancient Chinese society. It was decided on the requirements of training legal talent and the needs of managing and evaluating officials. Thus, it has its own characteristics.

4.2.1 Content of Legal Education

The legal education of the Chinese Legal Family was concerned with which members of the society could enter legal educational institutions to study law (admission qualifications), what main contents were involved in legal education, the examination system, and the whereabouts of the graduates, among others.

Admission Qualifications

Tang Liu Dian describes the qualifications for admission to legal education (the legal academy) in China as follows: "*Lvxue Boshi* is in charge of teaching the sons of the civil and military officials lower than eighth grade and commoners" (Li et al., 1992, 562). *Tong Zhi: Xuan Ju* (General Records—Selection of Officials, 通志·选举) also records that "In the 2nd year of the Longshuo Era (662), in *Guozijian* in the East Capital, the positions of a *Cheng* (head of *Guozijian*), a *Zhubu* (secretory), and a *Lushi* (recorder) were set up ... the first one is *Guozixue*; ... the fourth one is *Lvxue*. [Double lines of small letters] selecting the descendants of the eighth and ninth grade officials and commoners between 18 and 25 years old who are studying law" (Zheng, 1987, 723). Here, although not too detailed, general information about the conditions and qualifications for admission to the legal academy (*Myobo* subject) is provided; that is, the identification: descendants of the eighth and ninth grade officials and commoners who are studying law; the age: more than 18 and less than 25. As for other requirements, *Tang Liu Dian* also stipulates that the "rite of coaching (tuition), the supervision of classes, and the examination of students were similar to the rules applied to *Boshi* of the three divisions (Taixue, Guozi, and Simen)" (Li et al., 1992, 562). These provisions of the Tang Dynasty were also fully absorbed and borrowed by Japan.

In the book *Ryo-no-shuge* (published in 868) compiled by Koremune no Naomoto, a *Myobo Hakase*, in explaining the provision Ling on Officials: *Shikibu Sho–daigakuryo* of *Yoro Code*, he quoted Ge of the 2nd year of the Tenpyo Era. "The interpretation provides that according to memorial on the 27th day of the 3rd lunar month of the 2nd year of the Tenpyo Era (730), select four people for the position of direct lecturer [double lines of small letters]: one person as *Monjo Hakase* (literature doctors). Two people for *the position of Ritsugaku Hakase* ... Ten people as *Myobo* students. ... Simply selecting from low-ranking officials or talented commoners, no age limit should be imposed."[58] According to the other provisions of the *Yoro Code*, the qualifications for admission to the *Myobo* subject—low-ranking officials and talented commoners—were limited to officials lower than the Greater Initial Rank, those who were holding the lower official positions of attendant, secretaries, servants, handymen, guards, retainers, and assistants, and even the commoners—i.e., sons of nobles without the right to inherit peerages and ordinary males, if they were intelligent and over 17 and under 25 years old (Riko, 1967, 132).

In China, during the Song Dynasty, the Lvxue division mainly enrolled the sons of civil and military officials below the eighth rank, as well as good-looking or extraordinary commoners, to study law in the school. "All the officials and the imperial scholars are allowed to enter the school, and each has a room." The students were not limited to sons of officials, and imperial scholars from different counties also had to go to school and study law. The conditions used for selecting students were strict. Only imperial scholars with recommendations could enter the school. "The imperial scholars must be recommended by two officials. They have to first go to the school to listen to classes and read law, and then take an examination to be officially enrolled" (Toqto'a, 1985, 3673). Only those who passed the examination could continue their studies. The official legal education of *Mingfa* Ke was abolished in the Yuan Dynasty and never restored. Therefore, in the Ming and Qing Dynasties, most of those who studied law entered the local governments to learn from legal assistants to magistrates—study to be assistants to magistrates. Most of the students were from poor families or failed the imperial examinations. Since there was no formal institution or system for this kind of education, it also depended on the teacher-apprentice relationship. Therefore, if a person wanted to study law and be a legal assistant, there was no certain way; it all depended on the opportunities he could get, mainly relying on the introduction and support of relatives and friends (Guo, 1996, 127). If a legal assistant to a magistrate decided to accept a young man as an apprentice at the request of his friend or relative, the friend or relative had to arrange some rituals to show respect to the teacher. After that, the apprentice would move into the teacher's house, live and work together with him, and help him do some paperwork. In addition to teaching the knowledge of being an assistant and tutoring the practice, the teacher would also take care of the apprentice's life and discipline his behavior. During the period of study, the apprentice's daily expenses were also subsidized by the teacher, and the relationship between the teacher and the apprentice was very close (Zhang, 1988).

---

[58] (1966). *Newly Updated National History Series, Volume 23, Ryo-no-shuge I*, 80. Yoshikawa Koubunkan.

Content of Study

It is clearly pointed out in Volume 8 of the ancient Japanese book, *Important Issues of the Old Customs*, that "*Myobo* is Ritsugaku (the legal studies), including laws on official positions, laws on officials, and the three generations of shiki (supplementary laws)" (Riko, 1967, 103). From this understanding of Japanese academia, we know that in the education on the *Myobo* subject, the learning object and teaching content comprised legal norms such as Ritsuryo. The *Myobo* subject was equivalent to law school today. This understanding of Japanese legal circles originated from the transplant of the Chinese legal education system (*Mingfa*). In the Chinese Tang Dynasty, the main content learned by law students was Lv, Ling, Ge, and Shi. Guozijian says in Volume 21 of *Tang Liu Dian* records, "One position of *Lvxue Boshi*, junior eighth rank lower grade, …, specializes in Lv and Ling, and also knows Ge, Shi, and Fali (precedents)" (Li et al., 1992, 561–562). Ge and Shi were sources of law in the Chinese Legal Family, and Fali was a collection of precedents because there were already official and unofficial collections of precedents for law students to study and take examinations in the Tang Dynasty (Zhang, 1996). Therefore, in the Tang Dynasty, students of the *Mingfa Ke* were already required to study Ge, Shi, and precedents in addition to Lv and Ling. From the records of ancient Japanese texts, it is clear that students were under great pressure to study. The copy of *Ryo-no-gige* stored in the Japanese Momijiyama Library cited the lost words concerning *Konin shiki* on the back of the paper: "when learning *Konin shiki*: all content that should be taught, … *Zhou Li*, *Yi Li* (Ritual, 仪礼), *Mao Shi* (Poetry, 毛诗), and Lv, each for four hundred and sixty-five days, … *Shang Shu*, *Lun Yu*, and Ling, each for two hundred days" (Riko, 1967, 147). Lv was to be taught in 465 days, and Ling in 200 days. There were about 500 articles in Lv and 950 articles in Ling. Therefore, the average daily task of studying Lv and Ling was basically one article of Lv and five articles of Ling. The pressure of studying was quite high.

In addition to existing laws and precedents, if there were newly promulgated laws and orders, the Ministry of Punishment would immediately send them to law students for studying.[59] This is closely related to the continuous reforms of laws during the reign of Emperor Shenzong. The familiarity of law students with the new laws also provided many talents for these reforms. If there were questions about the legal provisions or judgments when learning the crimes, the students had to discuss these with the Court of Judicature and *Dalisi*. In the Ming and Qing Dynasties, the most important aspect of legal education was to study the laws and learn books about being legal assistants.[60] The second important aspect was to practice under the guidance

[59] There was a regulation in the Xining Era that as long as the imperial court promulgated new laws, the Ministry of Punishment would immediately send them to the law students. See Toqto'a (1985, 3673).

[60] A famous legal assistant, Chen Tianxi, said in his book *Chizhuang Hui Yi Lu* that "at the beginning of the study, my brother ordered me to firstly read Da Qing Lv Li … especially, I must be familiar with the contents of it. When studying the laws and precedents, Mingli should be studied carefully. Other sections should be studied in sequence according to the need for usage." See Guo (1996, 138).

of the teacher. Generally, the teacher would first retrieve some case files that had been decided, particularly concerning killing, theft, adultery, trafficking, household, marriage, and land. They would then give these to the apprentice to read so he can have a general understanding of the procedures for handling cases.[61]

Examination

The second volume of *Tang Liu Dian* records: "The *Mingfa* examination tests Lv and Ling once for each. If the candidate understands the meaning and reasons well and is able to answer without question or stop, he can be regarded as passed. [Small print] If the candidate only has a rough understanding of the outlines and examples and has no deep learning of the directions and reasons, he can be regarded as not passing. The Lv and Ling being tested have ten cloze tests for each. The examination also includes ten essay questions, seven for Lv and three for Ling. If the candidate answers all the questions, he will be rated an A. Those who answer eight or more will be rated as B. Others will be rated as not passed" (Li et al., 1992, 45). Regarding other subjects, such as *jinshi*, the content of law was not tested in the first-round examination at the Ministry of Rites. However, after passing this first-round examination, the candidates still had to take an examination of "*shen* (body), *yan* (speech), *shu* (writing), and *pan* (making judgment)" at the Ministry of Officials. After that, they could be appointed as officials. Among these, *pan* involved making judgments for two mock cases.

The examination system for *Mingfa* (*Myobo*) students was very strict. For example, in Japan, after entering the school, a *Myobo* student had to take an examination on the text of the law that he should memorize once every ten days. The "Law on Learning" in the *Yoro Code* records: "When testing the memorization of law (reciting the laws), a question of three words will be asked for every thousand words."[62] This provision was a succession of Tang law and was similar to the examination of the law in the Tang Dynasty. These examinations were oral tests, namely just answering the questions. If students were not able to memorize a text of a thousand words in ten days, the examination would be postponed. The test of lecturing the law—similar to the hermeneutics of the law in later times–was also first taken every ten days. Teachers would choose three articles and ask for their meanings. In the every-ten-day examination, those who could answer two questions out of the

[61] In the legal education for assistants of officials in the Qing Dynasty, in addition to studying books and practicing case handling, another important part was learning how to be a good legal assistant, that is, the so-called moral education (vocational education). In this regard, according to his own personal experience, Wang Huizu talked a lot in *Zuo Zhi Yao Yan* and *Xu Zuo Zhi Yao Yan* about the need to "cultivate one's mind and virtue" (conscientious mind and good morality), "cultivating the moral self and managing the family," "choosing the lords wisely," "supervising the officials and control the guards" (supervising and suppressing the illegal and corrupted behavior of the officials and guards), "dedicated to working and loving the people," and in a word: "benefit the people and combat the evils."

[62] (1966). *Newly Updated National History Series, Volume 23, Ryo-no-shuge I*, 450. Yoshikawa Koubunkan.

three were considered to have passed, while those who could answer one question or none were considered to have failed. Those who failed to pass the examination were subject to the "discretionary punishment" of *Myobo Hakase*.[63]

In the Song Dynasty, this kind of every-ten-day examination was more detailed and strictly regulated. For example, the supervision of the examination was recorded in *Song Hui Yao Ji Gao* (Collection of the Compendium in the Song Dynasty, 宋会要辑稿) thus: "On the examination day, the examiner concerning the edicts and the inspection of laws should be found in different government divisions by appointing two people from the officials that attend the examination; the examiner concerning making judgments should be provided by the Institution of Review of Judgments, the Ministry of Punishment, and *Dalisi* by appointing two guards; the examination concerning summary of codes, the compilation of Chi, Lv, Ling, Ge, and Shi, and the making of legal text should be provided by the related government institutions" (Xu, 2006, 2211). The whole examination process was very thorough, and cheating was strictly prevented.

In addition to the every-ten-day examination, the more important examination on the *Myobo* subject was the annual examination—i.e., the examinations attended by the president or vice president of *daigakuryo*. According to the "Law on Learning: Reading Classics First" in *Ryo-no-gige*, "The interpretation provides that: 'the end of the year' used here refers to the seventh lunar month of the year according to the arrangement of the examination. Why? It is for setting the examinations for Boshi. The 'Law on Bureaucratic Establishment' provides: the examination means that all civil officials and the military squad should be examined for their merit and demerit by the end of the year."[64] The "Law on Learning" records: "at the end of the year, the president and vice president of *daigakuryo* and officials from different divisions with good professional ability should test the students. The test should cover the knowledge taught in the whole year, and eight questions should be asked; those who can answer more than six are regarded as the top, those who can answer more than four are regarded as the middle, and those who can answer less than three are regarded as the worst. If a student is regarded as the worst three times in a row, he will be dismissed."[65] Here, the regulation is very clear. If the student was regarded as the "worst" three times in a row (frequency three), he would be charged with violating the rules concerning service duties of officials and would be dismissed.

---

[63] "The Law on Learning: Reading Classics First" in *Ryo-no-shuge* records: "*The Old Record* provides: ... Question: if the sons of nobles failed and get punishment, does the law allow them to be exempted? Answer: They can be exempted according to the law, but still have to undertake the punishment given by the order of daigakuryo." See (1966). *Newly Updated National History Series, Volume 23, Ryo-no-shuge I*, 451. Yoshikawa Koubunkan. It can be seen that around the 10th year of Tenpyo Era (738) when *The Old Record* was published, there had already been a customary law of punishing *Myobo* students who failed in the Q&A exam and the law hermeneutics exam.

[64] (1966). *Newly Updated National History Series, Volume 23, Ryo-no-shuge I*, 451. Yoshikawa Koubunkan.

[65] (1966). *Newly Updated National History Series, Volume 23, Ryo-no-shuge I*, 451–452. Yoshikawa Koubunkan.

Of course, the most important examination for a student of the *Myobo* subject is the *Myobo* examination before graduation; that is, the examination for admission as a judicial officer. The prerequisite for the *Myobo* examination is to be a successful candidate. In the "Law on Examinations" in the *Yoro Code*, there are two types of qualified candidates for the examination, namely, gong (贡) students and ju (举) students.[66] The "Law on Bureaucratic Establishment: Selecting the Wrong Scholars" in *Ritsu-no-shuge* provides: "Gong scholars are those who are selected by different districts according to Ling; Ju scholars are students selected based on edicts other than Chi and Ling and officials selected by *daigakuryo*."[67] From this regulation (officials selected by *daigakuryo*), it can be inferred that there were also two types of qualifications for the *Myobo* examination of *daigakuryo*, gong scholars and ju scholars. In Japan at that time, there were not many gong scholars, so the ju scholars attending the *Myobo* examination were almost the only members. They were recommended to Daijo-kan (the Great Council of State), who would then send a note to *Shikibu Sho*, and the examination would be held in the eleventh lunar month of every year. The examiners were officials higher than the vice minister in *Shikibu Sho*. According to the "Law on Examinations" in the *Yoro Code* and the interpretation of the text, we know that the *Myobo* examination would start at 8:00 a.m., continue at noon, and end at night. Regarding the questions of the examination, the "Law on Examinations" almost entirely copied the Chinese system of the Tang Dynasty: "The *Myobo* examination will test ten articles of the law, (double line of small letters note: according to this provision, there must be *Myobo Hakase* and *Myobo* students) including seven provisions of Lv and three provisions of Ling. If the candidate understands the meaning and reasons well and is able to answer without question or stop, he can be regarded as passed. (Small print) If the candidate only has a rough understanding of the outlines and examples and has no deep learning of the directions and reasons, he can be regarded as not passing. If the candidate answers all the questions, he will be rated an A. Those who can answer more than eight questions will be rated as B. Others will be rated as not passed."[68]

In addition to admission qualifications, study content, and examination systems, there were also corresponding regulations in China and Japan regarding the length of schooling for the *Myobo* subject, treatment of students during their studies, management of students, whereabouts of students after graduation, and others. For the sake of space, we will not go into the details here.[69]

---

[66] (1966). *Newly Updated National History Series, Volume 22, Interpretation of the Ritsuryo*, 167. Yoshikawa Koubunkan.

[67] (1966). *Newly Updated National History Series, Volume 22, Interpretation of the Ritsuryo*, 34. Yoshikawa Koubunkan.

[68] (1966). *Newly Updated National History Series, Volume 22, Interpretation of the Ritsuryo*, 166–167. Yoshikawa Koubunkan.

[69] For example, regarding the educational system, *History of the Chinese Educational System* edited by Cai Qinxiang provides that the study period of the official school in the Tang Dynasty was 9 years, and *Taixue* and *Simenxue* were the same as the *Guozixue*, while *Lvxue* students "graduated in six years." See Cai (1933, 47–48). This statement should come from the records of *Wen Xian Tong Kao*: the students of *Guozixue*, *Taixue*, and *Simenxue* "stay in school for nine years. Lv students stay for

4.2.2 Characteristics of the Legal Education

Observing the 1300-year evolution of legal education in the Chinese Legal Family, we can find some distinctive features in terms of its admission qualifications, learning content, examination system, length of schooling, treatment of students, management, and where graduates go afterward.

First, it had never reached the level of professional legal education provided in independent law universities but was clearly affiliated with Confucianism, and to a certain extent, it can be called *Confucianized* legal education in imperial China. This Confucianized legal education gradually formed since the Wei and Jin Dynasties. For example, during the Western Jin Dynasty, *Jin Lv* (Jin Code, 晋律) was highly respected by the Sima royal court as the first Confucianized code combining ritual and law. Legal scholars at that time studied it thoroughly from the perspectives of classics and theories and spread the influence of the Confucian ethical ideas that it contained, to the public, through lectures, which had great cultural significance. From the Wei and Jin Dynasties to the Sui and Tang Dynasties, the official legal academy gradually entered a mature stage. For example, the commentaries and interpretations of the legal texts in *Tang Lv Shu Yi* were developed mainly based on Confucian rituals, and the legislative ideas and main contents of the Tang Laws were inherited by the major codes of later dynasties.

On the one hand, even in the most glorious period of the Chinese Legal Family, the Tang and Song Dynasties—the Nara and Heian periods in Japan—legal education was subordinate to Confucian education. It ranked fourth in China as one of the subjects of *Guozixue*, *Taixue*, *Simenxue*, *Suanxue*, and *Shuxue*. In Japan, it belonged to *daigakuryo* under Shikibu Sho, alongside *Myogyo* (classics), *Kiden* (literature), and *San* (arithmetic). However, it was ranked after subjects such as *Myogyo*. After the Yuan Dynasty, official legal education was simply abolished. In Japan, after the establishment of the Kamakura shogunate in 1192, the education of the *Myobo* subject also declined due to the shift of the ruler's attention. By the promulgation of *Engi shiki* (implemented in 908), the examination of the *Myobo* subject was canceled (Yaheiji, 1966, 161). Meanwhile, in the West, Italy became the birthplace of independent university education in law from 1088, and it spread to all countries in continental Europe and even across the sea to England.

On the other hand, after the Middle Ages, the teachers of university education of law in Italy and other European countries were basically full-time, such as Azo (c. 1150–1230) and Accursius (c. 1182–1260) in the University of Bologna. In contrast, the teachers providing legal education in the Chinese Legal Family, both in China

---

six years old in law. Those who cannot afford it withdraw from the school." See Ma (2011, 1208). For another example, regarding student's holiday, etc., *Wen Xian Tong Kao* states that "every ten days the students are given one day off. ... Every year in the fifth lunar month, there is a leave for student to do farm work, and in the ninth lunar month, there is a clothes preparation leave, etc." See Ma (2011, 1208). Also, regarding the whereabouts after graduation, *Lvxue* students in the Tang and Song Dynasties could obtain official positions if they pass the final exam, and *Myobo student*s who were qualified in the Nara and Heian periods in Japan can hold judicial positions such as *Myobo Hakase*, Head Judge and Prosecutor.

(*Mingfa Boshi*, *Mingfa yuan*, etc.) and in Japan (*Myobo Hakase*, head judges, and prosecutors), were basically judicial or administrative officials. Additionally, in the Western universities of law after the Middle Ages, the relationship between teachers and students was equal, and even the teaching and daily management of the university was organized, centering on the students.[70] The universities were also independent and autonomous from the government. This was not the case in China and Japan. In my opinion, the root of the differences lies in the official policy of ruling the country by Confucianism in imperial China. In particular, during the Han and Tang dynasties, with the Confucianization of the law, Chinese classical studies gradually became the dominant study in society and occupied a dominant position in traditional academia. In the historical conditions of the Middle Ages, legal education was influenced by Confucianism and did not become a subject independent of it, thus, showing different characteristics from the Western legal education of the same period in many ways.

Second, the development of legal education was intermittent, and its affiliation and administration frequently changed, making it unstable. Unlike the legal education born in Italy after the Western Middle Ages, which developed steadily after its birth, the legal education of the Chinese Legal Family was intermittent and very unstable, even during the Sui and Tang Dynasties. For example, after the establishment of the Tang Dynasty, the legal academy was established under the formal educational administration, *Guozijian*, in the Wude Era (618–626) by Emperor Gaozu, Li Yuan. But it was soon abolished. Later, it was restored during the reign of Emperor Taizong Li Shimin. In "Taizong Ben Ji" (Annals of Emperor Taizong) of *Jiu Tang Shu*, it is recorded that "in the 6th year of the Zhenguan Era (632), the first legal academy was established on *wuzi* (chronometric method in ancient China) day" (Liu et al., 1975, 42). In "Gaozong Ben Ji" (Annals of Emperor Gaozong) of the same book, it is recorded that in the 9th lunar month of the 3rd year of the Xianqing Era (658), "the academies of classics, arithmetic, and law were abolished" (no reason is given). It is also recorded that in the 2nd year of the Long Shuo Era (662), along with the large-scale reform of the bureaucratic system, "the three academies of law, classics, and arithmetic were re-established on *yisi* (chronometric method in ancient China) day" (Liu et al., 1975, 78 + 83). Treatise on Hundreds of Officials in *Xin Tang Shu* (The New Book of Tang, 新唐书) records: "in the legal academy, there were three Boshi of junior eighth rank, lower grade… (small letter) there were 20 students" (Ouyang & Song, 1975, 1267). However, in the next year, that is, the 3rd year of the Longshuo Era, the legal academy was abolished again. The positions of *Lvxue Boshi* were set up under *Dalisi* (which had been renamed as the *Xiangxingsi* at that time) and were no longer under the leadership of *Guozijian*.[71] It is not clear when

---

[70] Since the universities were run by students, the term *Rector*—i.e., the student leader—became the prototype of the term *Rettore* today.

[71] The abolition of legal education was done in the third year of the Longshuo Era, which was not recorded in *Jiu Tang Shu* or *Xin Tang Shu*. *Jiu Tang Shu* only records that in the second lunar month of the third year of the Longshuo Era, "candidates of Lvxue are enrolled by Xiangxingsi." See Liu et al. (1975, 84). Riko Mitsuo, a Japanese scholar, believes that Ritsugaku Hakase in Xiansxingsi (i.e., Dalisi) was a judicial official position, not an education official in schools, so Lvxue in the educational sense was abolished at that time. See Riko (1967, 107).

the abolished legal academy was restored, but according to the records of events in the period of Wu Zetian and Tang Zhongzong in "Xuexiao (school)" of *Tang Hui Yao* (Institutions of Tang, 唐会要), it is clear that among the "three schools of apprenticeship" mentioned in the minister's memorial to Wu Zetian during the Shengli years (698–700), only *Guozixue*, *Taixue*, and *Simenxue* were included, not *Lvxue* (the legal academy) (Wang, 1955, 633–634). Later, in the 2nd year of the Shenlong Era during the reign of Emperor Zhongzong of Tang (706), the record of the legal academy appeared again: "In the 9th lunar month of the 2nd year of the Shenlong Era, the emperor issued an edict: … when students go to school, they have to give some gift to the teachers to show their respects. *Guozi* and *Taixue* students have to give 3 *pi* (measure word in ancient China, around 33.3 meters) of silk and *Simenxue* students have to give 2 *pi* of silk. Junshi students and students of legal, classics, and arithmetical schools, as well as students from the prefectures and counties, have to give one *pi* of silk. Parties will also be held" (Wang, 1955, 634). The establishment and abolishment of the legal academy and the frequent changes of its higher-level authorities, on the one hand, reflected the lack of attention paid by the state to legal education and the squeeze of Confucian orthodox on legal education, on the other hand, exerted influence on the successor to the system of the Tang Dynasty, Japan. As a result, the most important Japanese laws, the *Taiho Code* and *Yoro Code* (mainly the part concerning "Law on Officials" in them), did not provide for the *Myobo* subject, causing instability in legal education in Japan afterward. The reason for the unstable development of legal education in ancient China and Japan is that, given the dominance of Confucianism and the mainstream of Confucianism in academic research and education, legal education was only subordinate to Confucianism and could not be elevated to the state's highest-level study.

Third, in legal education in the Chinese Legal Family, although Lvxue (*Myobo* subject) was established, it was always a partial and uncultivated elementary school, as reflected by the small number of students enrolled in it and its low status as a subject in the education system. According to *Tang Liu Dian*, which records the rules and institutions in the prosperous Tang and was compiled by Li Linfu (683–753), who served as the prime minister for 19 years during the reign of Emperor Xuanzong of Tang, there was only one position of *Lvxue Boshi*. In the same period, there were two positions of *Guozi Boshi*, three positions of *Taixue Boshi*, and three positions of *Simen Boshi*. In terms of the ranking of Boshi in the Tang Dynasty, *Guozi Boshi* was of the "senior fifth rank, upper grade," *Taixue Boshi* was of the "senior sixth rank, upper grade," and *Simen Boshi* was of the "senior seventh rank, upper grade," while *Lvxue Boshi* was only of the "junior eighth rank, lower grade" (Li et al., 1992, 559–561). It was several grades lower than other Boshi in terms of the rank of the official positions. The situation was even worse when looking at the students enrolled in the legal academy. *Guozixue* recruited 300 students, *Taixue* recruited 500 students, *Simenxue* also recruited 500 students, but only 50 students were recruited by the legal academy.[72] This was the situation during the prosperous Tang Dynasty, and it was even worse in other dynasties.

In Japan, too, there were no institutions concerning legal academies in *daigakuryo* under Shikibu Sho, which was established in 649, and there were no regulations concerning legal academies in the *Taiho Code* (701) and *Yoro Code* (718). After the establishment of legal education (*Myobo* subject) in 728, the number and status of *Ritsugaku Hakase* (*Myobo Hakase*) and law students (*Myobo* students) were not as high as that of the other subjects. For example, according to the "Law on Officials: *daigakuryo*" in the *Yoro Code*, there were 20 Monjo students and 30 San students but only 10 *Myobo* students.[73] The age limits were also different. The Myogyo subject required students to be older than 13 and younger than 16. *Myobo* students were required to be older than 17 and younger than 25. Myogyo students must be selected from the sons of the officials higher than fifth rank, while *Myobo* students were normally selected from the sons of low-rank officials and commoners. The situation was the same for the graduates of *Myobo* subject. The graduates of the subjects such as *xiucai*, *mingjing*, and *jinshi* would start as officials of senior eighth rank and be automatically promoted to officials of senior fifth rank or above when they reached a certain age. For graduates of the *Myobo* subject, however, even the best ones could only start as officials of Greater Initial Rank (the lowest rank for officials). Therefore, Japanese legal researcher Riko Mitsuo sighed and said, "Hardly any sons of officials of higher than fifth rank from famous families would choose *Myobo* subject" (Riko, 1967, 141–142).

Fourth, there were many legal families with a long history. For example, in the Tang Dynasty, there were father and son Han Zhongliang and Han Yuan, uncle and nephew Dai Zhou and Dai Zhide, father and son Su Gui and Su Ting, and Di Renjie, Di Guangsi, and Di Jianmo from the Di's Family. After the Song Dynasty, there were father and son He Ning and He Meng, father and son Wang Qiao and Wang Kentang, and the Wang Mingde Family. In Japan, legal families were also a common phenomenon in medieval legal culture. The people from several families served as *Myobo Hakase* in successive generations. It is noteworthy that since the middle of the Heian period, *Myobo Hakase* in Japan has gradually become a monopoly position inherited by specific "families" from generation to generation, and this is a unique concept of the "position" in Japan in the history with characteristics of the Middle Ages—i.e., the integration of specific families with a specific official position and function, which gradually blurred the elements of the family system and the official system. For example, the Sanuki legal family continued for several generations, from Sanuki no Chitsugu, Sanuki no Hironao, Sanuki no Naganao, to Sanuki no Naganari. The Nakahara family lasted for dozens of generations and

[72] See Li et al., (1992, 555–556). *Wen Xian Tong Kao* (A General Research of the Literature, 文献通考) has a slightly different record from *Tang Liu Dian* concerning the education system in the Tang Dynasty. For instance, it records that the allowance for *Simenxue* students was "one thousand and three hundred" people. See Ma (2011, 1207).

[73] (1966). *Newly Updated National History Series, Volume 23, Ryo-no-shuge I*, 80–81. Yoshikawa Koubunkan.

hundreds of family members served as law experts (*Myobo Hakase*),[74] which is rare and spectacular in the world.

Fifth, unofficial schools were more developed. In Japan, as the subjects such as *xiucai*, *mingjing*, and *jinshi* were occupied by the sons of officials higher than the fifth rank, the sons of lower-rank officials and commoners had to compete for the *Myobo* subject, which had a lower threshold. The competition was fierce and the examination was extremely difficult because of the small number of places available for *Myobo* students. It was almost impossible to enter *daigakuryo* without a long period of basic learning and training of Ritsuryo (including ancient Chinese). On one hand, this led to fierce competition.[75] On the other hand, it also led to the prosperity of private legal education and legal families, leading to the formation of the above-mentioned legal families.

In the case of China, after the abolition of official legal education after the Yuan Dynasty, the study of law was basically a matter for low-rank individual officials or commoners. In the Ming and Qing Dynasties, legal education for grassroots officials was conducted by legal assistants to magistrates. Poor young people or those who failed in the imperial examinations studied under the legal assistants to magistrates. The situation was somewhat similar to the legal education of the Inns of Court in England in the Middle Ages, but it was far less than that with regard to their nature and actual status. In medieval England, those who learned from the masters of the Inns of Court could serve as lawyers and then judges of the state, becoming the main force in state governance and the legal profession. In contrast, in China, even if a student had finished the learning with good grades, he was at best a "clerk" instead of an "official," which was a personal assistant or a legal consultant to a magistrate.

4.3 Legal Education and the Rise, Fall, and Inheritance of the Chinese Legal Family

From the discussion above, we can see that the legal education and fate of the Chinese Legal Family were closely related and they interacted with each other. As an important part of the Chinese Legal Family, the development and prosperity or the decline and fall of legal education would in turn affect the rise and fall of the Chinese Legal Family. In particular, legal education was a special business. Through the transmission of legal knowledge from the predecessors to future generations, and through the accumulation of legal research, it became crucial to the survival, continuity, and development of the law and jurisprudence of the state and people. The fate of the

[74] Counting up to Mr. Nakahara, who was still active in the 5th year of the Jowa Era (1349), there were more than 100 people. See Yaheiji (1966, 301).

[75] After examining the relevant ancient Japanese documents, Riko Mitsuo believes that although the "Law on Officials" of the *Yoro Code* stipulates that ten students would be enrolled every year, in practice, only one person is enrolled per year due to various limits. "It was difficult to pass the entrance examination of *Myobo* subject if one had not been familiar with Chinese books since childhood and received legal education from his family." See Riko (1967, 142).

Chinese Legal Family, as a community of laws from several countries, mainly China, was obviously influenced by legal education. In other words, in the big picture, the Chinese Legal Family was at its peak in the Sui, Tang, and Song Dynasties, and legal education was also the most developed at that time; legal education provided the country with a large number of highly talented scholars. After the Yuan Dynasty, the Chinese Legal Family was on the decline as a whole. As a result, legal education in China also gradually declined. Legal talents trained by private schools and legal assistants to magistrates were mostly taking office at the grassroots-level judicial positions, or working as legal assistants in local governments. They lost the opportunity and the path to participate in major national decisions.

In addition, the soul of the Chinese Legal Family was Confucianism, its main part was the legal system consisting of Lv, Ling, Ge, Shi, Li, etc., and its operation was driven by a large number of legal experts practicing law—mainly administrative and judicial officials. However, the above-mentioned soul, main part, and motivation were all subject to the legal philosophy and legal literacy of the emperor and the top rulers under the real conditions and mechanisms of the Chinese Empire. The model adopted by the top ruler was the rule of man, not the rule of law. The rulers paid little attention to the law, using it only as one of the tools of ruling, and only as a last resort when moral preaching was ineffective. In such circumstances, it was common for rulers to ignore the rule of law, and was an exceptional for rulers to attach importance to rule of law—for example, in the early Sui and early Tang periods. Whether it was the legal education or the construction and operation of the Chinese Legal Family, all were measured by the ruling interests of the supreme ruler, and even changed according to the ruler's attention and mood.

The situation in Japan was the same. The emphasis on legal education in the Nara and Heian periods was necessary to strengthen the Ritsuryo state centered on the emperor. With the rise of the shogunate regime, the ruler's attention immediately shifted to the rule of the shogunate, focusing more on the politics and customs of the samurai society.

This explains why the legal education of the Chinese Legal Family was established in the early seventh century, but never developed, transformed, or raised itself into a modern legal education like that of a law university. More than 300 years later, this was realized by the University of Bologna in Italy, which became the first law university in the history of the world and pioneered the modern type of legal education. A truly independent legal education, especially a modern legal university education, requires not only institutions, subjects, teachers, students, and good prospects for graduates, but also, and more importantly, the autonomy of legal education, a democratic legislative environment, and the autonomy of the university. In China and Japan, these elements were missing. Observing the development of the political and legal institutions of the Chinese Empire and the Japanese Shogunate, the later the period, the higher the authoritarian centralization. The consequence was a disdain for the legal system (at that time, there was not yet the concept of rule of law) and the suppression and extermination of free thoughts. This is best illustrated by the rampant use of Dongchang, Xichang, and Jinyiwei —all three are secret police departments controlled by emperors—and their interference with and disruption of the normal judicial system in the Ming Dynasty, as well as the further aggravation and spread of the literary inquisition in the Qing Dynasty. Although both *Da Ming Lv* and *Da Qing Lv Li* emphasize strict compliance with the law, and even made it a legal obligation for officials and ordinary people to be familiar with the law, all of these were done to strengthen the emperor's autocratic centralization of power.

However, despite all these constraints, and despite the fact that legal scholars at that time lived in such an authoritarian and centralized environment without freedom of speech and academic autonomy, the vast majority remained faithful to their careers, adhered to their professional ethics, and devoted themselves to legal research, writing and education. Wang Kentang, Shen Zhiqi, Wang Mingde, and Xue Yunsheng in China, and Sanuki no Naganao, Koremune no Naomoto, Sakanoue no Akikane, and Nakahara no Norisada in Japan were among the leading legal scholars of this group. Thanks to their hard work, the legal education of the Chinese Legal Family continued. They played a great role in promoting the effectiveness of law and contributed to the development, continuation, and transmission of the Chinese Legal Family.

Specifically, first, legal education cultivated talents for the growth and continuation of the Chinese Legal Family. In China, the Sui, Tang, and Song Dynasties all adopted legal studies as a subject of the imperial examination system. Although the official legal education was intermittent and small in scale, it lasted for nearly 680 years and nurtured many talents for the country's legal system. It should be said that in ancient China, the Tang and Song Dynasties attached the greatest importance to the legal system, and the emperors and officials had the highest legal literacy, which is related to the relatively developed legal education. In Japan, the 200-year development of the *Myobo* subject in the Nara period and early Heian period was also indispensable for legal education in the *daigakuryo*. Although the number of graduates of the *Myobo* subject was small, they were awarded judicial positions, such as *Myobo Hakase*, Head Judge, and Prosecutor, and were engaged in both legal education and judicial work. They also performed as legal advisers to the emperors, providing *Myobo* Kanmon (legal advisory reports) for the imperial court. In the Middle Ages, a number of prominent legal scholars, such as Sanuki no Chitsugu, Sanuki no Hironao, Anou no Uchihito, Okihara no Miniku, Nukata no Imatari, Sanuki no Naganao, Misuke Nagamichi, Sakurai Yuhitsu, Koremune no Naomoto, Koremune no Tadamasa, Sakanoue no Norimasa, and Nakahara no Norisada, were all fostered by the education of the *Myobo* subject in Japan.

Second, legal education promoted the progress of legislation and a judicial career. It was a kind of practical and empirical education. Although the Four Books and Five Classics were also included in legal education and the Confucian theories were the soul of education, the education on law, such as Lv, Ling, Ge, Shi, and Li, was still the basic content of the study, recitation, and examination in the *Myobo* subject. "*Zhou Li, Yi Li, Mao Shi*, and Lv, each for four hundred and sixty-five days, ... *Shang Shu, Lun Yu,* and Ling, each for two hundred days" (Riko, 1967, 147). This provision of the Japanese *Konin shiki* was derived from the requirements of legal education in the Chinese Tang Dynasty. After such rigorous learning and training, the students of the *Myobo* subject would have been very familiar with the major codes of both China and Japan at that time, such as *Kaihuang Lv*, *Tang Lv Shu Yi*, *Taiho Code*, and *Yoro Code*.

In addition, there were the every-ten-day examination, annual examination, and final examination at the time of graduation. The graduates of the *Myobo* subject would have a solid legal foundation and were able to play an important role in the legislative and judicial work of the country. Sima Rui, who was involved in the compilation of *Tang Lv Shu Yi* in the 2nd year of the Yonghui Era (651) of the Tang Dynasty, Yamato no Nagaoka (689–769), and Kibi no Makibi (695–775), who received the education of *Mingfa* Ke in China, returned to Japan and took part in the compilation of the *Yoro Code*, were all outstanding representatives in this regard. In Japan, since the eighth century, Lv, Ling, Ge, and Shi promulgated by the state were basically the result of the hard work of experts in law, such as Shioyano Komaro, Anouno Uchihito, Sakurai Tanabe Sada Sho, and Koremuneno Naomoto, who were nurtured by the Department of the Law.

Third, legal education helped to pass down the jurisprudence. At the same time as serving the country's legislation, judiciary, and legal services, legal education also contributed to the inheritance of the jurisprudence of the Chinese Legal Family. A number of important works of Chinese legal commentaries after the Sui and Tang Dynasties, such as *Tang Lv Shu Yi*, *Lv Fu Yin Yi*, *Song Xing Tong*, *Lv Jie Bian Yi*, *Du Lv Pei Xi*, and *Da Qing Lv Ji Zhu*, were all results of legal education, which reached the ultimate standard due to the efforts of legal scholars. The same is true in Japan, where the education of the *Myobo* subject has both encouraged the passing down of Japanese legal traditions and greatly enhanced the level of legal studies. Through his own research, Riko Mitsuo demonstrated that the education of the *Myobo* subject in Japan was very successful. He pointed out that at the beginning of the Japanese *Myobo* subject education, Japanese legal studies were not comparable to those of China nor to those of the second-tier countries such as Silla (Korea). However, after more than 120 years of rigorous *Myobo* education, Japanese legal studies had reached a very high-level by the ninth century. According to the record on the 17th day of the 8th lunar month in the 4th year of the Jogan Era (862) in *The True History of Three Reigns of Japan*, during the Jowa Era (834–848), the Head Judge Okihara no Miniku, and *Myobo Hakase* Nukata no Imatari extracted ten difficult criminal law problems accumulated during regular trials, preparing to go to Tang to seek advice from Chinese legal experts. *Myobo Hakase* Sanuki no Naganao volunteered to answer these questions. As a result, the legal problems about which they intended to go to Tang to consult on were successfully answered by Sanuki no Naganao (Riko, 1967, 154–155).

References

Ando, T. (2016). *History of Japan: Ancient, Middle Ages, and Modern Times*. Toyo Keizai Inc.

Bai, J. (2006). *Ce Lin San:Yu Gongchen Zhi Shu* (Discussion on Policies III: Methods of Managing the Meritorious Liegeme, 策林三·御功臣之术). In *Bai Juyi Ji* (*Collection of Works of Bai Juyi, 白居易集)* (Vol. 47). Phoenix Publishing House.

Ban, G. (1962). *Han Shu* (Book of the Former Han, 汉书) (Vol. 56: Dong Zhongshu's Biography the 26th; Book 8). Zhonghua Book Company.

Bao, Z. (2008 photocopy version). *Bao Xiaosu Zou Yi Ji: Qi Buyong Zangli* (Begging for Not Using Corrupted Officials, 乞不用赃吏) + *Qing Anzhi Lupi Daozhe* (Begging for Punishing the Daoist Priest in Buckskin, 请安置鹿皮道者) + *Shangdian Zhazi* (Memorials to the Throne, 上殿札子). In *Si Ku Quan Shu* (Book 427, pp. 111 + 126 + 92). The Commercial Press.

Bihai, J., Ito, M., Murakami, J., et al. (Eds.). (1976). *History of Law*. Tokyo University Press.

Cai, Q. (Ed.). (1933). *History of the Chinese Educational System*. World Journal Book Store.

Chen, L. (2015). The Road to *Lv Shu* in the Yonghui Era of the Tang Dynasty. *Academic Monthly, 9*, 135–146.

Chen, S. (1982). *San Guo Zhi* (Records of the Three Kingdoms, 三国志) (Vol. 21: Book of Wei No. 21, Wei Ji; Book 3). Zhonghua Book Company.

Chen, Y. (edited and reviewed). (1962). *Hai Rui Ji* (Works of Hai Rui, 海瑞集) (Book I). Zhonghua Book Company.

(2010). *Ci Hai* (Book I). Shanghai Lexicographical Publishing House.

Dong, G., et al. (1990). Li Yu Ting Jian Shu (Suggestions on Judiciary and Hearing of Expostulation, 理狱听谏疏). In *Quan Tang Wen* (The Whole Collection of Tang Literature, 全唐文) (Vol. 140). Shanghai Classics Publishing House.

Du, Y. (1988). *Tong Dian* (Comprehensive Statutes, 通典) (Vol. 15, Book 1) (checked and revised by Wang, W., et al.). Zhonghua Book Company.

Editing Committee of Japanese Grand Dictionary of National History. (1993). *Grand Dictionary of Japanese History* (Vol. 14). Yoshikawa Koubunkan.

Edward, S. C. (1996). *The "Higher Law" Background of American Constitutional Law* (Qiang, S., Trans.). SDX Joint Publishing Company.

Fan, Y. (1965). *Hou Han Shu: Guo Chen Liezhuan* (Book of Later Han: Biography of Guo Chen, 后汉书·郭陈列传) (Vol. 46, Book 6). Zhonghua Book Company.

Fang, X., et al. (1973). *Sui Shu* (Book of Sui, 隋书) (Vol. 25: Punishment and Law; Book 3). Zhonghua Book Company.

Fang, X., et al. (1974). *Jin Shu* (Book of Jin, 晋书) (Vol. 30: Punishment and Law; Book 3). Zhonghua Book Company.

Gao, M. (2010). A Tentative Analysis of the Basic Legislative Principles of the Chinese Legal Family. In Y. Zhu (Ed.), *The Chinese Legal Family* (Vol. 1). Law Press·China.

Gao, X. (2007). *Korean Law*. Shinzansha Publisher.

Gu, Y. (2007). *Ri Zhi Lu* (Record of Everyday Learning, 日知录) (Vol. 6: Cherishing People So Punishment is Needed, p. 343) (Vol. 8: The Harm of Current System of Selecting Officials, p. 496) (Vol. 13: Honor and Shame) (Vol. 29: Customs of Foreign Countries, p. 1672). Anhui University Press.

Gu, Y. (2015). *Ming Shi Ji Shi Ben Mo* (History of the Ming Dynasty Chronicle Ins And Outs, 明史纪事本末) (Vol. 2). Shanghai Classics Publishing House.

Guo, R. (1996). *Local Governments, Legal Assistants and Scholars—Research on "Shaoxing Shiye."* China Social Sciences Press.

Han, F. (2010). *Han Feizi* (韩非子) (Nan Mian [Southern, 南面], No. 18) (translated and annotated by Gao, H., et al.). Zhonghua Book Company.

Han, Y. (2001). *Han Changli Wenji:Fu Chou Zhuang* (Works of Han Yu: Discussion on Revenge, 韩昌黎文集·复雠状). Shanghai Classics Publishing House.

He, L. (2010). A New Exploration of Traditional Legal Studies. *Journal of Xiangtan University (Philosophy and Social Sciences), 5*, 71–74.

He, M. (1992). Unofficial Interpretation of Law in the Qing Dynasty and Its Methods. *Chinese Journal of Law, 2*, 63–69.

He, M. (1994). Characteristics of the Study on Legal Commentary in the Qing Dynasty. *Chinese Journal of Law, 6*, 81–87.

He, Q. (1997). Research on the Legal Philosophy of the Early Qin Dynasty. *Law Science, 6*, 15–19.

He, Q. (1999). Research on Legal Studies in Qin and Han Dynasties. *Chinese Journal of Law, 5*, 121–133.

He, Q. (2003). *Japanese Legal Science in the 20th Century*. The Commercial Press.

He, Q. (2006). *History of Chinese Legal Science* (Vols. 1, 2 & 3). Law Press· China.

Hu, G., et al. (Eds.). (1962). *Ming Taizu Shilu* (Veritable Records of the Emperor Taizu of Ming, 明太祖实录) (Vol. 6, pp. 116 + 162 + 163). Institute of History and Philology, Academia Sinica.

Huai, X. (checked and revised). (1999). *Da Ming Lv* (The Great Ming Code, 大明律). Law Press·China.

Huang, Z. (2021). *Mingyi Daifang Lu:Yuan Fa*(Waiting for the Dawn: Exploration of the Essence of Law, 明夷待访录·原法) (annotated by Sun, W.). Yuelu Press.

Ikeuchi, Y. (Ed.). (1978). *Collection of Historical Materials on the Legal System of the Middle Ages·Special Volume·Collection of Commentaries on Enryaku kotai shiki*. Iwanami Shoten.

Inoue, M. (2004). Commentary Books on Japanese Ritsuryo. In Q. He (Ed.), *Research on the Legal Studies* (Yin, L., Trans.). The Commercial Press.

Jia, J. (1984). *History of Ancient Chinese Forensic Studies*. Qunzhong Publishing House.

Li, G. (2003 photocopy version). *Xu Jiang Ji: Xing Jin Disi* (Collection of Works of Mr. Xu Jiang: Punishment and Prohibition IV, 盱江集·刑禁第四). In *Si Ku Quan Shu* (Book 1095). Shanghai Classics Publishing House.

Li, G. (2005 photocopy version). *Xu Jiang Ji: Xing Jin Disi+An Min Ce Diliu* (Strategy to Ease People VI, 安民策第六) + *Li Lun Diyi* (First Discussion on Li, 礼论第一). In *Si Ku Quan Shu* (Book 366, pp. 27 + 45 + 3). The Commercial Press.

Li, L., et al. (1992). *Tang Liu Dian* (Vol. 2: Shangshu Libu [Ministry of Personnel, 尚书吏部], p.35, p. 45) (Vol. 18, pp. 501 + 555 + 556) (Vol. 21: Guozijian [Imperial College, 国子监], pp. 559–562) (checked and revised by Chen, Z.). Zhonghua Book Company.

Li, Z. (1985). *Chinese Legal Family*(Vol. I). Taiwan Hua Xin Cultural Business Limited.

Liu, D. (1996a). A Discussion on Zhang Fei's Legal Thought—With a Concise Discussion on the Relationship Between the Legal Studies and Metaphysics in Wei and Jin Dynasties. *Chinese Journal of Law, 6*, 150–158.

Liu, J. (1996b). *Tang Lv Shu Yi Jian Jie* (Notes on Tang Lv Shu Yi, 唐律疏议笺解) (Vol. I). Zhonghua Book Company.

Liu, X., et al. (1975). *Jiu Tang Shu* (Vol. 3: Annals of Emperor Taizong; Book 1, p. 42) (Vol. 4: Annals of Emperor Gaozong; Book 1, pp. 78 + 83 + 84) (Vol. 50: Punishment and Law; Book 6, pp. 2134 + 2138 + 2141) (Vol. 70: Biography of Dai Zhou; Book 8, p. 2532) (Vol. 80: Biography of Han Yuan; Book 8, pp. 2739–2740) (Vol. 88: Biography of Su Gui; Book 9, p. 2878). Zhonghua Book Company.

Liu, Z. (2021). Refutation to the Discussion on Revenge. In *Liu Hedong Ji* (*Collection of* Works of Liu Zongyuan, 柳河东集). Zhejiang University Press.

Lu, Z. (1988). *Lu Xuan Gong Ji (Collection of Works of Lu Zhi,* 陆宣公集) (Vol. 5: Edict Concerning Reward for Loyal Officials Trapped in the Rebellion) (checked and revised by Liu, Z.). Zhejiang Ancient Books Publishing House.

Lu, Z., et al. (2016). Amnesty After the Suppression of Zhu Ci's Rebellion and the Return to the Capital. In *Lu Xuan Gong Ji* (Vol. 1). Zhonghua Book Company.

Ma, D. (2011). *Wen Xian Tong Kao* (A General Research of the Literature, 文献通考) (Vol. II). Zhonghua Book Company.

Mao, H. (2002). *A Treatise on the History of Medieval Chinese Society*. Shanghai Bookstore Publishing House.

Miura, H., & Takikawa, M. (1982). *Interpretation of Ryo-no-shuge* (Interpretation of the Subject). Kokushokankokai Inc.

(1965). *Newly Updated National History Series, Volume 26, Enryaku kotai shiki, Konin shiki, and Engi shiki*. Yoshikawa Koubunkan.

(1966). *Newly Updated National History Series, Volume 22, Interpretation of the Ritsuryo* (Ryo-no-shuge, recital 1). Yoshikawa Koubunkan.

(1966). *Newly Updated National History Series, Volume 23, Ritsu-no-shuge I*. Yoshikawa Koubunkan.

(1966). *Newly Updated National History Series, Volume 23, Ryo-no-shuge I*. Yoshikawa Koubunkan.

(1966). *Newly Updated National History Series II:Continued Japanese Chronicle.* Yoshikawa Koubunkan.

(1972). *Newly Updated National History Series:Assorted Kyaku of the Three Generations I &II.* Yoshikawa Koubunkan.

The Official of Qing. (1985 photocopy version). *Qing Shilu: Shengzu Shilu* (Veritable Records of Qing: Emperor Shengzu, 清实录·圣祖实录). Zhonghua Book Company.

Ouyang, X., & Song, Q. (1975). *Xin Tang Shu* (The New Book of Tang, 新唐书) (Vol. 48: Treatise on Hundreds of Officials III; Book 4, p. 1267) (Vol. 157: Biography of Lu Zhi; Book 16, p. 4921). Beijing: Zhonghua Book Company.

Qian, J. (1979). Theory That There Were Only Lv Scholars, Lv Studies and Rule of Lv without Fa Scholars, Fa Studies and Rule of Fa in China's Fengjian Society. *Academic Monthly, 2*, 44–49.

Qiu, J. (1999a). *Da Xue Yan Yi Bu* (Additional Notes for the Explanation of Da Xue, 大学衍义补) (Vol. 1: Manage the Imperial Court—General Discussion on Politics in the Imperial Court) (Vol. 3: Manage the Imperial Court—Fair Rewards and Punishment) (Vol. 67: Respecting Education—General Discussion on the Methods of Education). Jinghua Publishing House.

Qiu, J. (1999b). Shen Xing Xian: Zonglun Zhixing Zhi Yi (Law of Prudent Punishment: General Discussion on the Significance of Making Punishment Law, 慎刑宪·总论制刑之义) I & II. In *Da Xue Yan Yi Bu: Zhiguo Ping Tianxia Zhi Yao Jiu* (The Ninth Point of Governing the Country and the World, 治国平天下之要九). Jinghua Publishing House.

Riko, M. (1959). *Research on the Ritsuryo System.* Meijishoin.

Riko, M. (1961). *The Study of Lv.* Meijishoin.

Riko, M. (1967a). *Research on the Ritsuryo System.* Keio Communications.

Riko, M. (1967b). *The Ritsuryo System and the Surroundings* (Chapter 1: Myobo Subject in *Daigakuryo* of the Nara Period). Keio Communications.

Shen, J. (1985). *Research on the Criminal Law of the Past Dynasties IV* (checked and revised by Deng, J., & Pian, Y.). Zhonghua Book Company.

Sima, Q. (1982). *Shi Ji* (Records of the Grand Historian, 史记) (Vol. 6: Annals of the First Emperor of Qin, No. 6; Book 1, p. 243) (Vol. 30: The Book of Prices Leveling Off VIII; Book 4, p. 1420) (Vol. 87: Biography of Li Si, No. 27; Book 8, p. 2546). Zhonghua Book Company.

Song, C. (1981). *Xi Yuan Ji Lu* (Collection of Grievance Relief Stories, 洗冤集录) (checked and revised by Jia, J.). Shanghai Scientific & Technical Publishers.

Song, L., et al. (2008 photocopy version). *Yuan Shi: Xuanju Yi* (Selection I, 选举一) + *Shizu Benji* (Annals of Emperor Shizu, 世祖本纪) I / IX. In *Si Ku Quan Shu* (Book 292, p. 551+ [35, 42, 55 / 155]). The Commercial Press.

Su, S. (1986). *Su Dongpo Quanji* (Complete Works of Su Dongpo, 苏东坡全集) (Vol. II: Reply to Edicts "Policy VI"). China Bookstore Publishing House.

Su, Y. (2005). The Discussion of the Rise and Fall of the Legal Studies. In *Proceedings of International Symposium on Shen Jiaben and the Chinese Legal Culture II.* China Legal Publishing House.

Su, Y. (2006). Analysis and Correction of "Using Li as the Standards for All" in Tang Lv. *Tribune of Political Science and Law, 3*, 116–141.

Sun, Z. (1934). *Research on Works of Legal Scholars from Various Dynasties in China.*

Tang, N., Zhang, N., Wang, Q., & Yan, Y. (Eds.). (1995). *Trace of exploration: Brief history of chinese legal education.* Law Press·China.

Tian, T., & Zheng, Q. (1999). *Da Qing Lv Li* (The Great Qing Code, 大清律例). Law Press·China.

Toqto'a. (1985). *Song Shi* (Vol. 157: Records of Official Selection III; Book 8). Zhonghua Book Company.

Toqto'a et al. (2008 photocopy version). *Song Shi:Fan Zhongyan Zhuan* (Biography of Fan Zhongyan, 范仲淹传) + *Renzong Benji* (Annals of Emperor Renzong, 仁宗本纪) + *Shenzong Benji* (Annals of Emperor Shenzong, 神宗本纪) + *Taizu Ben Ji* (Annals of Emperor Taizu, 太祖本纪) 1 & 3 + (Vol. 496). In *Si Ku Quan Shu* (Book 286, p. 160) +(Book 280, p. 187) + (Book 280, p. 232) + (Book 280, p. 93 *&* 108) + (Book *288*, p. 897). Taipei: The Commercial Press.

Wang, A. (1999). Duzhifushi Tingbi Timing Ji (Autographing the Wall of the Accounting Official's Home, 度支副使厅壁题名记) + Hongfan Zhuan (Biography of Hongfan, 洪范传) + Shang Huangdi Wanyanshu (A Long Memorial to the Throne [with more than ten thousand of words], 上皇帝万言书), In *Wang Anshi Quanji* (Complete Works of Wang Anshi, 王安石全集) (checked and revised by Qin, K., & Gong, J.) (pp. 309 + 207 + 1). Shanghai Classics Publishing House.

Wang, F. (2020a). *Du Tongjian Lun* (Comments on the Comprehensive Mirror, 读通鉴论) (Vol. 1: Emperor Ershi VI, p. 34) (Vol. 4: *Emperor Xuan* IV, p. 323) (Vol. 6: Emperor Guangwu III, p. 532). Zhonghua Book Company.

Wang, M. (1997). *Du Lv Pei Xi* (References for Reading Laws, 读律佩觿). In Editing Committee of Existing *"The Four Categories", Si Ku Quan Shu Cunmu Congshu (Series of Books of Existing "The Four Categories",四库全书存目丛书)* (the Classics Part, Book 37). Qilu Press.

Wang, P. (1955). *Tang Hui Yao* (Institutions of Tang, 唐会要) II. (Vol. 35: School). Zhonghua Book Company.

Wang, P. (2006). *Tang Hui Yao I*. Shanghai Classics Publishing House.

Wang, S. (2020b). *Wang Yangming Quanji:Chongxiu Yuetansi Jian Gongguan Ji* (Complete Works of Wang Yangming: Record of Re-construction of Temple Yuetan and Construction of the Mansion, 王阳明全集·重修月潭寺建公馆记). Democracy and Construction Press.

Wei, Z., et al. (1973). *Sui Shu* (Vol. 27: Officials II; Book 3, p. 756) (Vol. 28: Officials III; Book 3, pp. 775–776). Zhonghua Book Company.

Wei, Z., et al. (2019 checked and revised version). *Sui Shu:Xing Fa Zhi* (p. 132) + *Gaozu Ji* (Annals of Emperor Gaozu, 高祖纪) (part 2, p. 11). Zhonghua Book Company.

Wu, J. (1990). The Legal Studies of the Qing Dynasty and the End of Them. In *Proceedings of International Symposium on the History of Chinese Law*. Shanxi People's Publishing House.

Wu, J. (2011). *Zhenguan Zheng Yao* (Keypoints of Politics in the Zhenguan Era, 贞观政要) (Vol. 1: Theories on Being an Emperor, p. 1) (Vol. 3: Discussion on Selecting Officials, pp. 186 + 189) (Vol. 4, Lessons for the Princes, p. 261) (Vol. 5: Discussion on Benevolence and Righteousness, p. 314) (Vol. 8: Discussion on Decree for Pardon, p. 552) (Vol. 8: Discussion on Punishment and Law, pp. 525 + 538). Zhonghua Book Company.

Wu, J. (2015). *Zhenguan Zheng Yao* (Vol. 3: Discussion on Selecting Officials, p. 203) (Vol. 8: Discussion on Punishment and Law, p. 525). Zhonghua Book Company.

Xiao, Z. (1972). *Nan Qi Shu* (Book of the Southern Qi, 南齐书) (Vol. 48: Kong Zhigui; Book 3). Zhonghua Book Company.

Xu, D. (1975). *Collected Essays on the History of the Chinese Legal System*. Zhiwen Publishing House.

Xu, S. (1981). *Shuo Wen Jie Zi (Discussing Writing and Explaining Characters,* 说文解字) (annotated by Duan, Yucai). Shanghai Classics Publishing House.

Xu, S. (2006 reprint edition). *Song Hui Yao Ji Gao: Chong Ru San (Respect the Confucian III,*崇儒三*)·Lv Xue* (Legal Studies, 律学). Zhonghua Book Company.

Yaheiji, F. (1966). *Research on Myobodo*. Shinseisha.

Yan, A. (2005). *Research on Families in the Han and Jin Dynasties*. Shanghai People's Publishing House.

Yang, Y. (1984). *Research on Strict Codes of the Early Ming Dynasty*. Hunan People's Publishing House.

Zhang, J. (1992). Explanation of Unofficial Commentaries on Law in the Qing Dynasty. In J. Zhang, *Research on Qing Lv*. Law Press·China.

Zhang, J. (2019). *Zhang Taiyue Ji* (Collection of Works of Zhang Taiyue, 张太岳集) (Vol. 1: Memorial to the Throne on Six Things, p. 1) (Vol. 2: Reply to Governer Xiong Jinhu Concerning the Bandits in Guangdong and Guangxi, p. 25) (Vol. 3: Miscellaneous Issues, p. 304). China Bookstore Publishing House.

Zhang, T., et al. (1974). *Ming Shi* (History of Ming, 明史) (Vol. 93 & 94: Punishment and Law I & II; Book 8). Zhonghua Book Company.

Zhang, T., et al. (2008 photocopy version). *Ming Shi: Hai Rui Zhuan* (Biography of Hai Rui, 海瑞传) + *Xiaozong Benji* (Annals of Emperor Xiaozong, 孝宗本纪). In *Si Ku Quan Shu* (Book 300, p. 711) + (Book 297, p. 166). The Commercial Press.

Zhang, W. (1988). Legal Education in the Qing Dynasty. *Taiwan University Law Journal, 18*(01), 1–36.

Zhang, Z. (1996). *Long Jin Feng Sui Pan* (Judgments by Officials, 龙筋凤髓判) (checked and revised by Tian, T., & Guo, C.). China University of Political Science and Law Press.

Zhang, Z. (2015). *Principles and Significance: Exploring the Approaches of Chinese Legal Culture.* China University of Political Science and Law Press.

Zhang, Z. (2016). Why Discussing Traditional Chinese Legal Philosophy. In Y. Zhu (Ed.), *The Chinese Legal Family* (Vol. 8). Law Press·China.

Zhangsun, W., et al. (1983). *Tang Lv Shu Yi: Jin Lv Shu Biao* (*Report on the Submission of Lv Shu,* 进律疏表*)* (p. 578) (checked and revised by Liu, J.). Zhonghua Book Company.

Zhao, E., et al. (1977). *Qing Shi Gao:Shengzu Benji* (Draft of History of Qing: Annals of Emperor Shengzu, 清史稿·圣祖本纪) (Book 2, p. 165) + *Shizu Benji* (Annals of Emperor Shizu, 世祖本纪) (Book 2, p. 83). Zhonghua Book Company.

Zheng, K. (1981). Shi Yuan (Shang): Cao Shu Ming Cha (Acquit the Innocent, I: Cao Shu's Well Awareness, 释冤上·曹摅明察), In *Zhe Yu Gui Jian* (Mirrors for Making Judgments, 折狱龟鉴) (Vol. 1). Qunzhong Publishing House.

Zheng, Q. (1987 photocopy version). *Tong Zhi* (General Records, 通志) (Vol. 59: Selecting Officials II—Schools; Book 1). Zhonghua Book Company.

Zhu, X. (1996). *Zhu Xi Ji:Da Cheng Yunfu* (Works of Zhu Xi: Reply to Cheng Yunfu, 朱熹集·答程允夫) + *Da Deng Weilao* (Reply to Deng Weilao, 答邓卫老). Sichuan Education Press.

Chapter 3
Chinese Legal Family in Its Home Country

1 Forms of Law

1.1 Overview

Dozens of forms of law, such as *Xian* (laws), *Xing* (penalty laws), *Ze* (rules), *Lv* (laws), *Ling* (decrees), *Ke* (judgment), *Bi* (principles of comparison), *Ge* (rules), *Shi* (regulations), *Dian* (codes), *Zhao* (edicts), *Yu* (imperial orders), *Gao* (imperial orders), *Tiaoli* (regulations), *Zeli* (administrative law), *Shili* (temporary law), and *Tiaoge* (compiled rules), existed in traditional Chinese society. The diversity in the forms of law and their interplay to regulate various social relations in a uniform manner are noteworthy features of the Chinese Legal Family (Qu, 2007, 70). Other forms of law were also adopted because there were functions that could not be met by the legal codes (Yang, 2002).

Some scholars have pointed out that "the ancient Chinese forms of law structured since the Qin Dynasty as multi-level and interrelated categories. The different levels of forms differed in stability, effectiveness, and judicial application and formed an organic whole with each other. Of course, different forms of law in different periods have been highly valued and developed by the rulers. The judicial practice has proved that success in the legislation of a certain form of law does not necessarily bring success in judicial practice. Through long-term development, ancient Chinese forms of law developed two complementary legal structure patterns. One of them was more effective, provided greater stability, higher abstraction, and smaller quantity, and the other one was of greater accuracy, in larger quantity but less effective and more variable. They met the diverse and conflicting needs of stability and variability, abstraction and accuracy, and timeliness and continuance of law" (Hu, 2014).

The formation stage of the Chinese Legal Family comprised the Sui and Tang Dynasties, which was also the completion stage of the Confucianization of *fengjian* law. This continued to the Song, Yuan, Ming, and Qing Dynasties. In this process, the rulers summarized various experiences that were conducive to the construction

Q. He et al., *Chinese Legal Family*, https://doi.org/10.1007/978-981-96-6522-8_3

of the *fengjian* legal system and thus formed a situation in which various forms of law, such as Lv, Ling, Ge, Shi, Dian, Chi, and Li, were used together.

In summary, the forms of law used in the Tang Dynasty were mainly Lv, Ling, Ge, Gehou Chi, and Shi; in the Song Dynasty, mainly Lv, Ling, Bianchi, Ge, Shi, Li, and Tiao Fa Shi Lei; in the Yuan Dynasty, mainly Ge and Li; in the Ming Dynasty, mainly Lv, Ling, Gao, Li, and Dian; and in the Qing Dynasty, mainly Lv, Li, Zeli, and Dian.

1.2 Forms of Law in the Tang Dynasty

In summary of the legislative experience and achievements of the past dynasties in developing the legal system, the Tang Dynasty finished the Tang Lv, the earliest extant and most systematic and complete ancient statute law. It directly influenced the *fengjian* legislation of later generations and neighboring countries and became a representative work of the Chinese Legal Family.

The Tang Dynasty established Lv, Ling, Ge, and Shi as the dominant forms of law, as well as Gehou Chi after the mid-Tang Dynasty. Lv, Ling, Ge, and Shi all had their own structures and became independent laws (codes). From the perspective of the nature of these laws, Tang Lv was the criminal code and Ling and Shi were comprehensive administrative laws (codes), which also included civil, procedural, and military laws, as well as other legal branches. Ge and Gehou Chi were comprehensive laws (codes) of various legal norms, including criminal, administrative, procedural, and military laws. Lv, Ling, Ge, and Shi in the Tang Dynasty were interrelated and worked in harmony. Together, they constituted a complete legal system. The inception of these forms of law in the Tang Dynasty, especially Lv and Ling, played a great role in the formation of the Chinese Legal Family, with the legal system of Lv and Ling as an important formal feature.

1.2.1 Lv

Lv was one of the most basic and major forms of law in the Tang Dynasty. It was relatively stable. According to *Tang Liu Dian: Xing Bu*, "Lv is used to regulate crimes and impose proper punishment."

Xu Daolin believes that "Tang Lv has the highest status in the entire history of the Chinese legal system. This is because it assimilated the greatest achievements of the previous Qin, Han, Wei, and Jin Dynasties and set up an excellent model for the later Song, Yuan, Ming, and Qing Dynasties. Therefore, Tang Lv is unparalleled among the laws of all dynasties" (Xu, 1947, 6). Zhang Zhongqiu believes that "compared with other codes of the same period and type in the world, *Tang Lv Shu Yi* appears to be perfect and mature in terms of institutional settings and legislative techniques. Therefore, both from a comparative perspective of the legal history and from a legislative perspective of codification, *Tang Lv Shu Yi* is an excellent code" (Zhang, 2013b).

The legal system in the Tang Dynasty was a developed form of the Chinese *fengjian* legal system. According to Wu Jianfan's research, Tang Lv was founded in the seventh year of the Wude Era during the reign of Emperor Gaozu, and according to historical documents, it was subsequently revised six times. These revisions comprised an amendment in the Zhenguan Era; changes in the Yonghui, Chuigong, and Jinyun Eras; a change in the 7th year of the Kaiyuan Era; and an amendment in the 25th year of the Kaiyuan Era (Wu, 2003, 213–216).

Tang Lv Shu Yi[1] is a representative code of ancient China. Later generations used it as a blueprint for the revision of laws. It has been continuously reprinted. Until today, it has been preserved for more than 1300 years, becoming the earliest extant and complete *fengjian* statute law. The text, style, and contents of *Tang Lv Shu Yi* are believed to have been formed in the period from the first to the fourth year of the Yonghui Era (Pu, 1982, 18).

The existing *Tang Lv Shu Yi* consists of 12 chapters, 30 volumes, and 502 articles. Its chapter titles, style, and structure are the same as those of *Kaihuang Lv* of the Sui Dynasty.

The first chapter, "*Mingli*" (General Principles), consists of 57 articles in six volumes and introduces the whole law. The second chapter, "*Weijin*" (Guarding and Defense), comprises 33 articles in two volumes and is regarding the institutions and laws concerning the guarding of the royal palaces, halls, temples, and courts; the guarding of the garrisons of prefectures and towns; and fortress and border defenses. The third chapter, "*Zhizhi*" (System of Offices), consists of 59 articles in three volumes and is the law on the establishment of official positions, negligence of duty, corruption and bribes, and transportation. The fourth chapter, "*Huhun*" (Household and Marriage), consists of 46 articles in three volumes and is the law on household registration, land, taxation, marriage, and families. The fifth chapter, "*Jiuku*" (Stock and Storage), comprises 28 articles in one volume and is the law on the maintenance of public and private livestock, the management of warehouses, and the

[1] According to Wu Jianfan, the name *Tang Lv Shu Yi* was given by people from the Yuan Dynasty. It was called *Lv Shu* in the Tang and Song Dynasties. This was evidenced by Zhangsun Wuji's *Jin Lv Shu Biao*, the old and new *Tang Shu* (*Book of Tang*), *Song Shi: Yi Wen Zhi* (*History of Song: Treatise on Arts and Literature*), the *Chongwen General Catalogue*, and the *Guange General Catalogue* cited by *Yu Hai*. *Lv Shu* was used in all of them. The Song Dynasty incorporated all Tang Lv and Shu (commentaries) to it into *Song Xing Tong* (*Punishment Law of Song*) as its own Lv and Shu. Therefore, it was not called *Tang Lv* and *Tang Shu*. The Yuan Dynasty abolished the laws of the Tang and Song Dynasties and treated them as historical documents, so they were marked with the name of its dynasty. The copy published in the Taiding Era of the Yuan Dynasty had the name of *Gu Tang Lv Shu Yi* (*Old Tang Lv Shu Yi*). Thus, it was clear that the name of *Tang Lv Shu Yi* has appeared in the Yuan Dynasty. Why was it called *Tang Lv Shu Yi*"? This is because each paragraph of the commentaries starts with two characters "Yi Yue" (Discuss) (it is so in the Dunhuang remnants; the current circulated copy starts with three characters "Shu Yi Yue," which is not the original text), so Shu Yi was used as the name of this book. *Lv Shu* was written jointly, and the opinions in the book were discussed and settled together, so the text of the commentary starts with the characters "Yi Yue." See Wu (2003, 219–220).

income and expense control of official goods. The sixth chapter, "*Shanxing*" (Army and Construction), consists of 24 articles in one volume and is the law on military deployment, army mobilization, and construction, which is related to the control of military power and the management and use of labor. The seventh chapter, "*Zeidao*" (Thieving and Robbery), consists of 54 articles in four volumes and is divided into two parts: "thieving" and "robbery." The eighth chapter, "*Dousong*" (Fighting and Litigation), comprises 60 articles in four volumes and is the law on fighting and litigation. The ninth chapter, "*Zhawei*" (Fraud and Forgery), consists of 27 articles in one volume and is regarding the punishment of forgery and fraudulent crimes. The 10th chapter, "*Zalv*" (Miscellaneous Rules), consists of 62 articles in two volumes and is a collection of rules that could not be included in other chapters, and they cover a wide range of topics. The 11th chapter, "*Buwang*" (Catching Outlaws), comprises 18 articles in one volume and is the law on the hunting of escapees and fugitives by officials and commoners. The 12th chapter, "*Duanyu*" (Trials), consists of 34 articles in two volumes and is regarding trial, judgment, imprisonment, and execution.

On the basis of the contents of the Tang laws, the abovementioned 12 chapters can be grouped into three: the 1st chapter is analogous to the general principles of modern laws; the 2nd to 10th chapters, the subrules of modern laws; and the 11th and 12th chapters and some parts of the 8th chapter, the procedural regulation of modern laws.

Inheriting the legislative achievements of the past dynasties, such as *Fa Jing*, *Jiuzhang Lv*, *Bei Qi Lv*, and *Kaihuang Lv*, and the achievements of the Han and Jin legal studies, *Tang Lv Shu Yi* reflected the highest level of jurisprudential development of the time whether one considers the division of general rules to subrules or the compilation of various laws. With the guiding ideology of "moral guidance and supplementary punishment," it finally realized the unification and harmony of the *fengjian* Li (Ritual Propriety) and legal studies in the codification and put an end to the 700-year trial tradition since Emperor Wu of the Western Han Dynasty of "making judgments based on Confucian classics." It inherited the achievements of the legal commentary from Du Yu and Zhang Fei in the Jin Dynasty, making the *fengjian* legal interpretation more scientific and rigorous.[2]

1.2.2 Ling

Tang Liu Dian: Xing Bu states that "Ling is to establish institutions by setting up examples." Most of the Ling in the Tang Dynasty came from the emperor's single edict concerning the administration of the state. In terms of the nature of the law, Tang Ling included comprehensive laws (codes) that mainly consisted of administrative laws, but some civil, procedural, military, and other laws were also included. Since its promulgation in the seventh year of the Wude Era (624), Tang Ling was revised several times in the Zhenguan, Yonghui, Chuigong, Shenlong, and Kaiyuan

[2] For a detailed review of the achievements of the legal commentary in *Tang Lv Shu Yi*, see He (2006, 435–457).

Eras. Although these revisions were mainly changes in content, the available historical records prove that they also included additions and deletions to the titles and structures.

The earliest activity of establishing Ling in the Tang Dynasty according to *Jiu Tang Shu: Xing Fa Zhi* (*The Old Book of Tang: Treatise on Punishment and Law*, 旧唐书·刑法志) was made at the beginning of the reign of Emperor Taizong, when Pei Hongxian, a legal counselor of the King of Shu, "proposed more than forty issues that were not suitable for the time, and Taizong ordered him to lead the amendment of them." At the end of the Ming Dynasty at the latest, Tang Ling was already widespread and was not completely handed down. The only thing that we know now is the title and structure of *Kaiyuan Qinian Ling* (*Ling of the 7th Year of the Kaiyuan Era*) cited in the sixth volume, "Shang Shu Xing Bu," of *Tang Liu Dian*. The precise titles and structures of Ling of other eras in the Tang Dynasty are known. From the sixth volume, "Shang Shu Xing Bu," of *Tang Liu Dian*, it can be seen that there were 27 kinds of Ling, which were divided into 30 volumes.

1.2.3 Ge and Gehou Chi

Tang Liu Dian states that "Ge is to forbid violation of the law and stop evil conduct." Generally speaking, Tang Ge was a compilation of the emperors' edicts.

Qian Yuankai once wrote an article to carefully sort out the evolution of the form of law, "Ge," from the Qin and Han to Sui Dynasties (Qian, 1987). Academic circles have different views on the nature of Ge. Some scholars believe that Ge was a supplement and addition to Lv and Ling.[3] Some believe that considering the contents of Ge, most of them were administrative regulations (except for a small number of criminal regulations), which regulated specific and extensive matters and served as an important supplement to the systematic codes (Zhang, 2013a, 284). Some think that Ge was the state's special criminal law (supplementary law) and special regulations on major public affairs (Fan & Chen, 2007, 281). Some believe that Ge and Gehou Chi were comprehensive laws (codes) that included various legal norms, such as criminal law, administrative law, civil law, procedural law, and military law (Li, 2011, 171). In fact, Ge had undergone development and changes in the Tang Dynasty. In different periods, it had different focuses, and different types of Ge had different functions.

The earliest efforts of establishing Ge in the Tang Dynasty were the making of "twelve articles of the agreed law" during the reign of Emperor Gaozu and the making of 53 articles of Ge in the second year of the Wude Era (619).

In the late Tang Dynasty, Ge evolved into Gehou Chi. Its abolition, adoption, deletion, and amendment were timelier. Its contents were mostly regarding penalties and imprisonment. Gehou Chi became the main basis for determining crimes in the late Tang Dynasty and became the main form of law at that time. Ma Xiaohong

[3] Noboru Niida believed that Ge was a collection of the imperial orders at any time. After Kaiyuan Ge, there was Kaicheng Ge and others. See Niida (2011, 48).

summarized three differences in content and nature when Ge and Gehou Chi of that period were compared with Ge of the previous period (Ma, 1987).

First, because Ge and Gehou Chi of that period enjoyed a complete system of compilation and enforcement, their contents were updated more promptly. In terms of the nature of their specific provisions, they were similar to Linzhi Ge (Ge of the Linzhi Era) and Wude Ge (Ge of the Wude Era), which were temporary measures. However, as a whole, they formed a stable system.

Second, at that time, because of the advanced contents of the penalties and imprisonment, the Ministry of Punishment was in charge of the abolition, adoption, and enforcement of Gehou Chi and Ge.

Third, previously, the decision of guilty or not followed the following principle: if Ge provided a lighter punishment, Ge should be applied; if Lv provided a lighter punishment, Lv should be applied. This changed. The new principle was the following: Gehou Chi was superior to Ge, and Ge was superior to Lv.

Thus, it seems that Gehou Chi and Ge became the main basis for convictions in the late Tang Dynasty and became the main form of law at that time.

1.2.4 Shi

Tang Liu Dian: Xing Bu records that "Shi is to regulate and institutionalize matters." Shi consisted of regulations concerning the activities of administrative organizations at different levels and legal provisions concerning the formalities of official documents between superiors and subordinates. After compilation, Shi was called "Yong Shi" (permanent Shi) in the Tang Dynasty, which had a universal legal effect.

In the 11th year of the Zhenguan Era (637), Fang Xuanling and some others were ordered to make *Shi* with 33 chapters, which was *Zhenguan Shi*. Later, there were *Yonghui Shi*, *Chuigong Shi*, *Shenlong Shi*, and *Kaiyuan Shi*, each of which had 20 volumes. In the Tang Dynasty, Shi was normally revised following the revision of Lv and Ling. However, it was not revised after the Kaiyuan Era. *Kaiyuan Shi* included 34 chapters in 20 volumes. It was structured mainly based on the 24 divisions in the six ministries of the *Shangshu* Department, and some other authorities were covered.

Shi had considerable coercive power. Those who violated Shi were subject to administrative punishment. In addition, their conduct might constitute the crime of "*Weishi*" (Crime of Violating Shi), as provided in Lv, and they could be punished with 40 lashes (Zhangsun, 2008, 344).

The author agrees with Lv Zhixing's view that Tang Shi was a detailed regulation of Ling, which had the same nature as that of Ling, that is, legal norms concerning noncriminal and institutional matters. It included detailed rules for state organs to conduct administrative management and judicial activities, excluding official documents and procedures. The rules concerning the official documents and procedures of the Tang Dynasty were stipulated in *Gong Shi Ling* (Law on Public Procedures).

1.2.5 Tang Liu Dian

Following the order of Emperor Xuanzong of Tang, *Tang Liu Dian* was compiled after more than ten years of repeated revisions from the 10th year of the Kaiyuan Era (722) to the 26th year of the Kaiyuan Era (738).

In the 16th year of the Kaiyuan Era (728), Emperor Xuanzong ordered the *jixian-dian shuyuan* (the national book compilation institution) to compile *Tang Liu Dian*, following the structure of *liuguan* (six offices) stipulated in the Confucian classic *Zhou Li: Tian Guan: Da Zai* (*Rites of Zhou: Office of the Heaven: Head Officer*, 周礼·天官·大宰). The compilers included ministers Xu Jian and Wei Shu.

According to the Japanese scholar Kenkichi Naito, the compilation of *Tang Liu Dian* was largely motivated by Emperor Xuanzong's admiration for Confucianism and the emperor's vanity. In any case, it could be easily inferred that the purpose of the compilation was not to satisfy the need for the then legal codes (Naito, 2003, 362–363).

Tang Liu Dian consists of two parts: the main text and the commentary. The main text comprises 30 volumes. The chapters contain almost all of the official institutions of the Tang Dynasty during the Kaiyuan Era and record the official positions and duties in governments at different levels. In the commentary attached to the book, the historical development of the official positions from their creation to the Tang Dynasty and the related legal provisions (Lv, Ling, Ge, and Shi) are illustrated. The book does not include the contents of the amendment of the law in the 25th year of the Kaiyuan Era (737) concerning related institutions (Lv, Ling, Ge, Shi, and Commentary of the 25th year of the Kaiyuan Era). Therefore, it is about the old law, but some commentaries of the 26th year of the Kaiyuan Era can also be found in the book (Okumura, 2003, 331).

In addition, the nature of *Tang Liu Dian* has been a controversial issue since modern times among the researchers of the history of Tang law and even of the Tang Dynasty, and the debate has become more intense since the 1980s. Briefly, some scholars believe that *Tang Liu Dian* was the administrative code of the Tang Dynasty, whereas others disagree.[4] We believe that *Tang Liu Dian* was neither the administrative code nor the laws of the Tang Dynasty in terms of both the legislative process and its content. It was only an officially compiled classic following the style of *Zhou Li* to show the prosperity of the system of the Tang Dynasty (Li, 2004; Qian & Li, 1989; Qian, 1996b; Qian, 1996a, 157). Thus, obviously, the forms of law of the Tang Dynasty could not include Dian (*Tang Liu Dian*) (Li, 2011, 177–178).

---

[4] For a brief review of the different opinions on the nature of *Tang Liu Dian*, see Xu (1998).

2 Legal System

2.1 Overview

From the viewpoint of historical materialism, any type of law is a reflection and product of social relations. The diversity of social relations determines the diversity of the legal norms and legal instruments, thus forming some relatively independent legal departments and systems in a unified legal system. It is impossible for any country to have only one legal norm or one branch of law at any stage of historical development, and this is not determined by the subjective will of the legislators (Zhang, 1984). As far as the legal system of traditional Chinese society is concerned, aside from the criminal codes promulgated in the past dynasties, there were also several other forms of law from different historical periods, such as Ke, Bi, Zhao, Yu (imperial order), Gao (imperial order), Tiaoli, Zeli, Shili, and Tiaoge. The variety of these forms and their interplay with each other in regulating various social relations are noteworthy features of the Chinese Legal Family. Among these sources of law, other than the criminal code, there were a large number of provisions relating to various aspects of civil, administrative, economic, and procedural matters. Therefore, it can be said that the traditional legal system was composed of various legal parts, such as criminal law, civil law, procedural law, administrative law, and economic law, and the laws coexisted with each other (Qu, 2007, 70).

The legal system of the Chinese Legal Family had a strong Confucian ethical flavor. The Confucian ethics were incorporated into the law and gradually gained a dominant position. These core legal systems that were full of Confucian ethics were confirmed in Tang Lv and were inherited by the laws of the Song, Yuan, Ming, and Qing Dynasties, with only partial development and changes. This section selects some elaborations of the major criminal, civil, administrative, and judicial legal systems of the Tang Dynasty and discusses the evolution and changes of these systems.

The criminal legal system occupied the main position in the system of the Chinese Legal Family. Generally speaking, the criminal legal system consists of basic elements, such as types of punishment, crimes, and penalties. The criminal legal systems of different dynasties covered a wide range. They have both commonalities and new developments. In terms of the types of punishment, aside from the five major punishments, there were also punishments such as *cipei* (exile with tattoo), *lingchi* (death by a thousand cuts), *chongjun* (forced to serve in the army), *jiahao* (cangue), *tingzhang* (caning), and *faqian* (banishment). In terms of the principles for the application of punishment, there were privileges such as *yi* (for eight types of people, only the emperor can discuss and decide the punishment), *qing* (a report to the emperor and a petition for a deduction were needed before making decisions), *jian* (deduction), *shu* (evading punishment by giving money), and *guandang* (evading punishment by giving up official positions). The application principles also included reduction and exemption for the elderly and young, aggravation for "repeat offenders," distinction between prime culprits and accessories in joint crimes, surrender leading to commutation, combined punishment for several crimes committed by one person, differentiation between public and private offenses, cohabitators of the criminals being allowed to conceal their crimes, use of analogy for judgment when legal provisions were absent, special provisions on foreigners, heavier punishment for criminals from special areas, severe punishment for corruption, lighter punishment for minor crimes, and harsher punishment for serious crimes. In terms of the types of crimes, there were "ten abominations," "forbidden conducts," "six types of killing," "six types of property crimes," conspiracy, etc.

The civil legal system mainly includes the institution of household registration and identity, ownership, contracts, marriage and family, and inheritance. Among these, ownership, contracts, marriage and family, and inheritance are more distinctive, reflecting the characteristics of traditional Chinese legal culture. The institutions of marriage and family mainly include the contracts of marriage, the dissolution of marriage—"*qichu*" (the seven grounds for the husband to cast off his wife and send her back to her family), "*sanbuqu*" (the three situations where the husband was not allowed to cast off his wife), "*yijue*" (forced split-up based on righteousness), and "*heli*" (peaceful divorce)—and the restrictions to marriage (people having the same family name were not allowed to get married, relatives were not allowed to get married, ordinary people were not allowed to get married with outcasts, people were not allowed to use a false identity to get married, and some discussions regarding levirate marriage). Concerning the family, the focus is on the rights and duties of parents and husbands and wives. In terms of inheritance, two aspects are given the most attention: the inheritance of status and the inheritance of property.

The administrative legal system mainly includes the law on bureaucratic establishment and the administrative supervision system in the central and local aspects. This part systematically describes the development and changes of the central administrative structure and the evolution of the local administrative structure in Tang and examines the selection and appointment of officials, the examination of officials, and the administrative supervision of officials.

Judicial litigation and the trial system cover the evolution of the central and local judiciary in the Tang Dynasty, such as the structural system of the judiciary. This section also includes the evolution of the litigation system, such as the comprehensive regulations on proceedings and litigation of the Tang Dynasty. In terms of trial, the exchange of judges and the system of review of death sentences, such as the "three-time report" and "five-time report" systems in the Tang Dynasty, are examined.

2.2 Criminal Legal System

2.2.1 Types of Punishment

The five-punishment system is the basic punishment system in the Chinese Legal Family. It reflected the Confucianization of the legal system, the legalization of Confucian thoughts, and a high degree of integration of the two. Compared with the five punishments of *mo* (tattoo), *yi* (cutting the nose off), *yue* (cutting the foot off), *gong* (castration), and *dapi* (death) adopted in the slave society, the five *fengjian* punishments obviously made great progress. The former was mainly enforced by physical mutilation, whereas the latter was mainly enforced by restricting personal freedom. This reflected the gradual transition of the ancient Chinese penalty system from barbarism to civilization. It was also an affirmation of the inheritance of the results of the reform of the penalty system (abolition of corporal punishment) that began during the Wenjing Era of the Western Han Dynasty.

Some changes in the five-punishment system in the Tang Dynasty are worth noting. On the basis of the system adopted in *Kaihuang Lv*, *Tang Lv Shu Yi* adjusted the sequence of the stipulation on punishments from heavier punishment first to lighter punishment first. The five types of punishment were the following: *chi* (flogging), *zhang* (caning), *tu* (imprisonment), *liu* (exile), and *si* (death penalty). The punishments of *chi*, *zhang*, and *tu* were divided into five levels, i.e., floggings from 10 to 50, canings from 60 to 100, and imprisonment from 1 to 3 years, respectively. The punishment of *liu* was divided into three levels according to the distance of exile, ranging from 2,000 to 3,000 miles. Compared with the Sui Dynasty, each level of *liu* was increased by 1,000 miles, and all three levels of exile were accompanied by the obligation of serving 1 year of hard labor in the designated place. The death penalty was also divided into two levels, namely, hanging and beheading. The five punishments, except for the "ten abominations," could be redeemed by money. In *Tang Lv Shu Yi*, when explaining the meaning of "five punishments," classics were cited a lot. Tang Lv also adopted some reasonable methods of the past concerning the increase and reduction of the penalties. In addition, there was *jiayiliu* in the punishment of exile. This was exile without return, which was equivalent to the death penalty. However, *jiayiliu* was used only as a substitute for death and was not included in the five punishments.

2.2.2 Principles for the Application of Punishments

Heavy Punishment for the "Ten Abominations"

In the Northern Qi Dynasty, the "ten serious crimes" were incorporated into law, and based on it, *Kaihuang Lv* adopted a slight modification and formally established the system of the "ten abominations," which more clearly defined the key targets of the criminal law. Compared with the "ten serious crimes," the "ten abominations" had two changes. First, the two articles concerning treason and surrender were combined into one article on treason, and an article on discord was added. This change, in fact, reduced the content of national interest in the "ten abominations" and increased the content of family ethics. Tang Lv inherited this change. The second change was the addition of the word *mou* (plan) before the three crimes of *fanni* (rebellion), *dani* (great sedition), and *pan* (treason). After the change, they became *moufan* (plan on rebellion), *moudani* (plan on great sedition), and *moupan* (plan on treason).

The content of the "ten abominations" can be divided into three categories. The first covers the acts that directly threatened or damaged the emperor's person, power, and dignity, such as rebellion, great sedition, treason, and great irreverence, which were the core of the "ten abominations." These crimes directly violated the principle that "rulers guide subjects" and were punished with the heaviest penalties. The second category included the vicious crimes that seriously threatened the *fengjian* ruling order, mainly depravity; these crimes were generally punishable by death. In the third category were the acts that seriously undermined *fengjian* morality and moral relations, such as parricide, lack of filial piety, discord, unrighteousness, and incest, which accounted for half of the ten abominations. These reflected the guiding ideology for legislation in Tang Lv that "Li (Ritual Propriety) and Xing (Punishment) are combined." Here, Li was a ritual based on the Confucian classics.

Eight Deliberations

The "eight deliberations" were as follows: deliberation for the relatives of the emperor, old retainers of the emperor, the morally worthy, ability, achievement, high position, diligence, and guests of the state.

Kaihuang Lv implemented the principle of the hierarchical system that "rituals are different for different classes." It gave the nobles and officials privileges, such as the "eight deliberations," "general reduction," "redemption with treasure," and "redemption with official positions," which exerted a direct influence on later generations. Tang Lv inherited the *Kaihuang Lv* "eight deliberations" system. If the eight kinds of people, namely, relatives of the emperor, old retainers of the emperor, the morally worthy, ability, achievement, high position, diligence, and guests of the state, broke the law, the judicial organs were not allowed to follow the normal procedures of trial and the case must be reported to the emperor for the determination of their crime and the reasons that they should be deliberated. Usually, the emperor had to convene the public ministers to discuss the reduction or elimination of the penalty according to their status, identity, merits, and relationship with the royal family. However, "those who committed the ten abominations were not subject to this law."

Crimes Committed by "Foreigners"

During the Tang Dynasty, the economy was prosperous, and the culture was developed, so people from all over the world came to China for cultural exchanges or trade. At that time, there were more than 100,000 foreign people living and doing business in China, such as people from Tianzhu, Persia, Central Asia, and South Asia, and Jews. To settle the disputes that occurred in trade or among foreigners, Tang Lv adopted a provision of "foreigners' crimes." Thus, "if a foreigner commits an offense against a person who is also from his or her country, he or she should be punished following the law of their own country; if a foreigner commits an offense against a foreigner from another country, he or she should be punished following the Tang law."

According to Tang Lv, lawsuits between foreigners belonging to the same country should be handled according to the law of their own country, adopting the principle of personalism. Lawsuits between foreigners from different countries (including lawsuits between a foreigner and Chinese) should be adjudicated according to Tang Lv, adopting the principle of territoriality.

Analogy

Tang Lv adopted a provision concerning the "judgment when applicable laws were absent": "For crimes that deserve reduced or exempted punishment, judges should list the comparable provisions and impose lighter punishment based on them; for crimes that deserve increased punishment, judges should list the comparable provisions and impose heavier punishments based on them." It was clearly stipulated that "the circumstances of the crimes are so abundant, so analogy should be used." The premise of the application of this provision is that "applicable laws are absent." That is to say, in the absence of applicable laws, for those who deserve a reduced punishment, judges should list or compare the related provisions providing heavier penalties and imposing lighter punishment accordingly.

2.2.3 Types of Crimes

"*Liusha*" (Six Types of Killings)[5]

The "six types of killings" were the most representative of the scientific overviews at the time of Tang Lv and even of the traditional Chinese legal studies. Research on the "six types of killings" in Tang Lv can help in comprehensively analyzing the achievements of the traditional Chinese legal studies represented by Tang Lv in terms of legislative techniques, legal principles, and legal concepts.

According to the subjective state and specific behavior of the perpetrator, the "six types of killings" provided in Tang Lv include "*mousha*" (conspiracy to murder), "*gusha*" (murder not caused by fights), "*dousha*" (killing during fights), "*wusha*" (murder of the wrong person), "*guoshisha*" (negligent killing), and "*xisha*" (killing when playing).

"*Liuzang*" (Six Types of Property Crimes)

"*Liuzang*" were the six types of crimes related to economics, i.e., property crimes. The six types of property crimes were the standard for deciding the penalty for all property crimes. All property crimes other than the six were compared with them to

[5] Some people also added "*jiesha*" (killing when rescuing a prisoner) with the "six types of killings," making them the "seven types of killings." See Zhang (2013a, 303).

decide the judgment. Tang Lv classified the crimes against the government and private property into six categories, namely, *qiangdao* (robbery), *qiedao* (theft), *shoucai wangfa* (twisting the law after acceptance of bribes), *shoucai bu wangfa* (accepting the bribes but still following the law), *shousuo jianlin caiwu* (accepting bribes from subordinates), and *zuozang* (accepting property without justification). Among these, the subjects of the crimes of *qiangdao* and *qiedao* were general subjects, and the subjects of the crimes of *shoucai wangfa*, *shoucai bu wangfa*, *shousuo jianlin caiwu*, and *zuozang* were officials of the state.

2.3 Civil Legal System

2.3.1 Ownership Institution

Ownership is the most important form of property rights. Since ancient China was founded on agriculture, land ownership was the core of ownership.

In the Tang Dynasty, under the land-equalization system, the land was divided into two categories: state-owned land and privately owned land. The state-owned land included *koufen* (distributed to the people based on the number of people in their family), *zhifen* (distributed to officials based on official positions), and *gongxie* (distributed to different levels of government for public income). The privately owned land included *yongye* (permanently private) land and some house lots. Some scholars have summarized the status and structure of land ownership as "government–private duality, government-dominated, and diverse forms." The status and structure of land ownership were dynamic and changing, and the actual quantity and relative proportion were always varying both in terms of the specific forms of the land (state-owned or privately owned land) and the structure of the land ownership (duality of the state-owned and privately owned land) (Liu, 2006).

2.3.2 Contract Institution

In the Chinese Legal Family, there were contracts of sale, borrowing and loan, tenancy, pawn, and others. Among these, the main types were contracts of sale and loans.

Contracts of Sale

The contract of sale in the Tang Dynasty was the most important type of contract. Academic circles have classified the acts of sale and purchase in the Tang Dynasty. In his book *The History of Chinese Legal System: Land Law and Contract Law*, Noboru Niida classified sales and purchases in ancient China into trade in common movable property, trade in real estate, trade in slaves and livestock, trade with advance payment, credit sales, and permanent sales (Niida, 1991, 360–383).

The trade of slaves and maids was considered legal in the Tang Dynasty, but certain procedures were required. First, to prevent the trade of an ordinary person, the identity of the slave had to be confirmed, which was called "*guojian*" (examination of the slavery identity). Second, a written contract certified by the government was required, which was called "*liquan*" (establishment of the certificate).

Legal borrowing and loan relationships were protected by Tang Lv. It stipulated that a "*shiquan*" (contract) must be concluded for large transactions. Once the contract was concluded, both parties should abide by it and should prohibit the debtor from defaulting on the payment of the debt.

Borrowing and Loan Contracts

In the Tang Dynasty, both "borrowing" and "loan" had specific meanings. The term "borrowing" generally refers to "borrowing for use" (of a specific object). The term "loan" generally refers to a "loan for consumption" (of nonspecific objects). Borrowing and loan contracts were classified into two types: interest-bearing and interest-free contracts, which were, respectively, called "*chuju*" and "*fuzhai*" in ancient China (Zhang, 2013a, 318).

2.3.3 Marriage and Family System

Conclusion of Marriage

a. Monogamy was practiced, and polygamy was prohibited. However, concubinage was not forbidden at that time. Therefore, a monogamous institution with concubines permitted was adopted. However, it was forbidden to change the position of wives and concubines at will. The purpose was to clarify the distinction between the sons of the first and other wives to maintain the system of succession by the wife's first-born son.
b. The elders and masters had the right to arrange the marriage of the youngsters and slaves.
c. Matchmaking was also an essential element of legal marriages.
d. The marriage document and the offer of money were the prerequisites for the establishment of the marriage.

Dissolution of Marriage

a. "*Qichu*" (seven out, the seven grounds for the husband to cast off his wife and send her back to her family) and "*sanbuqu*" (three non-out, the three situations where the husband was not allowed to cast off his wife). According to current historical evidence, the introduction of "*qichu*" into the law was first seen in the Tang Dynasty. On the premise that men were not allowed to leave their wives at will, Tang Lv made "*qichu*" the condition for the husband to divorce and adopted "*sanbuqu*" to restrict "*qichu*," which objectively protected the stability of women's marriages.

Compared with Han Lv, the sequence of "*qichu*" in the Tang Dynasty was changed in the following order: childlessness, lasciviousness, disobedience to father-in-law and mother-in-law, garrulousness, theft, jealousy, and malady.

b. "*Yijue*." Tang Lv added "*yijue*" as a condition for the forced dissolution of marriage.
c. "*Heli*." The voluntary divorce of both spouses was called "*heli*," which originated from the Zhou Rites. It was incorporated into the code as a formal system since the Tang Dynasty and was developed in the Song, Yuan, Ming, and Qing Dynasties, becoming an integral part of the traditional legal divorce institution.

Restrictions on Marriage

a. Marriage between persons with the same surname was forbidden.
b. Marriage between relatives was forbidden.
c. Marriages between ordinary people and outcasts were forbidden.
d. Marriage shall not be contracted on the basis of false information. The term "false information" refers to a situation where a man or woman has a disability or is not the son/daughter of the legal wife, but it was not mentioned at the time of engagement.

Family Institution

a. The rights and obligations of parents. Tang Lv established the family institution according to the Confucian ethics of "fathers guiding sons" and "husbands guiding wives."
b. The rights and obligations of the husband and wife.

First, property rights. Family matters were decided by the husband. The property rights of the husband here were relative, and the concept was framed only in the relationship between the husband and wife, not in the whole family relationship. Generally speaking, in the relationship between the husband and wife concerning properties, the husband was free to dispose of the family property (including the wife's trousseau) without restriction. The wife did not have the right to own property, and if she did, she was guilty of "theft" of *qichu*.

Second, the right to teach. First, a husband could swear at his wife without being punished. Second, a husband might receive light punishment or no punishment for beating his wife. Third, a husband may not be punished for the negligent killing of his wife.

Third, the right to repudiate his wife.

Fourth, the right to sell his wife by marrying her to someone else.

Lastly, the obligations of the wife to her husband. The relationship between the husband and wife in the traditional society was based not only on the clear legalization of the husband's rights but also on the wife's obligations to her husband as a guarantee of the husband's rights. Meanwhile, no direct rights of the wife toward her husband were found in the law. The obligations of the wife to her husband mainly included the obligation of chastity, that the wife had to be loyal to her husband; the obligation of cohabitation, that the wife had to move with her husband; the obligation of concealing for her husband; the obligation of not marrying again during the mourning period after the husband's death; and the obligation of supporting the father-in-law and mother-in-law.

2.3.4 Inheritance Institution

Inheritance of Status

The inheritance of status was the core of the inheritance law. Tang Lv adopted the primogeniture succession system for status such as the ancestral domain and noble titles and made a strict distinction between the children of the wife and the concubines. In the rules of inheritance, the inheritance of status was the most emphasized. The first son of the wife would inherit the status, and the first son of the first son with his wife (the first grandson) would inherit the ancestral domain upon the death of the first son. If the wife had no son, the first-born son would inherit. According to Tang Lv, the eldest son of the wife would be the successor.

Inheritance of Property

In the Tang Dynasty, property was divided equally among the sons.

In addition to inheritance, the division of family property was important. According to Noboru Niida, in ancient Chinese society, whether according to the statute law or custom, the division of family property was always an even distribution among the sons in principle—none of the sons should have an advantageous position (e.g., see the provision on "how the property shall be divided" in the Law on *the Household* of the Tang Dynasty). However, it was sometimes accepted that the first son of the wife and the first son of the first son with his wife (the first grandson) had a slightly larger share. Such a custom of heterogeneous division among sons given birth by the wife and concubines was not uncommon as it varied from place to place (Niida, 2011, 182).

2.4 *Administrative Legal System*

2.4.1 Central Administrative System—Central Administrative Institutions in the Tang Dynasty

The central government of the Tang Dynasty had a system of Three Departments and Six Ministries, namely, the *Zhongshu* Department (中书省), *Menxia* Department (门下省), and *Shangshu* Department (尚书省). The Tang Dynasty followed the Sui system, i.e., the head officers of the three departments constituted a joint group of prime ministers.

Under the *Shangshu* Department, there were six ministries: *Li* (Ministry of Personnel), *Hu* (Ministry of Revenue), *Li* (Ministry of Rites), *Bing* (Ministry of War), *Xing* (Ministry of Punishment), and *Gong* (Ministry of Works). These were responsible for various administrative affairs, such as personnel, finance and civil affairs, education and rituals, military administration, judicial administration and review of major cases, and water conservancy and construction. They assisted the head officer of the *Shangshu* Department in forming the highest administrative executive body of the state and in exercising the administrative power of the state.

The central government of the Tang Dynasty also had consultant positions, which had a high status but no real power, such as the three *shi* (tutors, namely *Taishi*, *Taifu*, and *Taibao*) and three *gong* (excellencies; namely *Taiwei*, *Situ*, and *Sikong*). These are high advisory positions without real power. Nine *si* (court) were established: *Taichangsi* (in charge of sacrifice affairs), *Guanglusi* (in charge of daily affairs in the imperial court), *Weiyusi* (in charge of guarding the imperial court), *Zongzhengsi* (in charge of the affairs of the royal family), *Taipusi* (in charge of the traveling affairs of the emperor, especially goods in transit and horses), *Dalisi* (in charge of judicial affairs), *Honglusi* (in charge of the affairs of foreign envoys), *Sinongsi* (in charge of revenue, agriculture, and money), and *Taifusi* (in charge of trade and accounting). There were also five *jian* (supervisory body): *Guozijian* (in charge of educational affairs), *Shaofujian* (in charge of the expenses of the imperial court), *Jiangzuojian* (in charge of engineering), *Junqijian* (in charge of production and repair of weapons), and *Dushuijian* (in charge of water conservancy and river transportation). The nine *si* were equivalent to the nine ministers of the Han Dynasty, but their status declined because of the greater power of the six ministries. The five *jian* became subordinate agencies to the six ministries.

2.4.2 Local Administrative System

The local administration system in China was formally developed with the establishment of the county system in Qin. At the beginning of the Tang Dynasty, the state was divided into ten *dao* (circuit). Each province had inspectors, such as *anchashi* and *guanchashi* (supervisory officials), which were comparable to *cishi* (inspector) of the Han Dynasty. In the provinces, there was *zhou* or *jun* (prefecture). Under *zhou* or *jun* was *xian* (county). These constituted a quasi-three-tier system.

The local administrative system of the Tang Dynasty can be observed from two aspects. The first is the general system, i.e., *dao, zhou, jun,* and *xian. Dao* was the highest local division, the head of which was *xunanshi* (the name of the position was changed repeatedly later). The head of *zhou* was named *cishi,* and the head of *jun* was named *taishou.* The head of *xian* was named *xianling*. The second is the special systems. For example, *jiedushi* (*jinglveshi* [governor]), *dudufu* (military agency), and *duhufu* (inspector agency) were set up at the borders. A *zhaotaoshi* (military official) was appointed to command troops, and an *anfushi* (official for comforting people) was set up when there was a famine. A *xuanweishi* (consolation envoy) was sent when fiefdoms or vassal states had disagreements. A *zhuanyunshi* (official for transporting grain) was in charge of the transportation of grain, and a *nongshi* (official for agriculture) was established to encourage farming and textiles.

2.4.3 Law on Official Management

Selection and Appointment of Officials

The main method of selecting officials in the Tang Dynasty was through the imperial examination. The so-called *keju* (imperial examination) means "setting up examinations of different subjects to select from the scholar," which began in the Sui Dynasty. In the Tang Dynasty, there were a number of subjects, such as *xiucai, mingjing, jinshi, mingfa, mingshu, mingsuan, wuju* (examination of martial skills), *daoju* (examination of Daoism), and *tongziju* (examination for the underage). The examinations were divided into three levels, namely, examinations at the provincial level, central level, and imperial court level.

Examinations for Officials

In the Tang Dynasty, officials were assessed once a year by the head of their department or by the head officials of the local prefectures and counties. Every four years, a major assessment was conducted, with officials below the fourth rank being examined by the Division of Examination of the Ministry of Personnel and officials above the third rank being examined by the emperor himself. The assessment was characterized by the refinement of the standards using the so-called method of "four standards of good and twenty-seven standards of best." Another characteristic of the assessment in the Tang Dynasty was that strict standards were adopted and few people were considered the best.

2.4.4 Administrative Supervision System

In addition to the assessment and supervision of officials conducted by the Ministry of Personnel, there was a special organ, *Yushitai* (censorate), which exercised the power of administrative supervision in the Tang Dynasty. The officials of *Yushitai*, known as the *tai* officials, were the main team that strengthened the management of officials. On the basis of the experience of the previous dynasties, the Tang Dynasty had a more complete supervisory body. Its functions included the following: first, exercising the power of administrative supervision, which was equivalent to the present Ministry of Supervision; second, exercising the power of legal supervision, which was equivalent to the present Procuratorate. The highest official of *Yushitai* was the *yushi dafu*, whose status was second only to the prime ministers. The subdivisions of *Yushitai* included *taiyuan*, *dianyuan*, and *chayuan*. *Taiyuan* mainly supervised the civil and military officials in the imperial court and participated in hearing important cases. *Dianyuan* mainly supervised the court rituals and courtesy of the officials. *Chayuan* mainly visited the prefectures and counties and supervised the local officials performing their duties. The three divisions had their own duties and cooperated with each other in assisting the *yushi dafu* in exercising the power of supervision.

Emperor Taizong of Tang knew that the monarch's decisions were of great importance, and to reduce mistakes, he set up the *Menxia* department to hold the power of refutation. In addition, he set up special admonishers, including the left and right *jianyi dafu* (counseling officials), the left and right *shiyi* (proposer), and the left and right *buque* (adviser). They supervised the decision-makers and executors of the state, and sometimes, they could even advise and criticize the emperor. This was a check mechanism on the supreme power in the monarchical state, which was conducive to the healthy development of society.

2.5 Judicial, Litigation, and Trial Systems

2.5.1 Judicial Organs

Systematization of the Central Judicial Organs in the Tang Dynasty

In the Tang Dynasty, the judicial system consisted of three departments: *Shangshu Xingbu* (the Ministry of Punishment), *Yushitai*, and *Dalisi*. The emergence of this system broke the tradition since the Qin and Han Dynasties that *Tingwei*, i.e., *Dali* (the highest judicial officer), solely dominated the central judiciary. This also changed the tradition since the Sui Dynasty that the two departments, namely, the Ministry of Punishment and *Dalisi*, were in charge of law enforcement. The central judicial power was divided into three. This development of judicial institutions exerted great influence on the *fengjian* judiciary in later generations (You, 2003, 546). Among the central judicial organs, *Dalisi* was directly responsible for judgment and punishment,

Yushitai was responsible for administrative litigation, and the Ministry of Punishment was only responsible for legal and judicial review.

In the Tang Dynasty, *dalisi qing* (Head Officer of *Dalisi*), *xingbu shangshu* (Minister of Punishment), and *yushi zhongcheng* (Head Officer of *Yushitai*) were jointly responsible for the trial of major cases, which was called "judgment of the three ministers." It created the system of joint trial by the "three judicial departments" that was inherited by later generations. The emperor also often ordered nonjudicial organs to participate in the trial according to the facts of the case.

The division of the central judiciary into three was developed in the Tang Dynasty so that the three could check and balance each other and so that judicial effectiveness could be strengthened. In fact, under the autocratic system, the emperors had the supreme power to judge, review, and remit. This division also reflected the strengthening of the emperor's control over the judiciary.

Local Judicial Institutions in the Tang Dynasty

Xianling (magistrates of the counties, the lowest-level officials), *cishi* (governors of the prefectures), and judicial officials in *dudufu* (the higher-level officials) were all under the supervision of the central imperial supervising officials. Lower than the county level, there were *lizheng*, *fangzheng*, and *cunzheng* (i.e., township officials in the Tang Dynasty). These vacancies were filled by smart and competent people in the autonomous groups. Most civil lawsuits were judged by these township officials. If they failed to provide a solution, *xianling* would have to review the case. By contrast, the punishment in criminal lawsuits was directly decided by county-level officials. If someone directly brought a criminal case before prefectural authorities without going through county-level authority, it was called transgression. The person who brought the lawsuit and the person who received the lawsuit were both guilty. All criminals should be investigated and sentenced by officials in the county where the crime occurred.

2.5.2 Litigation and Trial System

Litigation System

The Tang Dynasty had comprehensive provisions for the filing of lawsuits. There were two types of lawsuits in the Tang Dynasty. The first type was filed by the supervisory organs or officials at all levels to report crimes to the government, which was called *juhe* (impeachment). It was similar to the modern public prosecution. These crimes should be reported, and if they were not reported or were not reported on time, the related officials would be criminally liable. The second type was brought to the governments by the parties or relatives, that is, private prosecution in modern times. However, for some criminal cases, there was a mandatory obligation to denounce. For example, "those who know about *moufan* (rebellion) and *dani* (great sedition) must confidentially report to the nearby governments; those who do not report will be hanged." If a relative was denounced, he was exempted from the collective punishment.

The civil litigation system was also developed in the Tang Dynasty. The steps, methods, and procedures for civil litigation began to be standardized. In the Tang Dynasty, there were official positions of *sihu canjunshi* (counselors on household affairs) in the prefectures and *hucao canjunshi* (counselors on household affairs) in border governments, which served as trial bodies for civil cases. Civil lawsuits were also handled by county-level administrative agencies. According to the principle of territoriality, criminal lawsuits were under the jurisdiction of the county where the crime was committed, whereas civil lawsuits were under the jurisdiction of the county where the lawsuit was received, i.e., the plaintiff's location (Li, 2012, 8). In addition, the jurisdiction of civil and criminal lawsuits in the Tang Dynasty was differentiated. *Sihuzuo* (household affairs officers) was responsible for civil litigation, *sifazuo* (judicial officers) was responsible for criminal litigation, and *xianwei* (the county lieutenant) was the superior officer of *sihuzuo* and *sifazuo*. In the Tang Dynasty, civil lawsuits were conducted on a self-representation basis, with bottom-up proceedings and with the county being the first level of trial. Most of the civil lawsuits were first tried by *xianwei* and finally decided by *xiancheng* (county deputy) or *xianling* (county magistrate).

Trial System

The trial system in the Tang Dynasty was relatively complete. To ensure the impartiality of trials, the Tang Dynasty further improved the recusal of trials, i.e., "the system of change." In the trial, the judge was required to "question in person" and "judge according to the pleadings." Matters that were not included in the pleadings should not be pursued. However, if the criminal was reported by someone or the judge found other crimes committed by him, this principle would not apply. Judicial officials needed to make judgments and penalties according to the law.

The Tang Dynasty had strict rules for appeals. Civil cases (including minor criminal cases) were mostly mediated before the trial in the Tang Dynasty. *Xianglao* (elderly wise men in the town), *lizheng* (chief of the town), *cunzheng* (chief of the village), and *fangzheng* (chief of the neighborhood) performed the function of mediating civil disputes that occurred in the area so that the civil disputes were resolved before litigation through mediation. After receiving a case, the judicial officials in the county could also settle the case by mediation.

In the Tang Dynasty, the death penalty system was characterized by a "three-time report" and "five-time report," but a one-time report was sufficient for felonies worse than parricide as well as for cases in which slaves or servants killed their masters.

In summary, as Zhang Zhongqiu argued, the methods for recording statutes, codification, institutionalization, and development of procedures of the traditional Chinese judicial system do reflect the civilized nature of the traditional Chinese judicature. First, as far as the statutes and codes of the traditional Chinese judicial system are concerned, we know that the judicature is a product of human dispute resolution and that the judicial system is an institutionalization of people's dispute resolution through the judiciary. Therefore, the emergence of the judicial system and the form it takes are a manifestation of human civilization in the culture of the judicial system. The judicial system in traditional China was statutory and codified early in history. Moreover, it has been uninterrupted and consistent for thousands of years. It is the only one of its kind in the history of human judicial culture. Second, regarding the institutions and procedures of the traditional Chinese judicial system, we can say that they began at the same time that the traditional Chinese judicial system became statutory and codified (Zhang, 2016).

References

Fan, Z., & Jingliang, C. (Eds.). (2007). *History of Chinese Legal System*. Peking University Press.
He, Q. (2006). *History of Chinese Law* (Vol.1). Law Press China.
Hu, X. (2014). A Study of the Structure of Ancient Chinese Forms of Law. *Northern Legal Science, 3*, 131–149.
Li, Q. (2012). *Research on Archives and Civil Litigation System in the Qing Dynasty*. China University of Political Science and Law Press.
Li, Y. (2004). Research on the Legal System in the Tang Dynasty. *The Jurist, 5*, 45–59.
Li, Y. (2011). A Summary of the Forms of Law in the Tang Dynasty. In Y. Yang (Ed.), *Research on the Forms of Law in Ancient China*. Social Sciences Academic Press.
Liu, Y. (2006). The Evolution of the Status and Structure of Land Ownership in the Tang Dynasty. *Journal of Shandong University, 2*, 73–80.
Ma, X. (1987). Evolution of "Ge" and Its Meaning. *Journal of Peking University (Philosophy and Social Sciences), 3*, 112–120.
Naito, K. (2003). The Implementation of Tang Liu Dian. In Y. Yang, & M. Okano (Eds.), *The History of Chinese Legal System—Volume 2 of Part C—Selected Translation of Japanese Scholars' Research on the History of Chinese Legal System—The Wei, Jin, Southern and Northern, Sui and Tang Dynasties*. China Social Sciences Press.
Niida, N. (1991). *Supplementary Study on the History of Chinese Legal System*. University of Tokyo Press.
Niida, N. (2011). *The History of Chinese Legal System* (F. Mou, Trans.). Shanghai Classics Publishing House.
Okumura, I. (2003). A Study of Da Tang Liu Dian. In Y. Yang, & M. Okano (Eds.), *The History of Chinese Legal System—Volume 2 of Part C— Selected Translation of Japanese Scholars' Research on the History of Chinese Legal System—The Wei, Jin, Southern and Northern, Sui and Tang Dynasties*. China Social Sciences Press.
Pu, J. (1982). Discussion on the Date of the Production of Tang Lv Shu Yi. In *Legal History Series*. China Social Sciences Press.
Qian, D., & Yusheng, L. (1989). Discussion on the Nature of Tang Liu Dian. *Social Sciences in China, 6*, 189–204.
Qian, D. (1996a). Discussion on the Legal System in the Tang Dynasty and the Nature of Tang Liu Dian Again. In D. Qian, *Research on Tang Lv and the Legal System in the Tang Dynasty*. Nanjing University Press.
Qian, D. (1996b). Tang Liu Dian is Not an Administrative Code—Reply to Mr. Ning Zhixin. *Social Sciences in China, 6*, 88–92.

Qian, Y. (1987). A Preliminary Discussion on the Evolvement of the Form of Law "Ge" from the Qin and Han Dynasties to the Sui Dynasty. *Quarterly Journal of Shanghai Academy of Social Sciences, 2*, 85–92.

Qu, C. (2007). Discussion on the Status of Song Law in the Chinese Legal Family. In Z. Zhang, (Ed.), *Proceedings of the International Academic Conference on the Chinese Legal Family*. China University of Political Science and Law Press.

Wu, J. (2003). Some Issues in the Study of Tang Lv. In *Editorial Board of Research on the History of Law, Editorial Board of China-Japan Cultural Exchange Series, A New Probe into the History of Chinese and Foreign Laws*. Shanxi People's Publishing House.

Xu, D. (1947). *Tang Lv Tong Lun* (General Discussion on Tang Lv, 唐律通论). Zhonghua Book Company.

Xu, Z. (1998). Comments on the Research Concerning the Legal System in the Tang Dynasty and Others. *Law and Social Development, 5*, 13–20.

Yang, Y. (2002). A Major Misunderstanding in the Study of the Chinese Legal Family—Questioning the Doctrine of "Integration of All Laws and No Differentiation of Civil and Criminal Laws". *Social Sciences in China, 6*, 78–94+206.

You, S. (2003). Key Points in Textual Research on Legal Systems in the Sui and Tang Dynasties. In Y. Yang, & S. You (Eds.), *Research on Chinese Legal System—Volume 4 of Part 1—Research on Legal Systems of Past Dynasties—Sui and Tang*. China Social Sciences Press.

Zhang, J. (1984). Re-discussion on Several Issues of the Chinese Legal Family. *Journal of CUPL, 2*, 6–16.

Zhang, J. (2013a). *The History of Chinese Legal Culture* (Volume on the Ancient Times). Law Press· China.

Zhang, Z. (2013b). Why Tang Lv Shu Yi is an Excellent Code. *Tribune of Political Science and Law, 3*, 121–126.

Zhang, Z. (2016). Traditional Chinese Judicial Civilization and Its Reference. *Law and Social Development, 4*, 81–89.

Zhangsun, W. (2008 photocopy version). Tang Lv Shu Yi: Za Lv (Commentary on Tang Code: Other Laws, 唐律疏议·杂律). In *Si Ku Quan Shu* (四库全书) (Book 672). Taiwan Commercial Press.

Chapter 4
Chinese Legal Family in Other Countries

1 Japanese Law

It is well known that traditional Chinese law has had a profound influence on Japanese law, and the existence of this influence provides us with richer material for understanding the inheritance and evolution of the traditional Chinese and Japanese legal systems. For example, Japan adopted the laws of the Sui and Tang Dynasties in China, which transformed its society and legal system. The legal historical materials handed down through adoption also provide a complementary perspective to modern people for understanding Chinese law in the past.

When Japan inherited Chinese law and its related ideas and institutions, it did not simply imitate them but made trade-offs and eventually developed a legal system of its own. During this process, the form of law and its effects were closely related to the expression of state power and the political environment of that country.

In ancient times, there were domineering powerful nobles at home and a gradually increasing threat of Silla abroad. The nominal supreme rulers thus turned their attention to the increasingly powerful China, hoping to establish a similarly centralized state. With the cultural dissemination of the envoys sent to Sui and Tang and a series of political preparations, the rulers began to make drastic reforms toward the goal of "the way of being emperor lasts forever." The reforms, which lasted for nearly a century, finally bore fruit in the early eighth century with the *Taiho Code* and the *Yoro Code*. They completely changed the situation in Japan, where powerful aristocrats had previously been in control of the court, and established a centralized state similar to the Tang Dynasty in terms of bureaucratic establishment and legal system. Moreover, in the adopted legal system, not only Lv and Ling were adopted, but also other forms of law, such as Ge and Shi, were inevitably adopted. Thus, a comprehensive system of Lv, Ling, Ge, and Shi was created. Although Lv and Ling served as the basic legal codes, the newly compiled Ge and Shi were adapted to the new political and social changes. There is no doubt that traditional Chinese legal thought profoundly influenced Japan during this period. However, as many scholars

Q. He et al., *Chinese Legal Family*, https://doi.org/10.1007/978-981-96-6522-8_4

have shown, although it can be said that Japan fully adopted the legal system of Lv, Ling, Ge, and Shi in the Tang Dynasty, it was not directly transplanted without adjustment. Instead, Japan made adaptations based on a thorough consideration of the legal provisions and the local conditions. It was because of this careful work that the legal system of Lv, Ling, Ge, and Shi, which was created and developed in China, became integrated into the political and social framework of Japan in ancient times.

However, political and social changes always lead to changes in the law. In medieval Japan, the rise of samurai power led to Japan's entry into an era wherein the aristocratic society centered on the emperors coexisted with the shogunate. Because the shogunate was more powerful than the aristocracy, it obtained part of the legal power that originally belonged to the aristocracy. In addition, because the Kamakura shogunate was established with the support and cooperation of many self-reliant local lords, the shogunate had to compromise with the local power and the local estates were given a part of the legal power within their territories. This political division led to changes in the form of law and its effect. The discussion on the laws of the Middle Ages had to be divided into three parts, namely, laws for the courtiers, the Honjo law (laws by the proprietor of the manor), and laws for the military houses. Although they had some parts in common, they differed greatly because of their different philosophies and interests.

It was inevitable that the system of Lv, Ling, Ge, and Shi that were adopted from the previous period changed during this period. The political foundation supporting the legal system was a strong centralized system, and that of the Middle Ages was characterized by decentralization. Thus, it became apparently impossible, and the Ritsuryo system established by the rulers in the previous period inevitably began to decline. However, our exploration does not stop here. The "arbitrary" interpretation of the law by *Myobo Hakase* in the cases showed that Lv and Ling were still regarded as the basis for adjudication during this time. More importantly, by examining the forms of law of the shogunate, we can see that after inheriting Chinese law in the previous period, Japan had already mastered and had become accustomed to the forms of law of the Ritsuryo system and the logic of making Lv, Ling, Ge, and Shi in traditional China reborn within the samurai law. This was manifested in the formulation of Shikimoku and additional Shikimoku. Accompanied by the changes in Japanese society and politics, the Ritsuryo system extended itself into the legal systems of Japan's emerging political forces.

In the early modern ages, as Shiro Ishii and Takeshi Mizubayashi pointed out, the small self-sustaining powers of the Middle Ages had largely disintegrated, and a centralized state centered on the monarch (shogun) was established (Ishii, 1966, 42).[1] At that time, the "law" was the orders of the monarch, as revealed by the statement, "human sentiments prevail over unreasonableness, law prevails over human sentiments, power prevails over law, and the emperor prevails over power." The "law" here is the same as the meaning of "law" in traditional China. In this regard, we can now divide the history of Japan's adoption of Chinese law into three stages:

[1] See the same as *The National Life of Japanese* (1986, Tokyo: University of Tokyo Press, 167) and Mizubayashi (1977).

the initial adoption of the Chinese legal system in ancient times (adoption of legal text), the integration of the Ritsuryo system and the samurai law in the Middle Ages, and the absorption of the Ritsuryo system by the samurai legal system (substantive adoption). In the final stage of substantive adoption, although Japanese laws were different from the original Tang (Ming) laws in terms of specific provisions and even guiding ideas, the meaning of "law" at that time was the same, i.e., the orders of the monarch.

However, it should be noted that although the centralized state was established, the legal power that had been scattered in the Middle Ages was unified in the early modern ages. The *hans* in the early modern ages could still be seen as small states with their own military, police, judicial, legislative, and taxing powers, thus giving rise to a dual structure of "law" consisting of orders from the central emperors and orders from local lords. The law that should be applied was determined by the specific relationship between the central and local levels. The problem of the general applicability of the law was not solved until the modern era.

In his discussion of the modernization of law, Hideaki Ishikawa proposed three elements of the modernization of law. Although this paper is not about the modernization of law from the perspective of time, it is useful to apply his theory in analyzing the influence of traditional Chinese law on Japanese law from the perspective of legal transplantation. Here we will first explain some of the key concepts used by Ishikawa. According to his definition, there is a "legal order" in a state. Under the legal order, there is a "legal system" (hereinafter referred to as ls) and a "legal base" (hereinafter referred to as lb). The "legal system" is a collection of substantive laws, whereas the "legal base" is a collection of legal concepts, legal consciousness, and even social customs. The "legal system" and "legal base" constitute what we call the "legal culture" (hereinafter referred to as lc).

On the basis of these definitions, Ishikawa cited three types of modernization of law. One is the ideal type, which is characterized by the fusion of indigenous law (hereinafter referred to as iL) and modern law (hereinafter referred to as mL) to produce a new legal culture, i.e., iL (lc) + mL (lc) → newL (lc). This style can evolve into iL (ls.lb) + mL (ls.lb) → newL (ls.lb). The second type is called the "strategic arrangement of law." This can be regarded as a transition to the first type, but Ishikawa understood it as a separate type with different characteristics from the first type. The formula is iL (lc) + mL (lc) → iL (lc) + mL (lc), i.e., a state in which the inherent legal culture and the modern legal culture coexist. The third type was named by Ishikawa as the "disguised modernization of law." The formula for this is iL (lc) + mL (lc) → new or mls, ilb, and a new "legal system" is created, but the old legal base continues to exist (Ishikawa, 2013).

Applying this three-element formula to the transplantation of law from one country to another, the adoption of Chinese law in Japan in the last century manifested the third type, i.e., the adoption of "legal systems" and the preservation of the "legal base." The incorporation of the system of Lv, Ling, Ge, and Shi, which was represented by the *Taiho Code* and the *Yoro Code*, seemed to be the full-scale flourishing of traditional Chinese law in Japan. However, from the perspective of legal concepts, consciousness, and the form of rule that supported the operation of the law, the adoption had yet to be completed.

In the Middle Ages, the adoption of Lv, Ling, Ge, and Shi seemed to have come to a standstill, and the national legal power was again divided, making the Ritsuryo system appear to be in a weakened state. However, the logic of Lv, Ling, Ge, and Shi had been accepted by Japan by this time. The new legal culture was being formed while simultaneously coexisting with the inherent legal culture. It became the second type of coexistence, as defined by Ishikawa.

In the early modern period, this adoption approached the first type, the so-called ideal state. It was at this stage that Japan really completed (almost completed) its adoption of traditional Chinese law, and a new "law" of its own emerged after the adoption. This process thus answers the question raised in the preface of this book, that is, what were the different characteristics of China and Japan during the period of Western law spreading to the East? The characteristics are rooted in Japanese indigenous law and the new legal culture (newL) that emerged from the adoption of traditional Chinese law. Japanese law was not the same as the traditional Chinese law that was once inherited.

In short, whether it is formal survival or substantive regeneration and whether it is the unification of the meaning of "law" or the creation of a new "law," the various discussions point to the same conclusion: the influence of traditional Chinese law on Japan is far-reaching, continuous, and gradual. As mentioned earlier, even in the Middle Ages, a period when the Ritsuryo system was in decline instead of a full adoption in the previous age, the Ritsuryo system continued to function effectively in society. In the Edo period of the early modern age, in the laws for the courtiers, the court still affirmed the use of traditional official positions and stipulated that "the punishment may be imposed in accordance with *Mingli* Lv."[2]

Moreover, the edicts issued in the 17th year of the Genroku Era (1704) and even in the 7th year of the Kaei Era (1854) at the end of the shogunate stated that "those who committed the eight crimes of abuse, intentional killing, conspiracy to murder, unauthorized coining, and robbery and theft cannot be exempted by the regular amnesty." These crimes were exactly the crimes stipulated in the text of Lv. This demonstrates that the effect of Lv was not abolished until the end of the shogunate.[3] Even after the Meiji Restoration, when Japan developed into a constitutional state, traditional Chinese law can still be found in the legislation. Discussing their content is certainly of great significance for understanding the establishment of the contemporary Japanese legal system.

---

[2] See *Research on Tokugawa Prohibitions*, Sobun Sha, 1959.

[3] *Hengyokushuu* collected by the Japanese Archives and Mausolea Department of the Imperial Household Agency (458–1, Mariner Volume), *Thoughts Before Sleeping*, "*Imperial Edict on the Change of the Designation to Ansei*," and *Outline of Historical Material on the Meiji Restoration*. Both of these are as cited in Yoshitaka (2009, 2–6). In addition, in the early modern ages, the direct application of Lv and Ling was limited to the imperial court. Outside the imperial court, the shogunate applied the shogunate law and the *han* applied the law adopted in that *han* in principle. However, in many cases, Lv and Ling were used as references. See Yoshitaka (2009, 7–8).

2 Korean Law

The transplantation of the Chinese legal system in the Korean Peninsula began in the era when states were established. From the earliest "eight forbidden laws" to the partial absorption of the Tang institutions during the unification of Silla, then later to the transformation and selective transplantation of the Tang Law by Goryeo, and finally, to the complete application of *Da Ming Lv*, Korea went through an extremely complicated path of legal transplantation for more than 2,000 years. The complexity it presents is extremely rare. However, for a variety of reasons, there is still a lack of basic understanding and attention to this process, which has led to insufficient research results.

The relationship between the legal system of the ancient peninsula and Chinese law is a process from "native customs" to "Chinese institutions." Although there were twists and turns during the long historical period, the general trend was that the "Sinicization" movement was deepened and broadened. In the Joseon Dynasty, *Da Ming Lv* was completely applied, and the process of "Sinicization" was completed. However, this does not mean that the peninsula's "native customs" disappeared. Instead, they were incorporated into the legal system, which seemed completely Sinicized in a more subtle way, resulting in a legal culture with a strong sense of ethics that is different from that of China in the peninsular.

Observing the Sinicization of the legal system in the peninsula over the millennia, before the Three Kingdoms period (unknown–918), the limited amount of historical material that has been preserved has led to a lot of ambiguities and confusion. For example, there are different opinions regarding the so-called "eight articles of prohibition" in ancient Korea. The author believes that they are probably distorted records created by people in the Han Dynasty based on their own legal reality and legal concepts, which were attached to the inherent customary laws of ancient Korean society.

In the four commanderies of the Han period, because of the influx of mainlanders that mainly consisted of merchants and officials, the social relations in the peninsula became increasingly complex. The simple customary laws were no longer sufficient to cope with the new situation, so the local governments intermittently issued some single-line written decrees. The law demonstrated a certain degree of Sinicization. After the demise of the four commanderies of the Han, local customary laws became the dominant legal norms again, and the "native customs" overwhelmed the "Sinicized institutions."

During the Three Kingdoms period, Goguryeo absorbed some elements of Chinese law left over from the four commanderies of the Han period. During the Sui and Tang Dynasties, the cultural "Sinicization" of Goguryeo was accelerated to a certain extent, but the legal system was still dominated by native customs. From the Northern and Southern Dynasties to the Sui and Tang Dynasties, Baekje had frequent interactions with the Chinese dynasties, and the influence of Chinese culture has penetrated to the level of its customs. However, this trend was not evident in the legal system, which was still dominated by the country's indigenous laws. The reason for such a situation is probably related to the legal lag.

Silla was the most backward of the three kingdoms. Its written law was mainly the codification of its own customary law, and Chinese law had little influence on it. In the Unified Silla period, although the Tang Dynasty legal system had some influence on the peninsula's legal system, the degree of "Sinicization" in Silla was not high and "native customs" were still the main focus.

The transplantation of the Chinese legal system by the Goryeo Dynasty went through an extremely tortuous process, and very complicated factors underlay this tortuous progress. The most important one was the inconsistency between the interests of the Goryeo royal power and the nobility, and the indigenous legal system, such as "native customs," was the institutional support of the noble society. To strengthen the autocracy, the rulers tried to introduce the Chinese system, which was based on the establishment and maintenance of the monarchy. However, it was resisted by the aristocracy, which led to the controversy between "Sinicization" and "native customs."

During the reign of Seongjong of Joseon, a compromise was reached between the royal power and the noble group. To respect the vested interests of the noble group, the royal power was able to transplant the Chinese system on a larger scale, but this also brought about a serious after-effect. In particular, the transplanted "Chinese system" had to accommodate the "native customs." Therefore, the Goryeo people made a large-scale and comprehensive reshaping of the system transplanted from China so that the Goryeo legal system showed a pattern of coexistence of the "Chinese institutions" and the "native customs."

At the very beginning of the Joseon Dynasty, it adopted a policy of comprehensive Sinicization. It declared that *Da Ming Lv* was adopted as its basic criminal code and popularized and promoted it in various ways to encourage its application and improve its status. In this process, the introduction of Chinese legal works was an extremely important aspect. By the time of Seonjo of Joseon (1567–1608), the task of full Sinicization was completed, and *Da Ming Lv* was deeply integrated into the society of the peninsula. However, after the destruction of the Ming Dynasty, the status of *Da Ming Lv* declined as the Koreans considered China to have been occupied by barbarians, and they believed that the flaws of Ming culture itself were a major cause of this outcome.[4] However, Korea was influenced by the centuries-old "Sinicization" policy and the strong belief in being a "Little China," and the cultural orthodoxy that strongly emphasized the "distinction between Chinese and foreigners" became mainstream in the late Joseon Dynasty. Although some fluctuations were experienced, the above reasons led to the consolidation of the status of *Da Ming Lv*, which is a symbol of respecting Chinese Zhou and Ming Dynasties and Chinese institutions and culture, from the time of Yeongjo of Joseon (1724–1776).[5] *Da Ming Lv* formed a complementary relationship with the Joseon Dynasty's own codes, such

---

[4] For a specific analysis of this issue, see Zhang (2011a, 2011b).

[5] For a specific analysis of this issue, see Zhang (2011a, 2011b, 61–73).

as the *Kyongguk taejon* (*Great Code of National Governance*) and the *Sok Daejeon* (*Supplement Great Code*), and became dominant in this complementary relationship.

In short, over a period of more than 2,000 years, the transplantation of the traditional Chinese legal system to the Korean Peninsula was an extremely tortuous process, with immensely complex contradictions and conflicts at various levels due to social structures, interest groups, power patterns, cultural differences, ideologies, and others. The complexity of this process is very rare. A more comprehensive and systematic comparative study of this overall history and complexity is not only of academic significance but also of practical value. It can encourage us to further consider certain realistic issues that we must face and provides us with a certain degree of reference for the construction of the current legal system.

3 Vietnamese Law

Vietnam is closely intertwined with China in terms of history and culture. Vietnamese historical records refer to themselves as the descendants of Shennong.[6] From the Qin and Han Dynasties to the beginning of the Song Dynasty, for most of the time, Vietnam was a dependency of the Chinese *fengjian* Dynasties, which Vietnamese historians called the "Era of Northern Domination." In 968, the Dinh Dynasty was established by Dinh Bo Linh, and Vietnam broke away from the direct rule of China and became an independent *fengjian* monarchy.[7] After the Dinh Dynasty was established, Vietnam maintained a "suzerainty relationship" with the Chinese *fengjian* dynasties. As a vassal state of China, Vietnam paid tribute to the Chinese dynasties constantly. Vietnamese history records and laws were written in Chinese characters. When a new ruler came to power in Vietnam, he could only be considered a legitimate ruler if he was enthroned by the Chinese central government. Then, in 1885, the Qing government signed the Treaty of Tientsin with France and was forced to recognize Vietnam's independence. From then on, Vietnam was completely independent of China and became a French colony (Guo & Zhang, 2001, 644).

Because of the special relationship between China and Vietnam in history, the Chinese legal system had an important influence on the legal system of Vietnam. During the Sui and Tang Dynasties, Vietnam, as a county of China, directly applied

[6] Ngo (1968), (Vol. 1) 97–98. It records, "Kinh Duong Vuong, whose name was Loc Tuc, was a descendant of Shennong." It also records, "earlier, Emperor Ming, the great-grandson of Yen Emperor Shennong, had a son, Emperor Yi; then he toured to the south in Wuling and married with a female immortal. They had their son, Kinh Duong Vuong." See Dao (1976, 34). The legends about the origin of our nation are truly uncanny. Let's just keep it with doubts. See Tran (1992, 32). From King Duong Vuong to Hung Vuong, the 18th generation, there were 20 kings in all. The duration was from 2879 B.C. to 258 B.C. or a total of 2,622 years. If counting averages, every king reigned for 150 years. Although these kings lived in ancient times, it is difficult for so many people to live so long. It is clear from this that the events of the Hong Bang Era are not necessarily accurate.

[7] See Minh (1958, 52–53). In 968, Dinh Bo Linh swept away all the governors and established a unified state.

the laws of the Sui and Tang *fengjian* dynasties. The content of the law was based on Confucianism, and it defended *fengjian* ethics, imperial power, and noble privileges. The form of law was also a combination of laws, with the main focus on punishment. It had various characteristics of the Chinese Legal Family (Ma & Shi, 2012, 119).

Vietnam's legal history is poorly documented and poorly researched, which is probably related to its long history of war and underdevelopment. Vietnam did not have official history books until after the thirteenth century.

3.1 Influence of the Chinese Legal System on the Legal System of Vietnam in Its Early Years

Although there were few historical records in the early period after the founding of Vietnam, the characteristics of the legal system during the Ngo, Dinh, and the former Le Dynasties can be summarized from the scattered sources. In the early years of Vietnam, the state institutions were simple, the laws were not perfect, and the influence of Confucianism was small. The legal system reflected brutality and harshness. Because the legislation was relatively backward at that time, village community rituals and customs, i.e., communal customs, still played an extensive and important role in regulating social relations in addition to the laws of the court. These customary laws had a widespread effect in the village community and were used to regulate land, marriage, family, and various other issues. At that time, the villagers lived mainly according to these laws and were less subject to the dictates of the court laws.[8]

However, Vietnam had just broken away from the direct rule of the Chinese *fengjian* dynasty. Thus, their legal system embodied many characteristics of the Chinese Legal Family:

1. The form of law was heavily influenced by the legal system of the Chinese *fengjian* dynasty, including Lv, Zhao, and Ling. Although there are no preserved written legal documents of that time, Vietnam must have had written laws then because the Vietnamese people began to accept Chinese characters from the Era of Northern Domination, and the kings, noblemen, monks, and Confucians of that time, all knew Chinese characters. There are also records of forms of law in historical books; for example, in *A Complete History of Great Vietnam*, there are descriptions such as "making court etiquette," "promulgating policies and orders," "making Lv and Li," and "issuing edicts."
2. The kings and nobles enjoyed legal privileges. Influenced by the Chinese *fengjian* imperial system, the rulers of the Ngo, Dinh, and former Le Dynasties also conferred official titles through edicts and decrees so that the kings and nobles enjoyed legal privileges. The emperors gave official titles to their sons, some

[8] The ancient communal customs were a summary of the existing customs of the ancient Vietnamese villages, covering all aspects of ancient village life, and the state power made certain concessions to this form of village autonomy. See Dao (2004).

of whom were assigned to guard and govern important areas of the country. During that period, each emperor would crown several queens. Emperor Dinh Tien Hoang had five queens, Le Dai Hanh had five queens, and Le Long Dinh appointed four queens. This system continued until the Ly Dynasty.[9]

3.2 *Influence of the Chinese Legal System on the Legal System of Vietnam in the Stage of Consolidation and Development of the* Fengjian *Dynasty*

Regarding the influence of the Chinese legal system on Vietnam in this period, Yang Honglie regarded it as "the era of imitating the laws of the Tang and Song Dynasties" (Yang, 1999, 416). Phan Huy Chu noted that "observing the punishment law of the Ly and Tran Dynasties, the provisions were extremely detailed and exhaustive. At the time when the law was made, the rulers wanted to follow the institutions of the Tang and Song Dynasties, with careful consideration sometimes concerning the degree of strictness."[10] It is clear that the Vietnamese legal system then was deeply influenced by mainland China. The influence covered a very comprehensive range, from legal thought to specific laws.

First, the emperor had supreme judicial power. Similar to other members of the Chinese Legal Family, the Vietnamese emperor also enjoyed such judicial power at that time. This power could be delegated by the emperor to the crown prince thus: "In summer, the first day of the fourth lunar month, it was decreed that from then on, disputes and litigation among people would be assigned to King Kaihuang to make decisions and report to the emperor. Guangwu Palace is ordered to be the King's court to hear the suits" (Ngo et al. 1984–1986, 229).

Second, it was deeply influenced by Confucianism. Although there are different views on the characteristics of the Chinese Legal Family, they are not entirely different. Several features are commonly recognized, one of which is the influence of Confucianism. The law under the influence of Confucianism presented a range of hierarchies and privileges. Meanwhile, because Confucianism emphasizes the protection of the people and regards the people as the foundation of the state, it also pays more attention to the people, particularly the disadvantaged groups. This is reflected in the following historical material: "In the 11th lunar month, the emperor decreed that those over 70 and under 80 years old, and over 10 and under 15 years old, and those with physical disabilities, as well as those from the royal family, with great meritorious deeds, and close relatives of the emperor were allowed to be redeemed when they committed crimes, except if they committed the ten abominations" (Ngo et al. 1984–1986, 231).

---

[9] See Trường Đại học Luật Hà Nội, Giáo trình Lịch sử Nhà nước và Pháp luật Việt Nam, NXB Công an Nhân dân, năm 2009, Tr 35.

[10] "Punishment Law" in *Lich trieu hien chuong loai chi* (Chronicle of Charters in the Past Dynasties), quoted from Yang (1999, 420).

Third, all laws were combined, criminal law was emphasized, and civil law was overlooked. Under the Chinese Legal Family, although the law covered a wide range of contents, including criminal law, civil law, economic law, and various other aspects, criminal law occupied a large proportion. The name of the code of the Ly Dynasty was the *Punishment Book*. Its relationship with criminal law is clear at a glance. According to historical records, it mostly concerns criminal affairs. "At the beginning of the Ly Dynasty, suits were numerous and law officials were harsh. Penalties and punishments were abusively imposed. Emperor Ly Thai Tong ordered the Secretariat to make the law, take into account the application of the law at that time, set the categories, and detail the provisions; this was developed into a criminal law. It covered the trafficking of underage children, theft of state-owned cattle, adultery with others' wives and concubines, and robbery or theft of money, among others, and made rules for atonement and desertion. The provisions were strict and clear" (Ngo, 1911, 43). Moreover, according to Zhang Jinlian's statistics, most of the legal materials in *A Complete History of Great Vietnam* were related to criminal matters (Zhang, 2008).

3.3 Influence of the Chinese Legal System on the Legal System of Vietnam During the Heyday of the Fengjian *Kingdom*

3.3.1 Deepening of Confucian Legal Culture

After the establishment of the Later Le Dynasty, Le Thai To set up hundreds of official positions, established schools, and recruited scholars on the two subjects of *jingyi* (scripture) and *shifu* (poetry), which were refined and influenced by China (Zhang et al., 2008, 654). Because of the sharp class contradictions in the country, the peasants were dispersed, and the land was desolate, which led to serious damage to the *fengjian* economy. To stabilize the rule of the new dynasty and restore the *fengjian* hierarchy, in the field of culture and thought, the Le Dynasty learned the lesson of paying equal attention to the three religions in the Ly and Tran Dynasties and only respected Confucianism and advocated Neo-Confucianism instead. The official selection system and school system of the Le Dynasty were particularly influenced by the Ming Dynasty, and the setting up of subjects and selection of officials were based on Neo-Confucianism. The Later Le Dynasty set up Confucian temples all over the country to worship Confucius. In the capital, the National Academy of Confucianism was established to enable the talents among the commoners to study. In the provinces, schools were established, teachers were invited to teach Confucianism, and the imperial examinations centered on Confucianism were continued and improved. After Emperor Chengzu of Ming reclaimed Vietnam as a prefecture of China, schools were widely established. According to statistics, 161 schools were established in different provinces, prefectures, and counties, including 14 provincial, 34 prefectural, and 113 county-level schools (Minh, 1960, 107). Meanwhile, the political, legislative, and cultural educational policies centered on Confucianism were fully implemented. Emperor Le Thanh Tong promulgated the *Hong Duc Code*, which referred to the laws of the Sui and Tang Dynasties. He also formulated the *Twenty-four Rules of Discipline*, which advocated loyalty, filial piety, morality, and righteousness. It defined the relationship between fathers and sons, husbands and wives, mothers-in-law and daughters-in-law, men and women, teachers and apprentices, party members, military, and civilians, among others. Confucian ethics were used to determine the hierarchical and inferior relationship between family members, community members, and even society as a whole. He decreed that all people, whether officials or commoners, must follow the law, and those who violate it would be heavily punished.[11]

3.3.2 State Institutions and Bureaucratic Establishment Based on Those of the Song and Ming Dynasties

In the central governmental system, there were various types of officials. Civil officials included officials in the six *Bu* (Ministries), such as *shangshu* (minister) and *zuo/you shilang* (vice ministers); in the six *Ke* (Official Supervising Authorities), such as *jishizhong* (consultant) and other officials; in the six *Si* (Courts), such as *siqing* (head officer), *shaoqing* (vice officer), and *sicheng* (assistant officials); in *Dongge* (East Cabinet), such as *daxueshi* (grand expert) and *xueshi* (expert); in *Zhongshujian* (Secretariat), such as *zhongshu sheren* and *zhengzi huawen zhiguan* (secretaries); in *Tongzhengsi* (Office of Transmission), such as *tongzhengshi* (head officer) and *tongzhengfu* (vice officer); in *Yushitai* (censorate), such as *duyushi* (head officer), *fu duyushi* (vice officer), *quan duyushi* (general officer), and *tixing shisandao jiancha* (supervisor for local criminal affairs); in *Chasi* (Supervisory Office), such as *xianchashi* (supervisor) and *xiancha fushi* (vice supervisor); in divisions under the six ministries, such as *langzhong* (director) and *yuanwailang* (deputy director); and in *Waichuizhengsi* (Office for Promoting Policies), such as *chengzhengshi* (implementer), *canzheng*, and *canyi* (consultants). Military officials included officials in the five *Fu* (theater) of *dong* (east), *xi* (west), *nan* (south), *bei* (north), and *zhong* (central), such as *shufududu* (commander-in-chief), *zuo/you dudu* (deputy commander), *tongzhi*, and *quanshi* (assistant officials); in the two secret troops of *Jinyi* and *Jinwu*, such as *zhangwei duzhihuishi* (commander), *tongzhi*, and *jinshi* (assistant officials); in the three guard troops of *Shenwu*, *Xiaoli*, and *Dianqian*, such as *tidu* (commander), *candu* (deputy commander), *dujiandian* (commander), and *zuo/you jiandian* (deputy commander); and in the border armies, such as *zongbingshi* (commander-in-chief), *zongbing* (commander), *tongzhi*, and *jinshi* (assistant officials) (Yang, 2007). At the local level, in the early years of the Later Le Dynasty, the country was divided into five *Dao* (areas) of *dong* (east), *xi* (west), *nan* (south), *bei* (north), and *haixi* (west of the sea) to manage the registered military and civilians. Under *Dao*, there were officials at the level *of Lu* (region) and *Zhen* (district).

[11] See Phan (1821), quoted from Yuan (2009).

Region-level officials included *anfushi* (governor) and deputies. District-level officials included *xuanfushi* (or *zhenfushi*, governor). *Anfushi* was in charge of civil affairs, and *zhenfushi* was in charge of military affairs. Under *Lu*, there were *Zhou* (provinces), the head official of which was called *fangyushi*. Under *Zhou*, there were *Xian* (counties), the officials of which included *zhuanyunshi* (transport official) and *xunchashi* (inspector) (Lv, 1994).

3.3.3 Administrative Division System Modeled on the Ming Institutions

The administrative division system of the Le Dynasty was modeled on that of mainland China. The Le Dynasty changed the name of the first level administrative regions from "*Lu*" used in the Tran and Ho Dynasties to "*Fu*," and "Zhen" (town) to "*Zhilizhou*" (province directly under the emperor's management). At the second level, the original *Fu* and *Zhou* were changed to *Shuzhou* (province). The third-level administrative regions, *Xian*, remained unchanged. In the seventh year of the Quang Thuan Era during the reign of Le Thanh Tong (1466), Vietnam imitated the Ming institutions and divided the whole country into the following 12 *Thua Tuyen Dao*: Thanh Hoa, Thuan Hoa, Nghe An, Quic Oai, Thien Truong, Nam Sach, Bac Giang, Tuyen bang, Hung Quang, Hung Hua, Thai Nguyen, and Lang San. In the second year of the Hong Duc Era, Quang Nam was added as a *Dao*, making it a total of 13 *Thua Tuyen Dao*. In the Later Le Dynasty, the system of administrative district names was completely consistent with the provincial administration commission established by the Ming Dynasty (Ngo, 1968, vol. 10, 657).

3.3.4 Criminal Law System and Codification with the Characteristics of the Chinese Legal Family

Various laws were adopted by the Later Le Dynasty. According to existing data, there were 22 laws promulgated in the Later Li Dynasty (Ma & Shi, 2012, 124). The relatively complete ones included *The Le Code* (also known as the *Hong Duc Code*) and *Regulations on the Investigation of Litigation of the Le Dynasty*. Most of the laws adopted by the Later Le Dynasty were based on or referred to Chinese laws. For example, the style of *The Le Code* was generally similar to Tang Lv, which was divided into 12 chapters, namely, Mingli (general principles), Weijin (guard of palaces), Weizhi (violation of rules), Junzheng (military affairs), Huhun (family and marriage), Tianchan (land), Daozei (robbery and theft), Dousong (disputes and litigation), Zhawei (fraud and forgery), Zalv (miscellaneous laws), Buwang (pursuing and capture of criminals), and duanyu (adjudication).[12] However, there were some differences. *The Le Code* added an additional chapter on land. The chapter on Mingli stipulated ten abominations, five punishments, eight deliberations, and so on. However,

---

[12] Quoted from *The Le Code*, Volume I—Chapter of Mingli, handwritten copy collected in the Institute of Han-Nom Studies, Vietnam.

the legal system of the Later Le Dynasty also had unique features, such as the proliferation of litigation institutions, which demonstrated a trend of distinguishing procedural law from substantive law. For example, the *Regulations on the Investigation of Litigation of the Le Dynasty* contained a large number of detailed provisions concerning the litigation system of the Later Le Dynasty.

3.4 Influence of the Chinese Legal System on the Legal System of the Nguyen Dynasty in Vietnam

Regarding the relationship between the legal system of the Nguyen Dynasty and the Chinese legal system, Yang Honglie made the following statement: "The Nguyen Dynasty took the 'Ming and Qing laws' as the blueprint, ... from which it can be seen that the laws compiled by them were still mostly the same as *Da Ming Lv*, except the regulations learned from *Da Qing Lv Li* and the regulations of the Hong Duc Era of the Le Dynasty during the reign of Le Thanh Tong (the 6th year of the Chenghua Era during the reign of Emperor Xianzong of Ming, i.e., 1470)" (Yang, 1999, 458). In the following text, Yang, after describing the legal system of the Nguyen Dynasty almost one by one, compared this legal system with *Da Ming Lv* and *Da Qing Lv* to find the corresponding articles in them. It has been recognized by the academic community that the legal system of the Nguyen Dynasty in Vietnam was deeply influenced by the Chinese legal system.

First, Confucianism was institutionalized. As the main legal code of the Nguyen Dynasty, Confucianism was incorporated into *Hoang Viet Luat Le* (the *Laws of Imperial Viet*) from the basic provisions to the practical implementation. In fact, it was a collection of ideas on the rule of morality, the rule of law, ritual and punishment, and the institutionalization of Confucian rituals. Confucianism advocated the use of moral rules to establish and maintain the *fengjian* social order. Confucian rituals were reflected in the relationship between the emperor and ministers, husbands and wives, and parents and children. The relationship was between superior and inferior, in which ministers must be absolutely loyal to the emperor, wives must be loyal and righteous to their husbands, and children must respect their parents. *Hoang Viet Luat Le* maintained the *fengjian* ethics and Confucian etiquette through the systems of ten abominations, five punishments, eight deliberations, and seven grounds for the husband to cast off his wife and stipulated extremely severe punishments for behavior that violated the moral norms, such as loyalty to the emperor, filial piety, and chastity.

Second, the form of law had all of the characteristics of the Chinese Legal Family. The main code of the Nguyen Dynasty, *Hoang Viet Luat Le*, included laws on criminal, civil, marriage and family, and litigation affairs. It was a combination of laws and regulated legal relations in all areas of society. Other than codes, there were also *huidian* (rules on institutions). The Nguyen Dynasty had the largest number of *huidian* in Vietnam. Ling, Zhao, Zhi, Yu, Chi, Zhi, and Gao were all forms of law at that time.

Of course, Vietnam had its own special circumstances. Thus, when the Chinese legal system spread to Vietnam, some twists were inevitable and developed into features that deviated from the parent law. In her article published in 2012, Nguyen Thi Thu Thuy compared *Hoang Viet Luat Le* and *Da Qing Lv Li* and summarized many differences between them (Nguyen, 2012). In addition, during the Nguyen Dynasty, the status of females in the law was improved. Although the ideas of male superiority, three obedience and four virtues, and preference for sons over daughters were more common at that time, female rights were improved in terms of the legal provisions.[13]

References

Dao, D. A. (1976). *Ancient History of Vietnam.* The Commercial Press.

Dao, T. U. (2004). The Role of Ancient and Modern Communal Customs in Building the Rule of Law in Vietnam. (Ji, Jianwen trans.). *Dongyue Tribune, 4*, 57–66.

Guo, Z., & Zhang, X. (Eds.). (2001). *General History of Vietnam.* China Renmin University Press.

Hao, T. (2008). *Discussion on the Characteristics of the Legal System in Vietnam During the Nguyen Dynasty.* Master's Thesis, Southwest University of Political Science and Law.

Ishii, S. (1966). *A Study of the History of the Japanese State System I—Power and Land Ownership.* University of Tokyo Press.

Ishikawa, Hideaki. (2013). Three Elements in Modernization of Law. *Kagoshima University Journal of Legal Studies, 47*(2).

Lv, S. (1994). The Influence of the Institutional Culture of the Ming Dynasty on the Vietnamese Le Dynasty. *Collected Papers of History Studies, 1*, 44–48.

Ma, X., & Shi, T. (Eds.). (2012). *The Extraterritorial Influence of Chinese Traditional Legal Culture: Export and Reaction.* China Renmin University Press.

Minh, T. (1958). *History of Vietnam (First Draft).* (Fan, Hongke et al. trans.). SDX Joint Publishing Company.

Minh, T. (1960). *History of Vietnam* (Fan, Hongke, & Gu Lv trans.). SDX Joint Publishing Company.

Mizubayashi, T. (1977). Introduction to Research on Laws and National Institutions in Modern Ages I: Material on Kishū. *Journal of the National Academy, 90*(1/2), 25.

Ngo, G. D. (1911). *The Essence of the History of Viet for Middle Schools (Summer Collection).* Backy Institute for Political Studies.

Ngo, S. L. (1968). *A Complete History of Great Vietnam* (Volume 1, Side Stories: Records of Hong Bang+Volume 10, Records of Le). (edited and checked by Chen, Jinghe). Institute for Advanced Studies on Asia, The University of Tokyo.

Ngo, S. L. et al. (1984–1986 i.e., Showa 59–61). *A Complete History of Great Vietnam.* (edited and checked by Chen, Jinghe). Oriental Studies Document Center, Institute for Advanced Studies on Asia, The University of Tokyo.

Nguyen, T. T. T. (2012). The Similarities and Differences between *Hoang Viet Luat Le* of the Nguyen Dynasty of Vietnam and *Da Qing Lv Li*. *Jianghan Tribune, 4*, 127–130.

[13] "The scope of Vietnamese women's role was not strictly limited within the family; within the family, Vietnamese women did not take all orders from men; it was also significantly more equal in terms of marriage between men and women in Vietnam; Vietnamese women's inheritance rights were protected." See Hao (2008).

Phan, H. C. (1821). *Lich trieu hien chuong loai chi* (Chronicle of Charters in the Past Dynasties, 历朝宪章类志) (Volume 26: Etiquette).
The National Life of Japanese. (1986). Tokyo: University of Tokyo Press, 167.
Tran, T. K. (1992). *General History of Vietnam.* The Commercial Press.
Trường Đại học Luật Hà Nội, Giáo trình Lịch sử Nhà nước và Pháp luật Việt Nam, NXB Công an Nhân dân, năm 2009, Tr 35.
Yang, H. (1999). *The Influence of the Chinese Law in the East Asian Countries.* China University of Political Science and Law Press.
Yang, J. (2007). *Relations between the Ming Dynasty and the Later Le Dynasty of Vietnam.* Master's Thesis, Yunnan Normal University.
Yoshitaka, S. (2009). *From Ritsuryo System to Constitutional System.* Seibundo Shinkosha.
Yuan, J. (2009). *Research on the Cultural Exchange between China and Vietnam in the 15th and 16th Centuries.* Master's Thesis, Zhengzhou University.
Zhang, C. (2011a). A Preliminary Research on the Status of the Da Ming Lv in the Late Joseon Dynasty. *Korean Studies*, (Book 19), 61–73.
Zhang, C. (2011b). Research on the Shaking of the Status of Da Ming Lv in Korea after the Destruction of the Ming Dynasty: An Examination Centered Around the "Ritual Litigation." *Jinan Journal (Philosophy & Social Sciences), 6*, 148–156.
Zhang, J. (2008). Legal Materials in *A Complete History of Great Vietnam. Information and Research of Legal Literature*, 2.
Zhang, T. et al. (2008 photocopy version). Ming Shi: Annan Zhuan (Biography of Annan, 安南传). In *Si Ku Quan Shu* (Book 302). The Commercial Press.

Chapter 5
Disintegration of the Chinese Legal Family

1 General Theories

"The Chinese Legal Family is a treasure trove of Chinese legal history and has attracted considerable attention from Chinese legal history scholars. Since the beginning of the Republic of China period, there have been a large number of monographs and papers concentrating on the Chinese Legal Family. The scope of the study has covered almost all aspects of the Chinese Legal Family, such as the ideological basis, history, characteristics, formation time, reasons for the formation, and development stages" (Zhang, 2007a, 2007b, 1–73). In contrast to the abovementioned aspects of the Chinese Legal Family, "the disintegration of the Chinese Legal Family" has not attracted much interest and attention from the academic community.[1] However, the disintegration is one of the major issues of the Chinese Legal Family, and it is necessary for legal historians to study and elaborate on this issue in depth. In this part, we explore the disintegration of the Chinese Legal Family from the perspectives of the key time points of the collapse, which provides a new exploration of the causes and process of the disintegration and puts forward some ideas.

The original version of the chapter has been revised. A correction to this chapter can be found at https://doi.org/10.1007/978-981-96-6522-8_6

[1] "The disintegration of the Chinese Legal Family" is also an important part of the Chinese Legal Family, which generally includes the causes, process, and effects of the disintegration. Although there have been some studies that focus on the disintegration of the Chinese Legal Family, they all only briefly mention the causes of the disintegration, for example, Han and Zhao (1983), Zhang (1991), Zhang (1999), Li (1999), He and Kong (2005), Zhang (2007a, 2007b). However, there are very few works that specifically elaborate on the causes, timing, and process of the disintegration of the Chinese Legal Family. Even if the abovementioned research results are available, some scholars have an inappropriate understanding of the causes and timing of the disintegration, which will be evaluated in detail in the following section.

Q. He et al., *Chinese Legal Family*, https://doi.org/10.1007/978-981-96-6522-8_5

1.1 General Introduction

Before starting the discussion, it is necessary to clarify and define some concepts to unify understanding.

The first concept is the understanding of "the Chinese Legal Family." The concept of "the Chinese Legal Family" was first put forward by Hozumi Nobushige in 1884, who believed that the legal families (legal systems) in the world could be generally divided into five major ones: Hindu law, Chinese law (the Chinese Legal Family), Islamic law (Sharia), English law, and Roman law (civil law) (He, 2003, 65). In recent times, different scholars have translated the term "Chinese Legal Family" in different ways, with some translating it as Chinese law family and some as the Chinese legal system. In fact, the content and scope of the terms are roughly the same. As to the concept and scope of the Chinese Legal Family, there are also many different opinions in academic circles. It is generally believed that "the so-called Chinese Legal Family refers to a collective name. It includes the legal system of the Chinese *fengjian* period, which was nurtured under the specific socio-historical conditions in ancient China, with the combination of Li (ritual) and Fa (law) as the fundamental feature, the written criminal code as the core content, and *Tang Lv Shu Yi* as the typical representative, and the legal systems of the East Asian countries that were modeled on the Chinese legal system" (He & Kong, 2005). In terms of scope, the Chinese Legal Family includes Chinese law before the modern era, Japanese law during the *fengjian* period, Korean law, Ryukyu law, Vietnamese law, and the laws of other minority regions in the vicinity, which has been largely agreed upon in the academic circles (Zhang, 2007a, 2007b, 103). It is necessary to emphasize that the Chinese Legal Family existed because there were both pre-modern Chinese law as the mother law and *fengjian* Japanese law, Korean law, Ryukyu law, and Vietnamese law as the subsidiary laws. If only the mother law or only the subsidiary laws existed, it could not possibly be called the Chinese Legal Family. Therefore, to examine the time, causes, and process of the disintegration of the Chinese Legal Family, one should take a macroscopic view of the Chinese Legal Family as a whole and not a microscopic view of only one or several particular aspects. Otherwise, the conclusion will be biased.

The second concept is the understanding of the "disintegration" of the legal family. From different perspectives, the understanding of "disintegration" is slightly different. On the one hand, from a macroperspective, the disintegration of a legal system means its death, like the termination of a living organism. On the other hand, from the perspective of the process of the disintegration in the member countries of the Chinese Legal Family, the change in the legal systems in East Asian countries in modern times is essentially the disintegration of the Chinese Legal Family in each country. Put differently, the process of modernization of legal systems in each country is the process of the disintegration of the Chinese Legal Family. "The main sign of the modern transformation of Chinese law is the destruction of the traditional Chinese legal system and the establishment of the civil law system in China … The outstanding achievement of the modern Chinese legal transformation is the establishment of a modern legal system modeled on that of Western countries" (Zhang, 2005, 429–430). For example, the modernization of Japan's legal system was the process of the disintegration of the Chinese Legal Family in Japan. The revision of laws at the end of the Qing Dynasty and the promulgation of *Liu Fa Quan Shu* (*Complete Book of Six Codes, 六法全书*) by the Nanjing National Government were the processes of the disintegration of the Chinese Legal Family in its home country. The changes in the legal systems in Korea and Vietnam in modern times were the processes of the disintegration of the Chinese Legal Family in Korea and Vietnam. Thus, we can understand the "disintegration" of a legal system from the above two perspectives.

1.2 Defining the Time of the Chinese Legal Family's Disintegration

The disintegration of the Chinese Legal Family was a procession, i.e., a period of time, not a point in time. Thus, there was a time of beginning and completion. Defining the time of the disintegration is the primary problem to be solved when studying the collapse of the Chinese Legal Family. Some of the existing research works studying the Chinese Legal Family have dealt with the definition of the time of the collapse of the Chinese Legal Family. For example, Li Gang believes that the collapse of the Chinese Legal Family originated from the New Policies at the end of the Qing Dynasty and was completed at the end of the Qing Dynasty (Li, 1999). Han Yulin and Zhao Guobin's view is that "it was the Xinhai Revolution led by the Chinese national bourgeoisie that basically broke the ancient tradition of the Chinese Legal Family. The *Provisional Constitution of the Republic of China* formulated by the Nanjing Provisional Government negated for the first time the long-standing *fengjian* hierarchical privilege system in the form of a fundamental law and broke the combination of ritual and law in the Chinese Legal Family. It was a great innovation in the history of China" (Han & Zhao, 1983). The above views hold that the Chinese Legal Family collapsed at the end of the Qing Dynasty and the beginning of the Republic of China. However, these two views are obviously somewhat inappropriate. The reason, as explained above, is that the collapse of the Chinese Legal Family should be understood from both macro- and microperspectives; that is, the Chinese Legal Family was composed of pre-modern Chinese law as the parent law and Japanese law, Korean law, Vietnamese law, and Ryukyu law in the *fengjian* period as the subsidiary laws.

The aforementioned definition of the time points only takes into account the dissolution of the parent law but ignores the dissolution of the subsidiary law. From this viewpoint, we agree with Zhang Zhongqiu that defining the time of the collapse of the Chinese Legal Family should take into account both "the process of the collapse of the Chinese Legal Family as a legal family" and "the process of change of the parent law of the Chinese Legal Family before its collapse at the end of the Qing Dynasty." In other words, the time of the collapse must be defined comprehensively in terms of the time of the collapse of both the subsidiary law and the mother law. It is further argued that "by the end of the nineteenth century, the Chinese Legal Family in its original sense has only Chinese law, as the mother law, actually maintained. Therefore, the collapse of the Chinese Legal Family was a process of gradual disintegration and contraction from extraterritorial to native and from subsidiary law to mother law, which took more than 40 years in total from the beginning to the end" (Zhang, 1999).

The beginning of the collapse should first be defined from the time of the disintegration in each country, signaled by the birth of the modernization of the country's legal system.[2] The modernization of the Chinese legal system began in the concessions because the concession authorities were the first to modernize the legal system in China by transplanting a large number of modern foreign legal systems. For example, the concessions' legal system had a modern statutory structure, modern legal language, modern trial system, and modern lawyer system (Wang, 2016a, 2016b, 21–32). The modernization of the legal system in the concessions began in the British concession in Shanghai. The "British concession in Shanghai was the starting point for the modernization of the Chinese legal system. It was the first to apply modern laws, the first to form a modern legal system, and the first to use a modern judicial system, etc." (Wang, 2015a, 2015b, 144–151). The modernization of the legal system in the concessions also presented different evolutionary stages. "The 100-year modernization of the legal system in the concessions included three stages: the stage of emergence and taking shape (1845–1893), the stage of expansion and maturity (1894–1925), and the stage of decline and death (1926–1945)" (Wang, 2015a, 2015b, 66–72). As the starting point, the modernization of China's legal system in the concession in Shanghai emerged and took shape from 1845 to 1893. From the perspective of legal systems, conflicts and the integration of legal systems first emerged in the concession in Shanghai, which also led to the disintegration of the Chinese Legal Family there. The modernization of the legal systems in Japan, Vietnam, Korea, and other member countries obviously came later than the concession in Shanghai. "Japan took the lead in 'changing the law' by promulgating the *Kaitei Ritsurei* (*Reformed Penal Code*, 改定刑律) in the 6th year of the Meiji Era (1873). It issued the *Old Penal Code* in the 13th year of the Meiji Era (1880), which realized the transition from the Chinese legal system to the civil law system. … After the Sino-Japanese War, Korea (later called the Korean Empire) gradually came under Japan's control until it was annexed by Japan in 1910, during which time, the *Penal Code* was promulgated, combining the Japanese and Western European systems, and beginning to abandon the Chinese legal system. Vietnam became a French colony in 1886, and the code developed since then became increasingly alienated from Chinese law" (Xu, 2012, 352). Thus, the initial sign of the collapse

[2] The academic circles have different names for the topic of "modernization of the legal system" since the late Qing Dynasty. Some scholars call it "jindaihua," whereas others call it "xiandaihua" (both mean modernization). However, they all centered around the legal reforms in the late Qing Dynasty. This book does not discuss these concepts and uses "modernization (jindaihua) of the legal system" uniformly for the convenience of writing.

of the Chinese Legal Family was the creation of the concession in Shanghai and the modernization of its legal system, in which a modern system of trials, lawyers, and laws and regulations was established. After that, the Chinese legal system began to collapse.

The second consideration is the time when the disintegration became complete. This was marked by the basic accomplishment of the modernization of the legal systems in countries in the Chinese Legal Family, i.e., the modernization characterized by the establishment of the principle of the rule of law, the emergence of elected legislators, the formation of a legal system for citizens featuring human rights protection, and the establishment of an independent judicial system (Xu, 2000). The time of the completion also cannot be judged by the disintegration in one country, but a macroperspective should be adopted. For example, the disintegration of the mother law of the Chinese Legal Family was roughly between 1927 and 1937, marked by the establishment of the six-code system by the Nanjing National Government. The disintegration of the subsidiary laws of the Chinese Legal Family came at different times. In Japan, the completion of the collapse was marked by the establishment of the six-code system of modern Japan around 1922. In Korea, it was after 1910 when Korea was forcibly and indirectly involved in the Japanese law system. In Vietnam, it was the establishment of the French colonial power. In fact, the collapse of the Chinese Legal Family in Korea and Vietnam was another manifestation of the breakup of its dependency relationship with China. In summary, the time of the disintegration of the Chinese Legal Family should be defined as between 1927 and 1937, and it is more reasonable to use the establishment of the Nanjing National Government's six-code system as a sign of the collapse.

1.3 A New Exploration on the Causes of the Disintegration of the Chinese Legal Family: Conflicts and Integration of Legal Systems

Some research has already been completed in the legal history field regarding the causes of the disintegration of the Chinese Legal Family. For example, Zhang Yaoming believes that in terms of external conditions, the direct causes of the disintegration were the invasion of capitalism and the introduction of the Western legal systems. In terms of the internal conditions, the main reasons for the disintegration were complex. They were mainly due to changes in the social and economic structure and the rise of the democratic revolutionary movement—the invasion of capitalism and the introduction of the Western legal systems played the role of the "catalyst" (Zhang, 1991). Han Yulin and Zhao Guobin believe that the changes in material living conditions and relations of production were the inherent and fundamental causes of the demise of the Chinese Legal Family, and the "importation of new laws from abroad" only played a "catalytic" role (Han & Zhao, 1983). According to He Qinhua and Kong Jing, the causes of the disintegration of the Chinese Legal Family included external and internal causes. The external cause was mainly the invasion of the Western powers, and the internal causes were the changes in the social and economic structure of the East Asian countries and the rise of the democratic revolutionary movement. The closed nature of the Chinese Legal Family was also an important factor leading to its disintegration (He & Kong, 2005). Li Gang argued that the disintegration of the Chinese Legal Family had profound external and internal causes. The direct cause was the revision of laws during the period of the New Policies in the late Qing Dynasty, and the external causes were the invasion of capitalism and the introduction of Western legal systems (Li, 1999). However, the above research results seem to have ignored the macroperspective. The disintegration of the Chinese Legal Family cannot be analyzed only from the perspective of Chinese law, which was the law of the home country, but the perspective of the legal family should be adopted. In other words, the disintegration should be examined from the perspective of the death of the legal family.

A legal family can be seen as a living organism (Wigmore, 2004, 953), because it also goes through various stages of creation, growth, and extinction. As mentioned above, the disintegration of a legal family is essentially its extinction. In *A Panorama of the World's Legal Systems* (1928), Wigmore examined six extinct legal families, five legal families that survived with integration, three legal families that survived without integration, and two legal families that underwent massive integration and renewal, and finally proposed that "the level of the legal profession" is the decisive factor for the survival of the legal families. He argued that "the most important factor determining the existence of legal systems is the emergence and survival of the legal ideological system in a strict legal sense, and this legal ideological system itself is the result of the existence of a legal profession. The legal thinkers and practitioners in the legal profession independently create and perpetuate the legal ideological system. … In short, the creation and survival of a legal system depend on the survival and development of a well-trained legal profession" (Wigmore, 2004, 957). The "determinism of the legal profession" does not seem to explain the disintegration of the Chinese Legal Family. On one hand, when Wigmore made this conclusion, he regarded the Chinese Legal Family as one of the "three largely unintegrated legal systems that have survived" and did not consider the disintegration of the Chinese Legal Family. On the other hand, in a strict sense, the legal profession in each country of the Chinese Legal Family did not disappear. It survived repeated regime changes. Thus, the disintegration of the Chinese Legal Family cannot be explained from this perspective.

It is better to return to the starting point of the analysis of the causes of the demise of legal systems. Wigmore regards six major legal systems as completely extinct, namely, the Egyptian, Mesopotamian, Greek, Hebrew, Celtic, and Canon legal systems (Wigmore, 2004, 955). The starting point is Wigmore's analysis and search for the causes of the demise of the dead legal systems.

In Table 1, Wigmore listed the causes of the demise of the six extinct legal systems. Except for the Canon legal system, which is a special case, the causes for the other five legal systems were related to invaders (or foreign conquerors), such as the Egyptian and Mesopotamian legal systems. Their disintegration was related to the occupation

Table 1 Disintegration of the six legal systems (Wigmore, 2004)

Name	Time	Causes of the disintegration	Current system
Egyptian	Starting from the eighth century BC	City wars and occupation of Assyrian, Persian, Greek, and Roman invaders successively	Civil law
Mesopotamian	Its demise was around the first century BC	Invasion of Persian, Greek, and other people	Sharia
Greek	Around 300 BC	Absorbed by the Roman system	Civil law
Hebrew	Starting from 1600	European nations began to converge	–
Celtic	16th Century	It was from a foreign conqueror (UK). Its own legal system was completely lacking; thus, it was difficult to adapt to the requirements of the new era	Common law
Canon	Starting from the thirteenth century	The jurisdiction of the church courts over secular issues was abolished by national legislation in various countries	–

by Assyrian, Persian, Greek, and Roman invaders. The Greek legal system was absorbed by the Roman system, so its demise was related to the Roman invasion of Greece. The disintegration of the Celtic legal system was due to the English conquest of Wales and Ireland. Hence, the Welsh and Irish laws were replaced by English law. The disintegration of Hebrew law was also related to the integration of the European nations. In summary, foreign invaders were the main cause of the collapse of legal systems. However, foreign invaders or wars were only the direct cause of the disintegration. The deeper reasons were the conflicts and integration of legal systems. For example, the disintegration of the Egyptian legal system was a result of the conflict and gradual integration of the Greek and civil law (Roman law) systems. The disintegration of the Mesopotamian legal system was an outcome of the conflicts between and integration of the Persian and Greek legal systems. The disintegration of the Greek legal system was the result of its conflicts and integration with the Roman legal system. The disintegration of the Celtic legal system was the result of the conflicts between and integration of the common law systems of Wales and Ireland. Essentially, the conflicts and integration of legal systems are the clashes and fusion of two different civilizations in a region because a legal system represents a civilization. For example, the Egyptian civilization produced the Egyptian legal system, the Mesopotamian civilization fostered the Mesopotamian legal system, and the Greek civilization created the Greek legal system. A legal system is a legal tradition that is an important part of the civilization, as well as an important means of political rule. Therefore, the disintegration of the five legal systems mentioned above is not so much the result of conquest by invaders but rather the process and result of the clashes and fusion of two civilizations in a certain region or, more precisely, the conflicts and integration of legal systems.

Moreover, the conflicts and integration of legal systems were the deep-seated reasons for the disintegration of the Chinese Legal Family. By observing the formation, development, and maturation of the Chinese Legal Family, it can be seen that only at the end of the Qing Dynasty did the Chinese Legal Family encounter its greatest challenge since its emergence. This led to unprecedented changes and, finally, to its collapse. Why did the Chinese Legal Family gradually form, develop, and reach maturity without collapse during the dynasties in Chinese history? This is a question worth examining. From the perspective of foreign invaders, there have been many times in Chinese history when foreign invaders ruled the Central Plain, such as during the Northern and Southern Dynasties, the Five Dynasties and Ten Kingdoms, the Yuan Dynasty, and the Qing Dynasty. However, there were no signs of the collapse of the Chinese Legal Family. Rather, the Chinese Legal Family continued to develop and mature in these dynasties. The Southern and Northern Dynasties were an important period for the formation of the Chinese Legal Family, and the Qing Dynasty marked the peak of the Chinese Legal Family. This means that foreign invaders cannot be considered the cause of the disintegration of the Chinese Legal Family. In fact, the disintegration at the end of the Qing Dynasty was manifested in the modernization of the Chinese legal system. "It has been widely agreed that the 'revision of the law at the end of the Qing Dynasty' was an important symbol of the modernization of the Chinese legal system. It 'widely involved local and foreign elements.' In less than a decade, a relatively complete modern legal system modeled on civil law took shape, completely breaking the 'Chinese system' that had been in place for thousands of years from normative content to a specific form" (Guo, 1992). From the perspective of comparative law, the modernization of the Chinese legal system comprised conflicts and integration of legal systems.[3] "The modernization

[3] Legal historians have different views on the reform of the legal system in modern China: the modernization (*jindaihua*) of the Chinese legal system and the modernization (*xiandaihua*) of the legal system. In fact, the main reason for this difference is the different translation of "modernization." "Modernization" can be translated as both "*xiandaihua*" and "*jindaihua*," which means that the term is often used to describe the phenomenon of social and cultural changes that take place in modern times. "According to Magnarella's definition, modernization is a global process of cultural and social changes experienced by developing societies in order to obtain some of the characteristics of developed industrial societies." See Haviland (1987, 575–585). This book makes no distinction between the two. From the perspective of modernization theory, the modes of modernization include endogenous and exogenous modernization. The driving forces of endogenous modernization (i.e., modern productive forces) are internally nurtured and grown, and have strong self-exploitation (i.e., ability). In exogenous modernization, especially the recent modernization in less developed countries, modern productive forces and modernized cultural elements are transplanted or imported from abroad. See Luo (1990). According to the different power sources of modernization, legal scholars categorized modernization into two basic modes—internal and external modernization of legal systems. See Lv and Yao (1995, 13–14). Both China and Japan's modernization of legal systems were considered exogenous modernization, i.e., due to the impact and strong pressure of external factors, the society is forced to implement sudden reforms on its legal system. Therefore, it can be said that the exogenous modernization model of China and Japan also confirms that the

of China's legal system was performed in the process of contradictory movements of Chinese and Western cultures, which was a unique product of the clashes and fusion of the two cultures" (Guo, 1992). Here, the clashes and fusions were between Chinese and Western cultures,[4] as well as between the Chinese Legal Family and civil law. The integration of law systems is the process of legal transplantation. "Without the transplant of foreign law over the past hundred years, there would be no modern Chinese law. The backbone of modern Chinese law is not the law of traditional Chinese society but foreign law, mainly Western law. The legal transplant is a fundamental historical phenomenon in the development of modern Chinese law" (He, 2002). Similarly, the disintegration of the Chinese Legal Family in Japan, Korea, Vietnam, and other countries was also correspondingly manifested in the process of modernization of the legal system and legal transplantation in each country.

Following this thread, another important question that needs to be explored in depth arises: Why did the conflicts and integration of legal systems emerge only at the end of the Qing Dynasty? Or, why did the clashes and fusion of the Chinese and Western civilizations arise at the end of the Qing Dynasty and not at other times? The development of a civilization has its own trajectory. Although a civilization lasts for a long time, it evolves all the time. Civilizations are dynamic in that they rise and fall and merge and split. Since the emergence of civilizations, the world has gone through the phases of encounter and impact and is now in a phase of interaction. The encounter phase of civilizations comprised the three millennia following the emergence of civilizations, during which interactions between civilizations were either nonexistent, very limited, or intermittent and tense. Thus, historians described the civilizational interaction of this phase as the "encounters" because civilizations in this phase were geographically separated from each other and maintained only minor ties with each other (Huntington, 2010, 27–28). Therefore, in this phase, world civilizations retained their own development trajectories and did not influence each other (it was difficult for a small connection among civilizations to generate a substantial impact on each other), and there were no clashes of civilizations at all. The second phase was a civilizational impact. It began with the rise of Western civilization in the fifteenth century and lasted for 400 years until the nineteenth century. In this phase, the impact was mainly the continuous, irresistible, and unidirectional impact of Western civilization on all other civilizations, which was directly rooted in technology: the invention of navigational tools to reach distant people and the development of military capabilities to conquer them (Huntington, 2010, 29–30). This doctrine of civilizational phases explained why the clashes between the Chinese and Western civilizations occurred at the end of the Qing Dynasty but not in other periods. The clashes between the two civilizations and the two legal systems at the end

conflicts and integration of the legal systems were the reason for the collapse of the Chinese Legal Family.

[4] American scholar Samuel Huntington listed contemporary civilizations as Chinese, Japanese, Indian, Islamic, Orthodox, Western, Latin American, and African civilizations, among which the Japanese civilization is the offspring of Chinese civilization. See Huntington (2010, 24–26).

of the Qing Dynasty just happened in the second phase in the history of civilization, that is, the "impact of Western civilization" phase.

2 Subtheories

Specifically speaking, during modernization, the change, or more exactly, the disintegration of the Chinese Legal Family followed approximately two ways. One is the evolution of the surface structure of law, which is centered on the legal system, including legal norms, legal organizations, and legal facilities. The other is the evolution of the deep structure of law, which is centered on legal consciousness, including legal thought, legal psychology, and legal values.[5] In the following text, the disintegration of the Chinese Legal Family is analyzed from two perspectives: the evolution of the surface structure of law and the evolution of the deep structure of law.

2.1 Disintegration of the Chinese Legal Family in China

On the basis of the evolution of the surface structure of law and the characteristics of legal modernization, the disintegration of the Chinese Legal Family in China can be roughly divided into four stages (Yang, 2012): (1) the beginning stage, which refers to the period of legal modernization in the concession in Shanghai, when the Chinese Legal Family directly faced conflicts of legal systems; (2) the gradual disintegrating stage, which refers to the period of legal reform at the end of the Qing Dynasty, when the Qing government began to transplant laws based on foreign laws and promulgated a series of draft departmental codes modeled on civil law codes; (3) the deepening stage, which refers to the period of legal establishment of the Nanjing Provisional Government and Beiyang government, where the two governments followed the tradition of transplanting the civil law system in the late Qing Dynasty and carried out a series of legal establishment based on the civil law system; and (4) the completing stage, which refers to the period of the Nanjing National Government's promulgation of *Liu Fa Quan Shu*, marking the completion of the collapse in China.[6]

---

[5] See Guo (1992). However, it should be noted that the modernization of the legal system and the modernization of the legal culture do not always coincide, i.e., the realization of the former does not represent the realization of the latter, and the realization of the latter seems to lag behind the realization of the former. Since the modernization of the legal system is a technical issue, it can be achieved through the government-led complete negation of the old system and formulation of new legal norms. This process can be completed in a short time. However, the modernization of legal culture is the modernization of legal spirit and legal thought, which is a cultural issue. The formation or transformation of legal spirit and legal thought cannot be achieved overnight but often requires a long-term process of inculcation and absorption. See Liu (2012, 79–80).

[6] After the establishment of the Nanjing Nationalist Government, on the basis of the laws revised by the late Qing Dynasty and the Beiyang Government, it completed the codification of various

2.1.1 Beginning Stage: Modernization of the Legal System in the Concession in Shanghai

The concession in Shanghai (British concession) was the starting point of the modernization of China's legal system because it was the first to imitate the modern Western parliamentary system, the first to establish a modern judicial system, the first to form a modern regulatory system, and the first to modernize the prison system.

Imitation of the Modern Western Parliamentary System in the Concession in Shanghai

In December 1846, one year after the publication of the *Land Regulations*, the British Consul Balfour convened a meeting of the leaseholders in the concession at the Richard Hotel to elect the expatriates to form the Road and Dock Committee. This was the first time that a meeting of the leaseholders was held after the establishment of the concession. Since then, the practice of holding a meeting once a year has been established. It was not until 1852 that the system of leaseholders' meetings began to take shape when the leaseholders' meeting in that year resolved that each leaseholder in the concession would have the right to vote at the leaseholders' meetings. Each leaseholder would have one vote regardless of the amount of land that he owned. Leaseholders who were absent from the meeting could also vote by proxy, creating a system of proxy voting for the leaseholders' meeting (Ma, 2009, 42). Thus, the embryonic form of the modern Western parliamentary system was born. In 1854, the system of leaseholders' meetings was further fixed in the form of clauses in the *Land Regulations of Shanghai Anglo-American and French Concessions*. It stipulated the duties of the leaseholders' meeting and further improved the system of the leaseholders' meeting. With this development, the leaseholders' meeting clarified the composition of personnel and the scope of powers and responsibilities, which had already taken the form of a legislative structure. On June 6, 1861, the resolution passed by the leaseholders' meeting stipulated that the number of leaseholders attending the meeting should be at least one-third of all leaseholders and that the resolution would have legal effect after it was approved by the consular corps in Shanghai and the Shanghai *Daotai* (governor) (Wang et al., 2012, 8). It can be seen that the leaseholders' meeting had the nature of a legislative body in Shanghai. Later, the taxpayers' meeting replaced the leaseholders' meeting and became more

important codes, individual laws, and regulations and completed the process of formulating each departmental law from draft to formal codes. The laws were implemented successively and became a typical representative of the peak of the development of the legal system in modern Chinese history. Between 1927 and 1937, the Nanjing Nationalist Government followed the European and Japanese practice of enacting various codes as its main task and gradually formed a six-code system with the Constitution, civil law, criminal law, civil procedure law, criminal procedure law, and administrative law as the main branches of law. See Wang (2007, 452–456).

of a legislative body in terms of rules, content of proceedings, taxation, and amendment of bylaws. At that time, the taxpayers' meeting had legislative, financial, and supervisory powers, which were no different from those of modern legislatures.

First Modern Judicial System Established in the Concession in Shanghai

In the British concession in Shanghai, the consular jurisdiction acquired under the unequal treaties was the first to introduce a modern judicial system in the concession. For example, a consular court was established in the British Concession's consulate. This system continued to be implemented in the Foreign Settlement until 1869 when the Mixed Court (Huishen Gongxie, 会审公廨) was established, and this modern judicial system was gradually applied to all cases that occurred in the concession (Wang, 2016a, 2016b, 68). The Mixed Court continued to exist for 63 years (1864–1927). It experienced a period of transition from a traditional to a modern society in China, and its development was not synchronized with the times. It combined Western legal elements in the traditional judicial system and affected almost all aspects of the municipal and economic life in the concession (Hong, 2005). The "Statutes of the Mixed Court" clearly defined the appointment of the court's personnel, the scope of jurisdiction, the competence of the court, and the system of sessions. At the same time, the "the Mixed Court" adopted the Western lawyer defense system, which allowed the Chinese to hire lawyers to defend themselves in both civil and criminal cases during the trial (Wang et al., 2012, 38). In summary, the first modern judicial institution and system in China were established in the concession in Shanghai (the British concession).

Formation of the Modern Regulatory System in the Concession in Shanghai

The concession was managed in accordance with the Western city management model. Except for full-time administrative departments and various advisory bodies, the concession also enacted and implemented administrative regulations to achieve good management results, which objectively contributed to the birth and formation of the modern regulatory system in the concession in Shanghai.

In the early stage of the Shanghai Municipal Council (Gongbu Ju, 工部局), it mainly regulated the behavior of the residents in the concession by issuing various notices. Later, the Council issued regulations on the social management of the concession. For example, at the beginning of the twentieth century, the Council issued the Regulation on the Public Security of the Foreign Settlement and the Regulation on the Public Constabulary of the Foreign Settlement (Ma, 2009, 40–41).

At the same time, in contrast to the traditional forms of law such as Lv, Ling, Ge, and Shi, the Shanghai concession promulgated several departmental regulations concerning various issues based on the 1845 *Land Regulations*, such as the *Duties of the Inspector of the Constabulary* in 1854, *Rules for the Punishment of Prisoners in Service* in 1866, and *Regulation for Officials of Courts in Yangjingbang* in 1869

(Wang, 2016a, 2016b, 67). Thus, a system of laws and regulations was formed in the British concession in Shanghai, which centered around the fundamental law, *Land Regulations*, and included a series of departmental regulations.

Modernization of the Prison System in the Concession in Shanghai

After the end of the Opium War, on November 17, 1843, Shanghai officially opened its port to foreigners in accordance with the provisions of the Treaty of Nanjing and the General Regulations for the Five Ports to Conduct Trade. A modern prison system was one of the manifestations of the modernization of the legal system in Shanghai. It was born in the concession in Shanghai.

The Municipal Council of the Foreign Settlement successively established Xiamen Road Prison and Tilanqiao Prison, and the Municipal Council of the French Concession established Masi South Road Prison. Tilanqiao Prison was built in 1901 with advanced hardware infrastructure and a modern Western prison management model. With the gradual development of the concession, the size of Tilanqiao Prison also gradually expanded and the number of prisoners it received increased yearly, reaching a maximum of more than 8,000. "Its huge size exceeded that of Bombay Prison in India and Sugamo Prison in Japan at that time, so it was known as the 'No. 1 Prison in the Far East'" (Ma, 2009, 64). Xiamen Road Prison was the first prison affiliated with the Municipal Council, but its size and management were not comparable to those of Tilanqiao Prison, and it was abolished in 1935. Masi South Road Prison in the French concession was built in 1910, and its size was smaller, covering an area of more than seven acres. In this regard, Tilanqiao Prison is undoubtedly the representative of the prisons in the Shanghai concessions in terms of size and management system. Tilanqiao Prison was the product of the transplantation of the Western prison system by the Concession Authority, which gradually modernized the prison system in the concession. The modernization of the concession had a profound impact on the Chinese community in Shanghai and even on the modernization of China as a whole.

(1) A Brief Description of Tilanqiao Prison. Tilanqiao Prison was originally called "Prison of the Police Department of Municipal Council of the Foreign Settlement in Shanghai" which was located at No. 117 Huade Road (now No. 147 Changyang Road). It was built by the Municipal Council of the Foreign Settlement in Shanghai in the 27th year of the Guangxu Era (1901). It was designed by the British Engineering Office in Singapore. The construction began at the end of 1901, and the prison started to operate in May 1903. It was called "Huade Road Prison," "Tilanqiao Prison," or "Tilanqiao West Prison."

Tilanqiao Prison was managed by the Municipal Council of the Foreign Settlement in accordance with various prison statutes, rules, charters, and regulations issued by the Municipal Council, such as the *Regulation of the British Prison in Shanghai* (1906.2), *Rules for Officers and Prisoners in the Shanghai Municipal Gaol* (1906), *Regulation on Detention Facilities in the Foreign Settlement in Shanghai* (1907.11), and *Rules for the Management of New Male and Female Detention Facilities in the Foreign Settlement in Shanghai* (1909). The main managers of Tilanqiao Prison were foreigners. "The top management officers include one head officer, one deputy officer, and two clerks, who were always appointed directly by the Municipal Council, mainly British. There were six Chinese constables and 54 Indian constables" (Pan, 2003, 185). However, the prisoners were mostly Chinese. "At the beginning, the prison mainly had two 4-story buildings with 480 cells, as well as cooking yards, office buildings, medical clinics, etc., covering an area of about 10 acres. Those who were imprisoned were mainly Chinese prisoners in the Foreign Settlement" (Xu, 1995). It is clear from its management system, officers, and detainees that Tilanqiao Prison was a prison where foreign rulers imprisoned Chinese people.

From its establishment, the prison absorbed the characteristics of Western prisons and was unlike traditional Chinese prisons. It was protected by iron fences and adopted a steel–concrete structure. On the basis of age and gender, the prison was divided into the male area, the female area, and the juvenile area. The prison also had hospitals, pharmacies, bathrooms, cooking rooms, and other living and sanitary facilities. Because Tilanqiao Prison was influenced by the concept of a modern Western prison system, it had excellent prison facilities and a modern prison management system.

(2) Tilanqiao Prison was the first prison in Shanghai to adopt a modern prison management system. The concept of a modern Western prison system originated from the Enlightenment Movement, influenced by modern ideas, such as natural human rights, freedom and equality, and humanitarianism, and focused on the idea of education and punishment. It was believed that prisons had the functions of encouraging transformation, technical training, restricting freedom, and eliminating evil characteristics, among others. At the beginning of the twentieth century, because of the spread and influence of the modern prison concept, the Municipal Council of the Foreign Settlement in Shanghai decided to establish a new prison with a modern prison system, replacing the previous police stations, detention houses, and detention centers to demonstrate the advanced, modern, and civilized Western management system. Tilanqiao Prison initiated the modernization of the prisons in Shanghai concessions. It not only paid attention to the protection and education of juvenile offenders but also modernized various prison institutions, such as weapon rationing and use, visits, admission, commutation, and release.

First, attention was paid to the protection and education of juvenile offenders. Minor offenders are still immature because of their intellectual development and age when their values and outlook on life are shaped and are easily influenced by the surrounding environment and people. Therefore, it is necessary to detain them separately from adult prisoners. At the same time, the prison set up a special reformatory to educate juvenile offenders with knowledge and culture to encourage self-rehabilitation. "Huade Road Prison has set aside 30 cells for juvenile offenders under the age of 19 as a reformatory. Thirty-one juvenile offenders were admitted that year. The juvenile offenders were kept separately from other prisoners, and the prison taught them manual skills and invited teachers from the Huayang Persuasion Institute to teach them cultural knowledge, and later the Chinese Young Men's Christian Association also participated in the education of juvenile offenders" (Compilation Committee of *Shanghai Concession Annals*, 2001, 304).

Second, weapon rationing and use were regulated. Modern Western prison systems have more mature and complete internal management rules, including detailed regulations on the distribution and use of weapons, to avoid prison officials' arbitrary and abusive use of weapons and instruments and to prevent the proliferation of illegal punishment in prisons. "In the Foreign Settlement, there was a gun store at Huade Road Prison. Each officer ranking higher than section chiefs or head guards was equipped with a pistol but was allowed to carry it only after passing target practice. When allowed to carry, the officer could get the gun from a room with a lock, and each officer had a fixed number. Usually, the gun should be returned on the same day of use, with signature needed all the way" (Compilation Committee of *Shanghai Concession Annals*, 2001, 228).

Third, a humane visiting institution was established. Tilanqiao Prison adopted a more humane visitation system, which allowed relatives to visit the prison after a certain sentence had been served and allowed prisoners to communicate with their relatives. The humane visitation system was conducive to the rehabilitation and education of the prisoners and reflected the humanitarian spirit. "At the beginning of the twentieth century, when prisoners in Huade Road Prison had served three months in prison, their relatives and friends were usually allowed to visit (to be received by) the prison." "During the concession period, prisoners in Huade Road Prison could communicate with their relatives once a month. Formerly, it was once every three months." In addition to visits from relatives, prisoners could contact their friends and make appointments with lawyers. In special circumstances, prisoners could send additional letters, which demonstrate the humane management of the prison visitation system in Tilanqiao Prison. "For prisoners who were in prison because of past due debts, the prison allowed them to contact their friends by communication and allowed them to write to their relatives and friends to request an appointment with a lawyer. In addition, prisoners might be given additional opportunities to write letters in case of serious illness or if the prisoners were about to be released from prison and needed clothes and other assistance, but this must be approved and reviewed by the warden." (Compilation Committee of *The Records of Shanghai Prisons*, 2003, 242).

Fourth, a modernized admission institution was established. A standardized, procedural, and modernized admission institution was good for the management of the prison and could help in eliminating the situations of arbitrary detention of prisoners. Modern admission institutions required complete legal documents and accurate records. Anyone who did not meet the legal requirements for admission could not be imprisoned; anyone who met the legal requirements for admission should be imprisoned in accordance with the law, and refusal was not allowed. Imprisonment was based on the courts' execution orders, verdicts, or imprisonment tickets, and Tilanqiao Prison had to check the personal information of the prisons and make a record of the prisoners' information to prevent impostors. "Huade Road Prison admitted prisoners in accordance with the execution orders, verdicts, or imprisonment tickets of the court. The prisoner's identity and name must be checked, and his/her fingerprint had to be recorded. The prison would search the prisoner's body, conduct a physical examination and take photos (for a period of time, three photos of the front, left, and right sides of the bareheaded prisoner must be taken). The prisoners would be required to have a haircut, cut their fingernails and toenails, and take a shower. The personal belongings and clothes of the prisoners would be put into cloth bags and recorded at the entrance of the prison, and they would be kept by the prison after steam sterilization. In addition, the prisoners would be given appropriate uniforms according to the length of their sentences" (Compilation Committee of *The Records of Shanghai Prisons*, 2003, 151).

Fifth, an institution of commutation was established. The commutation institution helped the rehabilitation of criminals. Educational commutation was only an adjustment to the original sentence, not a negation of it. It was helpful for the rehabilitation and education of criminals and helped them relieve the pressure of prison life. "On the 15th day of the 2nd lunar month of the 1st year of the Xuantong Era (April 5, 1909), in response to the large number of prisoners in prison and the overcrowding of detention facilities, David Randall, Chairman of the Municipal Council of the Foreign Settlement, proposed to D. Sifford, Consul General of the Consular Corps of the Foreign Settlement, that for prisoners sentenced to a fixed term of imprisonment, if they behave well in Huade Road Prison, a 'commutation institution' in accordance with European practice should apply to them, to reduce the prison's pressure" (Compilation Committee of *The Records of Shanghai Prisons*, 2003, 190).

Sixth, there were better living and sanitary conditions. Prisoners' uniforms were uniformly distributed by Tilanqiao Prison, which ensured the basic living needs of the prisoners. "Since the 29th year of the Guangxu Era (1903), each prisoner was given two sets of shirts and shorts in summer, three old linen blankets as bedding, and a set of cotton-padded jacket and trousers, and a quilt in winter" (Compilation Committee of *The Records of Shanghai Prisons*, 2003, 287). Hospitals (clinics) were set up in the prisons, and prisoners were sent to different hospitals according to the severity of their illnesses. "In the 29th year of the Guangxu Era (1903), a medical clinic was set up in Huade Road Prison. A three-story building with 36 beds for the treatment of general diseases of prisoners was established. Sick prisoners who needed surgery would be sent to the Huabu Hospital on Laobazi Road (now Wujin Road). Seriously ill prisoners would be sent to the Sacred Heart Hospital (a charitable institution located in today's Yangpu District). Lepers would be sent to the Dachang Leprosy Hospital, and mentally ill prisoners would be sent to the Minhang Neurological Hospital" (Compilation Committee of *The Records of Shanghai Prisons*, 2003, 297).

Tilanqiao Prison was also the first prison in Shanghai to adopt a modern prison management system. Although Xiamen Road Prison was literally the first prison established under the Municipal Council, its management system lagged behind that of Tilanqiao Prison. For instance, Xiamen Road Prison did not have a reformatory or an institution of commutation. The Shanghai County Jail was only renovated in the early twentieth century. Before the reform, a traditional Chinese management model was adopted. The prison was set up in *Yamen* (government office) and was not a prison in a modern sense. Rather, it was a place waiting for judgment, not a place for the execution of punishment. Other prisons were established later than Tilanqiao Prison, such as Masi South Road Prison (built in 1910), Shanghai District Procuratorate Model Prison (built in December 1911), and Caohejing Prison (built in May 1917). Therefore, the first prison in Shanghai to adopt the modern prison management system was definitely Tilanqiao Prison.

(3) Tilanqiao Prison was the largest prison in Shanghai. As the size of Tilanqiao Prison expanded from the initial 10 acres of land with only 480 cells to 60.4 acres of land with 4,000 cells in 1935, the title of "the No. 1 prison in the Far East" was true to its name.

First, compared with other prisons in the concessions, the size of Tilanqiao Prison was far larger. For example, Xiamen Road Prison was built in 1856 and was the first prison in the modern sense in the concessions. "Its main building was a two-story building, the main body of which was in the shape of '十,' including 72 prison cells plus a confinement cell and a hanging cell" (Xu, 1995). Masi South Road Prison was under the Municipal Council of the French Concession, and it was slightly larger than Xiamen Road Prison. "The prison had a total of 400 cells and could hold about 1,000 prisoners" (Xu, 1995).

Second, it can be compared with the prisons under the jurisdiction of China. The prisons in the modern sense in China were built in the late Qing Dynasty and early Republic years, including the Shanghai District Procuratorate Model Prison (later renamed "Shanghai Model Prison") and Caohejing Prison (later "Jiangsu No. 2 Prison"). Although the establishment of the prisons was influenced by the prisons in the concessions and the reform of the prisons in the late Qing Dynasty, their sizes were not comparable to that of Tilanqiao Prison. The Shanghai District Procuratorate Model Prison had only 200 cells. "The prison was renamed the 'Shanghai District Procuratorate Model Prison' in January of the 2nd year of the Republic of China (1913). In September of the following year, the Second Detention Center of the District Prosecutor's Office was abolished, and the prison cells were transferred to the Model Prison. The prison cut off the back street and converted it into a prison. The two blocks were connected, so the area was nearly doubled, and there were more than 200 cottage prison rooms" (Compilation Committee of *The Records of Shanghai Prisons*, 2003, 105). Caohejing Prison was a large prison under China's jurisdiction, but its size was still as large as that of Tilanqiao Prison. "At the end of the 12th year of the Republic of China, there were 550 prisoners; at the end of the 22nd year of the Republic of China, there were 2,300 prisoners, and at the end of the 24th year of the Republic of China, there were more than 3,000 prisoners" (Compilation Committee of *The Records of Shanghai Prisons*, 2003, 107).

(4) Tilanqiao Prison had a significant influence on the modernization of the prison system in Shanghai. Tilanqiao Prison was built in 1901 and is still in use today. It was the first prison in Shanghai to adopt a modern prison management system. Later, after continuous expansion and renovation, it also became the largest prison in Shanghai. "The Shanghai concessions transplanted the modern legal

system from the West before the areas under the jurisdiction of China and began to localize it, establishing its own modern legal system, making Shanghai begin to modernize its legal system. After this legal system took root in the concessions, it extended its influence to the areas around it under the jurisdiction of China, forming a pattern of extending from the center to the surrounding areas, i.e., a point-to-surface pattern" (Wang, 2006). The century-old Tilanqiao Prison has witnessed the development of Shanghai's prison system. It is a microcosm of the modernization of Shanghai's prison system and has had a significant impact on the modernization of Shanghai's prison system and even on the reform of China's traditional prison system.

At the end of the Qing Dynasty, in 1901, Empress Dowager Cixi issued an edict of "preparing for reforms" and began to introduce the New Policies. China began to pay attention to the reform of prisons and started a movement to reform the prison system in the late Qing Dynasty. Against this background, Tilanqiao Prison in Shanghai, as a representative of the modern Western prison system in the Shanghai concessions, gradually attracted the attention of the Qing government and the public. Newspapers such as *Shun Pao* (申报) reported on Tilanqiao Prison. Officials from the Ministry of Law of the late Qing Dynasty visited the prison themselves. In this regard, it is obvious that Tilanqiao Prison had a significant influence on the modernization of the prison system in Shanghai and the reforms of the prison system in the late Qing Dynasty.

The establishment of Tilanqiao Prison in the Foreign Settlement in Shanghai encouraged the spread of the modern concept of a prison system in Shanghai and throughout the Qing Dynasty. It was performed as a vehicle for the modern Western concept of a prison in the following three ways.

First, the Shanghai County Jail interfaced with Tilanqiao Prison.

As mentioned above, the modernization and transformation of the prison system in the concessions influenced China's modernization of the prison system in the late Qing Dynasty. With the establishment and use of the new prison system in the concessions, the reformers of the late Qing Dynasty also set out to reform the prisons under the guidance of the new prison model. The Shanghai magistrate, who accompanied Han Zhaofan, a minister in the Ministry of Law, to visit Tilanqiao Prison, began to reform the prisons in Shanghai after the visit. Initially, the lack of funds delayed the process. In the end, the Shanghai magistrate overcame the difficulties and completed the reform of the county prisons. "The reform of the county prisons has been completed. Yesterday, County Magistrate Tian arrived with the Shanghai Governor and the stand-by Prefectural Magistrate, Zhang Yan, who was sent by the higher-level government to inspect the local Justice Office. In the afternoon, they made an inspection tour and decided to order the constructor to hand over the project on the 20th day of this month. After that, the county will ask the superior to send people to examine and accept the project."[7]

Second, the acceptance and affirmation of the modern Western prison system by the officials of the late Qing Dynasty.

---

[7] Reform of Prisons Has Completed. *Shun Pao* (申报) (1911, January 18).

Since the operation of Tilanqiao Prison in 1903, because it was the epitome of the modern Western prison system, it attracted the attention of government officials in the Qing Dynasty. Not only did Shanghai *Daotai* (governor) personally inspect the prison, but officials from the Central Ministry of Law also visited Tilanqiao Prison to investigate. In April 1906, Han Zhaofan, a minister in the Ministry of Law, visited the prisons in Jiangsu (including Shanghai) and Zhejiang provinces and wrote a book entitled *Inspection of Prisons* after returning to Beijing. The book recorded the situation of Shanghai Tilanqiao Prison and introduced the reformatory. "The young people gathered in the reformatory. They are allowed to read books for about an hour a day. Their teaching was conducted by the traditional Chinese physicians" (Han 33rd year of the Guangxu Era, i.e., 1907). The new-style prisons in the Shanghai concessions, with their good sanitary and living conditions and humane management system, gave the officials of the late Qing Dynasty a refreshing feeling regarding the prison system. To promote the innovation of the prison system in the late Qing Dynasty, the Qing officials realized that the reformer of the prison system must first understand the operation and management of the Western prison system. Thus, they paid attention to the Western European and American countries, including their near neighbor Japan.

To make the country more aware of the modern prison system in the West, the Qing government sent officials to Europe, America, and Japan to study the prison system. In addition to Han Zhaofan's *Inspection of Prisons* mentioned above, Dai Hongci summarized his experience in a book *Diary of an Expedition to Nine Countries*, and Dong Kang wrote a book, *Record of Prison Visits* and *Report on Investigation of Japanese Judgments and Prisons*. These books introduced the modern prison management systems in Europe, America, and Japan in detail. Against this background, the Qing government supported officials and scholars to publish translations of Western prison systems and prison theories, such as *the Japanese Prison Law*, *Belgian Prison Law*, *Outline of Prison Issues*, and *Prison Science*. Fieldwork, writing, and translation of treatises implied that late Qing officials were slowly accepting and affirming the ideas of the modern Western prison system.

In addition, during the modernization and transformation of traditional prisons in the late Qing Dynasty, the greatest impact of modern thought on the Western prison system and on the traditional prison concept was the reconceptualization of the function of prisons. According to the traditional prison philosophy, the fundamental purpose of prison execution is to maintain orthodoxy and eradicate heresy, which can actually be regarded as "eliminating problems" and "forbidding evil" (Gao, 2008, 51). However, the modern Western concept of the prison system considers prisons as places for reforming and transforming prisoners, which devotes more attention to education and reformation, not the need to maintain the rule. The idea of the Western prison system began to change officials' understanding of the function of prisons in the late Qing Dynasty, which was incisively summarized by Shen Jiaben, an advocate of legal reform in the late Qing Dynasty, "prisons are for correcting people, not for making them suffer or humiliating them" (Shen, 2015, 207). His idea of prison reform was recognized by the Qing authority and was reflected in the subsequent reforms of the lawmaking and prison system.

Third, the people of Shanghai refreshed their understanding of the modern Western prison system.

At the beginning of its use, Tilanqiao Prison was questioned by the general public. "On February 6, 1901, the two major newspapers in Shanghai at the time, *Shun Pao* (申报) and *Xinwen Bao* (The News, 新闻报), published almost simultaneously the news that the adjudicators of the Mixed Court had retrieved the Chinese prisoners suffering from jaundice in the Western prison" (Zheng, 2009, 10). From the information provided by the newspapers, it is known that there were a large number of cases of jaundice and death in Tilanqiao Prison. After the news was released, the public spread rumors, and eventually, the hearsay was seriously inconsistent with the actual situation in Tilanqiao Prison. "There are even rumors that 'there is a Western prison in the concession which adopted cruel punishment that most of those who enter it die.'"[8] This once made the people of Shanghai have no good feelings regarding Tilanqiao Prison and generated questions regarding the Western prison system.

To let the people of Shanghai have an objective understanding of Tilanqiao Prison and better knowledge of the modern Western prison management system, the Shanghai Municipal Council once invited officials of the Mixed Court and journalists to visit Tilanqiao Prison. In 1906, after visiting the Tilanqiao Prison, a journalist from *Shun Pao* wrote a long article regarding the Western prison and published it on the second and third pages of *Shun Pao*. It mentioned that "although prisons are places where criminals are detained, the Eastern and Western countries attached great importance to two points. The first is to teach prisoners to be good and to teach them manual skills so that after they are released from prison, they can become good enough to support themselves. The second is to take people's lives as a priority, paying attention to hygiene" (Zheng, 2009). With the in-depth visits and reports of *Shun Pao* journalists, the people of Shanghai gradually gained a new understanding of Tilanqiao Prison. They reassessed the modern Western prison system and began to accept this new system, thus accelerating the modernization of the prison system in Shanghai.

The modernization of Shanghai originated in the Shanghai concessions, and Shanghai was the interface between traditional Chinese culture and modernization. Thus, the Shanghai concession was also the interface between the traditional Chinese prison system and its modernization. Tilanqiao Prison epitomized the modern Western prison system and was led by the Municipal Council of the Foreign Settlement's initiative to embrace a modern prison system. Its many institutions were the first in the history of Shanghai prisons, such as the institutions of reformatory and commutation. Tilanqiao Prison brought the Shanghai prison system into the modern era. It gradually improved people's awareness of the modern prison system, encouraged the spread of the humanitarian spirit in China, and helped the modern concept of punishment to be rooted. However, the Shanghai concession was a product of the Western powers' invasion of China and their violation of Chinese sovereignty. In modern times, the Shanghai concession was like a double-edged

[8] Comments on the Governor's Prevention of the Establishment of the Female Prison in the Concession. *Shun Pao* (1904, October 30).

sword that had multiple effects on all aspects of politics, economy, and culture in Shanghai and the whole of China. "To sum up, the impact of the Shanghai concession on modern Shanghai, and modern China, was multi-faceted, not singular. It is a mark of shame that China was bullied by the capitalist powers, but also a window to modern civilization" (Xiong, 1987). The same is true of Tilanqiao Prison, which objectively introduced a modern prison system to Shanghai but brought pain and shame. It was a product of the Western powers' violation of China's judicial sovereignty and an instrument for some states to oppress and enslave the Chinese. In the early days of Tilanqiao Prison, the prisoners were mainly Chinese, and until 1949, it had imprisoned many patriotic aspirants. "Before liberation, the prison had imprisoned many famous Chinese figures in modern and contemporary times, including Zhang Taiyan and Zou Rong, and Chinese communists Ren Bishi, Zhang Aiping, Cao Diqiu, Yang Paoan, Wang Lingbo, Xu Ya, Ah Ying, Yuan Yelie, Peng Kang, Jiang Shangqing, and Zhou Libo" (Records of Hongkou District Compilation Committee, 1999, 119).

Brief Comments

The process of modernization in China is a process of clashes and fusion between traditional and Western cultures, so it was not always smooth but always accompanied by some pain. The modernization of the legal system in the Shanghai concessions is no exception. It originated in the British concession in Shanghai and was deeply marked with a humiliating loss of sovereignty. However, it objectively contributed to the disintegration of the Chinese legal system and the spread and establishment of modern Western legal culture in China, which eventually stimulated the disintegration of the Chinese Legal Family.

2.1.2 Gradual Disintegrating Stage: Period of Legal Reforms in the Late Qing Dynasty

On January 29, 1901 (the 10th day of the 12th lunar month of the 26th year of the Guangxu Era), Empress Dowager Cixi, in the name of Emperor Guangxu, issued an edict adopting political reforms and initiated the New Policies of the late Qing Dynasty (Zhao, 2009, 91). In 1902 (the 28th year of the Guangxu Era), the Qing government established the Law Revision Institution, a specialized institution responsible for the revision of laws. Shen Jiaben, a deputy official of the Ministry of Law, and Wu Tingfang, a minister on mission to the United States, were appointed as the chief codifiers of the law revisions. This can be regarded as the official start of legal reforms in the late Qing Dynasty. In May 1904 (the 4th lunar month of the 30th year of the Guangxu Era), the Law Revision Institution formally started its work. Until the outbreak of the Xinhai Revolution in October 1911, under the leadership of Shen Jiaben and Wu Tingfang, the institution did a lot of basic legislative work and drafted some new codes based on the civil law systems of Europe and Japan. The legal institutions and legal system underwent significant changes during the period of legal reform in the late Qing Dynasty, particularly manifested in the disintegration of the Chinese Legal Family represented by the Tang Lv, the transplantation of legal models and legislative styles to China, which mainly came from the civil law system, and the gradual modernization of the legal system (Wang, 2007, 376–386). Specifically, the principle of the rule of law, a legislature representing public opinion, the legal system of citizens featuring human rights protection, and an independent judicial system were established. Moreover, the civil law system has always been characterized by a statutory code, and compared with other legal systems, its most typical manifestation is the complete legal system of the "six codes."[9] Therefore, in the modernization of China's legal system from the Chinese Legal Family to the civil law system, the first formal sign of the beginning of the disintegration of the Chinese Legal Family was the birth of the "six-code" legal system.[10]

Birth of a Modern Constitution

It is generally believed that there was no constitution in China during the period of the Chinese Legal Family.[11] The birth of a modern constitution came from the preparatory constitutional movement in the late Qing Dynasty. On September 1, 1906 (the 13th day of the 17th lunar month of the 32nd year of the Guangxu Era), Emperor Guangxu promulgated the *Edict of Declaration on Preparation for the Establishment of a Constitution with Preceding Collation of the Bureaucratic System*, which set the stage for the preparatory constitutional movement. After the declaration of the preparation for a constitution, the Qing government began to set up the Politics Inspection Bureau, a special office for the preparation for a constitution, which was changed to the Constitutional Affairs Bureau in the following year (Wang, 2007, 379). The bureau completed some tasks during the provisional constitution-making period. It played an active role in the birth of a modern constitution, such as drawing up a list

---

[9] According to Professor He Qinhua, the establishment of a six-code legal system centering around the six codes is not found in any other legal systems. Not only did the Common Law not have such a legislative feature, but also the previous Chinese Law Family, Hindu Law, and Sharia, which are still vibrant today, did not create such a system. This is a unique feature of the civil law system. See He (2013).

[10] Professor Zhang Jinfan also believed that the revision of the laws in the late Qing Dynasty was a major event in Chinese legal history. Thereon, the traditional *fengjian* legal system in China collapsed and the modern Chinese legal system was established, following the structure of the civil law system. See Zhang (2005, 387).

[11] The term "constitution" in the sense of the fundamental law of Western countries was first used in China in the mid to late nineteenth century. In the article "A Brief History of France" written by Wang Tao in the 9th year of the Tongzhi Era (1870), he mentioned that France "established a certain constitution in 1791 and spread it in the country." In particular, in his book *Postscript of Warnings in a Flourishing Age: Preface*, Zheng Guangying had already expressed the idea of adopting the constitution as the fundamental law of the state, saying "the constitution is the foundation of the state." See Zhang (2011, 27). Additionally, Professor Gao Fang believed that from the terminology to the actual content, China's modern constitutionalism was introduced from the West in the second half of the nineteenth century. He also clarified the implicit aspects and origin of constitutionalism in detail. See Gao et al. (2012, 1–5).

for a 9-year constitutional preparation, preparing the draft constitution, reforming the bureaucratic system, and guiding the establishment of a quasi-parliamentary organization (Peng, 2011).

In the process of preparing for constitutionalism after 1906, the Qing government also formulated some legal documents related to the constitution and constitutional organizations. They include *Regulations for the Constitutional Affairs Bureau* (the 16th day of the 7th lunar month of the 33rd year of the Guangxu Era, i.e., 1907), *Regulations for Ziyiju* (Local Advisory Council) (the 24th day of the 6th lunar month of the 34th year of the Guangxu Era, i.e., 1908), *Regulations for Electing Members of Ziyiju* (the 24th day of the 6th lunar month of the 34th year of the Guangxu Era), *Imperial Outline of Constitution* (the 1st day of the 8th lunar month of the 34th year of the Guangxu Era), *Regulations on Local Self-Governance in Towns and Villages* (the 27th day of the 12th lunar month of the 34th year of the Guangxu Era), *Regulations on Local Election for Self-Governance in Towns and Villages* (the 27th day of the 12th lunar month of the 34th year of the Guangxu Era), *Regulations for the Institute of Self-Governance* (the 16th day of the 3rd lunar month of the 1st year of the Xuantong Era, i.e., 1909), *Regulations for Zizhengyuan* (Advisory Council) (the 8th day of the 7th lunar month of the 1st year of the Xuantong Era), *Regulations for the Election of Members of Zizhengyuan* (the 13th day of the 9th lunar month of the 1st year of the Xuantong Era), *Regulations on Local Self-Governance in the Capital* (the 24th day of the 12th lunar month of the 1st year of the Xuantong Era), *Regulations on Local Election for Self-Governance in the Capital* (the 24th day of the 12th lunar month of the 1st year of the Xuantong Era), *Regulations on Local Self-Governance in Prefectures and Counties* (the 27th day of the 12th lunar month of the 1st year of the Xuantong Era), *Regulations on Local Election for Self-Governance in Prefectures and Counties* (the 27th day of the 12th lunar month of the 1st year of the Xuantong Era), *Bureaucratic Establishment of Bideyuan (Privy Council)*[12] (the 10th day of the 4th lunar month of the 3rd year of the Xuantong Era, i.e., 1911), *Regulations on Procedures of Bideyuan* (the 22nd day of the 6th lunar month of the 3rd year of the Xuantong Era), and *Nineteen Articles of Creed* (the 13th day of the 9th lunar month of the 3rd year of the Xuantong Era) (Huai, 2010a, 2010b, 114–190). These legal documents included the organizational charter of the quasi-parliamentary body, self-governance charter of local governments, and constitutional outline or documents, which constitute the prototype of the constitution in the modern sense.

During the birth of the modern constitution, both the *Imperial Outline of Constitution* and the *Nineteen Articles of Creed* were constitutional documents of great historical significance. This is because the *Imperial Outline of the Constitution* was the first document in history that was identified as "an outline of the constitution" (Gao et al., 2012, 509). Although it largely imitated the *Meiji Imperial Constitution*,

[12] Bideyuan was where the emperor personally consulted about the national affairs. It was set up following the model of the Japanese Privy Council, with a president and vice president, as well as 32 advisors. Lu Runxiang, Rongqing, and Yikuang served as the president of Bideyuan successively. However, a few days after the establishment of the council, the Xinhai Revolution broke out and the Qing Dynasty was overthrown. Thus, it actually did not effectively play its advisory role. See Zhang and Li (1991, 399).

adopted the Japanese model of constitutional dualism, and was characterized by "emphasizing the emperor's power over the people's power," it "established for the first time the supremacy of the constitution in China's legal system" (Xia, 2012, 146), and therefore, it was of progressive significance. Compared with the *Imperial Outline of Constitution*, the *Nineteen Articles of Creed* had more modern constitutional qualities because it was formulated and adopted by the quasi-parliament Council, the Advisory Council; thus, it can be regarded as the provisional constitution of the late Qing Dynasty. It was the first constitution in the history of the Chinese legal system. "This document was proclaimed by the Qing emperor and the regent in the imperial temple. The emperor vowed to observe it together with the people forever. Therefore, it can be seen as the only constitution adopted in the Qing Dynasty. It was also the first constitution in China's history" (Yang, 2012, 36). The *Nineteen Articles of Creed* adopted the British model of "constitutional monarchy" with its cabinet system. "Although the monarch still exists, the constitution is not based on the monarch's decision. The power to draft the resolution is vested in the Advisory Council, and the power to amend and initiate proposals belongs to the parliament, and this cannot be interfered with by the monarch. It is purely a constitution of parliamentary politics" (Yang, 2012, 38). For example, Article 8 provides that "the Prime Minister shall be elected by the parliament and appointed by the emperor. Other ministers of state shall be recommended by the Prime Minister and appointed by the emperor. Members of the royal family shall not be the Prime Minister, other ministers of state, or the governors of the provinces" (Huai, 2010a, 2010b, 190). Some provisions demonstrate vague features of modern constitutions, such as Article 11, which stipulates that "imperial edicts shall not replace laws. Except for emergency orders subject to specific conditions, edicts shall be limited to the execution of the law and those appointed by the law." Article 12 stipulates that "No international treaty shall be concluded except by resolution of the parliament. During the adjournment, decisions to make peace and declare war shall be ratified by the parliament afterwards" (Huai, 2010a, 2010b, 190). It even stipulates that the hierarchical effect of the Constitution was higher than that of the Imperial Code, such as in Article 16, which stipulates that "the Imperial Code shall not contradict the Constitution" (Huai, 2010a, 2010b, 190). These norms, which contain modern constitutional concepts, have never been found in the codes of the Chinese legal system. Of course, no matter how short the existence of the *Imperial Outline of Constitution* and the *Nineteen Articles of Creed* was, their historical status in the history of the Chinese legal system should not be underestimated. Their existence suggested the beginning of the establishment of the principle of the rule of law, which marked the birth of modern constitutional law. Therefore, their existence marked the birth of the modern Chinese constitution.

Birth of Modern Administrative Law

In the strict sense, there is no administrative law in the Chinese legal system. However, the governments of the various Chinese dynasties had a rich wealth of norms on state administration and management of officials. These can still be considered the administrative law of ancient China. After all, administrative law in ancient China was not administrative law in the modern sense.[13] The traditional Chinese administrative system was based on the "Three Departments and Six Ministries," whereas modern administrative law is centered on the rule of law based on the "separation of powers and checks and balances" (Weng, 2006, 85). The birth of modern administrative law demonstrates the trend of evolution from the traditional "Three Departments and Six Ministries" administrative system to the separation of powers, and it is the product of the reform of the bureaucratic system in the late Qing Dynasty. "In the process of preparing for the constitution in the late Qing Dynasty, the administrative structure was adjusted and corrected on a large scale... This process of adjustment and correction promoted the modernization of China's traditional administrative structure" (Xia, 2012, 212).

On September 1, 1906 (the 13th day of the 7th lunar month of the 32nd year of the Guangxu Era), the Qing government announced the preparation of the constitution and decided to first collate the bureaucratic system. It was proposed in the *Edict of Declaration on Preparation for the Establishment of a Constitution with Preceding Collation of Bureaucratic System* that "therefore, to eliminate the accumulated ills and clearly define the responsibilities, the starting point should be the bureaucratic system. It is urgent that the bureaucratic system should be collated, decided and adjusted, and the laws should be carefully defined" (Huai, 2010a, 2010b, 3). On November 6, 1906 (the 20th day of the 9th lunar month of the 32nd year of the Guangxu Era), Emperor Guangxu issued the *Edict of Declaration on Preparation for Establishment of a Constitution with Preceding Collation of the Bureaucratic System*, announcing the program for bureaucratic system reform, thus indicating the birth of the modern administration, as detailed in Table 2.

It can be seen from Table 2 that the focus of the reform of the bureaucratic system in 1906 was to "clarify responsibilities, eliminate the accumulated ills, seek truth from facts, and remove frivolity." Departments such as the Ministry of Civil Affairs, Ministry of Expenditure, Ministry of Rites, Ministry of Army, Ministry of Posts and Communication, Ministry of Tribal Affairs, Advisory Council, and the Auditing Court were established or reorganized. However, compared with the newly established or reorganized departments, there were still a large number of departments that "operate as usual and do not need to be changed," such as the Grand Council, Ministry of Foreign Affairs, Ministry of Official Personnel Affairs, Ministry of Education, Imperial Clan Court (宗人府), Grand Secretariat (内阁),

[13] Regarding the debate on whether there was administrative law in Chinese ancient times, Chen Quansheng believed that modern administrative law, as a product of democracy and the rule of law, made the constitution specific in the relationship between the government and citizens, thus becoming the continuation and supplement of the constitution. Although the ancient Chinese laws and regulations had provisions on administrative organization and functions, they were all compiled by the monarchs or officials, based on the practices of successive dynasties, to deal with administrative affairs that govern the people and officials. They were not the extension of the fundamental law and were not made by organs representing public opinion to achieve the purpose of democracy and rule of law. For a discussion on emergence and development of China's administrative law, see Chen (1995).

Table 2 Reforms of the bureaucratic system in the late Qing Dynasty (Huai, 2010a, 2010b, 194)

Before the reform	Reformed or not	After the reform
Grand council (军机处)	All established institutions remained the same	Grand council (军机处)
Ministry of foreign affairs (外务部)	All established institutions remained the same	Ministry of foreign affairs (外务部)
Ministry of official personnel affairs (吏部)	All established institutions remained the same	Ministry of official personnel affairs (吏部)
Patrol (巡警)	Patrol was one issue of civil affairs; hence, it was changed into the ministry of civil affairs	Ministry of civil affairs (民政部)
Ministry of revenue and population (户部)	It was changed into the ministry of expenditure, and the ministry of treasury (财政处) was integrated into it	Ministry of expenditure (度支部)
Ministry of rites (礼部)	Taichang (court of sacrifice affairs), Guanglu (court of imperial affairs), and Honglu (court of foreign envoys affairs) were integrated into it	Ministry of rites (礼部)
Ministry of education (学部)	All established institutions remained the same	Ministry of education (学部)
Ministry of war (兵部)	It was changed into the ministry of the army, and lianbingchu (bureau of military training) and *Taipusi* (court of imperial traveling affairs) were integrated into it	Ministry of army (陆军部)
–	Specialized bureaus for ships, railways, wires, and posts should be established	Ministry of post and communication (邮传部)
Council of tribal affairs (理藩院)	It was changed into the ministry of *Lifanbu* (tribal affairs, 理藩部)	Ministry of tribal affairs (理藩部)
Censorate (都察院)	It was changed into one censor and two vice censors	Censor and vice censor (都御史、副都御史)
–	To hear and learn from the masses, *Zizhengyuan* (advisory council, 资政院) was established	Advisory council (资政院)
–	To monitor expenditures, the auditing court was established	Auditing court (审计院)

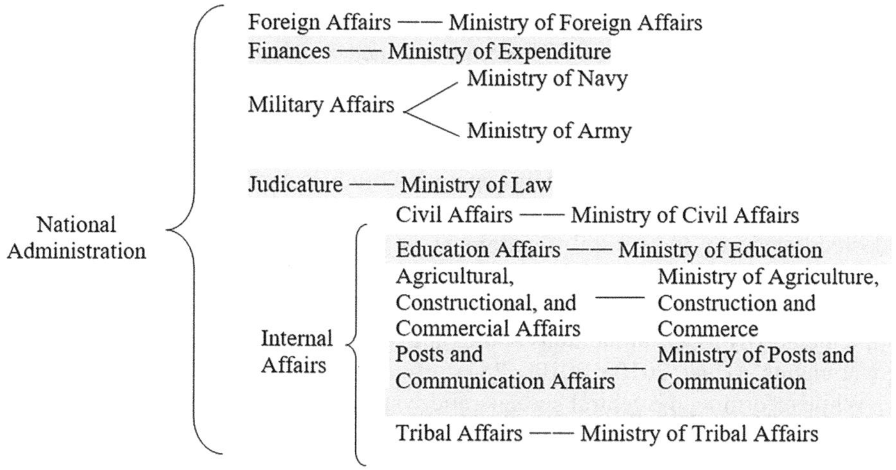

Fig. 1 Categories of national administrative affairs and divisions provided in *Qin Ding Xing Zheng Gang Mu* (*Categories of administration made by the imperial order*, 钦定行政纲目) (Huai, 2010a, 2010b, 283–284)

Imperial Hanlin Academy (翰林院), Directorate of Astronomy and Calendar (钦天监), Imperial Procession Guard (銮仪卫), Imperial Household Department (内务府), Imperial Institute of Medicine (太医院), various military of different banners (旗营), the Institute for Imperial Guards (侍卫处), Police and Guards (步军统领衙门), Shuntian Prefecture (顺天府), and Capital Granaries (仓场衙门) (Huai, 2010a, 2010b, 194).

As a product of democracy and the rule of law, modern administrative law specifies the relationship between the government and citizens, thus becoming the continuation and supplement of the Constitution. Although the ancient Chinese laws and regulations had provisions on administrative organizations and administrative functions, they were compiled by the monarchs or officials based on the practices of successive dynasties to deal with administrative affairs that governed the people and officials. They were not extensions of the fundamental law and were not made by organs representing public opinion to achieve the purpose of democracy and the rule of law (Fig. 1).

The birth of modern administrative law began in 1908 with the Qing government's *Qin Ding Xing Zheng Gang Mu.* On the one hand, it "clearly defined the administrative principles of the constitutional monarchy and the system of government in which the parliament, the government, and the courts, respectively, assisted the monarch in exercising legislative, executive, and judicial powers" (Xia, 2012, 213). On the other hand, it also clearly delineated the categories of state administrative affairs and the powers of each ministry and division (Huai, 2010a, 2010b, 284–311). *Qin Ding Xing Zheng Gang Mu* provided a detailed division of the categories and distribution of state administrative affairs, as shown in Fig. 1.

Qin Ding Xing Zheng Gang Mu also divided the state administrative affairs into four levels, the first being "direct governance," including "the administration of the central government, and the special officials in each province to carry out the decrees made by the central government." The second level is "indirect governance," including the situation where "the central government enacts decrees, but does not directly implement them by appointing officials, instead, appointing provincial governments to implement them." The third level is "local governance," including "decrees made by the central government or the provincial governments, which are followed by local officials." The fourth level is "local autonomy," including "decrees made by the central government or the provincial governments which are implemented by local autonomous bodies and appointed by the central or provincial governments" (Huai, 2010a, 2010b, 284).

While reforming the central bureaucratic system, in April 1906, the Qing government also began to reform the local bureaucratic system, which included abolishing the position of *xuezheng* (educational supervisor) and setting up *tixueshisi* (officials in charge of studying affairs), changing *anchashisi* (department of inspection on law affairs) into *tifashisi* (department in charge of law affairs), establishing the position of *jiaosheshisi* (department of diplomatic affairs), and setting up two divisions of *xunjing* (Patrol) and *quanye* (in charge of industry and commerce) (Zhang & Li, 1991, 401–402).

The Qing government also made a large number of administrative laws and regulations during the bureaucratic reforms, which covered a wide range of areas, with some related to public security management and urban management, and contributed to the gradual formation and development of the modern administrative legal system. Regarding public security management, there were the *Law on Association and Assembly* (1908), *Law on Violation of Police Orders* (1908), *Provisional Rules on Household Registration*, *Rules on Household Registration Management*, and *Law on the Enforcement of Household Registration Investigation*. On urban management, there were the *Modification of the Regulations of the Road*, *Rules for the Implementation of the Regulations of the Road*, *Special Rules for the Management of Handcart*, *Rules for the Management of Handcarts*, *Rules for the Management of Rickshaws*, *Regulations on the Punishment of Vehicles without Using Lights at Night*, and *Rules for Pandemic Prevention and Cleaning*, among others (Zhao, 2009, 157). The administrative legislation of the late Qing Dynasty was characterized by "a breakthrough from the traditional administrative system to the introduction of Western structures," "the development of departments in depth and breadth in administrative legislation," and "the proliferation of transitional regulations" (Zhang & Li, 1991, 404). Although these issued administrative laws and regulations were only shortly implemented or not implemented at all, they constituted the modern administrative law system, together with the laws promulgated during the bureaucratic system reforms, and laid the foundation for the administrative legislation of the Republic of China. In this regard, some scholars have given a fair assessment: "The emergence of a series of administrative laws and regulations centered on *Qin Ding Xing Zheng Gang Mu* at the end of the Qing Dynasty marked the emergence of a modern administrative legal system. Although most of the laws were only drafted and not actually promulgated, they had a certain degree of positive influence on the structure of the subsequent administrative legal system" (Cao, 2012, 304). The birth of modern administrative law and the emergence of many modern executive and legislative branches also suggested that a legislature representing public opinion began to appear.

Birth of Modern Civil Law

In the ancient Chinese legal system, there was no independent system of civil law rules and complete doctrine of civil law.[14] Thus, civil law did not exist as a law department.[15] The birth of modern civil law also originated from the revision of laws during the legal reforms in the late Qing Dynasty. Modern civil legislation began in 1907 (the 33rd year of the Guangxu Era) when the Ministry of Civil Affairs of the Qing government petitioned for the establishment of civil law (Yu, 2003, 24–28). The memorial pointed out:

"Examining the Eastern and Western countries, the laws are divided into public law and private law. Public law is to determine the relationship between the state and the people, that is, criminal law and so on; private law is to determine the relationship between people, that is, civil law and so on. The two are equally important, and neither

[14] Some present works have outlined the civil legal system in ancient China from the perspective of "civil law history," such as the *General History of Civil Law of China* edited by Zhang Jinfan and *History of Chinese Civil Law* edited by Kong Qingming, among others, which analyzed Chinese civil law from the aspects of the property rights relationship, debt relationship, contract system, inheritance, property division, and others. However, all of these works reconstruct the ancient Chinese civil law system based on the system structure of modern civil law, which is questionable. Therefore, they cannot provide an explanation for the existence of an independent civil law system in ancient China.

[15] As to whether there was civil law in ancient China, there are three different views in the academic circle since modern times: (1) Affirmation Doctrine. The leading exponents include Mei Zhongxie and Yang Honglie. The former is the author of *The Essentials of Civil Law*, and the latter is the author of *The History of Chinese Legal Development*. Both affirmed and agreed with the civil legal relationship in traditional society, holding that although there was no civil law in the formal sense in the Chinese Legal Family, there was substantive civil law. Li (etiquette) and customs constituted the ancient civil legal norms. (2) Denial Doctrine. The leading exponents include Liang Qichao and Wang Boqi. The former wrote *Evolution of Chinese Statutory Law*, and the latter wrote *Modern Legal Thought and China's Inherent Legal Culture*. They believed that ancient Chinese civil law does not exist, and no laws and regulations belong to criminal law and political law. (3) Unity Doctrine. The leading exponents include Pan Weihe and Dai Yanhui. The doctrine can further be divided into the unity doctrine of civil and criminal law (it is believed that the ancient codes did not differentiate between civil and criminal law, and public and private law; civil law is included in criminal law) and the unity doctrine of Li and civil law (civil law existed in the form of Li). See Zhao (2009, 157). We believe that when deciding whether there was civil law in ancient China, the characteristics, scope, and standards of modern civil law cannot simply be reversed into ancient civil law because, on one hand, it cannot be denied that the term "civil law" came from abroad and originated from ancient Roman law; on the other hand, there were indeed some norms or customs of civil rules in the Chinese Legal Family. Therefore, "civil law" has never existed as a law department in the Chinese Legal Family, but there were some civil rules and customs in the legal system of the Chinese Legal Family.

of them should be neglected, … the compositions of civil law in different countries are different, but the main idea and general structure are similar. Some major rules are important in civil law. For example, property law is to define ownership of properties, the law of obligations is to strengthen good faith in social interaction, family law is to clarify ethical relationships, and succession law is to solve inheritance disputes. All the civil laws are clear and detailed with categorized provisions. That's how they become clear and established laws. When matters occur, there are standards to follow. When making judgments, there are no ambiguous rules. Clear politics, harmonious rules, and peaceful society are largely due to this. In old China, the law did not differentiate between civil and criminal law. The name of civil law was borrowed from *Shang Shu Kong Zhuan* (comments attributed by Mr. Kong, 尚书孔传). In the laws of the past dynasties, provisions concerning household and marriage were actually approximate to civil law, but they were all deficient and incomplete. … we ask you to order the ministers responsible for making the civil laws to consider the worldly wisdom, politics, and customs with reference to the laws of various countries" (Li, 2001, 133).

The memorial proposed to draw lessons from the Western model of distinguishing between public and private law and to formulate a separate civil code. In the same year, "Shen Jiaben, Yu Liansan, and Ying Rui were appointed as ministers for the revision of laws, and the Law Revision Institution was established, recruiting students who returned from Europe, America, and Japan to make laws based on different law departments. A Japanese, Matsuoka Yoshimasa, was hired to draft the civil law" (Yang, 2012, 47). Eventually, in September 1911, the *Draft Civil Law of the Qing Dynasty* was finished, which was the first civil code in the history of the Chinese legal system (Wang, 2007, 389). The layout of the *Draft Civil Law of the Qing Dynasty* imitated the Pandekten System of the *German Civil Code*,[16] i.e., a five-part format. It comprises 1,569 articles, including 323 articles in Title I, General Provisions; 654 articles in Title II, Law of Obligations; 339 articles in Title III, Law of Property; 143 articles in Title IV, Families; and 110 articles in Title V, Inheritance (Huai, 2010a, 2010b, 510–810). It should be noted that the three titles, namely, General Provisions, Law of Obligations, and Law of Property, were drafted by Matsuoka Yoshimasa, a judge at the Tokyo Court of Appeals, and the two titles of Families and Inheritance were drafted by Chen Lu, Gao Zhong, and Zhu Xianwen. The difference in the drafters of each part demonstrated the Qing government's different attitudes toward the parts concerning the property and personal relations. This directly affected the

[16] Although the drafting of the *Draft Civil Law of the Qing Dynasty* was mainly undertaken by the Japanese, its content was more similar to the *German Civil Code* and was borrowed from the German civil law. For example, Professor Wang Limin believed that the content of Japanese civil law mainly came from German civil law, and German civil law was its main component; China actually absorbed German civil law, and the *Draft Civil Law of the Qing Dynasty* was very similar to the German Civil Code. Therefore, it is not difficult to see that although China studied civil law from Japan at the end of the Qing Dynasty, what it obtained was mainly German civil law. China only undertook the study of Japanese civil law as an indirect way of introducing German civil law. In the late Qing Dynasty, China absorbed the German civil law from the Japanese civil law. See Wang (1997).

different degrees of transplantation of foreign law in the two parts. Specifically, in the first three titles, many civil law theories of the civil law system were borrowed and transplanted. For example, "important principles such as the inviolability of private property, autonomy of will, freedom of contract, and liability for negligence were affirmed, and a series of institutions were systematically and completely transplanted, such as civil subjects, agency, legal acts, statute of limitations, real rights, and obligations" (Xia, 2012, 335). The latter two titles were drafted by the Li (Ritual) Institution, so some articles still inherited some contents of Chinese *fengjian* rituals, such as "marriage is decided by parents, polygamy, absolute authority of parents, and implied ancestral succession, which shows that the personal status law part of the draft was based on the *fengjian* patriarchal family institutions and did not recognize the independent personality and equal status of family members" (Li, 2001).

Overall, the publication of the *Draft Civil Law of the Qing Dynasty* was a milestone in terms of its ground-breaking status as it marked the birth of modern Chinese civil law. As some scholars have commented:

> The *Draft Civil Law of the Qing Dynasty*, as the first civil code, occupies a unique historical position in the history of Chinese civil legislation. The development from *Huhun Lv* (Household and Marriage Law) to the Western-style *Draft Civil Law of the Qing Dynasty* is, on the surface, a change in the form and name of the code, but in essence, a change from concept to content. It is also a facet of the modernization of traditional Chinese law. Particularly important, it put an end to the absence of civil law (the civil department law in the Western sense) in China and created a new civil law system. The historical significance of the *Draft Civil Law of the Qing Dynasty* lies in this. (Zhao, 2009, 206)

Moreover, although the *Draft Civil Law of the Qing Dynasty* was never formally adopted and implemented, its legislative content and style had an important influence on the civil legislation of the Republic of China. In terms of legislative content, both the *Draft Civil Law* proposed by the Beiyang government and the *Civil Law of the Republic of China* promulgated by the Nanjing National Government were influenced by the *Draft Civil Law of the Qing Dynasty* to varying degrees. As far as the legislative style is concerned, the two civil codes (drafts) during the period of the Republic of China were also heavily influenced by the Pandekten-style civil law system. It can be concluded that the publication of the *Draft Civil Law of the Qing Dynasty* marked the birth of modern civil law because "it was also the first specialized civil law codification document in Chinese legal history, which for the first time broke the old legal structure of indistinguishable civil and criminal law and established the independent status of civil law in China's legal system" (Zhao & Bi, 2006, 59). Moreover, the Pandekten-style civil law system chosen influenced the formation and complete establishment of modern civil law.

Birth of Modern Commercial Law

The *fengjian* Chinese law under the Chinese Legal Family was always influenced by Confucian thought, adhering to the policy of "emphasizing agriculture and restraining commerce" and "emphasizing agriculture and scorning commerce." Merchants had a very low social status in ancient Chinese society. After the Opium War in 1840, trade between China and foreign countries increased. National capitalism and its trading activities began to emerge and develop to varying degrees. The development of commercial law was closely related to commercial activities. Although there were some commercial rules and customs in *fengjian* China under the Chinese Legal Family, there was no commercial law in the modern sense. Stated differently, "there was no commercial law in ancient China. Unlike Western countries, where an independent concept and system of commercial law emerged in the Middle Ages, there was never the concept or system of commercial law in China before the end of the Qing Dynasty" (Guo, 2003). This situation changed only in the late Qing Dynasty during the legal reforms.

In 1903 (the 25th day of the 3rd lunar month of the 29th year of the Guangxu Era), Emperor Guangxu issued an edict: "A few days ago, Zhengwuchu (the general office) discussed and replied to Zai Zhen's request for the establishment of the Ministry of Commerce, and an imperial edict approving it has been issued. Now, I will first send Zai Zhen, Yuan Shikai, and Wu Tingfang to make commercial law as rules to follow. Once the commercial law is compiled and finalized, I will send specialized senior staff to establish the Ministry of Commerce, and officials should spare no effort to protect and maintain commerce, so that the revitalization and flourishing of business will come soon. In this way, building people's wealth and cultivating national capital can be realized. By command of the Emperor" (The Shanghai Compilation Office, 2010, 20–21). On January 21 of the following year, the Qing government issued the *Imperial Commercial Law of the Qing Dynasty*, which consisted of two parts: *General Regulations for Merchants* and *Company Law*. The former comprised 9 articles, and the latter comprised 131 articles. Although there were only nine articles in the *General Regulations for Merchants*, they all dealt with basic commercial issues, such as the scope of merchants, merchant qualifications, trade names, and trade books. The first article states that "anyone who conducts commerce, trade, buying, selling, or trafficking in goods is a merchant." This shows that the *Imperial Commercial Law of the Qing Dynasty* adopted subjectivism from the German Commercial Code as the legislative principle. *Company Law* identifies four types of companies: joint ventures, joint ventures limited, joint-stock companies, and joint-stock limited companies. It also covers content concerning shares, rights of shareholders, directors, auditors, meetings of directors, meetings of shareholders, accounts, change of articles of incorporation, closure, and penalties, among others (Huai, 2010a, 2010b, 865–872). The *Imperial Commercial Law of the Qing Dynasty* was indeed the first commercial law in the history of Chinese law in the formal sense, as it was the first law ever to be independently named "commercial law," and it established the subjectivist principle that came from the German Commercial Code. However, from a formal point of view, in the substantive sense, it was not the first commercial law in the history of the Chinese legal system because the majority of its legislative content was based on corporate law (93.6%) and did not constitute a commercial law system in the modern sense. Therefore, the *Imperial Commercial Law of the Qing Dynasty* was only the first single commercial regulation in the history of Chinese law, not the first commercial law. It marked the germination of modern commercial law. From the drafting year of the *Imperial Commercial Law of the Qing Dynasty* to 1907, the Qing government also promulgated other emergency commercial laws and regulations, such as the *Bankruptcy Law* (69 articles), *Trial Regulations for Company Registration* (18 articles), and *Regulations for Bank Registration* (8 articles). However, they did not form a complete commercial law system.

The birth of modern commercial law actually began in 1909 with the *Draft Commercial Code of the Qing Dynasty*. In September 1908 (the 8th lunar month of the 34th year of the Guangxu Era), the Law Revision Institution hired Japanese jurist Kotaro Shida to help in drafting the *Draft Commercial Code of the Qing Dynasty* (also known as the "Shida Act"). It was completed the following year. The draft was divided into five parts, namely, the General Provisions, Commercial Activities, Corporate Law, Shipping Law, and Negotiable Instruments Law, with a total of 1,008 articles, and it was the first commercial code in China's history (Xia, 2012, 380). Whether in terms of legislative style or content, the *Draft Commercial Code of the Qing Dynasty* was copied from the commercial laws of Japan and Germany, and the trace of legal transplantation was "obvious." "The structure was almost identical to that of the Meiji Commercial Code implemented in Japan at that time, which was divided into five titles: General Provisions, Companies, Commercial Activities, Bill of Exchange, and Maritime Affairs. In terms of content, it mainly imitated the Meiji Commercial Law of Japan and the 1900 *German Commercial Code*. Its provisions on the bill of exchange also referred to the *Hague Draft Uniform Regulations for Bill of Exchange*" (Li, 2001). However, the draft was criticized for excessive imitation. Therefore, in 1910 (the second year of the Xuantong Era), the Ministry of Agriculture, Construction and Commerce organized chambers of commerce to conduct a survey of commercial customs and took cognizance of the laws prevailing in other countries around the world in compiling the *Draft Revised Commercial Law*, which was more complete (Wang, 2007, 390). Nevertheless, it was "abandoned before it was passed." At that point, the commercial legislation of the late Qing Dynasty ended. The modern commercial legal system's birth was marked by the 1909 *Draft Commercial Code of the Qing Dynasty*.

Birth of Modern Criminal Law

In the Chinese legal system, criminal law during the imperial era was more developed (Wang, 2016a, 2016b, 8) and occupied a very important position in other legal systems of the Chinese Legal Family. The reform of criminal law in the late Qing legal reforms or the birth of modern criminal law can be considered the disintegration of the main part of the Chinese Legal Family. "The revision of criminal law in the late Qing Dynasty went through a difficult and slow process, which also essentially reflected the various contradictions and conflicts faced by Chinese law in the transition from the traditional model to the modern one" (Zhu, 2007, 344). The revision of criminal laws at the end of the Qing Dynasty and the birth of modern criminal law are two sides of the same coin, for the revision of criminal laws at the end of the Qing Dynasty was also the process of the birth of modern criminal law. From a macro point of view, the birth of modern criminal law can be divided into two stages, namely, the sunset stage of criminal law in the Chinese Legal Family and the new birth of modern civil-law-style criminal law. These are represented by the *Existing Criminal Law of the Qing Dynasty* and the *New Criminal Law of the Qing Dynasty*, respectively.

The first step in the revision of criminal law in the late Qing Dynasty was to delete and amend the old law. On the 20th day of the 3rd lunar month of the 31st year of the Guangxu Era, Emperor Guangxu promulgated the *Imperial Edict Concerning Permanent Abolition of Heavy Punishment Including Lingchi, Xiaoshou, Lushi* (*Insulting Corpses*) thus: "Now, I order to reform the law. From now on, the heaviest punishment will be beheading in the subsequent death penalties; the three punishments of *lingchi*, *xiaoshou*, and *lushi* should be forever abolished. ... We must follow the law and consider human sentiment, and appropriately balance them to comply with the firm intention of the imperial court to familiarize people with punishment laws well so that they will automatically follow them. This is publicly informed and should be well known by people. By command of the Emperor" (Huai, 2010a, 2010b, 3). Henceforth, heavy penalties in the criminal law of the Chinese Legal Family were removed and reduced.

The second step in the revision of the criminal law in the late Qing Dynasty was the revision of *Da Qing Lv Li*. The *Existing Criminal Law of the Qing Dynasty* was the product originated from Shen Jiaben's practice of imitating Japan by compiling an "existing criminal law" before the promulgation of a new criminal law. It was based on *Da Qing Lv Li* but slightly modified to solve the problem that *Da Qing Lv Li* had become old and had no appropriate amendments. On the 13th day of the 3rd lunar month of the 31st year of the Guangxu Era (1905), the Minister of Revision of Laws petitioned to first remove the articles that should be deleted from the law, determine the provisions, and divide them into three parts—121 articles in the first part, 137 articles in the second, and 86 articles in the third, for a total of 344 articles. Shen Jiaben and others later proposed a memorial to the Qing imperial court on the 29th day of the 1st lunar month of the 34th year of the Guangxu Era (1908)—*Petition for Making Existing Criminal Law to Establish the Basis for the Implementation of the New Law*—suggesting that the amendment of the Qing law should be restarted and proposing four basic principles for revising the existing criminal law. After more than a year of revisions, the first draft was completed in the eighth lunar month of the first year of the Xuantong Era (1909) and was corrected by the Constitutional Affairs Bureau (Xia, 2012, 254). Eventually, on May 15, 1910 (the seventh day of the fourth lunar month of the second year of the Xuantong Era), the Qing government issued the *Edict on the Promulgation of Existing Criminal Law* and said, "Last year, according to the petition of the Minister of the Revision of Law, *Existing Criminal Law* was compiled, and the Constitutional Affairs Bureau was ordered to review and report on it. According to the bureau and the officials, the existing criminal law was compiled into yellow books, and several articles were amended based on the new chapters. ... I order the immediate publication of the books, their worldwide issue, and that all people should comply with the law" (Huai, 2010a, 2010b, 4). The code comprised 389 articles in 36 volumes and 30 departments, with 1,327 bylaws. In addition, 12 articles of *Anti-Opium Regulations* and 165 articles of *Autumn Trial*

Regulations were attached (Cao, 2012, 223). The code was generally regarded as a transitional criminal code because it was only partially and formally changed, and the core aspects, such as the basic spirit, main principles, and content of the articles, remained the same as those of the *Da Qing Lv Li*. The "*Existing Qing Criminal Law* cannot be regarded as a new-style specialized criminal law, whether in terms of form, structure, or content" (Zeng, 2006, 252). Old stipulations such as the "ten abominations," "eight deliberations," and the diagram of the mourning system were all retained (Xia, 2009, 124). However, in this transitional criminal code, there were also many traces of modern criminal law. For example, the code first distinguished civil law from criminal law, selecting purely civil provisions from *Da Qing Lv Li*, such as provisions concerning inheritance, property division, marriage, mortgage and sale, land and house, and money and debts. These activities were no longer subject to punishment, and only fines were enforced, which showed the distinction between criminal and civil affairs (Wang, 2007, 387). Therefore, the *Existing Criminal Law of the Qing Dynasty* can be regarded as the late bell of the criminal law of the Chinese Legal Family.

The third step in the revision of the criminal law in the late Qing Dynasty was the writing of the *New Criminal Law of the Qing Dynasty*. While making the *Existing Criminal Law of the Qing Dynasty*, the Qing government also began to formulate a new criminal code. In 1906, Shen Jiaben hired Okada Asataro, a Japanese Doctor of Law, to help him review the criminal laws. He also selected a group of legal experts to compile the *Draft of New Criminal Law of the Qing Dynasty*, which was submitted to the Qing government in the second half of 1907. On November 5, 1910, the draft was reviewed, approved, and finalized by the Constitutional Affairs Bureau, and it was named the *New Criminal Law of the Qing Dynasty*. However, the new criminal code was strongly opposed and attacked by the ritualists, and the Law Revision Institution had no choice but to redraft it. Hence, it was not until January 25, 1911, after several revisions, that the Qing court finally published the *New Criminal Law of the Qing Dynasty*, according to the report of the Advisory Council and the Constitutional Affairs Bureau (Zhao, 2009, 309). Although the Qing government was replaced before the code could be implemented, the progressive significance of the new criminal code was still undeniable. First, in terms of structure, the new criminal code completely changed the previous pattern of using the "six ministries" to categorize the law and replaced it with the modern structure of a generalist criminal code, adopting the modern legislative style of general and subrules, as well as titles, chapters, and articles. It contains 53 chapters and 411 articles, with five articles annexed in the *Provisional Statute* (Xia, 2009, 124). Second, in terms of content, the *New Criminal Law of the Qing Dynasty* was almost completely different from the old code. For example, it established a new penal system based on free punishment, stipulated the principle of legality, deleted the proportional system in the old criminal code, reflected the humanitarian spirit in the systems of discretionary commutation of the death penalty, and so on; the spirit of equality before the law was embodied to a certain extent, the idea of prevention was implemented, and education by punishment was stipulated (Cao, 2012, 226–227). In short, the *New Criminal Law of the Qing Dynasty* made subversive changes to the traditional Chinese legal system of criminal law, both from the macroscopic and microscopic aspects, and marked the birth of modern criminal law in China. Thus, the modern criminal law system based on the *New Criminal Law of the Qing Dynasty* had its beginnings in the late Qing Dynasty.

Birth of Modern Procedural Law

In the traditional Chinese legal system, substantive and procedural laws were codified together, and there was no special procedural code. Meanwhile, the administrative and judicial institutions were united. During the legal reforms of the late Qing Dynasty, Shen Jiaben proposed that "criminal law should be the main body, and procedural law should be the instrument facilitating its implementation" and "the two complement each other and neither of them should be ignored," which initiated the drafting of the procedural code (Wang, 2007, 390). As an important part of judicial reform in the late Qing Dynasty, the codification of an independent *Draft of the Criminal and Civil Procedure Law of the Qing Dynasty* was formally started in 1905, and the first draft was completed in May 1906 (Zhu, 2007, 352). The draft comprising 260 articles can be divided into five chapters: general provisions, criminal rules, civil rules, general rules for criminal and civil matters, and the cases involving both domestic and foreign elements. It was the first independent draft of procedural law made in modern China. Specifically, it not only abolished the *fengjian* institutions of torture and evidence but also introduced many modern Western procedural institutions. For example, it distinguished criminal cases from civil cases, abolished *fengjian* punishments and interrogation, adopted the principle of discretional evaluation of evidence, and introduced the lawyer and jury systems (Zhao, 2009, 327). However, after the Qing government ordered the provincial governors to review the draft, it met with strong opposition and eventually failed to be promulgated.

After the *Draft of Criminal and Civil Procedure Law of the Qing Dynasty* was rejected, Shen Jiaben organized another drafting of criminal procedure law and civil procedure law in 1907. The following year, the Qing government hired Japanese jurists Matsuoka Yoshimasa and Okada Asataro to assist in making the two draft procedural laws. It was not until January 1911 that the *Draft Criminal Procedure Law of the Qing Dynasty* and the *Draft Civil Procedure Law of the Qing Dynasty* were completed successively. The *Draft Criminal Procedure La*w comprised 515 articles in six titles. It was the first draft code on criminal procedure in modern China and adopted the latest procedural principles and institutions of Western countries of the time. It provided specific and detailed regulations on criminal procedures. Th*e Draft Code of Civil Procedure* comprised 800 articles in four titles. It was the first Draft Code of Civil Procedure in modern China and was mainly based on the civil procedure laws of Germany and Japan. Although the two draft procedural laws were not implemented, they introduced the procedural law institutions from the civil law system and initiated the modernization of the litigation system in modern China. They marked the birth of modern procedural law and exerted an important influence on the litigation system of the Republic of China.

2.1.3 Deepening Stage: The Period of Legal Establishment During the Nanjing Provisional Government and the Beiyang Government

On January 1, 1912, the Provisional Government of the Republic of China was established in Nanjing, and China entered a new era with the establishment of the first democratic capitalist republic in its history. Later, the Beiyang government was established and replaced the Nanjing government. The Chinese Legal Family began to gradually dismantle at this stage, and the modern legal system began to form gradually. This was the stage of the gradual collapse of the Chinese Legal Family.

Formation of a Modern Constitution

(1) Promulgation and implementation of the *Outline of Organization of the Provisional Government of the Republic of China* and the *Provisional Constitution of the Republic of China.* Among the various constitutional documents promulgated by the Nanjing Provisional Government, the *Outline of Organization of the Provisional Government of the Republic of China* and the *Provisional Constitution of the Republic of China* were the two most influential ones. On December 3, 1911, the *Outline of Organization of the Provisional Government of the Republic of China* was promulgated with the approval of the "committee of provisional governors' representatives" and signed by all representatives present at the meeting. It comprised 21 articles in four chapters, stipulating that the Provisional Government was to be organized by the provisional president, the vice president, the executive ministries, the senate, and the provisional central judiciary. The *Outline* is modeled on the national system of the United States, establishing the Provisional Government as a presidential republic government and implementing the principle of separation of powers in political institutions. As it provides that "it shall be in force until the date of establishment of the Constitution of the Republic of China," it is obviously a government organization law with the nature of a provisional constitution. The *Outline* confirmed the birth of the capitalist republic in the form of law for the first time (Cao, 2012, 94). Because it did not contain provisions on the rights of the people and the design of the governmental system had many omissions, the Provisional Senate amended it and drafted the *Draft Provisional Constitution of the Republic of China.* After a month of drafting, discussion, and passage on the third reading, Sun Yat-sen signed and promulgated the *Provisional Constitution of the Republic of China* on March 11, 1912. It comprised 56 articles in seven chapters—General Outline, People, Senate, Provisional President and Vice President, State Council, Courts, and Bylaws. It adopted the constitutional principles of Western countries, such as "separation of powers," "private property being sacred and inviolable," and "equality and freedom," and for the first time, it stipulated that "the sovereignty of the Republic of China shall belong to all the people" (Article 2) (Zhao, 2009, 126–127). The *Provisional Constitution of the Republic of China* is the

first constitutional document in modern China with the nature of a democratic republic in the capitalist stage.

(2) Formulation of the *Tiantan Draft Constitution*. Because of the transitional and temporary nature of the Provisional Constitution, its contents were too simple to effectively limit the arbitrary power of the president and did not grant sufficient power to the parliament. Therefore, after the parliament was established on April 8, 1913, it planned to formulate a formal constitution to replace the Provisional Constitution. By October 31, 1913, the third reading of the *Tiantan Draft Constitution* was completed, and the draft was named the *Draft Constitution of the Republic of China*. It contained 113 articles in 11 chapters: Preface, National System, Territory, National, Parliament, Parliamentary Committees, President, State Council, Court, Law, Accounting, and Amendment and Interpretation of the Constitution. It maintained and developed the constitutional spirit of the *Provisional Constitution of the Republic of China* and was a constitution of a capitalist democratic republic. It had the following characteristics: First, it was guided by the concept of separation of powers followed by the capitalist nation-states. It designed a democratic republic model with a cabinet system. Second, it reflected a strong tendency to legislate on the basis of the person, i.e., the restraint on the power of the president. Although there were some shortcomings in the *Tiantan Draft Constitution*, it became the blueprint for the subsequent constitution because it largely completed the basic work of building a constitutional system (Xia, 2012, 168–173). Because the parliament was forcibly dissolved by Yuan Shikai, the *Tiantan Draft Constitution* became a dead letter before it was passed by the parliament and formally promulgated.

(3) Promulgation and implementation of the *Constitutional Compact of the Republic of China*. In March 1914, Yuan Shikai organized the Constitutional Conference in accordance with the *Regulations on the Organization of the Constitutional Conference*. As soon as the Conference was established, Yuan Shikai formally proposed a resolution to amend the Constitution to expand the powers of the president and fix it with the law. After more than 40 days of discussion and drafting, the *Constitutional Compact of the Republic of China*, also known as "Yuan's Constitutional Compact," was formulated. On May 1, 1915, Yuan Shikai formally announced the repeal of the *Provisional Constitution of the Republic of China* and issued the *Constitutional Compact of the Republic of China*. This comprised 68 articles in ten chapters. Its basic feature was that although it formally retained the provisions compatible with the republican government system of the Republic of China, it actually affirmed Yuan Shikai's dictatorship. At the same time, compared with the Provisional Constitution, the *Constitutional Compact of the Republic of China* greatly expanded the power of the president, practically abolished the principle of separation of powers, and replaced it with the dictatorial system, in which the president had the legislative, executive, and judicial powers simultaneously (Wang, 2007, 430). The *Constitutional Compact* was actually a retrograde step in the constitutional history of the Republic of China.

(4) Promulgation and implementation of the *Constitution of the Republic of China* (Yu, 2013). After the promulgation of the *Constitutional Compact of the Republic of China* in 1915, the republican government system was repeatedly damaged, and the head of the government frequently changed, resulting in intermittent and irregular constitutional activities. This did not end until the promulgation of the *Constitution of the Republic of China*. In 1922, the zhili clique called for "revitalizing the legal tradition" and restored the Provisional Constitution and the original parliament, regarding the formulation of a constitution as its primary task. On November 15 of the same year, the Constitution Drafting Committee held its 35th meeting and continued to draft the constitution based on the *Tiantan Draft Constitution*. On October 8, 1923, the Constitutional Convention completed the third reading of all of the articles of the draft constitution. Soon after, on October 10, the 12th anniversary of the Xinhai Revolution, the *Constitution of the Republic of China* was finally promulgated and implemented after having gone through many twists and turns (Zhu, 2007, 372). The *Constitution* contained 141 articles in 13 chapters, namely, the National System; Sovereignty; Territory; Nationality; National Right; Parliament; President; State Council; Court; Law; Accounting; Local Systems; and Amendments, Interpretation, and Effect of the Constitution. The distinctive contents of the *Constitution* included that the state system was clearly defined as a "unified and democratic state," the government system was stipulated as a republic government system with a responsible cabinet, and a unitary state structure with adequate local autonomy was established. The *Constitution* was characterized by a more complete system of constitutional norms, more provisions on national rights, and more skillful use of some technical norms. Therefore, it played a link-up role in the history of Chinese constitutional law (Xia, 2012, 178–180). Moreover, the promulgation of the *Constitution of the Republic of China* marked the birth of the first officially published constitution in the history of the Chinese legal system.

Formation of Modern Administrative Law

The new regime of the Nanjing Provisional Government was built according to the *Outline of Organization of the Provisional Government of the Republic of China* and the *Provisional Constitution of the Republic of China*. Although the Provisional Government survived for a short time, it made a fundamental contribution to the establishment of the administrative legal system and formed an initial administrative legal system.[17] By contrast, the development of administrative legislation during the Beijing government was outstanding because the disintegration of the Qing *fengjian* regime and the establishment of a new republic government had to rely on the adoption of relevant laws and decrees to establish the governmental bodies and clarify the division of powers. According to statistics, there were 852 laws, regulations, rules,

[17] Such as administrative regulations in the fields of military administration, internal affairs and police administration, education regulations, and economic management. See Zhao (2009,158).

ordinances, statutes, and orders enacted by the government during this period, which was considerable. Important laws and regulations concerning the organization of administrative organs promulgated in this period included the *Bureaucratic Establishment of the State Council* (1912), *Order to Unify the Organization of the Current Provincial and Local Administrative Offices* (1913), *Provincial Bureaucratic Establishment* (1914), *Prefectural Bureaucratic Establishment* (1914), and *County-Level Bureaucratic Establishment* (1914) (Cao, 2012, 306–307). In addition, legislation concerning the civil service was developed. For example, on civil service examination and appointment, the Beijing government promulgated various laws from 1913 to 1917, including the *Law on Advanced Examination for Civil Servants*, *Law on General Examination for Civil Servants*, *Law on Examination for Diplomatic and Consular Officials*, *Law on Examination for Judicial Officials*, *Rules for Implementation of Law on Advanced Examination for Civil Servants*, *Rules for Implementation of Law on General Examination for Civil Servants*, *Order on Appointment of Civil Servants*, *Law on Appointment of Civil Servants*, *Order on Selection of Civil Servants*, and *Execution Order on Appointment and Removal of Civil Servants*. Regarding the punishment of civil servants, the Beijing government promulgated the *Draft Law on the Punishment of Civil Servants*, *Law on the Correction and Impeachment*, *Order on Special Jurisdiction over Official Offenses*, *Order on Punishment of Official Offenses*, *Law on Punishment of Judicial Officials*, *Law on Punishment of Auditors*, *Regulations on Punishment of Civil Officials*, and *Regulations on Punishment of Corrupted Officials* (Zhang & Li, 1991, 407–408).

Therefore, the period of the Beijing government is, in fact, an important stage in the formation and establishment of the capitalist republic in China both in terms of quantity and scale.

Formation of Modern Civil Law

As mentioned earlier, the civil code formulated at the end of the Qing Dynasty had not yet been implemented and was still in its draft stage with no legal effect. At the start of the era of the National Government, there had not been any civil code during the establishment of the new country. To guide the civil rules and ensure the application of the law, the Beiyang government continued to adopt the basic principles of the late Qing legislation by presidential decree.

Meanwhile, the drafting of the various editions of civil law was also in progress (Zhao, 2009, 208). In 1915, Yuan Shikai instructed the Law Review Committee to compile a new *Draft Civil Code* based on the draft civil law of the former Qing Dynasty, incorporating the precedents made by *Daliyuan* (the highest judiciary body) of the Beijing government of the Republic of China in the past years. Later, from 1925 to 1926, its five parts were published successively: *General Provisions*, *Law of Obligations*, *Law of Property*, *Relatives*, and *Inheritance*, with a total of 1,745 articles (Zeng, 2006, 290). The *General Provisions* were drafted by Yu Chaichang, the *Law of Obligations* was drafted by Ying Shi and Liang Jingfu, the *Law of Property* was drafted by Huang Youchang, and *Relatives* and *Inheritance* were drafted by Gao

Zhong. The *Draft Civil Code* favored the protection of social interests, and there were various changes made to the title on obligations, adopting some principles and institutions of the *Swiss Law on Debts*. Unfortunately, when the *Draft Civil Code* was completed, the Beijing Coup occurred, and the parliament was dissolved, which prevented the draft from being promulgated and formally enacted (Xia, 2012, 337–338). Although the *Draft Civil Code* was not promulgated, its historical significance cannot be denied. It marked the formation of modern civil law and demonstrated that the Chinese Legal Family had gradually dismantled and the civil law system had begun to take shape. The draft also served a link-up function and paved the way for the formulation of the civil code of the Nanjing National Government, which greatly contributed to the establishment of modern civil law.

Formation of Modern Commercial Law

Modern commercial law was formed during the period of the Nanjing Provisional Government and the Beijing government. During this period, the governments promulgated and implemented a large number of commercial laws and regulations, which gradually built the prototype of the modern commercial law system.

Shortly after the establishment of the Republic of China in 1911, the government of the Republic of China made adopting commercial legislation an important task. In *Nanjing Provisional Government's Letter to Friendly Nations*, the government of the Republic of China clearly stated that it would revise the civil law, commercial law, and mining rules; would improve finance; and would temporarily apply the commercial law and bankruptcy law of the previous Qing Dynasty before the new laws were adopted. On May 14, 1912, the government stated in *Document to the Ministry of Commerce of the President's Secretary Office for Drafting Commercial Laws* that "the government should expeditiously investigate the mining methods and commercial customs in China and make reference to the mining and commercial laws of other countries to draft China's mining and commercial laws" (Cao, 2012, 192). In September 1913, after Zhang Rui, an industrialist, became the minister of agriculture and commerce in Yuan Shikai's government, he also proposed in an official document submitted to Yuan Shikai to "examine the drafts of the general rules of commercial law and the company law submitted by the former Qing Ministry of Agricultural, Constructional, and Commercial Affairs to the Advisory Council which should be adopted as the applicable regulations of the Ministry of Industry and Commerce, changing the general rules of commercial law to the general rules of merchants and changing the company law to the regulations on companies. I bravely report them to the President, asking the President to submit them to the parliament and promulgate them as the current regulations of the Ministry of Commerce." On the basis of *Investigation on Commercial Laws*, the Ministry of Agriculture and Commerce compiled the *Draft Company Regulations* and *Draft General Regulations for Merchants*. The former included 249 articles in five chapters: general provisions, unlimited companies, limited partnerships, companies limited by shares, and joint-stock limited partnerships. The latter included 73 articles in seven chapters:

merchants, merchant qualifications, commercial registration, trade name, commercial account books, commercial users and apprentices, and agents. On the basis of these two drafts, *Company Regulations* (6 chapters, 251 articles) and *General Regulations for Merchants* (7 chapters, 73 articles) were established with minor amendments. Yuan Shikai promulgated *Company Regulations* and *General Regulations for Merchants* by decrees issued on January 13 and March 2, 1914, respectively. They entered into force on September 1, 1914. Because they did not go through the procedures for making laws, they were called Li (regulations) instead of Lv (laws) (Ji, 2005, 60–62).

At the same time, the *Draft Law on Bills of Exchange* and *Draft Bankruptcy Law* were also formulated in this period. (1) The *Draft Law on Bills of Exchange* was formed on the basis of the revision of the former Qing *Draft Law on Bills of Exchange*. Five drafts were formed successively in 1913, 1922, 1923, 1924, and 1925. The 1925 draft consisted of four chapters and 117 articles. Nevertheless, none of the above drafts was promulgated. (2) The *Draft Bankruptcy Law* was compiled in 1915, including 337 articles in three titles: substantive law, procedural law, and penalty law (Wang, 2007, 447). In addition, the Beijing government promulgated some other commercial laws and regulations, such as the *Chamber of Commerce Law* (1914), *Rules for Commercial Registration* (1914), *Stock Exchange Law* (1914), and *Regulations on Interest Subsidies for Companies* (1914).

At that time, there was no unified commercial code containing all commercial legislation, and the drafts of laws often existed in the form of independent commercial regulations. The legislators seemed to oscillate between the unification and separation of civil and commercial laws. These commercial laws and regulations laid the foundation for commercial legislation during the Nanjing National Government.

Formation of Modern Criminal Law

Because of its short duration, the Nanjing Provisional Government had no time to revise the criminal law before it was changed. Therefore, the formation of modern criminal law was mainly under the Beijing government. However, the Beijing government had no significant achievements in criminal legislation. From 1912 to 1928, the official criminal law in force was the *Provisional New Criminal Law of the Republic of China*, which was renamed from the *Da Qing Xing Lv* (criminal law of the Qing Dynasty). Although two revisions were made in 1914 and 1918, neither was promulgated and implemented (Zhu, 2007, 382). In addition, a number of special criminal laws were issued.

(1) *Provisional New Criminal Law of the Republic of China*. At the beginning of its establishment, the Beijing government adopted the *Provisional New Criminal Law of the Republic of China*, which was made based on the deleted *New Criminal Law of the Qing Dynasty*. It included 52 chapters with two parts: General Provisions and Sub-Provisions. In this way, the progressive capitalist criminal law principles adopted during the lawmaking in the late Qing Dynasty were

implemented in the judicial practice of the Beijing government. On September 12, 1912, the Beijing government promulgated the *Rules for the Implementation of the New Provisional Criminal Law* to solve specific problems in judicial practice before and after the implementation of the new law (Wang, 2007, 439).

(2) Two amendments to the criminal law and the special criminal law. In 1914, the Law Review Committee formulated the *Draft Amendment to the Criminal Law*, which comprised 432 articles in 55 chapters of two titles. In 1918, the Law Revision Institution was established, which made the *Second Amendment to the Criminal Law*, with 377 articles in two titles. Because of many constraints, neither of the two draft amendments became a formal criminal code. In the same period, the Beijing government promulgated a large number of special criminal laws to meet the needs of its rule, such as *Martial Law*, *Regulations on the Punishment of the Army*, *Regulations on the Punishment for Administration of Public Security*, *Regulations on the Police for Public Security*, *Order on the Punishment of the Navy*, and *Law on Public Security, Theft and Robbery* (Cao, 2012, 231).

Therefore, the formation of modern criminal law was mainly centered on the *Provisional New Criminal Law of the Republic of China*, which constituted a legal system of modern criminal law with other special criminal laws.

Formation of Modern Procedural Law

The formation of modern procedural law can also be roughly divided into two periods: the periods of the Nanjing Provisional Government and the Beijing government. The procedural legislation during the Nanjing Provisional Government generally had little influence on the formation of modern procedural law, whereas the procedural legislation during the Beijing government had a decisive impact on the formation of modern procedural law.

(1) Legislation on litigation during the Nanjing Provisional Government. Because of the short duration of the Nanjing Provisional Government, many legislative procedures and work were not carried out. Two main aspects constituted the procedural legislation at that time.

First, in March 1912, the Provisional President Sun Yat-sen issued decrees prohibiting interrogation and corporal punishment, namely, the *Decree of the President on the Prohibition of Inquisition by Torture by the Ministry of Internal Affairs and the Ministry of Justice* and *Decree of the President on the Prohibition of Corporal Punishment by the Ministry of Internal Affairs and the Ministry of Justice*.

Second, on March 21, 1912, Attorney General Wu Tingfang proposed the application of the draft civil law, draft criminal law, and civil and criminal procedure law of the former Qing Dynasty. In response, the Senate passed the *Act on Temporary Application of the Old Law Before the Promulgation of the New Law* on April 3, 1912 (Zhao, 2009, 329). Unfortunately, after the official dismissal of Sun Yat-sen from office, the relevant institutions of the Nanjing Provisional Government ceased to function, and the legislative work ended abruptly.

(2) Legislation on litigation under the Beijing government. By contrast, the Beijing government made major breakthroughs in legislation on litigation. For example, in May 1912, the Beijing government promulgated the *Sections on Jurisdiction of the Draft Civil and Criminal Procedure Law* and *Provisional Regulations for the Trial of Proceedings by County Magistrates*. After that, on the basis of these documents, the Beijing government further compiled the *Civil Procedure Regulations* in 1921 and *Criminal Procedure Regulations* in 1922. Some useful explorations were also made of laws on court organization. For example, the *Trial Regulations for Courts at All Levels* and the *Organic Law of Courts* of the late Qing Dynasty were initially followed, and then, the government promulgated the *Provisional Law on the Organization of Local Courts in Counties* and *Regulations on the Establishment of Courts in Special Regions of Eastern Provinces* (Zeng, 2006, 291). It is noteworthy that because of the lack of legislation at this stage, the jurisprudence and interpretative examples compiled by *Daliyuan* became the legal source of procedural law.

Although the Beijing government made breakthroughs in legislation on litigation compared with the Nanjing Provisional Government, because of the constant change in governments and frequent wars among warlords, the legislation concerning the litigation system was generally lacking. It can be said that the modern procedural law system began to be gradually established, and the Chinese Legal Family continued to dismantle.

2.1.4 Completing Stage: The Promulgation of *Liu Fa Quan Shu* by the Nanjing National Government

After law revision in the late Qing Dynasty, the Nanjing Provisional Government and the Beijing government, the Chinese Legal Family continued to dismantle, and a legal system of "six codes" of the civil law system was gradually formed in modern China. However, until the Nanjing Nationalist Government, the modern civil law system of the six codes had not been fully established in China. Otherwise stated, the six codes had not been formally promulgated. Thus, the Chinese Legal Family had not yet completely collapsed in China. The full establishment of the modern constitution, administrative law, civil and commercial law, criminal law, criminal procedure law, and civil procedure law under the Nanjing National Government marked the complete disintegration of the Chinese Legal Family. The following text discusses the establishment of the six codes in modern times.

Formation of the Modern Constitution

After the Nanjing National Government was established, constitution-making activities resumed. Prior to 1937, they centered on "political tutelage" and mainly included *Guiding Principles for the Political Tutelage Period* and the *Provisional Constitution for the Republic of China During the Political Tutelage Period*.

(1) *Guiding Principles for the Political Tutelage Period*. The Second Five Central Executive Committee of the Kuomintang (KMT), held in August 1928, decided to implement "political tutelage" and promulgated the *Law on Organization of National Government*, that is, the *Law on Organization of the Five Branches*. On October 3, 1928, the standing body of the KMT Central Committee resolved to adopt the *Guiding Principles for the Political Tutelage Period*, which, by its nature, was a constitution (Jiang, 1988, 226). Thus, the status and main tasks of the KMT during the political tutelage period were legalized and institutionalized. The *Guiding Principles* had two distinctive features. First, they formally implemented the theory proposed by Sun Yat-sen that political and government power should be separated. Second, they highlighted the status of the KMT as the supreme authority of the state during the period of political tutelage (Xia, 2012, 182–183). According to the *Guiding Principles for the Political Tutelage Period* and *Law on the Organization of National Government*, the Executive Body, the Legislative Body, the Judicial Body, the Examination Body, and the Supervisory Body of the Nanjing National Government were established successively, and the basic structure of the government was formed.

(2) *Provisional Constitution for the Republic of China During the Political Tutelage Period*. In 1930, the internal opposition faction within the KMT, led by Wang Jingwei, set up the Constitution Drafting Committee and completed the draft of the *Constitution During the Political Tutelage Period* in October of the same year in Taiyuan. This was called the "Taiyuan Constitution." Later, on March 2, 1931, the executive meeting of the KMT Central Committee passed Chiang Kai-shek's proposal of "convening a national conference to formulate the *Constitution During the Political Tutelage Period*" and established the "Drafting Committee of the *Constitution During the Political Tutelage Period*." On May 5 of the same year, a national conference was convened, and the *Provisional Constitution for the Republic of China During the Political Tutelage Period* was adopted and promulgated on June 1, 1931. It comprised 89 articles in eight chapters: General Outline, Rights and Duties of the People, Outline of the Political Tutelage, National Livelihood, National Education, Competence of the Central Government and Localities, Organization of the Government, and Bylaws. As the fundamental law of the political tutelage period, it stipulated the long-awaited rights of the Chinese people to pursue freedom, which was also a progress in the history of legislation (Zhu, 2007, 410–411). Although academic circles have been somewhat negative regarding this *Provisional Constitution*, it cannot be denied that formally, the *Provisional Constitution* inherited the principles of democracy and freedom that were promoted by modern civil

law countries. The implementation of the *Provisional Constitution* marked the establishment of the modern constitution of China.

Establishment of Modern Administrative Law

To regulate the administrative activities of the new regime and strengthen the rule of the regime in general, the Nanjing National Government enacted a large number of administrative laws and regulations between 1928 and 1931 and a modern administrative legal system was established. In terms of content, it covered many aspects of administrative organization and management.

(1) Administrative organization. Xingzheng Yuan (the Executive Body) and its various divisions constituted the central administrative organ of the Nanjing National Government. On December 20, 1928, the National Government promulgated the *Law on the Organization of the Executive Body*. This stipulated the powers and functions of the Executive Body, its internal organization, and the rules for its activities. The Executive Body was composed of ministries and commissions of domestic affairs, foreign affairs, military affairs, finance, education, and transportation, among others. The specific settings varied according to the *Law on Administrative Organization* (which was revised several times later) in different periods (Cao, 2012, 311).
(2) Administrative management. The relevant laws included the *Copyright Law* (1928), *Nationality Law* (1929), *Trade Union Law* (1929), *Fishermen's Association Law* (1929), *Petition Law* (1930), *Law on the Handling of Labor Disputes* (1930), *Land Law* (1930), *Farmers' Association Law* (1930), *Law on Group Agreements* (1930), and *Household Registration Law* (1931) (Zhu, 1999, 614).

The Nanjing National Government also promulgated the *Civil Servants Appointment Law* (1933), *Civil Servants Retirement Law*, and *Civil Servants Disciplinary Law*, among others. Thus, a modern administrative legal system was formed.

Establishment of Modern Civil and Commercial Law

When the Nanjing National Government formulated the civil law, it adopted a completely different legislative method from that of the late Qing and Beijing governments, which integrated civil and commercial laws to conform to the historical trend. Therefore, The Nanjing National Government only enacted the civil code and formulated a number of individual commercial laws and regulations but not a separate commercial code.

The civil code adopted a method of separately drafting and passing different titles. On May 23, 1928, the Nanjing National Government promulgated the General Provisions of the Civil Code. In November 1929, two titles concerning Obligations and Properties were promulgated. At the end of 1930, two titles on inheritance and family were promulgated. Thus, the *Civil Law of the Republic of China* was born.

In total, it included 1,225 articles in five titles. Three basic characteristics can be identified: (a) a large number of legal terms from Western civil law were introduced, (b) obvious traces of male superiority over the female in marriage relations, and (c) the interests of creditors were protected, and high interest rates were adopted, facilitating exploitation (Zeng, 2006, 312–313). The *1930 Civil Law of the Republic of China* was the first civil code in the history of China; thus, it is of pioneering significance.

During this period, the Nanjing Nationalist Government also formulated and promulgated a series of single commercial laws and regulations, such as the *Company Law* (1929), *Negotiable Instruments Law* (1929), *Maritime Law* (1929), *Stock Exchange Law* (1929), *Insurance Law* (1929), and *Shipping Law* (1930) (Zhu, 2007, 404). Hence, the modern civil and commercial law system, centered on the *1930 Civil Law of the Republic of China* and supplemented by other individual commercial laws and regulations, was formally established. It changed the underdeveloped civil and commercial law of the old Chinese legal system.

Establishment of Modern Criminal Law

Under the Nanjing Nationalist Government before 1937, two criminal laws were enacted and implemented, namely, the *1928 Criminal Law of the Republic of China* and the *1935 Criminal Law of the Republic of China*, with the former being called the "Old Criminal Law" and the latter the "New Criminal Law."

(1) The *1928 Criminal Law of the Republic of China*. In April 1927, in response to the need for unification, the National Government settled in Nanjing and prepared to organize the legal system, of which criminal law was an important part. Minister of Justice Wang Chonghui made additions and deletions to the *1919 Second Amendment to the Reformed Criminal Law* and compiled it into the *Draft Criminal Law*. This was then sent by the National Government to State Councilor Wu Chaoshu and Supreme Court Chairman Xu Yuangao—together with Wang Chonghui—for review, and another 22 specific amendments were made. It was eventually submitted to the 120th executive meeting of the central government for discussion and resolution, and the *1928 Criminal Law of the Republic of China* was promulgated on March 10, 1928, and came into force on July 1, 1928. Later, because the *Criminal Procedure Law* was still under review, the date of operation of the 1928 *Criminal Law* was moved to September 1, 1928 (Xia, 2012, 261–262). However, because the special criminal law in force at that time was not incorporated into it, the Nanjing National Government began to prepare for the revision of the *1928 Criminal Law of the Republic of China* soon after its implementation.

(2) The *1935 Criminal Law of the Republic of China*. In 1932, the Second Plenary Session of the Fourth National Committee of the KMT put forward a Unified Criminal Act. Some of the latest foreign criminal legislation at that time was introduced into China, and the Legislative Body prepared to amend the *1928*

Criminal Law. In November 1934, the amendment to the *1928 Criminal Law* passed the third reading in the Legislative Body, and the Nanjing National Government promulgated the amendment on January 1, 1935, which became the *1935 Criminal Law of the Republic of China*. The law comprised 357 articles in 47 chapters with two titles (Cao, 2012, 232–233). The provisions and text of the new criminal law were more stringent. They involved the content of the special laws and regulations, introduced the institution of "security measures" stipulated in German and Italian criminal laws, and incorporated institutions such as "social crime prevention" and "reformatory education." Compared with the ancient Chinese hierarchical legal system mainly based on corporal punishment, which imposed different punishments for the same crime based on the offenders' identities and positions, the *1935 Criminal Law of the Republic of China* made radical changes based on principles such as the equivalence of crime and punishment and humanitarian punishment (Wang, 2007, 466–467).

In short, in the *1935 Criminal Law of the Republic of China*, the reform of criminal law in modern times was eventually completed, and the modern criminal law system and principles were established.

Establishment of Modern Criminal Procedure Law

Like the criminal law, the criminal procedure law under the Nanjing National Government also went through alteration from the old to the new. Two criminal procedure codes were enacted and implemented, namely, the *1928 Criminal Procedure Law* and the *1935 Criminal Procedure Law*.

(1) The *1928 Criminal Procedure Law*. Because the *Criminal Law of the Republic of China* was promulgated on March 10, 1928, the Nanjing National Government was in urgent need of a corresponding procedural law; there had been no national criminal procedure law before then. Therefore, the Ministry of Justice formulated the *Draft Criminal Procedure Law*, which consisted of 496 articles in seven titles, and sent it to the Legal Affairs Bureau for review. The Legal Affairs Bureau amended it and formed an amendments act, which included 513 articles. After being passed by the KMT Central Political Meetings, the *1928 Criminal Procedure Law* was promulgated on July 28, 1928. It entered into force on September 1, 1927, together with the *Criminal Law of the Republic of China*. The *1928 Criminal Procedure Law* was revised on the basis of the Beijing government's *Regulations on Criminal Procedure*, but there were no major changes in style and structure. There were some changes in content, such as the adoption of a four-level, three-trial system, the adoption of the national prosecution doctrine, the expansion of the jurisdiction of the primary courts, the adoption of the public defender system, and the abolition of the pretrial system (Zhao, 2009, 331–332).

(2) The *1935 Criminal Procedure Law*. The legislative work on the *Criminal Procedure Law* was in line with the legislation of the criminal law. As mentioned

above, the revision of the *1928 Criminal Law* started soon after its promulgation. Similarly, after entry into force of the *1928 Criminal Procedure Law*, its amendment began. In January 1935, the new *Criminal Procedure Law* was promulgated and came into effect in July 1935. This was the second *Criminal Procedure Law* of the Nanjing Nationalist Government, and it included 516 articles in nine titles. It incorporated provisions on the enforcement of security measures and admonitions. Regarding jurisdiction, a three-level, three-trial system was adopted. The Supreme Court was the first instance body for domestic strife, foreign aggression, and obstruction of national diplomatic relations, whereas the local courts were the first instance bodies for all other cases. In addition, the Nanjing Nationalist Government enacted a number of separate regulations on criminal procedures, such as the *Law on the Surrender of Communists* (1928), *Provisional Law on Jury in Counterrevolutionary Cases* (1929), and *Law on Arraignment* (1935) (Xia, 2012, 414).

By this time, the system of criminal procedure law was formally established by the Nanjing National Government.

Establishment of Modern Civil Procedure Law

After 1922, two civil procedure laws were actually in force in China. When the Nanjing National Government unified China, it decided to draft a unified procedural law as soon as possible to change this awkward situation.

(1) The *1932 Civil Procedure Law*. In 1928, the Legislative Body of the Nanjing National Government drew up the *Draft Civil Procedure Law*, with five titles. In September 1930, Title I to Chapter III of Title V of the *Draft Civil Procedure Law* was passed, and it was promulgated on December 26, 1930. Because of the influence of the titles concerning family and inheritance of the civil law, Chapter IV of Title V of the *Civil Procedure Law* was not formulated until the end of 1930, and it was promulgated on February 13, 1931. The *Civil Procedure Law* was thus completed and came into force on May 20, 1932. The *Civil Procedure Law* made in 1931 was modeled on the *1922 Civil Procedure Regulations* by the Beijing government. It consisted of 600 articles in five chapters. The main features of the law included the change from a four-level, three-trial system to a three-level, three-trial system; the expansion of preparatory procedures; the addition of institutions of trial in absentia and interim injunction with pledge; the abolition of the institution concerning proceedings on claims arising from a deed; the expansion of the application scope of the supervisory procedure; and the abolition of the participation of prosecutors in personnel proceedings. In terms of the effect and scope of implementation, the *Civil Procedure Law* adopted in 1931 was the first civil procedure code promulgated and enforced nationwide in China (Cao, 2012, 265–266).
(2) The *1935 Civil Procedure Law*. The revised *Civil Procedure Law* was promulgated on February 1, 1935. The new law consisted of 636 articles in nine titles,

namely, General Provisions, First Instance, Appeal, Complaints, Supervision, Precautionary Measures, Public Summons for Exhortation, and Personal Status Litigation. The new *Civil Procedure Law* had several characteristics: the adoption of the party-acting doctrine, cumbersome litigation procedures and obscure language, court mediation institutions for specific cases, and various restrictions on the initiation of litigation. In addition to the *Civil Procedure Law*, the Nanjing National Government enacted related laws, such as the *Law on Civil Procedure Costs* and *Compulsory Execution Law* (Wang, 2007, 486–487).

2.2 Disintegration of the Chinese Legal Family in Japan

From the Taika Reform[18] to the Meiji Restoration, Japanese law imitated the Chinese law of the *fengjian* period from the Tang and Song Dynasties and established a legal system of Lv, Ling, Ge, and Shi. Therefore, it was a subsidiary legal system in the Chinese Legal Family. In modern times, the Meiji Restoration became the turning point in the history of the Japanese legal system.[19] Japan promulgated its *Kaitei Ritsurei* (*the Reformed Penal Code*) in the 6th year of the Meiji Era (1873) and the *Old Penal Code* in the 13th year of the Meiji Era (1880), marking the transition from the Chinese Legal Family to the civil law system and the beginning of the disintegration of the Chinese Legal Family in Japan. In the following two or three decades, with the establishment of the modern legal system, the Chinese Legal Family completely collapsed in Japan, and Japanese law became a member of the civil law family. Therefore, the disintegration of the Chinese Legal Family in Japan can be divided into two stages, namely, prelude and manifestation. The Meiji Restoration period was the prelude to the disintegration of the Chinese Legal Family in Japan, which was specifically manifested in Japan's reception of modern laws. As shown in Table 3, the first signs of Japan's reception of laws began in 1880 with its enactment of a criminal code (i.e., the *Old Penal Code*), which transplanted French law. In addition, 1889 was a watershed year in which the *Meiji Constitution* started an era when foreign laws were completely transplanted. In the following half century (until 1922), legal transplants referring to French and German laws were carried out in the main Japanese legal system, and a system consisting of six main branches of law

[18] Some scholars also call it the "Taika Innovation," which was the product of the collision between the advanced *fengjian* system in China and the early slavery system in Japan. It played a significant role in the formation and development of Japan as a nation. The Japanese Ritsuryo system was developed based on this reform. See Zhao (2010, 12).

[19] Scholars generally divide the formation of Japanese law into three stages: the first being the prehistoric stage to the early seventh century AD, the second being the seventh century AD to the Meiji Restoration in 1868, and the third being the modern period. See Blackmore (1947, 635). The three-stage theory fits exactly with this paper. That is, the second stage was the stage of formation, development, and maturation of the Chinese Legal Family in Japan, and the Meiji Restoration in 1868 was the turning point, when the Chinese Legal Family began to collapse in Japan and the Japanese legal system began to modernize.

Table 3 Japan's transplantation of foreign laws (Han, 2000, 89–90)

Year	Code	Transplanted foreign law
8th century	Taiho code and Yoro code	Chinese law
1870	Shinritsu Koryo (Outline of the new criminal code)	Chinese law
1880	The penal code	French law
1880	Law on punishment of crimes (Criminal procedure law)	French law
1889	Meiji constitution	German law
1890	Civil law	French law
1890	Commercial law	German law
1890	Law on the organization of courts	German law
1890	Code of civil procedure	German law
1890	Code of criminal procedure	French law
1896	General rules of civil law, real rights, and claims	German law and French law
1899	Commercial law	German law
1905	Guarantee law	British law
1908	Criminal law	German law
1922	Criminal procedure law	German law
1922	Bankruptcy law	German law
1923	Trust law	British law
1946	Constitution of Japan	American law
1946	Regulatory law of labor relations	American law
1947	Anti-monopoly law	American law
1948	Criminal procedure law	American law
1948	Security law	American law
1950	Company law in commercial law	American law
1952	Law on corporate reorganization	American law

was established, namely, the constitution, civil law, commercial law, criminal law, civil procedure law, and criminal procedure law.[20]

2.2.1 Prelude to the Disintegration of the Chinese Legal Family in Japan: From the Meiji Restoration to 1888

The Meiji Restoration was a landmark in modern Japanese history and even in world history. For Japan, it was significant in two ways. On the one hand, the Meiji Restoration ended the rule of the Shogunate, re-established a strong central government,

[20] According to Professor He Qinhua, in 1928, the Iwanami Shoten began to compile and distribute the portable book *Roppo Zensho* (*Book of Six Codes*), thus laying the foundation of the modern book of six codes. See He (1998, 170).

abolished the *fengjian* regime, and abandoned the closed-door policy that had kept Japan isolated from the world (Blackmore, 1947, 636). It embarked on the development of capitalism, marking the beginning of Japan's modern history (Zhou, 1962). On the other hand, the Meiji Restoration had an impact on Japan's legal system. The Japanese emperor's government carried out a series of political reforms in the Meiji Restoration, which set off the disintegration of the Chinese Legal Family and was a first step toward the gradual establishment of the civil law system in Japan. In addition, the Japanese legal system at that time was characterized by an "interaction of the old and new legal systems." That is, the traditional legal system was still in effect, and at the same time, because of the new social environment and the requirements of the open legal structure, a large number of individual laws and regulations were enacted and promulgated to supplement the defects of the traditional laws. Therefore, the period from the Meiji Restoration to 1888 was a preparatory period for the formation of the new legal system (Han, 2000, 56),[21] as well as the prelude to the disintegration of the Chinese Legal Family in Japan. This embodies the reforms of the political system and the initial codification of the law.

Reforms of the Political System

From a macroperspective, the basic idea and ultimate goals of the Meiji Restoration were to abandon the traditional approach to governance, strengthen the state power, establish a centralized political system headed by the emperor, transplant the Western legal system, and transform Japan into a capitalist country, following the example of Western countries in Europe and the Americas (Xie, 2011, 99). From a microperspective, the Meiji Restoration began in 1868. On January 3, 1868, at the age of 16, Emperor Meiji, with the support of the anti-Tokugawa activists, such as Iwakura Tomomi, held a meeting attended by the imperial family, ministers, daimyo, and samurai and decided to carry out a coup. He issued an edict of "restoration of imperial rule," announcing that Tokugawa Yoshinobu's position of shogun and political power were annulled, everything should be restored to "the beginning years of Emperor Jinmu," and the emperor himself should be in charge of the government. In the following 17 days, the bureaucratic establishment of three positions and seven departments was formally developed. The president, legislature, and councilor were the three positions. On March 14, 1868, Emperor Meiji announced the

[21] As to the phasing of the formation of the modern Japanese legal system, the academic community generally divides it into the preparatory period (the founding period) and the codification period. However, there are different views as to the exact time point of demarcation. Some consider 1888 as the dividing point, such as Ding Xiangshun, who believed that the period before the promulgation of the Meiji Constitution in 1889 was the preparatory period for the codification in Japan and that this period was also when Japan went through a top-down modernization, which was more about creating the environment and conditions for the transplant of Western legal systems. See Ding (2011, 51). Some regard 1875 as the watershed year. For example, according to Professor He Qinhua, the period from the 1868 Meiji Restoration to 1875, when Emperor Meiji issued an imperial edict announcing the gradual establishment of a constitutional system of government, was the founding period (preparatory period) for the creation of a Japanese legal system. See He et al. (1999, 22).

Charter Oath of Emperor Meiji, and on April 11, 1868, the new government made the *Constitution* according to the *Charter Oath* (Zhao & Bi, 2006, 130–131). Its content included "frequently holding meetings and everything should be decided based on public arguments, economically revitalizing industry and commerce, diplomatically breaking old habits and acting in accordance with international public law, advocating the abolition of the social hierarchy, and affirming that the state power was wholly vested in the *Daijo-kan* (the Great Council of State) under the emperor. Concerning the reform of the land system, the land ownership of the occupants was confirmed, and land sales were permitted" (Han, 2000, 57). In the *Daijo-kan* system, "all the powers were vested in *Daijo-kan*. There were fewer problems if the policies and edicts were issued by the emperor and *Daijo-kan*. *Daijo-kan* was composed of three parts: legislative, executive, and judicial powers. Therefore, the problems of unbalanced power distribution also decreased" (Yasuoka, 1996, 123). The policy-making officials were in charge of legislation. Administrative, Shinto, accounting, military and foreign affairs officials were in charge of execution. Criminal law officials were responsible for justice. There were traces of the modern separation of powers. In the same year, the Meiji government accepted the territories and households given back by some of the *han* (domains) and ordered the other 30 *han* that had not yet done so to return their powers. The old *han* lords were renamed as "*han* officials," depriving them of their rights to land and people, making them local officials of the government, and abolishing their titles, such as *kogyo* (ministers) and *daimyo* (princes), while collectively calling them as *Kazoku* (exalted lineage) (Ding, 2011, 57). On July 14, 1871, the new government, in the name of the emperor, carried out the reform of "abolishing the *han* and creating the prefecture," that is, removing all *han* governors from their positions (Inoue & Suzuki, 1972, 80). The purpose of these political reforms was to eliminate separatism, establish a centralized system of government, and strengthen the power of the emperor. They also laid the political foundation for the modernization of the Japanese legal system and the adoption of the civil law system.

Preliminary Codification

After the smooth transition of power, the Meiji government began to prepare for the future codification of law. This was reflected in the preliminary codification of the constitution, civil law, and criminal law.

(1) Preliminary codification of the constitution. At the beginning of the Meiji government, the Left House[22] was established in 1871 as a legislative body to legislate for the Diet. In 1872, in the name of "stabilizing the foundation of the long-standing rule of the emperor," the Left House proposed a constitution and began to translate the "Six Laws" of France. It advocated the introduction of Western constitutional systems and sent officials to Europe and the United

[22] The *Daijo-kan* system at the beginning of the Meiji Restoration consisted of the Main House, the Right House, and the Left House.

States for study tours (Wu, 1997, 376). On April 14, 1875, Emperor Meiji issued the *Edict on the Gradual Establishment of a Constitutional Government*, which abolished the Left and Right Houses and created the Chamber of Elders, the Grand Auditors' Council, and the Council of Magistrates under the Main House. The newly established Senate was in charge of the drafting of a constitution. The *Draft National Constitution of Japan* was written in 1878 in accordance with the theories of the common rule and separation of powers between the emperor and the people, referring to the constitutions of Western European countries. However, Iwakura Tomomi, who was an important minister in the imperial court at the time, believed that the draft was heavily influenced by the 1831 Belgian Constitution and was "incompatible with the Japanese state system." Against this background, the draft was not implemented.

(2) Preliminary codification of the civil law. The first codification of the Japanese Civil Code can be traced back to the *1870 Draft Civil Code*. The initial codification of the civil code was closely related to Shinpei Eto, who was a head official in the *Daijo-kan* in 1870 and organized the codification of the civil code, focusing on human rights, property, and obligations. In April 1872, Shinpei Eto left the position of deputy speaker of the Left House and became the Minister of Justice. On the basis of the original translation of the French Code, the Japanese Civil Code was formulated. In 1873, the drafting of *Civil Code I: Personal Status*, *Provisional Civil Rules of Imperial Japan*, and *Provisional Rules of the Civil Code* was completed. It is noteworthy that *Civil Code I: Personal Status* was the first draft civil law in Japan and was modeled on the French Civil Code in terms of content. Although some articles differed from the French Civil Code, it was largely a product of the imitation of the French Civil Code (Zhao, 2010, 194–195). The work of drafting the civil code was transferred to the Ministry of Justice as the Left House was abolished in 1875, and in the same year, the Civil Law Division was established within the Ministry of Justice for better codification. The new Draft Civil Code was completed in January 1878, but because it was influenced heavily by the French Civil Code, many of the articles were purely translated from the French Civil Code, and there were many translation errors. Thus, the draft was opposed by public opinion and the government and was not enacted. Later, the Meiji government established the Civil Law Codification Bureau in the Chamber of Elders and restarted the codification of civil law (Zhao & Bi, 2006, 177–178). The Meiji government entrusted the drafting of the civil law to G.E.F. Boissonade (1825–1910), a French adviser to the Ministry of Justice (He et al., 1999, 31–33), but the codification and review of the civil law were slow. Until 1886, only the titles concerning property and acquisition of property had been drafted (He et al., 1999, 130).

(3) Preliminary codification of the criminal law. After its establishment, the new Meiji government attached great importance to the codification of criminal law to consolidate the Meiji regime under the emperor. In 20 years, from 1868 to 1888, the Meiji government promulgated four criminal codes, namely, the *Provisional Criminal Code* (1868), the *Shinritsu Koryo* (*Outline of the New Criminal Code*) (1870), the *Kaitei Ritsurei* (the *Reformed Penal Code*) (1873),

and the *Penal Code* (1880). These four criminal laws can be divided into two categories based on their nature, namely, summaries of the laws of the Chinese Legal Family and the first signs of modern criminal law.

First, they are summaries of Lv and Ling of the Chinese Legal Family. The three criminal laws, namely, the *Provisional Criminal Code*, the *Shinritsu Koryo*, and the *Kaitei Ritsurei*, were transitional in nature. They were only improvements or modifications of the *fengjian* laws. They did not contain any aspects of modern criminal law in terms of form, structure, and content. Specifically, the 1868 *Provisional Criminal Code* was formulated on the basis of the old laws, such as the *Yoro Code* and *Kujikata Osadamegaki.* It comprised 121 articles, and the penalties could be divided into four categories: flogging, imprisonment, exile, and death. It was never actually promulgated and was thus temporary and transitional in nature, which could not be applied in the long term (He et al., 1999, 338–339). In February 1870, the draft of the New Penal Code (i.e., the *Shinritsu Koryo*) was completed, which was promulgated to all prefectures in Japan on December 27, 1870.

The *Shinritsu Koryo* was based on the *Collection of Qing Laws and Criminal Cases.* It included 192 articles in 14 titles and in six volumes. In terms of penalties, it restored the five punishments of flogging, caning, imprisonment, exile, and death that had been practiced in the *fengjian* era. Because the *Shinritsu Koryo* was only a code that was hastily drawn up to replace the *Provisional Criminal Code*, many problems were revealed after its implementation. Hence, the Meiji government began to revise it soon after its promulgation by the Ministry of Justice (Zhao & Bi, 2006, 142–143). In June 1873, the Ministry of Justice promulgated another new criminal code, the *Kaitei Ritsurei.* This was actually a compilation and collation of a number of single laws, which complemented and improved on the *Shinritsu Koryo* and was essentially its special law. The *Kaitei Ritsurei* consisted of 318 articles in 14 titles and in three volumes. In terms of penalties, the *fengjian* five-punishment system was abolished. The new punishments included three types: servitude penalty, death penalty, and property penalty. The "no penalty without a law" principle in modern criminal law was still absent, but the principle that the law does not operate retroactively was adopted (Zhao, 2010, 123). The three criminal codes were more akin to the summaries of the laws of the Chinese Legal Family in Japan as they were drafted in a hurry to maintain social order and retained a strong *fengjian* Ritsuryo color in terms of style, structure, and content.

Second, they are the first signs of modern criminal law in Japan. The truly modernized criminal code would be the *1880 Penal Code* (also known as the "*Old Penal Code*"), which can be regarded as the prelude to modern criminal law. The making of the *Old Penal Code* started in 1875 when the Ministry of Justice amended the criminal law. In September of that year, the Ministry of Justice appointed Ohara Shigeya, Namura Taizo, and others as investigators for drafting a modern criminal code, with the guidance that "the draft would be based on the criminal codes of European countries and take into account the current situation and social relationship of the country." A year later, the Ministry of Justice submitted to the Main House a *Preliminary Draft of the Imperial Japanese Penal Code*, which was based on the *French Criminal Code*. However, it was considered premature. In January 1877, the Ministry of Justice carried out institutional adjustments, established the Criminal Code Codification Division, continued the work of compiling the Criminal Code, and entrusted the drafting work to the Frenchman Boissonade. At the end of that year, the 478-article *Draft Japanese Criminal Code* was finished and submitted to the Criminal Law Review Bureau under the *Daijo-kan* for review, revision, and amendments. An *Amendment to the Penal Code* was formulated and submitted to the Chamber of Elders in June 1879. The *Penal Code* was finally promulgated in July 1880 after a review by the Chamber of Elders (Ding, 2011, 132–133). This was the first modern criminal code in Japan and the first to be promulgated during the preparatory period of the new legal system. The *Penal Code* was modeled on the *1810 French Criminal Code* in terms of form and structure and consisted of 430 articles in four titles: General Provisions, Felonies, and Misdemeanors concerning Public Interest, Felonies and Misdemeanors concerning Human Body and Property, and Offenses against the Police. It was also deeply influenced by modern criminal laws, such as French law, in terms of content. For example, the code adopted for the first time the principle of "no penalty without a law" and the principle that "the law does not operate retroactively." It followed the trend of the criminal division in modern criminal law of the civil law systems, dividing crimes into felonies, misdemeanors, and crimes against the police. In terms of penalties, there were main and additional penalties. Surrender, attempted crimes, and self-defense were introduced (He et al., 1999, 344–345). In short, it had the characteristics of the modern civil law system, not only in terms of form and structure but also in terms of content. Thus, the *1880 Penal Code* was a modern criminal law and the first civil law system code to be established in Japan.

Brief Comment on the Preparatory Period for the New Legal System

It can be seen from the above discussion that both the reform of the political system in the early Meiji government and the preliminary codification of the law were riddled with twists and turns and chaos. For example, the codification authority was frequently shifted to different legislative departments; the drafts of the constitution, civil law, and criminal law were amended several times; and the persons in charge of the drafting of the relevant codes frequently changed. This also highlighted the problems in Japan in the early stage of legal transplantation, which were a series of side effects produced by the conflict and integration of the two major legal systems: the Chinese Legal Family and the civil law system. The two systems competed with each other. In this period, prior to its collapse in Japan, the Chinese Legal Family still stubbornly retained a certain vitality, but the civil law system had begun to be integrated into Japanese law. The complete disintegration and collapse of the Chinese Legal Family was the process of a complete transplant of modern laws in Japan.

2.2.2 Disintegration of the Chinese Legal Family in Japan: The Transplantation of Western Law (Establishment of Modern Japanese Law)

From 1888 onward, Japan entered a period of establishing a new legal system. The representative codes of this period were the 1889 *Meiji Constitution, 1898 Civil Code, 1899 Commercial Code, Law on Organization of Courts, Law of Administrative Courts, Criminal Procedure Law* adopted in 1907, and *1908 New Penal Code.* By 1914, Japan had established a relatively sound legal system, gradually established universal principles of the rule of law by legal practice in Japanese society, and formed a modernized legal culture (Han, 2000, 57). By 1922, when the *Criminal Procedure Law* and *Bankruptcy Law* were promulgated, Japan had formed a modern civil law system marked by the six-code system, which also meant the complete disintegration of the Chinese Legal Family in Japan.

Establishment of the Modern Constitution in Japan

In March 1882, Ito Hirobumi was ordered by the emperor to go to Europe to conduct a field constitutional survey. This 18-month survey was a landmark in the history of the *Meiji Constitution.* It had a significant influence on the formulation of the *Meiji Constitution* and even on the development of modern Japan because it was this constitutional survey in Europe that led Ito Hirobumi to believe that the German constitutional monarchy and secret constitutionalism were the most suitable for Japan (Zhao, 2010, 172). The most far-reaching impact of this survey was that it started an era when Japan comprehensively transplanted German law.[23] In 1883, the Institutional Review Bureau was established in the imperial court to research the reforms of the imperial court and the government. The *Edict on Kazoku* was formulated to establish five types of titles, which prepared the conditions for the future establishment of the House of Lords. In 1885, the *Daijo-kan* system was abolished, and the cabinet system was introduced.

In 1886, three senators, Ito Hirobumi, Inoue Kowashi, and Kaneko Kentaro, drafted the constitution (Wu, 1997, 376–377). It was drafted in secret and was not made public. With only the Privy Council having reviewed it, the *Constitution of*

---

[23] Regarding the reasons for the shift of Japanese constitutional thinking to the Prussian-German model, some scholars believe that there were four main reasons. First, there was a rise of nationalism in both Japan and Germany. Second was the Meiji government's basic estimation of its own power and the realpolitik considerations in response to the "crisis." Third was the fact that among the European countries, it was only in Germany that "the government is the imperial government," which was the ideal national system pursued by the Meiji government. Fourth, considering the history of philosophical thought, since the 20th year of the Meiji Era, German idealistic philosophy, i.e., German idealism, had replaced the British and French philosophy of "natural human rights," utilitarianism, and evolutionary philosophy that were popular from the 10th year of the Meiji Era, and became the mainstream philosophy of Japan. See Xiao (2007, 145–150).

the Great Japanese Empire was promulgated by the emperor to the cabinet ministers on February 11, 1889. Alongside, the *Law on the Diet*, *Law on the Election of Members of the House of Representatives*, and *Edict on the House of Lords* were also promulgated (Ding, 2011, 74).

In terms of structure, the *Meiji Constitution*, which was promulgated in 1889 and implemented in November 1890, was modeled on the 1850 Prussian Constitution and the constitutions of other German states. It comprised 76 articles in seven chapters: Emperor, Rights and Duties of Subjects, Imperial Diet, Ministers of State and the Consultants of the Privy Council, Judiciary, Accounting, and Supplementary Rules. It adopted the constitutional monarchy in form. However, it was, in fact, a constitutional code that compromised between absolutism and national liberalism (Zhao & Bi, 2006, 172). The *Meiji Constitution* had the following features: (1) the emperor's total rule was confirmed; (2) literally, the nationals enjoyed democratic freedom; (3) the Imperial Diet assisted and helped the emperor; and (4) the House of Lords and House of Representatives were established in the Diet (Wu, 1997, 377–379).

The contents of the constitution included the following: (1) extensive provisions on the emperor's powers: ruling, promulgation, and enforcement of laws (Article 6); convening, closing, and suspension of the Diet; and dissolution of the House of Representatives (Article 7); (2) the royal family's self-discipline: matters concerning the imperial family fell outside the constitution and were not subject to parliamentary intervention; (3) reservation of the laws: the liberties of the nationals were provided for and regulated by the laws; (4) superiority of the executive power: the executive power was exercised by ministers appointed by the emperor; (5) restraint on legislative power: the rights of the Imperial Diet to assist in legislation and to consider and recognize the budget were restrained by the great power of the emperor, who could make edicts that can replace laws; and (6) restraints on judicial power: special courts, such as the Administrative Court and the Military Justice Council, were not subject to the jurisdiction of the judicial courts (Yasuoka, 1996, 290). Although the *Meiji Constitution* heavily transplanted the German Constitution in terms of structure and content, the process of constitution-making reflected the clash and fusion of cultures (Han, 2000, 61). "The enactment and implementation of the *Meiji Constitution* not only changed the political consciousness of modern Japan to a great extent but also led to a revolutionary 'mutation' of the Japanese 'legal cultural DNA.' However, this change and breakthrough still had a certain scope and limit. The legal consciousness of modern Japanese people was still rooted in the past and maintained inextricable ties with traditional legal concepts" (Wei, 2012). In particular, the constitutionalism embodied in the *Meiji Constitution* did have some conflicts with traditional Confucian culture, but the drafters of the Constitution skillfully blended the two in the constitution-making process. The clash and fusion of cultures that appeared during the making of the *Meiji Constitution* were, in essence, a clash and fusion of legal systems.

The *Meiji Constitution* was not only the first modern constitution in Japan but also the first modern constitution in Asia, and thus, it had far-reaching significance. Because it was the product of the Meiji Restoration and the result of studying the Western legal systems, it played an important role in further breaking down the *fengjian* system and creating a modernized legal system in Japan, as well as modernizing Japanese politics.[24]

Establishment of Modern Civil Law in Japan

Before the *Meiji Civil Code* was enacted, there was a "controversy over the code." It resulted in the removal of the old civil code, which was transplanted from French law. The later drafts of Japanese civil law were all based on German law (Ding, 2002). The establishment of modern Japanese civil law began with the promulgation of the *Civil Code*, the preliminary compilation of which was discussed above. In March 1893 (the 3rd lunar month of the 26th year of the Meiji Era), the Meiji government set up the Code Survey Committee for the codification of civil and commercial law and other laws. In April, Prime Minister Ito became the president, Mitsukuri Rinsho and some others became the chief investigators, and the three members of the Committee, namely Hozumi Nobushige, Tomii Masaakira, and Ume Kenjiro, became the drafters. The committee began its work (Yasuoka, 1996, 311). The drafting of the Meiji Civil Code lasted for five years, starting from April 28, 1893 (when the first general meeting was held) to April 15, 1898. Different titles of the *Meiji Civil Code* were passed and promulgated at different times. Specifically, the three titles of General Provisions, Real Rights, and Claims were submitted to the Ninth Imperial Diet in December 1895, were passed in March of the following year, and were promulgated on April 27, 1896. The last two titles of the civil code, namely, Family and Inheritance, were submitted to the Twelfth Imperial Diet in May 1898, were passed in June, and published on June 21, 1898. Both titles came into force on July 16, 1898 (Zhao & Bi, 2006, 182). The civil law that became operational in 1898 was the *New Civil Code*, also known as the *Meiji Civil Code*, and it has been in force to this day.

The *Meiji Civil Code* was a transplantation of foreign law, both in structure and content. In terms of structure, the new civil law of Japan followed the German Civil Code. It included 1,146 articles in five titles: General Provisions, Real Rights, Claims, Family, and Inheritance. The General Provisions were modeled on the German Civil Code. The order of the titles concerning real rights and claims did not follow the German Civil Code (the Draft Bavarian Civil Code) but followed the Saxon Civil Code—placing the title on real rights before the title on claims, and statutory liens came from the French Civil Code (Xie, 1995). In terms of content, the General Provisions covered persons, legal persons, things, legal acts, periods of time and prescription, and others. The title on real rights covered possessory rights, ownership, superficies, farming rights, servitudes, rights of retention, statutory liens, pledge, and mortgages. The title on claims included contracts, benevolent intervention in another's business, unjust enrichment, and torts. The title on family dealt

[24] See He et al. (1999, 53). Meanwhile, some historians believe that the *Constitution of the Great Japanese Empire*, as the first modern constitution in the East, should be recognized for its progressive significance. See Feng (2008, 429).

with the head and members of a house, marriage, parents and children, parental power, guardianship, family council, and the duty of support. The title on inheritance (succession) provided for succession to a house, succession to property, the acceptance and refusal of a succession, separation of property, the absence of an heir, wills, and legal portions (Translation Academy of Nanyang Mission College, 2007, vol. 1, 255–262). To fully perform the functions of civil law, the Meiji government enacted several subsidiary laws during and after the promulgation of the civil code, including the *Law on Enforcement of the Civil Law* (1898), *Household Registration Law* (1898), *Trusteeship Law* (1899), and *Real Estate Registration Law* (1899) (He et al., 1999, 136).

In summary, the *1898 Meiji Civil Code* conformed to the characteristics of the civil codes of modern civil law countries in terms of both structure and content and was thus a modern civil law system civil code. It changed the old Ritsuryo legal system in Japan, beginning to take on the appearance of a modern legal system.

Establishment of Modern Japanese Commercial Law

Modern Japanese commercial law was formulated later than civil law, but the process was similar, going through the stages of the *Old Commercial Code* and *New Commercial Code* (*Meiji Commercial Law*). In 1881, the Meiji government entrusted K.F.H. Roesler (1834–1894), a German, with the task of drafting the commercial law. In March 1882, the Bureau for Codification of Commercial Law was established in the Chamber of Elders, and at the end of the year, the Regulations on Bills of Exchange and Promissory Notes were separated from the draft and promulgated ahead as a single law of commercial law. In January 1884, the drafting of the commercial law was completed, and Roselle submitted a detailed description of the draft to the government. After a few twists and turns, the final commercial law was completed in late 1889 and was promptly reviewed by the then Imperial Diet. The law was promulgated in April 1890 and was called the *Old Commercial Code* (He et al., 1999, 167–168). The *Code* consisted of 1,064 articles in three titles: General Commercial Rules, Maritime Law, and Bankruptcy. In terms of structure, the *Old Commercial Code* reflected the French law system (Zhao, 1994). The implementation of the *Old Commercial Code* was later delayed because of many factors and eventually became obsolete.

After the postponement of the *Old Civil Code* and the *Old Commercial Code*, the Meiji government set up the "Code Survey Committee" and started to revise the *Old Commercial Code*. However, the progress of the revision was slow. To speed up the legislative process, the government set up a committee to draft amendments to the commercial code, consisting of Okano Keijiro (1865–1925), a professor at the Imperial University, Ume Kenjiro, and other officials from the Ministry of Justice. It was not until May 1896 that the amendment to the commercial code was completed and immediately sent to the Code Survey Committee for consideration. After 13 meetings of the committee, it was eventually finalized in December 1896 and submitted to both houses of the Diet for consideration. However, because of the dissolution of the

House of Representatives, the consideration of the amendment was delayed (He et al., 1999, 171). Later, the revised commercial law was submitted to the Diet for the third time in December 1898 and was passed and promulgated on March 9, 1899. It came into effect on June 1, 1899, and was generally known as the "*New Commercial Law*" or "*Meiji Commercial Law*." The *Meiji Commercial Law* comprised 689 articles in five titles: General Provisions, Company, Commercial Actions, Bill of Exchange, and Maritime Law (Translation Academy of Nanyang Mission College, 2007, vol. 2, 1–111). The *New Commercial Code* was generally modeled on the old *German Commercial Code* and was enacted according to the needs of Japan's economic and social development (Zhao, 1994). Compared with the *Old Commercial Code*, the *New Commercial Code* had the following features: (1) It fully affirmed the existence of and highlighted the importance of business customs, (2) the merger of companies was stipulated, and (3) a normative system was adopted concerning the establishment of companies to meet the needs of Japan's economic development (Zhao & Bi, 2006, 192). After the *Meiji Commercial Law* came into force, the Meiji government also promulgated some individual laws and regulations on commercial law, such as the *Law on Enforcement of the Commercial Code* (1899) and *Law on the Scope of Small Businesses* (1899), which established the modern Japanese commercial law system.

Establishment of Modern Japanese Criminal Law

As mentioned above, the *1880 Penal Code* (also known as the "*Old Penal Code*") was the preliminary establishment of modern criminal law in Japan. The formulation of the *New Penal Code* also underwent many twists and turns. Before 1907, three drafts were rejected by the Diet because of various reasons. The first was drafted between 1883 and 1891, soon after the implementation of the *Old Penal Code*. The Ministry of Justice submitted an amendment to the *Daijo-kan*, who then sent it to the Senate for consideration, and the Senate asked the French adviser, Boissonade, to revise it. The new draft (which consisted of 414 articles in four titles) was first submitted to the Imperial Diet in 1891, but it was not passed because the draft was heavily influenced by the structure and content of the French Criminal Code (Zhao & Bi, 2006, 193). The second draft was completed during 1892–1901. In January 1892, the Ministry of Justice re-established the Commission for Examination and Revision of the Penal Code to draft new amendments to the Penal Code. The committee completed the new draft in 1897, but many lawyers and judges opposed the revision of criminal law at that time. The government had no choice but to reorganize the Code Survey Committee in March 1899 and leave the third group in charge of the revision of the Penal Code. In 1901, a new draft based on the 1897 draft, consisting of 300 articles in two titles, was submitted to the Imperial Diet. It was characterized by a shift toward an imitation of the German Penal Code. Unfortunately, the draft was not adopted because the Diet suspended its meetings in the middle of the year (Zhao, 2010, 232–233). The third drafting was made between 1902 and 1905. In 1902, the Meiji government submitted to the Diet, for the third time, a revised draft of the Penal Code. The main feature of this draft was the abolition of the division between felonies and misdemeanors; the rest of the draft followed the content of the 1901 draft. The House of Lords considered and amended the draft, but the session ended before the House of Representatives could complete its consideration. Later, several amendments were also proposed, but these were not considered because of the arrangement of the sessions in the Diet (He et al., 1999, 347).

Eventually, in 1906, the Meiji government set up a new committee to study the law and adopted a slight revision of the original amendment, which was submitted to the Diet and was passed in January 1907. It was promulgated in April of the same year and came into force on October 1, 1908. This Penal Code was referred to as the *1907 Penal Code* or the *New Penal Code* (He et al., 1999, 347). This *1907 Penal Code*, which was developed under the influence of German criminal law, is still in force today. It is characterized by an extremely broad range of crimes and a wide range of statutory penalties. In addition, the distinction between felonies, misdemeanors, and police offenses was ended, and the types of punishment were simplified. It goes without saying that it was rooted in revisionist liberalism that was popular in the late nineteenth century. This was the result of learning from the then criminal law theory and criminal policy (Otsuka, 2003, 50).

To implement the new criminal law, the Meiji government gradually promulgated some single criminal laws, such as the *Law on Enforcement of the Penal Law* (1908), *Prison Law* (1908), *Public Security and Police Law* (1900), *Law forbidding Smoking by Minors* (1900), and the *Law for the Suppression of Securities of Paper Money* (1906). Thus, a modern Japanese criminal law system was formed, with the *1907 Penal Code* as the centerpiece and other individual laws and regulations as supplements. Modern Japanese criminal law was formally established. This also meant the complete disintegration of the criminal law of the Chinese Legal Family in Japan.

Establishment of the Modern Japanese Civil Procedure Law

The drafting of the civil procedure law in Japan dates back to 1876. The Chamber of Elders was responsible for the survey of the draft. It completed a draft modeled on the *1806 French Code of Civil Procedure* in 1880. However, at that time, the drafting policy of Japanese law shifted from studying French law to studying German law, and just like the drafting of the constitution, civil law, and criminal law, the intention with civil procedure law was also to follow the trend and learn from German civil procedure law. Thus, the draft was not considered in the end (Zhao & Bi, 2006, 198). Later, Japan invited the counselor Techows from Prussia to make a draft code, imitating the *German Uniform Code of Civil Procedure*. Soon, Mosse, who was also a German, participated in the formulation of the code, thus forming a draft with a strong German flavor. In 1886, the *1890 Code of Civil Procedure* was officially approved as a government draft, and after consideration by the Chamber of Elders and the Privy Council, it was finally adopted and published in the Diet on April 21, 1890. It came into force on January 1, 1891 (Hukuyama, 2004, 496).

The *1890 Code of Civil Procedure* comprised 805 articles in eight titles: General Provisions, Procedural Rules for Proceedings before the Courts of First Instance, Appellate Remedies, Reopening of Proceedings, Proceedings on Claims Arising from a Deed in Which Only Documentary Evidence Is Submitted and Proceedings on Claims Arising from a Bill of Exchange, Compulsory Execution, Public Summons for Exhortation, and Arbitration Procedures (Translation Academy of Nanyang Mission College, 2007, vol. 2, 301–439). The code had the following characteristics in terms of content. First, it implemented the "party-oriented approach." Second, claims were necessary for the initiation of proceedings in a district court. The court would not recognize prelitigation settlements, but in principle, parties may orally sue and recognize prelitigation settlements before a district court. Third, evidence would generally proceed on the application of the parties, but the judge had the discretion to decide freely on the validity of the evidence. Fourth, the tradition of dealing with civil disputes through settlement was affirmed. Fifth, appellate hearings would be conducted only within the scope of the claims that were filed by the plaintiffs in the original trial and by the appellant in the appeal. Sixth, the enforcement of real estate would go through compulsory auction or compulsory administration (Zhao, 2010, 243). As mentioned above, the *1890 Japanese Code of Civil Procedure* was drafted after the *German Code of Civil Procedure*, i.e., the Prussian law was the core, and the 1802 Austrian draft law was referred to as well. Japanese scholars also admitted that "in general, it was almost a copy of the original German law, with only translations of the German code into Japanese" (Hukuyama, 2004, 496).

In addition, during and after the enactment and implementation of the civil procedure law, the Japanese government enacted some single civil procedure statutes, such as the *Regulations for the Enforcement of the Civil Procedure Law* (1890), *Law on the Cost of Civil Litigation* (1890), *Law on Family Bankruptcy* (1890), and *Personal Status Litigation Act* (1898) (Translation Academy of Nanyang Mission College, 2007, vol. 2, 440–464). Since then, Japan's modern legal system of civil litigation has been formed.

Establishment of Criminal Procedure Law in Modern Japan

The first code of criminal procedure in modern Japan was the *1880 Law on Punishment of Crimes*, drafted by the French. According to the provisions of this law concerning the organization of the courts, Japanese courts would be divided into four levels: the Grand Court, the Court of Appeals, the Court of First Instance, and the Magistrate's Court (He et al., 1999, 379). However, the *1880 Law on Punishment of Crimes* was not a pure code of criminal procedure in the strict sense but, at most, a prototype of modern Japanese criminal procedure law. The establishment of modern criminal procedure law in Japan was marked by the promulgation of the *Code of Criminal Procedure* in October 1890. This law was the product of Japan's learning from the German *1877 Criminal Procedure Law* (Wang, 2011, 91).

In terms of structure, the *1890 Code of Criminal Procedure* included 334 articles in eight titles and five bylaws. The eight titles were the following: General Provisions, Courts, Search and Prosecution of Crimes and the Preliminary Examination, Judgment, Appeal, Retrial, Litigation Procedures concerning the Special Jurisdiction of the Grant Court and Its Power of Judicial Execution Review, and Amnesty (Translation Academy of Nanyang Mission College, 2007, vol. 2, 581–630). In terms of content, it followed the content of the *1880 Law on Punishment of Crimes*. There were some main changes. First, the part on court composition in Title II was removed, making it a purely criminal procedure code. Second, a new title on appeals was created, stipulating that except for those falling under the special jurisdiction of the Grand Court, all general misdemeanors and felonies can be prosecuted and appealed against. Finally, the rules regarding jurisdiction were changed. In addition to the past trial jurisdiction based on the place where the crime was committed, the jurisdiction of the court where the defendant was located was recognized (Zhao, 2010, 244).

In summary, after the Meiji Restoration, by transplanting the systems of criminal procedure law from France, Germany, and other continental European countries, the Japanese criminal procedure law gradually broke away from the Chinese Legal Family and moved toward Western Europe's modern legal culture (Wang, 2011, 74). Japan transformed from the inquisitorial procedural model of the Chinese Legal Family to the *ex officio* procedural model of the civil law system.

2.3 Disintegration of the Chinese Legal Family in the Korean Peninsula[25]

Korea has been closely related to China since ancient times, and it was once a vassal state of China during the *fengjian* era. The most obvious manifestation of this is the name of the country, Choson (Joseon, in China, 朝鲜), which was decided by Emperor Taizu of Ming (Zhu Yuanzhang). "In 1390, Yi Seong-gye, who was in control of the military power of the Goryeo Dynasty, seized power through a coup on the ground that King Wang Chang was not a descendant of the Wang clan. In July 1392, Yi Seong-gye assumed the throne. In November, he wanted to change the name of the nation to 'Choson' or 'He Ning' and asked Zhu Yuanzhang to rule on it. Zhu Yuanzhang decided to adopt Choson because 'Choson is the most beautiful with a long history'" (Xie, 2011, 179). Thereafter, the peninsula entered the Choson era. The ancient legal culture of Korea was deeply influenced by the traditional Chinese legal

[25] From 1897 to 1910, Korea changed its name to the "Korean Empire." Moreover, after February 1945, according to the arrangements of the Yalta Conference, the Korean Peninsula was divided into two spheres, namely, "Choson (Democratic People's Republic of Korea)," under the influence of the Soviet Union, and "Korea (Republic of Korea)," under the influence of the United States. As a result, scholars in both nations have studied the modern history of the Korean Peninsula, but the titles of the books vary, i.e., "*Modern History of Choson*" and "*Modern History of Korea*." To avoid controversy, this book directly adopts the name of the "Korean Peninsula" to refer to modern Choson and Korea.

culture, and its political and legal systems were almost copies of the Chinese systems in the *fengjian* era. For example, "in the Goryeo Dynasty of Korea, the political and legal system of the Tang Dynasty was used as the model to establish the ruling order of centralization and autocratic monarchy. The system of Three Departments and Six Ministries and the imperial examination system were adopted. Also, imitating Tang Lv and Goryeo Lv was promulgated, forming a *fengjian* legal system with Lv, Ling, Ge, and Shi as the main body" (Cui, 2007, 158). Thus, both Chinese and Korean scholars agree that the ancient Korean legal system was part of the Chinese Legal Family.

However, in the nineteenth century, under the expansion and invasion of the colonial powers of the West, Korea faced the same difficulties as the suzerain, China. The *Treaty of Ganghwa* of February 27, 1876 (Cao, 1993, 51–52), was the most important turning point in the modern legal history of Korea as it severely undermined the sovereignty of Korea and brought it under the de facto control of Japan as a Japanese colony.[26] From thereon, Korea gradually became a Japanese colony, and the previous legal system of Korea was abolished. New laws were formulated under the guidance of the Japanese, including the *Categorization of Laws* (1896), *Categorization of Applicable Korean Laws* (1908), and *Applicable Korean and Japanese Codes* (1910). After 1910, the *Korea Criminal Order* (1912) and *Korea Civil Order* (1912) made by the colonial authorities were applied. At that time, Korea mainly accepted Japanese law and belonged to the civil law system (He & Li, 2002, 182).

According to the modern history of Korea, the two important demarcation points were the 1894 Political Reform and Japan's colonial rule of Korea in 1910. It is generally believed that the 1894 Political Reform was the starting point of the modernization of the Korean Peninsula's legal system and that the period from Japan's colonization of Korea in 1910 to the end of World War II was the period of the colonial legal system—or "the legal system of the Japanese Empire" (Han, 2000, 137 + 143). Thus, taking these two points as the dividing points, the disintegration of the Chinese Legal Family in Korea can be roughly divided into three stages: (1) The period of the first appearance of the disintegration, from the 1876 *Treaty of Ganghwa* to the 1894 Political Reform, during which the Korean government carried out a series of political reforms and the first signs of the disintegration appeared. (2) The beginning of the disintegration, from the 1894 Political Reform to 1910, when Japan colonized Korea. Korea began to modernize its legal system, marking the beginning of its contact with the Western European civil law system, and entered an era of legal and cultural integration. (3) The period of complete disintegration, from 1910 when Japan fully colonized Korea, and Korea was forced to accept the

[26] In the ninth year of the Meiji Era (on February 27, 1876), Joseon and Japan signed the treaty after "negotiation." Although the first article of the treaty stated that "the Choson State shall have equal rights with Japan as an autonomous state," the name of the treaty in Japanese showed the inequality: "The Treaty of Amity with the Choson State." This treaty was also known as the Treaty of Ganghwa Island, which was ratified by the Japanese government on March 22. From then on, under the cover of the beautiful words of "amity" and "equality," Japan's attempt to make Korea its colony was initially successful. See Feng (2008, 416).

Japanese legal system. This indirectly and forcibly made Korea a member of the civil law system and completely destroyed the Chinese Legal Family in Korea.

2.3.1 First Appearance of the Disintegration (1876–1894)

From 1876, when the *Treaty of Ganghwa* was signed, to 1894, before the political reforms, although Korea was no longer a hermit state and adapted to the world trend, it did not become a starting point for its establishment of a modern state and for carrying out an autonomous industrial revolution. Rather, it became an opportunity for the centralized power to cater to the external powers and to be politically and economically subordinated to them (Kang, 1993, 184). As a result, the traditional way of ruling in Korea was challenged during this period. The country's enlightened and conservative forces were constantly competing and conflicting. Politically, it was a choice between proactively welcoming foreign systems and maintaining the existing traditional rule. In terms of the legal system, it was whether to adopt the civil law system or stick to the old one. The most significant event in the history of the legal system in this period was the Enlightenment Policy from 1880 to 1882. This political change was the first manifestation of the disintegration of the Chinese Legal Family.

After the opening-up, the Korean government gradually formulated its Enlightenment Policy. They sent an envoy, Kim Hong-jip, to Japan. To stop the southward movement of Russia into the Korean Peninsula, the Korean government also formulated the "Choson Strategy" and proposed the policy of "pro-China, tying with Japan, and cooperating with America" (Kang, 1993, 185).

At that time, to adapt to the new situation of increasing complexity in diplomacy, trade, and domestic affairs after the opening-up and to further strengthen the political position of the Min group, Korea learned from the Qing government and set up a new office in charge of foreign affairs (Cao, 1993, 101). This was the "first stage of the reform." The reform of the administrative structure began in December 1880, and a General Administrative Institution was established, under which there were 12 divisions in charge of serving the great powers, relations with the neighbors, military affairs, border affairs, commerce, machinery, coast guard, ships, military supplies, official selection, language research, and accounting and finance (Yi, 1994, 281). From the tasks of these newly established divisions, such as the division of commerce, machinery, military supplies, and ships, it can be seen that the new administrative structure reflected Korea's attempt to adapt to the new situation that it was facing.

After the establishment of the General Administrative Institution, the government paid much attention to foreign exchange and study. In early 1881, a delegation of 12 persons was sent to Japan. They comprehensively inspected various government facilities, industrial and mining enterprises, and education affairs in Tokyo, Osaka, and the surrounding areas and made contact with 44 Japanese politicians, such as Iwakura Tomomi and Sanjo Sanetomi. Upon their return to Korea, the delegation submitted letters of reassurance and promoted the implementation of the Enlightenment Policy (Cao, 1993, 101). This study tour directly led to the "second-stage reform" in Korea. On November 9, 1881, the Korean government reorganized the General Administrative Institution, changing the 12 divisions into seven divisions, namely, language affairs, military affairs, commerce, accounting and financing, official selection, law, and supervision. The reform provided an opportunity for persons of the progressive party, such as Hong Yong-sik, Kim Yun-sik, Lee Jae-won, and Kim Hong-jip, to join the government and become high-ranking officials in each division (Cao, 1993, 102). The two-stage reform opened a gap in the old traditional system of Korea, and new Western systems began to appear in the Korean governmental structure, breaking the original pattern where the Chinese Legal Family was dominant in Korea.[27]

2.3.2 Beginning of the Disintegration (1894–1910)

It is generally believed that the 1894 Political Reforms marked the modernization of Korean law because it abolished the backward *fengjian* system and established a "modern absolute monarchy" from the political, legal, and economic aspects. The progressive party, which was supported by Japan and came to power, tried to change the dynastic system politically. The reform sought to modernize the country through democratic reforms in the areas of democracy, equality, and human rights, among others (Cui, 2007, 159). The Korean government enacted a large number of decrees during this period of political reforms. According to statistics, a total of 3,600 decrees were issued from 1894 to 1910 (Han, 1996, 522). The explosive increase in the number of decrees issued makes evident the severity of the legal changes at the beginning of the disintegration of the Chinese Legal Family in Korea.

The reforms were carried out in a specific context of the time. From the internal point of view, it was led by the demands of the peasant army. From the external point of view, it was an internal reform forced by Japan (Kang, 1993, 196). There is no certain general agreement in the academic community regarding the time frame of the political reforms.[28] However, it is generally believed that July to October 1894 was the most important period of the reforms, when the government was composed of pro-Japanese and neutral people, and the "cabinet" headed by Kim Hong-jip

[27] During this period, there was the 1884 Gapsin Coup led by the progressive party, which proposed a series of political reforms, such as abolishing *fengjian* gentry and implementing equality among the people, reforming land rents, abolishing interest on government loans, unifying the management of state finances, reforming the police and military systems, and introducing a cabinet system. However, their reform measures were suppressed by the Chinese army before they were announced. See Yi (1994, 289).

[28] Many scholars define it as the period from the establishment of the office of Military and National Affairs to the fall of the third Kim Hong-jip Cabinet (From July 27, 1894, to February 12, 1896), which was divided into three stages. The first stage was the period of the first Kim Hong-jip Cabinet (From July 27 to December 16, 1894). The second stage was the period when the second Kim Hong-jip Cabinet cooperated with the Bak Yeonghyo Cabinet (From December 17, 1894, to May 28, 1895) during the Bak Jeongyang Carbinet and the Bak Yeonghyo Cabinet (From May 29 to August 23, 1895). The third stage was the period of the third Kim Hong-jip Cabinet (From August 24, 1895, to February 12, 1896). See Cao (1993, 178–179).

carried out the 1894 political reforms almost completely independently. The new government established the Office of Military and National Affairs for the reforms (Yi, 1994, 302). This office introduced a series of reforms and formulated and issued more than 200 important decrees on internal affairs, covering almost all political, legal, and economic fields, including bureaucratic establishment, administration and justice, finance, personal status system, customs, and education.

The reforms included the following: (1) Reforming the bureaucratic establishment and promoting the modernization of the administrative system. On July 30, 1894, the Office of Military Affairs promulgated the *Act on the New Bureaucratic Establishment of the New Government*, consisting of 80 articles in nine chapters. It stipulated the organization and composition of the parliamentary government and changed the six departments of the cabinet into eight departments, namely, internal affairs, foreign affairs, accounting and finance, military affairs, legal affairs, academic affairs, industrial affairs, and agricultural affairs. At the end of August, 1894, Korea imitated Japan in the bureaucratic establishment of its imperial household agency and separated the court from the government. (2) Abolishing the imperial examination system and introducing a system of selection based on merit. (3) Social reforms, such as banning the sale of persons and allowing widows to remarry. (4) Implementing financial reforms. For example, measures were taken to unify the national financial management system, taxation in kind was abolished, weights and measures were unified, and the *Regulations on the Issuance of New Currency* was promulgated (Cao, 1993, 179–180). In addition, reforms were carried out to separate judicial power from administrative power, and the *Law on the Composition of Courts* was enacted, stipulating that all judicial issues were placed under the jurisdiction of the courts. Local courts included primary courts and high courts or circuit courts. The former included courts specially established in open ports, and the latter accepted appeal cases (Yi, 1994, 303).

After the 1894 Political Reforms, aside from the political reforms of the bureaucratic establishment, legal modernization also took place. Korea established the Law Drafting Committee and began to draft civil law, commercial law, criminal law, and political law. In January 1895, the basic program of the reforms, the *Fourteen Articles of Constitution*, was promulgated. The provisions covered both civil and criminal laws, including the prohibition of arbitrary imprisonment and punishment and the protection of people's lives and property. In August 1899, the *Constitution of the Republic of Korea*, which established an autocratic monarchy, was promulgated (Cui, 2007, 160). The promulgation of these laws gradually presented the outline of the modern civil law system.

Meanwhile, the Korean government codified and drafted many codes based on Japanese laws, such as the *1896 Categorization of Laws*, *1907 Categorization of Applicable Korean Laws*, and *1910 Applicable Korean Codes*. In the field of civil law, the Korean government promulgated separate regulations, such as the *Rules on the Issuance of Property Deeds*, *Civil Registration Law*, *Regulation on Interest*, and *Regulation on Civil Proceedings*. In the field of court organization law, the *Law on the Organization of Courts* was promulgated in 1908 (Zhao & Bi, 2006, 270–272).

Between 1894 and 1910, Korea carried out reforms and modernized its administrative system. In addition, it enacted a series of laws and regulations, gradually forming departments of laws in the civil law system, including the civil law, criminal law, procedural law, and constitutional law of the modern civil law system. The legal system of Korea gradually began to modernize. Meanwhile, the Chinese Legal Family, which was based on traditional *fengjian* Chinese law, began to dismantle in Korea.

2.3.3 Complete Disintegration (1910–1945)

In modern times, Japan had been trying to colonize Korea. After the Second Japan–Korea Treaty, Japan turned the Korean Peninsula into its de facto exclusive colony (Cao, 1993, 272). Korea became a Japanese colony in the legal sense when the *Treaty of Mergence Between Japan and Korea*[29] was signed on August 22, 1910, by Prime Minister Yi Wan-yong of the Cabinet of the Korean Imperial Government and Joseon Governor Terauchi Masatake. The document was issued on August 29, 1910, thereby completely making the Korean Empire a Japanese colony (Kang, 1993, 210). The name of Korea was then changed to Joseon, and the Joseon Governor's Office was established (Yasuoka, 1996, 388). Korea under Japanese colonial rule after 1910 marked the complete disintegration of the Chinese legal system in the Korean Peninsula. Korea was again compulsorily incorporated into Japanese law; that is, it indirectly became a member of the civil law system. Thus, "the legal system, which originated from the traditional society, came to a standstill after 1910 when the national and autonomous nature of the legal system was stifled due to Japanese colonial rule. The natural process of development of the legal system was disrupted, and the legal system of the Japanese colonialist was compulsorily accepted" (Han, 2000, 143).

Under the colonial rule of Japan, Korea's legislative, executive, and judicial powers were in the hands of the Japanese governor in Korea, and a Governor's Court was established. At that time, the hierarchical structure of the Korean legal system was mainly divided into two levels. One was the decrees issued by the emperor, the government, and the Diet of Japan, such as edicts and laws. The other was the decrees issued by the Governor's Office in Korea. In terms of legislation, Japan promulgated the *Korea Criminal Order* and *Korea Civil Order* in 1912, which stipulated that "except for the special provisions of this law and other laws, Japanese civil

[29] The treaty stipulates that (1) the Korean Emperor ceded all ruling rights concerning Korea to the Japanese Emperor completely and permanently. The Japanese Emperor accepted this cession and fully incorporated Korea into the Japanese Empire. (2) The Japanese Emperor agreed to give the Korean Emperor, the former Korean Emperor, the Crown Prince, and other members of the royal family the "dignity and honor" and treatment appropriate to their status. (3) The Japanese Emperor granted honorary titles and money rewards to Koreans with "merit"; the Japanese government employed as many Koreans as possible, who were loyal to the "new system," as officials of the Japanese Empire. See Cao (1993, 276).

law, commercial law, and civil procedure law should apply" (Zhao & Bi, 2006, 273–274). Therefore, through the referral function of this article, the civil and commercial activities of Korea could also be regulated by Japanese civil law, commercial law, civil procedure law, and other laws. Korea was indirectly included in the civil law system.

For Korea, the "legal system of the Japanese Empire" from 1910 to 1945 had a dual impact, thus creating a contradictory evaluation of the legal system during the colonial period. In terms of positive effects, this period was an important period for the modernization of the Korean legal system because "under the rule of the Japanese colonial policy, the historical process of legal modernization passively began, and the entire legal system of Korea, including the civil law model and some basic legal concepts, legal principles, and even legal institutions, were all formed at that time and have continued to this day" (Cui, 2007, 168).

During this period, the Japanese colonial rulers issued a large number of decrees. According to statistics, during the 36 years of colonial rule, more than 270 orders on criminal and civil matters were promulgated (Han, 1996, 524). This led to the complete disintegration of the Chinese Legal Family on the Korean Peninsula.

However, in terms of negative effects, "the legal system in the colonial period, as a tool of colonial rule, destroyed the structure and tradition of Korean society as a whole … ignoring legal procedures and implementing unequal policies" (Han, 2000, 144).

In summary, from the perspective of the legal family, the traditional Korean legal system was destroyed during the colonial period, and the Chinese Legal Family in Korea thoroughly and completely collapsed. Korea was forcibly and indirectly brought into the civil law system.

2.4 Disintegration of the Chinese Legal Family in Vietnam

Vietnam, another important member of the Chinese Legal Family, was historically known as Dai Co Viet, Dai Viet, and Annam. Only after Emperor Gia Long of the Nguyen Dynasty unified North Vietnam (1802) was it named Vietnam. As mentioned earlier, before the Sui and Tang Dynasties, Vietnam was a part of China and was under the rule of the Chinese *fengjian* dynasties. At the end of the Tang Dynasty, the local forces of Annam took advantage of the turmoil and became independent from the rule of the Chinese *fengjian* dynasties. Starting from the Yongle Era of the Ming Dynasty, Annam accepted the Chinese emperor's title and became a vassal state of China. It continued to follow the Ming calendar and use the Chinese script. The suzerainty continued until the Qing Dynasty. Vietnam was influenced by Chinese culture and adopted Chinese laws, such as the New Law of 1812, which was modeled on the Qing law. In addition, Nguyen Phuc Anh ordered his men to purchase the *Qian Long Yu Pi Tong Jian* (*Imperial Instruction of Emperor Qianlong*, 乾隆御批通鉴) and *Da Qing Hui Dian* (*Code of Institutions of the Qing Dynasty*, 大清会典) from China to study and use at all times (Xie, 2011, 165–166). Therefore, the ancient Vietnamese law was a subsidiary law of the Chinese Legal Family. However, in modern times, with the French colonial power's invasion, Vietnam gradually ended its suzerainty relationship with China and gradually became a French colony. Politically, the Sino-Vietnamese suzerainty relationship ended. Legally, it manifested the disintegration of the Chinese Legal Family in Vietnam.

2.4.1 Vietnamese Law During the French Colonial Period: The Disintegration of the Chinese Legal Family in Vietnam (Yang et al., 2017)

France was the first Western colonialist to invade Vietnam. In fact, the French culture and economy had already entered Vietnam in the seventeenth century when France sent missionaries and merchants to Vietnam. In 1858, under the pretext of protecting the missionaries, the French government cooperated with the Spanish fleet to shell Da Nang. The war of invasion started. In 1862 and 1874, the Nguyen Dynasty was forced to sign two Treaties of Saigon with the French government, which ceded Gia Dinh, Dinh Tuong, Bien Hoa, and Con Lon Islands to France and opened up Da Nang, Quang An, Hanoi, and Hai Duong as ports of commerce. The treaties also recognized the extraterritoriality of France in Vietnam, and the diplomatic power of the Nguyen Dynasty was handed over to France. Thereon, southern Vietnam fell into the hands of the French colonialists. Later, France attacked North Vietnam and entered Ha Noi and Hui. In 1884, the *Treaty of Hue* was signed, and Vietnam was officially recognized as a French protectorate. In 1885, the Qing Dynasty recognized France's protection of Vietnam in the *Treaty of Tianjin*, which ended the suzerainty relationship between China and Vietnam (Luo & Wu, 1998, 8).

Vietnamese Political System Under French Colonial Rule

In terms of the political system, although Southeast Asian countries were under different colonial powers, they all developed commonalities, such as the relative concentration of power, with the executive, judicial, legislative, military, and diplomatic powers in the hands of the governors or senior resident officers, who were subordinate to the monarchs or cabinet-related bodies of the colonizer. At the local level, the colonizers used the original ruling classes and institutions, such as the tribal chiefs and feudal aristocrats, in different degrees or retained them to help strengthen their rule. Of course, the level of capitalist development varied from one colonizer to another, and each brought some of its own domestic forms of rule to the colonies, so there were differences in the political systems of the colonies.

(1) Bureaucracy. In the early colonial administration, all officials were French, but from 1898 onward, local people were admitted to the administration, although they were middle and lower rank officials. In Cochinchina, the French abolished the traditional Chinese bureaucracy, and the Vietnamese had to be employed as

civil servants. In Annam and Tonkin, the traditional Chinese bureaucratic classes and positions were retained, and a new public service class, composed mainly of Frenchmen, was formed to complement the traditional bureaucratic rule. Of course, the involvement of local people in the bureaucracy was motivated by the need of the French colonialists to serve their interests, especially in the taxation and monopoly sectors, where the main task was to obtain economic benefits. Local knowledge was necessary to achieve these ends.

(2) Administrative structure. The French established colonies centered on Vietnam in Indochina. To strengthen the rule and administration of the colonies, France established a relatively complete system of administrative institutions in Indochina.

First, the governor. The governor was the central and full administrative head of the Federation. Before the governor became the administrative head with full power, it went through a process. In the beginning, the governor had little power and was only a general official. The power of the federal administration was in the hands of the French domestic rulers. The French National Assembly held the legislative power of the colonies. It could decide the general budget, tax quotas, economic policies, and even the construction plans of railways and highways. Through the Acts of 1891 and 1898, and especially the Acts of 1911, the powers of the governor were gradually expanded and fixed in all aspects. The governor obtained the power to determine the budget; manage the selection of civil and military officials; be responsible for internal affairs, public security, and defense; use and mobilize the garrison; and exchange views on foreign affairs with the French representatives or consuls in the Far East. The Governor's Office had a Chief Secretary to assist the governor and deal with daily affairs. Sixteen ministries and departments were established, including finance, construction, health care, agriculture, animal husbandry, forestry, customs, post and telecommunications, mining, geology, and education. Under the auspices of the governor, the Council of Government, Supreme Council of Finance and Economy, and Council of National Defense were established, of which the governor was the *ex officio* chairman or president. These institutions were only consultative, and the governor had the right to veto any proposal (Liang & Liang, 2005, 303).

Paul Doumer, the Governor of French Indochina from 1897 to 1902, created the so-called "Doumer System" to overcome the chaotic political situation and financial difficulties in the region. This integrated administrative system based on a highly centralized model is often referred to as "the beginning of modern Indochina" (Hall, 1964, 174). In the Doumer System, the governor was the centralized authority, and the European colonial and indigenous officials in each region were directly accountable to the governor; this held true all the way to the bottom of the colonial regime. Superiors required more obedience from their subordinates and gave them less autonomy. Subordinates were absolutely responsible to their superiors. "It abolished or disdained the traditional rulers and social institutions, and the personnel were directly assigned to form a bureaucracy. Europeans occupy an important place in this bureaucracy, and non-Europeans can only hold lower positions" (Fieldhouse, 1983, 31).

Meanwhile, in the Doumer System, there were a number of auxiliary bodies that mainly hired local people, such as the Indigenous Advisory Council and the Council of Nobles, which were established to enlist the prominent local gentry. The members of these bodies were ostensibly elected or recommended, but in fact, they had to go through a strict selection by the colonial authorities. For example, "the members of the Economic and Financial Council were not elected directly by popular vote, but by the parliamentary bodies of the regions; in the Indigenous Advisory Council, only local nobles, landowners, and wealthy merchants could be elected" (Pluvier, 1974, 19). In addition, "they were chosen from a small group of officials and those who were loyal to France. Even so, the councils could not discuss political issues. On other matters, they could only express opinions when a debate was permitted by the supreme resident officer. The budget of the protectorate was also reviewed at that council, but it was a mere formality" (Hall, 1964, 716). For example, the members of the Grand Central Council in Cochinchina could only provide consultative opinions on the local budget. Likewise, the Indigenous Advisory Councils in Annam and Tonkin were not allowed to discuss political issues. In Annam, Doumer abolished the Regency, removing any substantial power from the Nguyen regime without changing the status of the protectorate (Ennis, 1936, 88).

The Doumer System had two consequences: (1) It only considered the promotion of French interests instead of Indochinese interests. (2) It did not give room for or encourage the development of the native political and economic activities, resulting in the failure to defend the demands and interests of the natives, which, in turn, affected the rule of the French colonists.

Second, the Administration of Operations. The central colonial administration of the Federation was very large, and there were a number of authorities in charge of various operations. This book only introduces those that have played an important role in the central administration of the Federation.

a. Finance Bureau. This was established by the Decree of December 6, 1906. The bureau's tasks were the following: (1) to report directly to the Ministry of Finance and the Ministry of Colonial Affairs of France and receive instructions from them, (2) to prepare and execute the general budget of the Federation in accordance with the governor's instructions and report periodically on the financial situation of the Federation and the operations of the financial institutions, and (3) to supervise the expenditure of the central administration of the Federation and the operations of the Indochina Bank.
b. Tax Bureau and State Monopoly Bureau. These two administrations had a particularly important role in the central federal administration as they were the instruments of the French colonialists in exploiting and plundering the Indochinese people. They generated a large amount of monetary revenue every year, and this constituted an important part of the general budget of the Federation.
c. Directorate of Agriculture and Trade. This was established in 1898 to directly provide services for the French colonists and help them establish large plantations in Indochina. The directorate provided services for the French plantation owners to increase their production and reap huge profits by organizing research

in agricultural science and promoting advanced technology and good seeds. It also investigated and studied the socioeconomic characteristics of the Indochinese countries to better serve the French industrial and commercial bourgeoisie in rapidly transforming Indochina into its sales market and source of raw materials. Moreover, the directorate provided advice to the governor in formulating agricultural policies.

d. Bureau of Public Works. The bureau was established in 1898, and its tasks had both military and economic significance. Under the auspices of this bureau, several ports were built on the Indochina Peninsula; railways from Saigon to Hanoi, Haiphong, and Lao Cai were constructed; and ring roads connecting various parts of the Indochina Federation were built. All of these undoubtedly contributed to France's expansion and control of the Indochina economy and facilitated the military operations of the French colonists to suppress the uprising of the people in the region (Yang, 1989).

In addition, the colonial administration established various professional commissions to serve as advisers to the governor on professional matters. The early ones included the Committee on National Defense, which was set up in 1912, and the Committee on Social Work, which was set up in 1905, both of which were attended by senior officials of the French administrative bureaucracy and senior commanders of the French colonial forces in Indochina.

(3) Three regions. First, Cochinchina (The Southern Region). The administration of the Nguyen Dynasty was abolished in Cochinchina. A colonial body headed by a vice-governor was set up, and a Privy Council was established to be responsible for the administration. The colonial parliament served as an advisory body to the vice-governor, and the capital of the colony was located in Saigon. Cochinchina became a French colony in 1862. Until 1879, the admiral of the French naval fleet in the region also served as the governor of the colony. After 1879, a civil servant began to fill the post of the governor of the colony. Cochinchina was initially divided into 20 provinces. Later, the number of provinces was increased to 24. The colonial regime in this region at the provincial and county levels was rebuilt based on the destruction of the old *fengjian* regime and was a product of the specific conditions of the time. After the French colonialists invaded and occupied Cochinchina, the officials of the original *fengjian* regime at all levels of the Vietnamese Empire refused to cooperate with the French colonialists, most of them left Cochinchina, and the officials who stayed still acted according to the policies of the Vietnamese Empire. In this case, the French colonists had to resort to rebuilding, but the district and township levels of government still retained their original administrative agencies and officials.

Second, Tonkin (The Northern Region). Tonkin is located in the northern part of the Indochina Peninsula, and it was a bridgehead for the French colonialists to further invade and expand into southern China. Because of its strategic significance, the French colonists set up four military districts in Tonkin after occupying the region. The annexation of Tonkin by the French colonialists went through a gradual process. Initially, according to the preliminary agreement of August 25, 1882, the emperor of Vietnam was forced to agree to the establishment of a French protection system in Tonkin. In 1886, Tonkin was formally separated from Vietnam. Although the imperial governor sent by the Vietnam Empire was still formally in place, in reality, he was completely under the command of the French colonists. In 1893, the post of governor was officially abolished, but the local bureaucracy of the Nguyen Dynasty was retained, leaving Tonkin in a "semi-protected" state. "The decrees of 1899 and 1911 clearly provided that the French highest resident officer was the administrative head of the region. Tonkin was initially divided into 13 provinces, which were later increased to 23. The administrative power of each province was held by French administrative commissioners, who supervised the activities of the same-level officials in the region. In contrast with Cochinchina, the prefectural power remained in the hands of the local people, but the taxation, financial, and public utility organs were placed under the direct control of the French colonial officials.

Third, Annam (The Middle Region). In 1886, Annam was in the charge of an envoy under the French minister general. After the abolition of the post of the minister general, the envoy became the highest resident officer in Annam. Under the 1884 Treaty, a "protection regime" was established in Annam. Nominally, the Nguyen Imperial Court was allowed to administer the region, and the small Nguyen Imperial Court was retained. The nominal administrative head of Annam was the emperor, who was no longer the fully independent and supreme authority he had been, but a puppet subservient to the French colonial authorities, with no financial or military power and no power to develop diplomatic relations with foreign countries. If the emperor went against the wishes of the colonial authorities, he could be deposed, imprisoned, or exiled at any time. Under the emperor, there were a Privy Council, a Secretariat, and other bodies, but these were organs with little real power. According to the decree of November 27, 1897, the royal Council, which used to have great power, was replaced by the Council of Ministers, chaired by the highest French resident officer. Therefore, the actual head of the administration of Annam was the highest French resident officer. He had the power to handle the internal and external affairs of Annam and had the right to decide the general budget, meet the emperor when he deemed necessary, and supervise the activities of all administrative agencies and officials in the whole Annam territory. Annam was divided into 12 provinces. The local officials of each province were under the supervision of the French Commissioner of Administration, and the departments of finance, taxation, and public utilities were directly under the control of the French Commissioner of Administration.

(4) Parliament. In 1869, a parliamentary organization was set up in Cochinchina. Its members were mostly senior officials in the bureaucratic administration of the colony. Only four were the so-called "people's" representatives, two French and two locals, who were nominated by the provincial governor and appointed by the governor-general. The governor-general was the president of the parliament, and in his absence, the lieutenant governor or the secretary-general acted as the president. A consultative parliamentary organization was established under

the governor and the highest resident officer. However, these advisory councils could not debate political issues, and other issues could only be discussed with the permission of the governor or the highest resident officer. Moreover, the representatives of this parliamentary organization were appointed by the provincial governor or the highest resident officer. In 1898, Tonkin also established a parliamentary organization, which consisted of the following people: representatives of the senior officials of the colonial bureaucracy in the region, representatives of the senior commanders of the garrison in the region, and the highest resident officer who acted as the chairman of the organization. The parliamentary organization in Annam was roughly the same as that in Tonkin.

In terms of the formation of the parliament, there was a change from appointment to election. The 1880 decree stipulated that the parliament of Cochinchina, consisting of ten representatives, should be elected, four of whom should be French and six of whom should be locals. Universal suffrage was applied to the French in Cochinchina—all citizens over the age of 21 could vote. However, the natives were treated differently. Those who were called "enfranchised" were given the same treatment as the French in the election. Such "enfranchised" natives were obviously the loyal servants of the French colonizers and the enemies of the local people. As for the natives in general, especially the laboring people, they did not have any democratic rights, and the requirements for participation in the elections were very harsh, such as a higher age limit than the French, a higher education requirement, and a demand for certain fixed assets.

In 1922, Governor Long issued a decree to increase the number of local representatives in the colonial parliament and provide the taxpayers the right to vote. The members of the parliament should include 10 natives and 10–14 French. However, the decision of the parliament could be overridden by the Governor's Council, which consisted of 12 members, where only two were natives.

(5) Legislation and justice. The laws of French Vietnam were mainly enacted by the French Parliament and issued by the decree of the French Colonial Office. The French colonies were governed by a governor-general system. The governor exercised direct authority over the colonies on behalf of France. At the same time, because France was a republic, some French laws were also applicable to the colonies. This allowed the French colonies to send their own representatives to the French Parliament. However, because the number of citizens who held French citizenship was already very small, their seats in parliament were actually very limited. "In 1936, in a chamber with 612 seats, there were only 20 representatives from the colonies. Although their number was too small to have a sufficient influence on the formulation of policy, it was sufficient for the French government to claim that the colonies had approved the laws through their representatives" (Fieldhouse, 1983, 37). Thus, it is clear that the legislative work of French Vietnam was made by the French Parliament and that Vietnam as a colony did not play much of a role.

As for the judicial system and the judiciary, an attorney general was established to oversee all trials. From the beginning, the French colonialists in Vietnam had adopted separate litigation proceedings. The French and Europeans were prosecuted and tried according to French law, and the natives were tried according to the traditional local law.

2.4.2 Eventual Dissolution of the Chinese Legal Family in Vietnam

As mentioned above, after the French invaded Vietnam in 1858, Vietnam gradually became a French colony. The invasion of French law and the colonization ("Frenchization") of Vietnamese administrative, legislative, and judicial systems led to the collapse of the Chinese Legal Family and the demise of Chinese laws. Since the twentieth century, the colonization ("Frenchization") of the Vietnamese legal system was completed. For example, in 1921, the North Region promulgated the *Criminal Procedure Code of the Northern Region*, which comprised 21 articles in 13 chapters, and in 1922, the *Criminal Code of the Northern Region*, which comprised 328 articles in 30 chapters. Similarly, learning from the North Region, the Middle Region promulgated in 1933 and 1935, respectively, the *Criminal Code of the Middle Region* and the *Criminal Procedure Code of the Middle Region*.

Thus, like Japan and Korea, the disintegration of the Chinese Legal Family in Vietnam took place in the 1850s, but it was only in the 1930s or even after World War II that the process was completed, and Vietnam withdrew from the Chinese Legal Family altogether and embarked on the path of legal modernization (Yang et al., 2017).

References

Blackmore, T. L. (1947). Post-War Developments in Japanese Law. *Wisconsin Law Review, 4*, 635+636.

Cao, Q. (2012). *Textbook of the History of Modern Chinese Law (1901–1949)*. The Commercial Press.

Cao, Z. (1993). *Modern History of Korea (1863–1919)*. Orient Press.

Chen, Q. (1995). Discussion on Emergence and Development of China's Administrative Law. *Journal of Shanghai University (Social Sciences Edition), 2*, 20–26.

(1904, October 30). Comments on the Governor's Prevention of the Establishment of the Female Prison in the Concession. *Shun Pao*.

Compilation Committee of *Shanghai Concession Annals* (Ed.). (2001). *Shanghai Concession Annals*. Shanghai Academy of Social Sciences Press.

Compilation Committee of *The Records of Shanghai Prisons* (Ed.). (2003). *The Records of Shanghai Prisons*. Shanghai Academy of Social Sciences Press.

Cui, L. (2007). The Formation of the Modern Korean Legal System and Its Conservative Characteristics. In X. Zeng (Ed.), *Research on Legal Culture* (Series III). China Renmin University Press.

Ding, X. (2002). Historical Analysis of the "Code Debate" in Modern Japan. *The Jurist, 3*, 109–115+101.

Ding, X. (2011). *Transplant and Transformation: A Study of Japan's Modern Legal System*. China Fangzheng Press.

Ennis, E. (1936). *French Policy and Developments in Indochina*. University of Chicago Press.
Feng, W. (2008). *The History of Japan*. Shanghai Academy of Social Sciences Press.
Fieldhouse, D. K. (1983). *Colonialism 1870–1945*. Palgrave Macmillan.
Gao, F., et al. (2012). *History of Constitutionalism in the Late Qing Dynasty*. Sino-Culture Press.
Gao, F. (2008). *Observing the Traditional Chinese Prison Culture from Ti Lao Bei Kao*. Master's Thesis, Shandong University.
Guo, F. (2003, December 5). *The Evolution of Commercial Law and Its Fate in China*. Retrieved September 23, 2013, from official website of *China Civil and Commercial Law*.
Guo, Z. (1992). A Brief Introduction to the Modernization of China's Legal System. *Journal of Historical Science, 4*, 68–73.
Hall, D. G. E. (1964). *A History of Southeast Asia*. Macmillan Press.
Han, D. (1996). An Overview of the Modernization of the Korean Legal System. In the Legal Modernization Research Center of Nanjing Normal University (Ed.), *Study on Legal Modernization* (Vol. 2). Nanjing Normal University Press.
Han, D. (2000). *The History and Concept of the Rule of Law in East Asia*. Law Press· China.
Han, Y., & Guobin, Z. (1983). A Brief Discussion of the Characteristics of the Chinese Legal Family and the Ways of Its Formation and Demise. *Jilin University Journal Social Sciences Edition,4*, 59–64+76.
Han, Z. (Minister of Law). (1907). *Inspection of Prisons*.
Haviland, W. A. (1987). *Anthropology* (Wang, Mingming, Trans.). Shanghai People's Publishing House.
He, Q. (1998). *History of Legal Culture*. Law Press· China.
He, Q. (2002). On the Transplantation and Naturalization of Law. *China Legal Science, 3*, 4–16.
He, Q. (2003). *Japanese Legal Study in the 20th Century*. The Commercial Press.
He, Q. (2013). A Study of Evolution of Civil Law Family. *Modern Law Science, 1*, 3–17.
He, Q., & Kong, J. (2005). The Birth of a New Chinese Legal System? From the Three Legal Families to an East Asian Common Law. *Legal Forum, 4*, 44–52.
He, Q., Fang, L., Li, X., & Guan, J. (1999). *History of the Development of Japanese Law*. Shanghai People's Publishing House.
He, Q., & Xiuqing, L. (Eds.). (2002). *History of the Legal Development of the Seven Southeast Asian States*. Law Press· China.
Hong, J. (2005). *A Study on the Mixed Court of the Foreign Settlement in Shanghai*.East China University of Political Science and Law Doctoral Dissertation.
Huai, X. (Ed.). (2010a). *Historical Materials of Legal Reform in the Late Qing Dynasty* (Constitution, Administrative Law and Procedure Law Series). (proofread by Li, Jun et al.). China University of Political Science and Law Press.
Huai, X. (Ed.). (2010b). *Historical Materials of Legal Reform in the Late Qing Dynasty* (Criminal Law, Civil and Commercial Law Series). (proofread by Li, Jun et al.). China University of Political Science and Law Press (p. 3+4, pp. 510–810+865–872).
Hukuyama, T. (2004). *The Historical Evolution and New Code of Japanese Civil Procedure Law*. (Ding, Xiangshun, & Hepei Ding Trans.). In G. Chen, & W. Jiang (Eds.), *Procedural Law Review* (Vol. 9). Law Press· China.
Huntington, S. P. (2010). *The Clash of Civilizations and the Remaking of World Order* (revised version) (Zhou, Qi, et al. Trans.). Xinhua Publishing House.
Inoue, K., & Suzuki, M. (1972). *Modern History of Japan* (Yang, Hui. Trans.). The Commercial Press.
Ji, L. (2005). *Study on Commercial Legislation in the Late Qing Dynasty (1912–1937)*, Doctoral Dissertation, East China University of Political Science and Law.
Jiang, B. (1988). *A Brief History of China's Modern Constitutionalism and Constitutions*. Law Press· China.
Kang, M. (1993). *History of Modern Korea* (He, Jiancheng, Sichuan Zhou, Yongliu Yang, & Bo Liu, Trans.). Orient Press.

Li, G. (1999). The Disintegration of the Chinese Legal Family and the Preliminary Formation of the Modern Chinese Legal System. *Journal of Beijing Administration Institute, 4*, 42–45.

Li, X. (2001). The Forerunner of Modern Civil and Commercial Law: A Review of the Transplant of Foreign Civil and Commercial Law in the Late Qing Dynasty. *Studies in Law and Business, 6*, 126–140.

Liang, Y., & Liang, Z. (2005). *Modern History of Southeast Asia I*. Kunlun Press.

Liu, Y. (2012). *A Study of Foreign-Related Civil Cases in the No. 1 District Court of Shanghai Special Administrative Region—Centering on the 1940s Archive*. Master's Thesis, East China University of Political Science and Law.

Luo, R. (1990). The World Process of Modernization. *Social Sciences in China, 5*, 107–126.

Luo, S., & Chongbo, W. (1998). *Contemporary Political Systems in Southeast Asia*. Lanzhou University Press.

Lv, S., & Yao, J. (1995). A Brief Analysis on Concepts, Modes, and Categories of Modernization of Legal Systems. In the Legal Modernization Research Center of Nanjing Normal University (Ed.), *Study on Legal Modernization* (Vol. 1). Nanjing Normal University Press.

Ma, C. (2009). *The Concession in Shanghai*. Tianjin Education Press.

Otsuka, H. (2003). *Introduction to Criminal Law (General Theory)* (3rd ed.), (Feng, Jun, Trans.). China Renmin University Press.

Pan, J. (2003). *A Broad Scan of Chinese Prisons through the Ages*. Law Press·China.

Peng, J. (2011). *Research on Constitutional Affairs Bureau in the Late Qing Dynasty*. Peking University Press.

Pluvier, J. M. (1974). *Southeast Asia From Colonialism to Independence*. Oxford University Press.

Records of Hongkou District Compilation Committee (Ed.). (1999). *Records of Hongkou District*. Shanghai Academy of Social Sciences Press.

(1911, January 18). Reform of Prisons Has Completed. *Shun Pao*.

Shen, J. (2015). *Ji Yi Wen Cun* (Left Works of She Jiaben, 寄簃文存) (Volume 6, Records of Prison Visits, Preface). Zhonghua Book Company.

The Shanghai Compilation Office (compiled). (2010). *New Laws of the Qing Dynasty (1901–1911)*. (Vol. 1). (checked and revised by Li, Xiuqing et al.). The Commercial Press.

Translation Academy of Nanyang Mission College. (2007). *The New Translation of Japanese Regulations* (checked and revised version) (Volume 1, checked and revised by He, Jiaxin) (Volume 2, checked and revised by Li, Xiuqing). The Commercial Press.

Wang, L. (1997). In the Late Qing Dynasty, China Drew German Civil Law From Japanese Civil Law. *Law Science, 1*, 54–56.

Wang, L. (2006). Shanghai Concession and Its Modernization of the Legal System. *Law Science, 4*, 31–42.

Wang, L. (Ed.). (2007). *History of Chinese Legal System* (2nd ed.). Shanghai People's Publishing House, & Peking University Press.

Wang, L. (2015a). Changes in the Legal System of the Chinese Concessions in the Hundred Years—Focusing on the Changes in the Legal System of the Concession in Shanghai. *Tribune of Political Science and Law, 1*, 66–72.

Wang, L. (2015b). The Legal System of the Chinese Concessions and the Modernization of the Chinese Legal System. *Journal of Social Sciences, 2*, 144–151.

Wang, L. (2016a). *A New Probe into Tang Lv* (p. 8). Peking University Press (p.

Wang, L. (2016b). *A Preliminary Study on the Legal System of the Chinese Concessions*. Law Press· China.

Wang, L., Lian, Y., & Yao, Y. (Eds.). (2012). *Shanghai Legal System and Urban Development*. Shanghai People's Publishing House.

Wang, Z. (2011). *Research on the Changes of Models of the Criminal Process in Japan*. Sichuan University Press.

Wei, X. (2012). The Breakthrough of the Meiji Constitution on the Legal Consciousness of Modern Japan and Its Limitations. *ECUPL Journal, 4*, 66–73.

Weng, Y. (Ed.). (2006). *Administrative Law (I)*. Angle Publishing Co., Ltd.

Wigmore, H. J. (2004). *A Panorama of the World's Legal Systems*(I) (II). (He, Qinhua, Xiuqing Li, Guangdong Guo, et al. Trans.). Shanghai People's Publishing House.

Wu, T. (Ed.). (1997). *Studies on Modernization of Japan*. The Commercial Press.

Xia, B. (2009). *The Elegy under the Yellow Banner: A Historical Investigation of the Legal Reform in the Late Qing Dynasty*. Hefei University of Technology Publishing House.

Xia, J. (Ed.). (2012). *Conflict and Transformation: Legal Change in Modern China*. China Renmin University Press.

Xiao, C. (2007). *Modern Western Culture and Japan's Meiji Constitution*. Social Sciences Academic Press (China).

Xie, J. (2011). *The East Asian World and Modern China*. Shanghai People's Publishing House.

Xie, H. (1995). Research on the Civil Code of Civil Law Countries (Continued). *Translation and Commentary on Foreign Laws, 3*, 1–8.

Xiong, Y. (1987). Double Influence of the Shanghai Concession. *Historical Review, 3*, 103–110.

Xu, J. (1995). Exploration on Shanghai Prisons in the Old Times. *Min Guo Chun Qiu* (The Spring and Autumn Period of the Republic of China), *5*, 19–23.

Xu, L. (2000). A Comparative Study of the Modernization of the Chinese and Japanese Legal Systems. *Translation and Commentary on Foreign Laws, 1*, 41–49.

Xu, Y. (2012). My Opinion of the Signs and Causes of the Disintegration of the Chinese Legal Family. In the Legal History Research Center of East China University of Political Science and Law. In *The Growth of the Legal History* (II). Law Press· China.

Yang, C. (1989). An Overview of the French Colonial Administration in Indochina. *Journal of Minzu University of China, 2*, 84–89.

Yang, Y. (2012). *History of Modern Chinese Legislation* (proofread by Fan, Zhongxin et al.). China University of Political Science and Law Press.

Yang, C., Xiuyuan X., et al. (2017). *Modern Asian, African and Latin American Regional Law* (Volume I, Asian Law Part) (Chapter 6 written by Wu, Guanghong, & Haijun Wang). The Commercial Press.

Yasuoka, A. (1996). *Modern History of Japan*. (Lin, Hesheng, & Xinchun Li Trans.). China Social Sciences Press.

Yi, K. (1994). *A New Theory of Korean History* (Li, Fan, Trans.). International Culture Publishing Corporation.

Yu, J. (2003). *The Theory of Private Rights in Modern Chinese Civil Law*. Peking University Press.

Yu, M. (2013). Between Revolution and Constitution-Making: Wu Jinglian and the *Constitution of the Republic of China* (1923). *ECUPL Journal, 5*, 49–63.

Zeng, X. (Ed.). (2006). *History of Chinese Legal System* (2nd ed.). China Renmin University Press.

Zhang, Y. (1991). A Brief Discussion of the Disintegration of the Chinese Legal Family. *Journal of South Central Institute of Political Science and Law, 3*, 130–132.

Zhang, Z. (1999). *Review and Reflection: On the Study of the Chinese Legal Family* (pp. 79–96). Nanjing University Law Review.

Zhang, J. (2005). *The Tradition and Modern Transition of Chinese Law* (Second Edition). Law Press· China.

Zhang, J. (Ed.). (2007a). *Retrospect and Prospect of the Chinese Legal Family*. China University of Political Science and Law Press.

Zhang, Z. (2007b). From the Chinese Legal Family to East Asian Law—Legal Traditions and Changes in East Asia and Its Direction. *Journal of Nanjing University (Philosophy, Humanities and Social Sciences), 1*, 118–124.

Zhang, J. (2011). *History of Chinese Constitution*. People's Publishing House.

Zhang, J., & Li, T. (Eds.). (1991). *History of Chinese Administrative Law*. China University of Political Science and Law Press.

Zhao, X. (1994). The System of Japanese Civil and Commercial Law and Its Characteristics. *Contemporary Law Review, 3*, 76–81.

Zhao, X. (Ed.). (2009). *Special Issues Concerning the History of Modern Chinese Legal System*. China Renmin University Press.

Zhao, L. (2010). *History of the Japanese Legal System*. Intellectual Property Publishing House.
Zhao, L., & Bi, L. (2006). *Social Transformation and Changes of Legal System in Modern East Asia*. China Social Sciences Press.
Zheng, Q. (2009). *Shanghai Tilanqiao West Prison and Reform of Prison in the Late Qing Dynasty—Starting from the Public Opinion in the Newspapers (1901–1911)*. Master's Thesis, Fudan University.
Zhou, Y. (1962). Several Issues about the Meiji Restoration. *Journal of Peking University, 4*, 3–17.
Zhu, Y. (Ed.). (1999). *General History of Chinese Legal System* (Vol. 9). Law Press· China.
Zhu, Y. (Ed.). (2007). *History of Chinese Legal System* (2nd ed.). Law Press· China.

Correction to: Chinese Legal Family

Correction to:
Q. He et al., *Chinese Legal Family*,
https://doi.org/10.1007/978-981-96-6522-8

The original version of this book has been revised. Abstracts for Chapters 1, 2, and 5 have been removed as per the author's request.

The updated versions of these chapters can be found at
https://doi.org/10.1007/978-981-96-6522-8_1
https://doi.org/10.1007/978-981-96-6522-8_2
https://doi.org/10.1007/978-981-96-6522-8_5

Q. He et al., *Chinese Legal Family*, https://doi.org/10.1007/978-981-96-6522-8_6

Epilogue Historical Heritage of the Chinese Legal Family

The Chinese Legal Family has disintegrated, and rebuilding it is unlikely. The modern Chinese legal system, which was established after the modern era against the background of the eastward spread of Western laws, has transplanted almost everything from civil law countries such as France, Germany, and Japan, including the legal concepts, principles and theories, institutional content, forms of law, legal procedures, legal education, and jurisprudence. After the establishment of the People's Republic of China in 1949, law and jurisprudence were greatly influenced by the Soviet Union. At times, the legislature was even directly copied from the Soviet Union in the fields of jurisprudence, civil law, criminal law, and procedural law. After the reform and opening-up in 1978, China absorbed and introduced a large number of excellent laws and jurisprudence from common law countries, such as the United States, and jurisdictions of Greater China, such as Chinese Hong Kong and Taiwan. More importantly, the foreign laws and jurisprudence that China has transplanted since the "Opium War" in 1840 have become the backbone and foundation of contemporary Chinese law and jurisprudence (He & Li, 2003). In this situation, it is no longer possible to rebuild the Chinese Legal Family or establish a "new Chinese Legal Family" (a legal family requires several countries to imitate and follow the law of the mother country and form a legal community).

Therefore, how should we view the Chinese Legal Family today? As a dismantled ancient legal system, does it still have some value for the development of law and jurisprudence in China and the neighboring countries, such as Japan, Korea, and Vietnam? We believe that although the Chinese Legal Family has disintegrated, as one of the achievements of human legal culture and a legal system that has survived for more than 1,300 years, the Chinese Legal Family is still valuable today. As the mother law, Chinese law has an even longer history, dating back to earlier than 2700 BC, the legendary era of the Yellow Emperor. Rich legal experience and wisdom can be found in the Chinese Legal Family. Therefore, the Chinese Legal Family is a huge historical heritage that should be highly valued, cherished, inherited, and carried forward. Specifically, the following elements are noteworthy.

Q. He et al., *Chinese Legal Family*, https://doi.org/10.1007/978-981-96-6522-8

A. Understanding of Law

With regard to the understanding of law, the thinkers of the Chinese Legal Family particularly emphasized the normative, mandatory, equal, public, just, stable, and concise nature of law, as well as the evolutionary attributes of law. For example, the rulers and thinkers after the Tang and Song Dynasties emphasized that the law should change from time to time and that legislative reforms should be carried out continuously. They advocated that the law should be simple and straightforward so that the people could easily understand it and comply with it, and the judicial officials could be restrained. They also emphasized that the law was a public utility of the world and not of one family.

For example, in the eighth year of the Qingli Era (1048), Emperor Renzong of Song issued an edict to Hanlin Xueshi (Official Academician), Sansi Shi (Chancellor of the Treasury), Zhi Kaifengfu (Magistrate of Kaifeng), and Yushi Zhongcheng (Censor): "I want to know the mistakes I have made, the evils around me, the dangers and tricks in the central and local governments, the ruthless acts conducted in prefectures and counties, and the laws that are not for the sake of people. You have to report all of them to me" (Toqto'a et al., 2008, 187). Under this guiding ideology, during the reigns of Emperor Renzong and Emperor Shenzong, reformers such as Fan Zhongyan and Wang Anshi were engaged to carry out large-scale legislative reforms. During the reforms, the ruling group also put forward a series of ideas that laws should change over time. For example, Wang Anshi clearly stated, "To follow the ancestors' law is to follow the intention of the ancestors" (Wang, 1999, 1). "Adapt the law to suit the time, and then good governance can be achieved" (Wang, 1999, 207). He believed that the world was infinitely changing, and the legal system was no exception. The law could not be inherited from generation to generation, and only by abolishing the old laws and adopting new laws could it meet the needs of governance. He believed that the reason that the Song Dynasty was "poor and weak" was directly related to the fact that the ancestors' law was followed for generations. Therefore, to change this situation, the government must "change customs and establish laws and institutes." It was precisely because of the abovementioned ideas that Wang Anshi, Emperor Shenzong of Song, and others still unswervingly carried out the reforms despite the problems.

In the Ming Dynasty, in response to the changes in society after the mid-Ming Dynasty, Emperor Xiaozong and others adopted the important legal thought that the law should change with time. However, because of Zhu Yuanzhang's prohibition against "changing the law of the ancestors," Emperor Xiaozong and the others did not dare to directly amend the old law. It was by compiling the regulations of the past dynasties and revising and promulgating *Wen Xing Tiao Li* that Emperor Xiaozong finally modified the legal system of the Ming Dynasty to suit social development and changes. When guiding this work, Emperor Xiaozong once clearly stated: "Recently, there are so many laws for the Department of Law to interrogate prisoners that it is difficult for people to comply. Some of them are feasible, but the three law divisions should review and discuss them article by article and decide and report the appropriate provisions. Other laws that are redundant or difficult to apply should be completely removed" (Mao et al., 1962, 2547–2548). While emphasizing that the law should be changed according to the times, some insightful people in the ruling class in the middle of the Ming Dynasty also emphasized that the law should be simple, clear, and demotic so that ordinary people could easily know and abide by it and the judicial officials could be restrained. For example, after he examined the discussions concerning the complexity and simplicity of the laws in the previous dynasties, Qiu Jun pointed out in *Shen Xing Xian: Ding Lv Ling Zhi Zhi Xia* that at the beginning of the Shenlong Era (705–707), "Zhao Dongxi said: ... The most important thing for legislation is to make all people know it; then, they will not dare to violate it. ... Let Lv, Ling, Ge, and Shi use direct language to describe things without embellishment, ... Let ordinary people understand it as soon as hearing it, and they will follow each other and avoid violation. How can they clearly know it and still violate it deliberately? Therefore, it is said that if the law is clear, people will believe in it, and if the law is compatible, officials will respect it." "The minister's note: do not simplify its provisions, do not decorate its literary meaning, but directly write down the things and clarify its meaning; use common and simple words to provide full and detailed information. If the punishment is allowed to be increased or reduced, it should be decided according to the facts. Clear language should be provided; for example, what type of sentence a person deserves, how many lashes he should receive, or what punishment should be added or reduced. All people should be able to see, hear, and understand it ... In this way, the people will know what to do and what to avoid and will not fall into the trap."

The rulers of the Ming Dynasty also placed great emphasis on fairness, justice, and moderation in the use of law to correct Zhu Yuanzhang's preference for using punishment, especially heavy punishment. In the fourth year of the Hongzhi Era (1491), Emperor Xiaozong issued an edict to the Department of Justice and stated clearly: "From now on, all the criminal departments and judges in the world must be kind and forgiving, uphold the law fairly, and carefully examine what a criminal deserves based on sentiment, hoping that the lessons from the ancient sages are followed" (Zhang et al., 2008, 166). Zhang Juzheng also emphasized that "the law should be strict but not tough" and "the law should be simplified, not irritating and harsh." The key for the law to function lies in the fair and equal use of punishment: "punishment and reward should be just, not following personal feelings. The policies and orders must be decided by the emperor (the will of the emperor), not leading to disputes and controversy. When punishment should be imposed according to law, even nobles or close relatives cannot be forgiven. When unjust treatment is given, even acquaintances or lowly people should be provided with remedies" (Zhang, 2019, 1).

The late Ming and early Qing thinkers also emphasized that the law is a public utility of the world, not of one family. For example, Huang Zongxi clearly pointed out that the law should be "a public utility of the world, a tool to protect the entire people, not a tool for the ruler to exercise their power imperiously." "The law established in the Xia, Shang, and Zhou Dynasties was not adopted for any individual. However, for later rulers, once they gained the throne, the so-called law was the law of one family, not the law of the world." He believed that concerning the law of the world, "the looser the law, the fewer the crimes. This is the so-called law without laws. The law of later dynasties ... became strict, and crimes arose from it. This is the so-called law not performing as law." Therefore, he advocated that "I think there is first the rule of law, and then the rule of people. If the law is not performing as law, it shackles the people. Even if there are persons who can rule the world well, they are not able to get rid of the bad influence of the laws. If the law of the early three dynasties still existed, there would not be concepts falling outside the law. If the ruler is appropriate, he can implement his good policies, and if the ruler is inappropriate, he would not be able to impose strict punishment and would harm the world" (Huang, 2021, 29–31, 33–34). Gu Yanwu also pointed out that "the ruler cannot rule the world alone. Ruling alone, the punishment will be complicated. Ruling together, the law will be implemented" (Gu, 2007, vol. 6, 343). The law must be "for the sake of the whole world" (Gu, 2007, vol. 8, 496). Wang Fuzhi further emphasized that "an emperor is providing rewards and imposing punishments on behalf of the heaven. If personal strategies are involved, the heaven is betrayed, and the world will not obey ... Since the rewards and punishments are provided on behalf of the heaven, the emperor should publicize them worldwide and not include personal manipulation and 'the art of control,'" or stated differently, "practicing the selflessness of the heaven" (Wang, 2020, 532).

It should be said that the above understanding of ancient Chinese thinkers regarding the law is a summary of the experience and lessons of ancient Chinese law in governing the state. Like the concept of law of Western thinkers, they both arise from the ingenuity of man in understanding and applying law. However, ancient China had been under the rule of monarchy for a long time, and the monarch was both the lawmaker and the privileged person above the law. The implementation of the law was ultimately centered on consolidating the rule of the monarch rather than protecting the rights of the people. Therefore, when modern China transplanted Western law and built a modern legal system, the abovementioned understanding of ancient Chinese thinkers regarding law was no longer taken seriously. China and the West may have different historical traditions and cultural backgrounds, but their understanding of the law is the same. A concept of law that embraces both Chinese and Western understanding is certainly more progressive and practical than simply applying Western concepts of law. In particular, this understanding of law grew with difficulties in the authoritarian-centralized system. It was not easy, and more importantly, it carried the spirit of criticism of the authoritarian-centralized system. This is especially valuable for current China: to abandon the rule of man and build a country ruled by law. Therefore, after eliminating monarchical absolutism, we can fully integrate the ancient Chinese thinkers' concept of law with the modern concept of the rule of law and make it a guiding principle for building a socialist rule of law model with Chinese characteristics.

B. Tradition of Codified Law

According to historical records, the earliest written law in China was *Huang Di Li Fa* (*Punishment Law of Yellow Emperor*, 黄帝李法), which was finished around 2700 BC. After that, there was the law of Shi Gaotao, who was the great judge of the Shun Dynasty around 2100 BC, and *Yu Xing* (*Punishment Law of Yu*, 禹刑). After the Shang Dynasty (1600 BC), each Chinese dynasty enacted its own legal code, such as *Tang Xing* (*Tang's Punishment Law*, 汤刑) in the Shang Dynasty and *Jiu Xing* (*Nine Punishments*, 九刑) in the Zhou Dynasty. In spring and autumn and in the Warring States Periods, there were also written laws enacted by the states, such as the *Puqu Zhi Fa* (*Law Preventing Escape and Hiding*, 仆区之法) of the State of Chu, *Beilu Zhi Fa* (*Law of Beilu*, 被庐之法) and "the casting of a tripod with texts of law" in the State of Jin, "the casting of the book of punishment" and *Zhu Xing* (*Punishment Law on Bamboo*, 竹刑) in the State of Zheng, *Fa Jing* (*Law Classics*, 法经) written by Li Kui of the State of Wei, and the legislative works of Wu Qi in the State of Chu and Shang Yang in the State of Qin. In 221 BC, the first emperor of Qin unified China and established a strong centralized system of power while at the same time establishing a systematic and developed legal system, with written legal codes in all areas of criminal, civil, economic, and administrative law. Later, the Han, Wei, Jin, and Northern and Southern Dynasties also developed their own legal codes.

The Sui and Tang Dynasties were when the Chinese Legal Family was born, and the highest-standard written laws in ancient China finally appeared: *Kaihuang Lv* (581) of the Sui Dynasty and *Yonghui Lv* (651) of the Tang Dynasty. They formed the basis of the Chinese Legal Family in the ancient East. Later, the Song, Yuan, Ming, and Qing Dynasties continued to make progress in codification techniques. *Da Ming Lv* and *Da Qing Lv Li*, together with *Yonghui Lv* of the Tang Dynasty, became models of legislation for China's neighboring countries. For example, following China, Japan promulgated the *Taiho Code* and *Yoro Code*, Korea promulgated the *Great Code of National Governance*, and Vietnam promulgated The *Le Code*. Some scholars argue that the statutory codes of the Chinese Legal Family were mainly criminal laws, and all laws were integrated, so they are not very valuable for modern legislation. This view is one-sided. In ancient times, because of the limitations of people's knowledge and the level of development of law, almost all statutory codes were based on one of the law sectors, and all laws were combined. Even in Rome, the birthplace of the Western statutory tradition, its *Twelve Tables* promulgated between 451 and 450 BC and the *Corpus Juris Civilis* of the sixth century AD, which was based on Justinian I's systematic legislation, were combinations of all laws centered on civil law. Therefore, the legal cultural value of the ancient Chinese statute law tradition cannot be diminished by the fact that all laws were integrated with criminal law as the main body.

In fact, the ancient Chinese statute books not only have a tradition that distinguishes them from the laws of other ancient countries but are also an important historical and cultural resource for Southeast Asian countries in strengthening their legislative endeavors at present. First, the statutory codes of the Chinese Legal Family reached a very high level. They not only formed a relatively complete framework and structure but were also concise, abstract, clear, conceptually clear, and rich in content. Second, the statutory codes of the Chinese Legal Family paid more attention to substantive justice for the society, as well as the people's livelihood and people-oriented issues. For example, *Tang Lv Shu Yi* provided for the principles of reduction and exemption of punishment for the elderly, the young, the disabled, and the sick; equivalence of crime and punishment; no penalty without a law in the formal sense; false accusation leading to penalty; aggravation of punishment for recidivism; and reduction of punishment for voluntary surrender, among others. Third, the Chinese legal system's statutory code attached great importance to absorbing and adopting the essence of various legal doctrines created by people in the past and integrating them into the law. For example, *Tang Lv Shu Yi* (including the legislation of other member states) not only incorporated the Confucian ideas of people-oriented thoughts, such as moral guidance and supplementary punishment, and prudent penalty and light punishment, but also adopted the legalist views of governing officials according to the law, fairly deciding the punishment and rewards, and the law changing with time. Moreover, the Daoist thoughts of simplifying laws and limiting prohibitions and making simple and concise codes, as well as the Mohist advocation that "virtue must be rewarded and crimes must be punished," were involved. In this way, a national code actually became a culmination of the Chinese Legal Family, accumulating almost all of the legal wisdom of our ancestors.

C. Commentary and Interpretation of Laws

In recent years, the issue of legal interpretation has attracted more and more attention. Academic circles have published many treatises, as well as master's and doctoral theses on this topic. Among the practitioners, this issue is also very popular. Often, a great amount of legislative and judicial interpretation will be provided for each code. In the legal system of modern society, the interpretation of the law has become an important part of the operation of the law. In this regard, the achievements of legal interpretation in the Chinese Legal Family are especially worthy of our attention and reference.

In ancient China, to make the officials and commoners understand and grasp the law and effectively implement the law, the governments of Qin, Han, Wei, Jin, and North and South Dynasties started the interpretation of law early on. In the Tang Dynasty, the tradition of legal interpretation reached its peak. *Tang Lv Shu Yi*, promulgated in 652 AD (the third year of the Yonghui Era), provided a thorough, systematic, and complete interpretation of the texts of Tang Lv. Not only limited interpretation and extensive interpretation but also analogical interpretation, explanation by example, literal interpretation, sentence-by-sentence interpretation, analytical interpretation, question-and-answer explanation, and innovative interpretation are adopted. In addition, more than 190 legal terms used in the codes were given interpretations. The level of legal interpretation reached a high level. After the

Song Dynasty, the achievements of legal interpretation in the Tang Dynasty were inherited by legislators and legal practitioners. *Song Xing Tong*, *Da Ming Lv*, and *Da Qing Lv Li*, as well as a large number of legal commentaries, such as Sun Shi's *Lv Fu Yin Yi*, Fu Lin's *Xing Tong Fu Jie*, Lei Menglin's *Du Lv Suo Yan*, Wang Mingde's *Du Lv Pei Xi*, and S*hen Zhiqi's Da Qing Lv Ji Zhu*, made the ancient Chinese legal interpretation a discipline and a tradition of legal culture. In Japan, the situation was the same. After the promulgation and implementation of the *Taiho Code* and *Yoro Code*, a great number of legal interpretation achievements were also launched, such as the *Ryo-no-gig*e, *Ritsu-no-shuge*, and *Ryo-no-shuge*, as well as *Nukata's Commentary*, *Anou's Commentary*, *Kasuga's Commentary*, and *Okihara's Commentary*.

The legal interpretation activities of the Chinese Legal Family have some distinctive features. First, since the Western Jin Dynasty, it had been a practice in China for government officials involved in legislation to write and publish commentaries explaining the code when the code was promulgated. The legal commentaries of Zhang Fei and Du Yu were representative of this. These legal commentaries had almost the same effect as the code. By the time *Tang Lv Shu Yi* was promulgated, this feature had reached its height and became a tradition. *Tang Lv Shu Yi* consisted of 20% legal texts and 80% interpretation of the texts, which had the same legal effect as the code itself. The situation was the same in Japan, a member of the Chinese Legal Family. Soon after the promulgation of the *Taiho Code* in 701 and the *Yoro Code* in 718, the rulers and legal scholars began to compile commentaries and explanatory additions to the laws: *Ryo-no-gige*. After several generations of efforts, this work was finally promulgated in 834. As a law, its effect was the same as that of the *Taiho Code* and *Yoro Code*.

Second, from the perspective of technique, the interpretation of laws at that time had reached a very detailed and exquisite level. There were not only a large number of works of scholastic interpretation, such as Wang Mingde's *Du Lv Pei Xi* and Shen Zhiqi's *Da Qing Lv Ji Zhu*, but also works of songs and poems, such as Fu Lin's *Xing Tong Fu Jie* and Zong Jizeng's *Du Lv Yi De Ge*. In addition, there were a number of works of diagrammatic interpretation, such as *Chong Xiu Ming Fa Zhi Zhang Tu* (*Revised Tables to Interpret Laws*, 重修明法指掌图), which was written by Shen Xintian and revised by Xu Hao. It can be said that the ruling class and intellectuals in ancient China had exhausted all their wisdom in expounding the legal theories and explaining the meaning, significance, purpose, and spirit of the legal provisions to effectively enforce the law. The achievements were no less than the *Corpus Juris Civilis* finished in the sixth century AD in Eastern Rome and the works of the Italian School of Glossators in the eleventh century.

Moreover, after the Song Dynasty, in the field of legal interpretation, there were not only official commentaries but also a large number of private commentaries on the law. They numbered more than 110 in the Ming Dynasty and more than 160 in the Qing Dynasty. These made legal interpretation a spectacular movement. Among the Japanese exegetical works of the law, except for the *Ryo-no-gige*, which was an official work, all others were unofficial exegetical works.

It is generally believed that modern legal hermeneutics is a product of the Western legal tradition. Its historical origin is the early and late School of Glossators in medieval Italy, notably led by Irnerius (around 1055–1130) and Bartolus (1314–1357). Its direct sources were the French School of Exegesis in the nineteenth century, the German Pandektenwissenschaft, and the English Analytical School. These theories and techniques of legal interpretation were introduced into China and played a significant role in guiding Chinese legal interpretation (especially in terms of methodologies) and in helping implement the law. However, there are still differences between these Western achievements and the thinking and traditional mentality of Chinese legal practitioners. Therefore, in establishing a legal interpretation model suitable for Chinese conditions, the ancient Chinese experience deserves attention and emphasis. The achievements reached by the Chinese Legal Familyin legal commentary are a rich historical and cultural heritage. It is entirely feasible that scholars should break the *fengjian* authoritarian shell of the Chinese Legal Family and transform its rich and developed technical knowledge into resources that can be used for the development of modern law and jurisprudence.

D. Protection of the Environment and Resources

As early as 2,000 years ago, during the Xia Dynasty, the ancient people of China began to pay attention to the protection of the environment and resources. Legal provisions were used to regulate people's behavior. According to historical records, Yu the Great once issued a ban on cutting down trees on the hills in the third month of spring to "let the grass and trees grow" and on fishing in lakes and rivers in the third month of summer to "let the fish and turtles grow." During the Qin Dynasty, the protection of the environment and resources was further emphasized. *Qin Jian: Tian Lv* (*Qin Texts: Law on Land*, 秦简·田律) that was excavated in Shuihudi, Yunmeng, Hubei Province, in 1975 stipulates that in the second month of spring, people were not allowed to cut down trees on hills or block waterways. Before summer, it was forbidden to burn grass for fertilizer; pick newly sprouted plants; catch young animals, eggs, and young birds; poison fish and turtles; and set traps and nets to catch birds and animals. The ban could not be lifted until the seventh lunar month of the year. The Han Dynasty inherited the Qin institutions and continued to enforce the related provisions of the Qin Dynasty to protect the environment and resources.

The Sui and Tang Dynasties established the role of China as the mother country of the Chinese Legal Family. Established after more than 300 years of social upheaval and change during the Wei, Jin, and Northern and Southern Dynasties, Sui and Tang were richer and more mature than the previous dynasties in terms of both the ruling philosophy (the idea of the unity of heaven and man) and management experience. From *Tang Lv Shu Yi*, which was the basic code of the early Tang Dynasty, it can be seen that although relatively scattered, a well-designed system of rules concerning the protection of the environment and resources was adopted. For example, Article 404 of *Tang Lv Shu Yi* stipulates that no one was allowed to discharge dirt, waste water, or other garbage from his own household into the streets or alleys to pollute the public living environment. Offenders would be punished ("Persons who go out of their homes and discharge filth into the streets and alleys shall be punished with 60 times of caning"). Article 405 stipulates that the natural resources of the mountains, lakes, and rivers, which were common to all people, should be protected and enjoyed by everyone, and no individual had the right to encroach, destroy, or seize them for himself. Article 430 states that "anyone who burns a field during the prohibition period shall be flogged fifty times." The code further explained: "The prohibition period refers to the period after the first day of the second lunar month and before the 30th day of the tenth lunar month." This meant that anyone who burned grass for fertilizer outside the time specified in the law (the 1st day of the 11th lunar month to the last day of the 1st lunar month of the next year) would be punished by the law. This law was actually a continuation and development of the Qin law that forbade the burning of grass for fertilizer until summer. Article 442 stipulates that it was forbidden to destroy or cut down trees indiscriminately, and anyone who violated the law should be punished for theft. Although the purpose of this article was to protect public and private property, it objectively served the purpose of protecting the natural environment and resources by imposing severe sanctions on the destruction and indiscriminate felling of trees. It was the inheritance of the Chinese legal tradition since the Xia Dynasty. The laws of the Song, Yuan, Ming, and Qing Dynasties inherited these provisions of Tang Lv and made the protection of nature and the environment a target of the law.

A deep reason behind the protection of the environment and natural resources, which became one of the outstanding traditions of the Chinese Legal Family, was the ancient Chinese philosophy of the unity of heaven and man. This philosophy originated from the belief and worship of heaven (gods) in ancient times when productive forces were backward and people lacked knowledge. People (under the manipulation of rulers and shamans) made various rituals to achieve communication and harmony between humans and heaven. When the state and law came into being, especially after the Western Zhou Dynasty, the concept of the unity of heaven and man was further developed. The "heaven" became "the law of heaven," which was considered a self-contained system with perfect virtue and harmonious order of nature. From Mencius' theory of "the good nature of man" and Zhuangzi's theory of "the unity of heaven and man" to Dong Zhongshu's theory of "heaven and man united in the world" in the Han Dynasty and to Cheng Yi and Cheng Hao's theory that "heaven and man are essentially not different, so there is no need to speak of unity" and "heaven, earth, and man are the same," all emphasized that man must follow and obey heaven and that man cannot oppose heaven, go against heaven's will, or heaven's order. All human beings can do is to seek harmony with heaven through "heaven–human induction." Protecting the environment and natural resources around people was an important aspect of this seeking of harmony with heaven. Therefore, protecting the environment and resources through legislation and law enforcement was the result of both the ancient Chinese people's intuitive understanding of their own living conditions and their fear, worship, and reverence for the unmanageable nature (heaven), as well as their pursuit of living a stable and prosperous life by treating nature well and being sheltered by heaven.

At present, China is building a harmonious socialist society, and protecting the natural environment and resources is an important aspect of building this. It should be said that in the past 40 years of reform and opening-up, China has made great progress in environmental protection legislation, and legislation has been enacted in the relevant fields. However, a relatively complete legal system for environmental and resource protection has not yet been formed. Some important laws, such as laws on safety management of nature reserves, nuclear facilities, and toxic chemicals; laws on the protection of biodiversity, ecology, highland lakes, international rivers, and special mineral resources; and supporting laws and regulations for environmental and resource protection, such as control within a time limit, total control, ecological compensation, pollutant discharge permits, and environmental planning, are not yet in place. This will undoubtedly affect the development of a harmonious society. Therefore, the harmony between human beings and the natural environment, as well as the harmony between human beings and the social order, should be the focus of the laws. In this regard, the abovementioned historical heritage of the Chinese Legal Family should also be an important local resource for us to absorb and utilize.

E. Prudent Penalty and Light Punishment

As one of the historical legacies of the Chinese Legal Family, "prudent penalty and light punishment" shows Chinese ingenuity since ancient times and can be seen as the germination of humanism in modern law. According to *Kang Gao* (*Orders of Kang*, 康诰) and *Shun Dian* (*Law of Emperor Shun*, 舜典), which are two chapters of *Shang Shu*, one of the earliest preserved ancient texts in China, as early as the beginning of the Western Zhou Dynasty in 1000 BC, the ruler Duke Zhou already put forward the ideas of "advocating virtues and prudent punishment" and "cautious penalty and prudent punishment." It was emphasized that rulers should be as concerned regarding the people's hardships as they were regarding their own illnesses. Law enforcers should take the lead in abiding by it, handle the cases with care, and act strictly according to the law. Even if the emperor orders someone to be killed, the judge should not kill the one disobeying the law. This idea of Duke Zhou later became the theoretical basis for the pursuit of long-lasting social peace and one of the important criminal policies of the ruling class.

In the Tang Dynasty, when the Chinese Legal Family was formed, the idea of "prudent penalty and light punishment" was developed to an unprecedented extent. It became the consensus of the rulers and ministers in the early Tang Dynasty. The ruling group of the Tang Dynasty, led by Li Shimin, experienced firsthand how the powerful Sui Dynasty was overthrown in a few years because of its failure to deal with the people, extreme oppression of the peasants, destruction of the legal system, indiscriminate killing of innocents, and extremely luxurious and extravagant lifestyle. Therefore, they took "comfort the people and appease the nation" as the basic national policy and paid attention to improving the relationship of the ruling group with the people. "Prudent penalty and light punishment" is one important aspect of it.

To put it plainly, "prudent penalty and light punishment" means that the judiciary must be prudent, careful, and rigorous in convicting and sentencing, paying attention to human life and strictly following the law. Three elements underlie this: (1) In case there is doubt and the facts of the crime are not completely clear, do not rush to arrest people; if the suspect has been under arrest, do not rush to sentence the case. As stated by *Shang Shu*, "It is better to make ignorant mistakes rather than kill innocent people." (2) If the facts are clear but the penalty can be either heavy or light, apply the light penalty; if the offenders can either be punished or not, do not punish them. In the words of Confucius, "Leniency will win the hearts of the people, and kindness will be enough to move people." (3) In major cases of the death penalty, as people cannot be revived if killed, strict and thorough procedures must be adopted to minimize unjust death as far as possible. In this regard, the Chinese ancients made every effort to come up with ideas, and therefore, some further discussion will be given.

First, since the Han Dynasty, China explicitly provided by law strict trial procedures and appeal procedures for the correction of errors in cases where imprisonment or heavier penalties were imposed, such as *qiju* (retrial) and *luqiu* (review). In *qiju*, when a criminal case was decided, the prisoner would be summoned on the spot and told of his guilt. If the prisoner claimed to be unjustly treated, he was allowed to appeal and be heard in more detail. *Luqiu* means that the emperor, county magistrates, and inspectors would inspect the prisons in their respective regions on a regular or irregular basis to interrogate the prisoners who were already in custody, especially those on death row, to find out whether their convictions and sentences were lawful and appropriate. If injustice was found, it would "be dealt with immediately." These institutions were inherited by later generations (Shen Jiaben, a famous jurist in the late Qing Dynasty, had a detailed testimony on this) and became an important part of the principle of prudent penalty and light punishment.

Second, in addition, because the death penalty is related to human life and people cannot be revived after death, in ancient China, the handling of death penalty cases was even more cautious. There were multiple procedures of report and report again. In the Han Dynasty, this procedure was called *shangjuyu* (report the details regarding the sentence). In the Tang Dynasty, this procedure was better developed, and under the guidance of the ruling class's idea of "prudent punishment," the "three-time report" system was further improved (the death penalty re-report system was formed in the Northern Wei Dynasty, and the three-time report system appeared in the Sui Dynasty). In other words, after the death penalty was approved, there was a procedure for reviewing the death penalty before the execution of the condemned person. The emperor had to check and tick on the name of the condemned person before the execution. This procedure of report and approval had to be carried out three times. In the fifth year of the Zhenguan Era (632), Li Shimin, Emperor Taizong of Tang, in a fit of anger, mistakenly killed Zhang Yungu, the head official of *Dalisi*, whose behavior did not constitute a capital offense. To prevent further wrongful killings, he issued an edict stipulating that "all death sentences, although ordered to be executed immediately, must be reviewed five times." Later, *Yuguan Ling* (law for judicial officials, 狱官令) of Tang made an explicit stipulation on the three-time report, five-time report, and related issues. Death penalty cases that are executed in the capital must go through a five-time report before execution (two reports a day before the decision and three reports on the day of the execution). Cases that are executed outside the capital must go through the three-time report by the Ministry of Punishment (the day before the execution, the Ministry of Punishment had to report three times in a row to the emperor). The Tang Dynasty's three-time report and five-time report systems were inherited by the Ming and Qing Dynasties. On this basis, the Qing Dynasty also created the "autumn trial" system. It was a special review procedure wherein once a year, a nationwide review of cases sentenced to death and waiting for execution would be carried out to determine the life and death of the prisoner so that the wrong death penalty cases gained one more opportunity to be corrected.

Third, to ensure the strict implementation of the policy of prudent penalty and light punishment, in ancient China, officials who violated this policy would receive severe punishment. The article concerning "re-report and decision for prisoners sentenced to death" in *Tang Lv Shu Yi: Duan Yu* (*Commentary on Tang Code: Trial*) provides that "for all death penalty prisoners, officials who decide to execute without re-report will be sentenced to 3,000-*li* (a measurement in ancient China, approximately 300 steps) exile. After reporting to the emperor, the official should wait for three days before carrying out the execution. Those who execute the sentence before the time limit shall be imprisoned for one year; when the time limit is exceeded, the official will receive one hundred strokes of the cane one day after the due date and a high-level punishment two days after the due date." Here, the responsibility for the execution of the sentence before the due date was obviously greater than the responsibility for the execution of the sentence after the due date. The imperial court's firm position of prudent penalty and light punishment can be seen. Both *Da Ming Lv* and *Da Qing Lv Li* inherited the provisions of the Tang law and imposed severe penalties on judicial officials who did not comply with the legal procedures for the execution of sentences or violated the report duties.

In ancient China, the idea of prudent penalty and light punishment was introduced and stipulated in the code, which reflected respect for life and the humanitarian spirit in the implementation of criminal law. However, in real life, not many dynasties and emperors really followed it. This is mainly because, during the *fengjian* monarchy, the operation of the law and the observance of the institutions were all based on the rule of the monarch. Therefore, the policy of prudent penalty and light punishment was not consistently implemented, even during the most powerful and enlightened period of the Tang Dynasty. Nevertheless, the Chinese Legal Family's idea of prudent penalty and light punishment and the institutional design for its realization still have great theoretical and practical value. It is a precious legal and cultural heritage for today's China to strengthen the socialist rule of law, pay attention to the people's livelihood and the socially disadvantaged, and respect and protect human life as well as the basic human rights of citizens.

F. Respect for the Elderly, and Care for the Young and the Sick and Disabled

China has always been regarded as a nation of etiquette in the ancient East, with the greatest emphasis on family unity, parent–child harmony, and compassion for the sick and disabled. It was a model for ancient people in the thought and practice of human morality. The ancient Chinese people also incorporated this idea of human decency into the practice of law. In the ancient Chinese codes, there were legal provisions on respecting the elderly, loving the young, and compassionately treating the disabled and the sick. The elderly, young, disabled, and sick can be exempted, or their punishment can be mitigated, which is a typical expression of these human ethics in law. According to historical records, the provisions on respecting the elderly, loving the young, and showing compassion to the disabled and sick first originated from *Zhou Li: Qiu Guan—Si Li* (*Zhou Rituals: Judicial Officials—Si Li* [an official position], 周礼·秋官·司厉). It was clearly stipulated by the law in the Han Dynasty. In the Tang Dynasty, the law on respect for the elderly, and care for the young and the sick and disabled was further developed and improved, and the principle was clarified that the elderly, young, sick, and disabled could be exempted from or have their penalties reduced for crimes.

According to Tang Lv, the criminal liability of the old, young, sick (as "waste" in the legal provisions), and disabled was divided into three different cases and treated differently. In the first case, offenders who were over 70 years old or under 15 years old and who deserved punishment lighter than exile could pay money for a reduction of the penalty and did not have to serve the actual sentences. In the second case, those who were over 80 years old or under 10 years old, and those who were seriously ill (such as severe illness, madness, handicapped legs, and blind eyes) who committed crimes other than rebellion, murder, robbery, and assault could be exempted from serving. In the third case, if a person is over 90 years old or under 7 years old, "even if he has committed a capital crime, no punishment will be imposed." Tang Lv also stipulates that "those who were not old or sick at the time of the crime, but were old or sick at the time of the being found, shall be treated as being old or sick." This was also a more humane additional provision. The provisions of Tang Lv were inherited by the Song, Ming, and Qing Dynasties (*Song Xing Tong*, *Da Ming Lv*, and *Da Qing Lv Li*). Although the provisions were sometimes strict and at times lenient, it was always an important principle of the codes that the old, young, sick, and disabled could be exempted from or have their penalties reduced.

The legal concern for the elderly, young, sick, and disabled to be exempted from or have their penalties reduced is the ideological basis and jurisprudential spirit of the ancient Chinese thinkers (mainly Confucianists). They advocated the ethical spirit of maintaining the hierarchical order of a patriarchal society based on blood lineage and family relations, which was considered the norm of human nature and even the rule of survival of all things in the universe. In this way, such an ethical spirit paved the way for cultivating one's moral character, bringing order to the family, wisely ruling the country, and appeasing the world. Therefore, they provide that the elderly, young, sick, and disabled can be exempted from or have their penalties reduced. Then, on the one hand, the codes (as interpreted by *Tang Lv Shu Yi*) "take care of the old, the young, and the sick" and "demonstrate the righteousness of loving the old and nurturing the young," reflecting a humanitarian concern and promoting the moral values of ancient Chinese ethics. On the other hand, the codes clarified the people who were different from normal people, i.e., the elderly because they are old, the juveniles because they are young, and the disabled because they are mentally deranged or have other diseases (such as broken limbs, missing legs, and blind eyes), who "have little intelligence" and "cannot bear to be punished." Therefore, they should be exempted from criminal punishment, which is in line with the basic law of the growth and survival of natural things.

Because the above provision of the reduction or exemption of punishment for crimes against the old, young, sick, and disabled was contained in the ancient Chinese family ethics and was often confused with patriarchal ethics, parental authority, and the hierarchy of superiority and inferiority, their significance to the modern rule of law has not yet attracted enough attention. In fact, China is now building a system of laws for the protection of the rights and interests of the elderly, women, and children, as well as laws to protect minors, to create a harmonious and united family ethical order contributing to the building of a harmonious socialist society. China can eliminate the *fengjian*, hierarchical, and privileged elements contained in family relations and can carry forward the ancient Chinese legal provisions of respect for the elderly, and care for the young and the sick and disabled. In real life and legal practice, the elderly need more care than children and the disabled. Meanwhile, China still lacks strong legal protection measures for the rights and interests of the elderly. The current law on the protection of the rights and interests of the elderly is a "soft law" that lacks sufficient compulsory power, and people rarely apply it in legal practice. The ancient Chinese principle of remission for crimes committed by the old, young, sick, and disabled has been developed to the present day, and the latter three have been inherited by Chinese criminal law, which provides for the corresponding remission of criminal punishment. However, there is yet no remission for crimes committed by the elderly. This deserves some consideration.

In fact, our legislative and judicial bodies can provide more humane and ethical treatment for the elderly who committed crimes because, after all, the elderly over the age of 70 are physically and mentally different from the young and adults. Emperor Xuandi of Han once issued an edict in the fourth year of the Yuankang Era (62 BC): "I am mindful of the elderly, whose hair and teeth have fallen and who have been less courageous and less brutal. They may be put in jail till death without peaceful final years. I feel sympathetic for them." "From now on, all those who are 80 years old, if they did not commit false accusation, killing, or assault, they can be exempted from serving the sentences." Here, Emperor Xuandi of Han stated the reason for exempting the elderly from punishment, which is actually still twofold: one is that the ability of the elderly to commit crimes is greatly reduced, and the other is that by punishing them, they will die of old age in prison and cannot enjoy their remaining days, which is against the spirit of traditional Chinese ethics and morality. The reasonable considerations contained in this passage deserve attention and should be followed.

G. Criminal Law Principles and Institutions Accumulated Through Repeated Refinement

The successive codes of the Chinese Legal Family, which lasted for more than 1,000 years, have constantly provided principles and institutions of criminal law that have been repeatedly refined and accumulated. These are a precious historical heritage for the theory and practice of modern criminal law. This book looks at some examples of the principles and institutions of criminal law established in the Tang Dynasty.

1. Criminal Law Principles

(1) Principle of patriarchal ethics. Specifically included were that first, crimes committed by relatives were to be decided based on the mourning system; second, people living together were allowed to shelter each other.

(2) Principle of false accusations leading to penalties. In the Tang Dynasty, false accusations merited the imposition of the same punishment on the accuser. The principle of false accusations leading to penalties was an important principle established by Tang Lv, which had a significant influence on the judicial practice of the Tang Dynasty and the later dynasties.

(3) Principle of moral guidance and supplementary punishment. In the Sui and Tang Dynasties, the core content of the worldview of *fengjian* orthodox jurisprudence had been integrated with the specific legal provisions. Thus, the principle of moral guidance and supplementary punishment was not explicitly stipulated by a particular legal provision. It ran through the legislative purpose and spirit of the code, and it was reflected in the specific provisions. *Tang Lv Shu Yi* gave a theoretical elaboration of this.

(4) Principle of equivalence between crime and punishment. Another aspect of the principle of moral guidance and supplementary punishment was the principle of equivalence between crime and punishment, which was implemented by Tang Lv.

(5) Principle of legality (no penalty without a law). The *Duan Yu Lv* (*Law on Trial,* 断狱律) (Article 484) stipulates that "All judgments must be made according to the legal text of Lv, Ling, Ge, or Shi. Those who violate it will be flogged 30 times." When explaining the grounds of this article, *Tang Lv Shu Yi* pointed out that if the text of the law was not strictly and exhaustively cited in determining the sentence, it may lead to absurdities ("If it is not specifically cited, it may lead to misconduct"). From this provision of Tang Lv and the above explanation of *Tang Lv Shu Yi*, it can be seen that formally, Tang Lv also adopted the principle of legality.

(6) Principle of a specific law taking precedence over the general provisions. If there is a conflict between the principles determined by the *Mingli Lv* (*General Provisions*) and the specific provisions of each special law, the specific provisions

should be followed. In other words, in Tang Lv, the principle of *lex specialis* had been emphasized.

2. Criminal Law Institutions

When establishing the modern criminal law system, some important institutions developed in the Chinese Legal Family over the past 1,300 years also left a rich historical legacy. These institutions include the following:

(1) Additional punishment for recidivism. The term "recidivism" did not appear in Tang Lv and *Tang Lv Shu Yi*, but the concept of "recidivism" was similar to that of modern criminal law, such as "repeatedly committing a crime obviously violating the law" and "repeatedly in prison." The law also stipulated and illustrated the additional punishment for this.

(2) Combined punishment for several crimes. For several crimes committed at the same time, *Tang Lv Shu Yi* provided a categorization of three situations and stipulated different punishments. First, if more than two crimes were found, the "absorption doctrine" or the "aggravation doctrine" would be adopted. Second, if one particular act constituted two crimes, the "aggravation doctrine" would be taken. Third, if someone who had already been sentenced committed a crime again, a heavier punishment would be imposed based on his new crime, that is, using limited aggravation to measure the sentence.

(3) Joint crime. This is also known as a crime with an accomplice, which refers to a crime committed by two or more persons who conspire and commit the crime together. According to the provisions and interpretations of Tang Lv and *Tang Lv Shu Yi*, there were four main levels of joint crime. First, the general principle of punishment for joint crimes was that the first offender received the full punishment, and the accomplice received one-level reduced punishment. Second, there were some special cases concerning joint crimes (such as committing a crime of the ten abominations or crimes committed by a person with a specific identity). Third, Tang Lv also stipulated the punishment for offenders who were equivalent in nature to accomplices under *duress*. Lastly, provisions concerning an abettor can also be found in Tang Lv. It stipulated the relationships between the offenders when one offender conspired with the other to commit crimes.

(4) Surrender remission. According to the provisions and interpretations of Tang Lv and *Tang Lv Shu Yi*, the general principle of surrender was to give either an exemption or remission. The specific treatment is different depending on the following four situations: (a) If the offender admitted all of the crimes that he had committed, he should be exempted from punishment (the stolen goods should still be returned). (b) If the crimes admitted were untrue or incomplete, it was incomplete surrender, and the offender should not be completely exempted from punishment. Only the punishment related to the part that he admitted can be exempted. (c) If a person surrendered under the condition that he or she knew that someone was going to sue (or the judge wanted to raise the case), he or she was a passive surrenderer. He or she would not be exempted from

punishment, but the judge would "reduce the punishment by two levels." (d) If someone committed murder or rebellion and returned to surrender, it was called a surrender after the act. In accordance with the usual practice, the offender was not to be exempted from punishment, but the judge would "reduce the punishment by two levels" (Liu, 1996, 378–379).

(5) Intent and negligence. *Tang Lv Shu Yi* systematically absorbed the experience and research results of its predecessors in this area and developed the connotation of intent and negligence in the provisions of various specific crimes and penalties. For example, *Tang Lv Shu Yi* developed three categories of intent. First, the intentional pursuit of a consequence (in *Dousong Lv*, "intent to kill"); second, knowing that a consequence will occur but allowing it to happen (in *Zeidao Lv*, "selling poisoned meat"); third, not knowing at first, but knowing later and not reporting it (*Bu Wang Lv*, "concealing criminals"). In the case of negligence, *Tang Lv Shu Yi* often used the words "negligence," "miss," "by mistake," "unawareness," "unknown," "unaware," and so on. Specifically, it referred to three kinds of cases. The first was negligence and carelessness, such as "not being able to hear and see" and "not being able to consider." The second was overconfident negligence, such as "lifting a heavy object together, but unable to control the object." The third was accidents, such as "going together to a high and dangerous place and falling down by accident."

H. A Preference for Resolving Issues Without Going Through Litigation

A preference for resolving issues without going through litigation is also one of the historical legacies of the Chinese Legal Family. It is not only a major tradition in Chinese society, but it also continues to have a wide influence in real life. There are many discussions and various opinions in the law circle on this issue, so it is necessary to expand the discussion.

This preference was, first of all, a consistent idea of ancient Chinese thinkers. For example, Confucius, who once served as *Dasikou* (the highest judicial official) of the State of Lu, declared very clearly: "I have no difference with others when hearing cases, and the most important thing for me is to make these cases not occur at all" (Confucius, 2017, 185). Confucius' disciples further elaborated the idea of no litigation as "using rituals to create precious harmonization; the way of the previous emperors is the best."

The ideas of Confucius and his disciples influenced the thinkers of various dynasties. In the Song Dynasty, after the formation of the Chinese Legal Family, the great Confucian Zhu Xi further emphasized in his *Quan Yu Bang* (*List of Advice*, 劝谕榜) that it is advisable for the scholars, villagers, and affinities to be friendly and harmonious. If there are small conflicts, people should think twice. If not resolved, mediation and conciliation should be used, and litigation should not be easily pursued. This is generally because even if you have good grounds, it will cost you money and time. Then again, if you have no good ground, you may be found guilty and receive a penalty. Anyway, there will be some unwanted effects, and therefore, litigation should be avoided. Wang Yangming, who was active slightly later than Zhu Xi in the Ming Dynasty, also declared in his "Statement about the Ten-Household Collective Management Law" that monthly, each family in the same group should advise each other, making sure that everyone restores integrity, cultivates goodwill, avoids litigation, and stops disputes, getting better day by day. In this way, people will know the wrongs of disputes, and litigation can be simplified. Therefore, in ancient Chinese thought, the avoidance of litigation can be regarded as a basic demand.

Observing the ancient Chinese judicial practice, this preference was also a consistent practice of judicial officials. According to historical records, in the Tang Dynasty, when Wei Jingjun served as the magistrate of Guixiang, a mother and son pair accused each other. Wei Jingjun said to them: "I grew up as an orphan, so when I saw those who supported their parents, I often regretted that I have no such a blessing. You own such warmth, but you do not cherish it and even litigate with each other. It is really my sin that you are so disappointing." He whimpered and cried and took out *Xiao Jing* (*The Book of Filial Piety*, 孝经) for the mother and son to read. "Then the mother and son were enlightened, and both asked for repentance, and they praised each other for their love and filial piety" (Liu et al., 1975, 3263). Such stories could also be found in the judgments and notes of Ming and Qing judicial officials. Even some honest and upright officials who cared about people's hardships, such as Bao Zheng and Hai Rui, made it their ideal that there would be no litigation or not much litigation in the areas that they ruled. They did not believe that people should defend and fight for their rights through litigation. This preference also appeared in some emperor's instructions. For example, the "Six Orders of Emperor Shunzhi" of the Qing Dynasty, the "Sixteen Articles of the Imperial Orders" of Emperor Kangxi, and the "Imperial Orders for Wide Discipline" of Emperor Yongzheng. All of these elaborated on "the importance of filial piety and fraternity," "respect for human decency," "understanding courtesy," "harmony with relatives and clans," "harmony with the countrymen," and "avoidance of disputes."

In addition, this preference became a common opinion of ancient Chinese people. Some ancient Chinese proverbs and folk sayings reflect the common people's hatred and fear of litigation, such as "do not be contentious at home, do not talk too much in social life," "the courthouse is open, but do not come in without money," "understand some Confucius rituals and do not violate the law," "scholars who interfere with litigation are thought second rate," "it's better to ignore small disputes instead of pursuing litigation in the government, because you have to spend money on it and even if you win, the gains do not make up for the losses," and "people should be patient and not pursuing litigation, which is good for both parties; if you go to the court because of others' incitement, both you and the counterparty have to spend money." Unlike the ruling class and the scholar class, who were pursuing the social order and ideal situation of no litigation, the commoners' willingness to no litigation was out of helplessness. This is because, in real life, the commoners were struggling to make a living. Limited by poverty, the commoners were, in fact, trying to grasp every slight profit in daily life. This was fully demonstrated by Zheng Ke of the Song

Dynasty's book, *Zhe Yu Gui Jian*. A number of cases were recorded in which people were fighting for a needle, a little salt, or a few vegetables and went into litigation before the court. Whether because of willingness or helplessness, it is fair to say that this preference is the main value orientation of the ancient Chinese judicial system, an ancient Chinese culture, and a legal tradition.

In relation to this preference of ancient China, the rulers of successive generations also made every effort to advocate mediation. As early as the Western Zhou Dynasty, local officials were assigned to mediate disputes among the people, "managing the hardships of the people and harmonizing them." After the Qin and Han Dynasties, the suppression of litigation and the promotion of mediation further became important duties of the imperial court and officials at all levels. Wu Hu, the Minister of Jiaodong State, Han Yanshou, the Prefect of Dongjun, and Xu Jing, the Prefect of Guiyang in the Han Dynasty; Hu Zhi, the Prefect of Dongguan Prefecture of the Wei Dynasty; Cao Shu, the Magistrate of Luoyang in the West Jin Dynasty; Liu Huaiwei, the Prefect of the Dongyang Prefecture in the Qi Dynasty of the Southern Dynasty; Zhao Gui, the Inspector of Xiazhou in the Sui Dynasty (Now Yichang, Hubei); Yang Cheng, the Inspector of Daozhou, and Li Huideng, the Inspector of Suizhou in the Tang Dynasty; Liu Sui, a judge in the military of Yongkang (Now Guanxian, Sichuan Province), and Su Song, the Magistrate of Jiangning (now Nanjing, Jiangsu Province) in the North Song Dynasty; and Lv Sicheng, the Magistrate of Tiaoxian, Jingzhou (Now Jingxian, Hebei Province) in the Yuan Dynasty, were all "honest officials" and "uncorrupted officials" in ancient China, who were good at mediating and settling litigation. By the Ming Dynasty, mediation was prescribed by law as a preprocedure for civil litigation. At that time, the villages were equipped with "*shenmingting*" (declaration pavilion). Civil disputes were mediated by elders in the village. Those who did not want to settle were allowed to sue before the government. However, after being accepted by the government, the parties still had to first go through mediation. Any agreement reached during mediation had a legal effect, and the parties could not sue again for the same facts and reasons. The Qing Dynasty inherited this system from the Ming Dynasty.

While mediating disputes and persuading people to avoid litigation, ancient Chinese dynasties did not forget to crack down on lawyers who instigated lawsuits. For example, in the provision of "Punishment Law: Litigation" in *Da Ming Lv*, there were stipulations concerning the punishment for those who "instigate a lawsuit." Thus, "those who instigate a lawsuit make complaints for others and make up facts to falsely accuse others of a crime shall be found guilty of the same crime as the accused." *Da Qing Lv Li* adopted this provision without changing a word, and six articles were added, specifying in detail the various penalties for different situations of this kind of behavior. *Xing An Hui Lan*, a famous compilation of cases in the Qing Dynasty, contains many such cases. For example, "Governor of Anzhou Consulting: offender Chen Yutian, who had been found guilty by another court, wrote complaints on behalf of Zhang Mingyu and falsely accused Sun Yongsui of taking illegal interest. The complaint was written according to Zhang Mingyu's instructions. But Chen Tianyu had made complaints for others six times, and therefore, he should be punished according to military regulations as a habitual pettifogger. The final punishment would be demotion: *mantu* (a punishment, exile and forced labor for less than three years)" (a case in the 18th year of the Jiaqing Era, i.e., 1813). For another example, "offender Xu Xuechuan, who has been found guilty by another court, has made complaints about others five times. They were all ordinary cases, and there was no collusion with the officials, manipulating people, intimidation, or fraud. The punishment should be reduced a level on the basis of the punishment for a habitual pettifogger provided by military regulations: *mantu*. [Although] the offender was over 70 years old, he performed as a pettifogger harming the people, and therefore was not allowed to pay money for the reduction of punishment" (a case in the 25th year of the Jiaqing Era, i.e., 1820). In these two cases, in fact, the two offenders were not unruly litigators. Xu Xuechuan was even over 70 years old and should have been specially taken care of by the law, but they were still heavily punished. When explaining why he had to crack down so severely on the litigators, Emperor Jiaqing clearly pointed out that the purpose was to correct the litigious atmosphere and stabilize the social order to prevent the people from spending money for no reason.

This preference of the Chinese Legal Family was determined by the socioeconomic, political, cultural, and national psychological factors of the time. First, when litigation starts, there is a heavy financial burden for both the plaintiff and the defendant. Second, politically speaking, in ancient China, the administration and judiciary were not separate. A local official had to manage the financial issues, household register, taxation, litigation, and punishment. He was really overworked. Moreover, the imperial court assessed the performance of officials not based on how many cases they heard in a year but mainly on the amount of money, grain, and taxation collected, whether the population had increased, the local security, and how well the emperor's grace was disseminated (the so-called "enlightenment"). Under the strict "judicial accountability system" in ancient China, if something went wrong with the handling of a case, the official hearing the case would be held criminally responsible. Thus, it was only natural that officials almost invariably wanted to reduce the number of lawsuits. Third, because of the cultural factors, such as the strong propaganda and advocacy of the abovementioned Confucianists and rulers of successive generations, as well as the social characteristics of China's patriarchal family system, in which the family and state were integrated, the people's preference for litigation was considered a challenge to the authority of the emperor (the highest parent). The commoners were also psychologically more inclined to mediation than litigation in disputes.

As a *fengjian* legal tradition, the defects of no litigation were obvious. On the one hand, it hurt people's faith in the law, hindered the progress of Chinese law and jurisprudence, and seriously affected the development of China's legal profession. On the other hand, and more importantly, it seriously infringed on the private rights of the people (there was no concept of "citizenship" yet at the time) and stifled the growth of individual civil rights. A typical example of this is the handling of the case of "brothers' disputation over a piece of land" by Lan Dingyuan, a famous honest official and the magistrate of Puning, Guangdong, during the Kangxi Era. Chen Zhi, who had died, had two sons. "The eldest, Ah Ming, and the younger, Ah Ding, studied together when they were young, worked together when they grew up, and they loved each other. After marrying, they divided the fortune and lived apart." After the death of the father, the two brothers, in competing for the inheritance of seven acres of land, ignored the family's mediation and kept litigating with the government. When Lan Dingyuan failed to mediate for them, he had the guard lock the two brothers together and make them "sit together, eat together, lie down together, get up together, sleep together, go to the toilet together, and stand together. No one could separate them for a while." After some time, seeing that they had repented, Lan Dingyuan brought the four sons of the two brothers and said to them at the court, "If you had been the only son without your brothers, you would have had everything to yourselves, and your life would have been so happy, and there would not have been the lawsuit today. But unfortunately, your parents gave birth to two of you, and even more unfortunately, you each gave birth to two sons. So, instead of letting them compete for money in the future, you should kick out one of them now and keep only one son each. Ah Ming can keep the eldest son, Ah Ding can keep the younger son, and the remaining two children can be sent to the foster home and let the beggars adopt them. The beggars have no property, and there will be no trouble of litigation in the future." Hearing these words, the brothers Ah Ming and Ah Ding both kowtowed and cried, willing to repent and withdraw the lawsuit. The next day, the two brothers came with their wives and clan leaders to admit their mistakes. Lan Dingyuan made a decision that the disputed seven acres of land should be used as his father's sacrificial property, and the brothers took turns collecting rent for the sacrifice. The parties concerned "kowtowed seven to eight times in the court to thank and leave. Since then, the brothers and their wives were kind to each other a hundred times better than before."[1] Fairly speaking, seven acres of land in rural China at that time was a considerable amount of wealth. The two brothers fighting over property rights were not unreasonable. However, guided by the ideology of pursuing no litigation, Lan Dingyuan succeeded in mediating through strong power, but the sense of private rights, in this case, was suppressed.

Nevertheless, as a legal tradition that had lasted for more than 2,000 years with a great influence, this preference also had many reasonable influences. This has been agreed by most scholars. For example, the concept of no litigation is conducive to the establishment of a mediation system with Chinese characteristics, the integration of the rule of law with the rule of morality, and the ethical advocacy promoting the order and stability of the society, which contributes to the effect of preventing crime. It also helps with the cultivation of a sense of responsibility toward family, relatives, friends, and society, and the value of "putting righteousness over profit" contained in the idea of no litigation is helpful for the maintenance of legal justice. More importantly, the value pursued by the idea of no litigation is good for the building of a harmonious socialist society. Therefore, by eliminating the *fengjian* elements, the rich intention of the no litigation concept can be transformed into an excellent historical resource. This book holds that the legal tradition of no litigation demonstrates the ancient Chinese people's efforts to seek harmony in the natural order and their kind desire to live in a peaceful and stable social environment. This is the essential thing in the ideal of no litigation, and its roots are in the nature of

[1] The pronunciation of "曩" is "nǎng" in Chinese, and it means "Past."

human beings. This is why not only in Eastern societies that emphasize mediation and pursue no litigation but also in Western societies where the rule of law is well developed, people are now reflecting on the economic costs and social problems caused by excessive litigation and have begun to emphasize different mechanisms for resolving disputes instead of litigation. Various measures have been taken, such as the extensive use of summary proceedings, out-of-court and in-court mediation, the participation of social intermediary organizations in civil disputes, and the preference for arbitration in economic cases. The reason for this is that people have realized that, after all, litigation is only one way of resolving disputes, but in fact, there are many other ways for dispute resolution.

Appendix
Bibliography[2]

1. Books

Year of publication	Author	Book	Publishing house
1946	Ju Zheng 居 正	*Why We Need to Reconstruct the Chinese Legal System* 《为什么要重建中国法系》 *Weishenme Yao Chongjian Zhongguo Faxi*	Dadong Bookstore 大东书局 Dadong Shuju
1970	Chen Guyuan 陈顾远	*Chinese Culture and Chinese Legal System* 《中国文化与中国法系》 *Zhongguo Wenhua Yu Zhongguo Faxi*	San Min Book Co., Ltd 三民书局 Sanmin Shuju
1971	Li Zhongsheng 李钟声	*Chinese Legal Family (I) (II)* 《中华法系》(上、下) *Zhonghua Faxi* (Shang, Xia)	Huaxin Culture Center 华欣文化中心 Huaxin Wenhua Zhongxin
1977	Chen Guyuan 陈顾远	*Chinese Culture and Chinese Legal System* 《中国文化与中国法系》 *Zhongguo Wenhua Yu Zhongguo Faxi*	San Min Book Co.,Ltd 三民书局 Sanmin Shuju

(continued)

[2] * The Translator's Note: According to the requirements of the foreign press, the original Chinese Bibliography is reserved in Chinese with Pinyin attached, so that readers can query the corresponding references.

Q. He et al., *Chinese Legal Family*, https://doi.org/10.1007/978-981-96-6522-8

(continued)

Year of publication	Author	Book	Publishing house
1997	Hao Tiechuan 郝铁川	*Research on the Chinese Legal Family* 《中华法系研究》 *Zhonghua Faxi Yanjiu*	Fudan University Press 复旦大学出版社 Fudan Daxue Chubanshe
1997	Zhang Jianguo 张建国	*Formation and Development of the Chinese Legal System* 《中国法系的形成与发达》 *Zhongguo Faxi De Xingcheng Yu Fada*	Peking University Press 北京大学出版社 Beijing Daxue Chubanshe
2002	Guo Chengwei 郭成伟	*The Spirit of the Chinese Legal Family* 《中华法系精神》 *Zhonghua Faxi Jingshen*	China University of Political Science and Law Press 中国政法大学出版社 Zhongguo Zhengfa Daxue Chubanshe
2002	Liu Guangan 刘广安	*Re-understanding of the Chinese Legal Family* 《中华法系的再认识》 *Zhonghua Faxi De Zai Renshi*	Law Press·China 法律出版社 Falv Chubanshe
2005	Li Yusheng 李玉生	*Study of Tang Dynasty Legal Codes and the Chinese Legal System* 《唐令与中华法系研究》 *Tangling Yu Zhonghua Faxi Yanjiu*	Nanjing Normal University Press 南京师范大学出版社 Nanjing Shifan Daxue Chubanshe

(continued)

(continued)

Year of publication	Author	Book	Publishing house
2006	Fan Zhongxin 范忠信	*Chinese Culture and Chinese Legal System: A Collection of Essays on Legal History by Chen Guyuan* 《中国文化与中国法系—陈顾远法律史论集》 *Zhongguo Wenhua Yu Zhongguo Faxi—Chen Guyuan Falvshi Lunji*	China University of Political Science and Law Press 中国政法大学出版社 Zhongguo Zhengfa Daxue Chubanshe
2006	Pan Liping 潘丽萍	*Harmony Concept in the Chinese Legal System* 《中华法系的和谐理念》 *Zhonghua Faxi De Hexie Li'nian*	Law Press· China 法律出版社 Falv Chubanshe
2007	Zhang Jinfan 张晋藩	*Retrospect and Prospect of the Chinese Legal Family* 《中华法系的回顾与前瞻》 *Zhonghua Faxi De Huigu Yu Qianzhan*	China University of Political Science and Law Press 中国政法大学出版社 Zhongguo Zhengfa Daxue Chubanshe
2007	Zhang Zhongqiu 张中秋	*Proceedings of the International Academic Conference on the Chinese Legal Family* 《中华法系国际学术研讨会文集》 *Zhonghua Faxi Guoji Xueshu Yantaohui Wenji*	China University of Political Science and Law Press 中国政法大学出版社 Zhongguo Zhengfa Daxue Chubanshe
2009	Lv Zhixing 吕志兴	*Legal System of Song Dynasty and the Chinese Legal Family* 《宋代法律体系与中华法系》*Songdai Falv Tixi Yu Zhonghua Faxi*	Sichuan University Press 四川大学出版社 Sichuan Daxue Chubanshe

(continued)

(continued)

Year of publication	Author	Book	Publishing house
2009	Fan Zhongxin, You Chenjun, Gong Xianzhai, (Eds.) 范忠信、尤陈俊、龚先砦选编	*Why We Need to Reconstruct the Chinese Legal System: Selected Works on Ju Zheng's Legal and Political Ideas* 《为什么要重建中国法系:居正法政文选》 *Weishenme Yao Chongjian Zhongguo Faxi:Ju Zheng Fazheng Wenxuan*	China University of Political Science and Law Press 中国政法大学出版社 Zhongguo Zhengfa Daxue Chubanshe
2010	Deng Yong 邓勇	*On the Core Cultural Spirit and Historical Operations of the Chinese Legal System: Analysis of the "Emotional-Reasoning" Model in Ancient Legal Life* 《试论中华法系的核心文化精神及其历史运行—兼析古人法律生活中的"情理"模式》 *Shilun Zhonghua Faxi De Hexin Wenhua Jingshen Ji Qi Lishi Yunxing —Jian Xi Guren Falv Shenghuo Zhong De "Qingli"Moshi*	Law Press·China 法律出版社 Falv Chubanshe
2010	Zhang Jinfan 张晋藩	*Collection of Research on the Chinese Legal System* 《中华法系研究论集》 *Zhonghua Faxi Yanjiu Lunji*	China University of Political Science and Law Press 中国政法大学出版社 Zhongguo Zhengfa Daxue Chubanshe
2011–2017	Zhu yong 朱勇	*Chinese Legal Family (Vol. 9)* 《中华法系》(九卷) *Zhonghua Faxi*(Jiu Juan)	Law Press·China 法律出版社 Falv Chubanshe

(continued)

(continued)

Year of publication	Author	Book	Publishing house
2010	Li Yufu 李玉福	*The Form and Soul of the Chinese Legal Family* 中华法系的形与魂 *Zhonghua Faxi De Xing Yu Hun*	People's Public Security University of China Press 中国人民公安大学出版社 Zhongguo Renmin Gongan Daxue Chubanshe
2014	Gao Mingshi 高明士	*Chinese Legal System and Confucianism* 《中华法系与儒家思想》 *Zhonghua Faxi Yu Rujia Sixiang*	Taiwan University Press 台湾大学出版中心 Taiwan Daxue Chuban Zhongxin
2014	Ma Xiaohong, Liu Tingting 马小红、刘婷婷	*Research on Legal Culture(Vol.7): Symposium on the Chinese Legal System* 《法律文化研究第7 辑中华法系专题》 *Falv Wenhua Yanjiu Di-Qi Ji Zhonghua Faxi Zhuanti*	Social Sciences Academic Press (China) 社会科学文献出版社 Shehui Kexue Wenxian Chubanshe
2015	Zeng zhe 曾 哲	*Exploring the Roots of the Chinese Legal System: Selected Readings from Chinese Legal Classics* 《中华法系寻根:中华法学名篇选读》 *Zhonghua Faxi Xungen: Zhonghua Faxue Mingpian Xuandu*	China Renmin University Press 中国人民大学出版社 Zhongguo Renmin Daxue Chubanshe

(continued)

(continued)

Year of publication	Author	Book	Publishing house
2016	Yu Ronggen 俞荣根	*Ritual Traditions and the Chinese Legal System* 《礼法传统与中华法系》 *Lifa Chuantong Yu Zhonghua Faxi*	Press of Chinese Democratic Legal System 中国民主法制出版社 Zhongguo Minzhu Fazhi Chubanshe

2. *Journal Articles*

Year of publication	Author	Article	Journal	Issue No
1902	Liang Qichao 梁启超	The Development of the Chinese Jurisprudence 中国法理学发达史论 Zhongguo Falixue Fadashi Lun	*The New People's Gazette* 新民丛报 *Xinmin Congbao*	Issue 12 12 期
1903	Gong Fazi 攻法子	Comparative Study of the Five Legal Families in the World 世界五大法系比较论 Shijie Wu Da Faxi Bijiao Lun	*Political Science and Law Quarterly* 政法学报 *Zhengfa Xuebao*	Issue 2 of Guimao Year 癸卯年第二期 Guimao Nian Di'Er Qi
1918	Lu Fu 卢 复	Theories Concerning the Chinese Legal Family 中国法系论 Zhongguo Faxi Lun	*Journal of Law and Political Science* 法政学报 *Fazheng Xuebao*	Volume 1, Issue 1 1 卷 1 期
1926	Gao Weilian 高维廉	Establishment of a Chinese Legal Family 建设一个中国法系 Jianshe Yige Zhongguo Faxi	*The China Law Review* 法学季刊 *Faxue Jikan*	Volume 2, Issue 8 第2卷第八期

(continued)

(continued)

Year of publication	Author	Article	Journal	Issue No
1929	Xue Siguang 薛祀光	Characteristics of the Chinese Legal Family and Its Future 中国法系的特征及其将来 Zhonghua Faxi De Tezheng Ji Qi Jianglai	*The Monthly of Social Science Series* 社会科学论丛月刊 *Shehui Kexue Luncong Yuekan*	Volume 1, Issue 4 第1卷第四期
1930s				
1930	Li Cishan 李次山	The Chinese Legal Family in the World Legal Families 世界法系中的中华法系 Shijie Faxi Zhong De Zhonghua Faxi	*China Law Journal* 法学丛刊 *Faxue Congkan*	Issue 2, 3, 4 第 2、3、4 期
1930	Ma Cunkun 马存坤	Establishing a New Chinese Legal Family 建树新中华法系 Jianshu Xin Zhonghua Faxi	*Chaoyang Law Review (*published during the Republic of China period*)* 法律评论 *Falv Pinglun*	Volume 7, Issue 39 第 7 卷 39 期
1930	Jiao Yitang 焦易堂	New Chinese Legal System and the Great Harmony of the World 新中国法系与世界大同 Xin Zhongguo Faxi Yu Shijie Datong	*The China Law Review* 法学季刊 *Faxue Jikan*	Volume 1, Issue 1 第 1 卷第 1期
1931	Li Jingxi 李景禧	Chinese Legal System and Korean Legal System 中国法系与韩国法系 Zhongguo Faxi Yu Hanguo Faxi	*Chaoyang Law Review* 法律评论 *Falv Pinglun*	Volume 15, Issue 12 第 15 卷 第 12 期
1931	Wang Ruqi 王汝琪	Revitalization of the Chinese Legal Family (I) 中华法系之复兴 1 Zhonghua Faxi Zhi Fuxing 1	*The Monthly of Renaissance* 复兴月刊 *Fuxing Yuekan*	Volume 1, Issue 1 第 1 卷第 1 期
1933	Wang Ruqi 王汝琪	Revitalization of the Chinese Legal Family (II) 中华法系之复兴 2 Zhonghua Faxi Zhi Fuxing 2	*The Monthly of Renaissance* 复兴月刊 *Fuxing Yuekan*	Volume 1, Issue 10 第 1 卷第 10 期

(continued)

(continued)

Year of publication	Author	Article	Journal	Issue No
1933	Liu zhe 刘哲	Civil and Criminal Law in Classical Japan Dominated by the Chinese Legal Family 受中华法系支配的日本中古民刑事法 Shou Zhonghua Faxi Zhipei De Riben Zhonggu Min Xingshifa	*China Law Journal* 法学丛刊 *Faxue Congkan*	Volume 2, Issue 4 第 2 卷第 4 期
1933	Ruan Yicheng 阮毅成	Yang Honglie's "The Development History of Chinese Law" 杨鸿烈的中国法律发达史 Yang Honglie De Zhongguo Falv Fadashi	Book Review 图书评论 *Tushu Pinglun*	Volume 1, Issue 8 第 1 卷第 8 期
1934		Table of Contents for Lectures on the Chinese Legal System 中华法系讲稿目次 Zhonghua Faxi Jianggao Muci	*The Ten-day Periodical of Tongji University* (published during the Republic of China period) 国立同济大学旬刊 *Guo Li Tong Ji Da Xue Xun Kan*	Issue 39 第 39 期
1934		Schedule of Lectures on the Chinese Legal System at Shanghai Academy of Law 上海法学院函该院中华法系讲演日程 Shanghai Faxueyuanhan Gai yuan Zhonghua Faxi Jiangyan Richeng	*The Ten-day Periodical of Tongji University* 国立同济大学旬刊 *Guo Li Tong Ji Da Xue Xun Kan*	Issue 39 第 39 期
1934	Cheng Shude 程树德	A Discussion of the Chinese Legal System 论中国法系 Lun Zhongguo Faxi	*Chaoyang Law Review* 法律评论 *Falv Pinglun*	Volume 11, Issue 19 第 11 卷第 19 期
1935	Jiang Liquan 蒋澧泉	Evolution of the Legislation of the Chinese Legal Family 论中华法系立法之演进 Lun Zhonghua Faxi Lifa Zhi Yanjin	*Republic of China Journal of Law* 中华法学杂志 *Zhonghua Faxue Zazhi*	Volume 6, Issue 7 第 6 卷第 7 期

(continued)

(continued)

Year of publication	Author	Article	Journal	Issue No
1935	Lin Tingke 林廷柯	Unique Voluntary Surrender in the Chinese Legal System 中华法系特有之自首制度 Zhonghua Faxi Teyou Zhi Zishou Zhidu	*Fagui Journal*(published during the Republic of China period) 法轨期刊 *Fagui Qikan*	Volume 2, Issue 2 第 2 卷第 2 期
1935	He Xingxiang 何兴翔	On the Overview of the China's Legal System 试论我国法系之梗概 Shilun Woguo Faxi Zhi Genggai	*Minzhong Quarterly* (published during the Republic of China period) 民钟季刊 *Minzhong Jikan*	Volume 1 第 1 卷
1936	Chen Guyuan 陈顾远	Relationship between Confucian Jurisprudence and China's Inherent Legal System 儒家法学与中国固有法系之关系 Rujia Faxue Yu Zhongguo Guyou Faxi Zhi Guanxi	*Chinese Law Monthly* 中国法学杂志月刊 *Zhongguo Faxue Zazhi Yuekan*	Volume 1, No. 3 第 1 卷第 3 号
1936	Chen Peng 陈 鹏	Thoughts on Rights and Modernity in the Chinese Legal System 中国法系之权利思想与现代 Zhongguo Faxi Zhi Quanli Sixiang Yu Xiandai	*Chaoyang Law Review* 法律评论 *Falv Pinglun*	Volume 13, 40 第 13 卷,40
1937	Yang Honglie 杨鸿烈	History of Chinese Legal Development 中国法律发达史 Zhongguo Falv Fadashi	*Renwen Monthly (published during the Republic of China period)* 人文月刊 *Renwen Yuekan*	Volume 8, Issue 3 第 8 卷第 3 期
1937	Zhou Jingru 周敬如	Observing the Past and Present of the Chinese Legal System 中国法系之今昔观 Zhongguo Faxi Zhi Jinxi guan	*Gongyan Semimonthly* (published during the Republic of China period) 公言 *Gongyan*	Issue 74 第 74 期
1937	Chen Guyuan 陈顾远	Treatise II: Relationship between Confucian Legalism and China's Intrinsic Legal System 论著二—儒家法学与中国固有法系之关系 Lunzhu Er —Rujia Faxue Yu Zhongguo Guyou Faxi Zhi Guanxi	*Monthly Journal of Guangxi Judicial Office* (published during the Republic of China period) 广西司法办月刊 *Guangxi Sifaban Yuekan*	Issue 74 第 74 期

(continued)

(continued)

Year of publication	Author	Article	Journal	Issue No
1937	Chen Guyuan 陈顾远	Relationship between the Family System and China's Inherent Legal System 家族制度与中国固有法系之关系 Jiazu Zhidu Yu Zhongguo Guyou Faxi Zhi Guanxi	*Republic of China Journal of Law* 中华法学杂志 *Zhonghua Faxue Zazhi*	Volume 1 第 1 卷
1937	Chen Guyuan 陈顾远	Relationship between Natural Law and China's Inherent Legal System 天道观念与中国固有法系之关系 Tiandao Guannian Yu Zhongguo Guyou Faxi Zhi Guanxi	*Chinese Law Monthly* 中国法学杂志月刊 *Zhongguo Faxue Zazhi Yuekan*	New Edition in 1937 1937年新编
1937	Ding Yuanpu 丁元普	Chinese Legal System and National Renaissance 中华法系与民族复兴 Zhonghua Faxi Yu Minzu Fuxing	*Chinese Law Monthly* 中国法学杂志月刊 *Zhongguo Faxue Zazhi Yuekan*	Volume 1, Issue 7 第 1 卷第 7 期
1940s				
1940	Xie Zhiteng 谢志腾	Research on the Chinese Legal System 中国法系的研究 Zhongguo Faxi De Yanjiu	*Fayu Journal*(published during the Republic of China period) 法语 *Fayu*	Issue 3 第 3 期
1944	Liu Chengqing 刘澄清	Great Chinese Legal System 伟大的中国法系 Weida De Zhongguo Faxi	*Wenfeng Journal*(published during the Republic of China period) 文风杂志 *Wenfeng Zazhi*	Volume 1, Issue 6 第 1 卷第 6 期
1945	Li Jingxi 李景禧	Chinese Legal System and Korean Law 中国法系与韩国法 Zhongguo Faxi Yu Hanguofa	Chinese and Korean Culture (published during the Republic of China period) 中韩文化 *Zhong Han Wenhua*	Issue 1 第 1 期
1945	Zhang Tianquan 张天权	On the Chinese Legal Family 论中华法系 Lun Zhonghua Faxi	*Chinese Legal System Journal* (published during the Republic of China period) 中华法系杂志 *Zhonghua Faxue Zazhi*	Volume 4, Issue 8 第 4 卷第 8 期

(continued)

(continued)

Year of publication	Author	Article	Journal	Issue No
1948	Cao Decheng 曹德成	Exploration of the Chinese Legal Family: Objects and Tasks of the Research 中国法系研究发微—研究的对象与任务 Zhongguo Faxi Yanjiu Fa Wei —Yanjiu De Duixiang Yu Renwu	*Republic of China Journal of Law* 中华法学杂志 *Zhonghua Faxue Zazhi*	Volume 7, Issue 4 第 7 卷第 4 期
1948	Shang Aihe 尚爱荷	Reconstruction of the Legal System in New China and the Three Principles of the People 新中国法系的重建与三民主义 Xin Zhongguo Faxi De Chongjian Yu Sanmin Zhuyi	*Chinese Law Monthly* 中国法学杂志月刊 *Zhongguo Faxue Zazhi Yuekan*	Volume 7 第 7 卷
1980s				
1980	Chen Chaobi 陈朝璧	A Preliminary Study of the Characteristics of the Chinese Legal Family 中华法系特点初探 Zhonghua Faxi Tedian Chutan	*Chinese Journal of Law* 法学研究 *Faxue Yanjiu*	Issue 1 01 期
1980	Zhang Jinfan 张晋藩	Origins of the Features of the Chinese Legal Family 中华法系特点探源 Zhonghua Faxi Tedian Tanyuan	*Chinese Journal of Law* 法学研究 *Faxue Yanjiu*	Issue 4 04 期
1982	Zhao Changsheng 赵长生	A Brief Discussion on the Characteristics of "Preference of Criminal Law to Civil Law" in the Chinese Legal System 浅谈中华法系的重刑轻民特点 Qiantan Zhonghua Faxi De Zhongxing Qingmin Tedian	*Modern Law Science* 现代法学 *Xiandai Faxue*	Issue 1 01 期
1983	Liu Hainian, Yang Yifan 刘海年、杨一凡	Formation of the Chinese Legal Family and Its Characteristics 中华法系的形成及其特点 Zhonghua Faxi De Xingcheng Ji Qi Tedian	*People's Judicature* 人民司法 *Renmin Sifa*	Issue 1 01 期

(continued)

(continued)

Year of publication	Author	Article	Journal	Issue No
1983	Han Yulin, Zhao Guobin 韩玉林、赵国斌	A Brief Discussion of the Characteristics of the Chinese Legal Family and the Ways of Its Formation and Demise 略论中华法系的特点及其形成和消亡的途径 Luelun Zhonghua Faxi De Tedian Ji Qi Xingcheng He Xiaowang De Tujing	*Jilin University Journal Social Sciences Edition* 吉林大学社会科学学报 *Jilin Daxue Shehui Kexue Xuebao*	Issue 4 04 期
1984	Zhang Jinfan 张晋藩	Re-discussion on Several Issues of the Chinese Legal Family 再论中华法系的若干问题 Zai Lun Zhonghua Faxi De Ruogan Wenti	*Journal of China University of Political Science and Law* 中国政法大学学报 *Zhongguo Zhengfa Daxue Xuebao*	Issue 2 02 期
1986	Qiao Wei 乔 伟	Basic Characteristics of the Chinese Legal Family 中华法系的基本特点 Zhonghua Faxi De Jiben Tedian	*Literature, History, and Philosophy* 文史哲 *Wen Shi Zhe*	Issue 2 02 期
1987	Zhao Jianhua 赵建华	Brief Discussion on the Chinese Legal Family 浅谈中华法系 Qiantan Zhonghua Faxi	*Learning and Guidance* 学习与辅导 *Xuexi Yu Fudao*	Issue 2 02 期
1987	Zeng Hui 曾 慧	Harm in Practice of the Closedness of the Chinese Legal Family 中华法系封闭性的现实危害 Zhonghua Faxi Fengbixing De Xianshi Weihai	*Political Science and Law* 政治与法律 *Zhengzhi Yu Falv*	Issue 1 01 期
1987	Wang Zhantong 王占通	On the Criminal Liability Basis of Violating Etiquette in Tang Code: A Discussion on the Characteristics of the Chinese Legal System 论违礼是唐律的刑事责任依据—兼论中华法系的特点 Lun Weili Shi Tanglv De Xingshi Zeren Yiju —Jian Lun Zhonghua Faxi De Tedian	*Social Science Front* 社会科学战线 *Shehui Kexue Zhanxian*	Issue 4 04 期

(continued)

(continued)

Year of publication	Author	Article	Journal	Issue No
1988	Yan Qingyi 阎青义	*Commentary on Tang Code*: One of the Typical Examples of the Chinese Legal System 《唐律疏议》:中华法系的典型之一 *Tang Lv Shu Yi:* Zhonghua Faxi De Dianxing Zhi Yi	*Journal of Ancient Books Collation and Studies* 古籍整理研究学刊 *Guji Zhengli Yanjiu Xuekan*	Issue 1 01 期
1988	Fan Mingxin 范明辛	On Features of the Chinese Legal Family 论 "中华法系"的特点 Lun "Zhonghua Faxi" De Tedian	*Legal Learning and Research (The predecessor of The Jurist)* 法律学习与研究 *Falv Xuexi Yu Yanjiu*	Issue 1 01 期
1988	Xu Yongkang 徐永康	On the Disintegration of the Chinese Legal System 论中华法系的解体 Lun Zhonghua Faxi De Jieti	*Thesis Collection of Master of Laws in East China University of Political Science and Law* 华东政法学院法学硕士论文集 *Huadong Zhengfa Xueyuan Faxue Shuoshi Lunwenji*	
1989	Zhang Jinfan 张晋藩	New Achievements in the Study of the Chinese Legal System: *Research on the Clan Law in the Qing Dynasty* 中华法系研究的新成果—关于《清代宗族法研究》 Zhonghua Faxi Yanjiu De Xin Chengguo—Guanyu *Qingdai Zongzufa Yanjiu*	*China Book Review* 中国图书评论 *Zhongguo Tushu Pinglun*	Issue 1 01 期

(continued)

(continued)

Year of publication	Author	Article	Journal	Issue No
1989	Xu Xiaoguang 徐晓光	Doubts about the Mongolian Legal System: Discussion on the Relationship between Law Systems of Northern Ethnic Minorities during Ancient China and the Chinese Legal System “蒙古法系”质疑—兼论中国古代北方少数民族法律制度与中华法系的关系 “Menggu Faxi” Zhiyi—Jian Lun Zhongguo Gudai Beifang Shaoshu Minzu Falv Zhidu Yu Zhonghua Faxi De Guanxi	*Journal of Comparative Law* 比较法研究 *Bijiaofa Yanjiu*	Issue Z 1 Z1 期
1989	Li Zhu 李 竹	Revisiting the Characteristics of the Chinese Legal System 再论中华法系特点 Zai Lun Zhonghua Faxi Tedian	*Jorunal of Yunan University (Law Edition)* 云南大学学报(法学版) *Yunnan Daxue Xuebao (Faxue Ban)*	
1990s				
1991	Zhang Zhongqiu, Jin Mei 张中秋、金 眉	An Explanation of the Enclosed Nature of the Chinese Legal System 中华法系封闭性释证 Zhonghua Faxi Fengbixing Shizheng	*Journal of Nanjing University* 南京大学学报 *Nanjing Daxue Xuebao*	Issue 3 03 期
1991	Sun Yaoming 孙耀明	A Brief Discussion of the Disintegration of the Chinese Legal Family 略论中华法系的解体 Luelun Zhonghua Faxi De Jieti	*Studies in Law and Business* 法商研究 *Fa Shang Yanjiu*	Issue 3 03 期
1993	Wu Shuchen 武树臣	China’s Hybrid Law: Including the Status of the Chinese Legal System in the World 中国的 “混合法”—兼及中国法系在世界的地位 Zhongguo De “Hunhefa”—Jian Ji Zhongguo Faxi Zai Shijie De Diwei	*Political Science and Law* 政治与法律 *Zhengzhi Yu Falv*	Issue 2 02 期

(continued)

(continued)

Year of publication	Author	Article	Journal	Issue No
1993	Yu Ronggen 俞荣根	Characteristics and Values of Confucian "Middle Way" and the Chinese Legal System 儒家"中道"与中华法系的特点和价值 Rujia "Zhong Dao" Yu Zhonghua Faxi De Tedian He Jiazhi	*New Horizons from Tianfu* 天府新论 *Tianfu Xinlun*	Issue 6 06 期
1994	Da Tingxiu, Ma Xiaohong 大庭修、马小红	Evolution of the Ordinance Legal System and the Laws of Qin and Han Dynasties 律令法系的演变与秦汉法典 Lvling Faxi De Yanbian Yu Qin Han Fadian	*Peking University Law Journal* 中外法学 *Zhong Wai Faxue*	Issue 1 01 期
1994	Ma Xiaohong 马小红	Discussion on Features of the Chinese Legal Family Again 中华法系特征的再探讨 Zhonghua Faxi Tezheng De Zai Tantao	*Peking University Law Journal* 中外法学 *Zhong Wai Faxue*	Issue 2 02 期
1994	Li Xin 李 昕	The Closedness of the Chinese Legal Family and Its Reasons 中华法系的封闭性及其成因 Zhonghua Faxi De Fengbixing Ji Qi Chengyin	*Science of Law* 法律科学 *Falv Kexue*	
1994	Chen Guangguo, Xu Xiaoguang 陈光国、徐晓光	Historical Development Trajectory from the Penalties and Redemption of the Chinese Legal System to the "Compensating for Killing a Person" of the Legal System in Tibetan Areas 从中华法系的罚赎到藏区法制的赔命价的历史发展轨迹 Cong Zhonghua Faxi De Fashu Dao Zangqu Fazhi De Peimingjia De Lishi Fazhan Guiji	*Qinghai Social Sciences* 青海社会科学 *Qinghai Shehui Kexue*	Issue 4 04 期

(continued)

(continued)

Year of publication	Author	Article	Journal	Issue No
1996	Nan Yuquan 南玉泉	Origins and Development of Pre-Qin Thought and Culture in the Chinese Legal System 先秦思想文化与中华法系之源流 Xianqin Sixiang Wenhua Yu Zhonghua Faxi Zhi Yuanliu	*Tribune of Political Science and Law* 政法论坛 *Zhengfa Luntan*	Issue 3 03 期
1997	Yang Zhenhong 杨振洪	On the Formation and Development Conditions of the Chinese Legal System 论中华法系的形成和发展条件 Lun Zhonghua Faxi De Xingcheng He Fazhan Tiaojian	*Chinese Journal of Law* 法学研究 *Faxue Yanjiu*	Issue 4 04 期
1997	Hou Wenfu, Zhang Libo, Jia Guofa 侯文富、张立波、贾国发	A Brief Analysis of the Characteristics and Values of the Chinese Legal System 简论中华法系的特色与价值 Jianlun Zhonghua Faxi De Tese Yu Jiazhi	*Journal of Northeast Normal University* 东北师大学报 *Dongbei-Shida Xuebao*	Issue 3 03 期
1998	Fan Zhongxin 范忠信	Legalism of the Chinese Legal Family—Comments on *Studies on the Chinese Legal Family* 中华法系法家化驳议—《中华法系研究》之商榷 Zhonghua Faxi FaJiahua Boyi —*Zhonghua Faxi Yanjiu* Zhi Shangque	*Journal of Comparative Law* 比较法研究 *Bijiaofa Yanjiu*	Issue 3 03 期
1999	Zhang Jinfan 张晋藩	Some Thoughts on the Rebuild of the Chinese Legal Family: Discussion on the Chinese Legal Family for the Third Time 重塑中华法系的几点思考—三论中华法系 Chongsu Zhonghua Faxi De Jidian Sikao—Sanlun Zhonghua Faxi	*Nanjing University Law Review* 南京大学法律评论 *Nanjing Daxue Falv Pinglun*	Issue 1 01 期

(continued)

(continued)

Year of publication	Author	Article	Journal	Issue No
1999	Zhang Zhongqiu 张中秋	Review and Reflection: On the Study of the Chinese Legal Family 回顾与思考:中华法系研究散论 Huigu Yu Sikao: Zhonghua Faxi Yanjiu Sanlun	*Nanjing University Law Review* 南京大学法律评论 *Nanjing Daxue Falv Pinglun*	Issue 1 01 期
1999	Xu Zhongming 徐忠明	Rethinking the Study of the Chinese Legal System 中华法系研究的再思 Zhonghua Faxi Yanjiu De Zaisi	*Nanjing University Law Review* 南京大学法律评论 *Nanjing Daxue Falv Pinglun*	Issue 1 01 期
1999	Peng Fenglian 彭凤莲	On the Formation of the "Emphasis on Etiquette, Insignificance of Law" Feature in the Chinese Legal System 论中华法系 "重礼轻法" 特征的形成 Lun Zhonghua Faxi "Zhongli-Qingfa" Tezheng De Xingcheng	*Journal of Anhui Normal University* 安徽师范大学学报 *Anhui Shifan Daxue Xuebao*	Issue 2 02 期
1999	Fan Zhongxin 范忠信	Family Ethics in the Chinese Legal Family: A Comparative Study with the Ius Quiritium in Western Legal Systems 中华法系的亲伦精神—以西方法系的市民精神为参照系来认识 Zhonghua Faxi De Qinlun Jingshen—Yi Xifang Faxi De Shimin Jingshen Wei Canzhaoxi Lai Renshi	*Nanjing University Law Review* 南京大学法律评论 *Nanjing Daxue Falv Pinglun*	Issue 1 01 期
1999	Li Gang 李罡	The Disintegration of the Chinese Legal Family and the Preliminary Formation of the Modern Chinese Legal System 中华法系的解体与中国现代法律制度的初步形成 Zhonghua Faxi De Jieti Yu Zhongguo Xiandai Falv Zhidu De Chubu Xingcheng	*Journal of Beijing Administration Institute* 北京行政学院学报 *Beijing Xingzheng Xueyuan Xuebao*	Issue 4 04 期

(continued)

(continued)

Year of publication	Author	Article	Journal	Issue No
1999	Wang Shaotang 王绍棠	Revisiting Legal System and the Chinese Legal System 法系·中国法系再议论 Faxi· Zhongguo Faxi Zai Yilun	*Nanjing University Law Review* 南京大学法律评论 *Nanjing Daxue Falv Pinglun*	Spring 春季刊
1999	Zhang Jinfan 张晋藩	Global Position of the Chinese Legal Civilization and Several Issues Concerning Modernization 中华法制文明的世界地位与近代化的几个问题 Zhonghua Fazhi Wenming De Shijie Diwei Yu Jindaihua De Jige Wenti	*Speaking of the Legal System in Zhongnanhai and the Great Hall,* The Commercial Press 载《在中南海和大会堂讲法制》,商务印书馆 Zai *Zai Zhongnanhai He Dahuitang Jiang Fazhi,* Shangwu Yinshuguan	
Twenty-first Century				
2000	Rao Ai 饶艾	New Thoughts on the Chinese Legal Family: A Comparative Study with Civil Law and Common Law 中华法系新论—兼与西方两大法系比较 Zhonghua Faxi Xinlun —Jian Yu Xifang Liang Da Faxi Bijiao	*Journal of Southwest Jiaotong University* 西南交通大学学报 *Xi'nan Jiaotong Daxue Xuebao*	Issue 1 01 期
2000	Xia Jixian 夏吉先	An Exploration of the Cultural Transplantation of Criminal Law in the Chinese Legal System 关于中华法系之刑法文化移植的探索 Guanyu Zhonghua Faxi Zhi Xingfa Wenhua Yizhi De Tansuo	*Journal of Fujian Public Safety College* 福建公安高等专科学校学报 *Fujian Gongan Gaodeng Zhuanke Xuexiao Xuebao*	Issue 2 02 期
2000	Yu Ronggen 俞荣根	A Major Characteristic of the Chinese Legal System—Punishment for Crime is Both Statutory and Non-Statutory 中华法系的一大特点—罪刑既是法定又是非法定的 Zhonghua Faxi De Yi Da Tedian —Zui Xing Jishi Fading Youshi Feifading De	A Collection of Zhejiang University Guanghua Law School 浙江大学法学论集 *Zhejiang Daxue Faxue Lunji*	Initial Issue 创刊号

(continued)

(continued)

Year of publication	Author	Article	Journal	Issue No
2000	Guo Chengwei, Ma Zhigang 郭成伟、马志刚	Historical Circumstance and Legal System Construction: A Response from China 历史境遇与法系构建:中国的回应 Lishi Jingyu Yu Faxi Goujian: Zhongguo De Huiying	*Tribune of Political Science and Law* 政法论坛 *Zhengfa Luntan*	Issue 5 05 期
2000	Fan Zhongxin 范忠信	Characteristics of Small-Scale Agriculture and the Traditional Chinese Legal System 小农经济与中华法传统的特征Xiaonong Jingji Yu Zhonghua Fa Chuantong De Tezheng	*Journal of Henan Administrative Institute of Politics and Law* 河南省政法管理干部学院学报 *Henansheng Zhengfa Guanli Ganbu Xueyuan Xuebao*	Issue 6 06 期
2001	Zhang Jinfan 张晋藩	Reshaping the Chinese Legal System and the Great Rejuvenation of Chinese Nation 重塑中华法系与中华民族的伟大复兴 Chongsu Zhonghua Faxi Yu Zhonghua Minzu De Weida Fuxing	*Tribune of Political Science and Law* 政法论坛 *Zhengfa Luntan*	
2001	Wang Limin 王立民	Another Discussion on the Chinese Legal Family 也论中华法系 Ye Lun Zhonghua Faxi	*ECUPL Journal* 华东政法学院学报 *Huadong Zhengfa Xueyuan Xuebao*	Issue 5 05 期
2001	Zhang Xipo 张希坡	Communist Party of China has Created a New Era of Socialist Chinese Legal System 中国共产党开创了社会主义中华法系的新纪元 Zhongguo Gongchandang Kaichuang Le Shehui Zhuyi Zhonghua Faxi De Xin Jiyuan	*The Jurist* 法学家 *Faxuejia*	Issue 4 04 期
2001	Ren Yanping 任延平	An Overview of the Chinese Legal System and Its Development Trends 中华法系要览及其发展趋势 Zhonghua Faxi Yaolan Ji Qi Qushi	*Journal of Chongqing Three Gorges University* 重庆三峡学院学报 *Chongqing Sanxia Xueyuan Xuebao*	A Supplementary Issue 增刊

(continued)

(continued)

Year of publication	Author	Article	Journal	Issue No
2001	Yang Zhengrong 杨峥嵘	A Comparative Study of the Chinese Legal System and Continental Law System 中华法系与大陆法系比较研究 Zhonghua Faxi Yu Dalu Faxi Bijiao Yanjiu	*Contemporary Law Review* 当代法学 *Dangdai Faxue*	Issue 1 01 期
2002	Wang Xuwei 王旭伟	Evolution of the Regulation of Utilization of and Profiting from Land in the Chinese Legal System 中华法系土地用益制度的演进 Zhonghua Faxi Tudi Yongyi Zhidu De Yanjin	*Journal of Shenyang Normal University* 沈阳师范学院学报 *Shenyang Shifan Xueyuan Xuebao*	Issue 5 05 期
2002	Yang Yifan 杨一凡	A Major Misunderstanding in the Study of the Chinese Legal Family—Questioning the Doctrine of "Integration of All Laws and No Differentiation of Civil and Criminal Laws" 中华法系研究中的一个重大误区—"诸法合体、民刑不分"说质疑 Zhonghua Faxi Yanjiu Zhong De Yi Ge Zhongda Wuqu—"Zhu Fa Heti, Min Xing Bufen"Shuo Zhiyi	*Social Sciences in China* 中国社会科学 *Zhongguo Shehui Kexue*	Issue 6 06 期
2002	Long Daxuan 龙大轩	An Exploration of the Origins of Qiang Ethnicity Legal Culture with a Discussion on the Early Formation of the Chinese Legal System 羌族法文化渊源考—兼论中华法系的早期雏形 Qiangzufa Wenhua Yuanyuan Kao —Jianlun Zhonghua Faxi De Zaoqi Chuxing	*Thinking* 思想战线 *Sixiang Zhanxian*	Issue 6 06 期

(continued)

(continued)

Year of publication	Author	Article	Journal	Issue No
2002	Yuan Kaiyu 袁开宇	Family and Community: The Legal System under Tension—Reading Notes on Famous Works of Legal History 家与群:张力下的法律体系—法史学名著读书札记 Jia Yu Qun: Zhangli Xia De Falv Tixi—Fashixue Mingzhu Dushu Zhaji	*Tsinghua Forum of Rule of Law* 清华法治论衡 *Qinghua Fazhi Lunheng*	Issue 2 02 期
2002	Gao Xuchen 高旭晨	Tradition: Foundation of Integration between Different Legal Systems 传统—法系融合之基础 Chuantong—Faxi Ronghe Zhi Jichu	*A Collection of Essays on the Modernization of Chinese Legal History, China University of Political Science and Law Press* 载《中国法律史近代化论集》中国政法大学出版社 Zai *Zhongguo Falvshi Jindaihua Lunji,* Zhongguo Zhengfa Daxue Chubanshe	
2002	Zhang Jinfan 张晋藩	Evolution of the Chinese Legal History 中国法律历史的演进 Zhongguo Falv Lishi De Yanjin	Elite Forum 《世纪大讲坛》 *Shiji Da Jiangtan*	Volume 3 第3辑
2003	Zeng Daiwei 曾代伟	National Legal Culture and the Legal System of the Chinese Nation—Examples from the Jin Dynasty 民族法文化与中华法系—以金代为例 Minzufa Wenhua Yu Zhonghua Faxi—Yi Jindai Wei Li	*Modern Law Science* 现代法学 *Xiandai Faxue*	Issue 5 05 期
2003	Tang Junjie 唐俊杰	Roots of the Chinese Legal System: Reading *The Basic Spirit of Chinese Legal Tradition* 中华法系的寻根之作:读《中国法律传统的基本精神》 Zhonghua Faxi De Xungen Zhi Zuo:Du *Zhongguo Falv Chuantong De Jiben Jingshen*	*Legal Traditions of the West and China* 中西法律传统 *Zhong Xi Falv Chuantong*	

(continued)

(continued)

Year of publication	Author	Article	Journal	Issue No
2003	Yu Ronggen 俞荣根	Harmony of the Principle of Legality and Non-Legality: A Characteristic of the Chinese Legal System 罪刑法定与非法定的和合—中华法系的一个特点 Zui Xing Fading Yu Feifading De He He—Zhonghua Faxi De Yige Tedian	*Legal Traditions of the West and China* 中西法律传统 *Zhong Xi Falv Chuantong*	Issue 1 01 期
2003	Lv Shilun, Deng Shaoling 吕世伦、邓少岭	Beauty of the Chinese Legal System in the Harmony between Man and Nature 天人合一境界中的中华法系之美 Tianren-Heyi Jingjie Zhong De Zhonghua Faxi Zhi Mei	*Modern Law Science,* also published in *Essentials of Chinese Legal History* (2001–2003), Higher Education Press 现代法学又载《中国法史学精萃》2001—2003年卷,高等教育出版社 *Xiandai Faxue,* You Zai *Zhongguo Fashixue Jingcui* 2001—2003 Nian Juan, Gaodeng Jiaoyu Chubanshe	Issue 3 03 期
2003	Ma Xiaohong 马小红	Chinese Legal System and Rule of Law in the 21st Century 中华法系与21世纪法治 Zhonghua Faxi Yu 21 Shiji Fazhi	*Chinese Culture in the 21st Century,* *China Yan Shi Press* 载《中华文化与 21 世纪》,中国言实出版社 Zai *Zhonghua Wenhua Yu 21 Shiji,* Zhongguo Yan Shi Chubanshe	
2004	Ai Yongming 艾永明	Chinese Legal Family Is Not Punishment Based 中华法系并非"以刑为主" Zhonghua Faxi Bingfei "Yi Xing Wei Zhu"	*China Legal Science* 中国法学 *Zhongguo Faxue*	Issue 1 01 期

(continued)

(continued)

Year of publication	Author	Article	Journal	Issue No
2004	Ai Yongming 艾永明	Questioning the Characteristics of the Chinese Legal System's Emphasis on Criminal Law 中华法系 "以刑为主"特点质疑 Zhonghua Faxi "Yi Xing Wei Zhu" Tedian Zhiyi	*Philosophical Reflection on Legal History: Proceedings of the 2002 Annual Conference of the China Institute of Legal History,* Law Press· China 《法史思辨:2002 年中国法史年会论文集》,法律出版社 *Fashi Sibian: 2002 Nian Zhongguo Fashi Nianhui Lunwenji,* Falv Chubanshe	
2004	Chen Hongyi 陈鸿彝	*Book of Documents*: Providing a Prototype Framework for the Chinese Legal System 《尚书》:为中华法系提供原型构架 *Shangshu:* Wei Zhonghua Faxi Tigong Yuanxing Goujia	*Journal of Jiangsu Police Institute* 江苏警官学院学报 *Jiangsu Jingguan Xueyuan Xuebao*	Issue 2 02 期
2005	Zhang Jinfan 张晋藩	*A Review and Prospect of the Study of the Chinese Legal System* 中华法系研究的回顾与前瞻 Zhonghua Faxi Yanjiu De Huigu Yu Qianzhan	*Proceedings of the International Academic Conference on the Chinese Legal Family* 中华法系国际学术研讨会文集 *Zhonghua Faxi Guoji Xueshu Yantaohui Wenji*	September 16, 2009 2009年9月16日
2005	Zhang Jinfan 张晋藩	Re-discussion on the Features of the Chinese Legal Family 中华法系特点再议 Zhonghua Faxi Tedian Zaiyi	*Jiangxi Social Sciences* 江西社会科学 *Jiangxi Shehui Kexue*	Issue 8 08 期
2005	Zhang Jinfan 张晋藩	Humanism—One of the Features of the Chinese Legal Family 人本主义—中华法系特点之一 Renben Zhuyi—Zhonghua Faxi Tedian Zhiyi	*Hebei Law Science* 河北法学 *Hebei Faxue*	Issue 9 09 期

(continued)

(continued)

Year of publication	Author	Article	Journal	Issue No
2005	Zhang Jinfan 张晋藩	Historical Value of the Supervision Law of Ancient China—The Perspective of the Chinese Legal System 中国古代监察法的历史价值—中华法系的一个视角 Zhongguo Gudai Jianchafa De Lishi Jiazhi—Zhonghua Faxi De Yige Shijiao	*Tribune of Political Science and Law* 政法论坛 *Zhengfa Luntan*	Issue 6 06 期
2005	Yu Ronggen, Long Daxuan 俞荣根、龙大轩	Summary of Study on the Chinese Legal Family 中华法系学述论 Zhonghua Faxi Xueshu Lun	*Journal of Shanghai University of Political Science and Law* 上海政法学院学报 *Shanghai Zhengfa Xueyuan Xueba*	Issue 4 04 期
2005	Long Daxuan 龙大轩	Harmony: General Characteristics of the Chinese Legal System 和合:中华法系的总体特征 He He: Zhonghua Faxi De Zongti Tezheng	*Research on Legal Culture* 法律文化研究 *Falv Wenhua Yanjiu*	
2005	He Qinhua, Kong Jing 何勤华、孔晶	The Birth of a New Chinese Legal System? From the Three Legal Families to an East Asian Common Law 新中华法系的诞生?—从三大法系到东亚共同体法 Xin Zhonghua Faxi De Dansheng?—Cong San Da Faxi Dao Dongya Gongtongti Fa	*Legal Forum* 法学论坛 *Faxue Luntan*	Issue 4 04 期
2005	Xu Xiangmin, Chen Chen, Liu Yuanzheng, Zhang Hongjie 徐祥民、陈晨、刘远征、张宏杰	Similarities between the Continental Legal System and the Chinese Legal System 大陆法系与中华法系的相近性 Dalu Faxi Yu Zhonghua Faxi De Xiangjin Xing	*Journal of Ocean University of China* 中国海洋大学学报 *Zhongguo Haiyang Daxue Xuebao*	Issue 5 05 期

(continued)

(continued)

Year of publication	Author	Article	Journal	Issue No
2005	Shi Guangquan 史广全	A First Exploration of the Chinese Legal System Research by Chen Guyuan 陈顾远中华法系研究初探 Chen Guyuan Zhonghua Faxi Yanjiu Chutan	*Journal of Tianjin Administrative Cadre College of Politics and Law* 天津市政法管理干部学院学报 *Tianjinshi Zhengfa Guanli Ganbu Xueyuan Xuebao*	Issue 1 01 期
2006	Xu Xiaozhuang 徐晓庄	Da Ming Law and the System of "Voluntary Surrender" in the Chinese Legal System 《大明律》与中华法系 "自首" 制度 *Daming Lv* Yu Zhonghua Faxi "Zishou" Zhidu	*Journal of Tianzhong* 天中学刊 *Tianzhong Xuekan*	Issue 3 03 期
2006	Yu Ronggen, Long Daxuan 俞荣根、龙大轩	Summary of Study on the Chinese Legal Family 中华法系学述论 Zhonghua Faxi Xueshu Lun	*Legal Traditions of the West and China* 中西法律传统 *Zhong Xi Falv Chuantong*	
2006	Qu Chaoli 屈超立	Discussion on the Status of Song Law in the Chinese Legal Family 论宋代法律在中华法系中的地位 Lun Songdai Falv Zai Zhonghua Faxi Zhong De Diwei	*Proceedings of the International Academic Conference on the Chinese Legal Family* 中华法系国际学术研讨会文集 *Zhonghua Faxi Guoji Xueshu Yantaohui Wenji*	
2006	Li qing 李 青	Why Has the Chinese Legal System Become the Parent Law of East Asian Countries 中华法系为何成为东亚各国的母法 Zhonghua Faxi Weihe Chengwei Dongya Geguo De Mufa	*Proceedings of the International Academic Conference on the Chinese Legal Family* 中华法系国际学术研讨会文集 *Zhonghua Faxi Guoji Xueshu Yantaohui Wenji*	

(continued)

(continued)

Year of publication	Author	Article	Journal	Issue No
2006	Liu Gaoyong 刘高勇	Yang Honglie: Strengthening the World Position of the Chinese Legal System—Focusing on *The Influence of Chinese Law in East Asian Countries* 杨鸿烈:力树中华法系的世界地位—以《中国法律在东亚诸国之影响》为中心 Yang Honglie: Lishu Zhonghua Faxi De Shijie Diwei—Yi *Zhongguo Falv Zai Dongya Zhuguo Zhi Yingxiang* Wei Zhongxin	*Social Sciences Review* 社科纵横 *Sheke Zongheng*	Issue 10 10 期
2006	Su Jilang 苏基朗	"Chinese Legal System" in Modern Legal Interpretation: Focusing on Property Rights and Contracts 现代法学诠释中的"中华法系" ——以产权与合约为中心 Xiandai Faxue Quanshi Zhong De "Zhonghua Faxi"—Yi Chanquan Yu Heyue Wei Zhongxin	*Law Science* 法学 *Faxue*	Issue 12 12 期
2006	Liu Guang'an 刘广安	Development of Characteristics of the Chinese Legal System 中华法系特点的发展 Zhonghua Faxi Tedian De Fazhan	*Proceedings of the International Academic Conference on the Chinese Legal Family* 中华法系国际学术研讨会文集 *Zhonghua Faxi Guoji Xueshu Yantaohui Wenji*	
2006	Gao Mingshi 高明士	On the Characteristics of the Chinese Legal System 也谈中华法系的特质 Ye Tan Zhonghua Faxi De Tezhi	*Proceedings of the International Academic Conference on the Chinese Legal Family* 中华法系国际学术研讨会文集 *Zhonghua Faxi Guoji Xueshu Yantaohui Wenji*	

(continued)

(continued)

Year of publication	Author	Article	Journal	Issue No
2007	Zhang Jinfan 张晋藩	New Theory on the Chinese Legal Family 中华法系研究新论 Zhonghua Faxi Yanjiu Xinlun	*Journal of Nanjing University* 南京大学学报 *Nanjing Daxue Xuebao*	Issue 1 01 期
2007	Zhang Zhongqiu 张中秋	From the Chinese Legal Family to East Asian Law—Legal Traditions and Changes in East Asia and Its Direction 从中华法系到东亚法—东亚的法律传统与变革及其走向 Cong Zhonghua Faxi Dao Dongyafa—Dongya De Falv Chuantong Yu Biange Ji Qi Zouxiang	*Journal of Nanjing University* 南京大学学报 *Nanjing Daxue Xuebao*	Issue 1 01 期
2007	Ma Xiaohong 马小红	Purpose of Studying the Chinese Legal History—Reflections on *The Study of Tang Code and the Chinese Legal System* 中国法律史研究之目的—读《唐令与中华法系研究》有感 Zhongguo Falvshi Yanjiu Zhi Mudi—Du *Tangling Yu Zhonghua Faxi Yanjiu* You Gan	*Research on Legal Culture* 法律文化研究 *Falv Wenhua Yanjiu*	
2007	Zhang Baoshan, Ma Guotao 张宝山、马国淘	Tang Code, Representative Work of the Ancient Chinese Legal System 唐律,古代"中华法系"的代表作 Tanglv, Gudai "Zhonghua Faxi" De Daibiaozuo	*The People's Congress of China* 中国人大 *Zhongguo Renda*	Issue 3 03 期

(continued)

(continued)

Year of publication	Author	Article	Journal	Issue No
2007	Zhu Jingwen 朱景文	On Tribute System of Ancient China and Overseas Administrative Regions System of Ancient Rome 古代中国的朝贡制度和古罗马的海外行省制度—中华法系和罗马法系形成的制度基础 Gudai Zhongguo De Chaogong Zhidu He Guluoma De Haiwai —Zhonghua Faxi He Luoma Faxi Xingcheng De Zhidu Jichu	*Law Science Magazine* 法学杂志 *Faxue Zazhi*	Issue 3 03 期
2007	Yu Yongfan 余甬帆	Impact of Translating *Elements of International Law* on the Chinese Legal System: Supplement or Disintegration 《万国公法》的译入对中华法系的影响:补充抑或是瓦解 *Wanguo Gongfa* De Yiru Dui Zhonghua Faxi De Yingxiang:Buchong Yihuo Shi Wajie	*Journal of Suzhou Education Institute* 宿州教育学院学报 *Suzhou Jiaoyu Xueyuan Xuebao*	Issue 5 05 期
2007	Zhang Chi 张 翅	Pursuing the Tour of National Legal System, Remodeling the Spirit of the Chinese Legal System—Releasing the *General History of the Legal System of Chinese Minorities* and Summarization of the Symposium 追寻民族法制之旅 重塑中华法系之魂—《中国少数民族法制通史》出版首发暨研讨会综述 Zhuixun Minzu Fazhi Zhi Lv, Chongsu Zhonghua Faxi Zhi Hun—*Zhongguo Shaoshu Minzu Fazhi Tongshi* Chuban Shoufa Ji Yantaohui Zongshu	*Tribune of Political Science and Law* 政法论坛 *Zhengfa Luntan*	Issue 5 05 期

(continued)

(continued)

Year of publication	Author	Article	Journal	Issue No
2007	Xiao Guihua, Wang Ye 肖桂花、王烨	Discussions on the Chinese Legal System 刍议中华法系 Chuyi Zhonghua Faxi	Contemporary Legal Forum 当代法学论坛 *Dangdai Faxue Luntan*	Volume 3 第 3 辑
2007	Guo Shiyou, Li Zaiquan 郭世佑、李在全	Construction of the Discourse on "Chinese Legal System" as a Cultural Tool in Modern China 作为文化手段的"中华法系"—"中华法系"话语在近代中国的建构 Zuowei Wenhua Shouduan De "Zhonghua Faxi"—"Zhonghua Faxi" Huayu Zai Jindai Zhongguo De Jiangou	Rationality and Wisdom: Further Exploration of Chinese Legal Tradition—Proceedings of the 2007 Academic Symposium of the China Institute of Legal History 理性与智慧:中国法律传统再探讨—中国法律史学会2007年学术研讨会文集 *Lixing Yu Zhihui: Zhongguo Falv Chuantong Zai Tantao —Zhongguo Falvshi Xuehui 2007 Nian Xueshu Yantaohui Wenji*	
2007	Liao Zonglin, Wang Shumin 廖宗麟、汪树民	Characteristics of the Development of the Chinese Legal System from the Limitations of *Commentary on Tang Code* 从《唐律疏议》的局限性看中华法系发展的特点 Cong *Tang Lv Shu Yi* De Juxianxing Kan Zhonghua Faxi Fazhan De Tedian	*Journal of Hechi University* 河池学院学报 *Hechi Xueyuan Xuebao*	Issue 1 1 期
2007	Shao Fang 邵方	Confucianism's Middle Way and Its Influence on the Chinese Legal System 儒家中道及其对中华法系的影响 Rujia Zhongdao Ji Qi Dui Zhonghua Faxi De Yingxiang	*Journal of Shanghai University of Finance and Economics* 上海财经大学学报 *Shanghai Caijing Daxue Xuebao*	Issue 3 3 期
2007	Wang Fang 王芳	Several Speculations on Private Rights Protection in the Chinese Legal System 对中华法系中关于私权保护的几点猜想 Dui Zhonghua Faxi Zhong Guanyu Siquan Baohu De Jidian Caixiang	*Journal of Hotan Normal College* 和田师范专科学校学报 *Hetian Shifan Zhuanke Xuexiao Xuebao*	Issue 5 5 期

(continued)

(continued)

Year of publication	Author	Article	Journal	Issue No
2007	Zhou Ziliang, Wang Hua 周子良、王华	Social Basis Derived from the Ethical Characteristics of the Chinese Legal System 中华法系伦理法特质衍生的社会基础 Zhonghua Faxi Lunlifa Tezhi Yansheng De Shehui Jichu	*Journal of Shanxi University* 山西大学学报 *Shanxi Daxue Xuebao*	Issue 5 5 期
2007	Li Mijia, Sheng Chenhong 李米佳、生陈红	Japanese Factor in the Disintegration of the Chinese Legal System 中华法系解体下的日本因素 Zhonghua Faxi Jieti Xia De Riben Yinsu	*Legal System and Society* 法制与社会 *Fazhi Yu Shehui*	Issue 10 10 期
2007	Chen Xinyu, Xu Yamin 陈新宇、许亚敏	Legal Confucianization of the Chinese Legal System: A Jurisprudential Analysis 中华法系法律儒家化的法理分析 Zhonghua Faxi Falv Rujiahua De Fali Fenxi	*Journal of Science and Education* 科教文汇 *Kejiao Wenhui*	Issue 12 12 期
2007	Qian Ying 钱颖	An Introduction to the Chinese Legal System 简论中华法系 Jianlun Zhonghua Faxi	*Legal System and Society* 法制与社会 *Fazhi Yu Shehui*	Issue 12 12 期
2007	Ni Zhengmao 倪正茂	Comparison of Legal Systems and the Development of the Chinese Legal System 法系比较与中华法系发展 Faxi Bijiao Yu Zhonghua Faxi Fazhan	*Chinese Culture and the Rule of Law, Social Sciences Academic Press (China)* 载《中国文化与法治》，社会科学文献出版社 Zai *Zhongguo Wenhua Yu Fazhi*, Shehui Kexue Wenxian Chubanshe	
2007	Sun Yingluo 孙璎珞	Formation and Influence of the Chinese Legal System from the Perspective of Legal Culture 从法文化视角看中华法系的形成与影响 Cong Fawenhua Shijiao Kan Zhonghua Faxi De Xingcheng Yu Yingxiang	*Shandong University Law Review* 山东大学法律评论 *Shandong Daxue Falv Pinglun*	

(continued)

(continued)

Year of publication	Author	Article	Journal	Issue No
2007	Wang Hongzhi 王宏志	Confucian Classics: The Theoretical Basis of the Chinese Legal System—A Discussion on the Relationship between the *Commentary on Tang Code* and Confucian Classics 经学:中华法系的理论基础— 试论《唐律疏议》与经学的关系 Jingxue: Zhonghua Faxi De Lilun Jichu—Shilun *Tang Lv Shu Yi* Yu Jingxue De Guanxi	*Proceedings of the International Academic Conference on the Chinese Legal Family,* China University of Political Science and Law Press 载《中华法系国际学术研讨会文集》,中国政法大学出版社 Zai *Zhonghua Faxi Guoji Xueshu Yantaohui Wenji,* Zhongguo Zhengfa Daxue Chubanshe	
2007	Written by Ju Zheng, Compiled by Guo Jia 居正著、郭 嘉整理	Why do We Need to Establish a Chinese Legal System 为什么要建中国法系 Weishenme Yao Jian Zhongguo Faxi	*Research on Legal Culture* 法律文化研究 *Falv Wenhua Yanjiu*	Issue 00 00 期
2008	Li Qing 李 青	A Brief Discussion on the Value of the Chinese Legal System: Focusing on Sino-Japanese Legal Culture Exchange 简论中华法系的价值—以中日法文化交流为取向 Jianlun Zhonghua Faxi De Jiazhi —Yi Zhong Ri Fa Wenhua Jiaoliu Wei Quxiang	*Journal of Anhui Normal University* 安徽师范大学学报 *Anhui Shifan Daxue Xuebao*	Issue 1 01 期
2008	Xu Xiaozhuang 徐晓庄	*Da Ming Law* and the System of "Voluntary Surrender" in the Chinese Legal System 《大明律》与中华法系 "自首"制度 *Daminglv* Yu Zhonghua Faxi "Zishou" Zhidu	*Journal of Tianzhong* 天中学刊 *Tianzhong Xuekan*	Issue 3 03 期
2008	Ma Teng 马 腾	A Review of Valuation of the Chinese Legal Genealogy 中华法系价值论综述 Zhonghua Faxi Jiazhi Lun Zongshu	*Journal of the Graduates Sun Yat-Sen University* 中山大学研究生学刊 *Zhongshan Daxue Yanjiusheng Xuekan*	Issue 4 04 期

(continued)

(continued)

Year of publication	Author	Article	Journal	Issue No
2008	Zhang Baoshan, Ma Guotao 张宝山、马国淘	Tang Code, Representative Work of the Ancient Chinese Legal System 唐律,古代"中华法系"的代表作 Tanglv, Gudai "Zhonghua Faxi" De Daibiaozuo	*The People's Congress of Jilin* 吉林人大 *Jilin Renda*	Issue 3 03 期
2008	Guo Shiyou, Li Zaiquan 郭世佑、李在全	Construction of "Chinese Legal System" Discourse in Modern China "中华法系"话语在近代中国的建构 "Zhonghua Faxi" Huayu Zai Jindai Zhongguo De Jiangou	*Jiangsu Social Sciences* 江苏社会科学 *Jiangsu Shehui Kexue*	Issue 6 06 期
2008	Li Shifu 李世福	Preliminary Probing into Founding the State by Justice in Chinese Traditional National Character and Justice Legal System in the Chinese Legal System 中国传统国格之正义立国及中华法系之正义法系初探 Zhongguo Chuantong Guoge Zhi Zhengyi Liguo Ji Zhonghua Faxi Zhi Zhengyi Faxi Chutan	*Journal of Taiyuan Normal University* 太原师范学院学报 *Taiyuan Shifan Xueyuan Xuebao*	Issue 6 06 期
2008	Lai Junnan 赖骏楠	Constructing the Chinese Legal Family—Theory, Nationalism, Discourse and Practice (1900–1949) 建构中华法系—学说、民族主义与话语实践(1900—1949) Jiangou Zhonghua Faxi—Xueshuo, Minzu Zhuyi Yu Huayu Shijian(1900—1949)	*Peking University Law Review* 北大法律评论 *Beida Falv Pinglun*	Issue 2 02 期

(continued)

(continued)

Year of publication	Author	Article	Journal	Issue No
2008	Feng Shuxia 冯曙霞	Legislative Performance of Ethical Sentencing System in the Chinese Legal System 中华法系伦理量刑制度的立法表现 Zhonghua Faxi Lunli Liangxing Zhidu De Lifa Biaoxian	*Social Sciences Review* 社科纵横 *Sheke Zongheng*	
2008	Feng Shuxia 冯曙霞	Core Significance of Ethical Sentencing in the Chinese Legal System: The Historical Evolution of the Norms of "Filial Piety" 中华法系伦理量刑的核心意蕴—"孝道"规范的历史沿革 Zhonghua Faxi Lunli Liangxing De Hexin Yiyun—"Xiaodao" Guifan De Lishi Yange	*Journal of Zhengzhou University* 郑州大学学报 *Zhengzhou Daxue Xuebao*	Issue 5 05 期
2008	Feng Shuxia 冯曙霞	Historical Evolution of Ethical Sentencing Theory in the Chinese Legal System 中华法系伦理量刑理论的历史演进 Zhonghua Faxi Lunli Liangxing Lilun De Lishi Yanjin	*Huxiang Forum* 湖湘论坛 *Huxiang Luntan*	Issue 6 06 期
2008	Si Yiwen 司贻文	A Brief Discussion on the Cultural Support of the Chinese Legal System 中华法系的文化支撑浅论 Zhonghua Faxi De Wenhua Zhicheng Qianlun	*Cards World* 金卡工程 *Jinka Gongcheng*	Issue 12 12 期
2008	Peng Weiwei 彭威伟	Research on the Chinese Legal Family 中华法系研究 Zhonghua Faxi Yanjiu	*Study Monthly* 学习月刊 *Xuexi Yuekan*	Issue 20 20 期

(continued)

(continued)

Year of publication	Author	Article	Journal	Issue No
2009	Liu Guang'an 刘广安	Re-understanding of the Chinese Legal Family 对中华法系的再认识 Dui Zhonghua Faxi De Zai Renshi	Zhu Yong (Ed.), *Chinese Legal Family* (Volume 1), Law Press· China, 2010 朱勇主编的《中华法系》第一卷,法律出版社 2010 年版 Zhu Yong Zhubian De *Zhonghua Faxi* Di-Yi Juan, Falv Chubanshe 2010 Nian Ban	
2009	Yu Ronggen, Peng Yifei 俞荣根、彭奕菲	Confucian Legal Culture and the Chinese Legal System 儒家法文化与中华法系 Rujia Fa Wenhua Yu Zhonghua Faxi	*Research on Legal Culture* 法律文化研究 *Falv Wenhua Yanjiu*	
2009	Zhang Zhongqiu 张中秋	Comparison of the Principles and Philosophies between the Chinese Legal System and Roman Law: A Study of *Commentary on Tang Code* and *The Institutes of Justinian* 中华法系与罗马法的原理及其哲学比较—以《唐律疏议》与《法学阶梯》为对象的探讨 Zhonghua Faxi Yu Luomafa De Yuanli Ji Qi Zhexue Bijiao—Yi *Tang Lv Shu Yi* Yu *Faxue Jieti* Wei Duixiang De Tantao	Proceedings of the Fourth International Symposium on Roman Law, Chinese Law, and the Codification of Civil Law 第四届罗马法、中国法与民法法典化国际研讨会论文集 *Di-Si Jie Luomafa, Zhongguofa Yu Minfa Fadianhua Guoji Yantaohui Lunwenji*	
2009	Jiang Liquan, Zhang Jing 蒋澧泉、张 婧	Evolution of the Legislation of the Chinese Legal Family 中华法系立法之演进 Zhonghua Faxi Lifa Zhi Yanjin	*Research on Legal Culture* 法律文化研究 *Falv Wenhua Yanjiu*	
2009	Feng Hong 冯 红	Principles of Mid Criminal Law of the Xi Zhou Dynasty 中华法系罪刑相适应原则探源—试论西周中刑原则 Zhonghua Faxi Zuixing Xiang Shiying Yuanze Tanyuan—Shilun Xizhou Zhong Xing Yuanze	*Journal of Hebei University* 河北大学学报 *Hebei Daxue Xuebao*	Issue 2 02 期

(continued)

(continued)

Year of publication	Author	Article	Journal	Issue No
2009	Peng Min, Zhang Xijun 彭敏、张希君	A Brief Discussion on the Main Features of the Chinese Legal System 浅论中华法系的主要特征 Qianlun Zhonghua Faxi De Zhuyao Tezheng	*Science and Technology Information* 科技信息 *Keji Xinxi*	Issue 33 33 期
2009	Ge Zhirui 葛之蕤	On the Renaissance of the Chinese Legal System 论中华法系之复兴 Lun Zhonghua Faxi Zhi Fuxing	*Legal System and Society* 法制与社会 *Fazhi Yu Shehui*	Issue 23 23 期
2009	Wang Wei 王薇	Analysis of the Characteristics and Origin of the Chinese Legal System 中华法系的特点及成因探析 Zhonghua Faxi De Tedian Ji Chengyin Tanxi	*Study Monthly* 学习月刊 *Xuexi Yuekan*	Issue 22 22 期
2009	Meng Shuang 孟爽	Legislative Thought of the Chinese Legal System 中华法系的立法思想 Zhonghua Faxi De Lifa Sixiang	*Legal System and Society* 法制与社会 *Fazhi Yu Shehui*	Issue 28 28 期
2009	Wang Hongzhi 王宏志	Analysis of the Diverse Perspectives on the Influence of Legal Systems in the Contemporary Chinese Law 分析当代中国法 "法系影响"的多元视角 Fenxi Dangdai Zhongguofa "Faxi Yingxiang" De Duoyuan Shijiao	*Research on the History of Foreign Legal Systems* 外国法制史研究 *Waiguo Fazhishi Yanjiu*	
2009	Feng Shuxia 冯曙霞	Preliminary Discussion on the Classification of Sentencing Standards in the Chinese Legal System 中华法系量刑标准分类问题初步探讨 Zhonghua Faxi Liangxing Biaozhun Fenlei Wenti Chubu Tantao	*Fujian Tribune* 福建论坛 *Fujian Luntan*	Issue 4 4 期

(continued)

(continued)

Year of publication	Author	Article	Journal	Issue No
2009	Zhang Jinfan 张晋藩	Several Issues Regarding the Chinese Legal Civilization 论中华法制文明的几个问题 Lun Zhonghua Fazhi Wenming De Jige Wenti	*China Legal Science* 中国法学 *Zhongguo Faxue*	Issue 5 5 期
2009	Du Wenzhong, Wu Jie 杜文忠、吴 杰	On the Spiritual Characteristics of "Chinese Law" 论"中国法"的精神特质 Lun "Zhongguofa" De Jingshen Tezhi	*Proceedings of the 30th Anniversary Conference and 2009 Annual Conference of the China Institute of Legal History* 中国法律史学会成立30周年纪念大会暨2009年会论文集 *Zhongguo Falvshi Xuehui Chengli 30 Zhounian Jinian Dahui Ji 2009 Nianhui Lunwenji*	
2009	Nanjie· Long yingqiang 南杰· 隆英强	Value and Position of Tibetan Traditional Legal Culture in the Chinese Legal System from the Perspective of Legal and Cultural Studies 论法文化视域下藏族传统法律文化在中华法系中的价值与地位 Lun Fa WenHua Shiyu Xia Zangzu Chuantong Falv Wenhua Zai Zhonghua Faxi Zhong De Jiazhi Yu Diwei	*Proceedings of the 30th Anniversary Conference and 2009 Annual Conference of the China Institute of Legal History* 中国法律史学会成立30周年纪念大会暨2009年会论文集 *Zhongguo Falvshi Xuehui Chengli 30 Zhounian Jinian Dahui Ji 2009 Nianhui Lunwenji*	
2009	Zheng Yu 郑 宇	On the Significance of the Thought of Combining Rites and Laws in the Chinese Legal System for Building a Harmonious Society 论中华法系礼法结合思想对构建和谐社会的意义 Lun Zhonghua Faxi Lifa Jiehe Sixiang Dui Goujian Hexie Shehui De Yiyi	*Business China* 中国商界 *Zhongguo Shangjie*	Issue 8 08 期

(continued)

(continued)

Year of publication	Author	Article	Journal	Issue No
2010	Chen Chaobi 陈朝璧	Formation and Development of "Socialistic" New Chinese Legal System 试论社会主义的新中华法系的形成和发展 Shilun Shehui Zhuyi De Xin Zhonghua Faxi De Xingcheng He Fazhan	*Xiamen University Law Review* 厦门大学法律评论 *Xiamen Daxue Falv Pinglun*	
2010	Zhang Jinfan 张晋藩	Interpretation of the Locality of the Chinese Legal Family 解读中华法系的本土性 Jiedu Zhonghua Faxi De Bentuxing	*The Chinese Procurators* 中国检察官 Zhongguo Jianchaguan	Issue 1 01 期
2010	Zhang Jinfan 张晋藩	The Development of My Understandings of the Chinese Legal Family 我对中华法系认识的发展轨迹 Wo Dui Zhonghua Faxi Renshi De Fazhan Guiji	Zhu Yong (Ed.), *Chinese Legal Family* (Volume 1), Law Press· China 载朱勇主编《中华法系》,第一卷,法律出版社 Zai Zhu Yong Zhubian *Zhonghua Faxi,* Di-Yi Juan, Falv Chubanshe	
2010	Yu Ronggen 俞荣根	Getting to the Root and Compromising China with the West: Rebuilding the Chinese Legal System 正本清源折中融西—重建新的中华法系 Zhengben-Qingyuan Zhezhong-Rongxi—Chong Jian Xin De Zhonghua Faxi	*Journal of China University of Political Science and Law* 中国政法大学学报 *Zhongguo Zhengfa Daxue Xuebao*	Issue 2 02 期

(continued)

(continued)

Year of publication	Author	Article	Journal	Issue No
2010	Zhang Zhongqiu 张中秋	Comparison of the Principles and Philosophies between the Chinese Legal System and Roman Law: A Study of *Commentary on Tang Code* and *The Institutes of Justinian* 中华法系与罗马法的原理及其哲学比较—以《唐律疏议》与《法学阶梯》为对象的探讨 Zhonghua Faxi Yu Luomafa De Yuanli Ji Qi Zhexue Bijiao—Yi *Tang Lv Shu Yi* Yu *Faxue Jieti* Wei Duixiang De Tantao	*Tribune of Political Science and Law* 政法论坛 *Zhengfa Luntan*	Issue 3 03 期
2010	Shan Chun 单 纯	Characteristics of the "Harmony between Man and Nature" in the Chinese Legal System 中华法系的"天人合一"特色 Zhonghua Faxi De "Tianren-Heyi" Tese	*Journal of Cultural Criticism* 粤海风 *Yue Hai Feng*	Issue 1 01 期
2010	Han Lulu 韩璐璐	Reflections on Humanism in the Chinese Legal System 对中华法系中人本主义的思考 Dui Zhonghua Faxi Zhong Renben Zhuyi De Sikao	*Legal System and Society* 法制与社会 *Fazhi Yu Shehui*	Issue 20 20 期
2010	Feng Shuxia 冯曙霞	Analysis of the Formation of the Ethical Sentencing System in the Chinese Legal System 中华法系伦理量刑制度形成探析 Zhonghua Faxi Lunli Liangxing Zhidu Xingcheng Tanxi	*Academic Journal of Zhongzhou* 中州学刊 *Zhongzhou Xuekan*	Issue 5 05 期

(continued)

(continued)

Year of publication	Author	Article	Journal	Issue No
2010	Yang Shiqun 杨师群	Analysis of the Formation Causes of the Subject of Criminal Law in the Chinese Legal System 中华法系 "刑法"主体形成原因辨析 Zhonghua Faxi "Xingfa" Zhuti Xingcheng Yuanyin Bianxi	*Exploration and Free Views* 探索与争鸣 *Tansuo Yu Zhengming*	Issue 6 06 期
2011	Zhang Jinfan 张晋藩	Legal Culture of Pluralistic Integration: The Chinese Legal Family Condenses the Legal Wisdom of Ethnic Minorities 多元一体法文化:中华法系凝结少数民族的法律智慧 Duoyuan Yiti Fawenhua: Zhonghua Faxi Ningjie Shaoshu Minzu De Falv Zhihui	*Ethno-National Studies* 民族研究 *Minzu Yanjiu*	Issue 5 05 期
2011	Liu Guang'an 刘广安	Re-understanding of the Vitality of the Chinese Legal Family 中华法系生命力的重新认识 Zhonghua Faxi Shengmingli De Chongxin Renshi	*Tribune of Political Science and Law* 政法论坛 *Zhengfa Luntan*	Issue 2 02 期
2011	Wang Tao 王涛	A Postmodern Discourse Critique of the Research on the Chinese Legal System 中华法系研究的后现代话语检视 Zhonghua Faxi Yanjiu De Hou Xiandai Huayu Jianshi	*Tribune of Political Science and Law* 政法论坛 *Zhengfa Luntan*	Issue 4 04 期

(continued)

(continued)

Year of publication	Author	Article	Journal	Issue No
2011	Zhang Zhongqiu 张中秋	Spirit of Moral Culture in the Chinese Legal System and Its Significance for the Future Law of Greater China 中华法系道德文化精神及对未来大中国法的意义 Zhonghua Faxi Daode Wenhua Jingshen Ji Dui Weilai Da Zhongguo Fa De Yiyi	*Law Science* 法学 *Faxue*	Issue 5 05 期
2011	Wang Hongzhi 王宏志	Diverse Perspectives on the Influence of Legal Systems in Contemporary Chinese Law 当代中国法 "法系影响" 的多元审视 Dangdai Zhongguofa "Faxi Yingxiang" De Duoyuan Shenshi	*Academic Exchange* 学术交流 *Xueshu Jiaoliu*	Issue 1 01 期
2011	Shao Fang 邵 方	Inheritance and Innovation of the Western Xia Code on the Chinese Legal System: A perspective from the *Tiansheng Penal Code* 西夏法典对中华法系的传承与创新—以《天盛律令》为视角 Xixia Fadian Dui Zhonghua Faxi De Chuancheng Yu Chuangxin—Yi *Tiansheng Lvling* Wei Shijiao	*Tribune of Political Science and Law* 政法论坛 *Zhengfa Luntan*	Issue 1 01 期
2011	Zheng Xianwen 郑显文	About the Coincidence between the Chinese Legal System and Roman Law 中华法系与古代罗马法之 "暗合" Zhonghua Faxi Yu Gudai Luomafa Zhi "Anhe"	*Journal of Beijing University of Aeronautics and Astronautics (Social Sciences Edition)* 北京航空航天大学学报(社会科学版) *Beijing Hangkong Hantian Daxue Xuebao (Shehui Kexue Ban)*	Issue 4 04 期

(continued)

(continued)

Year of publication	Author	Article	Journal	Issue No
2012	Zhang Jinfan 张晋藩	Revival of Legal Culture and Rethinking of the Chinese Legal Family 法文化的复兴与中华法系的再思考 Fa Wenhua De Fuxing Yu Zhonghua Faxi De Zai Sikao	*Lessons Learned: Past and Present in the Research of Legal History,* Xiamen University Press 载《镜鉴心语:法史研究中的古与今》,厦门大学出版社 Zai *Jingjian Xinyu: Fashi Yanjiu Zhong De Gu Yu Jin,* Xiamen Daxue Chubanshe	
2012	Li Qing 李青	Uruma State and the Chinese Legal System 琉球国与中华法系 Liuqiuguo Yu Zhonghua Faxi	*Journal of Chinese Academy of Governance* 国家行政学院学报 *Guojia Xingzheng Xueyuan Xuebao*	Issue 5 05 期
2012	Yu Ronggen 俞荣根	Harmony: The Soul of the Chinese Legal System—Keynote Speech at the Fifth World Confucian Conference 和:中华法系之魂—在第五届世界儒学大会上的主题发言 He: Zhonghua Faxi Zhi Hun—Zai Di-Wu Jie Shijie Ruxue Dahui Shang De Zhuti Fayan	Academic Proceedings of the 5th World Confucian Conference 第五届世界儒学大会学术论文集 *Di-Wu Jie Shijie Ruxue Dahui Xueshu Lunwenji*	
2012	Hu Xingdong 胡兴东	Tradition of Case Law and the Chinese Legal System 判例法传统与中华法系 Panlifa Chuantong Yu Zhonghua Faxi	*Law Science Magazine* 法学杂志 *Faxue Zazhi*	Issue 5 05 期
2012	Ruan Zhigang 阮智刚	Cultural Conservative Complex in the Study of Chinese Legal History: A Review of Zhang Jinfan's Proposal for Reshaping the Chinese Legal System 中国法律史研究中的文化保守情结—评张晋藩的"重塑中华法系"主张 Zhongguo Falv Shi Yanjiu Zhong De Wenhua Baoshou Qingjie —Ping Zhang Jinfan De "Chongsu Zhonghua Faxi" Zhuzhang	*Legality Vision* 法制博览 *Fazhi Bolan*	Issue 1 01 期

(continued)

(continued)

Year of publication	Author	Article	Journal	Issue No
2012	Ma Zhiguo, Zhou Xingsheng 马治国、周兴生	A Textual Research of the Basic Role of the *Book of Documents* in the Building and Development of Chinese Rites Law—A New Argument on the Reliability of the *Book of Yu* as the Foundation of Research of the Authentic History of Rites Law 《尚书》在中华礼法形成与发展中的基础性地位考证—《虞书》作为礼法信史研究根基的可靠性新证 *Shangshu* Zai Zhonghua Lifa Xingcheng Yu Fazhan Zhong De Jichuxing Diwei Kaozheng—*Yushu* Zuowei Lifa Xinshi Yanjiu Genji De Kekaoxing Xinzheng	*Journal of Xi'an Jiaotong University (Social Sciences)* 西安交通大学学报(社会科学版) *Xi-an Jiaotong Daxue Xuebao (Shehui Kexue Ban)*	Issue 6 06 期
2012	Huang Zhen 黄 震	Chinese Legal System and Major Legal Systems in the World: An Historical Study from Legal Systems to Legal Styles 中华法系与世界主要法律体系—从法系到法律样式的学术史考察 Zhonghua Faxi Yu Shijie Zhuyao Falv Tixi—Cong Faxi Dao Falv Yangshi De Xueshushi Kaocha	*Law Science Magazine* 法学杂志 *Faxue Zazhi*	Issue 9 09 期
2012	Li Dongming 李东明	On the Warm and Humane Care in the Chinese Legal System 论中华法系中的温情与人性关怀 Lun Zhonghua Faxi Zhong De Wenqing Yu Renxing Guanhuai	*Legality Vision* 法制博览 *Fazhi Bolan*	

(continued)

(continued)

Year of publication	Author	Article	Journal	Issue No
2012	Li Li 李 力	To Look at the Chinese Legal Family from Another Perspective: Heritage and Judgment of Fa-Chia Legal Culture 从另一个角度审视中华法系:法家法律文化的传承及其评判 Cong Lingyige Jiaodu Shenshi Zhonghua Faxi: Fa Jia Falv Wenhua De Chuancheng Ji Qi Pingpan	*Law Science Magazine* 法学杂志 *Faxue Zazhi*	Issue 6 06 期
2012	Wu Shuchen 武树臣	On the Social Origins and Development Trajectory of the Chinese Legal System 论中华法系的社会成因和发展轨迹 Lun Zhonghua Faxi De Shehui Chengyin He Fazhan Guiji	*ECUPL Journal* 华东政法大学学报 *Huadong Zhengfa Daxue Xuebao*	Issue 1 01 期
2012	Zheng Yongliu 郑永流	China's Legal Circle: Cross-Cultural Contemporary Chinese Law and Its Future 中国法圈:跨文化的当代中国法及其未来 Zhongguo Faquan: Kua Wenhua De Dangdai Zhongguofa Ji Qi Weilai	*The Chinese Procurators* 中国检察官 Zhongguo Jianchaguan	Issue 19 19 期
2012	Zheng Yongliu 郑永流	China's Legal Circle: Cross-Cultural Contemporary Chinese Law and Its Future 中国法圈:跨文化的当代中国法及其未来 Zhongguo Faquan: Kua Wenhua De Dangdai Zhongguofa Ji Qi Weilai	*China Legal Science* 中国法学 *Zhongguo Faxue*	Issue4 04 期
2013	Deng Changchun, Yu Ronggen 邓长春、俞荣根	Confucian Legal Thought and the Chinese Legal System—Interview with Professor Yu Ronggen 儒家法思想与中华法系—俞荣根教授访谈录 Rujia Fa Sixiang Yu Zhonghua Faxi—Yu Ronggen Jiaoshou Fangtanlu	*Confucianism Today* 当代儒学 *Dangdai Ruxue*	Issue 1 01 期

(continued)

(continued)

Year of publication	Author	Article	Journal	Issue No
2013	Wu Shuchen 武树臣	On the Multi-Character and Significance of the Chinese Legal System 论中华法系的多元性格与时代意义 Lun Zhonghua Faxi De Duoyuan Xingge Yu Shidai Yiyi	*People's Tribune· Frontiers* 人民论坛·学术前沿 *Renmin Luntan ·Xueshu Qianyan*	Issue 2 02 期
2014	Yu Ronggen 俞荣根	Confucianism's Theory of Justice and the Chinese Legal System 儒学正义论与中华法系 Ruxue Zhengyilun Yu Zhonghua Faxi	*Research on Rule of Law* 法治研究 *Fazhi Yanjiu*	Issue 1 01 期
2014	Ma Xiaohong 马小红	Clarification on the Relationship between "Rites" and "Laws" in the Chinese Legal System—Questioning Certain "Conclusions" in the Study of Chinese Legal History 中华法系中"礼""律"关系之辨正—质疑中国法律史研究中的某些"定论" Zhonghua Faxi Zhong "Li" "Lv" Guanxi Zhi Bianzheng—Zhiyi Zhongguo Falvshi Yanjiu Zhong De Mouxie "Dinglun"	*Chinese Journal of Law* 法学研究 *Faxue Yanjiu*	Issue 1 01 期
2014	Ma Xiaohong 马小红	Proper Meaning of "Chinese Legal System" "中华法系"中的应有之义 "Zhonghua Faxi" Zhong De Ying You Zhi Yi	*China Law Review* 中国法律评论 *Zhongguo Falv Pinglun*	Issue 3 03 期

(continued)

(continued)

Year of publication	Author	Article	Journal	Issue No
2014	Fan Zhongxin 范忠信	"Lü" and "Ling", Ritual and Law: Evolution of Ritsuryō System in Ancient China 律令关系、礼刑关系与律令制法律体系演进—中华法系特征的法律渊源角度考察 Lvling Guanxi, Li Xing Guanxi Yu Lvlingzhi Falvti—Zhonghua Faxi Tezheng De Falv Yuanyuan Jiaodu Kaocha	*Science of Law (Journal of Northwest University of Political Science and Law)* 法律科学(西北政法大学学报) *Falv Kexue (Xibei Zhengfa Daxue Xuebao)*	Issue 4 04 期
2014	Liu Zhenyu 刘振宇	Inheritance and Innovation: Western Xia Legal System and Chinese Legal System from the Perspective of Legal Culture Exchange 继受和创新—法律文化交流视角下的西夏法制与中华法系 Jishou He Chuangxin—Falv Wenhua Jiaoliu Shijiao Xia De Xixia Fazhi Yu Zhonghua Faxi	*Theory Monthly* 理论月刊 *Lilun Yuekan*	Issue 12 12 期
2014	You Chenjun 尤陈俊	Understanding of "Great Ming Doctrine" in the Study of Chinese Legal System: An Academic History Perspective on Yang Honglie's Trilogy of Chinese Legal History Studies 中国法系研究中的"大明道之言"—从学术史角度品读杨鸿烈的中国法律史研究三部曲 Zhongguo Faxi Yanjiu Zhong De "Da Ming Dao Zhi Yan"—Cong Xueshushi Jiaodu Pindu Yang Honglie De Zhongguo Falvshi Yanjiu Sanbuqu	*China Law Review* 中国法律评论 *Zhongguo Falv Pinglun*	Issue 3 03 期

(continued)

(continued)

Year of publication	Author	Article	Journal	Issue No
2014	Zhang Jiaqi 张家祺	Review of the Chinese Legal System's "Synchronization Characteristic" 对中华法系"同步性特征"的检讨 Dui Zhonghua Faxi "Tongbuxing Tezheng" De Jiantao	*Chaoyang Law Review* 朝阳法律评论 *Chaoyang Falv Pinglun*	Issue 1 01 期
2014	Huo Dandan 霍丹丹	Historical Evolution and Revival of the Chinese Legal System: An Example of Legislative Thinking 中华法系的历史沿革与复兴—以立法思想为例 Zhonghua Faxi De Lishi Yange Yu Fuxing—Yi Lifa Sixiang Wei Li	*Journal of Mudanjiang University* 牡丹江大学学报 *Mudanjiang Daxue Xuebao*	Issue 1 01 期
2015	Zhang Liping 张丽萍	Structural Characteristics of the Chinese Legal System and the Two Major Western Legal Systems 中华法系和西方两大法系的结构属性 Zhonghua Faxi He Xifang Liangda Faxi De Jiegou Shuxing	*Journal of Chifeng University (Philosophy and Social Science Chinese Edition)* 赤峰学院学报(汉文哲学社会科学版) *Chifeng Xueyuan Xuebao (Hanwen Zhexue Shehui Kexue Ban)*	Issue 12 12 期
2015	Qian Ningfeng 钱宁峰	Interdependence of Morality and Rule of Law: Characteristics and Current Significance of the Chinese Legal System 德法互摄:中华法系的特质和现代意义 Defa Hushe: Zhonghua Faxi De Tezhi He Xiandai Yiyi	*Reality Only* 唯实 *Weishi*	Issue 12 12 期
2015	Shi Wenjuan 石文娟	On the Classic Systems of the Chinese Legal System and Their Influence on Future Generations 论中华法系经典制度及对后世的影响 Lun Zhonghua Faxi Jingdian Zhidu Ji Dui Houshi De Yingxiang	*Legal System and Society* 法制与社会 *Fazhi Yu Shehui*	Issue 33 33 期

(continued)

(continued)

Year of publication	Author	Article	Journal	Issue No
2015	Yu Jiang 俞 江	Some Issues about the Disciplinary Evaluation of Chinese Legal History: A Discussion Centered on the Status Quo of the Study of "Chinese Legal System" 中国法史学科评价中的若干问题—以"中华法系"研究现状为中心 Zhongguo Fashi Xueke Pingjia Zhong De Ruogan Wenti—Yi "Zhonghua Faxi" Yanjiu Xianzhuang Wei Zhongxin	*China Social Science Review* 中国社会科学评价 *Zhongguo Shehui Kexue Pingjia*	Issue 4 04 期
2015	Fang Yan 方 岩	Isomorphism of Ehrlich's Theory of "Life" and "Confucian" Practice of the Chinese Legal System 埃利希的"活法"理论与中华法系的"礼治"实践的同构性 Ai-lixi De "Huofa" Lilun Yu Zhonghua Faxi De "Lizhi" Shijian De Tonggouxing	*Journal of Jiamusi Vocational Institute* 佳木斯职业学院学报 *Jiamusi Zhiye Xueyuan Xuebao*	Issue 8 08 期
2015	Chen Jingtian, Geng Zhenshan, Lin Ping 陈惊天、耿振善 林 平	Reshaping the Chinese Legal System and Building a Rule of Law China—An Interview with Zhang Jinfan, Tenured Professor of China University of Political Science and Law 重塑中华法系建设法治中国—访中国政法大学终身教授张晋藩 Chongsu Zhonghua Faxi Jianshe Fazhi Zhongguo—Fang Zhongguo Zhengfa Daxue Zhongshen Jiaoshou Zhang Jinfan	*People· Rule of Law* 人民法治 *Renmin Fazhi*	Issue 8 08 期

(continued)

(continued)

Year of publication	Author	Article	Journal	Issue No
2015	Wu Meizhen 吴美珍	Comparison of the Spread of Indigenous Law in the Chinese and Roman Legal Systems 中华法系与罗马法系母法传播的比较 Zhonghua Faxi Yu Luoma Faxi Mufa Chuanbo De Bijiao	*Legal System and Society* 法制与社会 *Fazhi Yu Shehui*	Issue 12 12 期
2016	Huang Zongzhi 黄宗智	Past and Present of the Chinese Civil and Criminal Justice Systems: The Sinitic Legal Tradition from a Global Perspective 中国古今的民、刑事正义体系—全球视野下的中华法系 Zhongguo Gu Jin De Min, Xingshi Zhengyi Tixi—Quanqiu Shiye Xia De Zhonghua Faxi	*The Jurist* 法学家 *Faxue Jia*	Issue 1 01 期
2016	Huang Zongzhi 黄宗智	Civil and Criminal Parts in the Chinese Legal System 中华法系中的民事部分与刑事部分 Zhonghua Faxi Zhong De Minshi Bufen Yu Xingshi Bufen	*Social Sciences Digest* 社会科学文摘 *Shehui Kexue Wenzhai*	Issue 5 05 期
2016	Wang Feng 王凤	Analysis of Several Similarities between the Chinese Legal System and Ancient Roman Law 中华法系与古罗马法的几点相似之处小析 Zhonghua Faxi Yu Gu Luomafa De Jidian Xiangsi Zhi Chu Xiaoxi	*Science & Technology Ecnony Market* 科技经济市场 *Keji Jingji Shichang*	Issue 3 03 期
2016	Li Ping 李平	Succession and Flourishing of Daoist and Artistic Tradition in the Chinese Legal System 中华法系的道统与术统之代兴 Zhonghua Faxi De Daotong Yu Shutong Zhi Daixing	*Chinese Rule of Law Culture* 中国法治文化 *Zhongguo Fazhi Wenhua*	Issue 2 02 期

(continued)

(continued)

Year of publication	Author	Article	Journal	Issue No
2016	Qi Wenqi 奇文琦	A Brief Discussion on the Understanding of the Chinese Legal System 浅谈对中华法系的认识与理解 Qiantan Dui Zhonghua Faxi De Renshi Yu Lijie	*Chang'an Science Periodical· Philosophy and Social Sciences Edition* 长安学刊·哲学社会科学版 *Chang'an Xuekan· Zhexue Shehui Kexue Ban*	Issue 1 01 期
2017	Zhang Shiwe 张师伟	Confucianism and Legalism in the Construction of Chinese Legal System—The Confucianization of Law in the Theory System of Heaven-Man Human Induction in the Han Dynasty 中华法系体系构造中的儒家与法家—汉代天人感应理论体系下的法律儒家化 Zhonghua Faxi Tixi Gouzao Zhong De Rujia Yu Fajia—Handai Tian Ren Ganying Lilun Tixi Xia De Falv Rujiahua	*Journal of the History of Political Thought* 《政治思想史》 *Zhengzhi Sixiangshi*	Issue 1 01 期
2017	Liao Zhisong 廖志松	Discussing How to Solve Current Difficulties in Litigation from the Inheritance of the Chinese Legal System 从中华法系传承谈当前诉讼难题破解 Cong Zhonghua Faxi Chuancheng Tan Dangqian Susong Nanti Pojie	*Legality Vision* 《法制博览》 *Fazhi Bolan*	Issue 12 12 期

3. Newspaper Articles

Year	Author	Title	Newspaper	Date
1990	Wu Shuchen 武树臣	Features and Values of the Chinese Legal System 中国法系的特征及其价值 Zhongguo Faxi De Tezheng Ji Qi Jiazhi	*People's Daily* 人民日报 *Renmin Ribao*	January 15 1 月 15 日
2001	Fan Zhongxin 范中信	New Interpretation of the Issues in the Chinese Legal System 中华法系问题的新诠释 Zhonghua Faxi Wenti De Xin Quanshi	*Wenhui Daily* 文汇报 *Wenhui Bao*	April 7 4 月 7 日
2003	Yi Lin 一 林	Publication of the *Re-understanding of the Chinese Legal Family* 《中华法系的再认识》出版 *Zhonghua Faxi De Zai Renshi* Chuban	*Legal Daily* 法制日报 *Fazhi Ribao*	April 3 4 月 3 日
2005	Zhang Jinfan 张晋藩	Zhang Jinfan Proposes a New Proposition of Reshaping the Chinese Legal System 张晋藩提出了"重塑中华法系"的新命题 Zhang Jinfan Tichule "Chongsu Zhonghua Faxi" De Xin Mingti	*Beijing Daily* 北京日报 *Beijing Ribao*	May 16 5 月 16 日
2006	Wang Yingzhe, Sun Yan 王颖喆、孙 妍	Chinese Character Culture Circle and the Chinese Legal System 汉字文化圈与中华法系 Hanzi Wenhuaquan Yu Zhonghua Faxi	*People's Court Daily* 人民法院报 *Renmin Fayuan Bao*	April 3 4 月 3 日
2008	Staff Correspondent本报记者 Ben Bao Jizhe	Integration of Four Legal Regions to Construct a New Chinese Legal System 四法域融合构建新中华法系 Si Fayu Ronghe, Goujian Xin Zhonghua Faxi	*Wenweipo* 香港文汇报 *Xianggang Wenhui Bao*	October 17 10 月 17 日
2009	Chen Geng, Fu Dalin, Liu Tingting 陈 耿、傅达林、刘婷婷	Road to a New Chinese Legal System 走向新中华法系的道路 Zou Xiang Xin Zhonghua Faxi De Daolu	*Economic Information Daily* 经济参考报 *Jingji Cankao Bao*	September 22 9 月 22 日
2009	Zhang Jinfan 张晋藩	Unique Connotation of the Chinese Legal System: National Legal History 中华法系的特有内涵:民族法史 Zhonghua Faxi De Teyou Neihan: Minzu Fashi	*Chinese Social Sciences Today* 中国社会科学报 *Zhongguo Shehui Kexue Bao*	November 30 11 月 30 日

(continued)

(continued)

Year	Author	Title	Newspaper	Date
2009	Liu Hui 刘 卉	What does the "Revival of the Chinese Legal System" Refer to "中华法系复兴"意指何处 "Zhonghua Faxi Fuxing" Yizhi Hechu	*Procuratorate Daily* 检察日报 *Jiancha Ribao*	November 5 11 月 5 日
2010	Zhang Jingkai 张京凯	Outstanding and Unique Chinese Legal System 卓尔不群的中华法系 Zhuoer-Buqun De Zhonghua Faxi	*Legal Daily* 法制日报 *Fazhi Ribao*	September 7 9 月 7 日
2011	Staff Correspondent本报记者 Ben Bao Jizhe	One of the Main Characteristics of the Chinese Legal System Is "Hybrid Law" 中华法系主要特征之一就是"混合法" Zhonghua Faxi Zhuyao Tezheng Zhiyi Jiushi "Hunhefa"	*Jiangsu Legal News* 江苏法制报 *Jiangsu Fazhi Bao*	May 23 5 月 23 日
2011	Li Guogong 李国功	Revival of the Chinese Legal System Is a Necessity of the Times 复兴中华法系是时代的需要 Fuxing Zhonghua Faxi Shi Shidai De Xuyao	*Gansu Daily* 甘肃日报 *Gansu Ribao*	October 10 10 月 10 日
2012	Lin Hai 林 海	Ju Zheng: A Master of the Chinese Legal System Emerging from the Revolution of 1911 居正:辛亥革命中走出的中华法系大家 Ju Zheng: Xinhai-Geming Zhong Zouchu De Zhonghua Faxi Dajia	*Procuratorate Daily* 检察日报 *Jiancha Ribao*	February 9 2 月 9 日
2012	Ma Longping, Zhang Ting 马陇平、张 婷	Legalism—Origin of the Chinese Legal System 法家—中华法系的开源 Fajia—Zhonghua Faxi De Kaiyuan	*Gansu Legal News* 甘肃法制报 *Gansu Fazhi Bao*	February 15 2 月 15 日
2012	Ma Longping, Zhang Ting 马陇平、张 婷	Characteristics of the Chinese Legal Family 中华法系的特征 Zhonghua Faxi De Tezheng	*Gansu Legal News* 甘肃法制报 *Gansu Fazhi Bao*	March 30 3 月 30 日
2012	Staff Correspondent本报记者 Ben Bao Jizhe	The Influence of the Chinese Legal Family 中华法系的影响 Zhonghua Faxi De Yingxiang	*Gansu Legal News* 甘肃法制报 *Gansu Fazhi Bao*	April 18 4 月 18 日
2012	Lin Hai 林 海	Has the Chinese Legal System Disappeared 中华法系消亡了吗? Zhonghua Faxi Xiaowang Le Ma?	*Legal Weekly* 法治周末 *Fazhi Zhoumo*	May 16 5 月 16 日

(continued)

(continued)

Year	Author	Title	Newspaper	Date
2014	Zhang Jinfan 张晋藩	Zhang Jinfan: Pursuing the Original Appearance of History to Reshape the Chinese Legal System 张晋藩:追寻历史原貌重塑中华法系 Zhang Jinfan: Zhuixun Lishi Yuanmao, Chong Su Zhonghua Faxi	*Chinese Social Sciences Today* 中国社会科学报 *Zhongguo Shehui Kexue Bao*	January 13 1 月 13 日
2014	Huo Wenqi 霍文琦	Chinese Legal System: A Fusion of Laws from Various Ethnic Groups 中华法系由各民族法律融汇而成 Zhonghua Faxi You Ge Minzu Falv Ronghui Er Cheng	*Chinese Social Sciences Today* 中国社会科学报 *Zhongguo Shehui Kexue Bao*	January 17 1 月 17 日
2015	Chen Lizhu 陈立柱	How did Gao Tao Become the Ancestor of the Chinese Legal System 皋陶何以成为中华法系的鼻祖 Gao Tao Heyi Chengwei Zhonghua Faxi De Bizu	*Guangming Daily* 光明日报 *Guangming Ribao*	June 13 6 月 13 日
2015	Staff Correspondent本报记者 Ben Bao Jizhe	Traditional Rites and Law and Good Governance: Re-examining the Chinese Legal System 礼法传统与良法善治重新认识中华法系 Lifa Chuantong Yu Liangfa Shanzhi, Chongxin Renshi Zhonghua Faxi	Journal of Shenzhen University 深圳大学报 *Shenzhen Daxue Bao*	December 16 12 月 16 日
2016	Staff Correspondent 本报记者 Ben Bao Jizhe	Treasure of the Chinese Legal System: *Commentary on Tang Code* 中华法系的瑰宝《唐律疏议》 Zhonghua Faxi De Guibao *Tang Lv Shu Yi*	*Legal Daily* 法制日报 *Fazhi Ribao*	January 20 1 月 20 日
2016	Yu Ronggen 俞荣根	Take the Tradition of the Chinese Legal System Seriously 认真对待中华法系传统 Renzhen Duidai Zhonghua Faxi Chuantong	*People's Daily* 人民日报 *Renmin Ribao*	August 15 8 月 15 日

(continued)

(continued)

Year	Author	Title	Newspaper	Date
2016	Staff Correspondent 本报记者 Ben Bao Jizhe	Taking the Chinese Legal System Traditional Seriously, Drawing Wisdom and Nutrients for Good Governance 认真对待中华法系传统从中汲取良法善治智慧和营养 Renzhen Duidai Zhonghua Faxi Chuantong, Congzhong Jiqu Liangfa Shanzhi Zhihui He Yingyang	*Liaoning Daily* 辽宁日报 *Liaoning Ribao*	August 16 8 月 16 日
2016	Zhang Jinfan 张晋藩	Value of the Chinese Legal System and Reshaping of the Chinese Legal System 中华法系的价值与中华法系的重塑 Zhonghua Faxi De Jiazhi Yu Zhonghua Faxi De Chongsu	*Beijing Daily* 北京日报 *Beijing Ribao*	October 31 10 月 31 日
2017	Hua Wenjing 花文静	Guarding the Chinese Legal System and the Consciousness of Chinese Legal Studies 中华法系的守护与汉语法学的自觉 Zhonghua Faxi De Shouhu Yu Hanyu Faxue De Zijue	*People's Court Daily* 人民法院报 *Renmin Fayuan Bao*	February 24 2 月 24 日
2017	Ma Zuowu 马作武	Introducing Rites into the Law Lays the Foundation for the Chinese Legal System “引礼入法”为中华法系奠定基石 “Yin Li Ru Fa” Wei Zhonghua Faxi Dianding Jishi	*Shanxi People's Political Consultative Conference News* 山西政协报 *Shanxi Zhengxie Bao*	March 22 3 月 22 日
2017	Deng Changchun 邓长春	Global Influence of Chinese Legal Culture 中华法文化的世界影响 Zhonghua Fa Wenhua De Shijie Yingxiang	*Study Times* 学习时报 *Xuexi Shibao*	May 24 5 月 24 日

4. Dissertations

Year	Author	Title	University
2006	Li Jing 李 婧	*On the Characteristics, Development and Changes of the Chinese Legal System* 试论中华法系的特点及其发展变迁 *Shilun Zhonghua Faxi De Tedian Ji Qi Fazhan Bianqian*	Yunnan Normal University 云南师范大学 Yunnan Shifan Daxue
2006	Xie Minghui 谢明辉	*Weakness of Education Law under the Traditional Chinese Legal System and its Judicial Improvement* 中华法系传统下教育法的孱弱及其司法化改进 *Zhonghua Faxi Chuantong Xia Jiaoyufa De Chanruo Ji Qi Sifahua Gaijin*	East China Normal University 华东师范大学 Huadong Shifan Daxue
2007	Ruan Zhigang 阮智刚	*On Yang Honglie's Academic Construction of the Chinese Legal System* 论杨鸿烈对"中华法系"的学术建构 *Lun Yang Honglie Dui "Zhonghua Faxi" De Xueshu Jiangou*	Southwest University of Political Science and Law 西南政法大学 Xi'nan Zhengfa Daxue
2008	Shao Fang 邵 方	*Research on the Legal System of the Western Xia Dynasty: Based on the Perspective of the Inheritance and Innovation of the Chinese Legal System* 西夏法制研究—以中华法系的传承与创新为视角 *Xixia Fazhi Yanjiu—Yi Zhonghua Faxi De Chuancheng Yu Chuangxin Wei Shijiao*	Southwest University of Political Science and Law 西南政法大学 Xi'nan Zhengfa Daxue
2009	Deng Yong 邓 勇	*On the Core Cultural Spirit and Historical Operations of the Chinese Legal System: Analysis of the "Emotional-Reasoning" Model in Ancient Legal Life* 试论中华法系的核心文化精神及其历史运行—兼析古人法律生活中的"情理"模式 *Shilun Zhonghua Faxi De Hexin Wenhua Jingshen Ji Qi Lishi Yunxing—Jian Xi Guren Falv Shenghuo Zhong De "Qingli" Moshi*	Jilin University 吉林大学 Jilin Daxue
2011	He Xinding 贺新定	*Analysis of the Chinese Legal System and Reasons for Its Disintegration* 中华法系及其解体原因探析 *Zhonghua Faxi Ji Qi Jieti Yuanyin Tanxi*	Guangxi Normal University 广西师范大学 Guangxi Shifan Daxue

References

Confucius. (2017). *Lun Yu: Yan Yuan* (The Analects of Confucius: One of Confucius' Disciples Called Yan Yuan, 论语·颜渊) (translated and annotated by Xiao Wei). China Federation of Literary and Art Circles Publishing House.

Gu, Y. (2007). *Ri Zhi Lu* (Record of Everyday Learning, 日知录) (Volume 6: Cherishing People So Punishment is Needed, p. 343) (Volume 8: The Harm of Current System of Selecting Officials, p. 496). Anhui University Press.

He, Q., & Li, X. (2003). *Foreign Law and Chinese Law: Reflections on China's Transplant of Foreign Laws in the 20th Century*. China University of Political Science and Law Press.

Huang, Z. (2021). *Mingyi Daifang Lu: Yuan Fa* (Waiting for the Dawn: Exploration of the Essence of Law, 明夷待访录·原法) (annotated by Sun, Weihua). Yuelu Press.

Liu, J. (1996). *Tang Lv Shu Yi Jian Jie* (Notes on Tang Lv Shu Yi, 唐律疏议笺解) (Volume I). Zhonghua Book Company.

Liu, X., et al. (1975). *Jiu Tang Shu* (The Old Book of Tang, 旧唐书) (Volume 185 I: Good Officials I). Zhonghua Book Company.

Mao, J., et al. (1962 photocopy version). *Ming Xiaozong Shilu* (Veritable Records of the Emperor Xiaozong of Ming, 明孝宗实录). Institute of History and Philology, Academia Sinica.

Toqto'a et al. (2008 photocopy version). Song Shi: Renzong Benji (History of Song: Annals of Emperor Renzong, 宋史·仁宗本纪), In *Si Ku Quan Shu* (四库全书) (Book 280, p. 187). The Commercial Press.

Wang, A. (1999). Hongfan Zhuan (Biography of Hongfan, 洪范传)+Shang Huangdi Wanyanshu (A Long Memorial to the Throne [with more than ten thousand of words], 上皇帝万言书), In *Wang Anshi Quanji* (Complete Works of Wang Anshi, 王安石全集) (checked and revised by Qin, Ke, & Jun Gong). p. 207+1. Shanghai Classics Publishing House.

Wang, F. (2020). *Du Tongjian Lun* (Comments on the Comprehensive Mirror, 读通鉴论) (Volume 6: Emperor Guangwu III). Zhonghua Book Company.

Zhang, T., et al. (2008 photocopy version). Ming Shi: Xiaozong Benji (History of Ming, Annals of Emperor Xiaozong, 明史·孝宗本纪). In *Si Ku Quan Shu* (Book 297, p. 166). The Commercial Press.

Zhang, J. (2019). *Zhang Taiyue Ji: Chen Liushi Shu* (Collection of Works of Zhang Taiyue: Memorial to the Throne on Six Things, 张太岳集·陈六事疏) (Book I). China Bookstore Publishing House.

Q. He et al., *Chinese Legal Family*, https://doi.org/10.1007/978-981-96-6522-8

GPSR Compliance

The European Union's (EU) General Product Safety Regulation (GPSR) is a set of rules that requires consumer products to be safe and our obligations to ensure this.

If you have any concerns about our products, you can contact us on ProductSafety@springernature.com

In case Publisher is established outside the EU, the EU authorized representative is:

Springer Nature Customer Service Center GmbH
Europaplatz 3
69115 Heidelberg, Germany

Batch number: 10725800

Printed by Printforce, the Netherlands